DATE DUE

DEMCO, INC. 38-2971

American Pop

American Pop

c.1

Popular Culture Decade by Decade

VOLUME 4
1990–Present

Edited by Bob Batchelor

GREENWOOD PRESS
Westport, Connecticut • London

Library of Congress Cataloging-in-Publication Data

American pop : popular culture decade by decade / Bob Batchelor, set editor.
p. cm.
Includes bibliographical references and index.
ISBN 978-0-313-34410-7 (set : alk. paper)—ISBN 978-0-313-36412-9 (v. 1 : alk. paper)—ISBN 978-0-313-36414-3 (v. 2 : alk. paper)—ISBN 978-0-313-36416-7 (v. 3 : alk. paper)—ISBN 978-0-313-36418-1 (v. 4 : alk. paper) 1. Popular culture—United States. 2. United States—Civilization. 3. National characteristics, American. I. Batchelor, Bob.
E169.1.A4475 2009
973—dc22 2008036699

British Library Cataloguing in Publication Data is available.

Library of Congress Catalog Card Number: 2008036699
ISBN: 978-0-313-34410-7 (set)
978-0-313-36412-9 (vol 1)
978-0-313-36414-3 (vol 2)
978-0-313-36416-7 (vol 3)
978-0-313-36418-1 (vol 4)

First published in 2009

Greenwood Press, 88 Post Road West, Westport, CT 06881
An imprint of Greenwood Publishing Group, Inc.
www.greenwood.com

Printed in the United States of America

The paper used in this book complies with the Permanent Paper Standard issued by the National Information Standards Organization (Z39.48–1984).

10 9 8 7 6 5 4 3 2 1

The publisher has done its best to make sure the instructions and/or recipes in this book are correct. However, users should apply judgment and experience when preparing recipes, especially parents and teachers working with young people. The publisher accepts no responsibility for the outcome of any recipe included in this volume.

Contents

VOLUME FOUR, 1990–Present

2000s

Foreword: Popular Culture's Roots Run Deep

Ray B. Browne

Ray and Pat Browne Popular Culture Library
Bowling Green State University, Bowling Green, Ohio

Although *American Pop* focuses on popular culture as it developed in the twentieth century, it is critical that readers understand that most of these topics did not spring to life without roots running deep into the nation's past. In today's fast-paced, computer-dominated society, it is easy to forget history and innovation because so much of American idealism is based on looking toward the bright future. We are a nation obsessed with the idea that better days are on the horizon.

What one discovers when examining the development of culture over the course of the twentieth century is that each innovation builds off a predecessor. America has always had a popular culture, although what that means might change with each new technological breakthrough, national craze, or demographic shift. And, while defining culture is not an easy task, it can be seen as a kind of living entity. Similar to a growing garden, culture is the gatherings of community beliefs and behaviors, which depends on its roots for sustenance. As the plants grow both individually and collectively, they develop and influence the surrounding societies.

People in Colonial America, for example, had their cultural roots deeply implanted from the cultures of the lands from which they emigrated, but every people or group of individuals must harmonize the old with the new in order to justify one's culture. The unifying themes that emerged from the development of a new national culture enabled people to make sense of the world and their relationship to it. American colonists, therefore, adjusted to the old-world cultures of the people who were already settling the nation, while at the same time creating a new popular culture based on their lives as members of the new country.

The harmonization of the new with the old might be called *folk-pop* or *pop-folk* because the result led to a new everyday culture. This evolution is a neverending process in which the new is blended with the old and a new is born. Human nature demands cultural and individual cooperation for safety and advancement, which it achieves in various ways. Inventions and discoveries, for example, are not as helpful in shaping cultures as are innovation and dissemination of those inventions and discoveries. Culture must speak to its constituencies in their vernacular before it can be understood and fully appreciated. Cultures both lead and follow cultural politics, policies, and social movements.

The fields of entertainment from which the colonists could draw were rich: traveling acrobats, jugglers, circuses of various kinds, animal shows, "magic lantern" shows, group or individual singers, Black "Olios" (one-act specialties), drinking houses, card games, and other group activities.

In the conventional forms of culture development certain figures stand tall. Benjamin Franklin, after his move to Philadelphia, contributed in various ways through his writings in *Poor Richard's Almanac* (1732–1757) and others. He stated that his highest admiration was for "the people of this province... chiefly industrious farmers, artificers [skilled craftsmen] or men in trade [who] are fond of freedom." Inventor of the lightning rod and the Franklin Stove, and many more technological and cultural innovations, no one did more to advance popular culture in these early days than Franklin. In the twenty-first century, one finds similar figures who are much revered for their ability to create. Steve Jobs, Apple founder and executive, is a modern day Franklin in many respects, inventing products that transform popular culture, while at the same time, cementing his place in that history.

Less comprehensive but far more inflammatory were the political contributions of Thomas Paine (1737–1809). On January 10, 1776, he published *Common Sense* and sold it for a few cents so that everybody could own a copy. In a few months no fewer than 500,000 copies had been sold. Another of his great contributions was *The American Crisis,* which opens with the fiery words, "These are the times that try men's souls." Paine intuited and valued the power of the popular culture and wrote his works as if by a common citizen for other common citizens. Today's Thomas Paines may be the countless citizen journalists, primarily Internet-based, blogging, posting, and carrying out the kind of agenda Paine advocated. The writer turned to pamphlets as a method of keeping down price, just as today's bloggers use inexpensive tools to reach audiences nationwide.

Another powerful voice in popular culture was Harriet Beecher Stowe. Through *Uncle Tom's Cabin* (1852) Stowe alerted the public to the evils of slavery (with the help of the Almighty, in her words). After the enormous success of the work, the author claimed that God had dictated the book, with her merely writing down His words. Regardless of these claims, for the next 50 years the work was performed on stages worldwide more frequently than any other play in English (with the possible exception of Shakespeare's collected works).

A little more than a century later, racism still plagued the nation, but instead of being represented by a novel, two charismatic leaders took center stage. Dr. Martin Luther King Jr. and Malcolm X stood at opposite poles in the fight for equality, King preaching nonviolence, while Malcolm advocated "by any means necessary." As powerful as these leaders were, however, they became icons after their assassinations. As a result, their images transcend who they were as leaders, attaining a kind of immortality as popular culture figures.

Colonists loved professional plays. The first such presentation in America was "Ye Beare and Ye Cubbin Accomac County" staged in Virginia in 1665. The first theater in the Colonies was built in Williamsburg, Virginia, sometime between 1716 and 1718. *Romeo and Juliet* may have been presented in New York City in 1730 and *Richard III* in 1750, in addition to Williamsburg a year later. In 1752 the Charleston, South Carolina, theater presented 58 different offerings, including Shakespeare. Fourteen of Shakespeare's plays were staged 150 times in pre-Revolutionary Virginia, and from the 1850s to the Civil War Shakespeare was performed in all the major cities and several small ones.

For the second half of the nineteenth century one of the distributors of popular culture was widespread black-faced minstrelsy—thousands of such dramatics were presented on stage by whites with faces blackened by charcoal. No one can identify exactly when and why the first Negro minstrel show became so popular. Some authorities suggest that African Americans seem to be natural-born entertainers. Others are firm in their belief that the minstrel show flourished because blacks saw it as a means of social equality with whites who otherwise held them in slavery.

Minstrelsy was in its heyday from 1830 to 1870. So-called songsters, cheap songbooks running from 20 to some 50 pages and selling for 10–50 cents, were the main distributors of minstrel pieces, as well as songs from other sources. During the popularity of the minstrel show there were more than 100 shows running and some 2,000 songsters distributing at least 20,000 songs. Not all minstrel shows were black-on-white. Some were black-on-black, after black actors realized that white shows were exploiting them and they could in fact create their own shows. Minstrel shows were later eclipsed by vaudeville.

From these beginnings, one can trace the origins of Tin Pan Alley, which helped launch ragtime and jazz. In addition, the songsters and minstrel shows initiated a kind of crossover success that became the gold standard in the music business. "Crossing over," or scoring hit records in different genres, would come to define many of the industry's biggest stars from Elvis Presley and Johnny Cash to Chuck Berry and Little Richard.

The most enduring form of popular culture is the printed page, even though some observers feel that books, magazines, and newspapers are doomed in the Internet age. Books in particular, though, carry a special place in peoples' hearts, not only as tools for learning but as objects of affection. Many readers simply like to hold a book in their hands and feel the pages glide through their fingers. Even the most ardent techie does not get the same emotional lift from reading text on a screen, whether a laptop or handheld device.

The most influential literary form breaching the gap between the nineteenth and twentieth centuries has been the detective story. This form of literature has from its beginning satisfied deep interests of large groups. From the earliest times, people have wanted answers to the mysteries of life that keeps us continually looking back at history. Our fascination with the archaeological and anthropological past, for example, leads many to believe in monsters such as Big-Foot (Sasquatch) and the Loch Ness Monster. Many small towns and local villages have similar folktales of creatures frequenting dark mountains, forests, and deep lakes. Today, this love affair with fear and the unknown drives much of the current film and television industries. From the low budget sensation *The Blair Witch Project* to big budget movies filled with blood and gore, people thrive on their imaginations resulting from a collective indoctrination to fear.

These prehistoric beings supposedly living among us also help keep alive the mysteries and manifestations of the past, delivering some kind of answer in the form of explanations and comforting conclusions. Histories and mysteries need what scholar

Russel Nye called a "hook" to keep readers on the edge of their curiosity. But mysteries search more deeply into human existence and help explain us to ourselves. Einstein was certainly right when he said, "The most beautiful thing we can experience is the mysterious. It is the source of all true art and science." The enticement of the mysterious is a never fading light in the darkness of life's many anxieties.

Literary interest in horror developed in Europe in Mary Shelley's *Frankenstein* (1818) and pushed ahead vigorously in the *Memoirs* of Francois Eugene Vidocq, a reformed French thief who joined the police force and electrified Europe with publication of his underground activities in 1829. Edgar Allan Poe (1809–1849) caught the imagination of Americans beginning with *Murders in the Rue Morgue* (1841). Film scholars see Poe's writing inspiring the American film noir movement in the 1940s, 1950s, and 1960s.

The coals ignited by the interest in mystery and drama glowed especially in the publication of the adventures of Sherlock Holmes and Dr. Watson in 1887. Many Americans tried their pens at the art. Mark Twain published several works in the type, for instance, but found little success. But the door into the riches of mysteries had been opened to authors and readers of the twenty-first century. Mystery, having metamorphosed through the broadened titles of "Crime Fiction" and lately "Novels of Suspense," is the most popular form of fiction today, and is being used by historians for the true human emotions and actions contained in them. Historians a century or more from now may find themselves doing the same with the novels of Stephen King or James Patterson, novelists who sell millions of books, yet are taken less seriously by the cultural elite because they do so well.

One of the results of popular culture's interest in the make-believe and distortion of the minstrel show was the literary hoax, which flourished in such works as Poe's "Balloon Hoax," published in the *New York Sun* on April 13, 1844, an account of eight men crossing the Atlantic in a large balloon held up by coal gas. Others include Mark Twain's "The Petrified Man" (one of several by him), in which a character is discovered with his thumb on his nose in the timeless insulting gesture—the credulous public does not recognize the joke.

Other real-life hoaxes cropped up on every street corner. P. T. Barnum (1810–1891), famous for working under the philosophy that there's a sucker born every minute, opened his American Museum of Freaks in New York City, exhibiting all kinds of freaks and captivating the public especially with his Cardiff Giant, a plaster duplicate of the discovery on a farm outside Cardiff, New York. It was 10 feet long and weighed 3,000 pounds and had been proven a hoax, but still fascinated the public. The hoax, literary or physical, fed the American dreams of freedom and expansion and was an example of the American dream of personal fulfillment.

Another stalk growing from the same root included the works of the so-called Southwest humorists, who carried on in their stories and language the literature of the hoax. David Ross Locke (Petroleum V. Nasby), Henry Wheeler Show (Josh Billings), and George Washington and his Sut Lovingood stories created exaggerated physical and linguistic caricatures of their fellow citizens in a world they expected and hoped would be recognized as hoaxes. Instead of laughable hoaxes, however, they created a world of reality that is carried over in American popular culture today. The stereotype of the illiterate Southerner has a central role in the twenty-first century, particularly in television sit-coms and movies. The standup routines of Jeff Foxworthy and Larry the Cable Guy are built around the premise of the South being strangely (although often lovingly) different than the rest of the nation.

Another popular form of literature developed out of the idea of the hoax—graphic caricature and literature. Although the caricature had been common from the earliest days of America, the so-called common caricature known as the comic strip narrative, developed by the Swiss cartoonist Rodolphe Topfer in 1846, was probably introduced into America in the *San Francisco Examiner* on February 16, 1896, as "The Yellow Kid." Since then most newspapers have run their series of comic pages in the United States and abroad—especially in Japan, where they are read by all members of a family under the name *anime*. They are likewise pervasive in American (and world) culture, especially in animation, movies, and advertising, particularly when used to pitch products to children and young people.

Because of our growing knowledge of and interest in archaeology and anthropology, our interest in the 6,000 or so languages spoken worldwide, and the suspicion that humanity may be doomed to future space travel and colonization, more works are developing in comics and movies of the extreme past and the imaginative future. Such comic strips and books, now called graphic novels, to a certain extent feed on the hoax works of the nineteenth century and intellectually are not rocket science, as we freely admit.

Many of the ideas and artwork in today's comic books are useful in understanding modern popular culture and its influence. For example, graphic novels have been published for both political parties in the 2008 presidential campaigns. Furthermore, many of the ideas and artwork are highly suggestive to the genuine rocket scientist, and the art work is highly prized for its newness of ideas and execution of detail by comic book aficionados. One original picture of Mickey Mouse, for example, recently sold for $700,000. Many comic book fans live in a world of their own making, but to a certain extent in America's broad, rich, and complicated popular culture, each area is something of an island of culture all its own, justifying its existence.

Just as English poet William Wordsworth said that the child is father to the man, so a culture in one form and one power or another is always a product and variant of its predecessors. It grows and alters or breaks down the restrictions of its sometimes elite, sometimes popular predecessors as the force of the new development becomes overwhelming and suggestive. Sometimes the popular culture grows and sometimes fades, but, although it may diminish in use and memory, it seldom disappears. Popular culture is like animated wall murals and graffiti that permanently etches a record of the lifeblood of a culture of the moment.

The cornucopia of twentieth-century present and developing American popular culture has resulted from the free flow of opportunity provided by its predecessors. So it was up to the last century. The garden of popular culture seemed to the culture traditionalist a patch of weeds overwhelming the flowers. But a new culture in the process of finding and developing itself was not crowded. The new cultures were driven by the changing dynamic of a new people in a new land with opportunities for all men and women to live by and in the cultures they both desired and found satisfactory. Suggestions and opportunities will continue to be found and developed.

The power of the twentieth century continues to develop in the twenty-first as the richest and most energetic culture so far produced continues to flourish—sometimes to the bewilderment and consternation of the citizenry, but always irresistibly, Americans and non-Americans—as long as human nature insists that it wants or needs something new, improved, or just different and finds it in America. Popular culture is the voice of a worldwide, but especially American, growing insistence on democracy in all aspects of life, and the voices of the people—especially in America—will continue to flourish, be creative, and heard.

From the beginning, American popular culture, given a virgin land in which to grow, has developed fully and rapidly. Its influence has been especially forceful domestically and globally in the twentieth century as a result of its growth in the preceding century in the arts and extended cultures. American popular culture impacts the cultures of the world everyday, creating and resolving tensions that are labeled “Created and Made in America.” In the popular cultural world in all its manifestations the most influential label on world life at the present is and in the future will be “Lived in America.”

Preface

American Pop: Popular Culture Decade by Decade provides a survey of popular culture across America from 1900 to the present and presents the heart and soul of America, acting as a unifying bridge across time and bringing together generations of diverse backgrounds. Whether looking at the bright lights of the Jazz Age in the 1920s, the rock 'n' roll and lifestyle revolutions of the 1960s and 1970s, or the thriving social networking Web sites of today, each period in America's cultural history develops its own unique take on the qualities that define our lives. *American Pop* is a four-volume set that examines the trends and events across decades and eras by shedding light on the experiences of Americans young and old, rich and poor, along with the influences of arts, entertainment, sports, and other cultural forces.

Based partly on Greenwood's "American Popular Culture through History" series, this four-volume set is designed to give students and general readers a broad and interdisciplinary overview of the numerous aspects of popular culture. Each of the topical chapters stands alone as a testament to the individual decade, yet taken together, they offer an integrated history and allow readers to make connections among each of the decades. Of course, this organization also encourages readers to compare the sometimes striking differences among decades.

WHAT'S INCLUDED IN *AMERICAN POP*

The volumes in this set cover the following chronological periods.

- Volume 1, 1900–1929
- Volume 2, 1930–1959
- Volume 3, 1960–1989
- Volume 4, 1990–Present

Each volume, in turn, covers the popular culture of the decades through chapters focused on specific areas of popular culture, including:

An Overview of the Decade
- Advertising
- Architecture
- Books, Newspapers, Magazines, and Comics
- Entertainment
- Fashion
- Food
- Music
- Sports and Leisure
- Travel
- Visual Arts

In addition, each group of chapters is preceded by a timeline of events for the decade, which gives extra oversight and context to the study of the period.

Sidebars and Other Features

Within many of the chapters, the text is supplemented by sidebars that feature the significant, fascinating, troubling, or just plain weird people, trends, books, movies, radio and television programs, advertisements, places, and events of the decade. In addition sidebars provide lists of new words and phrases for the decade; new foods introduced during the decade; and "How Others See Us," information on how people outside of the United States adopted, reacted to, or disdained American popular culture. The chapters are enhanced with photos and illustrations from the period. Each volume closes with a Resource Guide, providing selected books, articles, Web sites, and videos for further research.

The appendices feature "The Cost of Products"—which spans from 1900 to the present and shows the prices of selected items from food to clothing to furniture—and a list of potential classroom resources of activities and assignments for teachers to use in a school setting. A carefully selected general bibliography for the set, covering popular culture resources of a general or sizeable nature, rounds out the final volume. A comprehensive index offers access to the entire set.

ACKNOWLEDGMENTS

American Pop is an audacious project that pulls together more than one million words about popular culture in the twentieth and twenty-first centuries. A series like this one owes a large debt to many wonderful authors, researchers, writers, and editors. First and foremost, my deepest gratitude goes out to Ray B. Browne, the series editor of the original "American Popular Culture through History" books. Like so many other popular culture scholars over the past several decades, I owe Ray more than I could ever hope to repay.

I would also like to thank all of the authors who poured their collective hearts into the series: David Blanke, Kathleen Drowne, Patrick Huber, William H. Young, Nancy K. Young, Robert Sickels, Edward J. Rielly, Kelly Boyer Sagert, Scott Stoddart, and Marc Oxoby. Their work provides the backbone of this collection. Several excellent writers contributed to the more than 300 sidebars that appear throughout this set: Mary Kay Linge, Ken Zachmann, Martha Whitt, Micah L. Issitt, Josef Benson, Cindy Williams, Joy Austin, Angelica Benjamin, Peter Lazazzaro, Jillian Mann, Vanessa Martinez, Jessica Schultz, Jessica Seriano, and Brie Tomaszewski.

Not even Superman could edit a collection like *American Pop* without a superstar team of editors. I have been lucky to benefit from the wisdom and leadership skills of

Kristi Ward and Anne Thompson throughout the project. *American Pop* would not exist without their enthusiasm, hard work, and dedication. Thanks also to Cindy Williams for her original editing of the project. She is wonderful.

My great honor in editing *American Pop* has been picking up where Ray left off. I have had the pleasure of writing three books in the series, so all told, I have spent more than five years of my life with this series. My sincere thanks go to my parents, Jon and Linda Bowen, and my brother Bill Coyle for their support. As always, my wife, Kathy, has lived this collection with me. I appreciate her sense of humor, sound advice, and thoughtfulness. My whole heart belongs to our daughter Kassie. Her smile, hugs, and kisses were always awesome diversions from writing and editing.

Bob Batchelor
University of South Florida
Tampa, Florida

Introduction

In the late twentieth and early twenty-first century, American popular culture is omnipresent. In earlier eras, it appeared that one had some ability to wade in and out of the pop culture machine at will. More important, there were opportunities for turning off the clutter. Today, once in the matrix, there is no escape.

This fundamental transformation has far-reaching consequences because of its complete totality. Not only are people in today's world unable to stop the pop culture noise; increasingly they are taught to believe that an "always on" mindset is typical. Rather than criticize people who carry on a variety of simultaneous conversations and odd jobs at once, multitasking is applauded. Children barely able to reach the mouse are urged to learn computer skills. Preschoolers, for example, can go online at Nick Jr. and interact virtually with the characters they watch on television. For an example of how we strive to create budding computer whizzes and future purchasing machines just visit the Disney, Sprout, or Nickelodeon/Noggin Web sites.

The critical assumption is that one accepts the idea that popular culture is as pervasive as the air around us. Perhaps it is more akin to a mighty river, usually rolling along swiftly, with powerful currents just under the surface. At other times, pop culture spills over its banks, sweeping away everything in its path.

Popular culture comes alive at the juncture of the entwined forces of mass communications, technology, political systems, and the economy. The mass communications industries that developed to support and disseminate culture require a seemingly endless supply of fact, fiction, gossip, illusion, and misinformation. Add a dash of national tragedy or smidge of political or economic intrigue and the pot boils over. The media/culture machine shifts into high gear, whether that means the evening news team at ABC, millions of bloggers, or a citizen journalist posting a grainy video on YouTube. People are overwhelmed by the overload, but at the same time taught to think that it is all okay. The result of countless pop culture impressions over the course of a lifetime produces a permanently heightened sense of sensationalism, chased with healthy doses of societal angst.

The 2000s have provided years of explosions and upheavals influencing American life, including the September 11, 2001, terrorist attacks and the ensuing wars in Iraq and Afghanistan; the nation's governmental response to natural and human-made phenomena, such as the devastation of Hurricane Katrina; and Wall Street's implosion at the hands of the real estate mess. These are serious issues that forced action, reaction, and interpretation, which then helped citizens comprehend the changes going on around them.

After September 11 the somber national mood led some experts to declare the end of popular culture based on irony and satire. Others wondered if future films and television shows would ever be able to feature exploding airplanes or buildings. Over time, however, popular culture played dual roles: first, helping the nation mentally transition through the aftermath of terrorism; and second, calling into question the rationale for war and the long-term occupation of foreign nations. Perhaps this ability to examine the actions of the government and other institutions of power is the most positive aspect of popular culture, although one could certainly argue that the fascination with pop culture diverts attention from important challenges the nation faces and serves as a kind of placebo, enabling people to feel good about the world around them without really confronting issues directly.

Many contend that popular culture is about individuals from across the celebrity spectrum, perhaps mainly because people interact with it from the standpoint of their favorite actor, band, or television shows. Others counter with the notion that culture is actually about the larger influences that drive society, such as technology, government, economic structures, and national ethos. For example, technology, economics, and innovation combine to produce culture-shifting products, such as the iPod and computers. These goods then set in motion a shift in popular culture as these products influence people far beyond their intended functions. In turn, users come to define themselves by them—the kinds of music they download, the movies they watch, and television shows they record via TiVo.

By examining popular culture within the following categories—leaders, money, innovation, and culture—an overview of the 1990–2008 period will emerge, which discusses the major issues driving everyday America during the era. Most instances of pop culture transformation, however, blur the lines between these topics. At what point, for instance, does the Internet move from an interesting communication medium to an online culture that completely alters the way people interact with one another and the world around them. Do we live in a Google world, as many pundits exclaim, or is Google just the latest version of the dozens of search engines that have captured users' imaginations?

At its essence, however, popular culture is about context. Studying the actions of political or corporate leaders provides the framework for understanding shifts in popular culture over time. It is impossible, for example, to quantify Bill Clinton's or George W. Bush's impact on the cultural developments of the 1990s and 2000s, but understanding them as leaders working within the mass communication structure enables one to grasp the broader meaning of culture during their time as president.

The ability to examine the actions of the government or a particular leader or group of leaders is arguably the most positive aspect of popular culture. Rooted in free speech, the rise of mass media enabled Americans to criticize their leaders and institutions, thus opening new opportunities for collective education and information. At the same time, free speech allows for humor. As a result, Jon Stewart can openly mock the president on *The Daily Show* and *Saturday Night Live*'s Darrell Hammond could impersonate Clinton weekly on the hit show without concern over his personal safety.

As millions of Americans interacted with mass media, whether watching the same movies or listening to radio programs, a common language developed that opened lines of communication between disparate groups. The downside to this unintended focus on mass communications, some argued, was that a growing fascination with pop culture actually diverted attention from important challenges the nation faced, ultimately serving as a kind of placebo. Therefore, popular culture enabled people to feel good about the world around them without really forcing them to directly confront critical issues.

LEADERS

Arguably, no president in history blurred the line between the office and popular culture more than Bill Clinton. He served as a kind of walking symbol of how society changed over the last several decades. After Clinton, for example, any vestiges of regality or luster the office held virtually disappeared. However, he was an incredibly popular president, routinely receiving high approval ratings.

Clinton was still "Mr. President," but for most people and the media, he was "Bubba" or "Slick Willy," a down-home, good ol' country boy from Arkansas—the kind of guy you would want to drink a beer with, listen to him tell jokes and stories, but never leave alone with your sister—wink, wink. Clinton's homespun image emerged despite his ties to Washington, D.C., and education at Georgetown University, Yale Law School, and a Rhodes Scholarship to University College, Oxford. Acknowledged as a masterful politician, both critics and admirers wondered which was the real Clinton. In hindsight, however, Clinton seemed simply too complex to put in a tidy box. He embodied traits of both the down-home country boy and big-city politician and used them strategically to achieve his goals.

The leadership rollercoaster ride took on new meaning after the September 11 terrorist attacks. Immediately after, the nation turned more patriotic. Firefighters and police officials across the nation became heroic figures, lauded for their bravery and willingness to serve the nation. President George W. Bush, with the backing of Congress, launched a series of military and economic programs designed to eliminate terrorist cells worldwide, particularly against members of Al-Qaeda, the organization headed by Osama bin Laden. The efforts culminated in the October 2001 military invasion of Afghanistan and its Taliban government, known partners of the terrorists. Despite the success of the military operations and overthrow of the Taliban regime, however, the United States could not capture bin Laden.

The Bush administration also initiated a series of domestic security programs designed to ease the public's fear regarding future terrorism on American soil. The president authorized the creation of the Department of Homeland Security and named former Pennsylvania Governor Tom Ridge as its first leader. Next, the administration worked with leaders in Congress to pass the USA PATRIOT Act (2001), which gave the federal government far-reaching power to carry out surveillance activities to weed out potential terrorism threats.

Homeland Security officials began a national alert status indicating potential threats, ranging in colors from red (severe risk) to green (low risk). Early in the system, the nation often found itself in orange (high risk) or yellow (significant risk) status. The new federal regulatory agency also set out to make the nation's borders safer, including its ports. Critics immediately questioned the resources it would take to inspect the millions of cargo containers arriving and departing the country's waterways. No terrorist activities, however, have taken place in this area of potential weakness.

In response to the attacks, the nation rallied around President Bush, officials in New York, including Mayor Rudy Giuliani, and the families of victims there and in Washington. Both Bush and Giuliani made high-profile appearances at "Ground Zero" amid the remains of the World Trade Center. Ground Zero transformed into a sacred area, with visitors later flocking to the site to pay their respects. And, "United We Stand" became a rallying cry for Americans, as well as a variety of peace symbols, including a "Support Our Troops" ribbon affixed to automobiles.

In the immediate years after September 11 the anniversary of the event dominated the airwaves. Television programming came to a standstill and refocused the viewing public on the tragic day. In 2002 CBS aired a documentary filmed inside the World Trade Center on September 11, watched by more than 39 million viewers. "All broadcast and many cable networks tossed out their normal programming schedules (and their advertising) on the anniversary," explained journalist James Poniewozik, "as if supersaturating the airwaves—turning September 11 into a virtual national holiday—could magically confine the terrible events to history, never to be repeated. There was mawkishness, anger, finger pointing, navel gazing, bathos, pathos—every possible response except forgetting."[1]

The hyperpatriotism did not last for long, however, and as the Iraq War dragged on it pulled Bush's approval ratings down with it. Critics started making analogies to Vietnam and wondered if the United States could ever leave the Middle East. One reason observers invoke Vietnam language is because the earlier war has also saturated popular culture. People understand that the word *Vietnam* is loaded with notions of America overstepping its bounds militarily and fighting a war that the indigenous population may not support.

MONEY

At one point in the recent past, observers held out hope that the Internet would serve as a democratizing force, allowing greater equality among users in a heated race toward greater information, education, civility, and wealth. The 2000s, however, have revealed a growing fracture in this idea—access issues actually contributed to a "digital divide" between those who could afford connectivity and those who could not.

The notion that popular culture is realized as a series of milestones in one's life is particularly vital in a world that can easily slip out of control or seem altogether frenetic. Still, popular culture holds remarkable power. The words, images, and communication vehicles that deliver this power have the potential to change the world. Bob Dylan's 1963 lyrics, imploring that "the times they are a-changin" remain significant, just as the artist himself is still important in a career spanning more than 45 years. Yet, when we look back at the hope and aspirations of those times, we see that the revolution failed. The "flower power" kids are now running the world. They morphed into their elders as they aged, replacing idealism with conservatism, and conducting a land-grab for all they could accumulate. Still, Dylan's words, and the dreams of a new and better day, live on.

The new millennium is a microcosm of the ways popular culture can be orchestrated to both impose order and initiate change. Discussing the aspirations of celebrity-obsessed online chatters, journalist David Samuels says, "A good number of readers seem to write in the openly delusional (yet not entirely impossible) belief that if their post is sincere or hateful enough, the walls separating their own lives from the lives of celebrities will dissolve, transporting them from the backlit world of their LCD screens to the super-pollinated atmosphere of the media daisy chain."[2]

The American Dream and popular culture are deeply knotted in the national psyche. Perhaps late in any decade, one senses that some cataclysmic change has either just taken place or is bound to occur in the near future. This feeling in itself is wholly American—

continually assessing the past for lessons and guideposts, while simultaneously peering into the future for glimpses of what may soon come. At this time, in this decade, the national mood is one of apprehension and menace.

The economic picture is cloudy and talk of recession mounts, despite the consolidated efforts of the Bush Administration, Congress, and various federal monetary agencies. Moreover, the United States is in the midst of a debilitating overseas war that seems to have no positive outcome. People long for good news from the real estate industry, but each new indicator leads to further concern. And, at the same time, the gap between wealthy individuals and the rest of the nation grows exponentially. All this leads to a volatility that, although not unprecedented, is far astray from what most people assume to be the American Dream.

So where is popular culture in this new era? My view is that popular culture is central not only to what Americans believe but how they interpret the world. The challenge is that many people use these forces to willingly allow themselves to be blinded to reality. If one is consumed by the latest films, television, or celebrity gossip, it is easier to put off thoughts of war, economic disparity, and melancholy. Thus, popular culture—literally the study of what influences people as they conduct their daily lives—can be a force for reinterpreting and changing the world. Or, it can mask reality in favor of a Hollywood version of life that emphasizes happy endings and rainbows. Wake up or tune out—the choice is yours.

INNOVATION

Welcome to Pop Culture 2.0!

In the new millennium, we are all members of "Generation eXposure," whether that means using social media Web sites, such as LinkedIn.com, to make business connections or keeping in touch with high school friends via Facebook. Every minute of every day, millions of people are using the Internet to connect. Today, regardless of a person's age, the explosion of Internet-based innovations essentially eliminates communications boundaries. Even for people who do not use social media sites on a personal basis, the fact that more and more corporations are using the channel to reach consumers is pulling them into the online conversation. A blue-haired grandma, for example, might receive coupons for products she buys via e-mail. At the same time, her tattooed granddaughter surfs MySpace searching for downloadable singles from the hottest emo band. Perhaps for the first time in human history, the old adage "it's a small world" is actually true.

The combination of technological innovation, economic factors, governmental forces, and cultural dynamics has created a new world—generation eXposure—in which nearly everyone manages a public image (the fastest growing segment of the population using MySpace, for example, consists of people over age 30). On a social network, like Facebook or MySpace, users create a persona that is both spectacle and truth in some odd amalgamation, which enables autonomy (if desired) and self-promotion simultaneously.

One of the most popular features on Facebook, for example, allows people to display what mood they currently exhibit, whether melancholy or looking forward to the weekend. When the user changes his or her mood, a new "Mini-Feed" alert is posted, so that "friends" (real or virtual) get nearly instant access to that new detail, spread by a news feed across the site. As a result, one's every impulse can be made public knowledge. Social media networks, whether designed for entertainment, business, or pleasure, provide users with a voice and a public persona that they can share across the street or around the world.

Scholars Stanley J. Baran and Dennis K. Davis explain the dramatic change taking place in the new millennium, saying, "We are in the midst of a revolution in communication technology that is transforming social orders and cultures around the world. Each new technological device expands the possible uses of the existing technology."[3] At the heart of this transformation is the American people, or as *Time* magazine dubbed its 2006 Person of the Year: You. "It's a story about community and collaboration on a scale never seen before," said journalist Lev Grossman, in outlining the magazine's rationale, "It's about the cosmic compendium of knowledge Wikipedia and the million-channel people's network YouTube and the online metropolis MySpace. It's about the many wresting power from the few and helping one another for nothing and how that will not only change the world, but also change the way the world changes."[4]

Every revolution inevitably contains a dark side and the spread of the Web is no exception. With the advent of social media and Web-based communications, many young people find that it is not enough to merely imitate Britney Spears or Paris Hilton. Following celebrity trends is done from the keyboard and a short trip to the nearest Target provides knockoffs that mimic designer brands. More important, technology gives everyone a platform to launch his or her own 15 minutes of fame. In the new millennium, Andy Warhol's famous maxim transformed the public yearning for fame into a spectator sport.

The negative aspect of this elusive search is that the fixation on self and celebrity acts as a diversion from more serious challenges the nation faces, including President Bush's "War on Terror" and a myriad of economic and socioeconomic problems that prevent millions of people from having any real share of the American Dream. Moreover, the same innovations that enable people to interact online also enable corporations to connect to consumers in a whole new way, extending their reach into people's wallets.

CULTURE

In the new millennium, popular culture is at the heart of most national debates. For example, the wars overseas sharply divided the country, after a period of unity in response to the September 11 terrorist attacks, which destroyed one of the world's most recognizable buildings. Our collective culture helped people process and interpret the world around them, from dramatic feature films to music and literature that addressed the national trauma head-on. Also, in the early years of the new century, the country watched as interest rates dropped to historic lows, but by late-decade "subprime" became one of the most searched terms on Google as the nation teetered on recession.

The low interest rates from that earlier era helped bring in an era focused on "big" like never before. Seemingly overnight, people across the country could buy or build their own McMansion—a giant-sized slice of the American pie. The fascination with the bigger the better had influence not only on supersized homes but also on gargantuan fast food meals, which became commonplace, new plasma and LCD televisions, which grew to epic sizes, and people themselves (or at least their waistlines), which seemed to grow bigger and bigger.

Whereas one part of pop culture centered on big, electronics and transportation advances proved that good things also came in increasingly smaller packages. Apple's iPod reinvented how people interacted with music and hybrid automobiles changed thoughts about fuel efficiency as a gallon of gas topped $4.00 and threatens to head much higher. And cell phone usage (many plans with "unlimited" minutes) ballooned in an "always on" society, while physically shrinking to the size of a deck of cards. Yes, Pop Culture 2.0, which pundits predicted would some day arrive, burst onto the scene:

always on—me-centric—and ultimately transforming the way we interact with one another and the world around us.

What is American popular culture? At the turn of the previous century, the answer seemed more straightforward. An awkward giant, the United States rode the presidency of Theodore Roosevelt to a position as world military and economic leader. The nation took these first aching steps toward global hegemony, however, still firmly rooted inward, a society dominated by its local outlook and nature. For most people, popular culture existed in a 10-mile radius from the place they were born or grew up.

During the twentieth century, the national outlook grew increasingly global. Overseas wars took Americans to the four corners of the world. Presidents and political leaders orchestrated a sea change in diplomacy, pushing the country into a role as the world's police force. Military supremacy prompted the expansion of cultural hegemony as the far reaches of the globe suddenly grew nearer.

In the midst of the new millennium, national and international borders are blurred, particularly as cultures blend and technology enables instant communications. Today, popular culture unites and intertwines technology, economics, and power relations—the epic forces shaping the modern world. The resulting tapestry enables people to situate themselves within society, among family, friends, neighbors, and communities.

As a result, despite being difficult to define because of its amorphous nature, popular culture is a type of unifying system. Using popular culture as a guidepost, people navigate among one another. We use its symbols, representations, and ideas to make sense of the world around us. The large-scale influences on people's lives are often difficult to understand or interpret, but popular culture provides a common language. The hottest television show or hit movie, for example, is a sort of guide or handbook that enables people to interact.

The power of popular culture today transcends discussions of low or high culture, which dominated interpretations of the topic for decades. As a fusing and interlacing force, popular culture allows for discussion that transverses barriers based on class, race, profession, wealth, or education. Of course, there are still societal breakdowns, especially in times of crisis. The aftermath of Hurricane Katrina, for example, reveals much about the fabric of society stitched together under the banner of popular culture. Under regular circumstances, however, popular culture seems to be a uniting influence. Perhaps it is during crises that the nation experiences the limitations of using popular culture as such a tool.

NOTES

1. James Poniewozik, "The Big Fat Year in Culture: So Much for the Post-9/11 Warm-and-Fuzzies. In 2002 the Pop World got Weird Again." *Time,* December 30, 2002, Expanded Academic ASAP. Thomson Gale. University of South Florida (accessed June 9, 2007).
2. David Samuels, "Shooting Britney," *The Atlantic,* April 2008, 37.
3. Stanley J. Baran and Dennis K. Davis, *Mass Communications Theory: Foundations, Ferment, and Future,* 4th ed. (Belmont, CA: Thomson Wadsworth, 2006), 2.
4. Lev Grossman, "Time's Person of the Year: You," *Time,* December 13, 2006, http://www.time.com/time/magazine/article/0,9171,1569514,00.html (accessed November 15, 2007).

1990s

Timeline

of Popular Culture Events, 1990s

1990

Iraq invades Kuwait.

Hubble telescope is launched.

AIDS activist Ryan White dies at the age of 18.

On TV: *Beverly Hills 90210, Seinfeld,* and *Twin Peaks* debut.

Henry and June becomes the first film released with the new NC-17 rating.

Luciano Pavarotti, Plácido Domingo, and José Carreras, as The Three Tenors, release the most successful classical recording in decades (reaches 43 on the pop music charts).

A Cincinnati museum director is brought up on obscenity charges for displaying work by photographer Robert Mapplethorpe.

The Clean Air Act passed.

2 Live Crew's *As Nasty as They Wanna Be* is ruled obscene by a federal judge in Florida.

By 1990, the U.S. government's ARPANET computer research network has been transferred to NSFNET, then connected to CSNET (the Computer Science Network) and then to EUnet (European research facilities) to form the very beginning of the Internet.

Tim Berners-Lee, working in Switzerland, who had proposed what he called the World Wide Web in 1989, develops his first web client and server.

1991

Persian Gulf War (Operation Desert Storm) air bombardment begins (January 16); Iraq accepts cease fire terms (February 28).

The Soviet Union regime collapses.

Nirvana's *Nevermind* is released.

First women's World Cup Soccer Tournament is held.

Earvin "Magic" Johnson announces that he is HIV-positive.

Street Fighter II arcade video game is introduced.

FDA approves ddl for AIDS treatment.

Supreme Court nominee Clarence Thomas is approved despite controversy over sexual harassment charges.

Coca-Cola advertising uses deceased stars resurrected through digital technology.

1992

Los Angeles race riots follow the acquittal of four police officers charged with the beating of Rodney King.

Bill Clinton is elected president.

Art Spiegelman's *Maus* becomes the first comic book to win a Pulitzer Prize.

America's largest shopping center, the Mall of America, opens in Minnesota.

Andrew becomes the most costly hurricane in U.S. history when it slams into Florida.

Boxer Mike Tyson is convicted of rape.

Johnny Carson retires from *The Tonight Show.*

Fubu (which stands for "For Us, By Us") line of hip hop clothing begins.

Image Comics begins publishing creator-owned comic books.

Superman dies and is reborn.

Id Software, creators of video games *Wolfenstein 3D* and *Doom,* begins business.

Rapper Ice T's heavy metal band sparks controversy with the song "Cop Killer."

Entertainment Weekly begins publication.

The Real World debuts on MTV.

1993

Ratification of the North American Free Trade Agreement (NAFTA).

The ATF (U.S. Bureau of Alcohol, Tobacco, and Firearms) and FBI conduct raids on the Branch Davidian compound in Waco, Texas; more than 80 members of the church group die.

The United States Holocaust Memorial Museum opens in Washington, D.C.

Steven Spielberg's Academy Award-winning film *Schindler's List* is released.

Widespread public access to the World Wide Web is created when CERN (the European Laboratory for Particle Physics) releases for free the technology initially invented by Tim Berners-Lee, who worked at CERN.

Bombs detonate at World Trade Center.

The *X-Files* debuts on TV.

The series finale of *Cheers* airs.

Chicago Bulls basketball player Michael Jordan announces his retirement, but returns to the sport the next year.

Stereograms come to the United States with the publication *Magic Eye.*

A series of floods cripple the rural Midwest.

Barnes and Noble booksellers forge an agreement to serve Starbucks coffee in their stores.

The Luxor, the world's third largest hotel, opens in Las Vegas.

The first 32-bit video game console, 3DO Interactive Multiplayer, is introduced by Panasonic.

1994

"The Republican Revolution" occurs; Republicans gain control of Congress.

Investigation of the Whitewater scandal within the Clinton administration begins.

Kurt Cobain of Nirvana commits suicide.

O. J. Simpson is arrested on two counts of first degree murder.

Congress abandons efforts to reform health care.

Friends debuts on TV.

Jacqueline Kennedy Onassis dies.

A massive 6.7 magnitude earthquake hits Los Angeles, causing $12.5 billion in damage. The quake and its aftermath kills 72 people and injures more than 12,000.

Dr. Bernard A. Harris becomes the first African American astronaut to walk in space.

Quentin Tarantino's *Pulp Fiction* is released in theaters.

The Netscape Navigator browser, a commercial upgrade of the NCSA Mosaic browser of 1992, is released.

Major league baseball players go on strike.

Olympic ice skater Nancy Kerrigan is attacked as part of a conspiracy involving rival Tonya Harding.

NHL hockey players are locked out following a labor dispute.

1995

Oklahoma City bombing takes place.

Amazon.com online book retailer begins operations.

Cal Ripken breaks Lou Gehrig's record for most consecutive games played in Major League Baseball.

The U.S. Government shuts down due to disputes between Congress and the President over the federal budget.

The O. J. Simpson trial ends with a verdict of not guilty for both murders for which Simpson was charged.

ESPN creates the *Extreme Games* (later called the *X Games*).

Toy Story, the first fully computer animated feature film, is released.

eBay online auction house is founded.

The San Francisco 49ers becomes the first football team to win five Super Bowls.

1996

The U.S. Government shuts down a second time as a result of budgetary disputes.
A welfare reform bill is passed.
Bill Clinton is reelected to the presidency.
Ted Kaczynski, the Unabomber, is arrested.
Oprah Winfrey begins an on-air book club.
The NAMES Project Foundation's AIDS Quilt is exhibited in its entirety for the final time in Washington D.C.'s National Mall.
Marvel Comics files for bankruptcy.
Tickle Me Elmo is introduced.
McDonald's restaurants and Walt Disney forge a 10-year licensing agreement.
Heavy-weight boxer Mike Tyson bites off part of Evander Holyfield's ear in the ring.
The Daily Show premieres, with Craig Kilborn as host.

1997

An antitrust suit is brought against Microsoft.
Maxim men's magazine debuts in the United States.
Dolly the sheep is cloned.
Tiger Woods wins the Masters Golf Tournament.
Fashion designer Gianni Versace is murdered.
Camel cigarettes retires its mascot, Joe Camel, in response to increasing public and political pressure.
Construction on Frank Gehry's Guggenheim Museum in Bilbao, Spain is completed.
The Volkswagen Beetle is reintroduced.
The Getty Center for art opens in Los Angeles.
Heaven's Gate cult commits mass suicide (38 people die) on the event of the passage of the Hale-Bopp comet.
Child beauty queen JonBenet Ramsey is found murdered.
California bans affirmative action.
Mars Pathfinder lands on Mars's surface.
World chess champion Gary Kasparov is defeated by IBM's computer opponent, Deep Blue.

1998

Newt Gingrich resigns as House speaker.
The scandal involving Bill Clinton's affair with intern Monica Lewinsky erupts.
School shootings take place in Jonesboro, Arkansas (March), and Springfield, Ohio (May).
U.S. Embassies in Kenya and Tanzania are bombed.
J. K. Rowling's *Harry Potter and the Sorcerer's Stone* is published in the United States.
Iraq is bombed by U.S. forces.
Bill Clinton is impeached by the U.S. House of Representatives, but later found not guilty of charges in the U.S. Senate in 1999.
Senator and former astronaut John Glenn, at 77, becomes the oldest man in space.
Seinfeld series finale is watched by 76.3 million viewers.
Titanic becomes the most successful motion picture ever made.
Viagra sexual stimulant is marketed.
Mark McGwire breaks Roger Maris's home run record.
The Furby toy is introduced.
America Online buys out Netscape.
A new Internet search engine company is formed, called Google, started by Larry Page and Sergey Brin, two Stanford graduate students.

1999

A massacre and suicide occurs at Columbine High School in Littleton, Colorado by two students who kill 12 students and one teacher and then kill themselves.
The women's U.S. soccer team wins the World Cup.
John F. Kennedy Jr. dies in a plane crash.
"Sensation" show at the Brooklyn Museum of Art opens to controversy.
Ricky Martin's "Livin' La Vida Loca" becomes the most successful single by a Latino artist.
Star Wars: Episode I: The Phantom Menace is released in theaters.
The Blair Witch Project, filmed on a budget of $35,000, becomes a box office smash hit.
Woodstock '99 music festival is marred by violence.
George W. Bush announces his presidential candidacy.

Overview of the 1990s

The Information Age
The Clinton Era

NICKNAMES FOR THE DECADE, 1990–1999

The United States was a distinctly different place by the end of the 1990s from what it was at the dawn of the decade. Politically, it had been a volatile era, and cynicism reached a new peak. Likewise, the technological innovations of the decade changed the world and how people viewed the world.

DEMOGRAPHICS

The age of the American populace began to receive an increased amount of attention in the 1990s. The birth rate in the United States declined in the 1970s, and remained low through most of the eighties and nineties, resulting in a significant increase in the average American's age. By the end of the 1990s, about 20 percent of the populace was over the age of 65, an increase from 8 percent in 1970.[1] The federal Medicare system and private medical care saw increases in costs, as did insurance companies. The changing age demographics of the country led many to worry that Social Security would not be able to provide what it promised, that the system could go bankrupt.

The loosening of immigration restrictions in the 1970s and 1980s contributed to a growing number of immigrant Americans in the 1990s. California, Arizona, New Mexico, and Texas saw jumps in the number of Latin American immigrants, and these populations became increasingly potent in shaping those states politically. But an even larger segment of the incoming immigrant population moved from Asia. Constituting more than 40 percent of new immigrants, people from China, Japan, Vietnam, Thailand, Cambodia, Laos, the Philippines, Korea, and India swelled the number of Asian Americans to more than 10 million, about 3.6 percent of the total U.S. population in 2000.[2]

The African American middle class also grew during the 1990s. Civil rights legislation that had started in the 1950s and 1960s contributed to growing opportunities for African Americans, and while race disparities in the professional world had not vanished, they were less pronounced. A larger portion of the African American populace attended college, and many made significant inroads in medicine, law, and education, as well as in other fields that had once been racially prohibitive. As a result, many black families moved into traditionally white neighborhoods, contributing to the growing trend of affluent African American neighbors.

There was also a large black underclass. Almost one-third of the nation's black populace lived below the poverty line, mostly in decaying urban neighborhoods. As middle class African Americans left these neighborhoods, the areas became increasingly impoverished. The remaining denizens grew increasingly desperate. Education and family life among inner city blacks were among the worst in the nation. Gangs, drugs, and violence became a way of life for much of the black underclass. Affirmative action programs largely focused on race as opposed to class, so many poor blacks were overlooked in favor of those of the middle class. Other social programs seemed just as futile to the poor black community.

This growing frustration and feeling of being trapped in poverty manifested itself in numerous ways. At its best, such anger was expressed through creative outlets such as rap music. At its worst, however, the negativity manifested itself in the form of senseless violence.

In April 1992, the anger of those living in poverty in Los Angeles exploded onto the streets. The year before, a black motorist named Rodney King had been stopped by police after leading them on a chase. A bystander with a video camera filmed the officers beating King with nightsticks. While some argued that King posed a direct threat to the officers, to most Americans, the beating appeared excessive, as King lay prone, unarmed, and outnumbered. Charges were brought against the officers, but they were acquitted in the initial trial by an all-white jury. The anger of poor blacks found its outlet in what would become the largest racial disturbance of the twentieth century. The riots, which fanned out from South Central Los Angeles's ghettos, left more than 50 dead and resulted in tremendous property damage from looting and arson.

ECONOMICS

Despite the rough early years, when a recession forced an increase in bankruptcy filings and mass layoffs in many industries, the 1990s will likely be remembered as an age of economic prosperity, although the economic gap between labor and management increased considerably. A study released in August 2000 showed that corporate executive salaries increased an average of 535 percent; during this same period, the average pay for workers increased a mere 27.5 percent, just over the inflation rate.[3]

Although the poverty rate was decidedly less that of the late 1980s, by the end of the 1990s, about 12.5 percent of the American population still lived below the poverty line. More than 6.6 million families and nearly 33.9 million individuals lived in poverty according to the 2000 Census Bureau.

Several developments fundamentally changed the economy of the nation, and, indeed, that of the world. One of the most important of these was the force of globalization, the linking of the American economy with the economies of other nations. From 1970 to 1994, the dollar amount of exported goods went from about $43 billion to $513 billion, and imports rose from $40 billion to $663 billion.[4] As industries lost a share of the market to foreign companies, and as numerous American corporations built factories in foreign countries with low wage labor, particularly Mexico and certain Asian countries, many American workers found their jobs threatened. However, many also saw globalization as a boom for the country. Certainly, increased importation created a wider selection of goods available to American consumers, which tended to keep prices low.

Many political leaders worked to stimulate global economic exchange by weakening trade barriers. In particular, two major trade agreements championed by the Clinton administration were passed by Congress in the 1990s. The North American Free Trade Agreement (NAFTA) was passed in 1993, and the General Agreement on Tariffs and Trade (GATT) was passed in 1994. Both were topics of fierce debate.

Certainly, the rapid advancement of computer technology contributed to major changes in the way business was conducted, and also in how personal finances were managed. Banking came to be almost entirely computer assisted, with most Americans engaging in some kind of computerized banking by the end of the decade. Computerized record keeping took over in all areas, from businesses and schools to government agencies. Libraries replaced card catalogues in favor of more efficient and user-friendly computer catalogues. Cash registers were widely replaced by new models that integrated computer processors and monitors with cash drawers. Also, increasingly, purchases were made with credit cards. Many stores instituted systems which allowed customers to swipe their own credit or debit cards into the computer. Even industrial manufacturing heavily utilized advanced computer technology, with computerized product design and robotic factory labor.

POLITICS

Politically, the U.S. populace was probably as evenly divided in the 1990s as it ever had been, but a growing number of Americans looked to politics with increased suspicion. Americans seemed increasingly tired of what they saw as governmental gridlock. George H. W. Bush, elected president in 1988, had difficulty with the Democratic Congress, especially when it came to domestic issues. Bush had inherited a dangerous economic condition, an enormous debt and deficit, which played a part in creating an economic recession in the late 1980s. Stumping in his bid for president, Bush promised "no new taxes," which resulted in frequent conflict with Congress over the implementation of any domestic programs that required increases in federal spending. And, in 1990, Bush approved a program to reduce the deficit, a program that required a considerable tax increase.

Despite this change of tone, as well as the fights with Congress over other issues, including a 1991 civil rights bill, Bush was a popular president for most of his term in office. Part of his popularity came from his involvement in several global conflicts that emphasized the United States' status as the only remaining superpower, a result of the Soviet Union weakening and then collapsing from 1987 to 1991.

The Gulf War 1991

The United States had great success with the ousting of Panama's leader Manuel Noriega, who was eventually convicted of drug trafficking. In 1991, the United States, along with an international military coalition, took action against Iraq, which had invaded Kuwait in an attempt to annex the oil-rich country. The United Nations demanded Iraq's withdrawal, even as the coalition gathered some 690,000 troops along the Saudi Arabia-Kuwait border. Iraq's leader, Saddam Hussein, failed to withdraw by the given deadline of January 15, 1991, and the next day, the U.S.-led coalition began a bombing campaign that lasted for six weeks, followed by a ground campaign. Ultimately, Iraqi forces were driven from Kuwait with relative ease. Coalition soldiers met little resistance on the ground, suffering a light casualty count of 141 fatalities. An apparent victory came when Saddam Hussein agreed to allied cease-fire terms on February 28, 1991, although the Iraqi regime remained intact.

Bush's popularity was at its highest point after the war, but economic woes hurt his approval ratings. The recession worsened and the public perceived that the administration was doing little to combat the downturn. The aristocratic, government insider Bush seemed out of touch to working class Americans who saw their paychecks spread thin. The mounting anger, combined a relentless barrage from Democratic challenger Bill Clinton led to Bush's defeat in the 1992 presidential election

The Election of Bill Clinton

Bill Clinton won a decisive victory in 1992, partly because George H. W. Bush had troubles trying to cater to the political right without alienating the left. But even more important, Bill Clinton's public persona played a major role in his victory. Clinton came across as affable and optimistic, a guy that the average person would want to hang out with at the local tavern. Clinton was also regarded as one of the finest public speakers that the U.S. presidency had ever seen. Clinton used his rhetorical skills to attack Bush on economic issues. He and his closest advisors, including political strategist James Carville, boiled their campaign motto down to one simple phrase, "It's the economy, stupid."

However, another election year development also revealed a great deal about the American public's view of politics. Texas billionaire Ross Perot entered the race as an independent candidate and, at times, appeared to be leading both Bush and Clinton in the polls. Although Perot was far richer than the vast majority of the populace, he came across as being outside of the establishment, not as tied down by the petty power politics of the major parties. His folksy style gave many Americans the sense that he was one of

A destroyed Iraqi tank rests near a series of oil well fires in northern Kuwait during the Gulf War in this March 9, 1991, file photo. AP Photo.

the common people, like themselves, and that he would represent the people, rather than any party line or corporate interests. Perot withdrew from the race in July in the face of media scrutiny and then reentered in October to much-diminished support. Nonetheless, he garnered 19 percent of the popular vote but failed to win any electoral votes. In truth, Perot offered few concrete ideas in his campaign, but the fact that he gained more support than any third-party candidate in 80 years demonstrated that much of the country was tired of partisan bickering and governmental bureaucracy.

The partisan struggles of the Bush administration paled in comparison to those experienced by Bill Clinton. Coming into office with a fairly liberal agenda, Clinton quickly found himself on the defensive. His efforts to eliminate the ban on gays in the military was countered so strongly by conservatives and military leaders that the result was a largely impotent "Don't Ask, Don't Tell" policy toward gay men and women serving in the armed forces. The congressional approval process on political appointments made by Clinton early in his administration was grew so contentious that he often had to withdraw the appointment. Clinton's efforts to dramatically reform national health care, so that every American had guaranteed affordable medical care, met with ferocious resistance. The attempts at medical care reform died in late 1994.

Clinton had his share of political victories—in part aided by his ideological move from the left to the center—including a new budget, which included significant new taxation of wealthy Americans. The conflicts of the government were seen by many Americans as nothing but party politics, Republicans fighting Democrats, and vice versa. This partisan combat became much more volatile with the elections of 1994, when Republicans took the majority in both houses of Congress.

The fights that ensued between Congress and the presidency in the years that followed reached their worst when the government shut down in November 1995 and again in January 1996 because of the two sides being unable to agree on a federal budget. To many, this case smacked more of election year posturing than true legislative debate, resulting in antipathy toward the federal government rising. The Republicans felt greater heat because their leaders refused to pass a "continuing resolution" that would have prevented the government from shutting down during Congressional debates.

This set the stage for Clinton's 1996 win of a second term over Republican Senator Bob Dole. The months before the election saw a major flurry of cooperation as Congress and the president grew concerned about how little legislation had been passed in the preceding two years. The legislation was largely economic, appealing to working class Americans. For the first time in over a decade, minimum wage increased. Congress also passed legislation that further protected workers from insurance companies, and it passed a major welfare reform bill, which reduced the amount of money available through welfare, and also turned much of the power to distribute those funds over to the states.

TIME MAGAZINE'S MAN OF THE YEAR*

1990 George H. W. Bush

1991 Ted Turner (Founder of CNN)

1992 Bill Clinton

1993 The Peacemakers: Nelson Mandela (anti-apartheid activist), F. W. de Klerk (President of South Africa), Yasser Arafat (PLO leader), and Yitzhak Rabin (Israeli prime minister)

1994 Pope John Paul II

1995 Newt Gingrich (Speaker of the House)

1996 Dr. David Ho (AIDS researcher)

1997 Andrew Grove (CEO of Intel)

1998 Bill Clinton and Kenneth Starr (Independent Counsel)

1999 Jeff Bezos (Founder and CEO, Amazon.com)

*Changed to "Person of the Year" in 1999

SCANDAL AND THE PRESIDENCY

In 1997, Bill Clinton proved that he could negotiate with the Republican Congress on a new budgetary plan. Subsequently, Clinton's popularity received a considerable boost. But the greatest challenge to his presidency was yet to come. From the start of his administration, rumors of scandal plagued Clinton, from alleged banking and real estate malfeasance (the Whitewater Scandal) to charges of corruption in his cabinet. Clinton even faced a sexual harassment suit filed against him by Paula Jones, who had worked for him when he was governor. Kenneth Starr, a former official in the Justice Department during Ronald Reagan's presidency, was appointed as an independent counsel for the Whitewater case, which had netted several convictions, but found no conclusive evidence of wrongdoing on the part of Clinton or his wife, Hillary. Starr was again appointed to investigate allegations that had arisen during inquiries into Paula Jones's accusations: that Clinton had been sexually involved with a White House intern, Monica Lewinsky. Moreover, it was claimed that, during his Paula Jones case deposition, Clinton had lied about the relationship and had encouraged Lewinsky and others to lie.

The Lewinsky affair cast a shadow over Clinton. He continued to vehemently deny the relationship. Many people regarded Clinton as an embattled victim and Starr as a vindictive villain seeking to derail a political opponent. During this time, Clinton's approval rating never dropped below 60 percent, reaching a record 79 percent at its peak. Then, Lewinsky struck a deal with Starr, testifying about the relationship; This chain of events forced Clinton to admit it happened. The report finally submitted by Starr created a media sensation, largely due to its graphic sexual details. It was published in full in many newspapers across the country and television newscasters recounted details. Americans seemed simultaneously fascinated and repulsed by the details of the case.

Many were distressed by the president's actions, but others were disturbed by what they saw as a clear-cut invasion of privacy. This latter impulse

President Bill Clinton, in a 1995 photo with White House intern Monica Lewinsky. AP Photo.

helped Clinton maintain a strong approval rating, even after the revelations. His ratings also stayed strong as Congressional Republicans called for his impeachment. On December 19, 1998, in a vote that largely fell along party lines, Clinton became the second U.S. president to be impeached. The president would eventually be acquitted by the Senate, but the whole affair had left an indelible mark on the country, and it disgusted many Americans.

The case was notable in that it seemed to do away with the line between private and public life, a line that many Americans held sacred. It was also important in how it brought scandal to the forefront of American politics. Many blamed the media for its almost morbid attention to detail, but in truth, the case fit in perfectly with the country's growing celebrity fixation. Getting a glimpse into the president's personal life served as a kind of reality television episode for the media and public, no new lurid detail seemed off limits.

CRIME

Despite the number of high-profile crimes that occurred in the 1990s, the decade actually saw a decline in the crime rate, reaching a 20-year low. The reasons for this decline were hotly debated. Some claimed that the decrease resulted from better crime fighting techniques, which allowed law enforcement to deter more crime, while others claimed that it was the result of an improving economy, wherein a greater number of people were financially stable. Some also claimed that tougher penalties led to fewer crimes. Certainly, the rapidly growing population in the United States' prisons suggested that more criminals faced incarceration and many served longer sentences than they might have a generation before. The growing prison population, however, was problematic. By the end of the 1990s, nearly two million Americans were in prison. Many new prisons were constructed, but they could not outpace the increased number of incarcerations, and prison crowding became an increasing challenge.

Central to the federal government's actions against crime of all sorts was the War on Drugs, a program that spent $16 billion annually to eradicate illegal drug use in the United States. The largest dollar amount of this war went to the Bureau of Prisons, a Justice Department agency that oversaw the operation of 90 prisons nationwide. State and local governments spent another $5 billion a year on drug user and dealer incarceration.

By the end of the decade, however, many questioned the efficacy of the War of Drugs. Use of illegal drugs did not diminish during the 1990s. Actually, the federal government's efforts to stifle the drug trade led, not to fewer drugs on the street, but rather to higher prices for those drugs, thereby making the drug dealing business even more lucrative. The War on Drugs also triggered an increase in violence, more so than had the drugs themselves. The crackdowns on drug solicitation prompted many dealers to arm themselves with more high power weaponry.

Certain crimes gained widespread media attention during the decade, creating a sense that the country was more dangerous than it ever had been. The murder trial of O. J. Simpson, a series of high school shootings, and a growing number of acts of domestic terrorism also caught the media's attention.

DOMESTIC TERRORISM AND THE MILITIA MOVEMENT

Ted Kaczynski, dubbed the Unabomber by the FBI, mailed a series of bombs from May 1978 to April 1995, killing several people and injuring many others. The Unabomber's identity remained a mystery for most of this time period, but in 1993 the otherwise silent Kaczynski began to write letters to the press and sometimes to his targets. In 1995, the *New York Times* published a 35,000-word essay by Kaczynski, which ultimately led to his arrest when a family member recognized his writing style. The essay published by the *New York Times* was a long political manifesto detailing Kaczynski's beliefs that American society was corrupt and rationalizing his desire to rebel against it. Most Americans who followed the story were convinced that he was mentally unstable, especially after a court-appointed psychologist deemed him a probable paranoid schizophrenic. In 1998, Kaczynski was sentenced to life in prison without parole.

Other acts of terrorism were less easily explained. The most striking of these was the bombing of a federal building in Oklahoma City on April 19, 1995. The bombing, which killed 168 people, including many children, was the worse act of terrorism in the 1990s. Initial speculation was that it was executed by Middle Eastern terrorists, but many Americans were shocked to find that it had been perpetrated by Timothy McVeigh, an American with ties to a militia group. The Oklahoma bombing was in part a response to a clash with a similar group, a well-armed religious cult calling itself the Branch Davidians, exactly two years earlier. The standoff with the Branch Davidians ended when the group's Waco, Texas, compound caught fire, killing most of the group. Many people agreed with federal officials that someone from within the compound ignited the deadly fire. But others, including McVeigh, believed that federal law enforcement officials deserved responsibility for the blaze.

Members in the country's growing militia movement viewed the tragedy at Waco as a sign that the federal government had overstepped its bounds. Centered mostly in rural areas, and composed largely of disaffected citizens, militias saw the federal government as a fascist institution, one that sought to trade in the rights of the common man in exchange for international power (though the concept of the "common man" was sometimes a narrow one given that some militia

Search and rescue workers gather at the scene of the Oklahoma City bombing, April 19, 1995. FEMA News Photo.

groups also exhibited strong white-supremacist tendencies). These notions bore some similarities to those presented in the Unabomber's manifesto, but here they were being extolled, not by a single man, easily dismissed as insane, but by a growing number of working-class Americans. Ultimately, the percentage of Americans involved in militia movements was quite small, but those militias made a name for themselves with acts like the Oklahoma City bombing.

MEDIA EVENTS AND O. J.

The political events that rocked the nation grabbed most of the populace's attention not merely for their inherent importance, but also for their significance as television dramas, nearly as compelling as programming network producers could come up with on their own. Certainly, the scandal that led to Bill Clinton's impeachment, with its salacious details, became a favorite story for television reporters. Likewise, the dynamic pictures from the front lines of the American invasion of Iraq kept viewers glued to their televisions. As important as these events were, as the media covered the stories, the manner of coverage itself became a major story.

The blurring of the line between journalism and entertainment grew even fuzzier in the case of former football great and actor, O. J. "The Juice" Simpson. Simpson's wife, Nicole Brown Simpson, and her friend Ronald Goldman had been found brutally murdered on June 12, 1994, outside of her Brentwood townhouse in Los Angeles. The murders immediately garnered considerable media attention, based on the location in Hollywood, the brutality of the slayings, and the celebrity connection to Simpson. However, the early attention soon seemed minute in comparison to the bizarre, almost surreal, events that followed.

Five days after the killings, Los Angeles police charged Simpson with two counts of first degree murder. Simpson's lawyer negotiated a time for his surrender at police headquarters, but when Simpson did show up, he became a wanted fugitive. That evening, Simpson was spotted, and then began the strange scene of Simpson riding in his white Ford Bronco, driven by his friend A. C. Cowlings, on Los Angeles freeways, followed by a parade of police cruisers. News helicopters covered the chase from the air. In fact, the whole convoy was traveling at well under the speed limit, resembling a ceremonial procession more than a high-speed chase. The television coverage was striking. Regularly scheduled programs were interrupted by newscasters presenting live video footage from the scene. Locals crowded the side of the freeway to watch, and even to cheer for Simpson, in some cases holding signs that read "Go, Juice, Go!" and the like. The cameras followed the chase along the freeways until the Bronco finally pulled into the driveway of Simpson's multimillion-dollar estate. The cameras stayed on the parked Bronco as Simpson spoke to police through a cell phone, with cameras still rolling after the sunset. Eventually, Simpson surrendered, but the "chase" interrupted hours of television programming.

The ensuing Simpson trial lasted for months, and ended in Simpson's acquittal, though he was later found guilty in a civil suit filed by Goldman's family. The trial became a sounding board about the justice system, media, celebrity, and domestic violence. The Simpson case brought commentators out in droves and became a major theme of discussion in all media.

Other crimes fell under public scrutiny in the 1990s, from the Menendez brothers' killing of their wealthy parents, to the high school shootings of the decade. The worse case of school violence came on April 20, 1999, when Eric Harris and Dylan Klebold conducted an assault on their Littleton, Colorado, high school. The boys were heavily armed, carrying a semiautomatic handgun, a semiautomatic rifle, two shotguns, and more than 50 bombs. By the time the rampage ended, with the two taking their own lives, they had killed 12 students, one teacher, and injured many others. Across the country, viewers watched television footage of students fleeing the school and law enforcement officials moving in. They saw footage of a bloodied student desperately escaping the school from a second story window.

In short, the media brought the shooting graphically into the homes of America, leaving the country in shock. No specific rationale was ever discovered for Harris and Klebold's actions, though they had been victims of hazing from certain classmates who were on the football team. As a consequence, many painted the shooting spree as a kind of war between cliques, though friends of the shooters pointed out that the cliques were not as strong as the media made them out to be. The shooters acted as individuals, not as members of a certain group.

The Gulf War also became a television spectacle. CNN's coverage played a significant role in boosting the station's influence and popularity. CNN led the way with its video footage of the initial U.S. air invasion of Iraq, enchanting television audiences with its video-game-like appearance.

These high profile events were newsworthy, but also packaged by the media to heighten the sensationalist aspects, particularly on television. Rather than simply relating the details of a given event, the media increasingly compartmentalized information. Many news stories went well beyond being mere reports, instead becoming "events," with television networks putting as much thought into their presentation as into the content of such presentations.

As hard news increasingly appeared as entertainment, many shows began blurring the line between reality and fiction. Shows like *A Current Affair* (1986–1996) and *Hard Copy* (1989–1999) presented themselves as news shows, yet even a casual viewer of these programs could tell that they were much different from the traditional network news broadcasts. Although the programs dealt with select important news items, their coverage focused on sensationalism. For instance, the details of Bill Clinton's sexual misconduct were a popular subject for these shows, while the rather dry details of impeachment proceedings garnered less attention. In short, the entertaining aspects of a story were emphasized more than the aspects that might prove educational.

THE AIDS EPIDEMIC

The 1980s saw a rapid spread of AIDS (acquired immune deficiency syndrome), both in the United States and overseas, but many Americans still considered it a virus that only affected the homosexuals and intravenous drug users. However, as the number of AIDS-related deaths increased in the 1990s, and as a growing number of high-profile figures, from sports stars to actors, contracted HIV (human immunodeficiency virus), the virus that led to AIDS, a different attitude developed. It became increasingly hard to dismiss AIDS as something that only affected promiscuous homosexuals and intravenous drug users. AIDS soon became one of the leading causes of death among Americans between the ages of 35 and 44. In 1997, the Centers for Disease Control estimated the number of Americans infected with HIV as being as high as 900,000. Moreover, they estimated that only about half of those infected were aware of their condition.[5] Worldwide, the number of HIV-infected individuals reached a staggering 22 million in 1997. Global concern about the epidemic increased accordingly. One problem with such estimates was that AIDS, despite growing education, was still considered by many to be a syndrome that should be hidden. In the 1990s, however, AIDS patients were less likely to be left untreated due to fears of contracting the disease, and generally, they were not as ostracized as they had been before.

The change in opinion about the disease took place as the public face of AIDS altered. In 1990, Ryan White presented a real problem to those who preferred to regard AIDS as a fringe disease. White, a teenager with all-American looks, had contracted the virus via a blood transfusion. In his short life, White became an important AIDS activist, showing that the disease's reach was far longer than some thought. In 1990, former president Ronald Reagan issued an apology for his administration's neglect of the AIDS crisis, signaling a change in official concern over the issue.

As the decade progressed, other well-known figures fell to AIDS, including actor Robert Reed, tennis pro Arthur Ashe, dancer Rudolf Nureyev, and rapper Easy-E. Perhaps the figure who most contributed to a change in the popular perception of AIDS was basketball great Earvin "Magic" Johnson, who announced in 1991 that he had contracted HIV. He retired from basketball and became a rallying figure for those who wished to show that AIDS could be contracted by anyone. Possibly the greatest change in perspective on the disease occurred when Johnson returned to professional basketball. The thought of an infected player on the court would likely have been scoffed at a decade earlier when most Americans had a lesser understanding of HIV, but now Johnson's return was celebrated, and his popularity remained undiminished.

COMPUTERS AND THE INTERNET

Undoubtedly, the most important technological innovations of the decade had to do with computers. Intel's introduction of the microprocessor in 1971 opened the door to increasingly compact and powerful computer systems. In the late 1970s, Apple Computer introduced the first mass-market personal computer (PC). In the 1990s, the proliferation of the personal computer accelerated to a new and astounding level. Computers changed the way the country operated. Few aspects of American life were untouched.

Throughout the decade, Microsoft served as the most powerful company in the computer industry. The company had devised the operating system MS-DOS for IBM's first personal computer. Microsoft's Windows operating system dominated the computer industry, and the company also produced highly popular software, turning itself into a giant corporation. As a result, CEO Bill Gates became one of the country's richest executives. Several smaller companies accused the corporation of unfair business practices. In 1997, the U.S. Department of Justice (DOJ) filed a number of antitrust suits against Microsoft, arguing that Microsoft's Windows '98 operating system worked so well with Microsoft programs, including its Internet Explorer, that it effectively stifled the market for other software products. After years of court proceedings and negotiations, the DOJ and Microsoft settled the case in late 2001. The agreement required the company to share some of its programming with outside companies, but most commentators felt the settlement equated to a slap on the wrist.

The Internet had existed in some form or another since the creation of the Arpanet for the government's Advanced Research Projects Agency in 1963. Expansion from that point had been gradual, but starting in the late 1980s, the Internet grew quickly. In 1984, there were fewer than a thousand computers hosting sites networked together, but by the mid-1990s, there were more than six million host computers, each servicing many individual personal computers, and an enormous number of individual users.

There were several reasons for acceleration in Internet use. The general proliferation of personal computers contributed considerably, as did the development of the World Wide Web (WWW), proposed by Tim Berners-Lee in 1989 in a lab in Switzerland. The WWW, frequently referred to simply as "the Web," allowed individual personal computer users an unprecedented opportunity to create their own sites online, and generally brought a greater sense of order, both for dissemination and retrieval of information. Most users accessed the Internet via phone lines, though with the growing amount of data on any given Web

THE GOOGLE EFFECT

Perhaps the seminal Web site of the 1990s, and possibly the history of the Internet, was (and still is) Google. Indeed, it is hard to fathom a world where one cannot log onto the Internet and Google a recipe for hummus, or the winner of the Kentucky derby in 1934, or the name of that funny painting where the androgynous woman looks like she just experienced a ménage à trois. Like "Kleenex" and "Coke," Google has become a universal word in the English lexicon meaning to look something up. "Just Google it" is a common response to anything that one does not know or is curious about. Merely by typing the keyword or phrase in the familiar rectangular space, one is instantly connected to a plethora of sites containing information about the subject. Google has taken the place of the old *Encyclopedia Britannica*. Rather than spend the time accessing heavy, thick bound encyclopedias, users can Google images, dictionaries, and, best of all, oneself. "In the afternoons, I enjoy googling myself" is already a stale joke. Certainly, those who have had the experience will never forget the moment they were googleable through an achievement, a publication, or even a blog. The Internet has made published writers and narcissists of many people.

site, many turned to fiber optics or other systems of information transference.

E-mail (or electronic mail) also contributed to the growth of the Internet by allowing individuals to communicate with ease and at little expense with other users across the globe. By the mid-1990s, observers estimated that the rate of e-mail use had overtaken that of the telephone and traditional mail. By decade's end, many phone companies offered Internet service. Media outlets particularly exploited the Internet. In 1998, there were more than 3,250 newspapers and 1,280 television stations with Web sites.

Commercial Internet service providers contributed the greatest boost to the Internet among users. America Online (AOL), CompuServe, and other companies provided customers with a user-friendly interface to the Internet, and helped the user search for and organize information more easily. AOL began as a self-contained online system. Users could send and receive e-mail from virtually any Internet user. They also accessed a greater number of features contained in America Online's host systems, but they were unable to browse the Web. AOL, however, quickly added Internet browsing software to later versions of their service. This helped make AOL the largest Internet provider in the world, as did its reputation as a "safe" way to access the Internet. AOL marketed itself as the most family oriented of the service providers, offering strong juvenile protections from potentially objectionable online content. By 1998, AOL reported that it had 14 million users.

COMMUNICATIONS

Besides e-mail, cellular phones, introduced publicly in the 1980s, became pervasive as their capacity grew and their size shrank. In 1994, there were about 16 million people in the United States using cell phones, but by 2001, there were 110 million users, according to the U.S. General Accounting Office. The increase was due to many factors, including the fact the phones became smaller. Likewise, as the phones became more popular, retailers like Motorola, Nokia, Verizon, and Erikson reduced prices both on the phones and service.

Early in the decade, having a cell phone was a distinct status symbol, but as the number of users increased, cell phones became less of a status symbol and more of a necessity. It became so pervasive that cell phone companies advertised not only to adults, but also teenagers. As the phone itself was no longer a means of self expression, the design of phones, now available in a multitude of colors, took over as a way for users to personalize the newfound accessory. The ring of a cell phone also became a means of self-expression. Early traditional digital tones were replaced by musical passages, at first a singular one and then by an electronically stored menu of selectable tunes. At decade's end, some cell phones could download musical ring tones from the Internet. The most advanced models offered e-mail capacity, direct Internet access, and even video games, becoming portable computers as well as telephones.

Advertising

of the 1990s

THE ADVERTISING BUSINESS

In the 1990s, the business of advertising became increasingly complex. The number of possible outlets for advertising increased dramatically, but so too did the fragmentation of potential audiences. Thus, advertisers had to explore many different avenues—television, radio, magazines, the burgeoning Internet, and others—in order to find the broadest possible audience. Nearly every venue for advertising seemed to flourish in the 1990s, with the possible exception of the billboard industry, which had to compete against a growing interest in highway beautification.

The sheer volume of advertising, as well as that of the money involved, was staggering. Advertising became so ubiquitous that some worried about the psychological effect it might have on the population at large. Advertising accounted for more than 60 percent of magazine revenue, some $30 billion a year, and the $40 billion generated by electronic media accounted for almost all of its revenues.[1] A 1991 estimate placed the number of ads targeted at the average American at a daily rate of 3,000.[2]

In general, the volume of spending on advertising by major corporations grew significantly each year. In part, advertising outlets charged more for space and airtime, but the larger companies also spread the word about their products with greater intensity. In addition, television commercials became, in essence, short movies peddling products. It was not uncommon for the actual production costs of a TV advertising spot to rival that of the television program during which it aired.

Certain big ticket broadcast events, like the Super Bowl or the Academy Awards, naturally made for prime advertising time. These events drew larger-than-normal audiences and, consequently, drew top dollar advertising. An ad for the Academy Awards, for instance, would typically cost more than $1 million for 30 seconds of airtime. Of course, these events also developed a reputation for the quality of their commercials because viewers knew that companies would be investing a great deal of money to make these commercials the best. It was not unusual to hear nearly as much about the commercials the next day in the media and in conversation than about the Super Bowl game itself.

American companies also marketed to other countries much more intensely in the 1990s. Particularly, Eastern Europe, after the widespread fall of Communism, provided fruitful advertising ground for companies like Procter & Gamble, Phillip Morris, and Coca-Cola.

GENERAL TRENDS

Several general trends accelerated in the 1990s. Many ads used the rugged outdoors to sell products.

Automobiles, especially trucks and sports utility vehicles, were frequently depicted tearing through the most hostile of environments. The 1996 Nissan Pathfinder, for instance, employed a campaign that took the vehicle on an African safari, while emphasizing the interior luxury and comfort that the would-be adventurer enjoyed. But other products also used the outdoors as a focal point in their ads. Food, clothing, telephone service, and virtually any other product could be sold by depicting individuals in the wilderness. Besides appealing to individuality, these ads to some degree endorsed the growing environmental concerns of consumers. These commercials and advertisements also provided an appealing setting for individuals who felt trapped by urban life.

Advertisers also exploited nostalgia. In general, American culture seemed to have a renewed interest in the recent past, as evidenced by a rise in "retro" fashions. Consequently, many ads sought to capture the look of the 1950s, 1960s, 1970s, or even, near the end of the decade, the 1980s. These eras were almost universally idealized in the ads, though the 1950s were often emphasized as kitschy rather than cool.

As young people of Generation X (generally considered to be those born between 1965 and 1980) and of the following generation developed their own sources of disposable income, advertisers targeted them by appealing to their specific interests. These young people had often been seen as defining themselves in opposition to mainstream society. As a result, the advertising directed at them exploited this concept, expounding on the idea that older individuals were somehow out of touch, and implying that the products under scrutiny were somehow rebellious. Extreme sports, like skateboarding and snowboarding, were frequent visuals used in these ads, even if they had little to do with the product being sold.

INNOVATION IN ADVERTISING

The common themes aside, advertising in the 1990s saw much experimentation. Many advertisers believed that startling, unusual ads would catch consumer attention far better than traditional approaches. A print ad for the Porsche 911 Turbo, for instance, downplayed the technical features and even the status of the car. Instead, it featured a photograph of the car with the slogan "Kills bugs fast."

One of the strongest advertising campaigns of the 1990s was for milk, which had never been considered a high-profile product. The California Fluid Milk Processor's Advisory Board (CFMPA), in seeking to improve the rather lackluster image of milk, created two wildly popular campaigns. The television campaign was kicked off by a commercial in which a young man sat eating a sandwich in a library filled with memorabilia related to Aaron Burr's shooting of Alexander Hamilton. He received a phone call from a radio station which offered him a chance to win $50,000 if he could answer a trivia question. The question was "Who shot Alexander Hamilton?" The man, with

ADVERTISING SLOGANS OF THE 1990s

"Generation Next," Pepsi-Cola, 1997

"Got Milk?" California Milk Processor Board, 1993*

"Always Coca-Cola," Coca-Cola, 1993*

"Think Different," Apple Computer, 1997

"Life is a journey. Enjoy the ride." Nissan, 1996

"Be like Mike" [Michael Jordan], Gatorade, 1991

"Can't beat the real thing," Coca-Cola, 1990

"Like a Rock," Chevrolet, 1991

"Beef: It's What's For Dinner," National Cattlemen's Beef Association, 1992

"Crave the Wave," Ocean Spray Cranberries, 1993

"Easy, breezy, beautiful Cover Girl," Cover Girl cosmetics, 1997

"Life is short. Play hard," Reebok, 1991

"Drivers wanted," Volkswagen, 1995

"You've got questions. We've got answers." Radio Shack, 1994

"Priceless," MasterCard, 1997

"The snack that smiles back," Goldfish crackers, 1997

"Moving at the speed of business," UPS, 1995

*Among *Advertising Age's* 100 Best Ads of 20th Century. http://adage.com/century/

his mouth full of sandwich and his milk carton empty, was unable to answer. The spot ended with the words, "Got milk?" More commercials followed with similar situations.

The print campaign was as simple as it was popular. The ads depicted various celebrities wearing milk moustaches, accompanied by brief descriptive copy. Celebrities clamored to be a part of the campaign, and soon actors, sports stars, musicians, and other celebrities sported the famous moustache.

TELEMARKETING AND INFOMERCIALS

There was considerable growth of telemarketing in the 1990s, a trend which also contributed to the growth in phone call screening devices and services. Calls from marketers selling phone service plans, magazines, credit cards, and other products and services gave telemarketing a reputation as one of the most infuriating forms of advertising. Additionally, consumer anger ultimately did little to reduce the sheer number of telemarketing calls. In fact, the industry grew during the 1990s, largely because it continued to be profitable. Telemarketing itself was an extremely inexpensive form of marketing, and therefore, returns did not have to be as high as for television and print ads. Annual sales for telemarketers reached $650 billion by 1999.[3]

Due to limited deregulation of commercial time restraints in the mid-1980s, the late 1980s and 1990s saw the rise of the infomercial, a television commercial expanded to 30 minutes or an hour. Infomercials for Soloflex, an exercise device, dominated late night broadcasts in the 1980s. Its success led to a flood of exercise equipment infomercials. Exercise books and videos proved popular subjects for these long advertisements. Exercise guru Billy Blanks made a name for himself and his Tae Bo exercise program through infomercials. Many other products were promoted as well. Over the course of 1991, juicers went from a $10 million industry to one that raked in $380 million a year. The key to the infomercial was that it tried, to some extent, to hide its ultimate purpose of selling a product. Certainly, the programs frequently showed an 800 number to call to order the product at alleged fantastic savings. But it also frequently exhibited a parade of celebrities chatting about the wonders of the product or conducting themselves like television talk show hosts. In short, the infomercial sought to entertain as well as sell because keeping the audience entertained for 30 to 60 minutes might well translate into a sale, or at least the imprinting of a brand name in the viewer's mind.[4]

CELEBRITIES

With the growth of advertising, there came an increased need to stand out from the crowd. The average American was exposed to advertisements so frequently that it was easy for ads to go all but unnoticed. In fact, a 1994 poll suggested that up to 74 percent of Americans switched channels during commercials, and that 50 percent occasionally muted the sound. Advertisers used celebrity spokespersons in an attempt to generate interest in products and services. One of the most commercially fruitful celebrity/advertiser relationships existed between Nike and basketball star Michael Jordan. Jordan was estimated to have been worth $5.2 billion to Nike, including the Air Jordan brand. During the time he appeared in Nike ads, the company went from earning 18 percent of the total retail sales market for sneakers to 43 percent.[5]

Naturally, celebrity advertising had a limited effect if viewers were not familiar with the personality in question. An ad featuring Denver Bronco John Elway, for instance, would carry little weight with a viewer uninterested in professional football. As a result, where and when celebrity-driven ads appeared was important. Ads with sports figures were used in greater volume in sports and men's magazines, while women's magazines typically featured more attractive television and movie stars. Likewise, television ads during sports programming were dominated by sports-related advertising and celebrities. An episode of *Seinfeld* might feature a credit card commercial featuring one of the show's stars. There were, however, celebrities who could successfully appear virtually anywhere, including Michael Jordan and Tiger Woods, who came to be recognized nationwide, even by those who did not follow professional golf.

Michael Jordan, right, a member of the U.S. Olympic basketball team and Sergej Bubka, a member of the CIS track and field team are all smiles during a news conference for Nike in Barcelona, July, 1992. AP Photo.

Celebrity endorsements didn't always work as well as planned. Madonna and Mike Tyson were both tapped to pitch for Pepsi, but the controversies that followed them forced Pepsi to discontinue their ad campaigns. Michael Jackson was a controversial figure, even before Pepsi sponsored his 1993 tour, but the soft drink company distanced itself from the singer after Jackson cancelled the tour due to dehydration.

PRODUCT PLACEMENT

A subtle form of advertising, that of product placement, infiltrated television shows and movies. Product placement involved the exclusive use of certain products in a show. For example, all of the characters in a given show might drink the same brand of soda. The products were not openly advertised, but it was assumed that these brand names would imprint themselves on viewers' minds, thereby increasing the likelihood that consumers would select that product. Linda K. Fuller cited 48 product placements in the 1990 Tom Cruise film *Days of Thunder*.[6] The practice gave rise to placement companies, who received scripts in advance of filming and could determine the best way to slip products into the scenes. The TV drama *Seven Days* featured a clearly placed can of Coca-Cola and a Wells Fargo Bank billboard. What made this particular case a standout over the ubiquitous product placement in the entertainment industry was that these images were actually digitally placed into the scene and were not there when it was first filmed.[7]

In 1991, advertisers utilized the same digital technology to exhume likenesses of dead stars to sell goods. A Coca-Cola ad seamlessly used old movie footage to compile a party scene featuring Louis Armstrong, Humphrey Bogart, James Cagney, Cary Grant, and Groucho Marx. The reanimated celebrities were depicted drinking diet Coke and having a wild and wonderful time. The commercial itself was a technological masterpiece, but many observers found the use of deceased personalities distasteful, and the technique was not widely embraced by advertisers.

CHILDREN AND ADVERTISING

There was considerable controversy about how ads for certain adult goods were geared toward children and young adults. Advertisements for alcohol, particularly beer, portrayed a life of parties, women, and rock 'n' roll. These ads typically featured people in their twenties, but certainly also celebrated a lifestyle that appealed to those in their teens. According to critics, such commercials were a thinly veiled invitation to underage drinking. Cigarettes were also attacked on these grounds. Many attributed the disturbing upward trend of teenage smoking to successful cigarette marketing. One advertising figure was attacked with particular vehemence. In its print and poster ads, Camel cigarettes employed a cartoon character named Joe Camel. Joe, an anthropomorphized camel, was the ultimate smooth character, dressed in a sharp suit, eyes hidden behind sunglasses. Ads depicted the cartoon character surrounded by beautiful women and fast cars, inevitably the center of attention. The fantasy of Joe Camel's life certainly appealed to a broad (if mostly male) demographic, but the fact that he was a funny animal cartoon character stoked fears that he also appealed to children. In fact, a 1991 study found that Joe Camel was as familiar to American six year olds as Mickey Mouse.[8] Camel staunchly denied that they were selling to minors, but in 1997, after much criticism from political leaders, advocacy groups, and the public, the company retired its mascot.

Billboard of Joe Camel smoking a cigarette. St Paul, Minnesota. Courtesy of Steve Skjold/Alamy.

Some attacked the advertising industry for its methods of advertising to children in general. Advertisers often hired psychologists to exploit the mental state of children in their ads. They emphasized the coolness of their products, understanding that children could be extremely persistent in their demands to their parents. Children also possessed more disposable income in the 1990s than ever before. Estimates place the amount of money spent by children and teens between the ages of 4 and 19 at $66 billion in 1992 alone, with $36 billion of that being parents' money.[9] Furthermore, advertisers understood the value in creating a desire on the part of children for certain events and activities, such as dining at fast-food restaurants.

A disturbing trend was the introduction of advertising into forums that had previously not allowed such efforts. Many school districts struggled in the 1990s, facing financial shortfalls and growing student bodies. Classes were getting larger and teachers were underpaid. In addition, with wealthier schools acquiring computers and other high-tech facilities, the financially strapped districts felt woefully inept. For some, advertising seemed the ideal means to improving conditions. In 1993, a Colorado Springs school district became the first to allow ads in hallways and on the sides of school buses. The initial ads for Burger King ended up making the district a disappointing $37,500 a year. However, in 1996, the district hired a marketing expert who negotiated a 10-year contract between the school and Coca-Cola for approximately $11 million.

The success of the Colorado Springs district enticed many other districts to follow suit. One school negotiated a deal with Dr Pepper to place an ad on the school's roof in order to market to overhead planes from the nearby airport.[10] The school district of Derby, Kansas, accepted $1 million from Pepsi, and in exchange, they agreed to serve only Pepsi products and name its elementary school resource center the GenerationNext Center, echoing the company ad slogan. Another school district in Texas was sponsored by the Dr. Pepper Bottling Company of Texas, and included this information on its administrative answering machine and elsewhere.[11] A Georgia school implemented an official "Coke in Education Day" after signing a deal with the Coca-Cola Company. At one point, the 1,200 students of the school, dressed in red and white, formed human letters spelling out the word "Coke." Their picture was taken by a photographer held overhead by crane, but one student revealed a Pepsi T-shirt just as it was shot. The student was suspended one day, amidst nationwide publicity and controversy, but the incident was a dramatic demonstration of the influence advertising could have on a school's administration.[12]

Advertising even found its way into textbooks. Math books, for instance, might include word problems designed around saving money to buy a certain name-brand product, or the number of trademarked food items able to fit into a package.[13] The 1990s also saw the widespread introduction of Channel One, a satellite-TV service ostensibly designed to bring students news and other features, but also riddled with advertising. Channel One typically charged as much as $200,000 for a 30-second spot, which gave advertisers access to its large, captive audience. At the end of the decade, a company called ZapMe! Corporation offered full computer labs, complete with Internet servers and teacher training, with the condition that the computers would contain "brand imaging spots" and marketing research software. In effect, the computers would conduct marketing focus groups in the schools. Around 6,000 schools signed up for the service by 2002.[14]

THE ANTI-DRUG CAMPAIGN

In 1998, Bill Clinton and a bipartisan Congress allocated $195 million a year for a five-year, anti-drug campaign, a large percentage going to advertising. One of the major forces behind the move was the Partnership for a Drug-Free America, which had earlier created a number of television advertisements in which a spokesperson held up an egg with the words, "This is your brain." The pan-fried egg represented "Your brain on drugs." As a part of the new campaign, a new variation appeared in which a young girl smashed the egg with the pan as a representation of "Your brain after snorting heroin." This was followed by a vigorous smashing of everything else in the kitchen as the girl swung her pan with fury and yelled, "This is what your family goes through! And your friends! And your job! And your self-respect! And your future!" At the end, she stared directly into the camera, making the same inquiry seen in those earlier ads: "Any questions?" These were probably the two highest profile ads of the more than 500 anti-drug ads produced by the Partnership for a Drug-Free America from 1989 to 1998. Other ads, however, were attacked for conveying misleading information about drugs and distorting the truth, particularly in their consideration of all drugs as equally harmful. Moreover, many questioned the ultimate effectiveness of scare tactics in advertising and pointed out that such advertising probably had more of an effect on parents than on the intended teen audience, and therefore, did little to reduce the demand for drugs.[15]

POLITICAL ADS

During the decade, there was increased concern about how corporations and individuals financed political candidates and campaigns. Questions increased about how campaign finance money was spent. Political advertising became a hot topic as politicians spent more on ads than ever before. A 1998 study conducted by the Annenberg School for Communication at the University of Southern California revealed that, in the three months leading to the gubernatorial election, major TV stations devoted an average of one half of one percent of their news broadcasting to the race. With so little time being granted them in the news, candidates naturally turned to paid advertising for publicity. Another 1998 survey found that the result was that viewers were four times more likely to see a political commercial than they were to see a political story aired on their local news.[16]

During the 1994 presidential election campaign, nearly $1 billion was spent on advertising for the candidates alone, most of it on television commercials and mailing circulars. That election also came to be seen as one of the sleaziest. Fewer ads argued the merits of the candidate and, rather, lambasted their opponent. Sensing the distaste felt by the American public toward such ads, the 1998 campaign's negativity was initially more tempered, but as the election neared, the advertising became increasingly negative.

NICHE MARKETING

Advertisers placed greater emphasis on niche markets in the 1990s to increase revenues by marketing to marginalized groups. Estimates at the end of the decade were that ethnic minorities would soon be making 30 percent of all consumer purchases.[17] African American-controlled media grew considerably in the decade, as did media directed toward black audiences. Television networks found tremendous success with sitcoms featuring blacks, as did the advertisers who bought commercial time during these shows. Likewise, an increasing number of magazines produced by African Americans and with large black audiences also provided to be excellent advertising territory. Advertisers diversified the types of people who appeared in their ads on the premise that the depiction of a multicultural world not only drew in an ethnic audience, but also made all consumers feel a little better about the world and, consequently, better about the product being pitched.

Asian Americans, Pacific Islanders, Hispanics, Arab Americans, and other ethnic groups, however, constituted smaller segments of the consumer market and had few unique outlets, but many advertisers nonetheless sought to reach those demographics. Spanish language television provided an opportunity for advertisers to reach the Hispanic community, and though some English language ads were dubbed, more were created in Spanish specifically for this outlet.

Advertisers also targeted the gay community as a valuable consumer demographic. Gay media in general grew during the 1990s, as did the number of gays depicted sympathetically in print and television entertainment, perhaps indicating the nation's understanding of the AIDS challenge. A 1998 campaign for Hartford Financial Services Group was created with the gay media in mind, but the growing visibility of gay media allowed it to cross over to the mainstream with relative ease. In 1997, American Express spent $250,000 researching the gay and lesbian market, and came to the conclusion that this was indeed a strong market.[18] Of course, the depiction of gays in advertising, as well as the depiction of ethnic minorities, was intended to accomplish one goal: sell products and services. If these weren't substantial consumer groups, it's unlikely that advertisers would pursue them so vigorously, but these ads did increase the visibility of gays and ethnic minorities, and they may have contributed to a more diversified perception of Americans.

ONLINE ADVERTISING

The rise of the Internet was a huge development in the world of advertising. For the first time since the birth of television, here was an altogether new advertising medium. The innovation of the Internet required advertisers to come up with new ways to market their wares. The great challenge of the Internet was that it was so thoroughly under the control of the user. Companies needed to draw consumers to their particular Web site. Many consumers went online specifically in order to seek out certain goods, but companies also wanted to grab the attention of consumers who were not looking for the specific product or service being sold. Several ways of marketing to this kind of surfing consumer developed.

Association proved to be the most popular of these. The best association a company could make was with one of the major Internet providers. For instance, if a company struck a deal with America Online, then AOL users might be exposed immediately to an advertisement for that company's goods when they signed on. Additionally, search engines might favor a site with which they had an agreement, so that a search for shoes, for example, would list their corporate associates first in their list of Web site hits.

Advertisers could also buy ads on sites that were related to the product they were selling. For example, someone browsing a Web site for a specific car model might see advertisements for the company that manufactured the car, for part suppliers, for books about the vehicle, for company memorabilia, and other related products and services. Small sites provided particularly fruitful ground for advertisers because they provided relatively inexpensive advertising rates and small but extremely focused interest groups. As it was likely that those online had some interest in computers, computer-related advertisements dominated the Web.

Nine of the top 10 online advertisers marketed computer products, including Microsoft, IBM, Digital Equipment, and Excite at the top of the list. Interestingly, many of the top advertisers were also among the top publishers of ads. Excite, for instance, advertised on other Web sites in order to bring surfers to their site, where Excite would, in turn, expose them to numerous other advertisements. In the first half of 1998, Excite spent nearly $5 million dollars on advertising, but brought in more than $47 million in revenues from publishing the ads of others. Yahoo, the top ad publisher, spent more than $3 million dollars on ads, but brought in $54 million.[19]

The Internet provided an unprecedented opportunity for companies to learn about their target audience. Typically, an advertiser could target a potential customer according to the region from which they accessed the Internet. In addition, Web sites could be used to keep track of how customers progressed though a site, thereby gauging what topics and displays had the most positive effect on an individual or specific groups. A number of Web sites and online surveys gave surfers questionnaires that frequently focused on public opinion. A survey might ask about politics or other issues in the news, or about entertainment and sports events. The surveys provided amusement for surfers who could compare their opinions and predictions to the online community at large. They also provided information to Internet service providers and other companies about the attitudes and demographics of their audience. Those companies then subsequently designed ads to appeal to those demographics. A 1998 government study discovered that out of the Web sites aimed at children, 89 percent asked for personal information in order to market to the demographic. This fact led directly to the April 2000 passage of the Children's Online Privacy Protection Act.

Ultimately, despite the trials that came with exploiting this new media, online advertising became as much a part of life to many Americans as the commercials on network television. Online advertising began in earnest about 1994, but by 1999, it had grown into a $1.8 billion industry.[20]

Architecture of the 1990s

Architecture has always experienced the conflict between art and commerce. At first glance, it might appear that, in the 1990s, commerce clearly won out over art, particularly with the rapid development of urban landscapes, not only on the fringes of large cities, but also in rural communities. Small communities expanded as national corporations came to realize the significant untapped markets in such areas, and, while shopping malls remained a force, superstores (most notably, Wal-Mart) entered new markets, changing landscapes enormously. The continued growth of the suburbs led to increased urban sprawl.

TECHNOLOGY AND ARCHITECTURE

For more traditional architects, the 1990s was a particularly challenging decade. The economic recession of the late 1980s and early 1990s made an already competitive employment market considerably worse, especially for new graduates. Many of those who found jobs were employed in the often creatively stifling world of corporate projects. The general dissatisfaction with such projects seems to have manifested itself in the 1999 American Institute of Architects Honor Awards, which only recognized two corporate buildings (the K. J. McNitt Building in Oklahoma City, designed by Elliott Associates Architects, and the FILA Corporate Headquarters in Maryland, whose award-winning interiors were designed by Shelton, Mindel & Associates), much in contrast to the 1980s, when such corporate works were the high-profile, high-prestige projects.[1]

Given the difficulties facing young architects, in a business climate that limited creative opportunities for all but the most established of architects, many turned to other avenues of self-expression. The entertainment world, especially the movie and electronic game industries, provided a new venue for some architects. As computer game environments became more sophisticated, thousands of new architecture graduates pursued careers in computer technology. Architects were allowed freedom not limited by corporate or fiscal concerns, and cyber-structures could flout conventional rules of structural soundness as well. Of course, one of the greatest draws was money. At the end of the century, the average pay for a newly graduated architecture firm intern was less than $40,000 a year. The architects working in the gaming field typically made $50,000. Moreover, as the movie industry came to use more and more computer graphics in film, the call from Hollywood for architects grew even more alluring, with greater pay opportunities.[2]

One reason that so many young architects proved so adept in computer graphic design was that computers had become as vital a tool for real-world architecture as for the virtual worlds. Architectural software became central to design of all sorts, including city planning and building construction. More than simply a tool for illustrating plans, computers allowed architects and city planners to gauge structural integrity and manage space. Traffic flow, for instance, could be modeled in virtual cities before the expensive work of constructing roads actually began. And even as computers came to prominence in architectural design, architects also found themselves in a position where they had to accommodate the growing technological functions of buildings. Such developments required designers, particularly those working on business buildings, to think about new configurations for computer work spaces, the reduced amount of space needed for filing systems, and the wiring of a structure for inter-office computerized communications.

FRANK GEHRY

For all the utilitarianism of 1990s architecture, there was room for structures that pushed the boundaries and redefined how Americans thought about buildings. One of the general trends, started in earlier decades but further emphasized in the 1990s, was toward a rather industrial, even incomplete look. Many newer buildings seemed to leave the nature of their construction apparent. Glass work, for instance, allowed one to see through the walls to the supports of a structure. Other buildings emphasized the steel and concrete instead of covering them, exposing the structural skeleton, as well as the duct systems. There was also a continuing move away from symmetry, toward a more fluid and chaotic look, as in the work of Frank Gehry (1929–).

The recipient of many international awards and honors over the course of the decade, Gehry stood as one of the 1990s most renowned

The Frederick R. Weisman Art Museum, by architect Frank Gehry, on the University of Minnesota Campus. Courtesy of Steve Skjold/Alamy.

architects. He won the Pritzker Prize for architecture in 1989, marking a turning point in his career. Critics claimed his work was structurally impractical and unrealistic, but Gehry continued to push the envelope with striking, expressionistic buildings that were still structurally sound. By the end of the 1990s, Gehry had earned the respect of his peers and much of the general public. In 1998, he was awarded the National Medal of the Arts, and in 1999, he was named a Gold Medalist by the American Institute of Architects, taking his place among such previous recipients as Thomas Jefferson and Frank Lloyd Wright.

More important, Gehry earned several high profile jobs. The Frederick R. Weisman Art Museum (1993) on the campus of the University of Minnesota, almost defied description, with a look that was simultaneously industrial and organic, constructed of stainless steel and orange brick, and exhibiting various structural angles that seem to follow no form. Perhaps Gehry's greatest structure was the Guggenheim Museum in Bilbao, Spain, begun in 1991, completed in 1997, and exhibiting the same kind of expressionistic freedom of design demonstrated by the Weisman Museum. Gehry also designed significant portions of the Paris, France, Disneyland in the late 1980s and early 1990s, which led to his commission to design the Disney Concert Hall (1989–2001) to house the Los Angeles Philharmonic.

I. M. PEI

The renowned architect I. M. (Ieoh Ming) Pei (1917–) was less widely visible in the 1990s than he was in the 1980s and in earlier years, but his firm of Pei Cobb Freed & Partners made a significant contribution to the American cultural landscape with the United States Holocaust Memorial Museum in Washington, D.C. The museum, completed in 1993, presented a considerable challenge. How could a mere building measure up to the historical importance, to the human tragedy of the Nazi concentration camps? Ultimately, a building could not, so the architects instead attempted to capture select elements of the Holocaust experience. The museum was a modular design, with different sections of the building hinting at different aspects of the concentration camp experience. The towers suggested the watchtowers of the camps, and the gantry-bridges suggested the Warsaw ghetto. High walls and narrow hallways with sinister doorways gave one the impression of a prison walkway, made all the more claustrophobic by the photographs of victims of the Holocaust covering every vertical surface.[3] The Holocaust Memorial Museum also included a stark and haunting central "Hall of Witness" lit by an overhead skylight. Although principally overseen by partner James Ingo Freed, Pei's interest in order and geometrical shapes was clearly noticeable in the museum's design, particularly in the pyramidal towers and the glass work of the Hall of Witness skylight.

Glass Architecture

Pei's work with glass provided a model for architects across the world. *Smithsonian* magazine, in fact, noting the large number of major glass buildings in the works, proclaimed a new age of glass construction. New technologies and building methods improved glass's standing considerably. For example, Design Alliance Architects designed the Alcoa Corporate Center, which opened in 1998 in Pittsburgh. The building appeared almost to be principally made of glass, with but a thin latticework of steel encasing it. The building was even more striking for its location, just alongside the Allegheny River. During the day, it catches the sunlight reflected off the water and sparkles. During the night, it reflects its own otherworldly glow off the surface of the river.

Even more striking was the work begun on the Rose Center for Earth and Space at the American Museum of Natural History in Manhattan. The Rose Center, designed by the firm of Polshek Partnership Architects, appeared as a 95-foot high glass cube encasing an aluminum sphere, which itself encases the Hayden Planetarium. The building was itself a marvel of scientific engineering and, like the Alcoa center, showed that glass could be used with at least as much freedom, if not more, than steel and masonry, as well as be structurally sound and energy efficient. Another of the many glass-heavy structures, the Sandra Day O'Connor U.S. Courthouse in Phoenix, Arizona, designed by Richard Meier, was notable not

The Rose Center for Earth and Space at the American Museum of Natural History in New York City. Courtesy of Richard Cummins/Alamy.

only for the complex use of steel and glass in its 120-foot-high structure, but also for its energy efficiency.

GREEN ARCHITECTURE

Green architecture developed as an area of specialization in the 1990s. These efforts sought not only to conserve resources, but to make structures coexist organically with the environment, so as not to appear like an environmental intrusion. At one end of the spectrum was architect Obie Bowman, who designed numerous buildings, like the Spring Lake Park Visitors Center in Sonoma County, California, which blended harmoniously with the landscape. The 2,000-square-foot building was constructed in something of a pyramid shape, looking like a small hill rising from the surrounding forest. Solar collectors provided warmth and suction ducts drew cool air inside during the summer months.[4]

Concerns about energy, the environment, and the physical and psychological well-being of citizens led some cities to commission environmentally conscious architects for urban projects. For environmentalist architects, the negotiation between nature and the costs of technology became paramount. Construction and building, regardless of the precautions taken, would necessarily involve some kind of cost to the environment.

One of the most notable ecologically conscious buildings erected in the 1990s was the Southern Progress Building in Birmingham, Alabama, designed by Jova/Daniels/Busby Inc., with the assistance of landscape architect Robert E. Marvin. The Southern Progress Corporation, a book and magazine publisher, long held to the idea of "responsible and enlightened use of the land," and the building to house the company was designed with this in mind. Built in 1991, within a 27-acre suburban forest setting, the architects and designers took care in its placement and design so that few trees were cut and little smoothing of the hillside site was necessary. In fact, the site was cleared by hand, rather than by heavy equipment, in order to spare the environment as much as possible. The five-story Southern Progress Building was expanded in 1994, but it remained so integrated with the environment as to be practically undetectable from the nearby highway.[5]

MUSEUMS

In the 1990s, museums seemed to become the new showcase for imaginative architects. In addition to Gehry's Guggenheim and Weisman museums, many other high-profile museums and exhibition halls were built. The buildings themselves became showpieces. Among these was the Getty Center, one of influential architect Richard Meier's most ambitious projects. Begun in 1984, the Getty Center opened in Los Angeles in 1997. More than simply a museum, the Getty Center was an art complex, almost a small city in itself. The center was perched upon a hill, an exclusive futuristic railway strung between it and the city. With its multiple massive buildings, including the J. Paul Getty Museum, and carefully landscaped and water-lined grounds, the Getty was touted as the first billion-dollar construction project in the country. Indeed, compared to the city below, the Getty Center did seem somewhat otherworldly, if not malevolent, and some accused it of being simply inappropriate for the locale, as if Meier had designed it without considering the environment, both urban and natural.

Other significant museums of the 1990s include the Seattle Art Museum (1991) and the San Francisco Museum of Modern Art (1994). The Seattle Museum, designed by Venturi Scott Brown and Associates and located between Seattle's business district and the waterfront, stretched to a height of five stories, made all the more striking by a series of vertical lines running the length of the building. Architect Mario Botta's San Francisco Museum of Modern Art was notable for its striking geometry, especially the enormous circular skylight, angled at 45 degrees, looking much like a gigantic eye peering skyward.

OTHER SIGNIFICANT BUILDINGS

In 2002, *USAWeekend* took the ambitious step of naming the five most important buildings of the twenty-first century, all of which were begun, and some finished, in the 1990s. The list included both the Rose Center and the O'Connor Courthouse. Also included was the Quadracci Pavilion of the Milwaukee Art Museum, which increased gallery space from 90,000 to 117,000 feet, but also proved to be a draw in and of itself with its 250-foot-long suspension bridge and flapping sunscreen. 3Com Midwest Headquarters, located in Rolling Meadows, Illinois, opened in 1999, also made the list. This structure bore some resemblance to a conventional office space, but it took those conventions and literally tilted them. Walls tilted at varying angles flouted the boxiness of most office designs, lending considerable charm to the 3Com Headquarters. This list was rounded out by the Westside Light Rail corridor in Portland, Oregon, which, upon its opening in 1998, offered the deepest transit station in North America, reaching 260 feet below ground. The winner of the White House Presidential Award for Design Excellence, much care was put into making the corridor environmentally and aesthetically friendly. The careful combination of glass, stone, and organic materials made the corridor an inviting and comfortable environment for travellers.[6]

One of the decade's largest architectural projects was the Denver International Airport Terminal Building, designed by Fentress Bradburn Architects, and erected in 1995. This massive terminal stretches 900 feet long and 240 feet wide, but more striking than its size was its external appearance. The roofing of the Terminal Building consisted of Teflon-coated fiberglass layers draped over steel masts placed 150 feet apart. The result was what appeared to be a series of white tents representing snow-covered mountain peaks.

URBAN SPRAWL AND SUBURBANIZATION

The beginning of urban sprawl and, indeed, of the suburbs, is generally thought to have been after World War II, as GIs, financed by government grants, moved away from the cities and into the newly developed suburbs. They typically sought to escape the older and, in many cases, declining areas, driven by the desire to have a fresh start and to improve their social status. The older areas came to be increasingly inhabited by the lower class and largely ignored by policy makers.

The decade saw the rise of a new kind of suburb. Earlier suburbs were largely designed as affordable housing, easily available to middle class families. But the newer suburbs were frequently of a different sort, both architecturally and demographically. The houses were larger than previous models, with 3,000 square feet or more not being unusual. The single story or small bi-level dwellings of prior generations were transformed to multi-storied mini-mansions. Such houses, sometimes referred to by detractors as *McMansions,* in reference to the McDonalds' fast-food chain, were frequently prefab, or modular, with parts largely built off-site and fitted together at the desired location. A study released by the Department of Housing and Urban Development reported that the number of prefab houses shipped in 1996 reached 363,000, more than double the number reported in a 1991 study.[7] While conformity had always been an aspect of the traditional suburbs, this seemed even more the case with the new version. An older suburban neighborhood might have houses that all conformed to the same basic floor plan and the same sized plot of land, but it did not exhibit the same monochromatic nature of the new suburbs, wherein no house, either on account of structure or color, would stand out. Suburban housing developments frequently would be divided into clusters of houses at different costs. A particular development, for instance, could have a cluster of houses all selling for $350,000, and a second cluster with $200,000 houses, and so on.

This separation helped contribute to a segregation of the populace on the basis of wealth. Thus, the new suburbs, especially the more affluent segments, came to be marketed not only for location and quality of construction, but also on exclusivity.[8] At the extreme, this exclusivity manifested itself in the form of gated communities, where residents needed special pass codes to enter the neighborhood. A 1997 survey placed the number of gated communities in the United States at approximately 20,000.[9] Among the general populace, the idea of gated communities, designed to keep out all but an elite few, met with considerable disapproval. Yet the new affluent suburbs were virtually as exclusive and protected from the masses by prohibitive housing costs and distance from urban areas. The class distinction between those who could afford the new suburbs and those left to the old suburbs and inner cities was marked. Most families in the new suburbs tended to be middle class families using credit to purchase a house. The ownership of such a house placed families somehow above those forced to live in cities or in the old suburbs that had once offered the top-notch homes.

When this previous generation of suburbia had first sprung up in the postwar years, there had been concern about how they drew money out of the cities, and this was also a challenge in the 1990s. Many businesses left the cities to relocate nearer the growing suburban areas, as well as the increased disposable income possessed by those living there. Likewise, government money that might be used in the cities shifted to construct and maintain suburban infrastructure, from sewers and plumbing to communication wiring and roads. Vitally important was the establishment of roads from the suburbs to the cities, where many of the suburban inhabitants worked. New highways were constructed to connect the urban centers with the suburban fringes. In areas that already had highway access, the increased commuter traffic necessitated roadway development, particularly involving the widening of roads.

URBAN RENEWAL

The 1990s saw a renewed fight against urban decay, as many cities attempted to revitalize downtowns and other urban areas that had come to be plagued by structural decay, poverty, and crime.

New York provides a good example. Although certain areas had experienced some significant revitalization, there were still areas that remained in relative ruin. The problem lies in the fact that the decay of urban buildings was part of a larger problem. Aggressive city planning and architectural repair needed to be supported by social services designed to combat poverty and crime. It was believed that the physical revitalization of an area—the refurbishing of buildings, and the substitution of irreparably dilapidated structures with new ones—would draw wealth, both in the form of consumers and businesses. This often led, however, to a mere relocating of the negative social elements of urban decay to neighborhoods still in a state of disrepair. In New York, the revitalization appeared to have helped the rich and middle class more than those living below the poverty line, about one-quarter of the city's population. Still, the city saw some truly desperate neighborhoods brought back to life. In 1997, President Clinton visited the South Bronx to celebrate its improvement. The South Bronx had once been renowned for its state of decay and disarray, but in the 1990s, significant portions were rebuilt, with buildings that had once been abandoned, or burned, or otherwise damaged, now reconstructed.[10] Likewise, other areas of New York, including downtown, were brought out of their state of disrepair. Other cities experienced similar patterns.

Of vital importance to revitalization was the drawing of big business to urban areas. But major corporations not only brought new wealth to urban areas, but effected an architectural change in developing communities as well, bringing a growing homogeneity across America's landscape. Smaller shops, like a Starbucks coffee shop or a McDonald's restaurant, could move into a community without overtly altering its look, but this was not the case for larger stores. Wal-Mart stores, for instance, could not fit easily into a pre-established strip mall. Utilitarian in their design, the superstores frequently gave the impression that a giant cube with few architectural frills and a vast spread of parking spaces had been dropped into the middle of a community. Moreover, Wal-Mart was accused of contributing to urban sprawl and urban blight because the stores were frequently constructed on the previously unbroken ground at the edges of developing cities. In addition, by having so many cheap goods under one roof, such stores took customers away from small businesses, including those located in downtown areas. With less incentive to go downtown, patrons of such stores dwindled, and small businesses vacated buildings, leaving them subject to eventual dilapidation, and, in some cities, the eventual need for more urban revitalization. As a result, in some communities, active efforts were made to keep stores like Wal-Marts out.[11]

Wal-Mart was not the only cause of the changing landscape of American cities. The 1990s saw the spread of a multitude of similar new buildings, including not only other department stores like Target and Super Kmart, but also specialty superstores like Barnes and Noble for books, Gart Sports for sporting equipment, and others.

With growing homogeneity and growing reliance on pre-fab buildings, the decade was somewhat difficult and creatively stifling for architects. The 1990s were an exciting, if difficult, period for the art of architecture, however. A March 2000 article in *Architectural Record* asked the question, "Is there a place for architecture?" The answer provided by the article was a resounding "yes," but it pointed out that the place for architects had changed and that architects would need to get involved in urban and suburban issues, well beyond the design and construction of single buildings.

Cities grew in the 1990s largely without the influence of architects; growth was instead handled primarily by city planners, developers, and political leaders. Firms became involved in the planning and design of communities, in considering the forces of the natural environment, traffic patterns, and surrounding urban areas. Other firms specialized in the renovation and revitalization of older buildings and neighborhoods.

Books

Newspapers, Magazines, and Comics of the 1990s

Perhaps more significant than the actual literary production of the 1990s were the tremendous changes occurring in the way literature was distributed. The book business experienced an unprecedented and unexpected boom.[1] This has largely been attributed to three factors. The first involved the changing image of the bookstore, particularly with the development of book superstores, led by Borders and Barnes & Noble. Second, the Internet stimulated the growth of the book industry as online bookstores, spearheaded by Amazon.com, provided the option of purchasing books from home. The third factor was an increased attention to literature in the mass media, best exemplified by Oprah Winfrey's televised reading group.

SUPERSTORES

Given the large scale of their operations, both as individually large stores and as part of large corporations, superstores gained several advantages in the marketplace. Their purchasing power with book distributors allowed superstores to offer discounts that smaller stores could not match. Moreover, the volume of sales, along with their large stock, allowed these stores to carry prestige items. The philosophy section of a Barnes & Noble superstore, for instance, might provide little revenue, but the presence of a well-stocked philosophy section added to the intellectual image of the store. Smaller stores needed to reserve their display space for items likely to sell well. Superstores also offered spaciousness and comfort. Liberally scattered chairs and sofas, along with low-pressure salesmanship, created a comfortable shopping (and browsing) environment that encouraged the idea of reading. Some stores offered videos, software, and music as well. Most offered cafés where patrons could purchase coffee concoctions, as well as pastries and light lunch foods. Barnes & Noble, for instance, formed a partnership with Starbucks coffee. These cafés, originally intended as just a supplement to the bookstores, quickly became a significant draw in and of themselves. Some stores even offered regular singles nights at their cafés.

Of course, with the rise of these superstores, smaller booksellers suffered. The struggle to keep up with the superstores' competitive prices and large selections eventually forced many bookstores to close. Those independent booksellers that survived generally filled a niche, such as focusing on mysteries or regional books.

ONLINE BOOK BUYING

Even as Barnes & Noble and Borders laid claim to a large segment of book buyers via their physical sites, a new avenue of sales debuted in cyberspace. In July 1995, Jeffrey P. Bezos launched an Internet site called Amazon.com with the stated mission: "to use the Internet to transform book buying into the fastest, easiest, and most enjoyable shopping experience possible."[2] The service proved an immediate success. Retail bookstores felt the crunch as consumers took advantage of Amazon's convenience. The online company's stock skyrocketed in the first few years of the company's existence, but Amazon itself was struggling, its expenses virtually eliminating its profits.

Despite its early difficulties, however, Amazon continued to experience astonishing growth. In 1999, for instance, the site's net sales were a full 169 percent higher than they had been for 1998. Moreover, in 1999, Amazon.com shipped some $16 million worth of merchandise in a single day, more than that for the entire year of 1996. Generally, Amazon managed to gain a degree of financial stability due to this growth, as well as its extension into music, software, video cassettes and DVDs, toys and games, and more. In addition, the company also offered access to auctions and other distributors of out-of-print and rare books, thereby providing a service not available from most book retailers. The site forged partnerships with several other non-book Internet companies, including pets.com, HomeGrocer.com, drugstore.com, and Gear.com (specializing in sporting goods).

The success of Amazon led other book retailers to exploit the Internet. Barnes & Noble launched its own Web-based business in March of 1997, which became the second largest online book distributor. Like Amazon.com, barnesandnoble.com did not limit itself to books. It also featured live online author chats and an archive of interviews with writers.

ONLINE PUBLISHING

The 1990s saw tentative forays into online publishing. Online journals and Web zines flourished as the Internet provided a new and inexpensive way for publishers, editors, and writers to reach wider audiences. Major publishers, however, only took minor steps into the field. Obstacles included the cost of digitizing existing texts, developing new technologies for e-book distribution, and the as-yet-undetermined method of handling e-book pricing and rights. In addition, the sheer mass of material on the Web made it difficult for a "small-press" online magazine to stand out. Some online publishers charged access fees, but publishers were limited by the amount most readers were willing to pay. These factors, combined with the fact that many of these publications were geared toward a rather select audience, largely limited Web publishing to a hobby or academic resource.

THE OPRAH EFFECT

As electronic publishing heated up, physical books nonetheless flourished in new ways. Television, long regarded as the greatest threat to literacy, sent hoards of shoppers into bookstores. Of all the television personalities recommending books, none came close to the influence of Oprah Winfrey. *The Oprah Winfrey Show* had long featured guests publicizing their books, but prior to 1996, these were generally nonfiction titles, frequently with a spiritual bent, like Sarah Ban Breathnach's *Simple Abundance* and Gary Zukov's *Seat of the Soul*. It became clear to booksellers and to producers of the show that sales on such titles experienced a notable, even phenomenal, growth. In some cases, distributors' supplies of a title were exhausted, and the publisher quickly went back to the presses.

In July 1993, Winfrey hosted a week's worth of shows featuring fiction writers she admired (or, as she phrased it, writers she would like to have dinner with). Included were Deepak Chopra, Maya Angelou, M. Scott Peck, Elie Weisel, and Andrew Vachss. While the authors did garner increased sales, the show itself sunk in the ratings, probably because viewers were not necessarily familiar with the work of the writers in question, and had little interest in the interviews. The solution came in September 1996 when Winfrey started her on-the-air fiction book club with *The Deep End of the Ocean,* Jacquelyn Mitchard's debut novel. In this new format, Winfrey began announcing the title of a novel far enough in advance so that viewers could acquire and read it before the broadcast of the discussion, commonly held over a dinner attended by lucky viewers (invited on the basis of their letters to Oprah regarding the book), the author, and the host.[3]

The ratings for the book club discussions proved to be steady, even improving as the club gained exposure and momentum. However, the real repercussions of Oprah's Book Club were felt in the literary marketplace. It soon became clear that such an endorsement would not only improve a book's sales figures considerably, but would invariably guarantee it a spot, usually the top spot, on the best seller lists. *The Deep End of the Ocean* achieved the top spot on the *New York Times* best-seller list almost immediately after being mentioned on Winfrey's show. Many of the books promoted by the club were new novels by first-time writers, like *White Oleander* by Janet Fitch and *Mother of Pearl* by Melinda Haynes, both of which were among the bestselling novels of 1999. The club also breathed new life into old books. Toni Morrison's 1977 novel, *Song of Solomon,* climbed up the paperback best-seller list when it was selected for the club in 1997, achieving sales numbers that dwarfed any the author had previously gotten, even after she was awarded the Pulitzer (for *Beloved*) in 1988 or the Nobel Prize for literature in 1993.

Of course, Oprah's Book Club generated critics. Winfrey clearly favored female authors, for instance, and while she made efforts to include more male writers, she kept in mind her largely female audience. Also, viewers complained that her selections tended to be too depressing. Winfrey responded that life itself was difficult, but that the way the protagonists of these novels dealt with such hardships was, in fact, uplifting. Both of these criticisms were ameliorated somewhat by the selection of Wally Lamb's *She's Come Undone,* as her club selection in January 1997. The book, a coming-of-age novel about a young

Nobel Prize-winning author Toni Morrison holds an orchid during "An Evening with Toni Morrison and Her Friends" at the Cathedral of St. John the Divine in New York, 1994. AP Photo/Kathy Willens.

NOTABLE BOOKS

Harry Potter series, J. K. Rowling (U.S.: 1998–2007)

Goosebumps series, R. L. Stine (1992–)

Jurassic Park, Michael Crichton (1990)

The Sum of All Fears, Tom Clancy (1991)

The Firm, John Grisham (1991)

A Thousand Acres, Jane Smiley (1991)

Loves Music, Loves to Dance, Mary Higgins Clark (1991)

Waiting to Exhale, Terry McMillan (1992)

The Bridges of Madison County, Robert James Waller (1992)

Men Are from Mars, Women Are from Venus, John Gray (1992)

Like Water for Chocolate, Laura Esquivel (1992)

Chicken Soup for the Soul, Richard Canfield (1993)

The Shipping News, E. Annie Proulx (1993)

Snow Falling on Cedars, David Guterson (1994)

The Celestine Prophecy, James Redfield (1994)

Angela's Ashes, Frank McCourt (1996)

The Horse Whisperer, Nicholas Evans (1995)

Midnight in the Garden of Good and Evil, John Berendt (1994)

Primary Colors, Anonymous (Joe Klein) (1996)

Tuesdays with Morrie, Mitch Albom (1997)

Cold Mountain, Charles Frazier (1997)

The Perfect Storm, Sebastian Junger (1997)

Holes, Louis Sachar (1998)

The Bad Beginning (Book 1 in A Series of Unfortunate Events), Lemony Snicket (1999)

woman, was such a popular choice that when Lamb published his second novel, *I Know This Much is True* (1998), Winfrey choose it as a book club selection. Perhaps a more serious criticism of the club came from book-sellers and publishers, who were regularly overrun immediately after the announcement of the latest books. Copies quickly sold out, and irate customers regularly had to place special orders, which were themselves delayed as publishers worked frantically to reprint the books. *Song of Solomon* publisher Plume, for instance, went back to press with that novel more than 10 times after its announcement on *Oprah.* To counter these problems, Oprah Winfrey made arrangements with publishers and booksellers to give them early notice on forthcoming selections.[4]

Despite these criticisms, Oprah's Book Club not only gave the book industry a shot in the arm, but also increased the market for literary fiction. Moreover, the club deserved praise for its infectious emphasis on the joys of reading, which likely brought previous non-readers to bookstores. *The Oprah Winfrey Show* also contributed to the increase of literary discussion groups throughout the decade, though the rise of the superstores had some effect as well. Oprah Winfrey was not the only celebrity to endorse books in the 1990s. Even politicians got into the act, such as Newt Gingrich spurring sales on such titles as *The Federalist Papers* and *Democracy in America.*

VETERAN BEST-SELLING AUTHORS

The greatest selling point for books is name recognition, and while some new writers made inroads during the 1990s, the old literary stalwarts—Stephen King, Mary Higgins Clark, Tom Clancy, Danielle Steel, Anne Rice, Sidney Sheldon, and others—continued to reign. The 1993 list of the top 10 longest-running best sellers, for instance, featured three novels by John Grisham and four by Michael Crichton.[5]

Stephen King had such clout in the publishing industry that he persuaded his publisher to experiment with format. One of King's novels, *The Green Mile,* was published in a series of six short mass-market (pocket book) paperbacks, once a month in 1996. Although the cost of six paperbacks was as much as the price of most of King's hardcover novels, *The Green Mile* was a tremendous success, inspiring other less successful attempts at the same format by others. Although King initially claimed that *The Green Mile* would not be published as a single volume, the decision was reversed, and the novel enjoyed a new life as a single item (bolstered further by the Academy Award–nominated film adaptation). Another King experiment involved the simultaneous publication in 1997 of two novels, *The Regulators* and *Desperation,* written under his early pen name Richard Bachman and under his own name, respectively. While each stood as a self-contained narrative, each also served as a kind of twisted mirror image of the other. Moreover, as the 1990s reached its end, plans were made to release a Stephen King novella, *Riding the Bullet,* exclusively over the Internet.

Most other best-selling authors largely stayed with the material that had won them their acclaim. Tom Clancy, for instance, continued to write the kind of political military techno thriller, which may have seemed more appropriate to the Cold War era, but continued to find a strong audience in the 1990s, with titles such as *The Sum of All Fears* (1991), *Without Remorse* (1993), *Debt of Honor* (1994), *Executive Orders* (1996), and *Rainbow Six* (1998).

FILM, TELEVISION, AND LITERATURE

Also important to the shaping of the best-seller lists were ties with other media. Naturally, many books were boosted in sales by the release of cinematic adaptations. In some cases, such as with *The Green Mile,* books adapted to the screen were already successful. Films, however, enhanced the sales of Patricia Highsmith's *The Talented Mr. Ripley,* John Irving's *The Cider House Rules,* and Susanna Kaysen's *Girl, Interrupted.* The enormous popularity of the James Cameron-directed movie *Titanic* not only spurred sales of official movie books and merchandise, but of virtually any books related to the sinking of the ocean liner. Walter Lord's account of the Titanic, *A Night to Remember,* climbed back onto the best-seller list some 40 years after its original publication.

The media probably had the largest impact on science fiction and fantasy. For many science fiction fans, the event of the decade was the release of a new *Star Wars* movie. But the literary fervor started earlier, with Bantam's release of Timothy Zahn's *Heir to the Empire,* the first in a trilogy, and the first new *Star Wars* novel since 1983. Each of Zahn's novels rode the best-seller lists for weeks. Ultimately, the *Star Wars* publishing franchise became a force on the scale of the ever-popular *Star Trek* franchise. Both franchises increased in popularity during the 1990s, and books from both series made the best-seller lists. Other movies and television shows also found success on the science fiction shelves, including *Stargate, Babylon Five,* and *The X-Files.* Publishers now realized that these movie and TV tie-ins had a serious audience that would pay hardcover prices for materials that it was previously believed could only be sold successfully as mass market paperbacks.

SCIENCE FICTION AND FANTASY

The gaming industry also gave a big boost to the science fiction genre. For instance, TSR, the company best known for creating the Dungeons & Dragons role-playing game, started several lines of fantasy novels. Though related to their role-playing games, TSR novels also stood on their own, accessible to readers with no gaming experience. The novels featured a variety of stories occurring in several shared fantasy universes, the most successful of which were the *Forgotten Realms* and *Dragonlance* series. What may have once been considered disposable, escapist literature now experienced an extraordinary shelf life; all books in these two series remained in print throughout the decade. Although initially published in paperback, their success led TSR to release a growing number of hardcover editions, including *Dragons of Summer Flame,* a *Dragonlance* novel with an impressive 200,000–copy first printing.

There was also growth in computer-game-based literature, including books based on *The Dig, The 7th Guest,* and several titles based on two popular CD-ROM games, *Doom* and *Myst.* Bantam also published a series of novels based on the *Star Wars: X-wing* computer game.[6]

Of course, the science fiction and fantasy market was not all about licensed universes and offered unprecedented opportunities for new writers. Science fiction publisher Tor, for instance, published approximately one first novel per month in 1996. Other publishers followed suit, and many authors enjoyed a level of promotion from their publishers that would have been far less likely for earlier generations of first-time science fiction and fantasy novelists. The 1990s also proved beneficial to established writers, with particular success for Kim Stanley Robinson's *Mars* trilogy, Terry Pratchett's *Discworld* series, and Marion Zimmer-Bradley's *Darkover* series. One of the most successful fantasy series of the

Like so many best-selling books of the twentieth century, *Jurassic Park,* by Michael Crichton (published in 1990), was made into an even more popular movie. The film, released in 1993 and directed by Steven Spielberg, featured spectacular scenes and well-crafted dinosaurs, including the terrifying velociraptor. Courtesy of Photofest.

decade was Robert Jordan's *Wheel of Time* series. Begun in 1990, the projected 10-volume series of high fantasy novels struck a chord with readers who eagerly awaited each new book.

As the genre broadened, publishers marketed books in a way that downplayed the traditional ideas about fantasy and science fiction. Cover art moved away from the typical images of spaceships and dragons toward a more sophisticated look. Certainly, works of science fiction and fantasy had proven to be potential best seller material. Michael Crichton's *Jurassic Park,* a novel about the genetic recreation of Cretaceous dinosaurs in the modern world, was science fiction, but written by an author known for less fantastic works of fiction, and it was clearly marketed as mainstream fiction. Its success as a novel and as a series of films, suggested that there was a large audience for such stories. Understandably, then, many publishers marketed fantasy and science fiction as simply "fiction." Longtime science fiction publisher DAW launched such a line in 1996 with *Killjoy* by Elizabeth Forrest, and then the first in a four-book series (*Otherland*) by its most popular author Tad Williams, under this imprint as well.[7]

MYSTERY AND CRIME FICTION

In the 1990s, the debate about what actually constituted a mystery novel intensified, with many readers, critics, and publishers claiming a distinct difference between the traditional Victorian tales of crime investigation and what might be called procedurals and hard-boiled crime fiction.

Perhaps most notable of these related genres is the legal thriller. Two authors in particular propelled the genre to new heights: Scott Turow and John Grisham. Both authors, trained lawyers, began their writing careers in the late 1980s and quickly became major players on the best-seller lists. Turow published numerous novels, the first, *Presumed Innocent* in 1987, followed by *Burden of Proof* (1990), *Pleading Guilty* (1993), and *The Laws of Our Fathers* (1996). The moral character of the protagonists of these novels varied, from devious and manipulative to decent and dedicated to justice. But Turow always emphasized the psychological elements of their individual strengths and weaknesses over the actual details of any mystery.

John Grisham's first novel, *A Time to Kill,* was published, after numerous rejections from publishers, in 1989 with a first run of 5,000 copies. His second novel, *The Firm* (1991), landed him at the top of best-seller lists. In fact, every Grisham book published thereafter—nine in the 1990s alone—enjoyed long runs on the best-seller lists. Moreover, Grisham's books made for easy cinematic adaptation, resulting in the filming of several of his books: *The Pelican Brief* (1992), *The Firm* (1993), *The Client* (1993), and *A Time to Kill* (1996). *The Rainmaker* (1995) was actually billed as *John Grisham's The Rainmaker,* confirming his place as a literary superstar. Detractors, however, claimed that Grisham's books were formulaic, with a young idealistic lawyer fighting against corruption in giant corporations, government, and the legal profession. The success of Grisham and Turow inspired the publication of legal thrillers by Richard North Patterson, Philip Friedman, Jay Brandon, Steve Martini, and others.

Women writers were well represented in the mystery genre during the 1990s. They had long dominated the subgenre of cozy mysteries, perhaps best represented by Agatha Christie's Miss Marple mysteries. Related to this subgenre was the culinary mystery that also experienced considerable popularity during the decade, with titles like Lou Jane Temple's *Death by Rhubarb* (1996) and Diane Mott Davidson's *The Main Corpse* (1997). These mysteries used a domestic setting and mixed usable recipes into the crime solving. Likewise, animal mysteries continued in popularity. The cat was an especially popular sleuth, including novels by Carole Nelson Douglas, Lydia Adamson, and Lilian Jackson Braun's long-running *The Cat Who...* (e.g., *The Cat Who Said Cheese, The Cat Who Blew the Whistle,* etc.) series.

Female writers also made inroads into the darker side of the field. Patricia Cornwell had repeated best seller success with sometimes gruesome novels, including *The Body Farm* (1994) and *Cause of Death* (1996), about a fictional medical examiner. Sara Paretsky had continued success with her hard-boiled detective, V. I. Warshawski. Sue Grafton's alphabetic series about a tough, bitter private investigator named Kinsey

Millhone began in 1984 with *A is for Alibi,* with an expected conclusion around 2015 with *Z is for Zero.* The 1990s saw the publication of *G is for Gumshoe* through *O is for Outlaw* with each new volume appearing on the best-seller lists. *N is for Noose* broke the one million first print mark for Grafton.[8]

Another novel that was more of a clear-cut mystery (as opposed to crime fiction or a thriller) was David Guterson's first novel, *Snow Falling on Cedars* (1995). The novel involved the trial of a Japanese American man for the murder of a fellow fisherman near Puget Sound in 1954, and the investigation surrounding the death. Despite this rather classical murder-mystery set up, there was much more to the book, including an interracial romance, lush treatments of the landscape, and, perhaps most importantly, significant historical detail involving the defendant's time spent in an American internment camp during World War II. *Snow Falling on Cedars* managed to draw a considerable audience among mystery readers and readers of historical fiction. It also drew a sizable mainstream audience, especially after it won the PEN/Faulkner award. The hardcover sold quite well, but the paperback edition surpassed the 2.5 million sales mark by the end of the decade.[9]

ROMANCE

The romance genre also saw the steady continued success of traditional styles—from demure period pieces to steamy contemporary works—even as the bounds of what could be published changed. As a result, the lines between romance and what has typically been called women's fiction by publishers and retailers began to blur. Authors like the always-popular Danielle Steel and Eileen Goudge could be considered either romance or mainstream, and bookstores might shelve them in either section. Even in those books whose labels might be less disputable, changes took place.[10]

For a 1990s audience, the stereotypical virginal romance protagonist who swoons into the arms of her lover proved problematic. Many modern women found the naiveté of these characters cloying and unrealistic. Consequently, many authors pushed what had generally been fairly strict categorical boundaries. Catherine Coulter, for instance, developed protagonists who were smart and independent of a male hero. Likewise, Diana Gabaldon developed a large and fanatical following with her *Outlander* series. Gabaldon's lead character was a strong, tough-minded woman who was not above playing the part of the seducer of the young virginal man. Moreover, Gabaldon's books—*Outlander* (1991), *Dragonfly in Amber* (1992), *Voyager* (1994), and *Drums of Autumn* (1997)—introduced a level of fantasy largely unknown to the genre prior to the *Outlander* series. The protagonist of Gabaldon's novels began in the series during World War II, but time-traveled to eighteenth century Scotland. Her successes inspired romance writers to incorporate adventure into their books or to use devices traditionally found in science fiction or horror novels, such as time travel, magic, or ghosts.

Other romance writers, such as Sandra Brown, Jayne Ann Krentz, Johanna Lindsey, and Fern Michaels also found crossover audiences. Also reaching the best-seller lists was the 1992 novel, *Scarlett,* a sequel to *Gone with the Wind,* which had more in common with author Alexandra Ripley's roots in the romance genre than with Margaret Mitchell's original novel.

Romance publishers began to broaden their scope to include African American and Hispanic audiences, and to provide modern issues in a romantic context. This broadening successfully drew in new readers to the point that, at the end of the 1990s, an estimated 45 to 50 percent of mass market paperbacks were romances.

At least one best seller, however, walked the line between romance and mainstream. Robert James Waller's 1992 novel, *The Bridges of Madison County,* was a romance in which an Idaho farmer's wife met and fell in love with a *National Geographic* photographer sent to document the title landmarks. Part of the appeal of the book, written in a mixture of spare and purple prose, was that the romance involved an older couple (played by the Meryl Streep and Clint Eastwood in the movie version directed by Eastwood in 1995). The novel sold more than four million copies in a year and claimed a spot on the best-seller list for a year and a half. Waller's second novel, *Slow Waltz at Cedar Bend,* made him the first author to hold both the first and second slots on the hardcover best-seller lists simultaneously. Waller also opened the door to a new popularity for mainstream romances, which covered similar ground as traditional genre romances, but were shelved with general fiction instead, such as Nicholas Sparks's *Message in a Bottle* (1998) and Nicholas Evans's *The Horse Whisperer* (1995).[11]

LITERARY FICTION

Several established literary authors also made the best-seller lists in the 1990s, including Don DeLillo's *Underworld* (1997), Edward Rutherford's *London* (1997), Salman Rushdie's *The Moor's Last Sigh* (1995), and Thomas Pynchon's long-awaited *Mason & Dixon* (1997). Certainly, name recognition made for stronger sales than for similar fiction by relative unknowns (the name Pynchon, for instance, drew a large chunk of the audience for such challenging literature).

Some new writers did create a stir. Leaving behind the gimmicky, hip tones associated with 1980s authors like Bret Easton Ellis, Jay McInerney, and Douglas Coupland, a new breed of young writers created considerable critical stir. *The Secret History* (1992), Donna Tartt's debut novel, took many of the ideas of her predecessors about identity and morality, and infused them with extensive allusions to classical literature. The plot dealt with a group of classics students who reenact a Greek Bacchanal, and, under the influence of drugs and alleged Dionysian frenzy, murder a farmer. The fairly straightforward story of crime and secrets is conveyed with almost overwhelming classicisms. Other writers reinvented the postmodernism of earlier generations. David Foster Wallace, often compared to Pynchon, published a 1,000-page novel *Infinite Jest* (1996), a chronicle of drug abuse and tennis. Likewise, Rick Moody published three novels in the 1990s—*Garden State* (1992), *The Ice Storm* (1994), and *Purple America* (1997)—that demonstrated skillful experimentation with narrative forms and points of view.

POETRY AND MEMOIR

By 1990, poetry had become something of a marginal art form. Cowboy poetry, both live and in print, garnered some attention, though such attention was usually regional. Likewise, poetry slams, a kind of high-energy recitation contest, proliferated, although this was generally confined to college campuses and clubs catering to artistic patrons. The most successful book of poetry of the 1990s was not by an established poet, but by singer-songwriter Jewel Kilcher. In 1995, PBS broadcast *The Language of Life with Bill Moyers,* an eight-episode series featuring 18 poets. The program was critically praised and well-received by those who saw it, but it remains the only one of its kind to be produced in the 1990s. Yet despite this, more poetry books were being published than ever before, suggesting that, small as the audience might be, it was a committed one. Notably, publication of poetry by traditionally marginalized groups—African Americans, Latinos, homosexuals, and so forth—increased, bolstered by small presses devoted to such groups.[12]

Many poets also delved into other genres to express themselves, a strategy that often opened them up to larger audiences. Memoir writing proved to be the genre most inviting to many poets, including Mary Karr whose memoir, *The Liar's Club,* was widely read and well-received. Several memoir titles were among the bestselling nonfiction books of the decade. Two of the most successful were Mitch Albom's *Tuesdays with Morrie* (1998), detailing the author's interaction with an elderly man who served as a kind of life advisor, which sold about a million copies in its first year, and Frank McCourt's *Angela's Ashes* (1996), about the author's childhood in a Irish ghetto, which spent more than 100 weeks on the best-seller list.

SELF-HELP

Self-help books enjoyed continued popularity during the decade. Aside from the Oprah-assisted *Simple Abundance,* a number of self-help books made it to the best-seller lists. Most were of the relationship subgenre, and the most popular of these was John Gray's *Men Are From Mars, Women Are From Venus,* which argued that men and women had very different psychological make-ups, and that the genders needed to accept this difference in order to make their relationships work. The book claimed a spot on the nonfiction lists for more than 200 weeks. Gray came out with numerous variations and elaborations of his blockbuster, such as *Mars and Venus in the Bedroom* (1995) and *Mars and Venus Starting Over* (1998).

Then Richard Canfield's successful series began with the volume *Chicken Soup for the Soul.* These collections of inspiring stories were geared to virtually every possible audience: *Chicken Soup for the Woman's Soul, Chicken Soup for the Teenager's Soul, Chicken Soup for the Pet Lover's Soul, Chicken Soup for the Veteran's Soul,* and so on. A similar, though more limited, series was spawned from William Bennett's *The Book of Virtues* (1993), followed by *The Moral Compass* (1995), and *The Book of Virtue for Kids* (1995).

Begun as a series of books to assist individuals with the varying aspects of computer technology, the...*for Dummies* series soon expanded beyond its initial confines. Even as books like *Windows 98 for Dummies* continued to dominate the computer book market, publisher IDG successfully introduced titles like *Success for Dummies* (1997) by Zig Ziglar. Macmillan/QUE publishers followed suit with their *The Complete Idiot's Guide to*...series, and between them and IDG, an astonishing number of topics were covered, from *Diabetes for Dummies* to *The Complete Idiot's Guide to Hypnosis.*

RELIGIOUS LITERATURE

The 1990s saw a resurgence in books on religion and spirituality. Some titles were assisted by mentions on Oprah Winfrey's show, such as Gary Zukov's *Seat of the Soul* (1998) and Neale Donald Walsch's *Conversations with God* and its sequels. Deepak Chopra's books, which expounded the ideas of "mind-body medicine," included best sellers *Ageless Body, Timeless Mind* (1994) and *The Seven Spiritual Laws of Success* (1996), just two out of more than a dozen books published by the author starting in 1987.

Also experiencing tremendous growth in the decade was the market for books about angels, ranging from art books to inspirational story collections and canonical guides to angels in religion. A 1993 report estimated that since 1990, some 200 books about angels had been published.[13]

A series of religious novels by Jerry B. Jenkins and Tim LaHaye, begun with *Left Behind* (1995), competed with mainstream literature on the best-seller lists. The books detailed the coming of the end times, beginning with the rapture, in which those in God's good graces are taken away. Thereafter, some of those left behind form a "tribulation force" (the title of the second novel, published in 1996) to battle the devil. Aside from espousing a religious philosophy, the novels also provided exciting supernatural adventure stories, which garnered them readership not only among the devoutly religious, but through a much larger segment of the American Christian population.

CHILDREN'S BOOKS

In the 1990s, sales of children's books stayed consistent, but they did not achieve the growth of other areas of the book industry. Part of the slump may have been due to natural market slowing as the children's book market settled and matured. Children's books were also hurt as the computer, as well as electronic gaming systems like Playstation, rose to greater prominence. Book tie-ins did help maintain stability in the market. Tie-ins to Disney films remained popular, with books published for every reading level, from every one of its feature films. Likewise, books featuring television and video game characters, as well as characters from the *Pokémon* collectible card game, had a strong reception, even if books from entirely original concepts struggled.

Despite the slowdown, however, the children's market did have successes. In the first half of the 1990s, one of the greatest of these was R. L. Stine and his *Goosebumps* series. This series of horror novels aimed at young readers started in 1989 and continued steadily into the 1990s. The series became an immediate success with readers, largely due to a deft combination of safe scares and humor. The series continued to grow in popularity until 1996 when it experienced a marked decline in sales, contributing largely to an overall 25 percent sales slump for publisher Scholastic.[14] Still, the success of the series cannot be denied, as more than 160 million copies of *Goosebumps* books were printed, with more than 100 different novels printed. Stine also made a successful foray into young adult literature with his Fear Street line, which inspired numerous imitators. Stine's first adult novel, *Superstitious* (1995), was a critical and commercial flop.

Series books, especially young reader series, proved popular during the decade, particularly *The Baby-Sitters Club* and *American Girls* series, geared toward a female audience. The *American Girls* series was, in fact, several series, each following a particular young, female protagonist, living in a particular time period and region of America. Another successful series—and the series that would help lift Scholastic up after the *Goosebumps* decline—was K. A. Applegate's *Animorphs,* which told the story of a group of youths who could transform into various animals. The power was given to them by an alien who hoped to recruit them to stave off the invasion of Earth by another hostile alien race. The series appealed to a number of interests: thriller, science fiction, and animals.

Of course, no discussion of children's books in the 1990s would be complete without mention of J. K. Rowling's Harry Potter books, about a boy who discovers that he is heir to a family of sorcerers. The first volume, *Harry Potter and the Sorcerer's Stone,* was released in the United States (it was originally published in Rowling's native England as *Harry Potter and the Philosopher's Stone*) in September 1998. It became a quick success and enchanted many readers with its richly drawn fantasy. Book two in the seven-book series, *Harry Potter and the Chamber of Secrets,* was published in the United States in June 1999, and the third volume, *Harry Potter and the Prisoner of Azkaban,* later that same year. At decade's end, the first three *Harry Potter* books occupied three spots on the best seller lists simultaneously. In 2000, prior to the publication of the fourth novel, the *New York Times* began a separate best seller list for children's books, thereby freeing four slots in the fiction list for adult works.

MAGAZINES AND NEWSPAPERS

The magazine market grew significantly in the 1990s, despite fears that online magazines might stifle the demand for the print variety. In a few cases, this was true. Online news cut into newspaper profits, forcing many independent publishers to close their doors or to sell out to media conglomerates. By 1995, eight companies, Gannett, Knight-Ridder, Advance Publications, Times Mirror, Tribune Company, Cox Newspapers, Hearst, and the Washington Post Company owned more than 185 daily newspapers. In 1995, these eight conglomerates formed a national network of online newspapers.[15]

Some men's magazines suffered as a result of the Internet's growth. *Penthouse* and other adult periodicals found that the easy accessibility of pornography online undercut their sales considerably. *Playboy,* which did not rely strictly on nudity for its content, fared considerably better, and so too did a new breed of men's magazine. *Maxim,* originally published in Britain, made its U.S. debut in 1997 to immediate success. The magazine bridged the gap between *Playboy* and magazines like *GQ* and *Esquire* with its mix of fashion, news, sports, entertainment, and, especially, scantily clad women.

NEW MAGAZINES

Entertainment Weekly, 1990

Martha Stewart Living, 1990

Allure, 1991

FamilyFun, 1991

SmartMoney, 1992

Wired, 1993

Vibe, 1993

In Style, 1994

Marie Claire, 1994

George, 1995

Time for Kids World Report, 1995

Newsweek en Espanol, 1996

People en Espanol, 1997

Jane, 1997

Maxim, 1997

ESPN–The Magazine, 1998

Stuff, 1998

CosmoGIRL!, 1999

National Geographic Adventure, 1999

WORDS AND PHRASES

air quotes

babelicious

bedhead

Benjamins (meaning cash, for the face of Benjamin Franklin on the $100 bill)

blamestorming

blended family

bling

blog, blogging, blogger

bootylicious

celebutante

cookie (in computing)

cyberpet

da bomb (excellent)

down-low

e-commerce

e-learning

fashionista

going postal (term for mass murder in the workplace)

google (as a verb, to research on an Internet search engine)

grrrl

metrosexual

mini-me

mixy-matchy and matchy-matchy

muggle

netcast

peeps (hip-hop slang for people)

phat

props (thanks or congratulations)

shout-out (as a noun)

spam (as a verb)

stalkerazzi

Webzine

Wi-Fi

Y2K

Because the women were less risqué than other men's magazines, *Maxim* could be carried in a wider number of locations, even in supermarkets. Moreover, famous actresses and models unwilling to pose nude for other magazines would pose for *Maxim,* which gave the magazine a further boost in sales. The formula was repeated by numerous other magazines, including *Stuff, Bikini,* and the most successful after *Maxim, FHM* (*For Him Magazine*).

Like newspapers, many magazines coupled their paper content with online publications. Advances in desktop publishing also made it easier than ever for individuals to create hard-copy publications, and magazines seemed to cover every possible niche: parents, Christians, hip-hop enthusiasts, rock collectors, and so on. A few new titles deserve mention. In 1992, Time Warner began publishing *Entertainment Weekly,* an entertainment/celebrity magazine. A new major beauty and fashion magazine, *Allure,* first published in 1991, attempted to set itself by emphasizing a nontraditional approach to beauty. One of the most popular periodicals to begin publication during the decade was *Martha Stewart's Living.* Launched in 1991, the magazine's focus on house and home, cooking and entertaining, and crafts, propelled Martha Stewart, already widely known for her books, to even greater fame.

COMICS

The 1990s were a volatile decade for the comic book world. The first years of the decade saw the rise of several new and unprecedented successful independent comic book publishers, as well as some of the greatest sales that the top two publishers, Marvel and DC, had ever seen. In addition, comic books became more respectable, with perhaps the high point being the 1992 awarding of a Pulitzer Prize for Art Spiegelman's graphic novel of the Holocaust, *Maus: A Survivor's Tale* (serialized and published in two volumes from 1980 to 1991). The late 1980s and early 1990s also saw a continued rise in the number of speculative comic book buyers and comic book specialty stores. But by the mid-1990s, partly due to the surplus of product (Marvel at one point was releasing over 150 titles a month), partly due to unsuccessful

HOW OTHERS SEE US

Peanuts

By the time creator Charles Schulz died in 2000, his daily comic strip "Peanuts" was featured in a record 2,500 newspapers around the world. In the five decades since its debut, the strip and its cast of characters, including Charlie Brown and his dog Snoopy, had made its way into public consciousness in 26 different languages. Schulz, declared Italian semiotician and novelist Umberto Eco, was a "modern poet" whose subject was "all the neuroses of a modern citizen of the industrial civilization."

He was also a marketing genius who licensed his characters to the tune of millions of dollars a year. Asia was an especially fertile ground for "Peanuts" merchandising. Products featuring Snoopy were introduced to Japan in 1966, two years before the strip itself appeared there, and the imaginative beagle would prove to be equally popular in South Korea, Singapore, Hong Kong, and the Philippines.

A new Snoopy-related marketing opportunity arises every 12 years, when the Year of the Dog is celebrated in Asia. Japanese author Masuhiko Hirobuchi took advantage of the occasion in 1993 to publish the book *Snoopiology,* which explored "Peanuts" as a tool that Asians could use to understand American culture. The strip, Hirobuchi said, gives such a clear picture of U.S. culture that a solid grounding in its sensibility would help Asian politicians and businesspeople communicate smoothly and clearly with Americans.

Hirobuchi's message resonated with some Asians, but it seemed that just as many people appreciated the strip's "unassuming nature," the clean lines of Schulz's art, and Snoopy's cute cuddliness. In 1998, "Snoopy-mania" ensued when tens of thousands of people in Hong Kong lined up at McDonald's outlets to buy Snoopy figurines dressed in kimonos and other Asian garb, and that same year, the first "Snoopy Place" restaurant opened in Singapore, becoming an instant tourist destination.

speculators, many new publishers and comic shops closed. It has been estimated that from 1993 to 1998, comic book profits dropped some 60 percent, from $800 million to $325 million.[16] Even the major publishers were not immune, with Marvel filing for bankruptcy in 1996. Most comic book distributors ceased business, leaving Diamond Comics Distributors as the only one left by 1997, and comics no longer found their way into non-specialty stores—supermarkets, convenience stores, and mom-and-pop shops.

In 1990, Marvel went public, and the company's stock, as detailed in their first annual report, cleverly disguised as a comic book, quickly skyrocketed. However, a part of this rapid inflation of stock value was the result of an artificially inflated market. In 1991, financier Ron Perelman bought a controlling share of the Marvel stock, which eventually led to financial and corporate wrangling about ownership and control of the company. Meanwhile, the early 1990s saw Marvel launching numerous new comic series, several which garnered record-breaking sales and contributed to a significant change in the look of superhero comics. In 1990, Marvel released a new *SpiderMan* title, written and drawn by fan favorite Todd McFarlane. This was followed in 1991 by Rob Liefeld's *X-Force* and a new *X-Men* title illustrated by Jim Lee, the first issue of which was released in five editions with variant cover art and sold 8 million copies, making it the best-selling comic book of the twentieth century.[17]

These three artists, though of different style and quality, helped to usher in a new look in comics. Their dynamic art tended toward high detail, or in some cases, the impression of high detail. Even more significantly, these artists also tended to use much larger panels, thereby giving the average comic book fewer (though frequently more complex) individual pictures per page and per comic book. Although larger panels had been used on occasion by artists before, the enormous popularity of Lee, Liefeld, McFarlane, and others made this technique, along with the over-rendered line, almost a standard in mainstream comics.

The popularity of these artists also led to industry shake-ups. Dissatisfied with the comics publishers' work-for-hire system, which denied creators ownership rights to their creations, Lee, Liefeld, and McFarlane, along with other favorite artists, Eric Larsen, Marc Silvestri, and Jim Valentino, left Marvel en masse. In 1992, they began publishing their own creator-owned books under the banner of Image Comics. The venture was a commercial success and proved the draw of individual artists. Image quickly became a worthy competitor to the two major publishers, DC and Marvel, with huge sales on books like Liefeld's *Youngblood,* McFarlane's *Spawn,* Lee's *WildC.A.T.s,* Valentino's *Shadowhawk,* Larsen's *Savage Dragon,* and Silvestri's *CyberForce. Youngblood* #1 sold about 1 million copies and *Spawn* #1 sold almost 2 million, well beyond the sales of most comics, even those published by the majors.[18]

While some argued that these books were derivative of Marvel superhero comics, they delivered exactly what fans desired. The successes of Image, however, were somewhat offset by early difficulties. Frequently late shipment of comics and generally poor management strategies chafed with fans, retailers, and distributors. In addition, internal conflicts would eventually lead to the departure of many key members of the Image team. Several artists set up their own production companies, and Liefeld established a separate company, Maximum Press, to publish his own work. In time, Image settled into a pattern of consistent sales, taking its place as a major independent publisher, although it no longer posed a threat to DC or Marvel.

The 1990s saw the birth of many new publishing imprints, a number of which were formed by former Marvel and DC creators encouraged by Image's success story. The most popular of these was Valiant, which, in addition to developing new superhero characters, resurrected heroes from the Gold Key comics line published from the 1950s to the 1980s. Despite considerable early critical and commercial praise, however, Valiant would not survive the decade due in part to a drop off in the quality of Valiant titles, as well as the loss of solid artists like Barry Windsor-Smith and Bob Layton, but Valiant's demise must also be credited to the drying up of the comics market in the latter half of the 1990s.

There were independent publishers that survived the 1990s. Companies such as Drawn & Quarterly, Slave Labor Graphics, Fantagraphics, and Dark Horse Comics catered to a smaller niche market with experimental and alternative titles. Even Dark Horse, which found considerable mainstream success with its movie-licensed titles featuring the likes of the Terminator, Aliens, and Predator, maintained their commitment to alternative comics. Alternative publishers also managed to make considerable inroads in terms of comics' respectability, with their books gaining notable attention in the popular and book trade press and finding their ways into chain bookstores like Barnes & Noble and Borders. Dan Clowes grabbed attention with stories like *Ghost World* (1993–1997), about two teens, recently graduated from high school and trying to find their place in the world, which was made into a movie in 2001.

The success of many alternative titles led DC to create its Vertigo imprint, which specialized in comics geared toward an older, more sophisticated audience. Central to this line was *The Sandman* and related books, in which writer Neil Gaiman created a metaphysically complex universe with the assistance of popular artists like Dave McKean, Kent Williams, and Sam Keith. Additionally, a number of DC's older properties, like *Swamp Thing* and *Doom Patrol* were reborn into the Vertigo line as new spins on traditional horror or superhero comics. The Vertigo line was a success, though sales were somewhat limited because the core comic book market still consisted of younger adolescents. Other imprints started by DC failed, like Helix, their science fiction line, and Milestone, an attempt to cater to African American youths with a line of black superheroes.

Of course, DC stuck with the properties that had put the company into the top tier of comic book publishers, with several comic book events garnering the company nationwide publicity. In 1992, Superman died at the hands of the aptly named villain Doomsday (Superman later came back to life), and in 1993, Batman was temporarily crippled, his back broken by the bad guy Bane. Superman's death, particularly, started a media coup. DC published the issue featuring the hero's death in two editions: a collectors' edition, specially bagged with a black armband, and a standard newsstand edition. The event brought many people into comic shops for the first time, many of them who hadn't read a comic book since their childhood. Some six million issues were sold of these first editions, and they were followed by three additional printings.

Entertainment of the 1990s

TELEVISION

Spurred by the continued success of the Fox network, two major studios, Warner Brothers and Paramount, started their own networks in 1995. WB and Paramount (UPN) networks each started rather slowly before finding its niche. The WB network found large markets for its teen-oriented dramas and its African American sitcoms. The Paramount network, spearheaded by its successful *Star Trek* properties, also found success with these genres and became a major outlet for TV science fiction.

Dramas retained their position as the prestige broadcasts of the networks, leading to a great variety of critically acclaimed shows. Many of them, especially police and medical dramas, cultivated a gritty realism. There were also dramas that were decidedly unrealistic, like filmmaker David Lynch's bizarre *Twin Peaks* (1990–1991), which often baffled its audiences. Science fiction and teen dramas saw unprecedented success, and among all this, there was still room for David Hasselhoff's lifeguard drama, *Baywatch* (1989–2001). The show, whose main draw was attractive people in bathing suits, developed into an international phenomenon, highlighting the importance of the overseas market for American television programming.

The 1990s are also notable for the number of filmmakers, including Lynch, Oliver Stone, Steven Spielberg, Barry Levinson, and George Lucas, who ventured into network television. The decade also saw the continued growth of the news magazine show and the rise of reality TV.

SCIENCE FICTION TV

Science fiction television experienced a renaissance in the 1990s. There was always at least one *Star Trek* series on the air. *Star Trek: The Next Generation* (1987–1994) completed its television voyages, and moved to the big screen. *Star Trek: Deep Space Nine* (1993–1999) set the crew, led by African American Avery Brooks, aboard a space station. *Deep Space Nine* involved considerably more political intrigue than prior *Star Trek* series, but never had as large a viewership as *The Next Generation.* By the series' last season, some critics were calling this the best and most ambitious of the *Star Trek* series. *Star Trek: Voyager* (1995–2001) featured a starship flung by a spatial anomaly to a galaxy far from its own. The crew attempts to return to their home galaxy, impeded by technical crises and hostile alien races. Like all *Star Trek* shows, *Voyager* presented a multicultural crew, featuring an Asian, a Latina, and a Native American, as well as a black Vulcan.

HOW OTHERS SEE US

Jerry Springer and "Reality" TV

The Jerry Springer Show premiered in the United States in 1991 and quickly became a pop-cultural phenomenon there. Regarded by many critics as the harbinger of reality television, the hour-long syndicated talk program featured sensational real-life stories of ordinary people caught up in affairs, drug use, violence, and kinkiness of every description. It was, in the host's own words, a "freak show" that reveled in Americans at their worst, willing to expose themselves for a few minutes of notoriety.

The freak show also proved equally fascinating to audiences outside the United States as TV networks around the world picked it up. At its height, *The Jerry Springer Show* could be seen by viewers in 200 countries, giving them, they were convinced, a look at the way Americans really lived. In 2003, Australian-born writer DBC Pierre claimed that he based the dialogue in his Booker Prize-winning novel *Vernon God Little* on his viewings of *The Jerry Springer Show.* It was the only way, he said, to capture the "American trailer-trash vernacular" of his Texas-based characters. That same year, *Jerry Springer: The Opera* opened in London's West End and caused a furor over its profanity (a rumored, and probably impossible, 8,000 unprintable words were spoken or sung in the show) and religious irreverence.

Religious authorities and intellectual elites excoriated *The Jerry Springer Show* wherever it aired. As an editorialist in a London daily put it, "To Europeans and higher-minded Americans, the people on 'The Jerry Springer Show' look like an American nightmare . . . His programme is a pure democracy of confession, where freedom of speech is extended to its logical conclusion, and every possible lifestyle has equal value." His show, said that same daily, was an "American folly," but nevertheless "changed the way people speak and think."

The show also starred the first female lead in the *Star Trek* franchise, Captain Kathryn Janeway, played by Kate Mulgrew. There were also numerous imitations of *Star Trek,* particularly *Babylon 5* (1994–1995), which quickly garnered a cult following, *SeaQuest DSV* (1993–1995), and *Earth: Final Conflict* (1997–2002), created by Star Trek creator Gene Roddenberry.

The X-Files (1993–2002), produced by Chris Carter, quickly became one of the Fox network's cornerstone shows. The show focused on two FBI agents, Fox Mulder (David Duchovny) and Dana Scully (Gillian Anderson), investigators of the supernatural. Scully, a generally skeptical medical examiner, served as a foil to Mulder's quick intuitive leaps to the most outlandish of conclusions, which often proved to be true. Yet, despite the inherent antagonism between the pair, the series also showcased a growing friendship, which ultimately proved as central to the series as the investigations into reports of vampires, werewolves, aliens, and killer insects. While the moody cinematography, clever writing, and skillful performances garnered the show praise, some attributed its success to how it tapped into a general state of paranoid malaise. A running storyline suggested that elements within the government not only knew about the existence of extraterrestrials but were also running alien genetic experiments on humans. Mulder and Scully's investigations into extraterrestrial activities would consequently bring them into conflict with the authorities they served. Thus, while the two were clearly the good guys, the agency they worked for was shadowy and menacing, reflecting an attitude toward the government held by a sizable segment of the American population. The catchphrases "Trust no one" and "The truth is out there" thereby found a warm reception from viewers. The success of *The X-Files* inspired considerable imitation, like *Dark Skies* (1996–1997) and another Carter show, *Harsh Realm* (1999–2000).

The success of the science fiction genre also encouraged the development of the fantasy genre, which had long been retired from the small screen. The earliest of these was *Hercules: The Legendary Journeys* (1995–1999). This series starred Kevin Sorbo as Hercules and featured elaborate

The X-Files. David Duchovny (as Agent Fox Mulder), Gillian Anderson (as Agent Dana Scully). Courtesy of Photofest.

Entertainment

NOTABLE TV SHOWS

Beverly Hills, 90210

Buffy the Vampire Slayer

Cheers

ER

Everybody Loves Raymond

Frasier

Friends

Home Improvement

L. A. Law

Law & Order

Murphy Brown

NYPD Blue

Seinfeld

Sex and the City

The Simpsons

The Sopranos

fight sequences and special effect-laden action reminiscent of the old Hercules and Sinbad. The series swung from melodrama to slapstick, capturing some of the spirit of the B-horror movies of the series' producer Sam Raimi. Xena was introduced early in the show and soon had her own series: *Xena, Warrior Princess* (1995–2001), which would become the most successful series ever produced in the genre. Xena (Lucy Lawless) was a character torn between her violent, mercenary upbringing and her desire to do good, cultivated by her young companion, Gabriel (Renée O'Connor). *Xena* demonstrated a skillful blend of melodrama, action, humor, and revealing costumes, as well as a playful twist on world history and mythology. The closeness of the relationship between the two women soon lent itself to lesbian readings of the series, which was embraced by gay and straight viewerships alike. The producers of *Xena* played up the angle, alluding to, but never confirming nor denying, the exact relationship between Xena and Gabriel. These shows were followed by imitators such as *Conan* (1998), *The Epic Adventures of Tarzan* (1996), *Beastmaster* (1999–2002), and *The New Adventures of Robin Hood* (1997–1999). By the time *Xena* bowed out in 2001, few other examples of the genre still aired.

RELIGION IN TV DRAMA

The 1990s saw a number of new series featuring a religious angle. Foremost among these was *Touched by an Angel* (1994–2003), starring Roma Downey and Della Reese as angels. Each week, Downey's character would come down to Earth to help people and inspire faith. Although the show was criticized for its pat solutions to social troubles, from alcoholism to racism, and for its sentimental portrayal of angels, it won a sizable viewership by virtue of its wholesome, uplifting storylines.

On a more earthly front, *7th Heaven* (1996–2007) detailed the day-to-day life character Eric Camden (Stephen Collins), a minister in the heart of the Bible Belt, and his family. While the show and its conservative values were highly praised by some, others criticized its lack of realism and general didacticism. Nonetheless, its success suggests that there was a definite audience for family-oriented shows with uncomplicated morals.

POLICE AND MEDICAL DRAMA

The police drama continued to be a staple of television production. The bulk of the police shows of the 1990s owed much to their greatest predecessor, *Hill Street Blues* (1981–1987), but there was also innovation. Of the many such dramas to air during the 1990s, three particularly stood above the rest, both critically and commercially.

Produced by Steven Bochco, David Milch, and David Mills, among others, *NYPD Blue* (1993–2005) garnered much early attention on ABC, mostly because it pushed the boundaries of what a network could show on television. Profanity and brief partial nudity were both common. In fact, actors' contracts often included a clause stating that they would disrobe for the camera if necessary. Responding to the violence, language, and nudity, nearly one-quarter of the network's 225 affiliates refused to carry the first episode, and ABC instituted a "viewer discretion advised" warning before each episode. *NYPD Blue* soon proved to be much more than skin and swearing, however. The show cast a harsh light on the lives of detectives in the New York City police department depicting men and women who, while following their noble vocations, were themselves flawed human beings.

The show saw numerous cast changes, including a rotation of leading men—David Caruso, Jimmy Smits, and Rick Schroder—but one of the show's stalwarts, Dennis Franz, a *Hill Street Blues* alumnus, became one of the most fascinating characters ever to appear on the small screen. Franz's Andy Sipowicz began the show as a violent, brutish, and mean cop. He frequently peppered his profanity-laden speech with racism, homophobia, and sexism. But as the character's life and relationships with his fellow detectives developed, he made an effort to change, controlling his temper and his intolerance, and even becoming a loving family man. Such transformations had been seen on television before, but never had they unfolded so gradually and so realistically. Franz won four Emmys, and the show received numerous awards and recognitions, including Emmys for actors Gordon Clapp and Kim Delaney, as well as Outstanding Dramatic Series.

NBC's *Homicide: Life on the Streets* (1993–1999) was another important contributor to the police drama genre. The show was created by Paul Attanasio and was based on David Simon's book detailing a year in the life of the Baltimore police department. It was produced by Tom Fontana and noted filmmaker Barry Levinson, a Baltimore native who frequently set his films there. The show featured a top-notch cast, including Yaphet Kotto, Ned Beatty, Daniel Baldwin, and Andre Braugher. *Homicide* quickly became a critical success, although it struggled in the ratings. The show continues to be hailed for realistically depicting the lives of homicide detectives and concentrating on the cerebral and emotional pressures of the job far more than on gunfire and sensationalism. It also paid close attention to the victims of violent crime, with the survivors sometimes taking center stage as much as the regular cast. Praised for its stylish verité cinematography and sharp writing, *Homicide* also earned acclaim for its portrait of minorities. At times, nearly half the cast was African American, rare for a television drama, though quite representative of urban Baltimore.

Homicide: Life on the Streets enjoyed several crossover episodes with NBC's *Law & Order,* the third of the major police dramas of the 1990s. *Law & Order* (1990–) functioned in two parts, the first half hour dealing with New York City police detectives investigating a crime, and the latter half following the district attorney's office prosecuting the crime. Thus, *Law & Order* allowed the viewer to see the ultimate results (or lack thereof) of police work in a way less often seen in other police dramas. The show regularly resorted to twist endings, and frequently advertised its storylines as ripped from the headlines. Although *Law & Order* focused less on the private lives of its characters, they nonetheless were subject to emotional turmoil, personal problems, injury, and death. *Law & Order* saw constant cast changes; no actor was on the show for the entire run. While the show starred many highly acclaimed actors, including Jerry Orbach, Sam Waterston, Jill Hennessy, and Paul Sorvino, its success was based on consistently solid storytelling. It had two spin-offs: *Law &*

Order: Special Victims Unit (1999–) and *Law & Order: Criminal Intent* (2001–). No legal thriller came close to matching *Law & Order's* success until ABC's *The Practice* (1997–2004). This David Kelly law firm drama shot to prominence when, in its first year, it won a number of major Emmys, including Outstanding Drama Series.

WELCOME TO COUNTY GENERAL . . .

One of the highest-rated dramas in television history, *ER* is an Emmy Award-winning series created by bestselling novelist Michael Crichton and producer John Wells. The show premiered on NBC September 19, 1994, and is set in the fictional emergency room of County General Hospital in Chicago.

Throughout the years, the series has served as a building block or jumping off point for a number of actors, notably George Clooney, who is now considered one of the biggest film stars in the world. Other original cast members included Noah Wyle, Julianna Margulies, Eriq La Salle, Anthony Edwards, and Sherry Stringfield. The 2008 cast includes Maura Tierney, Mekhi Phifer, John Stamos, and Goran Visnjic. Several *ER* guest stars used their appearances to bolster (or in some cases revive) their careers, including Sally Field, Ray Liotta, Don Cheadle, Bob Newhart, Alan Alda, and Forest Whitaker. Each of these guest performances won Emmy nominations, while Liotta and Field won Emmys, the latter for her portrayal of Dr. Abby Lockhart's schizophrenic mother, and the former for his portrayal of a dying alcoholic.

ER has earned 22 Emmy Awards and received 123 nominations—making it the most Emmy-nominated drama in history. In early 2008, NBC announced that *ER* will end after its 15th season in 2009. The show already enjoys widespread syndication. The enduring popularity of ER has had a significant influence on how the public views emergency room settings and their interactions with doctors and nurses. The dramatic elements of ER portray life in all its gritty, sometimes evil, elements but also in all its moments of joy, awe, and miracles.

The medical drama also proved popular, with two shows, both debuting in 1994, rising to considerable heights: *ER* and *Chicago Hope*. *ER* (1994–) focused on the emergency room operations of County General, a fictitious Chicago hospital. Created by novelist Michael Crichton, the show was unflinching in its camera work, making it one of the bloodiest shows on television. As the series progressed, however, the emphasis gradually turned away from emergency room procedures and focused more on interpersonal relationships. The persistently well-rated series helped propel a number of actors to stardom, including Eric LaSalle, Julianna Margulies, Anthony Edwards, and George Clooney, who became a top film star after his departure from *ER*. *Chicago Hope* (1994–2000) starring, among others, Mandy Patinkin and Hector Elonzo, was a darker show, with a less realistic portrayal of hospital life. The show seemed to bask in the unusual and employed a much greater degree of gallows humor.

YOUTH DRAMA

Fox's *Beverly Hills 90210* (1990–2000) and *Melrose Place* (1992–1999), both produced by Aaron Spelling, enjoyed tremendous popularity. *Beverly Hills 90210* began as a high school-based soap opera, and had immediate appeal to young viewers. *Melrose Place's* stories of betrayal, seduction, and infidelity were aimed at an older audience. Although many of the actors in *Beverly Hills 90210* were in their 20s at the show's start, Jason Priestley, Shannen Doherty, Luke Perry, and others gained renown as the most famous "teenagers" of their time.

The late 1990s also saw the rise of a new kind of teen drama, perhaps best exemplified by *Dawson's Creek* (1998–2003), *Party of Five* (1994–2000), and *Felicity* (1998–2002). These three staples of the WB network's lineup featured realistic teenage characters from middle class backgrounds played by talented teen actors, rather than adults. While these shows were criticized for their alleged depiction of teen promiscuity and the whiny self-importance of the characters, the troubles faced by the young protagonists often echoed the issues facing the young audience.

A new spin on the teen drama was introduced with *Buffy the Vampire Slayer* (WB, 1997–2003), in which Sarah Michelle Geller played the title character, defending her town of Sunnydale from vampires and other forces of darkness. The series, created by Joss Whedon, was based on a minor movie of the same name.

The series was a twist on the traditional horror film, in which the young blonde girl was menaced by some horror. In *Buffy,* the young blonde was more than able to take care of herself. The show skillfully mingled teen drama, horror movie thrills, and considerable humor with clever writing and often stunning cinematography. And while the show was largely ignored for major awards, most likely because of its genre, it regularly landed on critics' lists of best TV shows, and became the WB network's top series. Similar genre-mixing experiments were undertaken, including *Roswell* (WB 1999–2001, UPN 2001–2002), featuring teen extraterrestrials; *Charmed* (WB, 1998–2006), about young witches; and the *Buffy* spin-off, *Angel* (WB, 1999–2004), about a moral vampire who fights evil.

OTHER DRAMAS

Not all of the TV dramas of the 1990s were derivatives of traditional genres. *Twin Peaks* set a precedent for bizarre television in its blending of small-town strangeness with murder-mystery and supernatural occurrences. The show's critical praise and cult following inspired other producers to push the bounds with shows such as *Picket Fences* (CBS, 1992–1996), centered on the sheriff of an off-kilter small town. Another popular series was *Northern Exposure* (CBS, 1990–1995), which told the story of a physician, played by Rob Morrow, sent to an Alaskan town filled with endearingly odd characters.

The end of the decade also saw important developments in cable broadcasting with a number of made-for-cable movies and cable TV series. The most notable of these were HBO's *Sex and the City,* (1998–2004), which detailed the daily lives of a number of young urban professional women, and HBO's *The Sopranos* (1999–2007), which focused principally on the family and professional life of a mobster, Tony Soprano, played by James Gandolfini. Unrestricted by network censors, *The Sopranos* employed violence and coarse language, which offended some, but most took as appropriate to the show's subject matter. *The Sopranos* also became the first cable broadcast to win an Emmy for Best Drama Series.

TELEVISION COMEDY

While the typical domestic and workplace situation comedy continued to thrive, there were important steps forward in the genre. Two shows in particular dominated the world of TV comedy in the 1990s. The first of these, *The Simpsons* (Fox, 1989–) was the first successful prime-time animated series since the *Flintstones* (ABC, 1960–1966). Like that show, its creators modeled *The Simpsons* on the traditional family sitcom. The series, developed by cartoonist Matt Groening, featured Homer Simpson, the dull-witted father, Marge, the straight-laced mother with tall blue hair, Lisa, the super-intelligent daughter, Bart, the mischievous son, and the perennially silent baby, Maggie. The show began by focusing mostly on Bart, but Homer gradually became the prime vehicle through which it mocked ignorance and mob mentality.

The Simpsons turned into one of the wittiest satires on television, taking swipes at conservative and liberal values alike. The world of the series, the town of Springfield, was populated with numerous other characters, including the incompetent police chief, the apathetic reverend, and the town drunk, who added to the variety of issues available for satire. Moreover, in exposing the foibles of these various characters, the show ultimately made the dysfunctional title family the moral center of the series. Remarkably then, while the series displayed a scathing wit, viewers nonetheless sympathized with the characters, even as those same viewers might be the target of the show's satire. The show spawned an enormous marketing franchise, but none of the many animated series to follow in its footsteps, including *The Critic* (ABC, 1994; Fox, 1995), *Family Guy* (1999–2002, 2005–), and Groening's *Futurama* (Fox, 1999–2003), came close to approximating its consistently high ratings.

Two other animated series that aired on cable created quite a stir in the 1990s. The first of these was Mike Judge's *Beavis and Butt-Head* (MTV, 1993–1997), which focused on the two adolescent stars as they watched and mocked music videos. On the occasions that they left the sofa, they typically inflicted some kind of self-injury with the use of fire, a chainsaw, and so on. There was considerable outrage about the series, particularly after a five year old set fire to his house, killing his sister, apparently imitating the characters. The pair had a hit movie based on their adventures, *Beavis and Butt-Head Do America* (1996). Following in their footsteps was the Comedy Central series *South Park* (1997–). The foul-mouthed third-graders of this series, Stan, Kyle, Kenny, and Cartman, were the creations of Matt Stone and Trey Parker. Although laced with toilet humor, the series offered frequently smart social satire, particularly in its indictment of moral hypocrisy in America. Propelled by animation nearly as crude as that of *Beavis and Butt-Head,* as well as by running jokes, like a talking piece of excrement named Mr. Hankey and Kenny dying in nearly every episode, *South Park* reached the big screen in *South Park: Bigger, Longer & Uncut* (1999).

Along with *The Simpsons,* the other cornerstone sitcom of the 1990s was NBC's *Seinfeld* (1990–1998). Created by stand-up comedian Jerry Seinfeld and Larry David, the show focused on four friends, Jerry, George, Elaine, and Kramer, living in New York City. The characters simply went about their day's business, talking about the minutia of their day-to-day lives. Viewers applauded the reality of the show, but the characters of *Seinfeld* were anything but typical Americans, or even typical New Yorkers. The show was an acute satire of modern life's banality by pushing this banality to such extremes that it became quite surreal. The most inconsequential things—a tuna on rye sandwich, the board game Risk, Pez candy dispensers—ended up having extraordinary ramifications. The show frequently made fun of its own conventions and those of the sitcom in general. This practice reached its height with a series of episodes involving the creation of a TV pilot called *Jerry* by George and Jerry. This show-within-a-show closely approximated *Seinfeld,* with fictional actors cast to play the part of the *real* characters, themselves the fictional constructs of *Seinfeld.* The ultimate bizarreness of *Seinfeld* would not be imitated, which is a credit to the skill of the shows' writers and producers, and also to the chemistry between the show's principal cast, Jason Alexander, Julia Louis-Dreyfus, Michael Richards, and Seinfeld. The show's final episode in 1998 garnered 76 million spectators, the largest viewership ever for a sitcom.

There were other significant entries into the sitcom genre, including *Friends* (NBC, 1994–2004) created by Marta Kauffman and David Crane. This series detailed the relationship between a group of six friends in their twenties and early thirties. The show garnered consistently good ratings due to the chemistry between the characters. Moreover, it helped propel the careers of its young cast, Jennifer Aniston, Courtney Cox (Arquette), Lisa Kudrow, Matt LeBlanc, Matthew Perry, and David Schwimmer. It received numerous awards and nominations, including Kudrow's 1998 Emmy win for Outstanding Supporting Actress. Another noteworthy sitcom was *Frasier* (NBC, 1993–2004), a spin-off of *Cheers* (NBC, 1982–1993). In this show, Kelsey Grammer's *Cheers* character, the barfly psychologist Frasier Crane, relocated from Boston to Seattle where he began a call-in radio psychology show. The real focus of the show, however, was Crane's relationship with his father, Martin (John Mahoney), a retired police officer, who moves in with him, as well as with his father's caretaker, Daphne (Jane Leeves), and his brother Niles (David Hyde Pierce). *Frasier* offered unusually cerebral writing for a sitcom and made light-hearted fun of the intellectual, adding to its popularity among an educated, middle class audience. The show won numerous awards, including Emmys for Outstanding Comedy Series every year from 1994 to 1998. *Mad About You* (NBC, *1992*–1999), followed Paul Reiser and Helen Hunt through their quick courtship, their marriage, and the birth of their daughter. Another important series was *Will and Grace* (NBC, 1998–2006) significant for its positive portrayal of homosexuals. The title characters were a gay man and a straight woman who initially shared an apartment. The show explored new comic ground and made a political point about the real place of gays in American culture and society.

The 1990s also saw major activity in the production of African American sitcoms, with the

RADIO DEBUTS OF THE 1990s

"The Michael Reagan Radio Show" (1992): news and political commentary from the Republican strategist, son of U.S. President Ronald Reagan.

"Imus in the Morning" (1993): politics, headlines, guests, and commentary from shock-jock-turned-pundit Don Imus.

"The Jim Bohannon Show" (1993): evening interview show focusing on politics and current events.

"The Dr. Laura Schlessinger Program" (1994): no-nonsense, culturally conservative advice for callers with personal, relationship, and ethical problems.

"The Tom Leykis Show" (1994): "hot talk" afternoon drive-time show featuring crude comedy and sexual themes.

"This American Life" (1995): essays, short fiction, memoirs, and audio features, thematically based.

"The Michael Medved Show" (1996): politics, social issues, pop culture, movies, and entertainment news, with a conservative bent.

"The Jim Rome Show" (1996): "smack-talking" sports talk, along with entertainment news, offbeat headlines, listener call-ins, and interviews.

"Wait, Wait...Don't Tell Me" (1998): news-based quiz show in which comedian panelists try to stump listeners with questions on current headlines and also answer questions themselves.

"The Neal Boortz Show" (1999): interviews and call-in discussions with the libertarian commentator, author, and attorney.

WB and UPN networks leading the way. These included *The Fresh Prince of Bel-Air* (WB, 1990–1996), starring Will Smith; *Moesha* (Nickelodeon, 1996–2001) starring singer Brandy; *Hangin' with Mr. Cooper* (ABC, 1992–1997); and *The Jamie Fox Show* (WB, 1996–2001). They did find large audiences among African Americans, and many claimed that the shows offered funny variations on the true lives of the African American communities. Others believed that these shows exploited long-held racial stereotypes of buffoonish blacks. Among these critics was filmmaker Spike Lee, who offered his critique of them in his movie *Bamboozled* (2000).

COMPUTERS AND CINEMA

The 1990s saw the growth of many new studios and the introduction of numerous young, exciting directors. But perhaps the most significant developments in cinema were technological. The 1990s saw the dramatic influence of digital technology, with the bulk of movie theaters turning to digital sound. In 1990, *Dick Tracy* became the first major release with a digital soundtrack.

Advances in technology allowed for special effects imagery unlike anything previously. In 1993, the technologically groundbreaking *Jurassic Park* hit theaters. This Steven Spielberg thriller about a zoo filled with prehistoric creatures was notable for the dinosaurs that seemed to truly come alive. In fact, these realistically rendered beasts were digitally modeled and animated and placed seamlessly onscreen with live-action performers and settings. The long-awaited new movie in the *Star Wars* series, *Episode One: The Phantom Menace* (1999) was loaded with computer-generated effects, including one character, Jar Jar Binks, who was entirely computer created. (Despite the eye-popping complexity and sophistication of the special effects, however, many diehard fans were disappointed with the script and performances.)

Computer technology led to other startlingly new methods of filmmaking. *Toy Story* (1995) was the first full-length computer-animated feature, from the backgrounds to all the characters, primarily living children's playthings. Each fully computer-animated film that followed (including the 1999 sequel, *Toy Story 2*) featured more convincing computer animation.

The 1994 Robert Zemeckis film, *Forrest Gump,* also demonstrated new uses of computer technology in film. The movie used computer technology to show simple-minded Gump (Tom Hanks) meeting such historical figures as John F. Kennedy and Lyndon B. Johnson. Computer imagery placed Hanks into existing footage of these figures, which was itself computer manipulated to make the figures appear to be interacting with Gump. This technique stirred up considerable controversy about the appropriate use of such technology. The debate was propelled by the advent of commercials featuring dead stars, such as James Cagney, Louis Armstrong, and others, appearing in Diet Coke ads, and John Wayne's image used to hawk Coors Light beer.

Another important use of computers in special effects could be seen in *The Matrix* (1999) directed by the Wachowski brothers. The filmmakers used a new kind of digital effect, which they called "bullet time." Using multiple still cameras, special effects teams could effectively photograph scenes in rapid sequence from multiple angles, and then, assisted by computers, seamlessly animate these still photos. A kind of stop-action animation using live actors, bullet time allowed the makers of *The Matrix* to create stunning action scenes in this science-fiction thriller, in which time seemed to bend at the will of the directors, without any of the artificiality of sped-up or slowed-down film.

The most commercially successful movie of the 1990s, *Titanic,* directed by James Cameron, retold the story of the sinking of the luxury ocean liner. The 1997 film was a triumph of computer and other special effects, but the production of *Titanic* seemed to hearken back to the classic era of cinematic spectacle. The director used a submersible craft to view and film the actual wreckage of the Titanic, and he erected elaborate sets that duplicated sections of the ship. The cost of the project reached some $200 million, which evoked such concern on the part of 20th Century Fox that Cameron forfeited his salary and percentage of the gross. In the end, the film, which featured a rather traditional star-crossed love affair amidst the ocean liner's voyage and destruction, not only made back its money, but broke all box-office records and won several major awards, including Best Director and Best Picture Academy Awards.

INDEPENDENT FILM

In the 1990s, independent producers proved that there was a market for independent film, and many big studios started their own "independent" divisions, such as 20th Century Fox's Fox Searchlight line. The independent film market was further bolstered by the growth of the indy film festival circuit, spearheaded by the Sundance Film Festival. By the end of the decade, however, many were raising red flags about how the major film corporations, with their coopting of independent talent, their purchases of major independent studios (like Columbia TriStar's purchase of Miramax), and their domination of distribution channels, threatened to stifle independent film.

One of the most significant, as well as most debated, independent films of the 1990s was *The Blair Witch Project* (1999), a faux documentary about three film students who go into the woods to make a film about a local legend, and then are assaulted by forces beyond their comprehension. The film was produced on a shoestring budget of $35,000 and looked it. The camera work was handled by the principal actors, the film students, so it appropriately appeared amateurish. The ultimate quality of the film was debatable, but *The Blair Witch Project* became one of the top-grossing films of the year. After its release, much attention was cast on the guerilla publicity campaign as on the film itself. Directors Daniel Myrick and Eduardo Sanchez marketed the film on the Internet and elsewhere as a true story, producing a sizable amount of extra documentation, so that seeing the film was only a part (albeit, a major part) of the Blair Witch experience.

Henry and June (1990), which detailed the affair between writers Henry Miller and Anais Nin, was the first movie to receive the new NC-17 rating, which was meant to designate a film with strong adult, but not pornographic (i.e., X-rated), content. Although *Henry and June,* directed by Phil Kaufman, was rated NC-17, distributors, theaters, and video outlets nonetheless resisted the film just as if it were X-rated. Consequently, the film, though critically praised, remained largely unseen by the bulk of American moviegoers. This movie proved that there was no real restriction on the content of cinema, although it also proved there was also no way of forcing the industry to show such a film.

NEW TALENT

Pulp Fiction (1994), written and directed by Quentin Tarantino, was one of the most significant films of the decade. In 1992, Tarantino directed his first feature, *Reservoir Dogs,* an ultra-violent, low-budget picture that told of the aftermath of a bank robbery gone bad. The script had an almost theatrical patter, stylized, hip, and retro in tone. Moreover, as in *True Romance* (1993), written by Tarantino, the dialogue was filled with references to popular culture, from film, TV, comic books, and pop music.

With the success of *Reservoir Dogs* behind him, Tarantino cut loose with a nonlinear movie that traced the interweaving threads of numerous narratives. Critical praise, Tarantino's reputation, and considerable star power (including Bruce Willis, Uma Thurman, and John Travolta, whose career was reinvigorated by *Pulp Fiction*), brought viewers in droves. Some complained that Tarantino's overwhelming references to pop culture suggested a lack of original ideas. Others criticized Tarantino's use of extreme violence. Certainly, *Pulp Fiction* was much imitated by other filmmakers, and, frequently, in their shallow celebration of violence and "hipness," these imitations demonstrated the excellence of *Pulp Fiction,* which won Tarantino and Roger Avary an Academy Award for their screenplay. Tarantino followed *Pulp Fiction* with *Jackie Brown* (1997), starring Pam Grier in the title role. Though still filled with violence and snappy dialogue, *Jackie Brown* was decidedly less flashy, with a single linear storyline and a single character's plight.

There were other important young filmmakers. Paul Thomas Anderson's first feature *Hard*

The poster for *Pulp Fiction* (1994). Directed by Quentin Tarantino. Shown: Uma Thurman (as Mia Wallace). Courtesy of Photofest.

TOP ACTORS

Tim Allen (1953–)
Sandra Bullock (1964–)
Nicolas Cage (1964–)
Jim Carrey (1962–)
Kevin Costner (1955–)
Tom Cruise (1962–)
Robert De Niro (1943–)
Harrison Ford (1942–)
Jodie Foster (1962–)
Mel Gibson (1956–)
Tom Hanks (1956–)
Helen Hunt (1963–)
Holly Hunter (1958–)
Tommy Lee Jones (1946–)
Mike Myers (1963–)
Julia Roberts (1967–)
Meg Ryan (1961–)
Arnold Schwarzenegger (1947–)
Will Smith (1968–)
Kevin Spacey (1959–)
Denzel Washington (1954–)
Bruce Willis (1955–)

ACADEMY AWARD WINNERS

1990 Picture: *Dances with Wolves*

Director: Kevin Costner, *Dances with Wolves*
Actor: Jeremy Irons, *Reversal of Fortune*
Actress: Kathy Bates, *Misery*

1991 Picture: *The Silence of the Lambs*

Director: Jonathan Demme, *The Silence of the Lambs*
Actor: Anthony Hopkins, *The Silence of the Lambs*
Actress: Jodie Foster, *The Silence of the Lambs*

1992 Picture: *Unforgiven*

Director: Clint Eastwood, *Unforgiven*
Actor: Al Pacino, *Scent of a Woman*
Actress: Emma Thompson, *Howards End*

1993 Picture: *Schindler's List*

Director: Steven Spielberg, *Schindler's List*
Actor: Tom Hanks, *Philadelphia*
Actress: Holly Hunter, *The Piano*

1994 Picture: *Forrest Gump**

Director: Robert Zemeckis, *Forrest Gump*
Actor: Tom Hanks, *Forrest Gump*
Actress: Jessica Lange, *Blue Sky*

1995 Picture: *Braveheart*

Director: Mel Gibson, *Braveheart*
Actor: Nicolas Cage, *Leaving Las Vegas*
Actress: Susan Sarandon, *Dead Man Walking*

1996 Picture: *The English Patient*

Director: Anthony Minghella, *The English Patient*
Actor: Geoffrey Rush, *Shine*
Actress: Frances McDormand, *Fargo*

1997 Picture: *Titanic***

Director: James Cameron, *Titanic*
Actor: Jack Nicholson, *As Good As It Gets*
Actress: Helen Hunt, *As Good As It Gets*

1998 Picture: *Shakespeare in Love*

Director: Steven Spielberg, *Saving Private Ryan*
Actor: Roberto Benigni, *Life Is Beautiful*
Actress: Gwyneth Paltrow, *Shakespeare in Love*

1999 Picture: *American Beauty*

Director: Sam Mendes, *American Beauty*
Actor: Kevin Spacey, *American Beauty*
Actress: Hilary Swank, *Boys Don't Cry*

*Highest grossing of decade
**Highest grossing movie of all time

Entertainment

Eight (a.k.a., *Sydney*) was released in 1997. His next film *Boogie Nights* (1997), which took place in the late 1970s and early 1980s, explored the rise and fall of a male porn star. The film's content was startling for mainstream audiences, but it weaved a multi-layered story about love and fidelity and employed remarkable cinematographic techniques to capture the mindsets of his characters. Anderson followed *Boogie Nights* with *Magnolia* (1999), an elaborate tapestry of many interrelated narrative threads. The film, which starred Tom Cruise, Jason Robards, and Julianne Moore, earned a number of Academy Award nominations, including Best Actor for Cruise and Best Original Screenplay.

Another major new directing talent in the 1990s was Steven Soderbergh, who first gained widespread attention in 1989 with *sex, lies and videotape.* While much of Soderbergh's output in the early 1990s was only moderately well-received, *Out of Sight* (1998) and *The Limey* (1999) offered strikingly original visual experiences. In these films, Soderbergh displayed a sense of visual timing that seemed almost musical. Though a frequently experimental director, Soderbergh proved himself an effective commercial director with such films as *Erin Brockovich* and *Traffic* (both 2000).

ESTABLISHED FILMMAKERS

Already established major directors came back to the cinema with restored vitality in the 1990s. Two Steven Spielberg films deserve particular

NOTABLE MOVIES

Not including Best Picture.

Ghost (1990)
Goodfellas (1990)
Home Alone (1990)*
Pretty Woman (1990)
Beauty and the Beast (1991)
Boyz N the Hood (1991)
JFK (1991)
Thelma and Louise (1991)
A Few Good Men (1992)
A League of Their Own (1992)
Wayne's World (1992)
The Fugitive (1993)
Jurassic Park (1993)*
Mrs. Doubtfire (1993)
Sleepless in Seattle (1993)
Groundhog Day (1993)
Hoop Dreams (1994)
The Lion King (1994)*
Pulp Fiction (1994)
Speed (1994)
Apollo 13 (1995)
Toy Story (1995)
The Usual Suspects (1995)
Fargo (1996)
Independence Day (1996)*
Jerry Maguire (1996)
Mission Impossible (1996)
Men in Black (1997)*
Armageddon (1998)
Saving Private Ryan (1998)
There's Something About Mary (1998)
American Pie (1999)
Austin Powers: The Spy Who Shagged Me (1999)
The Blair Witch Project (1999)
The Matrix (1999)
The Sixth Sense (1999)*
Star Wars: Episode I: The Phantom Menace (1999)*
Toy Story 2 (1999)

*Highest grossing of decade.

attention. The first is *Schindler's List* (1993), an unflinching retelling of the Holocaust and of the title character who attempted to lessen its devastating effect. The film, shot mostly in black and white, was Spielberg's masterpiece, and it received multiple Academy Awards, including those for Best Picture and Best Director. The second film is *Saving Private Ryan* (1998), a film notable for its first 20 minutes, which depicted the invasion of Normandy on D-Day, June 6, 1944. Never before had World War II been depicted so viscerally, with jerky cinema verité camera work, and considerable gore. *Saving Private Ryan* was nominated for a Best Picture Oscar, and Spielberg won the award for Best Director. Spielberg also stuck close to his roots in the 1990s with movies designed for pure escapist entertainment, the two *Jurassic Park* films foremost among them.

Other major directors also made their mark in the 1990s, including Martin Scorsese, who directed numerous films, including *Goodfellas* (1990) and *Casino* (1997), both regarded by many as his masterpieces. Scorsese also proved himself quite an adventurous director, with an adaptation of the Edith Wharton novel, *The Age of Innocence* (1993); *Kundun* (1997), about the Dali Lama; and *Bringing Out the Dead* (1999).

Robert Altman added to his already illustrious career with *The Player* (1992), about the surreal life of a Hollywood film producer; *Short Cuts* (1993), an interweaving of numerous storylines based on the short stories of Raymond Carver; and others, like *Pret-á-Porter* (1994) and *Cookie's Fortune* (1999). Oliver Stone explored several real-life figures in such films as *The Doors* (1991), *JFK* (1991), and *Nixon* (1995). He also made *Heaven and Earth* (1993), *Any Given Sunday* (1999), and *Natural Born Killers* (1994), a graphically violent film that owed much to the spate of ultra-violence in the wake of *Pulp Fiction.* Clint Eastwood, who had made a name for himself principally as an actor in Westerns and movies about tough, even brutal police detectives, directed eight features in the decade. Although many of these films garnered critical acclaim, including *A Perfect World* (1993) and *Absolute Power* (1995), Eastwood's greatest triumph in the 1990s was *Unforgiven* (1992). With this picture, Eastwood helped temporarily revitalize the Western, while also offering an acute commentary on the violent nature of the genre. The movie, which won Oscars for Best Picture, Best Director, and Best Supporting Actor (Gene Hackman), solidified Eastwood's status as a director.

The vitality (and material wealth) of American cinema, drew many foreign directors to the United States, much as had happened early in the "golden age" of American film. The Taiwanese director Ang Lee, for instance, brought his subtle eye for family relationships to *The Ice Storm* (1997) and made a movie of the American Civil War, *Ride with the Devil* (1999). John Woo, known for his ultra-violent Hong Kong action movies, contributed to American film with *Hard Target* (1993), *Broken Arrow* (1996), and *Face/Off* (1997). Meanwhile, Swedish director Lasse Hallström brought his off-beat sensibilities to films like *What's Eating Gilbert Grape?* (1994) and *The Cider House Rules* (1999). Germany's Wolfgang Petersen made such films as *In the Line of Fire* (1993), *Outbreak* (1995), and *Air Force One* (1997), about the hijacking of the president's aircraft.

Late in the decade, The American Film Institute released a list of history's 100 greatest movies. Several movies from the 1990s proved worthy of inclusion, a noteworthy accomplishment given that the Institute only considered movies made prior to 1997. The list included *Schindler's List, Forrest Gump, Goodfellas, Pulp Fiction,* and *Unforgiven.* It also included Jonathan Demme's serial-killer thriller, *The Silence of the Lambs* (1991), Kevin Costner's Western about a Civil War soldier living among the Lakota Sioux, *Dances with Wolves* (1990), and Joel and Ethan Coen's updated film-noir, *Fargo* (1996). Since the list came out, opinion on these specific films has shifted somewhat, even as other overlooked films have climbed in estimation.

THEATER

As the century came to a close, the theater came to be seen as something of an elitist form of entertainment. In part, this had to do with the shift from light entertainment to more thematically serious drama. Another reason was that the cost of tickets, which frequently broke the triple digits dollar amount, particularly on Broadway, proved prohibitive to many. This said, the theater was not dead in the 1990s, which saw the rise of numerous small theater companies.

MUSICAL THEATER

The most popular theatrical form in the 1990s was the musical. However, the shows that met with the most success were not new. Englishman Andrew Lloyd Webber, the top producer of Broadway musicals in the 1990s, enjoyed continued success with shows like *Cats* and *Phantom of the Opera,* which started their runs in 1981 and 1986,

NOTABLE THEATER

Miss Saigon, 1991 (4,092 perfs.)

Crazy for You, 1992 (1,622 perfs.)

Guys and Dolls (revival), 1992 (1,143 perfs.)

Beauty and the Beast, 1994 (5,461 perfs.)

Grease (revival), 1994 (1,505 perfs.)

Smokey Joe's Café, 1995 (2,036 perfs.)

Chicago (revival), 1996 (4,700+ perfs.*)

Rent, 1996 (5,000+ perfs.*)

Jekyll and Hyde, 1997 (1,543 perfs.)

The Lion King, 1997 (4,300+ perfs.*)

Cabaret (revival), 1998 (2,377 perfs.)

Fosse, 1999 (1,093 perfs.)

Bring in 'Da Noise, Bring in 'Da Funk, 1999 (1,135 perfs.)

*Still running as of mid-2008.

respectively. Webber's new musical, *Sunset Boulevard,* based on the Billy Wilder film, opened in 1994 with record-breaking advanced ticket sales of $37.5 million but closed as a financial failure.

One of the most successful musicals of the 1990s was based on the 1994 Disney film, *The Lion King.* The Broadway musical version, launched in 1998, was produced by Disney with music by Elton John and lyrics by Tim Rice. Another of the great musical success stories of Broadway was *Rent,* written by Jonathan Larson and directed by Michael Greif. *Rent,* which opened on Broadway on April 29, 1996, was inspired by Puccini's opera, *La Bohème,* though it brought the story to a contemporary, New York City setting. It proved to be one of the most successful Broadway musicals ever, earning a place among its longest-running shows, and also winning the Tony Award and Pulitzer Prize. *Rent* is scheduled to end its Broadway run in September 2008.

Several major dance musical shows also met with resounding success, although many of these were European imports. Started in 1991 in England by Luke Cresswell and Steve McNicholas, *Stomp* combined percussion, industrial noise, dance, and visual comedy in a lively, adrenaline-pumping approach. By the second year, the *Stomp* performers were making commercials across the globe, including a high-profile Coca-Cola television ad. By the time the troupe came to the states, they sold out shows across the country.

Another form of dance that inspired much imitation was Celtic. *Riverdance* was the trailblazer in this form, combining the traditions of Irish dance with a modern sensibility. With the success of *Riverdance,* a number of other Irish dance troupes came to the fore, most notably, *Lord of the Dance,* headed by dancer Michael Flatley.

THEATRICAL DRAMA

During the 1990s, it became difficult for nonmusical plays to find a reception on Broadway. One of Broadway's most renowned productions in 1999 was Arthur Miller's *Death of a Salesman,* first produced in 1949. It celebrated its 50th anniversary with Brian Dennehy in the lead role.

On and off Broadway, many established playwrights continued fruitfully. Neil Simon, long a Broadway favorite for his nostalgic comedies, continued his successful career with *Lost in Yonkers* (1991), which won the Tony Award and a Pulitzer Prize and was recognized as one of the best works of his career. Simon followed this with *Jake's Women* (1992), *Laughter on the 23rd Floor* (1993), *London Suite* (1995), and *Proposals* (1997), none of which gained the same acclaim. Other more successful players in the 1990s included David Mamet with *Oleanna* (1992), *The Cryptogram* (1995), and *The Old Neighborhood* (1997), and Wendy Wasserstein, who wrote *The Sisters Rosensweig* (1992) and *An American Daughter* (1997).

Ultimately, the place for most serious playwrights, and especially new playwrights, was off Broadway, in New York, and elsewhere. The number of new plays and playwrights in the 1990s was large, but some specific figures deserve particular attention. Among these is Tony Kushner, who made his debut in 1991 with *A Bright Room Called Day,* about the rise of fascism in 1932 Berlin. The play ran for two weeks and met with mixed reviews, but Kushner would achieve considerable fame for his *Angels in America,* the first installment of which, *Part I: Millennium Approaches,* first appeared in London and Los Angeles, and then debuted on Broadway in May 1993. Set during the Reagan era, the play involved three overlapping storylines and numerous characters, from a former drag queen to a conservative Mormon lawyer. The play commented on politics, race, and religion, but it was most notable for its frank treatment of AIDS and homosexuality, and it won several Tonys and a Pulitzer. *Part II: Perestroika* appeared in November 1993. Although Kushner was not the first playwright to address the AIDS epidemic (Larry Kramer and others preceded him), his plays opened the floodgates, and many others followed his lead in addressing the issue.

The prohibitive costs of producing a play led to a rise in the number of one-man or one-woman shows. John Leguizamo, also known for his film acting, created three of the most highly regarded one-man shows, starting with *Mambo Mouth* (1990). This show was followed by *Spic-O-Rama* (1992) and *Freak* (1998). In the plays, Leguizamo explored various aspects of Hispanic culture, alternately playing various characters from his family and the American Latino community in general. Spalding Gray, a master of the one-man monologue since the mid 1980s, continued in this vein as well, writing and performing *Monster in a Box* (1990), *Gray's Anatomy* (1993), *It's a Slippery Slope* (1996), and *Morning, Noon and Night* (1999). Ana Deavere Smith was also a major figure in the one-person show, starting with *Fires in the Mirror* in 1992, which dealt with the 1991 Crown Heights riots, during which violence broke out between local African Americans and Jews. Another series of riots would provide the source for Smith's next presentation, *Twilight: Los Angeles, 1992* (1994). The success of these performers, and the fact that they were able to put their productions on with such a limited budget, stimulated the one-player show considerably, and many followed in their footsteps.

Fashion

of the 1990s

The 1990s saw considerable variation in fashion, particularly as previous fringe elements of popular culture came into the mainstream. Thus, while a certain kind of high fashion might have been in vogue at any given time, alternative fashions constituted a rejection of these styles. American media came to depict a much wider range of people, bringing with it a newfound diversity. Fashion was still important, but the interest turned increasingly to how fashion could serve the individual, and the notion of the "slave to fashion" waned.

The 1990s were described by many as a decade of minimalism. Many designers suggested that this was the result of a significant change in concepts of fashion. Design seemed to be increasingly dictated by consumers rather than by creators. Consumers were less interested in the flash of the 1980s, so designers implemented simple, elegant lines to their clothing. Black, which famed designer Giorgio Armani went so far as to call the most "elegant and intellectual" color in 1995, became the dominant color for women's clothing, and a trend developed favoring longer skirts. Some saw this subtlety in dress as a statement about the role of women in general. Women did not have the same need to attract attention as they had in the 1980s. Additionally, as women became a stronger force in public life, fashions were sought that, while retaining some femininity, did not detract from a woman's substantial role.

In general, young people had more money of their own in the decade, and a large amount of this money went toward clothing. As a consequence, manufacturers of children's apparel catered increasingly to children's tastes, rather than to the tastes of parents. Thus, the fashions worn by high school students could also be found in elementary school classrooms.

Fashion was big business in the 1990s, netting more than $100 billion a year annually. Late in the decade, sales topped $170 billion. The growth of the industry itself consumed much of the profit, as the natural metamorphosis of fashion trends seemed to accelerate. One estimate placed the average fashion trend at the end of the decade as lasting about 6 to 12 weeks.

FORMAL AND BUSINESS ATTIRE

Formal wear sought simplicity and elegance. The ruffles and garnishes of the 1980s were replaced by long, sleek dresses. Black seemed the preferred color, although other colors were also popular, particularly neutral or earthy colors. The pastel colors of the previous decade were replaced by brighter colors, such as bold reds and blues.

FASHION HIGHLIGHTS OF THE 1990s

The big hair and power dressing of the 1980s were replaced by more casual and natural styles. Many women felt more comfortable following their own styles and tastes, and considered themselves "anti-trend."

Women—Take on a more tailored, menswear look with straight-sided jackets, straight-cut pants, unadorned blouses, or Capri pants.

Men—Cargo pants, khakis.

Young women—Filmy baby doll dresses with leggings or bare legs; oversized sweaters or T-shirts with leggings; Capri pants; tousled, slightly shaggy "Rachel" haircuts.

Young men—Grunge look of flannel shirts, torn jeans, layered T-shirts; backward baseball caps in the mid/late decade; baggy beltless pants with boxers showing, or hip hop look with baggy jeans and sports jerseys.

Business suits stayed largely the same with relatively minor variations throughout the century, but the 1990s saw a decline in popularity of the business suit. This has been attributed, in part, to the growth of the computer industry, with its relatively young workforce and young management. This new industry encouraged a more casual approach to dress, and the traditionally formal industries became increasingly casual. This development largely began with the implementation of casual Fridays, but for many companies, this led to the adaptation of a looser, more casual overall dress code. In 1992, about seven percent of U.S. companies had a casual dress code, but by 1998, this number had increased to 53 percent.[1]

HIGH FASHION

The world of haute couture, or high fashion, seemed to grow continually more flamboyant in the 1980s and 1990s. Haute couture designers clearly worked on designs that were not really meant to be worn anywhere but on the catwalk. However, the general populace did have a distinct effect on high fashion. Many designers moved away from flashy and unwearable, as well as away from the overly casual, instead tapping into the desire for uncomplicated, yet graceful, even classical, styles of dress. Chanel and Yohji Yamamoto championed a revival of the black dress and classical lines. By the end of the decade, even guests at the Academy Awards were opting for elegant simplicity over audacious flash.

Gianni Versace reached new heights in popularity in the early 1990s, with a line of clothing influenced by underground fetish-wear. The look gained popularity in some circles, though naturally, the average American shied away from the leather and latex designs. Versace did not stick solely to this kind of fashion, but it helped his name became a household word, along with his friendships with other celebrities, like Elton John. Versace's murder in July 1997 in Miami, Florida, created quite a sensation in the news media. His company continued with his sister, Donatella, at the helm.

Other important designers of the decade included Anna Sui, Alexander McQueen, Isaac Mizrahi, Gucci, Donna Karan, and Miuccia Prada. Japanese designers, especially Yohji Yamamoto and Rei Kawakubo, also had significant influence on high fashion globally.

CASUAL WEAR

For everyday wear, T-shirts and jeans continued to be popular. Many of the T-shirts served the dual purpose of clothing and advertising. A less obvious means of self-expression, jeans nonetheless suggested much about their wearers. More than any other decade since their introduction, a variety of jean designs were simultaneously in vogue, depending on which crowd the wearer wanted to be identified with. In the grunge style, jeans had tears riddling the knees or upper thighs, thereby revealing boxer shorts. Many labels even sold pre-tattered jeans. The display of boxers was also associated with the trend of wearing large, ill-fitting pants that hung at the lowest part of the hips, whereas the boxer shorts still clung to the waist. Boot cut jeans became popular among urban women because of how they highlighted footwear, especially high-heeled boots. In 1998, hard jeans became quite popular. Wearers of these pants treasured the new, untouched look, and frequently took to ironing tight creases into the front of the legs, held well by the denim's stiffness.

Italian designer Gianni Versace along with his sister and business associate, Donatella Versace Beck, strolled through an exhibit of their work at the Fashion Institute of Technology, 1992. AP Photo.

Denim overalls, considered rather unfashionable a decade before, also became popular, especially with girls.

Clothing made of khaki became increasingly popular into the 1990s. Not as casual as T-shirts and jeans, khaki clothing could be worn in a variety of situations; by the end of the decade, entire suits made of khaki hit the market. Part of khaki's revival was due to a series of advertisements that depicted khaki as hip and exciting. The most popular line of TV ads, produced by The Gap, involved young, attractive dancers. The first in this line, which debuted in 1998, showcased khaki clothes in an elaborate dance to Louis Prima's swing classic "Jump, Jive, an' Wail." The ad was followed by similar displays to techno, hip hop, and other musical styles.

Clothing with professional sports team logos continued to be popular, including T-shirts, shorts, jackets, and socks. In addition, sports stars were hired, with great success, to publicize certain lines of clothing. Perhaps no company benefited more from ties to professional sports than the shoe company Nike, which associated itself with two of the highest profiles sportsmen of the decade, Tiger Woods and Michael Jordan. Jordan proved especially profitable for Nike, which created a shoe called the Air Jordan in 1984. In its first year, the Air Jordan brought in $130 million for Nike and continues to be sold late into the first decade of the 2000s.

CONTEMPORARY CASUAL RETAIL

The turn toward more casual fashions breathed new life into some retail establishments, most notably, Gap Inc., which owned The Gap, Old Navy, and Banana Republic stores. The company had its strongest decade ever, ranking as the country's largest apparel retailer, earning $1.93 billion in 1990, but jumping to $11.64 billion by the end of the decade. The company marketed simple, comfortable, casual, good-looking clothes, such as khaki clothes, polo shirts, and even quality T-shirts and jeans. The Old Navy stores grabbed consumer attention with a line of kitschy television commercials and a semi-retro look. However, perhaps due to the dying down of the retro fad and the company's hesitancy to change the general look of its clothes, profits began dropping significantly for Gap Inc. in the early 2000s.[2]

Target department stores also gained a considerable reputation in the 1990s. The stores started as a competitor to Kmart and other discount department stores, but as the decade progressed, Target developed its own unique image. Like The Gap, Target exploited the somewhat retro look, emphasizing casual but fashionable apparel. As the decade ended, Target avoided the pitfalls of The Gap, successfully keeping its image fresh with a line of sharp, stylized TV commercials and continued innovation in its clothing lines. In the early 2000s, Target hired famed designer Todd Oldham to design a new line, thereby demonstrating that even fashion makers like Oldham still found Target a vital outlet.

HIP HOP

Hip hop fashion took hold in the 1990s, finding its largest market, not in the ghettos where it originated, but among middle-American suburban youth. Hip hop fashion allowed individual expression within an identifiable framework. Common elements included baggy denim pants and overalls, wool and baseball-style caps, and sports-style jerseys and jackets. Likewise, shoes were vital to the hip hop look, with Nike being the most popular brand.

One clothing label, Fubu, was formed by Carl Brown, Daymond John, J. Alexander Martin, and Keith Perrin, all under 30 years old, who came from a lower-middle-class background in Hollis, Queens, New York. Formed in 1992, Fubu, an acronym for "for us by us," quickly gained popularity, partly due to well-placed publicity. Fubu clothes were worn by rappers like LL Cool J and Busta Rhymes and pop stars like Mariah Carey. They also appeared on television programs.

The company also flourished due to the work of the four founders. Many consumers of hip hop clothing found an honesty in the founders who attempted to bridge street style with mainstream style. These men believed enough in their clothes to wear them regularly, rather than suits and ties. In 1998, the company's men's line made around $200 million. The founders of Fubu intended to reach an African American consumer base that had largely been ignored by most clothing manufacturers, but they were surprised when their clothing line found such an enthusiastic reception among white youth.

Fubu was not the only success in the field of hip hop fashion. Other companies, including Ecko Unlimited, Enyce, Mecca, Pelle Pelle, and Phat Farm also thrived. Phat Farm was founded by Russell Simmons, who had been instrumental in the creation of the major hip hop record label Def Jam. Another line, Sean John,

Rap star MC Lyte (sometimes credited as Lana Michele Moorer) wearing a hip hop style of the 1990s, with knit cap, oversized jacket, and baggy pants. Courtesy of Photofest.

was started by rapper Sean "P. Diddy" Combs. In all, hip hop fashion, sometimes called urban sportswear, brought in an estimated $5 billion a year by the end of the decade.

The Tommy Hilfiger brand also became associated with hip hop fashion, although by different means. Hilfiger had started in the 1980s with a line of preppy designs, but in 1992, these clothes were mentioned in a Grand Puba rap, and found new life in urban neighborhoods. So, too, did Ralph Lauren and Fila. However, in finding a new audience, these clothes also found a new aesthetic, which led to the clothes being worn in a different way than they traditionally had been (most commonly in oversize), or mixed with more common street-level urban clothing.[3]

GRUNGE, SKATE, RAVE, AND GOTHIC FASHION

Hip hop design was part of the growing trend in the 1980s and 1990s of developing street style into major markets. Next to hip hop, the most popular adapted style was grunge. The grunge look was most popular in the early years of the decade, though it held significant sway well into the new millennium. The look mimicked musicians of the Seattle grunge movement. In addition to low-riding, tattered jeans, flannel shirts were a major part of the style. Flannel shirts were worn loose over T-shirts, or tied around the waist. The original emissaries of grunge style were not trying to make a fashion statement; they were simply wearing the most comfortable shirts and pants. The trend faded mid-decade as designers like Marc Jacobs took the look to the high fashion catwalks.

The skater look was also popular with young people. One of the most significant companies exploiting this look, which had the bagginess of hip hop, but also the T-shirt and jeans look of grunge, was X-Large. In addition to describing how its oversized clothes fit, the name X-Large was a merging of the phrases "Gen-X" and "Living Large." The line started in 1991 with the opening of a Los Angeles X-Large store, which sold the company's own clothing, as well as other brands. The line quickly became popular among skateboarders, but it also got significant publicity from other celebrities. Mike D of the rap-rock group The Beastie Boys invested in the company and helped bring it to nationwide attention. The company opened a store in Tokyo in 1992 and one in New York in 1993. In 1994, it introduced the x-girl line for women.

The raver look, named after the culture of underground, after-hours dance parties, had started in England, but began waning in popularity there in the early 1990s. In the United States, its influence on fashion stayed strong throughout the decade. Most influential was the rave tendency toward loose-fitting clothing, from oversized T-shirts to baggy trousers worn low on the hips. A great deal of rave clothing emphasized bright colors, which matched well with the spirit of fun and high energy that raves represented, and the look also frequently drew from 1970s club fashions.

A girl wearing cyber-rave style, featuring a plastic look born from earlier club styles. Shutterstock.

Gothic, or Goth, clothing gained considerable attention, although the trend was not especially widespread. Rather, the publicity came as a result of the spate of high school shootings in the late 1990s. Several of the youths who had committed the violence were fans of bands like Marilyn Manson, who bore some similarities to the Gothic bands of the 1980s. In addition, the youths seemed to have a kind of common uniform, consisting of black clothes and dark trench coats.

Media, parents, and school officials looked for an explanation for the violence and found a scapegoat in the music and fashion enjoyed by goths. As a consequence, nearly any youth who listened to dark, aggressive music or wore black clothes or a trench coat, came under suspicion, despite the fact that few who did so entertained vicious thoughts of the magnitude of the shooters'. Although the fervor over Goth style died down as school shootings diminished, it added considerable energy to an ongoing debate about school uniforms.

SCHOOL UNIFORMS

Fears of a growing gang problem among American youths led many to endorse the idea of traditional school uniforms. They feared clothing might be a sign of gang affiliation, and felt that uniformity would reduce the potential for school violence. Additionally, it was believed that uniforms would diminish class distinctions, and keep students, particularly young girls, from wearing inappropriately revealing clothes, which became a growing issue in American schools in the 1990s, especially with the popularization of scantily clad singers like Britney Spears, the Spice Girls, and Christina Aguilera.

Proponents argued that uniforms would create a less distracting environment, that students would relate to each other on more legitimate grounds than fashion sense, and that they would have an easier time concentrating on academic pursuits. The trend toward school uniforms gained a considerable boost in 1996, when President Clinton announced his support. It did seem that uniforms produced a greater sense of order in school, but critics noted that they also reduced children's ability to make their own choices, which was part of the learning process. Others argued that uniform guidelines stripped students of a vital sense of individuality and identity. Uniforms were most widely adopted by private schools. Although a growing number of public schools adopted uniforms in the 1990s, most continued without, though many maintained some sort of dress code.[4]

TECHNOLOGY

Technological developments in fabrics influenced fashion. Gore-Tex, a synthetic material designed to be breathable and water- and windproof, was introduced in 1989 by W. L. Gore & Associates, and became very popular in the 1990s. Also in 1989, microfibers were introduced by I. E. duPont de Nemours & Company. This revolutionary development of fibers about one one-hundredth of the thickness of human hair, finer than the finest silk threads, served to refine polyester, nylon, acrylic, and other synthetic materials. Another important development was Lyocell, released under the trade name Tencel. Lyocell was developed as an environmentally safe fiber made from the pulp of trees grown specifically for this purpose.

Although the advances in actual clothing materials were tremendous, perhaps a greater technological advancement could be found in the fashion industry's relationship to ever-advancing computer technology. The apparel industry only began fully exploiting computer technology in the mid-1990s, but ultimately, the technology improved the distribution of goods. Computers proved invaluable for keeping track of shifting inventories. An important name in this dimension of the industry was SAP, a software developer that modified its existing systems to suit the needs of major companies, including footwear company Reebok and the VF Corporation, the force behind the Wrangler, Lee, JanSport, and Vanity Fair lines of apparel. The installation of the system increased both companies' revenues by streamlining their sales and distribution. Designers also used the Internet as a showroom and sales floor for their goods. At decade's end, virtually every major designer had a Web site on which consumers could browse products and order to size.[5]

Naturally, fashion design schools, including major institutions like the Parsons School of Design and the Fashion Institute of Technology, increasingly taught computer use to students. Computers became instrumental to the process of designing clothes. While some stuck to traditional methods, clothing designers began to use CAD computer systems to design more and more. Gap, Banana Republic, Polo Ralph Lauren, Calvin Klein, Tommy Hilfiger, and numerous others all used CAD.

JEWELRY

With the turn toward simplicity in dress came a new emphasis on accessorizing. Jewelry played an important role in the world of fashion, as it allowed individuals to truly express themselves. An "anything goes" attitude seemed to take hold during the decade when it came to jewelry. A great deal of modern jewelry borrowed its look from the jewelry of the past, but no specific era dominated. Brooches and chokers echoed the jewelry of the nineteenth and early twentieth centuries, while jewelry of the 1960s was also influential. Peace signs, for instance, made a comeback. So, too, did jewelry utilizing hemp twine and wooden beads. Christian iconography was popular, but so were images from other religions and cultures, from African, to Asian, to Celtic. There was an increased use of synthetic material, especially polymer clays, which could easily be formed and hardened into virtually any desired shape.

There was also considerable growth in the home manufacturing of jewelry. It was easier than ever to make one's own jewelry, given not only a number of home-jewelry kits on the market, but also the availability of home kilns, stationary torches, and low-temperature soldering torches. These made it easier for home jewelers to create their own beads and use metal work to create necklaces, earrings, bracelets, and other forms of jewelry.

COSMETICS

As fashion drifted toward simplicity, and muted colors dominated, the cosmetic industry offered earthier tones. For many women, natural tones were preferred when it came to lipstick and nail polish. However, there were times when women wished to use makeup as a way to express themselves. Several women became makeup entrepreneurs in the 1990s, largely driven by their dissatisfaction with the limited palette of cosmetics available to them. Dineh Mohajer started her company, Hard Candy, as a 22-year-old premed student. Her inability to find the nail polish colors she wanted led her to start mixing her own. She developed four bright pastels, called Lime, Sky, Sunshine, and Violet. Her customer base grew quickly as the line expanded. By the end of the decade, Hard Candy was a million dollar company. Mohajer also started a men's line of nail polish called Candy Man.[6] The same kind of dissatisfaction with available makeup prompted Sandy Lerner, who had co-founded the technology company Cisco Systems, and Wende Zomnir to launch their own company, Urban Decay, in 1996. Urban Decay created colors with an urban, industrial edge, including greens, purples, and grays. It began with 10 lipstick colors, 12 nail polishes, and an advertising slogan, "Does Pink Make You Puke?" The company also selected caustic names for its colors: Acid Rain, Frostbite, Oil Slick, Ozone, Shattered, Smog, Rust, and Roach. Urban Decay also expanded into other cosmetics.[7] The success of these companies led even venerable cosmetic lines, like Channel and Revlon, to experiment with edgier colors.

The cosmetic industry grew dramatically in the 1990s. Department stores had been the dominant retailer of such items in earlier decades, but now the industry was strong enough to support specialized outlets. Sephora was one of the first to enter the market, and it remained the most popular throughout the decade. The first Sephora store was opened in France in 1993 and was later acquired by the company Louis Vuitton Moet Hennessy (LVMH). The first American store was opened in New York City in 1998. Sephora's success was driven by its emphasis on wide selection, a knowledgeable staff, and the customers' ability to try products before purchasing them. By the decade's end, there were more than 70 Sephora stores in the United States and more than 400 internationally.[8]

HAIR

Hair also provided an outlet for self-expression. Hair extensions increased in popularity, particularly with African American women, in part driven by their use by a number of African America singers, including Patti LaBelle and Queen Latifah. Elaborate hair pieces, straight or braided, were weaved into the natural hair of many women.

Hair coloring continued to be popular as well, with use increasing about 70 percent over the course of the decade. This growth was in part attributed to aging baby boomers, but also younger women. Men increasingly turned to hair color as well. While gray hair might have been considered distinguished in certain circles, a growing number of men reacted negatively to the thought of going gray, and the market for men's hair color surged as a result. On television, advertisements for products to color men's hair, including facial hair, aired nearly as often as similar ads for women's hair color products.

Hair coloring was also popular for those simply seeking to change their look, either subtly or radically. Red was a popular hair color choice for women in the 1990s, which may have been driven in part by models and actresses. Actress Gillian Anderson of *The X-Files* contributed to an increase in the number of women with brassy red hair. Blonde was popular, particularly among teen and pre-teen girls. This was partially driven by the styles of Britney Spears and other young, blonde pop singers. Many of these singers, and their fashion followers among the general public, didn't hide the fact that their hair was dyed, frequently allowing their darker roots to show freely.

There was less of a tendency toward dramatic change among men, though younger men and boys frequently turned to coloring or bleaching their hair. In the early 1990s, surf-bum bleaching of longish hair took hold with followers of the grunge movement, but by the end of the decade, it was more popular to wear bleached hair short, lightly spiked, and with apparent dark roots. This look was popular among skaters and other extreme sports athletes, as well as among musicians. It could be seen on the heads of punk and hard rock musicians, as well as in more mainstream music, sported by such top acts as Ricky Martin and members of the singing group 'N Sync. Fashion has always been influenced by how celebrities dressed, but in the 1990s, this was far truer of hair. The average hairstyling magazine was filled with photos of celebrities, or models sporting styles deliberately copied from celebrities. Each new season of the sitcom *Friends* drew almost as much comment about actress Jennifer Aniston's hairstyle as the storylines.

TATTOOS AND PIERCING

Another important component of 1990s fashion was body scarring and adornment. Pierced ears had long been popular in the United States, but piercing of the nose or navel were considered fringe practices. However, in the 1990s, these

Young woman with mohawk hair styling, and piercing. Shutterstock.

kinds of piercings became increasingly popular. Young people embraced nose and navel piercing rather quickly, but the practice also grew among adults. More extreme piercings, like the impaling of the tongue with a small bar or metal ball, were less widely embraced, but still grew in popularity.

Tattooing also became a mainstream practice throughout most of the nation, in part encouraged by a growing number of celebrities, from sports stars to movie and TV actors. For many Americans, tattoos became just another means of self-expression and adornment. Of course, young Americans most frequently sported tattoos, but the practice even took hold among the middle-class, suburban professionals. More extreme forms of bodily mutilation, like body scarring, remained rare, but nonetheless experienced small growth, largely among those who saw the mainstreaming of tattooing and piercing and sought new forms of cultural rebellion.

THE BREAST ENHANCEMENT INDUSTRY

A multi-billion dollar industry developed in the 1990s centered on the size of women's breasts. The Wonderbra, designed to lift and pad a woman's breasts, was introduced in the United States in 1994 by Bali Brassiere Company, and spawned numerous copies and imitations. In 1998, retail sales of the Wonderbra and other makes exceeded $100 million. A silicone bra insert, called Curvec, also spawned numerous imitations, and this industry made $50 million in retail sales.[9]

Of course, these products merely created the illusion of size. Surgical breast augmentation provided for the actual increase in size that many women desired. Silicone pouches surgically implanted in breasts became enormously popular, even with the hefty $3,000–$4,000 price tag. To some detractors, the implants made breasts look unrealistic, while simultaneously raising serious health concerns. Frequently, implants resulted in the hardening of the breast, making it difficult for a recipient to lie down or raise her arms. The surgery carried the additional risk of reduced sensitivity, and the biological creation of fibrous tissue around the implant as a foreign body. Furthermore, the fear of saline or silicone leakage into breast tissue became real to many in the health community. In all, health experts estimated the chance of developing serious health risks from breast augmentation at between 30 percent and 50 percent. Despite these concerns, the demand for enlarged breasts continued, not at all surprising considering the continuing portrayal of women perpetrated by the TV and film industries and both men's and women's magazines. In 1999, more than 167,000 breast implants were performed, more than a 50 percent increase from just three years earlier.[10]

COSMETIC SURGERY

Cosmetic also surged in popularity by the end of the decade. With such surgery being so common, and even something that celebrities frequently spoke about openly, its stigma was reduced. A survey by the American Association of Plastic Surgeons suggested that as much as 57 percent of women and 58 percent of men approved of plastic surgery.[11] For many, the numbers were shocking and disturbing in their revelation of the number of women who felt that they needed surgery to improve their appearance. In 1999, about 2.2 million cosmetic surgery procedures were performed, a 153 percent increase from 1992. The most common procedure was liposuction, which was performed 230,865 times in 1999, an increase of 264 percent from 1992. The second most popular procedure was breast augmentation, and the third was surgery on the eyelids, called blepharoplasty. Also popular were face-lifts, which surgically tightened facial skin, and chemical peels, which stripped the top layers of facial skin away altogether. Perhaps one reason why cosmetic surgery was approved of is that it was a sign of affluence. All of these procedures were quite expensive, with a facelift commonly costing more than $5,000, and a chemical peel, the simplest of these procedures, costing roughly $1,300.[12] There was also burgeoning interest in Botox, a form of botulism injected into people's faces with the intention of paralyzing the muscles, thereby reducing the appearance of wrinkles. While the treatment did indeed lessen wrinkling, it also limited facial expressions.

BODY IMAGE

The rise of the supermodel continued throughout the 1990s, setting an unrealistic ideal to which many women aspired. Supermodels provided an utterly impractical model for most women, especially as the new supermodels seemed to get thinner and thinner, with a much lighter natural bone structure. The extreme case of thinning models came in a trend toward advertising with emaciated, almost skeletal models. A series of Calvin Klein print ads was credited with starting what came to be known as the "heroin chic" look. In these ads, the models were so thin that they looked like extremely unhealthy drug addicts. Calvin Klein's intention had been to counter conventional ideals of beauty, as suggested by the campaign slogan, "Just Be." Many Americans were repulsed by the ads, but they nonetheless had an impact. These were, after all, fashion models, and if sickly thin appeared in a fashion magazine ad, then some readers would certainly take sickly thin as fashionable.

In 1990, the average fashion model weighed 23 percent less than the average American woman, compared to a mere 8 percent difference from a quarter-century earlier.[13] There were two reasons for this. First, the 1980s and 1990s saw an increase in obesity. By 1990, the average American woman weighed more than she did 25 years earlier. At the same time, however, the average fashion model was getting lighter. The curves on fashion models of the 1950s, for instance, fell to the wayside in favor of a much narrower, sleeker look. The result was that a greater number of women than ever before fell short of the ideal being depicted in fashion magazines and also in movies, television broadcasts, and the world of pop music. In response, there was an increased emphasis placed on accepting one's body for what it was, and for acknowledging that the media image was only one standard of beauty. This was especially geared toward teenage girls, among which there were skyrocketing rates of anorexia and bulimia. The decade experienced a flood of articles and books that examined the beauty industry and its effects on the psychology of women and girls, most notably Naomi Wolf's *The Beauty Myth: How Images of Beauty Are Used Against Women* (1991).

The number of boys becoming obsessed with body image greatly increased in the 1980s and 1990s as well. The hyper-masculine men of action films and pro wrestling created as much of a gap between the ideal and the average male body as there was for women. As a result, many men, especially young men in their teens and early twenties, turned to bodybuilding. More disturbingly, more turned to the use of supplements and steroids. Some experts in youth psychology suggested that boys who failed to live up to the masculine image were more likely to see themselves as outcasts, which may have contributed to the rise in suburban teen violence during the decade.

Ultimately, for both men and women, body image became a much greater concern than ever before. Ironically, some who pursued dramatic means of matching the supermodel or muscle man ideal sought not to be extraordinary, but to match the image that was, in their eyes, normal. The normal bodies possessed by many of these individuals were regarded as inferior because the norm had been redefined by the carefully photographed, meticulously lighted, and sometimes airbrushed (or otherwise altered) images on magazine pages and TV and movie screens.

Young children were frequently exposed to exceptional ideals of beauty, partly in the media, but parents also played a part. Perhaps the most notable example of this was the growing world of children's beauty pageants. Pageants of this sort were quite popular at the beginning of the 1990s, and the popularity continued to grow until there were approximately 3,000 being held in the United States annually, with around 100,000 participants. The pageant business became a billion-dollar-a-year industry.[14] Children's beauty pageants suffered a sharp decline in 1997, however, largely due to the JonBenet Ramsey murder case. The six-year-old Ramsey was murdered in late 1996 in a case that was sensational enough for its brutality and mysteriousness. Contributing to the sensation was the fact that Ramsey had been a child beauty queen. The wide media coverage repeatedly showed footage of Ramsey strutting across stages, wearing garish makeup and scanty outfits, exuding sex appeal that seemed completely inappropriate for a six-year-old girl. Almost overnight, the growing fad of children's beauty pageants became something that many Americans found distasteful.

Food

of the 1990s

In the 1990s, traditional fast food chains continued to expand their influence and new, higher class chain restaurants found their way into cities from coast to coast. Celebrity chefs, like Wolfgang Puck and Emeril Lagasse, got into the franchise game, not only with restaurants, but also with packaged foods in major supermarket chains.

However, the decade saw contradictory movements in nutrition. On one hand, eating healthy grew in popularity. A flood of low-fat, low-calorie packaged goods reached the supermarket shelves, restaurants paid more attention to the nutritional value of their offerings, and diet books and videos experienced increased sales. Yet, the decade also saw notable increases in nutrition-related health risks and growing obesity across all demographics.

The trend away from meals prepared from scratch continued unabated as the century came to a close. Many Americans were working longer hours and had a greater number of commitments. As a consequence, anything that made preparing meals easier seemed to sell. About 90 percent of the money spent by Americans on food in the 1990s went to processed goods—canned, frozen, or dehydrated. This was also true of the processed food found in fast food and other restaurants employing prepared goods. Americans seemed to be eating out much more, and as a consequence, the restaurant industry expanded considerably. Restaurants remained among the hardest small businesses to make succeed, but with the growth of chain restaurants and the change in Americans' dining patterns, the industry nonetheless found itself the largest employer of the 1990s. A 1998 report released by the National Restaurant Association projected total sales for the food service industry at $336.4 billion. By the end of the decade, the industry employed more than nine million people.[1]

Greatly influencing people's everyday diets, the consumption of sugar skyrocketed in the 1990s, particularly in the latter half of the decade. A study by the Department of Agriculture estimated that, by the decade's end, the average American consumed about 150 pounds of sugar annually, an increase of nearly 30 pounds from two decades earlier. As the American public became increasingly diet-conscious, the number of fat-free foods on the market also increased. However, in many cases, manufacturers simply replaced fat with sugar. Dieters looking for low-fat foods tended to overlook the high sugar content. The sugar increase was not merely the result of increased consumption of sweets; sugar was a common additive to many different kinds of food. Potato chips (and other potato products), meats, and even packaged vegetables saw sugar becoming a common additive. A bestselling diet book called *Sugar Busters!,* published in 1998, brought considerable attention to this. The craze for fat-free food tempered somewhat as consumers paid increased attention to sugar content.[2] Nabisco even created a sugar-free version of its highly popular low-fat Snackwell cookies as awareness of sugar content increased.

READY-MADE FOODS

By the end of the decade, more than 9,000 new food products launched annually, but the percentage of food bought at supermarkets—as opposed to specialty stores, warehouse clubs, or chain stores like Wal-Mart—declined during the 1990s. The trend toward pre-packaged and prepared food continued to accelerate. A 2000 survey conducted by the Food Marketing Institute found that 62 percent of shoppers bought precut and ready-to-eat packaged vegetables once a month or more. Thirty-nine percent bought frozen side dishes, and 26 percent purchased pre-cooked or marinated, pre-seasoned ready-to-cook meat.[3]

One important development in the packaging of food was a new packing method sometimes called modified atmosphere packaging. This technique was instrumental in the increased prevalence of packaged salad mixes. The prewashed and prepared mixes ranged from simple iceberg lettuce varieties to more unusual mixes that included more exotic greens, dressing, croutons, and other toppings, giving consumers everything needed to prepare an elaborate salad. The Food Marketing Institute survey found that nearly half of all shoppers bought packaged salad mixes at least once a month.

For many children, the Oscar Mayer Lunchable became a popular substitute for the traditional parent-made school lunch. Lunchables offered a boxed lunch of crackers and cold cuts, cold burgers, hotdogs with buns, cold pizza, or nachos, with a drink (soda or juice), a dessert (cookies, chocolate bars, etc.), and occasionally, a small, cheap toy. In creating these simple food packages, Oscar Mayer exploited both the tastes of children and also parents' increasingly busy schedule. More than simply a desire for the food enclosed, children demanded Lunchables because marketing trained them to respond to the packaging.

Frozen diet foods saw a surge in popularity as well, with brand names like Lean Cuisine, Smart Ones, and Healthy Choice offering relatively healthy variations on the classic TV dinner. With the swell of vegetarians and vegans in the United States, many in the food industry sought to diversify so that they could cater to vegetarians as well as to meat eaters. Frozen vegetarian burgers, like Garden Burger and Boca, reached a wider audience, with products made of grain, vegetables, tofu, and texturized vegetable protein. Consumers could find vegetarian hot dogs, sausage, chicken nuggets, and other goods. Many restaurants added vegetarian entrees to their menus. In 1990, McDonald's changed the way it cooked its French fries. The chain switched from a high beef tallow cooking oil to a pure vegetable oil and used additives to simulate the flavor that had long made McDonald's fries so popular.[4]

By 1999, sales of frozen foods were overtaken by ready-made meals, prepared by supermarket delis and kept chilled and ready for reheating. These ready-made meals typically approximated a home-cooked meal better than did frozen foods, yet required little work in the kitchen. Many could be microwaved, but some required basic use of ovens or stove-tops. Although these products were all but finished, consumers could feel that they were actually cooking, which reduced the guilt behind instant foods. Moreover, consumers tended to think of these as fresher and healthier than frozen meals, though top quality frozen foods were flash-frozen using a process that maintained freshness and nutritional content.

The 1990s were also a golden age for that most portable of foods, the bar. Bars were nothing new, given the long-lived popularity of candy bars. But consumption of various bar-shaped foods increased notably in the decade, as did the variety. Cereal bars were among the most popular, catering to people who missed breakfast and those who simply wanted a sweet, relatively healthy snack. The bars were frequently modeled on the flavors and ingredients of traditional cereals, particularly those consisting of oats, nuts, and honey. The Kellogg Company was one of the strongest competitors in this market, particularly with their Nutri-Grain line of bars. General Mills and Quaker, well-established makers of traditional granola bars, also came out with cereal bars. Diet bars, such as Slimfast, were designed to simulate the sweetness of a candy bar, thereby satiating the urge without imparting the caloric content. Moreover, these bars were often marketed as a high-nutrition meal substitute. Similarly, energy bars, such as PowerBars and Balance bars, found a considerable audience, especially among athletes and would-be athletes. These were seen as an excellent supplement to a high-protein diet.

The decade also saw an increase in the popularity of energy drinks. Traditional sports drinks like Gatorade were joined by new products like Red Bull and KMX. These energy drinks typically came in cans that were much smaller than a traditional soda can, but usually twice the price. Rather than simply offering a refreshing beverage, they promised to "vitalize the body and stimulate the mind," as Red Bull marketing claimed. Red Bull, originally from Austria, topped the energy drink market, due in part to a highly successful line of animated commercials praising Red Bull for "giving you wings" with its formula of high caffeine and taurine, an amino acid touted as a metabolic transmitter and detoxifier.[5]

Bottled iced teas also experienced a growth in popularity, largely due to an aggressive marketing campaign by the leading brand in the field, Snapple. Snapple iced teas incorporated a great variety of fruity and sweet flavors to attract a new type of tea drinker. Snapple packaging and advertising downplayed the old-fashioned image of iced tea, and for the first time in many years, tea became chic. Snapple and other companies were helped by the growing desire on the part of many Americans to develop healthier eating habits. People viewed tea as healthier than sodas or coffee, particularly green tea, which garnered praised for its high level of antioxidants. Hot teas, traditional and herbal, also experienced considerable market growth, with Lipton, Bigelow, and Celestial Seasonings dominating. Many tea manufacturers exploited the rising interest in herbal supplements. Celestial Seasoning, for example, developed a line of special Wellness Teas using increased amounts of ginseng, Echinacea, valerian root, and other herbal additives. The claims made by these teas and other herbal remedies were not evaluated by the Food and Drug Administration, but this lack seemed to have little effect on consumers.

FOOD HIGHLIGHTS OF THE 1990s

1990 Birmingham, Alabama, is home to more than 60 Chinese restaurants.

1991 Sales of salsa are reported to outpace those of ketchup.

1991 The USDA replaces its "Basic Four" nutritional pie chart with a food pyramid that places new importance on vegetables, legumes, fruits, and grains.

1994 The FDA reports that the Flavr Savr, a tomato developed through biotechnology, is as safe for human consumption as conventional hybridized tomato varieties.

1995 Kraft Foods brings out DiGiorno, the first frozen pizza with a self-rising crust.

1996 Leroy, New York, the birthplace of JELL-O, opens the JELLO-O Museum, which features artwork by Maxfield Parrish and Norman Rockwell.

1997 *Emeril Live,* hosted by celebrity chef Emeril Lagasse and showcasing his "New New Orleans" cuisine and animated cooking style, debuts on the Food Network.

1997 Coca-Cola estimates that it sells one billion servings of its product worldwide on a daily basis.

1997 Scribner publishes the sixth edition of the bestselling *Joy of Cooking,* by Irma S. Rombauer, Marion Rombauer Becker, and Ethan Becker, and promises that, in the new edition, "every chapter has been rethought with an emphasis on freshness, convenience, and health."

1999 Lipton invents "Cold Brew" and calls it "the ultimate ice-tea time saver," tea that can be brewed in cold water.

1999 General Mills introduces Go-Gurt, "portable" yogurt that's squeezed and eaten from a plastic sleeve.

FAST FOOD

By the end of the 1990s, Americans were spending about $110 billion dollars on fast food. In his book, *Fast Food Nation: The Dark Side of the All-American Meal,* Eric Schlosser suggested that "Americans now spend more money on fast food than on higher education, personal computers, computer software, or new cars. They spend more on fast food than on movies, books, magazines, newspapers, videos, and recorded music—combined."[6]

Children had long been a prime target for fast food marketing. Advertisers realized that the ability to coax a child into a restaurant meant not only a sale of food to that child but also to one or more parents. Certainly, McDonald's, by employing its clown mascot Ronald McDonald and building restaurants with playgrounds, appealed to children. McDonald's further encouraged visits to the restaurants with Happy Meals, a child-sized meal that included a toy, often a tie-in from a popular children's movie or cartoon character. In the 1990s, Happy Meals experienced unprecedented popularity. More than simply including traditional toys featuring the McDonald's cast of characters—Ronald, the Hamburglar, Grimace, and others—the company joined with major toy manufacturers in the 1990s to boost their sales. McDonald's association with Disney proved successful, as movie-related toys in Happy Meals not only boosted McDonald's sales but also served as vital promotion of Disney movie productions. In 1996, McDonald's and the Walt Disney Company forged a 10-year agreement, giving the fast food chain exclusive rights to Disney film characters for the purpose of promotions like Happy Meal toys. With these and other toys, McDonald's emphasized the "collect them all" mentality, thereby tapping not only into children's interests, but also into a collectors' market. Indeed, the collectors' market for McDonald's toys grew enormously in the 1990s, with the publishing of at least five different price guides devoted to McDonald's paraphernalia. Even adults bought them. In 1997, McDonald's Happy Meals sales leapt when they featured highly popular, collectible Beanie Babies. Whereas McDonald's typically sold about 10 million Happy Meals a week, a 10-day period in April 1997 saw about 100 million Happy Meal sales.[7]

Food

As much as competing fast food chains fought for market shares, they were also battling to have exclusive rights to tie their products to the latest blockbuster movie, popular television show, or toy craze. Taco Bell introduced several new food items in the 1990s, but none of these came close to the marketing boon that accompanied the chain's association with the long-awaited new *Star Wars* movie. Television ads for Taco Bell, as well as for KFC (Kentucky Fried Chicken) and Pizza Hut (all three owned by Tricon Global Restaurants, Inc.), essentially served as ads for the movie. Taco Bell sales increased due to the various *Star Wars* goodies that could be attained at the restaurants.

McDonald's forged ties with the Fox Kids Network and Klasky-Csupo, the producer of *Rugrats* and *The Simpsons,* while Burger King linked with Nickelodeon and *Pokémon.* Restaurant chains also allied themselves with sports leagues and events: for example, McDonald's with the National Basketball Association and the Olympics; Wendy's with the National Hockey League' Denny's with Major League Baseball; and the triumvirate of KFC, Pizza Hut, and Taco Bell with the National Collegiate Athletic Association.[8]

Restaurants were not the only sector of the food industry to build associations with non-food businesses. Products from chips, to cereal, to sodas attempted to gain an edge in marketing by displaying, for instance, sports stars or cartoon characters on their packaging. As in the case with the Happy Meal, traditional cereal box toys increasingly had some larger association, and many products had some kind of mail-in offer, in which toys or other goods would be rewarded with a certain number of proofs-of-purchase.

It was clear by the start of the decade that fast food had, for all intents and purposes, conquered the United States; now it was time to conquer the world. American fast food chains expanded internationally like never before. In 1993, McDonald's opened 193 new restaurants, but of these, only 50 were opened within the United States. Taco Bell also successfully opened locations in Mexico.

OTHER CHAINS

The growth of the market for chain restaurants was not limited to fast food. Other major chains grew considerably in the 1990s. Increasingly, cities across the country came to have the same restaurants, much as they came to have the same department stores, the same hardware stores, and the same bookstores. Many of these chains had their start in earlier decades, but the 1990s saw an unprecedented acceleration in their growth. T.G.I. Friday's is one example whose first location opened in 1965, its second in 1970, and its 169th restaurant in 1990, including several international locations. In 1998, it opened its 500th restaurant.[9]

The decade saw an explosion in the number of Outback Steakhouses, Red Lobsters, Olive Gardens, and other chain restaurants. The success of these restaurants relied on the quality of the food and atmospheres, which took a large step beyond anything available at fast food restaurants, or even the coffee-shop style of Denny's and the like. These restaurants provided a casual sit-down atmosphere, with menus that offered variety, but were familiar. Visitors to a town might not know which of the local restaurants to choose, but they could certainly walk into a familiar chain restaurant with a good idea of both the quality and the selection. Of course, the proliferation of chain restaurants diminished the individuality of a given locale, creating a kind of culinary homogeneity nationwide. Naturally, local restaurant owners also resented the competition of the chains, which made it harder to entice diners into trying someplace new. The chains also had a competitive advantage because the volume of their business allowed them to offer large meals at affordable prices. The larger portions served at these restaurants contributed to a trend as many independent restaurants were forced to offer larger portions in order to compete.

Many of the restaurant chains were part of a single parent company. KFC, Pizza Hut, and Taco Bell all fell under the auspices of Tricon Global. Brinker International, known as Chili's, Inc. until a name change in 1991, owned not only the Chili's restaurant chain, but also Romano's Macaroni Grill, On The Border, and others. By the end of the decade, Brinker owned more than 1,000 restaurants, more than 700 of which were Chili's. Likewise, Darden Restaurants owned Red Lobster, The Olive Garden, and others. By 1994, Darden made more than $1 billion in revenue. At the end of the century, the company operated more than 1,000 restaurants.

However, the largest non-fast food restaurant group was the Advantica Restaurant Group, which acquired the Denny's restaurant chain in 1987. At the time, Denny's suffered a serious image problem, plagued by high-profile charges of racism. In 1993, these charges reached a peak when six black men accused an Annapolis Denny's of discrimination. Worse still, the six men were Secret Service officers who were to protect the president later that day. The publicity was a public relations disaster, affecting the entire company. In the following years, Denny's instituted high-profile efforts to clean up their tarnished image, including the hiring of a greater number of minorities both in individual restaurants, and in all levels of company management. Denny's also instituted a program of sensitivity training for all employees. By the end of the decade, the racism charges were largely forgotten, and Denny's netted record-breaking revenues.[10] And, by the end of the decade, Advantica owned thousands of restaurants across the United States and internationally.

CELEBRITY CHEFS

Chefs frequently became celebrities starting in the 1980s. The trend accelerated in the 1990s as chefs had unprecedented access to mass media. Emeril Lagasse, for instance, attracted viewers to his cooking show, not only through his culinary skills, but also by his boisterous presentation, punctuated with shouts of "Bam!", a catchphrase that would become more associated with Lagasse than any of his signature dishes. Lagasse's popularity grew rapidly in the 10 years that followed the opening of Emeril's Restaurant in March 1990. He opened his second restaurant two-and-a-half-years later, and in 1993, he published his first cookbook, *Emeril's New New Orleans Cooking*. That year, he began hosting his own cooking show, *The Essence of Emeril*, on the new cable television Food Network. In the years that followed, Lagasse opened several new restaurants and published numerous books. His television show gained unrivalled popularity for a cooking show, with *Time* magazine calling it one of the 10 best shows in 1996. In 2001, Lagasse was the first chef ever to be given his own television sitcom. The NBC show *Emeril* flopped, but the fact that executives thought it worth producing in the first place demonstrated just how popular Lagasse had become, and it also served as notice to the new status of the celebrity chef.[11]

In addition to running their own restaurants and appearing on their own television shows, celebrity chefs marketed products through supermarket outlets. Wolfgang Puck pioneered this movement. The chef behind the famed restaurant Spago used his fame to sell a line of frozen pizzas in the late 1980s and later branched out with a popular line of canned soups. Emeril Lagasse sold his jarred pasta sauces, as did Paul Prudhomme, with his line of Cajun spices and seasoning blends. Other restaurateurs also got into the supermarket game. For instance, California Pizza Kitchen brought something new to the world of frozen pizzas. In a market that seemed already overcrowded, the small company, originally started as a Southern California restaurant, offered pizzas with unusual toppings: Thai Chicken, Portobello Mixed Mushroom, BBQ Chicken, and others. They created a sound niche, aided by a major distributor, Kraft Foods.

Emeril Lagasse was one of the first celebrity chefs of the 1990s, helping to make the new Food Network on cable television a success. In later years, he also began appearing on ABC's *Good Morning America*. Courtesy of Photofest.

Some fast food companies got into the supermarket business. Taco Bell, for instance, began selling its own brands of hot sauce and taco shells in major American supermarkets. These products were immediate successes due to brand familiarity.

COFFEE CULTURE AND STARBUCKS

One of the greatest culinary forces in the 1990s was a coffee company started in Seattle, Washington. The company, Starbucks Coffee, opened its first location in 1971 and started a gradual expansion in the 1980s, changing its approach in the hopes of nurturing a coffee bar culture similar to that in Europe. In the late 1980s and 1990s, the number of independent coffee shops seemed to grow exponentially, but Starbucks quickly became the powerhouse in the market. At the end of the 1980s, the company had 55 locations. In 1991, Starbucks opened its first airport location in Seattle. In 1993, it received enormous assistance in its climb to become the nation's most successful coffeehouse chain through its alliance with Barnes & Noble bookstores. Barnes & Noble built numerous chain bookstores in the 1990s, and with their emphasis as much on atmosphere as on product, the stores frequently included a Starbucks cafe. Partnerships with other corporations were significant to Starbucks' success, such as its partnership with Dreyer's Grand Ice Cream to produce what would quickly become the number one brand of coffee-flavored ice cream in the nation; with Pepsi to market a bottled version of Starbucks' Frappuccino beverage, and with other companies, including Kraft Foods and Albertson's grocery stores. Starbucks also expanded overseas, establishing locations not only in Europe, but in such unlikely

Customers sip coffee, read the morning papers, and work on their laptop computers at a Starbucks in New York City. AP Photo.

places as the Philippines, Thailand, Kuwait, and Lebanon. By the end of the decade, Starbucks had 2,135 locations, a number that would more than double in the first two years of the new millennium.[12] Starbucks coffee also appeared on many grocery stores' shelves. Starbucks was the target of the same sort of criticism leveled against most major chain retailers: it forced independent coffee houses out of business, and that it contributed to an unhealthy national homogeneity.

CRAFT BEER

The late 1980s and early 1990s were an era of beer connoisseurship, as reflected by the number of microbreweries spreading across the country. In the 1990s, the major beer sellers—Coors, Budweiser, and Miller—continued to dominate, but not without a surge in the market for lesser-known brands of beer, coming from every corner of the country. Some microbreweries proved so successful that they could no longer truthfully consider themselves micro, the term "craft beer" proving much more suitable. The largest of these was the Boston Brewing Company, makers of Samuel Adams Lager. Brewer Jim Koch once suggested that the cutoff for being considered a microbrewery should be 15,000 barrels a year, believing that "Sam Adams will never get that big." But, as the new millennium began, about 1.2 million barrels were being produced by the Boston Brewing Company.[13]

Other companies that surged to the top of the craft brew market were Sierra Nevada Brewing Company, New Belgium Brewing Company, Deschutes Brewery, Alaskan Brewing Company, Redhook Ale Brewery, and Harpoon Brewery.[14] While many craft brewers had their start in the 1980s, some of the strongest had much earlier origins, including Jacob Leinenkugel and FX Matt, both of which started in the late nineteenth century. The popularity of craft beer in the latter decades of the twentieth century gave these older companies a market boost. The late 1990s, however, saw a significant slowdown in the popularity of microbreweries. Many small brewers folded, but others persevered, largely because microbrewers were frequently not people who got into the business to make a quick profit, but because of their love of beer and brewing. Still, a 2000 survey by the Institute for Brewing Studies in Boulder, Colorado, found that 21 new microbreweries opened that year, while 31 folded. As a result of this trend, many microbreweries returned to an older strategy of catering to a regional customer base.

SODA

Soda consumption continued to grow in the 1990s, reaching an estimated annual rate of 56 gallons a person at the end of the decade. Fast food chains provided a considerable outlet for soda companies, giving them exclusive rights to their restaurants. Such arrangements were extremely profitable to both the restaurant chains and the soda companies, as soft drinks offered the highest profit margin of all goods sold. Soft drink companies targeted every possible outlet, even some elementary and high school campuses. (See Advertising of the 1990s.) The soft drink market became fiercely competitive and an actively hostile one for smaller soda producers. By the decade's end, more than 90 percent of the soda market was controlled by Coke, Pepsi, and Cadbury-Schweppes.[15]

The increased soda consumption marked a disturbing trend, especially among the nation's youth. A 1997 study showed that sodas constituted more than 27 percent of Americans' beverage consumption, averaging out to the equivalent of more than 576 cans of soda a year per person. Males age 12 to 24 were the greatest consumers of sodas, averaging two and a half cans per day. This was particularly alarming when it came to children and young teens. As soda consumption increased, consumption of other more nutritious beverages, such as milk and juice, decreased. Soda's high sugar and calorie content and low nutrient count, led many to raise warnings about the poor dietary habits of American youths.[16]

DIET AND NUTRITION

Nutrition in general seemed under siege in the 1990s, as more and more Americans consumed a great deal of soda, fast food, high-fat snacks, and packaged foods. Warnings abounded about the accelerating trend of obesity in Americans, especially in children—a rate far outpacing that of Europeans. Poor diets led to increases in heart disease, bone loss, dental problems, and other health challenges frequently attributed to eating habits. A 1996 survey of American youth found that they fell far short of government diet recommendations. Only 36 percent of boys and 14 percent of girls consumed the recommended daily calcium intake. Only 34 percent of boys and 33 percent of girls ate the recommended serving of vegetables.[17] Poor diet combined with a decrease in the amount of physical exercise produced an embarrassingly unhealthy condition for the wealthiest nation in the world.

For many, it became nearly impossible to maintain a healthy diet in the 1990s. Certainly, it became far easier for many Americans to purchase fast food or packaged microwavable meals than it was to prepare a full meal from scratch. This was particularly true in the increasing number of households in which all adults worked. Many Americans turned to dietary and vitamin supplements to make up for the nutrients they did not get in the food they ate. The industry also produced special packaged pill cocktails, advertised as providing energy or boosting mental prowess, which frequently consisted, not only of vitamins and minerals, but also of herbal compounds. Companies marketed dietary supplements at athletes as a healthy alternative to steroid use.

The growing rate of obesity in the nation notwithstanding, Americans put themselves on diets in unprecedented numbers. This can be in part attributed to the images of both men and women in the media. Thin fashion models and actresses had long provided an unrealistic exemplar of beauty and health. (See Fashion of the 1990s.) Increasingly at the end of the century, this was also true of the depiction of men.

The 1990s began as a time of anti-fat paranoia. The most popular diets were those that called for a dramatic reduction in fat intake. Consumption of chicken and other fowl increased, largely due to the lower fat content than that in beef and other red meats.[18] However, a small but growing number of diet books argued that fat-free diets were problematic, ultimately not working well. Rather, these diets proposed that carbohydrates were the real source of a fattening public, and called for a severe reduction, along with increased protein consumption. Among these books were Robert C. Atkins's *New Diet Revolution* (actually introduced in a somewhat different form in the 1970s), Barry Sears's *The Zone,* Rachael F. Heller and Richard F. Heller's *The Carbohydrate Addict's Diet,* and Michael R. Eades and Mary Dan Eades's *Protein Power.*

The market for dietary drugs boomed during this period, but there were considerable concerns about the safety. Few felt that they provided as beneficial weight reduction as adjustments in diet and exercise, and some diet drugs were proven actively harmful to their consumers. Some dietary drugs that actually led to weight loss, but several were linked to liver disease, kidney disease, respiratory and coronary damage, and other problems. One of the more notorious dietary drugs "Fen-Phen," a cocktail of Pondimin and Redux (which individually were targeted for health risks), was found to result in high blood pressure, irregularities in heart rate, insomnia, tremors, nervousness, headaches, seizures, heart attacks, strokes, and other symptoms in certain consumers. First introduced in 1996, Fen-Phen later became the subject of several major class-action suits. So, too, did the diet drug Meridia, which was introduced in 1998 and soon came under suspicion of causing, in combination with other factors, many deaths. Despite warnings, consumption of these drugs continued, as did the obsession with thinness on the part of consumers, and the lure of profit on the part of manufacturers outpaced health concerns.

BIOENGINEERING

The advent of bioengineering altered the way people thought about food and nutrition. The most significant name in bioengineering in the 1990s was the Monsanto corporation, which took pioneering steps in the genetic manipulation of crops. Essentially, Monsanto examined how foreign DNA could be introduced into crop species, thereby altering crops. With the growing world population, there was considerable interest in producing food at a greater rate. Moreover, geneticists hoped that their efforts could not only increase food production but also make engineered vegetables more nutritious. Or perhaps crops could be engineered so that their growth and harvest would not strip soil of its nutrients, or so that they could grow in otherwise hostile environments, thereby using farm land more efficiently. Crops could also potentially be made extra-resistant to harsh weather or insects. Maybe different subspecies could be engineered based on the eventual uses of a crop: a subspecies of corn, for instance, engineered for human consumption, another for animal feed, and another for processed foods like corn syrup. In short, the possibilities for bioengineered food were staggering. And these possibilities prompted Monsanto to turn the whole of the company's assets to biotechnology, investing $8 billion dollars in seed processing.

The company's efforts were met with ideological opposition, not unlike the opposition facing the advances in animal cloning during the 1990s, particularly the 1996 cloning of Dolly the sheep. Many were worried about the risks of "playing God" that they saw as inherent in tampering with nature. Fears likewise arose about the potential damage that altered plant life might have on the natural environment, on other plants and animals, and on entire ecosystems.

These fears were amplified as evidence mounted that some bioengineered corn produced a natural pesticide harmful to monarch butterflies and other beneficial insect populations. Opposition also came from certain nations. Japan ruled that genetically altered foodstuff would have to be labeled as such, and several corporations, such as brewers Kirin and Sapporo, announced that they would not use genetically engineered materials. This was also true of several Mexican companies that traditionally imported corn from the United States. Within the United States, companies like Gerber and H. J. Heinz, producers of baby food, also refused to use genetically engineered corn or soy. Kraft taco shells containing modified corn that had not been approved for human consumption were part of a high-profile, high-publicity recall. Worst of all for the bioengineering business was the European Union's decision to stop importing any American corn, coming on the heels of its ban on American beef raised using growth hormones.

These events ultimately resulted in the dissipation of Monsanto. Its resulting financial troubles forced it to merge with Pharmacia & Upjohn, a major drug company that sold off much of the company's agricultural assets.

Milk also came under unusual scrutiny in the 1990s, even as it hit upon its most popular advertising campaign ever. Print advertising showing various celebrities sporting a milk moustache spurred consumption of milk (See Advertising of the 1990s), but many were questioning just how healthy milk actually was. Monsanto had developed a hormone (IGF-1) to increase milk production in cows. Some claimed that the hormone increased risks of breast and prostate cancer. These claims were disputed, especially by Monsanto, but they still carried enough weight that many other nations, including Canada, refused to use it, making the United States the only major developed nation to allow it. Consequently, many consumers turned to organically produced milk, but even this raised worries. Even without the hormone, critics attacked milk for its high fat content. A study by the Center for Science in the Public Interest claimed that one cup of whole milk carried as much detrimental fat as five strips of bacon, and a glass of two percent milk as much as three strips. Those who criticized milk made a case for calcium intake through the consumption of green vegetables.[19]

Music of the 1990s

NIRVANA

In its May 13, 1999, issue, *Rolling Stone* magazine proclaimed singer/songwriter Kurt Cobain its "Artist of the Decade."[1] Perhaps there is no better place to begin a treatment of music in the 1990s than with Cobain, not only for his popularity as the front man for the band Nirvana but also as a representative of changes happening in the music industry. A great deal of music that had previously been directed to a niche audience—not only alternative rock and pop, but also soul, country, rap, and more—turned mainstream. Although Nirvana was not the sole reason for this, the band greatly influenced the opening up of mainstream media to new kinds of music.

Alternative rock, which had its roots in the punk rock and new wave of the 1970s and early 1980s, had, by the start of the 1990s, established a strong outlet, mostly through college radio and a few commercial stations. It is primarily through these alternative commercial and college stations that bands like Nirvana were first heard by many listeners, but it is a single song, with an aggressive guitar riff, bleak lyrics, and Cobain's screaming voice that made much of America sit up and take notice. The single, "Smells Like Teen Spirit," from the 1991 album *Nevermind,* seemed to become an anthem virtually overnight for the nation's malaise and particularly for America's youth. The song also signaled that supposed niche music could indeed find a wider audience, and even, as was the case with *Nevermind,* achieve enormous commercial success.

Nirvana formed in the late 1980s, as part of Seattle's Sub Pop scene. The Sub Pop record label had made a name for itself by working with numerous bands whose inspirations came in part from punk, but also infused other musical styles, especially the melodies of 1970s hard rock, into the mix. The most notable of these bands was Soundgarden, which predated Nirvana.

Nirvana's first album, *Bleach* (1989) was immediately well-received by alternative radio, but lacked the spirit and the catchy songwriting that would later bring the band its great acclaim. Two years and two EPs later, Nirvana released *Nevermind,* which eventually sold more than seven million copies. On this record, original members Cobain and Chris (later Krist) Novoselic were joined by drummer Dave Grohl, and the music coalesced into a melodic wall of sound. "Smells Like Teen Spirit," the opening track, demonstrated a hallmark of Cobain's writing style, alternating between clean guitar chords, with lyrics sung in a lazy, mumbled style, and then an explosion of distortion and shrieking. Formula aside, the key to the song and the band's success was Cobain's sense of melody. Behind the aggression and the noise was a remarkably well constructed pop song. Listeners found themselves humming along based on the strong melody. The Cobain formula resulted in numerous hits from *Nevermind* and its follow-up album, *In Utero.*

Part of Nirvana's appeal was the implied lack of control suggested by Cobain's lyrics. Self-deprecation, paranoia, disassociation, and even a sense of contempt for the world of pop music and its fans haunted his songs. That lack of control manifested itself in Nirvana's music and Cobain's life. The less commercially successful *In Utero* seemed more fragile and lacked the self-control of *Nevermind,* which also likely reflected the instability of Cobain's mental and emotional state. Although the band's performance on the TV show *MTV Unplugged* would later be released as a CD, *In Utero* would be their final studio record. Cobain fell further under the thrall of drug, health, and emotional problems, and in April 1994, he killed himself in his Seattle home.[2]

Cobain's death sent shockwaves across the country. His suicide at the age of 27, followed by a fan-based funeral vigil and an around-the-clock tribute on MTV, led many to proclaim Cobain the latest in a long line of rock 'n' roll martyrs. Those associated with Nirvana went on to other projects: Novoselic formed a band called Sweet 75. Grohl found enormous success with his new band, Foo Fighters. Cobain's widow, Courtney Love, found continued fame as the front woman for the band Hole and as a minor film actress in movies like *The People vs. Larry Flynt* (1996).

GRUNGE AND ALTERNATIVE HARD ROCK

The term *grunge* came to be applied to numerous bands that came to light during the early 1990s, especially those coming out of Seattle's Sub Pop label. Several grunge bands, including Soundgarden, Alice in Chains, and Stone Temple Pilots, found considerable commercial success, in part due to Nirvana's trailblazing. Second only to Nirvana in fame was Pearl Jam, led by singer Eddie Vedder. Pearl Jam's melodies drew more from heavy metal and 1970s rock than Nirvana's. They opted for pseudocerebral existential sensitivity rather than Cobain's self-deprecating humor. The real appeal of Pearl Jam was Vedder's almost hyper-emotive vocals. Pearl Jam's 1991 debut *Ten,* which sold more than 6 million copies, offered up a sense of seriousness and profundity. It was clear from *Ten* and the records that followed, including *Vs.* (1993) and *Vitalogy* (1994), which both entered the charts at number one, that Pearl Jam took itself seriously and warmed up to its commercial success far more easily than Cobain.[3]

The success of grunge also opened doors for bands with an equally aggressive sound that might not be strictly considered grunge. Smashing Pumpkins, for instance, melded grunge, 1970s rock, and the gothic rock sound of the 1980s. Smashing Pumpkin's songs on their debut *Gish* (1991) and their two-disc concept album *Mellon Collie and the Infinite Sadness* (1995) were marked by deep (and often bleak) introspection and rage, but what particularly stood out was front man Billy Corgan's thin and reedy, yet hypnotic, voice.

Rage Against The Machine, a multiethnic band, mixed hardcore punk, hip hop, and heavy metal with a dash of reggae and fiery political lyrics, literally raging against the establishment. Political polemics were not widespread in the pop music of the 1990s, making Rage Against The Machine an anomaly. The band's self-titled debut in 1992 introduced themes to which it would return frequently: social injustice, power politics, and especially racism. Rage Against The Machine often played benefit concerts and openly protested what they saw as unjust, such as the imprisonment of Native American activist Leonard Peltier.[4]

Similar in sound, if not in politics, to Rage Against The Machine were a number of new hard rock bands that blended crunching guitars with hip hop beats and vocals. Korn gained a large following among men in their late teens and early twenties. Korn's unrelentingly aggressive music and lyrics, along with occasional interesting instrumentation—singer Jonathan Davis played bagpipes—made them a mainstay of hard rock radio. Their third album, *Follow the Leader* (1998), debuted at the top spot of *Billboard* magazine's list of top 200 albums and spawned the hit singles "Got the Life" and "Freak on a Leash." Leaning more heavily on rap were rap-rock performers like Insane Clown Posse, known as much for their costumes and makeup as for their music,

IT CAME FROM SEATTLE

Grunge came roaring out of the American Northwest in the mid-1980s and peaked in the early 1990s as a rejection of the dominant glam metal look and sound of the "hair bands." The music fused the raw energy and lyrical content of punk with the edgy angularity of metal, and it drew on such seminal 1980s rock acts as the Pixies, Sonic Youth, and the Melvins to create a raw new style. Grunge was also identified with the slacker chic image of ripped denim, flannel shirts, knit caps, and work boots. As the music's popularity spread, so did grunge style, even reaching the runways of the world's fashion capitals. The punk ethic of the bands and the Seattle fans that helped birth the scene made many of them denounce the worldwide spread of their city's sound. Interestingly, it wasn't until the British music paper *Melody Maker* described the burgeoning Seattle sound in 1989 that many Americans took notice.

While grunge became popular worldwide, Britpop emerged in the mid-1990s as, in part, a self-conscious rejection of the dour lyrics and introspective moodiness of the grunge bands. British acts such as Blur and Oasis brought Beatles-esque sunshine to the rock landscape, while acknowledging that their sound was in part inspired by and reaction against the grunge aesthetic.

Meanwhile, Australian youth were heavily exposed to the Seattle sound and look, and they took to it. Australian rockers Silverchair are counted among the more notable early successes of the post-grunge movement. That genre tended to be more slickly packaged and produced but was indebted to the intense heart of grunge.

Lead singer of the shock rock band Marilyn Manson performs at OzzFest '97 at Giants Stadium, in 1997, in East Rutherford, New Jersey. AP Photo.

and Kid Rock, who also threw a country twang into the mix.

The music of Marilyn Manson incorporated the same power guitar riffs, musical noise, and distorted vocals often found in the noise-laden industrial pop of the late 1980s. Marilyn Manson (born Brian Hugh Warner), the man whose stage name leant itself to the band, became as well known for his costuming, which combined drag queen with horror movie walking undead, and onstage antics. The sex-and-death motif of their music, shows, appearance, and stage names earned Marilyn Manson widespread publicity, but they also raised the ire of parents and community leaders. Performances by the band were barred in several areas, and its music was linked to several acts of high school violence. The criticisms spread to include all gothic music, and although Marilyn Manson had little to do with the gloomy gothic rock that was born in the 1980s, the term gothic came to be identified with similar bands.[5]

THE MAINSTREAMING OF ALTERNATIVE ROCK

Prior to the 1990s, alternative rock had largely been the domain of the college radio stations and commercial alternative stations that were mostly confined to coastal urban areas, such as Los Angeles and New York. But the 1990s saw large corporations coming to control local stations, with stations playing the same alternative rock from region to region. Alternative rock festivals, like Lollapalooza and several festivals starting in 1994 under the name "Woodstock," became some of the most successful live music events in the nation. The crass commercialism of Woodstock '99 and the widespread violence and vandalism that took place at the festival, however, proved it to be much different than its namesake.

MTV, corporate radio, and rock festival tours contributed to a growing homogeneity, even in the traditionally eclectic and localized world of alternative rock. This encouraged the popularity of bands that were only mildly alternative, veering closer to an adult-contemporary sound, such as Hootie & the Blowfish.

The Dave Matthews Band, led by Matthews, a South African relocated to Charlottesville, Virginia, garnered much attention for its multicultural, multi-ethnic lineup, including a saxophonist and a violinist. The band's base was acoustic rock, but its influences included folk, jazz, and world music. With early independent releases, including its debut, *Remember Two Things* (1993), the Dave Matthews Band developed a fanatic following, even though they had yet to gain much radio airplay. With *Under the Table and Dreaming* (1994) and *Crash* (1996), the band established itself as a one of the most popular bands in the world, reflected both on radio and the band's near-constant touring. By the end of the decade, the group's musical virtuosity, catchy songs, and its front man's affable nature routinely packed venues.

WOMEN IN ROCK

The strong female presence in alternative music during the 1990s is perhaps best represented by the establishment of an annual festival primarily devoted to women's music: Lilith Fair. The festival was primarily the brainchild of Sarah McLachlan. Her first album, *Touch* (1988), made her a pop star in her native Canada; her follow-ups *Solace* (1991) and *Fumbling Towards Ecstasy* (1994) established her in the United States. These layered, guitar- and piano-driven records prominently featured McLachlan's rich, airy voice, and introspective and frequently melancholy lyrics. McLachlan became a strong proponent of women's music and argued that the music industry, particularly in terms of live performance, was not kind to female artists other than those whose prime asset was their sex appeal, like the Spice Girls and Britney Spears. Lilith Fair was her attempt to rectify this, at least in part.

The popularity of Lilith Fair, as well as that of McLachlan and other female singers, like Tori Amos, inspired other women and created a more welcoming environment in the music industry. While there were many McLachlan imitators, other women developed their own distinct sound. Alanis Morissette, another Canadian, had made several innocuous pop albums before the 1995 release of *Jagged Little Pill,* a multi-platinum album of often cynical, frequently angry, yet catchy pop songs. Jewel (surname Kilcher) released her first record, *Pieces of You,* in 1995. A highly skilled vocalist, Jewel drew from traditional folk music and the pop world. Sheryl Crow, initially as popular for her good looks as for her music, proved herself with folk- and blues-based rock 'n' roll and an appealing mixture of tough and vulnerable vocals. Fiona Apple, a teenaged singer with a voice that sounded much older, released her debut *Tidal* (1996) to critical and commercial acclaim.

HEAVY METAL

Heavy metal, while still limited in its radio appeal, continued to accumulate a significant following, particularly among young men in their teens and twenties. A Grammy Award for best hard rock/heavy metal act was introduced in 1989, and while its first recipient, the classic rock group Jethro Tull, raised the ire of many heavy metal fans, the award marked a change in the general conception of the genre. The 1980s and 1990s saw the genre spread into a number of sub-genres, such as thrash metal, speed metal, and death metal. Death metal received considerable criticism for its frequent use of violent imagery and its attention to death and decay.

Despite its growing sales, most heavy metal failed to garner much radio play, as stations instead latched on to grunge-derived sounds. But there were exceptions, such as Metallica. From its beginnings with the 1983 speed metal record *Kill*

'Em All, Metallica built the strongest following, winning the 1990 heavy metal Grammy. Throughout the 1990s, the band continued to prosper as it became more melodic, while never losing its often bleak and always aggressive outlook. While heavy metal may have influenced grunge bands, Metallica remained unarguably the most successful true metal band of the decade, meriting high sales for its albums *Metallica* (1991), *Load* (1996), *Re-Load* (1997), *Garage Inc.* (1998), and *S&M* (1999).

RAP AND HIP HOP

Like heavy metal, rap and hip hop largely went ignored by most commercial radio, even as the sales figures for the genre shot sky high. Many Americans first became aware of rap through the relatively accessible and non-controversial rapping of MC Hammer, Run-D.M.C., and the like in the 1980s. However, in 1990, the group 2 Live Crew attracted attention when a federal judge in Florida ruled its album *As Nasty as They Wanna Be* (1989) to be obscene, due to its explicitly sexual lyrics. The ruling gave 2 Live Crew the dubious distinction of being the first musical group of any kind to have a record legally declared obscene in the United States, but the added notoriety increased the group's sales.

Authorities, especially those in Florida, continued to target the group and their music, raiding live shows and arresting and prosecuting record store owners and clerks for selling the record. After the arrest of several members of 2 Live Crew at an adults-only show at a Florida night club, the group went to trial. Some questioned the merits of the trial, noting that equally explicit material could be found in other musical forms, as well as in literary works. This led some to suspect that 2 Live Crew were singled out in part because they were black, and therefore more threatening than a white comedian with equally lascivious material, like the popular Andrew Dice Clay. Ultimately, 2 Live Crew was acquitted and the obscenity ruling on their album reversed, but the controversy surrounding rap was far from over.

Particularly targeted for attack on counts of misogyny and encouraging violence was the Gangsta Rap genre. This rap form can arguably be said to have its source in the music of Public Enemy, whose records, including *It Takes a Nation of Millions to Hold Us Back* (1988), *Fear of a Black Planet* (1990), and *Apocalypse 91... The Enemy Strikes Black* (1991), brought a new political consciousness to rap. But it was groups like N.W.A. (Niggas With Attitude) that dragged their listeners deep into the realistic world of African American communities. N.W.A. painted a brutal picture of their home, Compton in South Central Los Angeles, as their lyrics detailed drug deals and gang wars in explicit and violent terms. While some critics lambasted them for the violence and disrespect toward women in their lyrics, others applauded the group for their honest portrayal of life in the lower class African American neighborhoods. Several individual members of the group would go on to their own solo success during the course of the decade. Ice Cube had a string of critically praised albums, starting with *AmeriKKKa's Most Wanted* (1990), and he started a successful career as an actor. Eazy E began a successful solo stint but died of AIDS in 1995. Meanwhile, Dr. Dre co-founded his own label, Death Row Records.[6]

The name Death Row was chosen in part because of the criminal background of many of the executives and recording artists on the label, and the label was plagued with violence and run-ins with the law. Co-founder Marion "Sugar Beat" Knight openly admitted to ruling by intimidation as much as by business acumen, an attitude that may have contributed to a major rivalry with Sean "P. Diddy" Combs and his Bad Boy label. Meanwhile, Death Row's top artist Snoop Doggy Dogg was being tried on murder charges. Though treating the usual themes of gangsta violence, womanizing, and drug use, Snoop Doggy Dogg was unusual in his oddly sing-song, playful raps. Employing the more traditional swagger and aggression of gangsta rap, Tupac "2Pac" Shakur was recruited from his jail cell by Knight, even as his record *Me Against the World* (1995) was selling phenomenally, topping the charts. This all lent credence to the accusations of rap's violent nature, as did the growing rivalry between Death Row and Bad Boy.

Although it was never proven that the conflict resulted directly in violence, the period saw the murders of several involved with the labels,

Dr. Dre, left, and Snoop Dogg, both featured in *Rolling Stone '93: The Year in Review,* shown on television in December 1993. Courtesy of Photofest.

including Tupac Shakur in 1996 and Bad Boy's most popular artist, the Notorious B.I.G., in early 1997. Death Row eventually dissolved after it was abandoned by Snoop Doggy Dogg and by Dr. Dre, who formed his own label, Aftermath Entertainment. Knight was ultimately incarcerated for violating parole.[7]

Another important figure in gangsta rap was Ice T who, like Ice Cube, would eventually take up acting as well. Ice T spent his early years engaged in gang and criminal activity in Los Angeles. He released his first album in 1987 and developed a considerable following, as well as stirred up controversy, both of which would hit their peak in 1992 with the formation of his heavy metal band, Body Count, and the release of the band's self-titled album. The band was an anomaly: heavy metal, the traditional domain of young middle class white men, was now being performed by an angry black man from the 'hood.

Body Count's songs made it clear that Ice T was not one to steer away from controversy. A song called "Cop Killer" sparked hostility toward the rapper-cum-rocker from the law enforcement community, and Vice President Dan Quayle blamed the song for encouraging violence against police officers. The Body Count album would eventually be re-released without "Cop Killer," a move criticized by other artists who derided Ice T for caving in to external pressure.

The Gangsta label had long been questioned by many of the rappers whose work was being labeled as such, but calling something gangsta was a wise commercial move. Many rappers viewed gangsta as having become more concerned with fashion than with personal and political expression.

Because of this, as well as the violence and misogyny in so much of the music, there was a backlash against gangsta and hardcore rap from within the hip hop community. The Native Tongues family, a loose-knit conglomeration of rap artists coming originally out of New York in the mid-1980s, eschewed themes of violence and criminality. Native Tongue bands like De La Soul, the Jungle Brothers, and A Tribe Called Quest explored political issues, frequently drawing from soul, blues, and jazz for their melodic and rhythmic structures. This style of rap also tended to be friendlier to women. Queen Latifah's first record, released in 1989, received immediate critical and commercial success, which she used as a springboard in the 1990s to further musical success, as well as an acting career and significant activism in support of AIDS research and ecology.[8]

This kinder, gentler rap sound reached its commercial peak in a Georgia group called Arrested Development. This group not only celebrated their African roots, but also their Southern upbringing, both in their clothing and their sung and rapped vocals. Their first record, *3 Years, 5 Months and 2 Days in the Life of....* (1992) marked the time it took for the band to be signed to a record label. The album went platinum within the year. Arrested Development showed many hip hop artists and the general American populace that rap need not be simply about black anger.

With the success of rap, it was only natural that whites would venture into the world of hip hop. Many of the newer white rappers were copying the styles of black music but expanding it to capture their own experiences. The Beastie Boys, for instance, developed a sound on *Check Your Head* (1992), *Ill Communication* (1994), and *Hello Nasty* (1998) that relied significantly from rap—rhythmically spoken lyrics and heavily layered samples, for instance—but was almost a new genre unto itself. The Beastie Boys started their own label, Grand Royal, which allowed them full creative freedom and provided an avenue for others, like the all-female group Luscious Jackson.

By following a similar pattern, Beck, a singer-songwriter, sprang to nationwide popularity with the single "Loser," which despite its lo-fi sound and sloppy vocals (by design), became a surprise hit. The single was re-released on Beck's debut, *Mellow Gold* (1994), an entertaining but uneven record. On his *Odelay* (1996), Beck left behind the amusing childishness of "Loser" in favor of surprisingly intelligent songs that only bore the slightest resemblance to traditional rap. Beck's popularity exploded, based on his fusion style and willingness to change styles with each new CD.

At the end of the decade, Eminem stole the crown as the most popular white rapper, and as his fame grew, he developed into one of the most popular performers in the world. By then, much of the controversy about rap had died down, as rappers expanded into new musical territories and the gangstas had largely dissipated. However, with *The Slim Shady LP* (1998), Eminem brought the controversy back to the front page. Eminem, born Marshall Bruce Mathers III, became a target almost immediately, even as album sold 480,000 in its first two weeks. Eminem was accused of encouraging violent behavior, particularly against women and homosexuals. The lyrics presented some of the most brutally graphic images to appear in all of pop music. Eminem also received early flack for being a white artist performing black music, but Eminem was soon largely accepted, if not always approved of, by the hip hop community. His debut album, after all, had been released on a real hip hop label, Dr. Dre's Aftermath Entertainment, with the brilliant Dre producing the album and appearing in Eminem music videos.

African American performers also found success in rhythm and blues (R&B). R&B performers like Janet Jackson and Mariah Carey successfully stuck to the familiar dance-pop sound that had carried their careers thus far. By the end of the 1990s, Macy Gray had become one of the top selling R&B performers, with a brassy soul sound that could well have come from decades earlier.

LATINO POP

Latinos also experienced success in the 1990s in genres from punk to heavy metal to hip hop, but the greatest successes were those in mainstream pop, with Latin American influences. Although performers like Gloria Estefan had garnered a certain amount of attention for Latin pop, no such performer had ever come close to Ricky Martin. Martin, originally a member of mid-1980s boy band group Menudo, had already established himself in Latin America, especially his birthplace of Puerto Rico, when, in 1999, he released his first English language album, *Ricky Martin.* Propelled largely by the energetic dance single "Livin' La Vida Loca," the album shot to the top of the pop charts. The song itself became virtually inescapable.

Martin opened doors for other Latino performers, including Marc Anthony, Enrique Iglesias, and singer/actress Jennifer Lopez. Martin's attempt to crossover followed in the footsteps of singer Selena, who had made significant moves to expand her fan base to include non-Latinos, before her 1995 murder put a premature end to her promising career.

Ultimately, the growth in Latin music's popularity was phenomenal, with annual sales reaching more than $570 million in 1998.[9] The success of Latin music in America was not surprising, given the rapid growth of the Hispanic population in the United States. What is perhaps more surprising is that performers like Ricky Martin found such a warm welcome with a white, English-speaking audience, although certainly in Martin's case, his movie star good looks and dance moves played a large role in his success. Consequently, record companies began to market their wares to both Hispanic and Anglo audiences.

COUNTRY MUSIC

Country music also continued the move into the mainstream with the upsurge of younger performers and the shift to an adult-contemporary pop sound. 1989 saw the rise of country superstars like Travis Tritt, Clint Black, Vince Gill, Mary Chapin Carpenter, and Garth Brooks. Both rock and country influences were clearly audible in Brook's music, which, if stripped of his country twang vocals and the occasional country instrumentation (i.e., slide guitar and fiddle), could easily be mistaken for mainstream soft rock. Brooks later became the bestselling recording artist of the 1990s, selling more than 100 million records.[10]

Some country purists complained that, as these artists moved toward a stronger pop sound, they stripped country of its soul, taking away its unique qualities. There was still an audience for traditional country, and, fortunately, old stalwarts, such as Johnny Cash and Waylon Jennings, still made that kind of music. Although possessing definite pop sensibilities (as evidenced by a later duet with Elton John and her subsequent recordings), 13-year-old singer LeAnn Rimes shot to stardom in 1996 with "Blue," a song that clearly nodded to country music legend Patsy Cline and helped Rimes win a Best New Artist Grammy.

Others also stuck to the traditions of the country genre, in a movement referred to as Americana, roots revival, and (ironically, given its closer adherence to traditional sounds) alternative-country. One of the most notable groups in this vein was the Dixie Chicks, a trio of women who flaunted their looks and fashion sense, but who also had a keen interest in preserving country's heritage.

HIT SONGS OF THE 1990s

"Friends in Low Places"—Garth Brooks (1990)

"Nothing Compares 2 U"—Sinéad O'Connor (1990)

"Smells Like Teen Spirit"—Nirvana (1991)

"Nuthin' But a 'G' Thang"—Dr Dre featuring Snoop Doggy Dogg (1993)

"Wonderwall"—Oasis (1995)

"Ironic"—Alanis Morissette (1996)

"Don't Speak"—No Doubt (1996)

"I'll Be Missing You"—Puff Daddy and Faith Evans featuring 112 (1997)

"My Heart Will Go On"—Celine Dion (1998)

"...Baby One More Time"—Britney Spears (1998)

MAINSTREAM POP

Even as record companies became more adventurous with their releases in the 1990s, there was no shortage of traditional pop. Bubblegum pop had an enormous resurgence during the decade, with the music of young, mostly blonde girl singers and boy bands becoming virtually inescapable, although it could be argued that these youths were largely being sold on their image, not their music. The boy bands, for instance, provided fans with non-threatening heartthrobs and playful, never sexual, love songs. The girl singers, on the other hand, were frequently overly sexualized, raising both controversy and record sales.

Certainly, sex appeal was a large part of the Spice Girls' success. This British group of five singers, bearing monikers like Sporty Spice, Baby Spice, and Ginger Spice, were almost immediately showered with criticisms: that they were style over substance, that they were more marketing than musical, that they catered to feminine stereotypes, even that they were racially inequitable (the one black member was called Scary Spice). Whatever the criticisms, however, the group's debut album, *Spice* (1996), and the first single, "Wannabe," quickly reached the number one spot on the charts.

The Spice Girls found a considerable audience among young teen and pre-teen girls, and given this audience, some felt troubled by their sexed up image, especially that of Baby Spice, who was in her early twenties. By the end of the decade, there would be a new breed of sexed-up teen singer that would make Baby Spice's sexuality seem tame.

In 1999, singer Britney Spears released her debut album, *... Baby One More Time,* which sold more than 10 million copies before the end of the year. The buoyant dance pop music tapped into the young teens and pre-teens audience to whom the Spice Girls' music appealed. Also like the Spice Girls, Britney Spears's image was equally important to her appeal. But at the time of her debut, Spears was 17 years old, and some thought she provided a bad example for young girls, while also appealing to prurient interests among adults. Spears denied that her scanty outfits were worn in the interest of sex appeal, claiming that the clothing simply reflected the fashion of the day.

Spears began slightly downplaying her sexuality, albeit still with considerable bare skin, but her popularity continued into the next decade, along with that of similar performers, such as Christina Aguilera and Jessica Simpson.

The boy bands of the late 1990s were almost diametrically opposed to the image created for most of the young female pop singers. Instead of being highly sexualized, these groups were largely presented as non-threatening. Thus, the Backstreet Boys might come across as fun-loving and mischievous but never dangerous. The image paid off, as the group would be named Artists of the Year in *Rolling Stone*'s 1999 readers' poll, followed closely by similar groups, especially 'N Sync. The Backstreet Boys were formed in 1993, the product of an open audition in Orlando, Florida, held by businessman Lou Pearlmen, but it wouldn't be until 1997, after considerable touring and moderate success in Europe, that the group would finally break through in the United States. They had repeated success with songs like "Quit Playing Games (with My Heart)," "As Long As You Love Me," and "I'll Never Break Your Heart." The Backstreet Boys would eventually break from Pearlman and successfully venture forward on their own, but not before Pearlman had put together a similar group, 'N Sync.[11] As another five boys in their late teens and twenties, singing similar love songs, 'N Sync could be seen as simply a carbon copy of the Pearlman era Backstreet Boys, but 'N Sync (who would also break from Pearlman) sold more than nine million copies of their self-titled debut album by the end of the 1990s.[12]

Of course, veteran pop divas continued to prosper. Madonna pursued an acting career, especially in *Evita* (1996). She experimented with electronica and other musical forms on her albums *I'm Breathless* (1990), *Erotica* (1992), *Bedtime Stories* (1994), and *Ray of Light* (1998). Another diva, Celine Dion, had one of the most popular singles of the decade with "My Heart Will Go On," recorded for the soundtrack of *Titanic* (1995). The song won an Oscar and enjoyed virtually inescapable radio airplay.

Sports

and Leisure of the 1990s

A growing American population and increased concerns about health and fitness contributed to an overall growth in sports participation during the 1990s. A growing environmental impulse also prompted an increase in the number of Americans seeking outdoor experiences, like hiking, camping, backpacking, and bicycling. Moreover, sports appeal was cultivated by the media and big business, as advertisers exploited sports imagery in commercials. The growth of supply superstores made sporting gear easily attainable, affordable, and fashionable as well. Retail sales for sporting gear had the fastest growth ever in the nineties, as did spending on recreational team sports and gym memberships.

A 1995 survey found that more than 24 million people participated in in-line skating, also called rollerblading, in which the wheels were placed in a single row that simulated the straight blade of an ice skate. One reason for the popularity of in-line skating was that people could skate on any paved surface. In-line skate sales hit a plateau as other vehicular fads, like the scooter craze of the early 2000s, cut into the demand for roller blades among the youths who had constituted 62 percent of skaters according to the 1995 study.[1]

Another athletic trend of the 1990s was an exercise program called Tae-Bo, which had a fairly limited pool of participants. The program, a combination of martial arts and aerobics, was largely propelled by a series of TV ads and infomercials featuring its energetic creator and spokesman, Billy Blanks and also by its reputation as a celebrity exercise program. Tae-Bo had, according to Blanks, evolved out of his experimentation with the traditional martial art Taekwondo. Experts were divided about whether or not Tae-Bo offered more than traditional aerobic and martial arts training, but the program was notable for the media blitz that brought it into American homes.

EXTREME SPORTS

While traditional sports continued to enjoy widespread participation, a growing segment of the populace began looking for something that stimulated an adrenaline rush well beyond that provided by conventional athletics. Many of these individuals turned to activities that had at least some semblance of danger, or sports that had previously enjoyed something of an underground following, such as skateboarding. Snowboarding, once a fringe hybrid of skiing and surfing, enjoyed widespread growth especially. A 1995 study found that there were about 2.3 million snowboarders in the country, a growth of 800,000 since 1990. The study also noted that most snowboarders were under the age of 18, suggesting that the sport was still very much in its growth stage.[2]

Extreme sports also frequently involved using traditional sporting equipment in a new and more exciting way. Traditional skiing mutated into free-style and aerial skiing, wherein what a skier did while in the air, flung by jumping ramps, was at least as important as what he or she did while in contact with the snow. Likewise, bicycling, particularly BMX (bicycle motocross) bikes, became an extreme sport, as riders performed acrobatics while balanced on the bike frame, spinning the handlebars, or soaring off of ramps.

While many of these activities had existed in some form before the 1990s, now they became a popular spectacle, flirting with mainstream success. Snowboarding and free-style skiing became official Winter Olympic sports. White-water rafting, skateboard bungee jumping, and other extreme sports appeared in many advertisements as companies tried to tap into a market of young people with disposable income.

Many of these sports were brought together by an annual tournament, the X Games, created by and broadcast on the cable network ESPN. First held in 1995 as the Extreme Games, the competition featured 350 participants in 27 events, and both numbers increased every year thereafter. The growing extreme sports culture spawned its own celebrities, including skateboarder Tony Hawk, who appeared on numerous TV shows, was signed to advertising contracts on par with other sports stars, and had his name pasted on a multitude of products, from clothing to Hot Wheels toy cars.

PROFESSIONAL WRESTLING

On February 9, 1989, the New Jersey Senate proclaimed that, for purposes of regulation, big-time professional wrestling was *entertainment* rather than a sport. The senate's legislation removed some of the restrictions placed on wrestling matches, but it also acknowledged that the activity, which always depicted itself as an authentic athletic contest, was one in which matches were, to some extent, choreographed, and participants often trained to avoid serious injury. Other states followed New Jersey's legislative lead.

The World Wrestling Federation (WWF) in the 1990s. Shown: Ultimate Warrior. Courtesy of Photofest.

However, rather than stifling enthusiasm, this proclamation breathed new life into pro wrestling. In fact, the World Wrestling Foundation (WWF) had requested the legislation. The major wrestling organizations, the WWF, headed by Vince McMahon, and the smaller World Championship Wrestling (WCW), founded in 1994 by Ted Turner, became increasingly flamboyant.

Wrestlers developed striking personas and acted out elaborate dramas of betrayal, jealousy, and revenge, both in the ring and in the locker rooms. There was frequently a kind of mythic quality to the dramas, with good pitted against evil, and heroes fallen and redeemed. Pro wrestling featured celebrities like "Stone Cold" Steve Austin, Dwayne "The Rock" Johnson, and Mankind (Mick Foley). As always, wrestling still featured over-the-top action, and as a matter of fact, greater risks seemed necessary to generate fan interest. In a September 1999 WWF bout, for example, Austin beat up an opponent, dragged him out of the ring and backstage, and then threw him into the back of an ambulance. Next, Austin climbed into a semi and smashed into the ambulance. Few adults saw such a spectacle as a real fight, but worries abounded about young people who watched these events. The WWF did, after all, market to youth, and it even issued a line of WWF action figures for sale in toy stores. Desensitization to violence was the primary fear, but there was also concern about imitation. Among teenagers, the popularity of backyard wrestling, in imitation of the WWF and the WCW, grew enormously, and a number of teens suffered serious injuries as a result of their imitations.

The success of pro wrestling in the 1980s and 1990s spawned similar athletic entertainments, like *American Gladiators* (1989–1997). In the TV show, contestants, who were real athletes, rather than trained performers, competed in odd events against each other and the Gladiators, muscle-bound men and women whose primary goal was to prevent the contestants' success. The events included climbing rock walls with Gladiators in hot pursuit, or rolling around in giant cage-like balls. *Battle Dome,* which debuted in 1999, offered similar entertainment, increasing the amount of physical contact, as well as the flamboyancy of their costumed gladiators, called Warriors. However, the feuds between the Battle Dome Warriors bore a stronger resemblance to those of pro wrestling.

WOMEN'S SPORTS

In 1972, Title IX, guaranteeing gender equality in educational programs, was instituted. The legislation mandated that women be given the equal opportunity to participate in high school and college sports. Title IX was never without controversy, and many athletic directors and administrators continued to hold the beliefs that sports were primarily the realm of men, and that women's sports just couldn't bring in the same kind of revenue that men's sports did. The Women's Sports Foundation conducted a study in 1998 that found these attitudes still running strong, even though, in the same year, the Supreme Court declined to hear an appeal to overturn Title IX.[3]

Even as Title IX had been increasing the number of women taking part in amateur sports, professionally, women were making a name for themselves like never before. Moreover, they were making a name for themselves in sports that were not traditional women's sports. Instead, they were playing basketball in the Women's National Basketball Association (WNBA). The league was conceived in 1996, after U.S. women won Olympic gold earlier in the year, and the first WNBA tip-off took place on June 21, 1997. Women's soccer received a considerable boost in popularity as well. In 1991, the U.S. team won the first women's World Cup. While that first triumph received relatively little press, more attention was given to it in 1999. The U.S. women's World Cup team took home the trophy again, much in contrast to the 1998 men's World Cup tournament, in which the U.S. team ranked dead last. The spectacular performance of the women's team created several high-profile celebrities, including Mia Hamm and Brandi Chastain. Chastain gained widespread publicity for celebrating a goal by sliding on the playing field and pulling off her jersey, revealing a sports bra, upon winning the tournament. Even hockey opened up to women in the 1990s. The first Women's World Hockey Championship, won by Canada, was held in 1990, and in 1998, the U.S. team won the first Olympic gold medal in women's hockey. However, despite the growing popularity of women's sports, they continued to receive considerably less publicity than men's events.

PROFESSIONAL SPORTS

Auto Racing

The 1990s were a golden age for auto racing, particularly for the National Association for Stock Car Auto Racing (NASCAR). Directed in the 1990s by Bill France Sr. and Bill France Jr., NASCAR was the fastest-growing spectator sport of the decade. Started in the late 1940s, NASCAR-sanctioned stock car racing experienced gradual growth, but in the 1980s, sponsorship from major corporations and growing television coverage brought NASCAR to new audiences. NASCAR-licensed merchandise, an $80 million industry in 1990, brought in more than $950 million in 1998. Racers such as Dale Earnhardt, Jeff Gordon, Dale Jarrett, and Sterling Marlin became celebrities on par with those of football, basketball, and baseball. Of course, fame did not diminish the danger of high-speed racing. The 1990s saw the loss of several racers, including J. D. McDuffie, Clifford Allison, Rodney Orr, Neil Bonnett, and John Nemechek. Earnhardt, perhaps the most popular driver in NASCAR history, died in a crash at the Daytona 500 in February 2001.

Basketball

Basketball's popularity grew rapidly in the 1990s, propelled by fast-paced action and a marketing campaign designed to emphasize the sheer entertainment value of the sport. Numerous players had tremendous appeal well beyond their skills on the court, such as Earvin "Magic" Johnson, Charles Barkley, David Robinson, Karl Malone, and Shaquille O'Neal. Michael Jordan stood first and foremost among these greats. Jordan's on-court skills made him arguably the greatest player ever, while his enormous popularity grew based on his charisma and geniality. He proved to be the highest-profile player in the strongest team of the decade, the Chicago Bulls. Despite his retirement during the 1993–1994 season, Jordan was instrumental in leading the Bulls to six NBA championships (1991–1993, 1996–1998). Jordan's skills were also supplemented by a top-notch team, which included Scotty Pippen, Dennis Rodman, and Toni Kukoc.

Football

The National Football League added three teams: the Carolina Panthers and the Jacksonville Jaguars in 1995, and the Baltimore Ravens in 1996. These teams increased the number to 31, making it the largest league in pro sports. Attendance at NFL games continued to rise, with the Super Bowl consistently rating as the most popular annual event in spectator sports. One of the top teams of the decade was the Dallas Cowboys, which won Super Bowls XXVI (1993), XXVIII (1994), and XXX (1996). But there were other champions, including the San Francisco 49ers, winner of the Super Bowl in 1990 and in 1995, becoming the first team to win five Super Bowls. The Green Bay Packers won the Super Bowl for the first time in 29 years in 1997. They returned to the Bowl the next year but were defeated by the Denver Broncos. In winning Super Bowl XXXII, Denver became the first AFC team to win in 13 years. They won their second consecutive Super Bowl in 1999.

Hockey

The 1990s were a good decade for American hockey, although American teams were heavily stocked with players from other countries, primarily Canada. Nonetheless, never before had U.S. teams earned such good standing in the Stanley Cup hockey championships. The Pittsburgh Penguins won back-to-back in 1991 and 1992, as did the Detroit Red Wings in 1997 and 1998. Other American teams winning the cup in the 1990s were the New York Rangers in 1994, the New Jersey Devils in 1995 (who again won in 2000), the Colorado Avalanche (formerly the Quebec Nordiques) in 1996, and the Dallas Stars (formerly the Minnesota North Stars) in 1999. These championships certainly contributed to the growing popularity of hockey in the United States, despite a 1994 labor dispute that resulted

Wayne Gretzky, playing in the late 1980s. Courtesy of Photofest.

WAYNE GRETZKY (1961–)

Few athletes have had a larger impact on their sport than Wayne Gretzky has had on hockey. The Canadian native, dubbed "The Great One," is widely considered the greatest hockey player of all time. His stellar play and positive celebrity image helped popularize the sport in the United States during his playing days, and he continues to influence hockey as a coach and an icon.

Gretzky holds or shares 61 records, including most career goals (894), most career assists (1,962), and most total points (2,856). Gretzky began his career in the World Hockey Association in 1978 at the age of 17. Gretzky later played for the Edmonton Oilers and moved to the National Hockey League (NHL) when that team joined the league.

In 1988, Gretzky joined the Los Angeles Kings. The move, known by hockey fans simply as "The Trade," disheartened Canadians who watched as their national hero moved south. In response, Nelson Riis, a Canadian New Democratic Party House Leader, demanded that the government block it. Gretzky remained with the Kings until 1996 when he was traded to the St. Louis Blues. That same year, Gretzky made his final move to the New York Rangers, where he played three years before retiring in 1999.

Gretzky played his final game against the Pittsburgh Penguins, April 18, 1999, in Madison Square Garden. He left a legacy of winning four Stanley Cups, nine Hart Trophies as MVP, 10 Art Ross Trophies as the NHL's top scorer, and two Conn Smyth Trophies as playoff MVP. Gretzky appeared in every All-Star Game of his 20 years in hockey. His number 99 was retired by the league in 1999, the same year of his induction into the Hockey Hall of Fame. The Great One is currently head coach and part owner of the Phoenix Coyotes, married to American actress Janet Jones, and they have five children.

in a 103-day lock-out of National Hockey League players. Also adding to the popularity was the growing number of American teams in the NHL. In the course of the decade, professional hockey welcomed the San Jose Sharks, the Tampa Bay Lightning, the Florida Panthers, the Anaheim Mighty Ducks, and the Nashville Predators.

Baseball

Several longstanding baseball records fell during the decade, including that for the most consecutive games played. The 56-year-old record, set by New York Yankee Lou Gehrig, fell on September 6, 1995, when Baltimore Orioles shortstop Cal Ripken stepped onto the field for his 2,131st game. And to confirm his place as a quality player, Ripken hit home runs in both the record tying and breaking games.

Later in the decade, however, an even more sacred baseball record was broken. In the 1998 season, two players were poised to break New York Yankee Roger Maris's long-standing homerun record, set in 1961. As St. Louis Cardinal Mark McGwire and Chicago Cub Sammy Sosa came closer to the mark, game attendance and television ratings rose. In the end, McGwire would break the record and hold it for the season,

WORLD SERIES

1990 Cincinnati Reds (NL) 4 games; Oakland A's (AL), 0 games

1991 Minnesota Twins (AL), 4 games; Atlanta Braves (NL), 3 games

1992 Toronto Blue Jays (AL), 4 games; Atlanta Braves (NL), 2 games

1993 Toronto Blue Jays (AL), 4 games; Philadelphia Phillies (NL), 2 games

1994 Cancelled due to players' strike

1995 Atlanta Braves (NL), 4 games; Cleveland Indians (AL), 2 games

1996 New York Yankees (AL), 4 games; Atlanta Braves (NL), 2 games

1997 Florida Marlins (NL), 4 games; Cleveland Indians (AL), 3 games

1998 New York Yankees (AL), 4 games; San Diego Padres (NL), 0 games

1999 New York Yankees (AL), 4 games; Atlanta Braves (NL), 0 games

though Sosa would also exceed Maris's record. Although there was some grumbling that steroid use—which many believed was rampant in pro sports in general and in baseball in particular—had played a role in the fall of Maris's record, for most fans, this was a welcome return to the glory days of the sport.

Although two long-standing Yankee-held records fell, the New York team had little to feel bad about in the 1990s. The team reached the World Series three times in 1996, 1998, and 1999, winning each time. Atlanta had less luck. Although the Braves played in five of the nine 1990s series, they only won in 1995. The Toronto Blue Jays proved themselves by taking the pennant in 1992 and 1993, while the Cincinnati Reds, Minnesota Twins, and Florida Marlins rounded out the list of champions for 1990, 1991, and 1997, respectively.

SCANDAL AND CONTROVERSY IN PRO SPORTS

Professional sports saw many scandals in the 1990s. The most high-profile case was that of retired football great O. J. Simpson (See Overview of the 1990s), but drugs and violence infected nearly every major pro sport. Scandal even infected women's ice skating in 1994, when Olympic figure skater Nancy Kerrigan was attacked, her knee severely beaten after a practice session, in a conspiracy that involved Kerrigan's rival Tonya Harding.

Boxing came under particular fire. Never a gentle sport, boxing had long been criticized for its violence and its exploitation of athletes. However, in the 1990s, the accusations of barbarity focused principally on Mike Tyson, the heavyweight champion. Tyson developed a reputation as a strong and ferocious fighter, but his antics outside the ring drew considerable publicity as well. High-profile accusations of abuse by his wife, actress Robin Givens, and conviction of rape charges destroyed the fighter's reputation.

After his release from prison in 1996, Tyson fought Evander Holyfield, then current heavyweight champ. The fight was stopped by the referee after Holyfield clearly had Tyson at a disadvantage. A rematch was cut short by referee Mills Lane after Tyson twice bit his opponent, literally tearing off part of Holyfield's ear with his teeth. The spectacle invigorated renewed condemnation of boxing. Though Tyson was barred from the sport (only to return in 2002), the criticisms of boxing continued to be largely ignored. Boxing remained big business, bringing large revenues to the host cities and proving extraordinarily popular on pay-per-view cable TV.

Baseball also suffered, morally if not commercially, in the 1990s, with numerous player run-ins with the law. Most of these cases were drug-related, a fact that tarnished the image of a game that traditionally had great family appeal. The image was also damaged by Atlanta Braves pitcher John Rocker, who let loose a tirade of racist and bigoted slurs in a *Sports Illustrated* interview. The league did not take kindly to Rocker's outbursts, but the short suspension and fine Rocker received seemed a mere slap on the wrist, his prowess on the field clearly ranking as more important than his ethical conduct. What hurt baseball the most, however, was a player strike in the 1994–1995 season. For many fans, the suspension of the season seemed an affront because already highly paid players were demanding still higher pay. Defenders of the strike noted that professional baseball made huge amounts of money, and that the money not going to the players was going to already wealthy executives and owners. But combined with the ever increasing cost of game tickets, the strike signaled that baseball's tradition and history had been buried under the mounting commercialism of the sport. In short, baseball suffered a confidence crisis among fans, and the popular 1994 PBS TV series, *Baseball,* produced by Ken Burns, seemed to signal how far baseball had fallen.

Sports also suffered some major losses due to AIDS and the HIV virus. In 1991, basketball superstar Earvin "Magic" Johnson announced that he had contracted HIV and was retiring from the game (he briefly returned later). (See Overview of the 1990s.) In 1993, tennis legend Arthur Ashe died of AIDS contracted from a blood transfusion. In 1996, boxer Tommy Morrison was barred from the sport upon the revelation that he was HIV-positive. These cases woke many athletes and young people to the risks of sexual promiscuity, and also drew national attention to AIDS, which could no longer been seen as a fringe disease if it was affecting the country's sports heroes.

SPORTS AND MONEY

Professional sports also suffered as spiraling costs made attending sports events prohibitive for many Americans. This was especially true of newly constructed sports arenas, many of which devoted part of their space to catering to wealthy spectators and corporate interests, with private clubs and luxurious boxes for rent from $75,000 to $300,000. Even the less glamorous seats became increasingly expensive. This was due to the widespread introduction of permanent seat licenses, which consumers would have to purchase just to have the right to buy tickets. Therefore, the additional license fee charged by stadium owners could jack up the price of a $40 ticket to several hundred dollars. Stadiums also continued to rely on corporate sponsorship. Advertising became omnipresent within stadiums, and arenas forged special arrangements to only serve a particular brand of beer, hotdog, or soda. In 1995, 3Com Corporation purchased the rights to San Francisco's historic Candlestick Park, and it officially became 3Com Park. Most San Franciscans continued to call the stadium Candlestick.

As ticket prices and advertising increased, many sports fans also looked with disdain at players' increasing wealth. Few fans would deny that players deserved high compensation, as they did in fact entertain millions and brought in high revenues, but to many, salaries seemed to skyrocket to ridiculous levels.

Aside from ticket prices, sports leagues charged an ever increasing rate for broadcast rights. The amount of money in professional sports broadcasts was staggering. In 1993, the NBA negotiated four-year deals with NBC for $750 million and with cable's TNT for $352 million. In 1994, the NFL entered into deals with ABC, NBC, Fox, and ESPN, which garnered the league $4.4 billion (approximately $39.2 million per team). There was prestige connected with sports broadcasts, especially such events as the Olympics, the Super Bowl, and the World Series, but the monetary payoff sometimes fell short of expectations.

Networks were spending a great deal of money to acquire broadcast rights, but they had also to make back their money, and the primary source of revenue was advertising. Getting advertisers to buy airtime at a high enough cost to cover the acquisition expenses, however, was a challenge. CBS had some of the greatest losses, particularly early in the decade, with the 1992 Winter Olympics broadcast and a $1.06 billion arrangement with Major League Baseball from 1990 to 1994. Even as the networks were struggling to afford broadcast rights for sports, cable providers were exploiting the pay-per-view system of subscription television. Pay-per-view had considerable success with broadcasting relatively inexpensive, and typically regional, sporting events, like hockey and college football. But the service's greatest success came with boxing and professional wrestling matches. A 1993 fight between Evander Holyfield and Riddick Bowe, for instance, brought in $33 million dollars for pay-per-view broadcasters.[4]

Top athletes made a good deal of money on endorsements. In some cases, product sponsorship even outpaced their salaries. In 1997, for instance, basketball star Michael Jordan earned $31.3 million in salary, but $47 million on product sponsorships, making him the highest-paid athlete of the year. Tiger Woods, who earned a salary of $2.1 million in 1997, earned $24 million in sponsorships.[5]

CELEBRITY ATHLETES

Sports celebrities became major commercial assets. Basketball spawned perhaps more superstars than any other sport in the 1990s, none more popular than Michael Jordan. His skill and clean image, as compared to far too many other sports figures, made Jordan an ideal role model, and consequently an ideal product spokesman. He became the most sought after basketball player by advertisers, making commercials for Hanes underwear and Nike's Air Jordan shoes. (See Advertising of the 1990s.) He also appeared on the large screen in 1996, playing basketball with Warner Brothers cartoon characters in the blockbuster *Space Jam.* Jordan, however, was hardly alone in his commercial success. Other basketball players also made it to the big screen. Shaquille O'Neal starred in *Kazaam* (1996) and *Steel* (1997), and Dennis Rodman appeared in *Double Team* (1997) and a short-lived TV series, *Soldier of Fortune, Inc.* (1998).

Another major sports celebrity was golf hero Tiger Woods. Young, charming, handsome, and black, Woods was not the kind of person typically associated with the game of golf. Woods hit the professional circuit with a vengeance, winning the Master's Tournament in 1997, the youngest player to do so, at 21 years old. In 1999, he ranked first five times in the PGA tour. Woods broke major ground in a sport that had long been regarded as the elite realm of white men. He was not only the first African American to win a major tournament, but also, as his mother was Thai, the first Asian-American to do so. As a result, Woods became another highly sought after advertising property, and subsequently made ads for Titleist golf gear, Nike, American Express, Rolex, and others. Clearly, he was the most widely-recognized celebrity ever to emerge from the game of golf.

LEISURE ACTIVITIES

Studies have suggested that Americans spent more time working in the 1990s than ever before, but they still seemed to have plenty of time for leisure activities. More toys than ever were being produced, and the average child tended to have more toys than children of earlier generations. Many adults also turned to toy collectibles. The market for games boomed, especially that for computer games, which developed astonishing sophistication. Sports also provided plenty of opportunities to pass the time, either as participant or spectator.

TOYS

The continued increase in the toy market can be attributed, in part, to the increase in disposable income held not only by parents, but also by children themselves. Also important to the growth of the toy market was the continued success of chain retail outlets, like Toys R Us, which accounted for about 20 percent of the retail toy market.

To a large extent, the toy market was driven by licensed properties based on characters and situations on TV or in movies, such as the *Mighty Morphing Power Rangers, Pokémon,* or *Star Wars.* For example, a *Star Wars* Lego series proved popular, but also posed a problem for the Lego Company. It now had to follow up with something

HOW OTHERS SEE US

China Hoops It Up

The hula hoop debuted in 1958 as one of the most explosively popular fads of all time. More than 50 million of the hollow plastic hoops were sold in the United States in the toy's first year, and by 1960, 50 million more had been sold worldwide in Japan, Britain, Australia, and elsewhere. The hoops lost their fad status by 1960, and over the next few decades, manufacturer Wham-O conducted periodic re-launch efforts to temporarily boost sales. However, even the company was surprised when, 35 years later, the hula hoop finally became a craze in mainland China.

Largely isolated from popular culture by its communist government, China seemed immune to fads that swept the rest of the world. In early 1992, however, the official New China News Agency signaled official approval of the *hula quanr* as "part of the new trend of keeping fit and slim," despite the activity's Western origins—a rarity at the time.

The multicolored hoops, which sold for the equivalent of $1.20, were already so popular that shops in China's major cities were unable to keep them in stock. According to one report, a shop in Beijing sold an entire shipment of 350 hoops in 10 minutes. More than 500,000 were sold in China in the fad's first three months. Workers on their midmorning breaks would pull out their hoops and gyrate, and on their way home in the evenings, adults and children alike could be seen with hoops slung over their shoulders or balanced on their bicycle handlebars.

The fad was not without its dark side, however. Soon the Chinese press was warning hoopers to warm up properly and to avoid hooping after eating, when reports emerged that three people had suffered "twisted intestines" as a result of overly vigorous sessions with the toy.

equally exciting; it could no longer count on a child's own creativity for its popularity.

Except for Barbie, most doll sales slumped in the 1990s. However, the collectors' market picked up considerably, becoming one of the 1990s fastest-growing hobbies. Just as she dominated the general doll market, Barbie dominated the collectors' market. A series of international Barbies showed off meticulously-designed ethnic costuming. Barbie also appeared in movie-themed costumes, covering classic films like *The Wizard of Oz* and *Gone with the Wind.*

The Beanie Baby craze centered on a line of small stuffed animals produced by Ty Inc. This large line of many different cute animals soared in popularity. The competition to attain Beanie Babies was fierce, especially among adult collectors, who would sometimes pay outlandish prices for specific ones. Ty stoked the fires by releasing especially rare toys, produced well under the demand level of the market.

In 1996, Tickle-Me Elmo stimulated a buyers' frenzy, not unlike that seen for Cabbage Patch Dolls in the 1980s. This plush version of the character from the Sesame Street children's television program laughed hysterically when tickled on its tummy. The doll's success led to numerous imitators, and *Sesame Street* licensed the creation of similar dolls of other characters from the show.

ACTION FIGURES

Action figures also found a considerable market among adults. Prior parallels like G. I. Joe notwithstanding, the action figure came into its own in the 1970s, particularly with the release of the *Star Wars* action figures line. In the 1990s, *Star Wars* experienced a new surge in popularity due to the release of several *Star Wars* novels and the anticipation of new films in the series. Naturally, the action figures also saw a rebirth. But this time, there were adults who had grown up on the movies and who fondly remembered playing with the toys. Therefore, the acquisition of action figures served as a nostalgic reclamation of the past. *Star Trek* figures also flourished, as did many others tied to various movies and television programs. With the growth of the collectible toy market, the stigma of adults owning action figures was reduced, spurring collectors on, and manufacturers began catering more to this audience.

Todd McFarlane poses with his action figure creation, Spawn, at his office in Tempe, Arizona, April 1999. AP Photo.

One of the groundbreaking companies in this field was McFarlane Toys, founded by Todd McFarlane, creator of the comic book series *Spawn.* McFarlane oversaw the production of figures based on his comic book designs. The result was the most meticulously detailed and gruesome figures to ever hit toy stores. McFarlane's zombies, demons, and monstrosities introduced a new aesthetic to action figure production. McFarlane Toys produced high quality figures for such non-children-oriented properties as the *X-Files* TV series, Austin Powers, and the rock band KISS.[6] These changes in the market also ushered in a new era of sexuality in action figure production. McFarlane Toys had produced several figures of scantily-clad, well-endowed women, principally characters drawn from comic books. Other companies followed suit, creating figures, again mostly based on comic book characters, whose proportions made Barbie's look quite natural. These figures did merit some criticism, but the outcry was limited, given that most figures were sold in comic shops and stores specializing in collectibles.

COMPUTER GAMES

The decade also saw a rise in the popularity of video games. Advances in graphics, complexity, and sophistication of computer gaming engines far outpaced the advances for the prior history of computer gaming. Several major breakthroughs occurred in 1989 with the development of two 16-bit (a unit of memory) gaming consoles, NEC TurboGrafx 16 and Sega Genesis. Much more sophisticated than prior game systems created by companies like Amiga, Atari, and Coleco, these consoles immediately gained wide acceptance despite the price tag of nearly $250. Genesis sales generally outpaced those of the TurboGrafx 16, largely due to the wider selection of games available for the system, particularly those made by Electronic Arts, which began by specializing in sports-related games, but in 1990, began buying out other game publishers. Sega also benefited from the exclusive rights to its own popular line of arcade video games. One of the decade's biggest names in electronic gaming, Nintendo, a software developer known primarily for its best-selling *Super Mario 3* game and Game Boy handheld video game console, introduced its Super NES system in 1991. In 1992, Sega released the first CD-driven console, a technology that would revolutionize not only electronic games but computer operations in general. The system was highly touted, but Sega failed to release the tools that would allow other companies to produce games. These tactics hurt Sega sales as they limited the number of games available to consumers. Nonetheless, other companies, including Sony and Nintendo, began creating their own CD systems. Before long, CDs would replace software cartridges except those in handheld systems.

In 1993, Panasonic released the first 32-bit console, the 3DO Interactive Multiplayer. The system was a limited success, held back by the $699 price, as well as by the looming release of Atari's Jaguar, a 64-bit gaming system. Although the Jaguar suffered from internal hardware limitations, it made clear how rapidly obsolescence could set in. Naturally, it didn't take long for other companies to leap into the 64-bit fray, though the 32-bit console still dominated, with particular success for Sony's 1995 release of a 32-bit PlayStation console. Sony also gained market share by reducing the PlayStation price to $199 in 1996, making it far more affordable than similar systems. That year, Nintendo also released its first 64-bit system. In Japan, where it was first released, the Nintendo 64 sold 500,000 units in the first day, and the 350,000 shipment to the United States sold out in less than three days. By the end of the decade, the games were astonishingly sophisticated with elaborate virtual environments. In 1999, Sega announced plans to release a 128-bit system using CD-ROM technology and with built in modem play support.

Nintendo's Game Boy system provided another major venue for electronic gaming, spawning numerous imitators in the handheld console market. In 1995, Nintendo released its Virtual Boy 32-bit portable system, which, along with continued advances in the Game Boy systems, left the company dominant in this niche for the duration of the nineties. Portable game systems never reached the level of sophistication displayed by non-portable systems, but they still saw considerable advances in technology.

Of course, with the proliferation of video games, concerns about their effects increased considerably. The growing popularity of video games encouraged children to spend even more time in front of screens. Most experts agreed that this contributed to a decrease in physical activity, thereby contributing to obesity and other physiological problems. Moreover, many were concerned about the kinds of games being played by children, many of which seemed to celebrate violence without showing the consequences. Shooting games were popular, as were hand-to-hand combat games.

Street Fighter II, introduced in 1991 in arcades and later for home systems, was one of the most popular video games ever. It involved one-on-one combat between colorful characters modeled on Japanese animation (*anime*). The goal of the game was to beat opponent after opponent into submission. The violence of the game was reasonably non-realistic, but flecks of blood and the fact that players were encouraged to hurt others in the gaming world troubled critics. Parents shocked by *Street Fighter II*'s violence, however, were in for an even bigger shock with Midway Games' 1993 introduction of *Mortal Kombat,* which used photographic instead of cartoonish characters in similar combat situations. Furthermore, the violence became much more graphic. Blood flowed freely, and players could execute maneuvers such as yanking the hearts out of opponents' chests, beheading them, or stripping them of their spines. Outrage over the violence led to the creation of a rating system for video games, but this did little to deter the flow of violence. Ultimately, despite criticisms, no definitive relationship between video game violence and real-world violent acts committed by youths was ever proven.

One of the most significant names in the realm of personal computer gaming was id Software, founded in 1992. The company's first big success was *Wolfenstein 3D,* in which the player raced around various levels of an old castle shooting down aggressive Nazi soldiers. The game introduced the first-person shooter style of computer gaming. *Wolfenstein 3D* was followed by *Doom,* a similarly oriented game in which the player assumed the role of a space marine battling zombies and hellish monsters. The game was a resounding success, and imitators leapt on the first-person shooter bandwagon. Id Software itself soon released the sequel *Doom II,* and then *Quake,* which offered a greater flexibility of character movement. Each of these games, all released within the first five years of id's existence, was more successful than its predecessors, with *Quake* selling more than 1.7 million copies in its first year (compared to sales of about 100,000 for most PC games). These games were not without controversy, given their graphic violence and the fact that the storylines seemed little more than excuses for simulated killing. The games were accused of desensitizing youths, and some directly blamed the games for the increase in suburban high school shootings.[7]

Created by Robyn and Rand Miller in 1994 for the Broderbund software company, *Myst* offered a very different gaming experience. *Myst* involved an exquisitely rendered 3D environment through which players roamed, solving puzzles to further the storyline. With about four million units sold, *Myst* became the top selling computer game. *Myst* and similar games, including *The 7th Guest* and its sequel *The Eleventh Hour,* were primarily puzzle oriented, but the environments, along with the narrative structures of the games, made them as popular as most action games.

Perhaps the ultimate computer game of the 1990s, however, was a contest between machine and the human mind. The game was chess, and the participants were the master of the game Garry Kasparov and the IBM RS/6000SP, named Deep Blue. Kasparov was regarded by most not only as the top current chess player but as the best there had ever been. He went into the match with Deep Blue having won the World Championship for 11 years running. The man and machine met in February 1996. The multi-game match began on a startling note, with Deep Blue defeating the world champion handily. Thereafter, Kasparov seemed to take the match more seriously and soundly defeated Deep Blue, winning four games to the computer's two. The opponents met for a rematch a year later. This time Kasparov won the first game, but the second, third, and fifth games ended in draws. The fourth was won by Deep Blue. Then, in the final game, Kasparov crumbled under an aggressive and unpredictable assault by Deep Blue, conceding the game and match to the computer after the loss of his queen. By the time the final game had commenced, the media turned more attention to the match than it ever had to a chess game, aware that something truly remarkable took place. Millions watched as man at his best was defeated by a synthetic mind. Kasparov defenders accused the programmers of designing Deep Blue to not play a fine chess match per se, but to defeat Kasparov's specific style of play.[8]

COLLECTIBLE CARD GAMES

The game field also saw the rise of collectible card games. The games tapped into two potential markets: game players and collectors. The first popular card game to hit the market was *Magic: the Gathering,* a fairly complex fantasy-oriented game. It featured cards representing characters or weapons, events or powers. The basic unit of this and similar games was the starter deck, a set of cards that included everything that players needed to play the game. The real money for companies in this market, however, was in booster packs. The packs of, typically, 10 to 15 cards allowed players to supplement their starter deck with more powerful cards, which were also usually rare and highly collectible, as well. Detractors criticized the fact that the amount of money paid directly influenced the strength of a player's deck, but the booster cards also let players customize their decks, and with thousands of different cards available in the many types of booster packs, a player could develop a seemingly infinite number of combinations. Such possibilities made for an unpredictable and exciting game.

Similar card games followed. Among the most successful were those tied in with other media. The *Star Trek* game cards snared both gamers and science fiction fans, who were delighted by the attention to detail shown in the cards, which depicted not only major characters and events, but also the minutia that added to their atmosphere. Similar sets featuring *Star Wars, Hercules: The Legendary Journeys, Babylon 5,* and *Xena, Warrior Princess* also appeared, as did other independent collectible card games. With simpler rules, geared toward a younger audience, the *Pokémon* collectible card game became, for a time, the hottest such game on the market.

Although started as a game, *Pokémon* quickly grew into an empire, manifesting itself in television programs and movies, as well as on sneakers, backpacks, food products, T-shirts, and many other items. The game had broad appeal. Children could enjoy the colorful creatures featured on the cards, yet also learn it fairly quickly. The cards also found an audience among adult collectors, especially those interested in Japanese culture, out of which *Pokémon* was born. The game utilized very basic rules, but many of the rules could be bent based on text printed on the cards in play, which allowed for simplicity that could grow complex as play unfolded.

THE INTERNET

An important part of the collectors market was the development of online auctions. The search for antiques and collectibles once involved scouring thrift and antique stores and communicating via phone and letter writing. With the rise of the Internet, and especially with the birth of the Internet's largest auction house, eBay, collecting took on a different dynamic. Collectors could easily search a wide database of items with photographs and contact sellers via e-mail. EBay was founded in September 1995, and it maintained its dominant status throughout the decade. By decade's end, it had more than 40 million registered users, and in 2000, it facilitated more than $5 billion in merchandise transactions.

The Internet in general quickly became a hobbyist paradise. Seemingly, no matter how obscure a hobby, at least one Web site could be found devoted to it. Sites devoted to various collectibles, from stamps to Beanie Babies, flourished as both dealers and collectors showed off their wares. Surfers could easily compare the completeness of their own collections to those of others or to definitive catalogues. Likewise, those more interested in craft hobbies could easily find tips and ideas online. Perhaps most importantly, the Internet allowed hobbyists around the world to communicate via e-mail or real-time chat rooms.

The Internet itself became something of a hobby for many Americans. Chat rooms provided millions with a form of relatively inexpensive entertainment, and, in its way, revived the art of conversation. Stories of romance born of online interaction became increasingly common as the decade progressed.

The Internet also provided a medium for game playing. Individuals could easily find simple games like card games and puzzles online from the earliest years of the Internet. And, as technology advanced, many games became increasingly complex. Game players could network their systems to play multiplayer games of popular software titles, like *Doom.*

Perhaps the biggest source of Internet amusement was the simple act of Web surfing. The increase in Internet users during the decade was staggering. Largely made public in 1992, by 1994 about 3 million people went online regularly. By 1998, more than 100 million were online with many simply typing topics of interest into search engines and following where they led. Most Web sites were linked to other sites of similar interest and so on, and by following these links, surfers could easily spend hours online. For some, the Internet became more compelling than television. The lure of the Internet was, at least in part, the semblance of control. Television largely dictated what a viewer could watch and when. The choices on the Internet were seemingly infinite and were typically available when the consumer wanted them. Naturally, television networks and movie studios, as well as radio stations, noted this shifting audience and frequently implemented their own Web sites, complete with online broadcasts.

Travel of the 1990s

The 1990s were a boom decade for travel and the tourism industry. Yet, it was also a volatile decade, with new challenges brought about by developing technologies, competitive business practices, and new notions on the part of many Americans about the nature of travel. The travel industry, heavily reliant on service workers, was notable in its hiring of non-white female immigrants, who, frequently working for minimum wage, accounted for as much as 80 percent of the new hires of the 1990s.

In 1999, the number of international arrivals to the United States reached 663 million, although during the decade, the United States slipped a spot on the list of top travel destinations, coming in third place behind France and Spain. Still, this created limited concern in the travel industry given the steady increase in the sheer number of tourists, and the United States maintained its position as the top tourism income earner. A 1998 study showed that U.S. tourism receipts equaled some $74 billion; Italy, the second place on this list, made more than $30 billion.[1]

The first few years of the 1990s were difficult ones for the airline industry, with losses of approximately $12.8 billion. The increase in the sheer number of travelers, as well as low fuel costs, helped turn around the industry.[2] By 1997, the industry launched more than 22,350 flights a day and attained record profits of more than $5.2 billion. By the end of the 1990s, the industry consisted of about 800 different airlines employing more than three million people and carrying more than one billion passengers a year. These airlines were complemented by some 14,000 airports across the world, including giant new constructions, like the Denver International Airport, which, in 1995, became the first major new U.S. airport to be built in 20 years.

Business travel grew in the decade, due in part to improvements in communication technologies, especially the Internet and the ability to transmit so much information via computers. This technology allowed businesses to function smoothly in numerous locations, even locations overseas. The greater dispersion led to an increase in business travel for important face-to-face interaction within a company and with clients.

Travel itself became an object of conspicuous consumption for some, with tales of travels and adventures amounting to a status symbol. The travel book industry expanded considerably in the 1990s, with new publishers leaping into the fray and older publishers printing more books than ever before. While much of the market tapped into actual travelers, the sheer quality of many of the books, in terms of photography and textual content, also garnered a significant share of armchair travelers. There was also a growth in specialization in the travel book industry, with books geared specifically to families, the elderly, ecotourists, or gay and lesbian travelers.

WORLD TRAVEL

In the United States, major cities began to resemble one another as the same kind of large chain businesses moved in. This brought about the question as to how a city could remain distinct—thereby remaining a worthwhile tourist destination—even as it acquired the same retailers and restaurants to be found from city to city. This was also a factor internationally, as much more of the world came under the shadow of American corporations.

The Berlin Wall came down in 1990, which led to the reunification of Germany. This opened what had been East Germany to a whole new tourist market that had largely been stifled due to its Communist regime and internationally imposed travel restrictions. The fall of the Berlin Wall was also symbolic of the general collapse of Communism in the late 1980s and early 1990s. Some formerly Communist countries, as well as former Soviet Republics, remained dangerous places to visit as political and social power struggles, even civil war, filled in the gap left by Communism's fall. However, many others, including Poland and Russia, became popular tourist destinations, driven largely by a curiosity about these nations that had not been easily accessible in the past.

THE DANGERS OF TRAVEL

On September 11, 2001, terrorism thrust itself into the public consciousness, delivering a mighty blow to the airline industry and tourism as a whole with attacks on the World Trade Center in New York and the Pentagon. Terrorism also concerned travelers in the 1990s as several high-profile incidents increased the awareness of the dangers of flying overseas (though domestic flights were still considered relatively safe). Notably, since the 1991 Gulf War (and 1998's Desert

HOW OTHERS SEE US

EuroDisney: The Mouse Invades Europe

Mickey Mouse had been a welcome fictional resident in his American birthplace ever since the 1955 founding of the Disneyland theme park in Anaheim, California. When he landed in Paris in 1992, though, French citizens largely reacted as if they'd seen a rat. A big one.

The advent of Disneyland Paris, first known as EuroDisney, was heralded by some as a "cultural Chernobyl" and a Trojan horse from an American corporate goliath. Some French observers saw the resort as an opportunity for profit and economic stimulation in the countryside northeast of the capital, but predictions that the theme park would never last were widely publicized early on. During its first months of operation, labor disputes periodically cut off the rail line that led to the Magic Kingdom, and farmers frequented the gates with protest signs decrying the misuse of valuable farmland. Visions of doom remained plausible in 1994, when the park reported a loss of $493 million.

However, before the entertainment spot marked its fifth birthday, the company had reversed its record and announced it had become the biggest "paid for" tourist attraction in France, with 11.3 million visitors—three times that of the Louvre. The turnaround was attributed to several changes in Disney's strategy, including the jettisoning of the rankling "Euro" prefix, the addition of wine to its restaurants, and a wide-ranging international menu that included, among other fare, fine French cuisine at the *Auberge de Cendrillon*—Cinderella's Inn.

While retaining American features from burger shops to a Wild West show, and the cute and sanitized characteristics associated with Disney and its critics' neologism, "Disneyization," Disneyland Paris also incorporated French cultural content, with Jules Verne-inspired rides and such characters as Victor Hugo's Hunchback of Notre Dame.

Fox operations), there was a sharp increase in terrorist activity, especially in the Middle East. Strife in some former Soviet republics made these equally dangerous travel destinations, along with regions of Northern Africa, Latin America, and the Baltic states, among others. Furthermore, much of this accelerated terrorism was directed toward American targets. Tourists and tourism hot spots became what have been described as "soft targets:" easy objectives, difficult to defend, yet high-profile enough to garner terrorist groups the attention they desired.

Unlike the terrorist attacks of September 2001, however, the terrorism of the 1990s slowed tourism to particular destinations. Suffering more from terrorism were the countries that relied on tourism for a significant amount of their national revenue. Egypt, for instance, felt a considerable economic loss in the wake of a November 1997 terrorist attack on tourists visiting a historic temple. The attack killed 58 people. One study, however, suggested that the effects on some tourist sites was fleeting, with tourism returning to full visitation within six weeks.

Perhaps one of the strangest developments out of the increasingly threatening world was a book series issued by notable travel book publisher Fielding, Robert Young Pelton's *The World's Most Dangerous Places.* Though prefaced with stern warnings that the destinations listed in the book were indeed dangerous and should not be considered as tourist destinations, the book was marketed as a travel handbook, and it became a *New York Times* best seller. Ultimately, the annual editions of the books served mostly as interesting reading for people who would never actually see the destinations in question. But even if few of the purchasers of this book actually ever considered visiting the war zones and such listed therein, the book's mere existence and success suggests an important aspect of travel and the tourist mentality of the 1990s.

ADVENTURE AND SPORTS TRAVEL

For many Americans, the desire now was for adventure or travel off the beaten track. Many travelers pursued vacations involving hiking, camping, bicycling, rock climbing, boating, skiing, river rafting, and numerous other physical activities. The number of American's engaging in outdoor sports increased notably in the 1990s, as did travel of this sort. (See Sports and Leisure of the 1990s.) Camping and backpacking trips became increasingly popular as Americans sought temporary solace from the hustle of urban life. One survey found that more than 53 million people went camping in the 1994–1995 season, roughly 10 million more than a decade before. Rather than simply visiting established camping areas, Americans were seeking out areas that were as far as possible from civilization. Indeed, the 1994–1995 study found that the number of primitive area campers had almost doubled from the 1982–1983 season.[3] Likewise, skiing vacations increased in popularity, with snowboarding's growing popularity (driven by the rise in popularity of extreme sports, as well as by its induction into Olympic competition) adding significantly to ski resorts' revenues. There was a boom in the number of visitors to the country's national parks. Additionally, there was a significant increase in the number of tourists who pursued marine activities like swimming with dolphins or close-quarters whale watching. These attractions proved problematic for marine biologists, who saw the opportunity to educate the public about ocean life, but also how these activities could infringe upon the natural environments and behaviors of sea creatures.

Many travelers took a new approach to international travel. The 1990s saw a significant increase in travel to less developed (or third world) nations, which included much of the South American and African continents. Similarly, many took to backpacking across Europe or the Orient or any other destination they might reach. Adventure travel in the 1990s tended toward less developed but fairly known lands. The goal of adventure travel was not to accumulate knowledge of the world for the benefit of mankind, but to experience to personal growth or enrichment. Interaction with native populaces outside of well-worked tourist destinations, it was reasoned, must be more enlightening than the usual tourist traps. Likewise, firsthand experience with exotic locales certainly must be more personally enlightening and invigorating than simply reading about such places in *National*

Geographic. Critics noted that adventure travelers often lacked contextual understanding of the cultures they visited and upon whom they passed judgment. Additionally, adventure travel was also unquestionably a status builder, offering bragging rights, rather than enlightenment, to those who visited the most exotic locales.

Adventure travel was especially appealing to a fairly young segment of the population, those labeled Generation X. The individuals of this generation came into their own as independent consumers, and consequently were, for the first time, planning their own vacations. This was also the generation seemingly most dissatisfied with the growing urbanization of the United States, as well as the growing homogeneity of America's urban spaces, which were perceived as instituted by earlier generations.

ENVIRONMENT AND SUSTAINABLE TOURISM

One of the major problems of tourism is that tourist destinations experience the wear and tear that comes with increased traveler traffic. The latter decades of the twentieth century seemed to demonstrate an increased awareness of the damage that could be inflicted by tourism. England's Stonehenge, for instance, saw increased levels of protection. The ancient monument, which could once be viewed by visitors close up, even touched by them, was cordoned off in 1989. Ultimately, the separation of traveler from artifact diminished the experience of visiting Stonehenge and similar destinations, but so, too, would the gradual degradation of the monument.

Naturally, the concern about manmade destinations was echoed in consideration of natural attractions, including natural parks and preserves. Visits to federally owned natural sites increased some 40 percent from 1986 to 1996, often outpacing the parks service's efforts both to provide accommodations and to reduce the detrimental environmental effects of the crowds.[4] The infrastructure of many parks fast became insufficient for the tourist load. Increasing the size of roads and build more tourist accommodations, however, infringed upon the natural environment, the very attraction drawing visitors.

As concern over the state of the environment increased, so, too, did the attention given to tourism's impact on the environment. Thus, environmental tourism, also called "green" tourism and, from the travel industry side, sustainable tourism developed. The early 1990s saw several pioneering books espousing the ideas of environmental tourism, particularly *Ecotourism: The Potentials and Pitfalls* (1990) by Elizabeth Boo, which outlined the problems and set a precedent for exploring ways to sustain both the desires of travelers and the environments to which they traveled.

On a global level, tourism's environmental impact was indirectly addressed at a 1992 Earth Summit, where government representatives from 179 countries unanimously endorsed an agenda designed to address the problem. This agreement, Local Agenda 21, encouraged the sustaining of destination lands with additional funding, land grants, and tax incentives on the part of host governments. While the initial agenda did not specifically name tourism, a 1999 meeting of the U.N. Committee on Sustainable Development refined Local Agenda 21, calling for further government efforts in this matter, and also calling on the travel industry itself to educate travelers—through in-flight videos and publications, for instance—about how to reduce their environmental impact.

Of course, one important issue addressed how tourism, even ecotourism, might affect local populations. Tourism certainly had an effect on native populations. Some experts expressed their concerns about how sustainable tourism was being applied to the environment of destinations without consideration of other factors.

Ultimately, the number of eco-tourists increased, as did the number of general travelers with an eye for the environment. This growth became apparent in the increased attention on the part of transportation services and hotels to the environment, and, perhaps more importantly, to making their attention to the environment visible to the consumer. Hotels spearheaded the move by posting signs encouraging lodgers to reuse towels to reduce water use and minimize dissemination of laundry detergents into the environment. Additionally, many tourists sought to lessen their impact by camping, rather than staying in hotels, or relying increasingly on hiking and biking, rather than on less environmentally friendly modes of vehicular travel.

GAMBLING DESTINATIONS

Traditional gambling destinations—Atlantic City, Las Vegas, and Reno—suffered in the 1990s on several counts. First, legalized gambling grew as an industry, with many states allowing limited casino development and the installment of state lotteries. Moreover, in 1988, Congress passed the Indian Gaming Regulatory Act, which limited how states could regulate Native American–run casinos on Indian lands. As a result, hundreds of largely unregulated and untaxed Indian casinos sprouted up across the country. Spurred in part by the growth of Indian casinos, many states instituted limited legalized gambling. In 1990, Colorado, Illinois, and Mississippi enabled some degree of gambling. These were followed by Louisiana, Missouri, Indiana, and Michigan. Canada also relaxed its gambling restrictions in the early 1990s. While many of these regions limited gambling to waterways or rural locations, the casinos still reduced the need for gamblers to travel to Nevada or Atlantic City. The 1990s also saw the development of Internet gambling, which allowed wagering from home. Early online casinos were fairly simplistic, but later models offered elaborate virtual casino environments.[5]

Still, even with the rise of online gambling, a study revealed that, in 2000, some 72.8 million travelers, about 7 percent of domestic travelers, made trips that involved significant gaming.[6] A large part of this success was due to the development of new luxury hotel casinos, such as the Luxor Hotel, Treasure Island, Mandalay Bay, and others in Las Vegas and the Silver Legacy in Reno. These new casinos marketed themselves differently than the gambling industry had in the past by promoting non-gaming entertainment, particularly spectacular shows with big name entertainers. Moreover, many of these hotels emphasized the family aspect of the casinos, a precedent set by the Circus Circus hotels back in the 1970s. A casino like the Luxor, opened in 1993 as the world's third largest hotel, could market itself by its elaborate Egyptian theme, complete with pyramid and sphinx. Treasure Island offered an extravagant pirate spectacle designed to appeal to the entire family. The draw of these new hotels, however, resulted in the closing of smaller, older casinos, leaving much of downtown Reno, for instance, filled with vacant buildings by century's end.

AUTOMOTIVE TRAVEL

A 1996 study found that auto travel (including rental cars, trucks, and recreational vehicles) accounted for about 80 percent of personal travel in the United States. Air travel accounted for 17 percent, with bus and train travel registering barely one percent each. The sense of personal control and flexibility offered by personal vehicles amplified in the 1990s. Car models often reflected a driver's desire for freedom and individuality.

The popular sports utility vehicle (SUV) of the 1990s bridged the gap between the family car and the truck, and it was sporty. SUVs were rugged, large, four-wheel drive autos, designed to take on all kinds of terrain. Advertisements typically showed them climbing mountains, racing through mud, and in other adventurous settings. The names given these vehicles frequently tapped into the adventure notion as well: Blazer, Cherokee, Expedition, Tahoe, Yukon, and Bronco. Cadillac added a luxury SUV to the market in 1999, the Escalade. SUVs were significantly more expensive than the average pickup truck, and consequently, the SUV appealed to better-off buyers, mostly urban.

SUVs also found a major market among professional women with families and with suburban housewives because it could accommodate many passengers and goods. Moreover, it may well be that such large vehicles also gave the drivers a sense of power and safety. Critics questioned the need for such a vehicle on well-paved city streets and noted their truly awful gas mileage. Whatever their disadvantages, however, the SUV craze continued. There were 7 million SUVs on American roads in 1993, but at the end of the decade, this number had risen to 20 million.[7]

Several car manufacturers also tapped into the nostalgia held by baby boomers. The prime example of this is the reintroduction of the Volkswagen Beetle in 1997. Sales of the classic Beetle

The 1999 Cadillac Escalade, shown in this 1998 photo in Detroit, was Cadillac's first sports utility vehicle (SUV). AP Photo.

in the United States ended in 1978, although production continued in Mexico into the 1990s. The reintroduced Beetle was only superficially similar to earlier models, bearing more resemblance under its shell to the more conventional VW Golf. But that shell, a modernized variation on the classic Beetle, made all the difference. The Beetle became one of the most popular small cars of the late 1990s, and it was followed by other nostalgia vehicles, most notably Chrysler's PT Cruiser, a combination of 1930s style and 1990s minivan engineering, which was introduced in 1999 to widespread popularity.

Of course, more traditional designs continued to flourish, with plenty of sport cars and economy cars. But many of the automotive advances vastly improved automotive safety, especially in terms of body design and the increased use of airbags, which was one of the reasons for the elimination of a federally-mandated maximum speed law. This change allowed states and cities to determine their own speed limits, or in one area of Montana, to do away with a posted speed limit altogether. Additionally, auto makers began incorporating more elaborate computer systems into vehicles. Some cars had computerized security systems, some had digital dashboard instruments, and some had entertainment systems, complete with television for those in the back seat.

Perhaps most significant was the incorporation of a Global Positioning System (GPS) in some vehicles. When used in conjunction with a computerized map system, the GPS could inform a driver as to his or her exact location, and offer directions to the desired destination. In 1997, OnStar linked the GPS with cellular technology, connecting drivers with live operators using wireless cellular technology. The data conveyed to the human operator included the car's exact location. Consequently, operators could inform customers of not only their location, but of nearby roadways or businesses and of current traffic conditions. Additionally, the OnStar system had connections to various parts of the car, and was thereby able to relay information about the car's status and unlock doors. Sensors connected to airbags reported when the bags were inflated, so that operators could attempt to contact drivers and authorities in the event of a crash.

Road construction also accelerated during the decade, although clearly road building failed to keep up with increased traffic. Observers realized that roads inefficiently funneled far more vehicles into traffic patterns than the roads were designed to handle. Much of the construction focused on growing cities, but established urban areas lacked space to expand their roadways significantly. In 1999, the transportation institute of Texas A&M University studied 75 urban areas and found that the average driver spent about 60 hours in traffic, up from 16 hours in 1982, when the last similar study was conducted. Another traffic study the following year found that time in traffic increased to 62 hours. Additionally, the study found that the weekday high traffic period referred to as rush hour had grown from less than five hours long to about seven hours. The study recommended the building of more roads, but also noted that better management of roadways and better promotion of alternative transportation would also be necessary.

The condition of roads also became an important issue in the 1990s, with many older roadways falling into serious disrepair. For example, in California, it is estimated that the number of urban highways in need of serious repair doubled in the 1990s, and that roads in poor condition were costing the average Californian $140 a year in auto repairs. Likewise, the growing dilapidation of California bridges became a major concern.

TRAINS, BOATS, AND BUSES

Railways continued to flourish as a domestic means of travel in other countries, but the United States had seen a long downward slide in train travel since its peak in the 1920s. Most rail companies turned away from passenger transport, concentrating on cargo shipping, which left Amtrak essentially unopposed. Despite the decline in rail travel, Amtrak still saw significant revenues. In 1997 alone, Amtrak carried 48 million travelers, including many business commuters, and garnered a record-breaking $1.67 billion. Amtrak was, however, still subsidized by the federal government, as an economic and relatively environmentally friendly means of transportation. Amtrak strived in the 1990s to reach a level of self-sufficiency, particularly with the production of high-speed Acela Express, which was unveiled in 2000 as the American answer to Japan's and France's high speed trains.[8]

In 1993, The White House Conference on Global Climate Change reported that intercity bus service was the most energy-efficient commuter transportation mode, more efficient than air, automobile, and even train service (including subways). Estimates at the end of the 1990s placed the number of buses in service at between 26,000 and 28,000. While many were confined within city limits, bus services flourished not only in cities, but over longer distances as well, with companies like Greyhound. and the Trailways National Bus System offering charter and tour "motorcoach" services. The continued stability of the charter bus industry was aided by replacing older vehicles with luxury buses, complete with reclining seats and climate control.

The cruise liner industry was one of the most rapidly growing travel industries at the end of the century. In 1980, an estimated 1.4 million people took cruise ship vacations, but by 1997, that number reached over 5 million. The Caribbean accounted for about 48 percent of cruise ship vacations according to 1998 figures, but other destinations, especially the Mediterranean, Alaska, Northern Europe, and the Bahamas, were also popular. Disney made a great stir when it established the Disney Cruise Line, which geared cruises toward the whole family, providing at least as much for children to do as for adults. Additionally, Disney offered a package vacation including not only the cruise, but also time at Florida's Walt Disney World or Disney's Animal

The *Carnival Destiny,* a huge cruise ship, dwarfs a smaller cruise vessel, background, as it arrives at the Port of Miami in 1996. The ship has a passenger capacity of 3,400 people, is higher than the Statue of Liberty, and is too wide to pass through the Panama Canal. AP Photo.

Kingdom, a new 500-acre, $800 million park that opened in April 1998.

Pleasure boating also grew in popularity. Although the expense of boating kept it as an activity for the wealthy and upper-middle class, an increase in disposable income for many Americans led to an increase in boat sales. Technological advancements changed boating significantly. In 1985, a sailboat could travel some 20 miles in two hours. By 1998, high-speed catamarans could travel 75 miles in the same amount of time. Consequently, boat tourism increased significantly. A given tropical island that once took a full day to reach just 15 years earlier could now be visited in a matter of hours.

Visual Arts of the 1990s

ART AND CONTROVERSY IN THE EARLY 1990s

The 1980s ended with considerable controversy about the appropriate subject matter for art. This controversy came to a head with the debate over federal National Endowment for the Arts (NEA) funding of artists considered by some as obscene. Specifically, the work of such artists as Robert Mapplethorpe and Andres Serrano had become the battleground over which the NEA, the artists, and their supporters fought against such groups as evangelist Donald Wildmon's American Family Association. In July 1989, Senator Jesse Helms snuck an amendment through the sparsely attended Senate, that proclaimed that public funds (including, but not limited to, NEA funds) could not be used to support art that featured "depictions of sadomasochism, homoeroticism, the sexual exploitation of children, or individuals engaged in sex acts and which, when taken as a whole, do not have serious literary, artistic, political, or scientific value."

In 1990, the NEA's president vetoed grants to several performance artists, Karen Finley, John Fleck, Holly Hughes, and Tim Miller, claiming their work was too political. That the performers were gay males, lesbians, and feminists—and politically on the left—was not lost on many observers. A lawsuit filed by the artists reinstated the grants three years after the vetoes, and also undercut the potency of the anti-obscenity pledge that NEA grant recipients were required to sign in the wake of the Helms amendment.

The NEA found itself embattled not only by the political right, but also by the left, which felt that the organization's recent attempts to restrict artistic content amounted to an assault on the first amendment's guarantee of free speech.

POLITICAL ART

AIDS had had a terrible impact on the art world in the 1980s and 1990s, taking the lives of Mapplethorpe (in 1989), Scott Burton, Keith Haring (both in 1990), David Wojnarowicz (in 1992), and many others. Not surprisingly, then, many artists created works that directly engaged the AIDS epidemic. Frequently, this work was among the most direct of the artists' work, backed as it was by a desire to educate. Ultimately, the most famous work of art addressing the AIDS epidemic, however, was more properly qualified as folk art. The AIDS Memorial Quilt, by the NAMES Project Foundation, with each panel representing a different AIDS victim, was started in 1987. The quilt included 1,920 panels when first displayed, and by 1996, the last time it was displayed in its entirety, it included about 38,000 panels and covered the entirety of Washington, D.C.'s National Mall. The quilt continued to grow, reaching in excess of 46,000 panels and 91,000 names, which only represented 17.5 percent of American AIDS deaths. The 1996 display was likely the last such presentation of the whole quilt, which, at some 50 tons, was far too large for more than partial exhibition.[1]

Art that advanced feminist and homosexual politics continued to thrive within the world of art, but more notable was the growth in exhibitions featuring work by ethnic minorities. In 1990, the New Museum of Contemporary Art in New York launched "The Decade Show: Frameworks of Identity in the 1980s," a groundbreaking exhibition devoted to ethnic diversity and multiculturalism. Many of the artists of color featured in the exhibit were brought out of obscurity by the show. In the years that followed, major art museums added a great deal of work by ethnic minorities to their permanent collections, and held numerous shows highlighting their work. One of the most notable of these shows was the 1994 Whitney Museum exhibition titled the "Black Male," which took to task representations of black men in popular culture.

PUBLIC ART

In the United States, public art projects seemed to be erected at an accelerated pace late in the century. A central force in the creation of public art—mostly sculptures and murals, but also architecture and museum exhibits—was the attempt on the part of many cities to revitalize urban areas. (See Architecture of the 1990s.) Proponents claimed that public art would help add a sense of life to an area, bringing businesses and patrons back to the abandoned urban areas of a city. Whereas prior public art, more accurately thought of as civic art, had been frequently placed without regard to area residents, the late 1980s and 1990s saw public officials seeking to allow the local populace some say in the kind of art that would decorate their town.

Several cities instituted art education programs in conjunction with the development of public art projects. An example of this is a statue of the Aztec winged-serpent god Quetzalcoatl erected in San Jose, California. While the statue had its detractors, it nonetheless served as a significant work for a city with such a large and active Latino populace.

ART AND TELEVISION

One of the most important figures in bringing high art to a popular audience was also one of the most unlikely. Sister Wendy Beckett, a tiny nun with an animated and passionate way of talking about art, found a wide audience through her BBC/PBS television shows that traced the history of art. Sister Wendy, born in South Africa and later relocated to England, made her first television appearance in 1991 on the BBC, and was shortly re-aired in the United States to critical and popular acclaim. She hosted numerous art documentaries, including *Sister Wendy's Story of Painting* (1997). She not only explored ancient arts, but also delved into the world of modern art in such a way that the average audience could begin to understand avant-garde art. Sister Wendy simply didn't come across as an art critic. There was no jargon and no pretense to her commentary, simply a knowledge of art history, a keen eye for detail, and an obvious passion for art. Her television success was supplemented by some 15 books on art authored by Sister Wendy, along with numerous articles in art magazines.

Though none quite matched Sister Wendy in sheer charm, other art series appeared on PBS. Among these were the series *American Photography: A Century in Images* (1999) and *American Visions* (1997) hosted by renowned critic Robert Hughes. The art critic for *Time* magazine, Hughes wrote and narrated the eight-part series, which took the viewer to more than 100 locations in the United States. Hughes sought to explore how art reflected the point of view of various people in various parts of the country at different times in history.

PHOTOGRAPHY

David LaChapelle and France's Jean-Baptiste Mondino shaped the look of the decade's fashion and celebrity photography. Their photography frequently relied on high stylization, unusual and deliberate posing of the subjects, and garish colors. LaChapelle produced particularly conspicuous celebrity photography, as one of the most commonly employed cover photographers for *Rolling Stone* and other major magazines like *The Face* and *Interview.* Mondino worked in many areas of photography, from fashion shoots, to album and magazine covers. Both photographers also directed music videos. Other major photographers working in the field of fashion and celebrity photography included Steven Klein, a frequent contributor to international editions of *Vogue,* and Greg Gorman, who also produced movie posters. The German-born former model, Ellen von Unwerth, also made a name for herself in the 1990s with her own brand of fashion and celebrity photography, which appeared in major magazines like *Vogue,* as well as in several books.

Working in a decidedly different vein, Anne Geddes was perhaps the most popular photographer of the decade. Her best-known work involved babies dressed as various natural objects, including animals, insects, vegetables, and especially flowers. Detractors claimed that her work was more interested in being cute than being substantive. Geddes's many books (particularly the 1996 collection *Down in the Garden*) were photography best sellers, and they spawned a cottage industry. Her distinctive baby photos could be seen on note cards, journals, calendars, photo albums, advertisements, and more. In addition, numerous children's books were produced using her photographs.

Similarly criticized for their lack of substance were a series of photos by William Wegman, who became enormously popular in the 1990s on the basis of his dog photos. He dressed Weimaraners in various costumes and photographed them, as in his picture-storybook adaptation of Little Red Riding Hood, complete with Weimaraner wolf and Weimaraner Red Riding Hood. This 1993 publication was followed by the like-minded *Cinderella* in 1999. Wegman's highly successful photography albums included *William Wegman's Farm Days* (1997), *My Town* (1998), *What Do You Do?* (1999), and *William Wegman's Pups* (1999). Interestingly, even as critics lambasted Geddes and Wegman, their technique was quite strong. Wegman, particularly, was less known for his edgier non-dog photography, wherein his sense of composition served a more pointed, less commercial purpose.

As in other areas of visual art, photography was the subject of considerable controversy, particularly the work of several photographers whose focus was the youthful human body. San Francisco Bay area photographer Jock Sturges had several books that contained nude photos of young people, particularly girls, just coming into sexual maturity. Defenders of Sturges's work argued that his photos were artfully composed depictions of a natural part of adolescence. Detractors claimed they were no better than child pornography. Sturges was charged, and later cleared, as a pornographer.

Other photography books with similar content also received condemnation. Among these were those of Lexington, Virginia, photographer Sally Mann, whose photos were collected in *Immediate Family* (1992) and *Still Time* (1994). A well-regarded photographer, Mann's photos were moodier than those of Sturges, with shapes and shadow almost in abstraction. Thus, many considered Mann's work decidedly less sexualized than that of Sturges. Barnes & Noble and other outlets took to keeping these photography books behind the counter, and eventually making the books available only through special order. The controversy about the books and their photographers eventually diminished, having affected little more than an increase in the sales of the books.

An altogether different kind of controversy developed around the digital manipulation of photographs. Although the practice of altering photographic evidence was nothing new, computer technology made the practice much easier and much harder to detect. While this practice did have some worthwhile practical effects—such as the use of computer-generated age progressions in the search for missing persons—it also caused concern because even a photograph could not be taken as irrefutable proof.

Digital photo alteration became commonplace. Photo technique magazines regularly featured articles on how to manipulate photographs, to center an image, to sharpen (or even alter) a background, and to brighten or mute colors.

Moreover, these powers were not only granted to the professional photographer but also came within the reach of the average amateur. The 1990s saw the development of affordable digital cameras, which captured images in a computer memory, allowing them either to be printed or downloaded onto a home computer. In addition, many models allowed for instant review of a photograph, so that only successful photos needed to be kept, and these could be digitally manipulated for various purposes or easily e-mailed or posted on Web sites.

COMPUTER ART

The 1990s saw the development of several new avenues of artistic production using the computer itself for the creation of art, alternately called cyberart, digital art, or simply computer-generated art. Indeed, works frequently might exist strictly within the memory of a computer, without any true source material for manipulation. In addition, the computer allowed for the creation of art that could not be approximated with any other medium.

One prime example of this was the creation of digital stereograms, also known as Magic Eye pictures. Stereograms existed in some form long before the 1990s, with early postcards using duo images. The idea was that, by bringing these images into the same visual space and relaxing the eyes, sometimes with the assistance of vision distorting lenses, the pair of 2D images would appear as a single 3D image. In the 1960s, the application of computers to this concept took place. By the 1990s, the stereogram techniques had advanced amazingly, and individuals like Dan Dyckman and Mike Bielinski saw the aesthetic potential

In this example of fractal art, a representation of a complex mathematical iteration looks both beautiful and strange. Courtesy of Shutterstock.

of the stereogram. Advanced computer technology simplified the mathematical processes used in stereogram creation, resulting in images of increasing complexity. Most stereograms appeared, at first glance, as chaotic abstract patterns, but with the relaxing of the eye, now without the need for special lenses, previously unseen 3D images came into focus. Other stereograms used non-abstract repeated images—of coins, insects, flowers, and so on—which could create a similar illusion of depth. The stereogram phenomenon first exploded in Japan, and its popularity quickly reached the United States. In 1993, the book *Magic Eye: A New Way of Looking at the World,* which featured images created by N. E. Thing Enterprises, hit bookstores and quickly became a best seller. The book's success led to many other books of stereograms. Additionally, such images began appearing more frequently in advertising, on posters and greeting cards, and even in a few art gallery showcases.

Fractal art also became popular during the decade. These designs, the visual representations of complex mathematical formulas, began to appear with greater frequency on posters, cards, and more. Several books of fractal art were published. Critics contended that it was not true art because the images were the simple playing out of mathematical algorithms. Defenders claimed that, because the artist made certain selections in launching a fractal, that determined the ultimate pattern.[2] The works, with their complex mingling of both natural patterns and high tech computations, quickly found an audience, with successful video-cassettes and books, such as *Fractal Cosmos: The Art of Mathematical Design* (1994).

Fractals and stereograms were among the most high-profile works of computer art, but they were not the only modes of digital creativity. Even the average home computer included illustration software, and those in the business of art used such software to create representational art that, in some cases, was difficult to distinguish from straight photography. The perfection of textural modeling allowed computer artists to closely approximate the look of different materials, from metal to human skin. Also significant was the rise to prominence of computer collages and mosaics. For a collage, the artist simply used the computer to juxtapose illustrations, photos, and other images (including backgrounds and color schemes) to create a unified whole. Mosaics took this process further, using perhaps thousands of photos and placing them in such a way that, with some digital manipulation of color and shadow, these small photos formed a larger picture. As these new innovations shaped the way people thought aesthetically, age-old

FROM STREET TO NET

Graffiti has a long history, going back all the way to the cave art of ancient humans. One of its most recent forms, spray-painted graffiti (or, as some would call it, aerosol art), emerged in New York City in the late 1960s. By the mid-1980s, the form had been adapted by the art world, and painters like Jean-Michel Basquiat and Keith Haring, who had gotten their start as graffiti street artists, were showing their work in high-end galleries in North America and Europe. New York's street graffiti practitioners continued to create their (usually illegal) displays on walls and subway trains until police crackdowns in the 1990s began to discourage them.

At that point, though, taggers and aerosol artists in Europe, Africa, and South America injected new life into the subculture, united by technology: the Internet. What was formerly an ephemeral and local art form suddenly could take on an extended life and find a wider audience. Artists and crews in Buenos Aires, Cape Town, Copenhagen, Oslo, Toronto, and many other cities set up Web sites where they could show off pictures of their tags and murals to inspire their peers and teach new techniques. E-mail chains and message boards allowed graffiti writers to connect with one another, arrange collaborations and visits, and share tips and tricks.

Some of the old-school graffiti makers disdained such high-profile activities, maintaining that "true vandals" needed to keep a low profile for fear of prosecution. But the newer artists reveled in the chance to establish a global movement, to join the "classroom on the Net" that could show them how to emulate the South Bronx taggers who had started it all.

debates arose about what, exactly, constituted art. Could a Web page be art, with its mingling of images and texts? Could computer games be considered art?

ART AND CONTROVERSY IN THE LATE 1990s

Just as the decade opened with controversy about what was appropriate in art, so, too, did it end. Of particular note was the Brooklyn Museum of Art show, "Sensation: Young British Artists From the Saatchi Collection." This show, which began in October 1999, was combated not only by the usual decency groups, especially the Catholic League, but also came under fire by then-New York Mayor Rudolph Giuliani. The exhibit, first opened at London's Royal Academy in 1997, offered such viewings as Marc Quinn's self-portrait carved out of eight pints of the artist's own frozen blood and Damien Hirst's macabre work featuring such things as a bisected pig and a 14-foot tiger shark floating in formaldehyde. But the center of the controversy was Chris Ofili's stylized painting of the Virgin Mary, notable for the lump of elephant dung affixed to the portrait and the clippings from pornographic magazines surrounding it. Proclaiming the exhibit "sick," Giuliani announced that he would withhold the $7.2 million in city funding to the museum unless the show was cancelled. He also threatened to disband the museum's board of directors and filed a lawsuit on behalf of the city, which claimed that the museum had violated its lease.[3] The Brooklyn Museum countersued, claiming that the denial of funding was an infringement on free speech. Artists across the world and much of the mainstream press jumped to the museum's defense. Respected news commentator Hugh Downs reported that, although he found the show disgusting, it was neither his nor Giuliani's place to decide for others what was appropriate viewing. However, these legal matches (settled some months after the exhibit had closed in early 2000) had little effect other than to raise awareness of the show. Those putting on the show were well aware that controversy sells. Even the advertising seemed to bear this out. One poster, for instance, presented itself as a health warning: "The contents of this exhibition may cause shock, vomiting, confusion, panic, euphoria, and anxiety. If you suffer from high blood pressure, a nervous disorder, or palpitations, you should consult your doctor before viewing this exhibition." Such copy served a dual purpose, laying ground for the claim that no one who had viewed the exhibit had done so without full knowledge of the nature of its content, as well as enticing attendees with a lurid promise of forbidden sights.

Chris Ofili's *The Holy Virgin Mary,* created in 1996, a controversial painting of the Virgin Mary embellished with a clump of elephant dung and two dozen cutouts of buttocks from pornographic magazines, is shown at the Brooklyn Museum of Art in 1999, in New York City. AP Photo.

ENDNOTES FOR THE 1990s

OVERVIEW OF THE 1990s

1. See http://www.census.gov.
2. See http://www.census.gov.
3. Sarah Anderson, John Cavanagh, Chuck Collins, Chris Hartman, and Felice Yeskel, "Executive Excess 2000:

Seventh Annual CEO Compensation Survey," (August 30, 2000), http://www.tni.org/archives/cavanagh/ceo2000.pdf.

4. For more information, see William Julius Wilson, *When Work Disappears: The World of the New Urban Poor* (New York: Knopf, 1996).
5. Chandler Burr, "The AIDS Exception: Privacy Vs. Public Health," *The Atlantic Monthly* 279 (June 1997): 57–63, 64–67.

ADVERTISING OF THE 1990s

1. Jean Kilbourne, *Deadly Persuasion: Why Women and Girls Must Fight the Addictive Power of Advertising* (New York: The Free Press, 1999), 34–35.
2. Roy F. Fox, *MediaSpeak: Three American Voices* (Westport, Connecticut: Praeger, 2001), 108–10.
3. Fox, *MediaSpeak,* 110.
4. James B. Twitchell, *Twenty Ads That Shook the World: The Century's Most Groundbreaking Advertising and How it Changed Us All* (New York: Crown Publishers, 2000), 194–203.
5. Twitchell, *Twenty Ads That Shook the World,* 215.
6. Linda K. Fuller, "We Can't Duck the Issue: Imbedded Advertising in the Motion Pictures," *Undressing the Ad: Reading Culture in Advertising* ed. Katherine Toland Frith (New York: Peter Lang, 1998), 109–29.
7. Fox, *MediaSpeak,* 133.
8. Eric Schlosser, *Fast Food Nation: The Dark Side of the All-American Meal* (New York: Houghton Mifflin, 2001), 43.
9. Fox, *MediaSpeak,* 108–9.
10. Schlosser, *Fast Food Nation,* 51–53.
11. Fox, *MediaSpeak,* 93–95.
12. Schlosser, *Fast Food Nation,* 55.
13. Fox, *MediaSpeak,* 95–96.
14. Fox, *MediaSpeak,* 101–4.
15. "This is Your Government on Drugs," editorial, *Rolling Stone* 794 (September 3, 1998): 43–44.
16. Paul Taylor, "Stumped Speech," *Mother Jones* (May/June 2000).
17. Kilbourne, *Deadly Persuasion,* 37–38.
18. Kilbourne, *Deadly Persuasion,* 39.
19. Robbin Zeff and Brad Aronson, *Advertising on the Internet,* 2nd ed. (New York: John Wiley & Sons, 1999), 7–10.
20. Zeff and Aronson, *Advertising on the Internet,* 4.

ARCHITECTURE OF THE 1990s

1. Andrea Oppenheimer Dean, "Our Critic Goes Behind the Scenes at This Year's AIA Honor Awards," *Architectural Record* 187 (May 1999), 5.
2. Michael Cannell, "Brain Drain," *Architecture* 88 (December 1999): 125–27.
3. Hugh Pearman, *Contemporary World Architecture* (London: Phaidon, 1998), 61–62.
4. James Wines, *Green Architecture* (New York: Taschen, 2000), 172–76.
5. Kidder Smith, *Source Book of American Architecture,* 629.
6. Dennis McCafferty, "Breaking New Ground," *USA Weekend* (August 30–September 1, 2002), 6–7.
7. James Parsons, "A New World (Made To) Order," *Architecture* 88 (May 1999), 5.
8. Andres Duany and Elizabeth Plater-Zyberk, *Suburban Nation: The Rise of Sprawl and the Decline of the American Dream* (New York: North Point Press, 2000), 43–45.
9. Edward Blakely and Mary Gail Snyder, *Fortress America: Gated Communities in the United States* (Washington, DC: Brookings Institute Press, 1997).
10. Thomas Angotti, "New York: Challenges Facing Neighborhoods in Distress," in *Rebuilding Urban Neighborhoods,* ed. W. Dennis Keating and Norman Krumholz, 177–90 (Thousand Oaks, CA: Sage Publications, 1999).
11. Roberta Brandes Gratz and Norman Mintz, *Cities Back from the Edge: New Life for Downtown* (New York: Preservation Press, 1998), 152–56.

BOOKS, NEWSPAPERS, MAGAZINES, AND COMICS OF THE 1990s

1. A report published at the end of the 1980s attested some 45 million Americans were functionally illiterate. Mortimer B. Zuckerman, "The Illiteracy Epidemic." *U.S. News & World Report* 72 (June 12, 1989).
2. See http://www.amazon.com/exec/obidos/subst/misc/company-info.html.
3. Bridgete Kinsella, "The Oprah Effect," *Publishers Weekly* (January 20, 1997), 276.
4. Daisy Marlyes, "Connecting the Dots," *Publishers Weekly* (January 20, 2000), 25.
5. *Publishers Weekly* (January 3, 1994).
6. Robert K. J. Killheffer, "Inter-Galactic Licensing," *Publishers Weekly* (September 25, 1995), 27–31.
7. Robert K. J. Killheffer, "Creative Experimentation Reigns," *Publishers Weekly* (June 17, 1996), 34–41.
8. Jonathan Bing, "Sue Grafton: Death and the Maiden," *Publishers Weekly* (April 20, 1998), 40–41.
9. John Blades, "David Guterson: Stoic of the Pacific Southwest," *Publishers Weekly* (April 5, 1999), 215–16.
10. Lucinda Dyer, "Love, Thy Magic Spell is Everywhere," *Publishers Weekly* (May 13, 1996), 41–47.
11. Daisy Maryles, "The Medium Makes the Sale," *Publishers Weekly* (January 3, 1994), 55.
12. Mallay Charters, "The Different Faces of Poetry," *Publishers Weekly* (March 3, 1997), 38–41.
13. Kenneth Woodward, "Angles," *Newsweek* (December, 27 1993), 57.
14. Jim Milliot and Diane Roback, "1996 a Difficult Year for Children's Publish-ers," *Publishers Weekly* (November 3, 1997), 35–38.

15. Fredric A Emmert, "U.S. Media in the 1990s" (November 7, 2002), http://usinfo.state.gove/usa/ infousa/ media1rd.htm.
16. Ron Goulart, *Great American Comic Books* (Lincolnwood, IL.: Publications International, 2001), 328.
17. Goulart, *Great American Comic Books,* 315.
18. Goulart, *Great American Comic Books,* 315.

FASHION OF THE 1990s

1. William Hamilton, "Suitably Attired," *The Atlantic Monthly* 288 (September 2001): 122–25.
2. Amy Merrick, "Tired of Trendiness, Former Shoppers Leave Gap, Defect to Competitors," *The Wall Street Journal* (December 6, 2001).
3. Jancee Dunn and Patti O'Brien, "How Hip-hop Style Bun-Rushed the Mall," *Rolling Stone* 808 (March 18, 1999): 54–57, 59.
4. Ruth P. Rubinstein, *Society's Child: Identity, Clothing, and Style* (Boulder, CO: Westview Press, 2000), 259–60.
5. Nancy Rutter and Owen Edwards, "Ready to Ware," *Forbes ASAP* (April 5, 1999), 30–32.
6. "The Name Game" (July 25, 2002), http://www.pbs.org/newshour/infocus/fashion/namegame.html.
7. Urban Decay Web site (July 25, 2002), http://www.urban decay.com/aboutudframe.html.
8. "Sephora—Liberating Beauty Products," Corporate Design Foundation Web site, (July 25, 2002), http://www.cdf.org/7_2_index/sephora.html.
9. Mim Udovitch, "Breasts, Reassessed," *Esquire* 131 (February 1999): 86–89.
10. Debra L. Gimlin, *Body Work: Beauty and Self-Image in American Culture* (Berkeley: University of California Press, 2002), 75.
11. Deborah Caslav Covino, "Outside-In: Body, Mind, and Self in the Advertisement of Aesthetic Surgery," *Journal of Popular Culture* 35, no. 3 (Winter 2001): 91–102.
12. Gimlin, *Body Work,* 75.
13. Gimlin, *Body Work,* 5.
14. Rubinstein, *Society's Child,* 249.

FOOD OF THE 1990s

1. Charles R. Goeldner, J. R. Brent Ritchie, and Robert W. McIntosh, *Tourism: Principles, Practices, Philosophies,* 8th ed. (New York: John Wiley & Sons, 2000), 178.
2. Melinda Fulmer, "Food Firms Hope You Can Never Have Too Much of a Sweeter Thing," *Los Angeles Times,* April 28, 2002, http://www.proquest.com.proxy.usf.edu.
3. Food Marketing Institute Web site, http://www.fmi.org.
4. Eric Schlosser, *Fast Food Nation: The Dark Side of the All-American Meal* (New York: Houghton Mifflin, 2001), 120.
5. Red Bull Web site, http://www.redbull.com.
6. Schlosser, *Fast Food Nation,* 3.
7. Schlosser, *Fast Food Nation,* 47–48.
8. Schlosser, *Fast Food Nation,* 47–48.
9. T. G. I. Friday's Web site, http://www.tgifridays.com.
10. Jim Adamson, *The Denny's Story: How a Company in Crisis Resurrected Its Good Name* (New York: John Wiley & Sons, 2000).
11. Emeril Lagasse Web site, http://www.emerils.com.
12. Starbucks Web site, http://www.starbucks.com.
13. Andy Murray, "Microbreweries Focus on Close-to-Home Connoisseurs," *Eagle-Tribune* online (March 3, 2002), http://www.eagletribune.com/news/stories/20020303/BV_ 001.htm.
14. "Craft-Brewing Industry Keeps Growing" (July 13, 2002), http:/www.beertown.org/PR/ industry_growth.htm.
15. Schlosser, *Fast Food Nation,* 53–54.
16. Michael F. Jacobson, "Liquid Candy: How Soft Drinks are Harming Americans' Health," http://www.cspinet.org/sodapop/liquid_candy.htm.
17. Jacobson, "Liquid Candy."
18. Schlosser, *Fast Food Nation,* 140.
19. Elizabeth Larsen, "Bossy's Lament," *Utne Reader* 100 (July–August 2000): 18–19.

MUSIC OF THE 1990s

1. Greil Marcus, "Kurt Cobain: Artist of the Decade," *Rolling Stone* 812 (May 13, 1999): 46–48.
2. See also Gina Arnold, *Route 666: On the Road to Nirvana* (New York: St. Martin's, 1993) and Rolling Stone, *Cobain* (Boston: Little, Brown, 1994).
3. Ira Robbins, *The Trouser Press Guide to '90s Rock* (New York: Fireside, 1997), 549–50.
4. David Fricke, "The Battles of Rage Against the Machine," *Rolling Stone* 826 (November 25, 1999): 42–50.
5. For further analysis, see Robert Wright, "'I'd Sell You Suicide': Pop Music and Moral Panic in the Age of Marilyn Manson," *Popular Music* 19, no. 3 (October 2000).
6. Steven Stancell, *Rap Whoz Who* (New York: Schirmer Books, 1996).
7. Robert Marriott, "Gangsta, Gangsta: The Sad, Violent Parable of Death Row Records," in *The Vibe History of Hip Hop,* ed. Alan Light (New York: Three Rivers Press, 1999), 319–25.
8. Joe Wood, "Native Tongues: A Family Affair," *The Vibe History of Hip Hop,* 187–199.
9. Ed Morales, introduction, "Hey, Latin Lovers!" *Andy Warhol's Interview* (June 1999), 98–105, 118.
10. Robert K. Oermann, *A Century of Country: An Illustrated History of Country Music* (New York: TV Books, 1999), 297–98.
11. Jancee Dunn, "The Backstreet Boys Year in Hell," *Rolling Stone* 813 (May 27, 1999): 42–47.

12. Anthony Bozza, "Nsychronicity," *Rolling Stone* 837 (March 30, 2000): 52–58.

SPORTS AND LEISURE OF THE 1990s

1. Alison S. Wellner, *Americans at Play* (Ithaca, NY: New Strategist Publications, 1997), 114–16.
2. Wellner, *Americans at Play,* 265–68.
3. Lynette Lamb, "Can Women Save Sports?" *Utne Reader* 97 (January–February 2000): 56–57.
4. David Deardorff II, *Sports: A Reference Guide and Critical Commentary, 1980–1999* (Westport, CT: Greenwood Press, 2000), 31.
5. BBC News Online, "Business: The Economy: Woods Holes $90m" (August 25, 1999), http://news.bbc.co.uk/1/hi/business/the_economy/429698.stm.
6. See http://www.mcfarlane.com/.
7. Cynthia True, "Master of the Game," *Rolling Stone* 800 (November 26, 1998): 94, 99–101.
8. Haynes Johnson, *The Best of Times: America in the Clinton Years* (New York: James H. Silberman, 2001), 11–16.

TRAVEL OF THE 1990s

1. Charles R. Goeldner, J. R. Brent Richie, and Robert W. McIntosh, *Tourism: Principles, Practices, Philosophies,* 8th ed. (New York: Wiley, 2000), 10–11.
2. Goeldner, Ritchie, and McIntosh, *Tourism,* 138.
3. Alison S. Wellner, *Americans at Play* (Ithaca, NY: New Strategist Publications, 1997), 3.
4. H. Ken Cordell and Gregory R. Super, "Trends in Americans' Outdoor Recreation," in *Trends in Outdoor Recreation, Leisure and Tourism,* ed. W. C. Gartner and D. W. Lime, 133–44 (New York: CABI Publishing, 2000).
5. Valene L. Smith and Maryann Brent, eds. *Hosts and Guests Revisited: Tourism Issues of the 21st Century* (New York: Cognizant Communications Corporation, 2001), 72.
6. Smith and Brent, *Hosts and Guests Revisited,* 55.
7. Haynes Johnson, *The Best of Times: America in the Clinton Years* (New York: James A. Silberman, 2001) 150–51.
8. Goeldner, Ritchie, and McIntosh. *Tourism,* 143–45.

VISUAL ARTS OF THE 1990s

1. See http://www.aidsquilt.org/quiltfacts.htm.
2. Carl Machover, "Is It Technology or Art?: The New Tools," *Cyber Arts: Exploring Art & Technology,* ed. Linda Jacobson (San Francisco: Miller Freeman, Inc., 1992), 39–40.
3. Cristopher Rapp, "Dung Deal," *National Review* (October 25, 1999), 69–70.

2000s

Timeline

of Popular Culture Events, 2000s

2000

December 12: The Supreme Court votes 5–4 to halt presidential election recounts, essentially declaring Bush the winner.

Stock market jitters turn more widespread, signaling the end of the dot.com boom.

Computers around the world are infected with the "I love you" virus attached to spam e-mail.

Six-year investigation into the Clintons regarding Whitewater allegations ends with no indictments.

Presidential election pitting Vice President Al Gore versus Texas Governor George W. Bush gridlocked over turmoil regarding outcome of Florida vote. The recount is hindered by fraud allegations and legal wrangling. Bush later declared winner by 537 votes.

2001

September 11: Islamic terrorists under the direction of al-Qaeda leader Osama bin Laden hijack four passenger airliners in the United States. They deliberately crash them into the World Trade Center in New York City and the Pentagon in Washington, D.C. The fourth plane crashes in a rural area outside Shanksville, Pennsylvania, while thought to be headed for the White House or U.S. Capitol Building. The attack on the World Trade Center destroys the buildings and inflicts major damage to the surrounding areas. Some 3,000 people are killed overall.

October: There are national worries over anthrax scare after drug-laced letters sent to media and governmental figures.

December 2: The Enron Corporation files for bankruptcy in a spectacular flameout after years of winning critical acclaim from the media for its successes in corporate America.

George W. Bush is sworn in as nation's 43rd president.

President Bush advocates and Congress passes $1.35 trillion tax cut over 11 years.

In response to the September 11 attacks, the U.S. and British armies invade Afghanistan in October in search of bin Laden, to destroy al-Qaeda terrorist camps, and overthrow the Taliban government.

2002

March: Fox airs the show *Celebrity Boxing*, pitting celebrities against one another in the ring. The first program featured former child actors Danny Bonaduce versus Barry Williams and former Olympic ice skater Tonya Harding versus Paula Jones, a woman infamous for alleging an affair with Bill Clinton.

October: Congress votes to authorize President Bush to use force, if necessary, to disarm Iraq.

Former president Jimmy Carter wins the Nobel Peace Prize.

In his State of the Union address in January, President Bush labels Iraq, Iran, and North Korea an "axis of evil" that threatens world peace.

Dave Thomas, founder of the fast food chain Wendy's dies. He had gained widespread fame from starring in the company's television commercials.

The Homeland Security Advisory System is introduced in March. The color-coded scale links the threat against the U.S. based on a five-point range, from red ("severe") to green ("low").

At the 74th Academy Awards, actress Halle Berry becomes the first African American female to win the "Best Actress" award.

Lisa "Left Eye" Lopes, a prominent female rapper and member of the hip hop group TLC, is killed in La Ceiba, Honduras, in a car accident while on vacation.

FBI agent Robert Hanssen sentenced to life in prison without parole for selling secrets to Russia over a 22-year period in exchange for money and diamonds.

Baseball great Ted Williams dies. After his death, his family battled over his remains, with his son eventually having the body placed in cryonic suspension.

A series of shootings take place in the greater Washington, D.C., area with 10 people killed and three more critically injured. The gunman is labeled the "Beltway sniper." Residents are urged to use caution and stay away from some areas. Two men orchestrated the attacks, which they had carried out earlier in the South and West. In total, they are known to have killed 16 people.

2003

February 1: The Space Shuttle *Columbia* explodes upon reentry. All seven astronauts inside are killed.

March: President Bush says in a primetime news conference that he is prepared to go to war against Iraq, with or without United Nations or other international support.

The U.S. launches a predawn missile attack in Iraq in March, targeting sites of "military importance," according to President Bush. Saddam Hussein appears on Iraqi television to denounce the attacks and rally his people.

Dixie Chicks lead singer Natalie Maines sets off a national controversy when at a London concert she exclaims that the group members feel "ashamed" that President Bush is a fellow Texan.

The DaVinci Code, a novel by Dan Brown, reaches the top of the best-selling fiction lists and stays there for three years. (The movie version is released in 2006, starring Tom Hanks.)

Allied forces rescue Army Pfc. Jessica Lynch, a prisoner of war held at an Iraqi hospital, who becomes a patriotic symbol.

After the fall of Baghdad and Tikrit, the Pentagon declares an end to major fighting in Iraq and begins withdrawing troops, warships, and aircraft from the Gulf region. In May, President Bush stands in front a banner announcing "Mission Accomplished."

President Bush signs $350 billion tax cut bill.

Federal and local authorities raid the BALCO offices owned by Victor Conte. The raid sets in motion the investigation of professional athletes with ties to BALCO.

2004

The CIA admits in February that no imminent threat from weapons of mass destruction existed prior to the 2003 invasion of Iraq.

The city of San Francisco begins issuing marriage licenses to same-sex couples.

Dove launches "Celebrating Curves" campaign, featuring real women as models in print and television ads, in contrast to young, beautiful, slender models that dominated most advertisements.

Former president Ronald Reagan dies in his Bel-Air, California, home at the age of 93.

The Boston Red Sox win the World Series. The victory breaks the supposed "Curse of the Bambino," said to haunt the franchise since it last won a title and then later sold the rights to Babe Ruth in 1918 to the New York Yankees.

After a long investigation and trial, a jury finds Scott Peterson guilty of the murder of his wife Laci and unborn son Conner. The case dominated the news headlines after Peterson reported his wife missing on Christmas Eve in 2002.

President George W. Bush is re-elected, beating John Kerry, the Democratic nominee.

Social networking Web sites Facebook and My Space are launched.

2005

May: W. Mark Felt reveals that he is the famous "deep throat" informant who leaked information to Bob Woodward and Carl Bernstein regarding Watergate.

June: Pop singer Michael Jackson is acquitted of 10 charges, including molesting a child, conspiracy, and providing alcohol to minors, in a California courtroom.

July: Sandra Day O'Connor, the first woman on the U.S. Supreme Court, retires after serving for 24 years.

August: Hurricane Katrina ravishes part of Florida, Louisiana, and Mississippi. The storm surge causes the levees to break in New Orleans, resulting in widespread damage as 80 percent of the city is flooded. The Bush administration is criticized for its slow response and mismanagement of disaster relief efforts.

September: Millions of people are left homeless or displaced due to Hurricane Katrina. Thousands of stranded people are evacuated to the Astrodome in Houston and to other locations around the country. President Bush signs emergency $10.5 billion relief bill for the region.

The United States and other countries around the world donate supplies and assist with relief efforts in January after a tsunami devastates 11 Asian nations in late December 2004.

Jennifer Aniston and Brad Pitt announce their separation, setting off a popular news media frenzy.

NHL Commissioner Gary Bettman cancels the season after owners and players fail to reach agreement on a new contract and salary cap for players.

Lifestyle celebrity Martha Stewart is released from a West Virginia prison after serving a five-month sentence for lying to federal investigators about the questionable sale of stocks.

Terri Schiavo, a woman in a persistent vegetative state for 15 years, serves as a political lightning rod after her husband decides to remove the feeding tube keeping her artificially alive. While activists argue the morality of such a decision, the House and Senate vote to allow a federal court to rule on the case. Federal judge James Whittemore refuses to order that her breathing tube be reinserted. The U.S. Supreme Court does not hear the case. Schiavo dies on March 31, 13 days after the tube is removed. An autopsy revealed that she had no chance for recovery.

The House Government Reform Committee holds hearings to investigate steroids use in baseball. Ten players, including Mark McGwire and Sammy Sosa, testify.

Pfc. Lynndie England pleads guilty to seven criminal counts related to her role in torturing Iraqi prisoners of war held in Abu Ghraib.

Musicians in nine countries hold Live 8 concerts in July to raise money and awareness in the global fight against poverty in Africa.

The Colbert Report, a mock news show debuts, satirizing right wing news shows and general pomposity. It is a spin-off from another satirical news show, *The Daily Show with Jon Stewart,* and both are critical and popular successes, especially with young people.

2006

Former Enron executives Ken Lay and Jeff Skilling are convicted of conspiracy and fraud for their roles in the company's downfall.

For the first time in his presidency, President Bush uses his veto power, declining legislation that would have expanded stem cell research that uses federal financing.

Bob Dylan's *Modern Times* album debuts at Number One on the Billboard chart, his first work to hit the top spot since 1976's *Desire.*

The Democrats gain control of the House and Senate in the midterms elections.

Technorati, the first blog search engine, estimates that there are 28.4 million blogs online.

2007

April: Shock jock Don Imus sparks a national controversy after making derogatory racial remarks about the Rutgers University women's basketball team. The fallout includes Imus losing his CBS Radio and MSNBC television shows. However, by December he is back on the air with different networks.

Former vice president and senator Al Gore wins the Nobel Peace Prize for his work on global climate change.

After the Democrats win a majority of seats in the 2006 midterm elections, California Democrat Nancy Pelosi becomes the first woman Speaker of the House of Representatives.

Harvard University names its first female president when historian Drew Gilpin Faust takes over for embattled former leader Lawrence Summers.

Two articles by *Washington Post* reporters Dana Priest and Anne Hull investigating medical negligence at Walter Reed Army Medical Center in Washington set off a national controversy over treatment of returning and injured American soldiers who fought in Iraq.

A lone student gunman goes on a killing rampage on the campus of Virginia Tech University, killing 32 people.

The final episode of the HBO hit drama series *The Sopranos* airs. Fans and critics debate the open-ended finale.

Price Is Right host Bob Barker retires from the show at age 83 after 35 years of helming the show. Barker is replaced by comedian Drew Carey.

Apple Computer launches the iPhone, a high tech cellphone with a sleek black design and virtual keyboard that enables users to easily surf the Web and download music as well as actually make a telephone call.

"I Got a Crush... on Obama," a YouTube video posted by "Obama Girl" Amber Lee Ettinger, gains wide popularity. Although Barack Obama criticizes the video, it gets more than three million viewings by the fall.

A bridge spanning the Mississippi River outside Minneapolis collapses, killing 13 people and injuring hundreds more. The tragedy begins a national conversation regarding bridge safety and other problems with the country's infrastructure.

San Francisco Giants slugger Barry Bonds hits his 756th home run to pass Henry Aaron as the all-time home run king. Many consider Bonds's feat tainted by allegations that he used steroids.

Atlanta Falcons' star quarterback Michael Vick pleads guilty to charges of operating a dog-fighting operation and participating in killing dogs.

Britney Spears lip-synchs and dances awkwardly through a live performance at the MTV Video Music Awards show. Her hopes for a "comeback" are foiled, but the shoddy performance keeps her in the celebrity news cycle.

Former football star and actor O. J. Simpson is arrested in Las Vegas and charged with robbery with a deadly weapon and other charges after attempting to steal some of his sports memorabilia items owned by a collector.

A panel of international experts upholds the decision to strip the 2006 Tour de France title from Floyd Landis, an American cyclist accused of doping violations.

Fueled by the Santa Ana winds, a wildfire rages across Southern California. The flames scorch more than 400,000 acres, destroy 2,000 homes, and force the evacuation of one million people before being contained.

2008

Presidential primary race gets officially underway with Iowa caucuses. Democrat Barack Obama and Republican Mike Huckabee win in Iowa. In the New Hampshire primary, Democrat Hillary Clinton is victorious, as is Republican John McCain.

Louisiana Republican Bobby Jindal becomes the first Indian-American governor in the United States.

President Bush proposes a $145 billion economic stimulus package in response to the sluggish economy, including the housing market crisis and rising oil prices. The plan features rebate checks for individuals. The House votes 385 to 35 in favor of the plan.

The Federal Reserve cuts interest rates by .75 percent, the largest single-day reduction in Fed history.

The Senate votes 81 to 16 in favor of the revised $168 billion stimulus package.

The Senate votes 68 to 29 to extend for six more years a law passed in August 2007 that permits government eavesdropping on telephone and e-mail conversations of American citizens and people overseas without a warrant. The bill also provides immunity to telecommunications companies that assist the government in its eavesdropping efforts.

A strike that began in November 2007 between Hollywood production companies and the Writers' Guild of America ends. The strike is estimated to have cost the industry more than $2 billion and forced an overhaul of the television season.

A student gunman opens fire on a classroom at Northern Illinois University, killing 6 students and himself and wounding 15 others.

Propelled by primary victories in Texas, Vermont, Rhode Island, and Ohio, John McCain appears to have won the Republican presidential nomination.

New York Governor Eliot Spitzer admits to his role in a prostitution ring and resigns from office. A former state attorney general, Spitzer had gained fame as an aggressive crusader against white collar crime.

Neil Diamond, age 67, becomes the oldest performer to reach #1 on the Billboard album chart with *Home Before Dark*, produced by music impresario Rick Rubin.

Citigroup Chairman Win Bischoff predicts that "we're through the worst" caused by the collapse of the subprime mortgage market. Citigroup, the largest bank in the United States, booked more than $40 billion in credit losses.

May: Myanmar is hit by a cylone, killing at least 84,000, with another 50,000 missing, and the province of Sichuan in Western China is hit by devastating earthquakes killing an estimated 80,000 people.

June: Barack Obama finally secures enough primary votes to be the Democratic nominee for the presidential election and the first African American to win from either party. Hillary Clinton concedes and campaigns with him to strengthen his support.

June: Floods in the Midwest cause billions of dollars in damages, severely damaging many towns, cities, and valuable farm land, with predictions of resultant higher food costs.

October: Congress approves, after first rejecting, a bailout package to buy up to $700 billion dollars in bad assets at financial institutions in order to stabilize markets, including preventing a massive number of home mortgages from defaulting.

On November 4, Barack Obama, the son of a man from Kenya and a woman from Kansas, wins the presidency of the United States.

Overview of the 2000s

Google Nation

NICKNAME FOR THE DECADE, 2000–2008

In the twenty-first century, American popular culture is omnipresent. Sometimes it flows like a mighty river, slowly rolling along, but with powerful currents just under the surface. In other instances, pop culture spills over its banks, sweeping away everything in its path.

Popular culture comes alive at the juncture of the entwined forces of mass communications, technology, political systems, and the economy. The industry that developed to support and disseminate culture requires a seemingly endless supply of fact, fiction, gossip, illusion, and misinformation. Add a dash of national tragedy or smidge of political or economic intrigue, and the pot boils over. The popular culture machine shifts into high gear, whether that means the evening news team at ABC or a citizen journalist posting a grainy video on YouTube. The result of countless pop culture impressions over the course of a lifetime produces a permanently heightened sense of sensationalism, chased with healthy doses of societal angst.

The 2000s have been a decade of popular culture explosions, from the September 11 terrorist attacks and the nation's military response to natural and manmade phenomena, such as the devastation of Hurricane Katrina and Wall Street's implosion at the hands of the real estate mess. These are serious issues that forced action, reaction, and interpretation, all of which helped citizens comprehend the world around them.

After September 11, the somber national mood led some experts to declare the end of popular culture based on irony and satire. Others wondered if future films and television shows would ever be able to feature exploding airplanes or buildings. Over time, however, popular culture played dual roles: first, helping the nation mentally transition through the aftermath of terrorism; and second, calling into question the rationale for war and the long-term occupation of foreign nations. Perhaps this ability to examine the actions of the government and other institutions of power is the most positive aspect of popular culture. However, one could certainly argue that the fascination with pop culture diverts attention away from important challenges the nation faces and serves as a kind of placebo, enabling people to feel good about the world around them without really confronting issues directly.

Many contend that popular culture is about individuals from across the celebrity spectrum, perhaps mainly because people interact with it from the standpoint of their favorite actor, band, or television shows. Others counter with the notion that culture is actually about the larger influences that drive society, such as technology, government, economic structures, and national ethos. For example, technology, economics, and innovation combine to produce culture-shifting products, such as the iPod and computers. These goods then set in motion a shift in popular culture as these products influence people far beyond their intended functions. In turn, users come to define themselves by them—the kinds of music they download, the movies they watch, and television shows they record via TiVo DVR. Each of these larger forces acts like the wind on our climate, transforming the weather without really being seen or even felt. All the roots of popular culture trace back to technology, governmental systems, economic influences, and culture.

TECHNOLOGY

Technology is a critical component of popular culture, weaving through virtually every aspect of society. Although the Internet is a major factor in how pop culture develops, technology goes beyond the Web. For example, plasma and high definition (HD) televisions are changing the way people watch programs and buy content. Cell phones seem to constantly evolve, not only getting smaller, but adding new capabilities that expand far beyond linking users by voice.

THE INTERNET

U.S. Internet activity reflects and expands on what is happening in the offline world. Perhaps one could argue that there really isn't even much of a distinction between the real world and the virtual world at this point. Unique visitors at political Web sites, for example, jumped 35 percent between December 2006 and December 2007 to 8.38 million. Furthermore, while pundits debated whether or not the nation sat in the midst of a recession, 31 percent more Web users visited online classifieds and career training and education sites over the same timeframe. In addition, Craigslist.org, which features both classifieds and job ads, increased unique visitors by 74 percent to reach 24.5 million.[1]

The search market continued to grow at an astronomical clip in 2007. Total searches eclipsed 113 billion for the year, with Google gaining a 56 percent market share. In December 2007 alone, Google recorded 5.6 billion searches, up 30 percent from a year earlier. Yahoo! sites accounted

LOVED AND HATED: CELL PHONES AND OTHER GADGETS

In the 1987 film *Wall Street,* Gordon Gekko, a Wall Street tycoon played by Michael Douglas, conducts his business on a mobile phone the size of a high school band's wood block, cementing in the minds of millions the notion that cell phones were synonymous with money and power. Fast forward just two decades later, and the cell phone has become as ubiquitous as a billfold, for many people, obsolescing the need for land lines altogether. Today's cell phone is also a computer, camera, stereo, and little black book filled with all the information that links human beings to society. Cells have permeated all classes and ages and have become boons in times of crisis. Everyone from elementary school children to octogenarians carry around their phones, and most take advantage of added features such as text messaging. Cell phones have become major players in the crisis narrative of modern times. Who can forget the calls from terrified students to their parents during the Columbine massacre? Or the tragic calls during September 11? Perhaps the only lamentable aspect of the cell phone age is the necessary evil of having to listen to the shameless caller who forgoes the etiquette of public space and bellows into his or her phone to the chagrin of everyone in the vicinity.

No doubt, like every other instance of conspicuous consumption, it's all about the image. Nevertheless, the age of personal gadgets is upon us, from hands-free devices that enable cell phone users to gesticulate in a full range of motions, to Blackberries, to GPS devices in cars, whose multifaceted functions would make the 1980s television character MacGyver drool (who was always scientifically inventive when getting out of tight spots). The positive side is that those in the know are walking information databanks, having instant access to the Internet, organizing applications, phone services, mapping services on the go, instant messaging, and camera applications.

for 2.2 billion, but it dropped 4 percent from its mark 12 months earlier.[2]

The downside of more widespread Internet activity is that the number of scammers and cyber criminals multiply as well. The battle against hackers and others who hope to exploit people's personal identity is like a vicious cycle, with government agencies, corporations, schools, and organizations spending greater time and effort putting up firewalls and installing antispyware software. The bad guys, however, are working just as hard to thwart these systems.

According to several observers, the number of records lost, such as credit card or social security numbers, increased 300 to 400 percent from 2006 to 2007. For example, the San Diego-based Identity Theft Resource Center estimates that the number of records compromised jumped from 20 million to 79 million over that period. One of the highest profile cases involved discount retailer TJX Companies, which admitted that hackers accessed some 46 million customer credit card numbers. After further examination, though, banks involved in this fraud estimated that the number of records actually reached 94 million. TD Ameritrade, the online broker, had its records hacked as well, resulting in 6.3 million customer files breached.[3]

DOT.COM "REVOLUTION"

The dot.com "revolution" referred to the period spanning from the late 1990s through the spring of 2000 when Wall Street, corporate America, the general public, and the media caught a wave of euphoria generated by the Internet and the use of advanced technology for business purposes. Numerous factors all came together to create an "Internet bubble" of market speculation and frenzied investment, primarily small investors who could use Web-based trading sites to easily buy and sell stocks online.

The ensuing stock market boom revolutionized the way businesses operated by providing the capital to invest in new technology. Perhaps more importantly, the dot.com revolution fundamentally changed the way people communicated through Internet-based technologies, such as e-mail, message boards, chat rooms, and others. Thus, despite the failure of most dot.com companies, the transformation continued through the use of technology and the Internet for business purposes.

In its broadest sense, the dot.com revolution served as a massive growth engine for the American economy. For the first time in recent history, the power and mystique of small, entrepreneurial companies began to dwarf that of established corporations. Given the public's willingness to invest in Internet-based startups, their valuations soared.

Finally given the chance at riches gained from stock options and participation in initial public offerings (IPO), workers flocked to dot.coms, despite the risk involved. When added to the possibility for quick riches, the quirky, decentralized culture of Web companies drew Generation X (born 1965 to 1980) workers in droves. The media added fuel to the mass exodus from the Fortune 500 by reveling in stories of office foosball tournaments and game rooms, company-sponsored espresso machines, and a constant state of business casual clothing. Tech entrepreneurs were also able to promote work as a way of achieving a more spiritual or fulfilling state, which appealed to the sullen masses of workers awash in endless rows of drab, gray cubicles in the nation's large companies. Startups were seen as anti-authoritarian and laid back, mirroring the lifestyle exuded in Northern California since the 1960s. Some of the early companies included: PayPal, pets.com, eToys.com, dot.com incubator Internet Capital Group, and a slew of service firms to publicize and advertise these entities, such as Organic Online, Scient, and USWeb/CKS.

Dot.com mania reached a peak in the late 1990s when venture capitalists started funding dot.coms based on the ability to take the company public, thus cashing in on the IPO shares. Seemingly ludicrous businesses started getting millions of dollars in seed money from a variety of investors, despite having little more than a bright idea. The list of now defunct dot.coms reads like a comedy sketch, ranging from fashion site Boo.com, which burned through its $135 million investment before declaring bankruptcy, to online toy retailer eToys, online newspaper LocalBusiness.com, and the self-descriptive FurnitureAndBedding.com.

Online grocer Webvan may be the biggest failure in Internet history, burning through an estimated $1 billion before shutting down.

Soon, large companies started to get in on the rush. Corporations such as America Online, Cisco Systems, Sun Microsystems, and Oracle began publicizing their Net wares and purchasing startups that could add innovative technology to their portfolios. Microsoft, which had been slow to grasp the importance of the Web, debuted its Internet Explorer, MSN Web sites, and an online service. Fortune 500 corporations also rushed to implement e-commerce capabilities, put up Web sites, and search for methods to sell their products and services online.

The dot.com revolution coincided with and was stimulated by the Year 2000 (Y2K) problem that gripped businesses worldwide. The necessity for purchasing and updating computer systems hinged on the belief that computers would not function properly when the New Year changed from 1999 to 2000. Although the switch did not cause global panic, greatly increased expenditures on corporate information technology systems added to the rationale for Internet spending.

DOT.COM BUBBLE BURSTS

The companies that flamed out at the tail end of the New Economy bubble were like kindling for the recession wildfire that gripped the United States at the dawn of the new century. Over the course of one month (March 10, 2000, to April 6, 2000), the NASDAQ stock market lost $1 trillion in value. The figure then jumped to nearly $1.8 trillion by the end of the year.[4] Then, a tsunami destroyed the dreams of many dot.coms in its wake and startled tech investors back to reality. For employees at startup companies, from the CEO on down, stock options ended up "under water," worthless scraps of paper that would never regain their luster.

Today, economists contend that people have seen the downfall coming sooner. Flying in the face of multiple warning signs, too many people still sought a shot at Web wealth and glory, unable to pass on the gamble, despite the long odds. Even after NASDAQ crashed in spring of 2000, investors rushed in to buy shares of depressed stocks, many of which would rebound slightly before falling for good. The media (fueled by business cable stations, like CNBC, which turned Internet CEOs into celebrities, and the plump, ad-soaked tech magazines) made folk heroes out of people like Amazon.com's Jeff Bezos and Yahoo's Jerry Yang. So many Internet legends were tales of rags-to-riches glory or college students coming up with an idea in their dorm rooms that, by focusing on them, the media made it seem easy.

By the end of 2001, thousands of dot.com companies went bankrupt and countless tens of thousands of employees lost their jobs. The massive failure of the New Economy and the subsequent trickle of new investments in technology companies, combined with corporate governance scandals and the September 11 terrorist attacks,

GOOGLE: SEARCH ENGINE AND ADVERTISING GIANT

Google is, by far, the most popular Internet search engine in the world, carrying a lofty 71 percent market share as of July 2008. That overwhelming lead (Yahoo! stands at a distant second with 19 percent), gives life to Google as a vehicle for advertising. In the 2006 fiscal year, for example, Google's ad revenues hit $10.5 billion. Advertisers buy space on Google search result pages based on user searches. Similarly, Google operates its own popular e-mail service (Gmail) and allows advertisers to buy space there with results often tied directly to the subject matter of one's e-mail messages.

For users of Google's search engine, the company's goal is to provide relevant ads that complement the search results. Google helps advertisers further target their ads to interested consumers. The advertisers pay for the space through an auction for certain keywords related to their products or services.

Several high-profile acquisitions allowed Google to extend its advertising prowess. For example, Google purchased YouTube in October 2006, for $1.65 billion, which helped the company become the leader in online video. In turn, Google gets to put its ads in front of YouTube's vast audience, which watches hundreds of millions of video each day.

sparked a recession that plagued businesses in the early years of the twentieth century. High tech centers, such as Silicon Valley, San Francisco, Austin, Texas, Washington, D.C., and New York were especially hard hit by the failure of the dot.com revolution.

Despite the meltdown, the high tech revolution continued, though on a more modest scale, as traditional businesses used e-commerce and the Internet to meld online and physical storefronts. Companies used Web-based services and technologies to become more efficient and profitable. It is nearly impossible to find an industry that has not been improved through Internet-based technology, whether it is in education and nonprofit organizations or financial services and manufacturing.

The dot.com revolution ended in early 2000, but innovation continued to propel companies into novel areas that mix business and the Internet. Figures released by the United Nations revealed that there were 655 million registered Internet users worldwide in 2002 and that global e-commerce topped $2.3 billion, doubling the figure from 2001.[5]

BIG MEDIA

The Internet did not remain the "Wild West" domain that many observers imagined it in its early days. Small companies and startups continued to drive innovation, but most often they would grow to a certain size and prominence, and then a large corporation would come in and gobble them up. In the new millennium, much of the consolidation took place among media conglomerates, which had the stock price and cash reserves to purchase upcoming technology-based firms. The trend continued from the mass empire building that took place in the wake of the Telecommunications Act of 1996, which loosened ownership regulations across mass media. With the federal government more lenient, large organizations had the freedom to buy up additional channels in various markets.

The traditional fear is that a handful of media moguls will wind up owning the majority of the voice that consumers hear across radio, television, newspapers, and the Web. Rupert Murdoch, the founder and CEO of the global corporation News Corp., is the living embodiment of critics' fears, owning Fox Broadcasting, the *New York Post*, London's *The Times*, and the *Wall Street Journal*. He purchased *WSJ* in December 2007 for $5 billion, adding its 2 million readers worldwide to his global news network.

While Murdoch's vast reach is symptomatic of the challenge of monopolistic ownership, harkening back to earlier barons, such as William Randolph Hearst, in today's media world, about a dozen corporations own roughly 33 percent of the nation's 1,400 daily newspapers, according to journalist Samantha Levine. The largest is Gannett Co., which owns *USA Today*, followed by the Tribune Company.[6] Gannett revenue surpassed $8 billion in 2006 among its 20 TV stations, approximately 100 daily newspapers, magazines, and Internet properties.

One of the most intriguing and mind-boggling media conglomerates is Time Warner. Through a series of high-profile mergers and acquisitions, the company built a network of television networks, a cable system, movie companies, magazines, and Internet companies. In 2006, the company ranked number one in the media business with $44.2 billion in revenues, up from $37 billion in 2005. Despite its size and reach, however, Time Warner never lived up to its $164 billion acquisition of AOL in 2001, ranking as the largest media deal in history.

By mid-decade, it became evident that the company, renamed AOL Time Warner, could not take advantage of or exploit the synergies inherent in the merger. Executives struggled to find a strategy. Not helping matters, the company combated the triple-whammy of an economic recession, the dot-com implosion, the terrorist attacks on America and the subsequent war on terror. No one cried crocodile tears for AOL Time Warner, though. Not when the combined entity dropped in value to become worth less than the sum of its own parts. Stockholders were left in the bag—they watched as more than $100 billion in shareholder value wiped off the board.

In 2008, media watchers project that new chief executive Jeff Bewkes will slice and dice the company, selling off many units and spinning off AOL. Drastic measures are necessary given that company shares rose a meager 13 percent in the preceding five years. A former business exec at HBO, Time Warner's highly-successful premium cable network, Bewkes discussed his vision for the company, stating, "I believe strongly in trial and error, and Time Warner needs to move faster, take more risk, and change course more often."[7] The parts of the Time Warner puzzle most frequently rumored for sale are its cable business, AOL's access division, along with a significant number of magazines.

GOVERNMENT

If one thought in early 2000 that the polarizing force of the Clinton administration would dissipate and lead to a friendlier political atmosphere post-Clinton, they would have been sorely mistaken. The 2000 presidential election fractured the nation even further as Al Gore and George W. Bush squared off. The contentious environment peaked in the weeks after the hotly contested election, in which Gore won the popular vote by about 540,000 votes, but Bush won the Electoral College: 271–266.

The furor over voting ignited in Florida, where officials disputed the outcome of the election and who should win its critical 25 electoral votes. The inconsistencies in results included the now-famous "hanging chads," or partially punctured voting cards. In the end, the resulting court battles over recounts took 35 days past election day. In his first speech as president-elect shortly after Gore's concession, Bush said, "I know America wants reconciliation and unity. I know Americans want progress. And we must seize this moment and deliver. Together, guided by a spirit of common sense, common courtesy, and common goals, we can unite and inspire the American citizens."[8]

In the 2004 presidential election between President Bush and Massachusetts Senator John Kerry, both political parties and affiliated groups supporting them took part in a race that became increasingly divisive and mean-spirited. In the end, the election was again so close that one state determined the outcome. Ohio's 20 electoral votes went to President Bush, giving him a 286 to 252 win in the Electoral College, to go along with his 62 million to 59 million win in the popular vote (51 percent to 48 percent).

A personal bitterness developed between the two candidates, the political parties, and special interest groups that did not exist in the 2000 campaign. The supposed moral gulf between the two candidates fueled a great deal of this acrimony. Much of the rhetoric that developed during the contest centered on what would happen in the "war on terror" depending upon who won the election. Some of the barbs were direct, such as Bush's labeling Kerry a "flip-flopper" and "Massachusetts liberal." Both terms painted the challenger as someone who would not be tough enough to lead during wartime. Another example of the personal attacks that characterized the 2004 election is the work of a group called the Swift Vets and POWs for Truth. In a national television campaign, the members called Kerry's military service and combat medals into question. Summing up the Bush victory, historian Eric Foner said, "I suspect that the attacks of September 11 and the sense of being engaged in a worldwide 'war on terror' contributed substantially to Bush's victory. Generally speaking, Americans have not changed presidents in the midst of a war. The Bush campaign consistently and successfully appealed to fear, with continuous warnings of imminent and future attacks. Land of the free? Perhaps. Home of the brave? Not anymore."[9]

GEORGE W. BUSH

Rarely do historians garner the headlines the way Sean Wilentz did in early 2006 when he rhetorically questioned whether President George W. Bush could be considered "The Worst President in History" in a headline that appeared on the cover of *Rolling Stone* magazine with a caricature of the president sitting in a corner wearing a dunce cap. The Princeton University professor ignited a media frenzy, including countless blog posts and television appearances. Wilentz cited a 2004 survey of 415 historians by the nonpartisan History News Network (HNN) that revealed some 81 percent considered the Bush administration a "failure." And, as Wilentz notes, HNN took the pulse of America's historians prior to the "debacles over Hurricane Katrina, Bush's role in the Valerie Plame leak affair, and the deterioration of the situation in Iraq."[10]

The Plame affair, for example, occurred when Vice President Dick Cheney's aide Lewis "Scooter" Libby leaked Plame's name to newspaper columnist Robert Novak, who then revealed her as a

CIA officer.[11] Libby, as well as other administration officials, slipped the information to Novak in retaliation for the role Plame's husband, former ambassador Joseph C. Wilson IV, had played in a highly-publicized op-ed in the *New York Times* claiming that the Bush administration relied on shoddy information to support its theory that Iraqi officials purchased uranium from Niger. A jury convicted Libby, but others thought that the blame should have reached Bush strategist Karl Rove or other high-ranking members of the administration. President Bush commuted Libby's prison term in June 2007.

Wilentz's article and ensuing discussion point to Bush's role as a polarizing force in American society. Soon after the terrorist attacks on September 11, for example, the president received the highest approval ratings in history, reaching about 90 percent. As the Iraq war dragged on with no end in sight after 2006, his ratings dropped to historic lows, hitting 26 percent in mid-2007.[12] Wilentz sees the downturn as the culmination of Bush's "disastrous domestic policies, foreign-policy blunders and military setbacks, executive misconduct, crises of credibility and public trust." Moreover, the historian explained, "He has also displayed a weakness common among the greatest presidential failures—an unswerving adherence to a simplistic ideology that abjures deviation from dogma as heresy, thus preventing any pragmatic adjustment to changing realities."[13]

Despite his flagging numbers over his last four years in office, Bush remains upbeat and convinced of the correctness of his administration, from its handling of the economy to the wars in Iraq and Afghanistan. As he prepared for his final State of the Union address to Congress in 2008, Bush borrowed from the playbook of Ronald Reagan, another lame duck Republican president who faced falling approval ratings. Bush focused on what he still had left to accomplish, including a $150 billion economic stimulus package.[14]

While historians will debate the Bush presidency far into the future, they will be forced to acknowledge the wins in his early years in office, including tax-cutting measures and his support of the "No Child Left Behind" education plan. However, the narrow victory over Massachusetts Senator John Kerry in 2004 and the disastrously executed handling of the Hurricane Katrina disaster in the Gulf region in 2005 started a chain reaction that weakened public support for programs at home and abroad and enabled the Democrats to win back Congress in the midterm elections of 2006.[15]

The ultimate turning point for the Bush administration took place when the president ordered the invasion of Iraq based on what was later found to be faulty (and perhaps fabricated) intelligence that outlined Saddam Hussein's potential nuclear capabilities and the now-infamous "weapons of mass destruction," which could be turned on the United States. Many political and military experts believe that by drawing Iraq into the "War on Terror" and linking Hussein to Al Qaeda, Bush and members of his cabinet, including Vice President Dick Cheney and Defense Secretary Donald Rumsfeld, took the country in a direction that committed America to a military quagmire that cost the nation more than $500 billion to conduct (as of March 2008). After the public learned of the faulty rationale for the war in Iraq and as further atrocities came to light, such as the torture of Iraqi prisoners in Abu Ghraib and Guantanamo Bay, Bush's approval ratings dropped like a rock.[16]

SEPTEMBER 11, 2001

In the blink of an eye, the terrorist attacks that took place September 11, 2001, transformed the Bush presidency. In responding to Al Qaeda and its leader Osama bin Laden, the president directed a massive retaliatory attack on Afghanistan to root out the terrorist group and topple its power.

President George W. Bush in the documentary *No End in Sight* (2007), which investigated the Bush administration's engagement in the Iraq War. ©Magnolia Pictures. Courtesy of Photofest.

The terrorist attacks on the World Trade Center in New York took place on a beautiful morning, marked by clear blue skies and bright sunshine. No one could have imagined that on such a morning, 19 Al Qaeda operatives set out on four separate planes to launch a coordinated attack on New York and Washington, D.C. Before the morning ended, three planes had crashed into American landmarks, while another—potentially heading for the nation's capital—crashed in a Shanksville, Pennsylvania, field before it could reach its target. Nearly 3,000 people died in the attacks.

Aftermath

Immediately after the September 11 attacks, the nation turned more patriotic, while firefighters and police officials across the nation became heroic figures, lauded for their bravery and willingness to serve the nation. President Bush, with the backing of Congress, launched a series of military and economic programs designed to eliminate terrorist cells worldwide, particularly against members of Al-Qaeda and bin Laden himself. The efforts culminated in the October 2001 military invasion of Afghanistan and its Taliban government, known partners of the terrorists. Despite the success of the military operations and overthrow of the Taliban regime, however, the United States could not capture bin Laden.

The Bush administration also initiated a series of domestic security programs designed to ease the public's fear regarding future terrorism on American soil. The president authorized the creation of the Department of Homeland Security and named former Pennsylvania Governor Tom Ridge as its first leader. Next, the administration worked with leaders in Congress to pass the USA Patriot Act (2001), which gave the federal government far-reaching power to carry out surveillance activities to weed out potential terrorism threats.

Homeland Security officials began a national alert status indicating potential threats, ranging in colors from red (severe risk) to green (low risk).

A view of the twin towers of the World Trade Center burning on September 11, 2001. Prints & Photographs Division, Library of Congress.

Early in the system, the nation often found itself in orange (high risk) or yellow (significant risk) status. The new federal regulatory agency also set out to make the nation's borders safer, including its ports. Critics immediately questioned the resources it would take to inspect the millions of cargo containers arriving and departing the country's waterways. However, no terrorist activities have taken place in this area of potential weakness.

In response to the attacks, the nation rallied around President Bush, officials in New York, including Mayor Rudy Giuliani, and the families of victims there and in Washington. Both Bush and Giuliani made high-profile appearances at "Ground Zero," amid the remains of the World Trade Center. Ground Zero transformed into a sacred area, with visitors later flocking to the site to pay their respects. And, "United We Stand" became a rallying cry for Americans, as well as a variety of peace symbols, including a "Support Our Troops" ribbon affixed to automobiles.

In the immediate years after September 11, the anniversary of the event dominated the airwaves. Television programming came to a standstill and refocused the viewing public on the tragic day. In 2002, CBS aired a documentary filmed inside the World Trade Center on September 11, watched by more than 39 million viewers. "All broadcast and many cable networks tossed out their normal programming schedules (and their advertising) on the anniversary," explained journalist James Poniewozik. "As if supersaturating the airwaves—turning Sept. 11 into a virtual national holiday—could magically confine the terrible events to history, never to be repeated. There was mawkishness, anger, finger pointing, navel gazing, bathos, pathos—every possible response except forgetting."[17]

In response to questions about intelligence failures leading up to the terrorist attacks, Congress created a 10-member National Commission on Terrorist Attacks upon the United States in November 2002. The Bush Administration fought the creation of such a panel, though the president eventually signed the bill into law. On July 22, 2004, the group released its public report,[18] which created a media spectacle of finger-pointing and accusations. In preparing the report, the panel interviewed more than 1,200 people in 10 countries and inspected 2.5 million pages of documents, including classified national security briefs. The report recommended significant changes to the national security model, which included greater shared resources and interaction between agencies.

In December 2004, the passage of the Intelligence Reform and Terrorism Prevention Act reorganized the American intelligence community, though critics have observed that the results of the bill have not fundamentally transformed the disparate groups for the better. According to Jack Devine, a former CIA acting deputy director of operations, the centralized power created by the bill diminished the role of the CIA, which he believes has actually weakened national security, despite the budget for security growing to $43 billion. More importantly, he said, American agents have not penetrated the terrorist organizations that pose the greatest threats: Iran, North Korea, Russia, China, and Pakistan.[19]

TIME MAGAZINE'S PERSON OF THE YEAR

2000 George W. Bush

2001 Rudolph Giuliani (Mayor of New York City)

2002 The Whistleblowers: Cynthia Cooper (Worldcom), Sherron Watkins (Enron), and Coleen Rowley (FBI)

2003 The American Soldier

2004 George W. Bush

2005 The Good Samaritans: Bill Gates, Melinda Gates, and Bono

2006 You (Internet contributions by the general public)

2007 Vladimir Putin (President of Russia)

AMERICA AT WAR

On March 20, 2003, the United States and a multinational coalition force invaded Iraq with the intent of stopping Saddam Hussein's building of weapons of mass destruction, as well as the terrorism threats Iraq posed, which President Bush linked to the September 11 attacks. In May, aboard the USS *Abraham Lincoln,* the president declared victory in Iraq, a swift win in an overwhelming battle between good and evil. The rhetoric of the

A Marine shares some gum with children his patrol encountered in the Garmsir city district of Helmand Province in Afghanistan in August 2008. Marines have been training and conducting joint patrols with Afghanistan National Border Patrolmen to help prepare them to take over security operations once the Marines redeploy. Photo by Cpl. Alex C. Guerra. The U.S. Marine Corps Web Site. www.marines.mil.

event ran at an all-time high, given that Bush flew onto the aircraft carrier on a jetfighter and stood before a televised audience in a Navy flight suit with a banner in the background blazing the now infamous phrase: "Mission Accomplished."

The reality of the situation, however, turned, and the public realized that the country was far from finished in Iraq. Many political observers believe that the victory declaration touched off a downward spiral for the Bush Administration. According to one journalist, "As American casualties mount and bombs shake Baghdad, the image of Bush's flight suit strut under a banner proclaiming 'Mission Accomplished' is so discordant, his opponents believe, it said more about the administration's arrogance and incompetence than any stump speech could."[20]

According to a survey conducted by the Pew Research Center, some 72 percent of Americans viewed the military efforts in Iraq as the "right decision" in early 2003 and 88 percent saw the war going "very/fairly well." This early support is accentuated by the president's reelection in 2004 and the many symbols of national unity that sprung to life in support of the war, from patriotic "Support Our Troops" car magnets to a rise in the number of American flags purchased. In the post–September 11 world, no politician, civic leader, or business executive could leave the house without an American flag lapel pin.[21]

In the ensuing five years, more than 4,000 American soldiers lost their lives in the fighting, along with more than 29,500 wounded. Most of the last 1,000 to die were killed by an improvised explosive device (IED), the most sinister piece of jargon to emerge from the War on Terror. According to journalists Lizzette Alvarez and Andrew Lehren:

> The year 2007 would prove to be especially hard on American service members; more of

> them died last year than in any other since the war began. Many of those deaths came in the midst of the 30,000-troop buildup known as "the surge," the linchpin of President Bush's strategy to tamp down widespread violence between Islamic Sunnis and Shiites, much of it in the country's capital, Baghdad. In April, May and June alone, 331 American service members died, making it the deadliest three-month period since the war began.[22]

The fallout from the War on Terror in both Afghanistan and Iraq continues to threaten the feelings of national unity experienced after September 11. Certainly, as the war grew more hotly contested, President Bush suffered an extraordinary drop in his personal approval rating. Furthermore, the Democrats were able to use discussion of a war with no end in sight to regain control of the House of Representatives and the Senate after the 2006 midterm elections. The Democratic Party's election triumph not only swept them into power, but led to the election of Nancy Pelosi as the first woman to serve as the Speaker of the House.

The national approval rating for the war in Iraq dropped to a low of 47 percent in February 2005 and remained below 50 percent until rebounding slightly to 54 percent three years later. In early 2008, some 48 percent of Americans surveyed declared that the war in Iraq was going very/fairly well, while the same number said that the effort went not too/not at all well. These figures indicate that the war in Iraq continues to be a divisive issue.[23]

Troubles for Vets Back Home

The challenges facing veterans who served in the war on terror remained virtually hidden after the warfare ensued. Most commentators remarked that the national feelings of patriotism resulting from the terrorist attacks would ensure that people would not treat these veterans with disdain, as many Vietnam vets were treated. In early 2007, however, *Washington Post* reporters Dana Priest and Anne Hull exposed the horrific treatment many wounded and ailing veterans received at the Army's top medical facility, the Walter Reed Army Medical Center in Washington, D.C. For penetrating the secretive world of the army facility, the paper received a 2007 Pulitzer Prize.[24]

The article by Priest and Hull provided graphic details of black mold, cockroaches, mouse droppings, rotten ceilings, and other horrible conditions, which caught the nation's attention. At the heart of the investigative work, however, stood a more sordid story of the neglect that faced the wounded soldiers, from bureaucratic logjams to overcrowded conditions that forced the less wounded to care for their more sickly comrades. According to the journalists, "The soldiers say they feel alone and frustrated. Seventy-five percent of the troops polled by Walter Reed last March said their experience was 'stressful.' Suicide attempts and unintentional overdoses from prescription drugs and alcohol, which is sold on post, are part of the narrative."[25]

Since the conditions at Walter Reed surfaced, veterans groups have kept up the pressure on the federal government. Two nonprofit organizations filed a class-action lawsuit that went to trial in April 2008 against the U.S. Department of Veterans Affairs claiming that the federal agency is not doing enough to prevent suicide among returning soldiers or providing adequate medical care. Statistics that came to light during the pretrial investigation revealed that an average of 18 military veterans commit suicide each day, including five under VA care. In addition, a RAND Corp study released in early 2008 estimated that some 300,000 troops, or 20 percent of those deployed in the war on terror, suffer from depression or post-traumatic stress disorder after serving in Iraq or Afghanistan. In response, the VA counters that the number of claims have grown tremendously, from 670,000 in 2001 to 838,000 in 2007, primarily from veterans aging, not the current war efforts. Regardless of who wins the lawsuit, such claims continue to tug at the national consciousness and call into question the postwar status of the heroes who return home after serving overseas.[26]

HURRICANE KATRINA AND THE AFTERMATH

On August 29, 2005, Hurricane Katrina slammed into the Gulf Coast as a Category 5 storm. While many areas of Louisiana, Mississippi, and Alabama suffered mightily, New Orleans could not withstand the onslaught. Levees designed to protect the city broke, which inundated the area with devastating flood waters. An estimated 1,836 people died in the storm and its aftermath, which also caused $81.2 billion in damages, the most costly hurricane in the nation's history.

The national tragedy of Katrina soon took on a life of its own as a barometer of race relations in the United States. Critics quickly placed blame on the Bush Administration and Federal Emergency Management Agency (FEMA) Director Michael D. Brown for not responding quickly enough to help those without the means to escape the waters.

As a result, desperate citizens, primarily African Americans, took shelter in the Louisiana Superdome—also called the crown jewel of the New Orleans skyline—which quickly became a cesspool of waste and sewage. More importantly, people died while at the Superdome. The city's poor who flocked there for relief had no food, running water, or air conditioning. The ill-equipped emergency shelter, like the nearby Convention Center, became a symbol of the storm's devastation and the Bush administration's failure to aid the people suffering in the drowned city.

The news media scurried to broadcast the lurid tales of mayhem amid the flooded ruins. The plight of disadvantaged African Americans left behind to virtually fend for themselves in the wake elicited a national outcry. Millions of viewers sat spellbound as the news filtered out of the city. Rapper Kanye West summed up the private thoughts many dared not speak publicly, proclaiming that "George Bush doesn't care about black people" on a nationally-televised hurricane relief program. Katrina put race back on the national agenda.

Unfortunately, many Americans are quick to dismiss racism as simply a defective character trait or a sign of overt stupidity. But many believe

Hurricane Katrina caused devastation across the Gulf Coast, especially New Orleans and the gulf towns of Mississippi. iStockphoto. ©Chad Purser.

CELEBRITIES AND HURRICANE KATRINA RELIEF

Hurricane Katrina destroyed the lives of many Gulf Coast residents. The national tragedy led to a series of high-profile benefits to raise money for relief efforts. Similar to the efforts after the terrorist attacks on September 11, celebrities responded to the call for help, donating both time and money to the cause.

Musicians from across genres participated in a series of benefit concerts. MTV held one of the star-studded events, showcasing the Rolling Stones, Neil Young, Kanye West, Paul McCartney, and the Neville Brothers. Others across the entertainment industry donated millions of dollars and created foundations to serve the Gulf region. Writer John Grisham donated $5 million to help rebuild Mississippi. Rapper David Banner started an organization, Heal the Hood. Actress Rosie O'Donnell pledged $3 million over three years to provide emergency child care services. Celine Dion and business partners, along with George Clooney, Nicolas Cage, and Oprah Winfrey's Angel Network each gave $1 million.

Celebrities were not above getting dirty either. Many went right to the ravaged areas and pitched in. Country music star Faith Hill and her superstar husband Tim McGraw loaded up her tour bus and a semi hauler with supplies and drove them to Mississippi. Actor Jamie Foxx and singer Macy Gray helped distribute clothes, food, and toiletries. John Travolta personally flew 400 tetanus vaccines to the survivors, while Sean Penn pulled victims from the floodwaters in a borrowed boat. Although there was some sniping at them for giving money or donating time and money simply to improve their images, in general, celebrities made the statement that they were genuine in helping the less fortunate and that they did not want it to appear that the nation forgot about the victims.

it runs deeper, straight to the heart of the country's national fabric. Historian John Hope Franklin told the Associated Press, "The New Orleans tragedy speaks in a loud but eloquent voice that racial inequities in the United States persist. As far as race in America is concerned, Katrina was just another example of the failure of the people of the United States to come to terms with a centuries-old problem...and make a forthright effort to solve it."[27]

The chaos in New Orleans revealed the depths of racism that exists in the United States, but many hoped the catastrophe would touch off a renewed national dialogue on racism and possibly eliminate it once and for all in the post-Katrina America. However, when the immediate chaos and governmental finger-pointing devolved into a post-storm bureaucratic nightmare of red tape, and the sensationalist images and stories disappeared, so too did the discussions of racism.

Some observers note that Americans are so ashamed of the heritage of slavery and the current state of those living in poverty that the nation can only examine race if it comes from the mouths of cartoon characters (think of Token Black, the African American on South Park), standup comics like Chris Rock and Dave Chappelle, or rap musicians. But though West's audacious claim touched off a media frenzy, frank dialogue never really materialized, and today, despite the fact that Barack Obama has been elected president of the United States, most observers believe that America still has a long way to go in solving race problems.

Looking back, the failure of a national dialogue regarding race proves West's point yet again. Race slipped from the national agenda in part because George W. Bush did not keep the issue at the forefront. Of course, politicians going back to the Founding Fathers have failed to adequately address race. Many argue that Bush had the opportunity to use the Katrina tragedy to reinvigorate the race discussion on a national level.

RACE IN AMERICA

Although President Bush is criticized for routinely flubbing multisyllabic words, he is a master of modern American corporate speak, in which a CEO is applauded for focusing on looking to the future without ever acknowledging current or past errors. For example, the president played up his post-Katrina discussions with NAACP CEO Bruce Gordon without conceding any slip-ups on the part of his administration: "We talked about the challenges facing the African American community after that storm. We talked about the response of the federal government. And most importantly, we talked about the way forward. We talked about what we can do working together to move forward." At another point in the speech, he revealed the real reasons he finally addressed the organization: "You must understand I understand that racism still lingers in America. It's a lot easier to change a law than to change a human heart. And I understand that many African Americans distrust my political party. I consider it a tragedy that the party of Abraham Lincoln let go of its historic ties with the African American community. For too long my party wrote off the African American vote, and many African Americans wrote off the Republican Party."[28]

Political strategists assert that the black vote could be critical in the 2008 presidential race. However, Bush won the southern vote across the Dixie South (and subsequently both elections) by appealing to white southerners with coded language, including his "tough on crime" stance.

Despite his lip service and political pandering in this speech, Bush has done little to help African Americans. According to NAACP statistics, blacks are twice as likely to be unemployed compared to whites, significantly less likely to own homes (75 percent for whites compared to 48 percent for blacks), and have an average median net worth of $10,000 versus $81,700 for whites.

Many experts agree that a president who cares about African Americans would look out on the nation and be disgusted by what is happening in black communities. He would place race on the national agenda. If the weight of the office can push terrorism and security to the top of the agenda, then it can do the same for racism. Though the Bush administration has "czars" for everything from cyberterrorism, to AIDS, there's no czar for racism, no money behind completing the "unfinished story of freedom." The National Priorities Project estimates that the war in Iraq has cost more than $300 billion, yet poverty-stricken Americans at home slip further into despair.

But, as easy as it is to blame the president for the current state of racism in America, the lack of leadership within the African American community must be cited as well. The fact that West—a musician—stood as the most significant black political figure to emerge from the devastation in New Orleans reveals the paucity of leadership among blacks.

Barack Obama, elected president of the United States on November 4, 2008, from his U.S. Senate Web site.

Some observers are hopeful that Barack Obama, as president of the United States, will be able to put racism on the national agenda, though it is clear that dealing with critical economic problems, the wars in Iraq and Afghanistan, and other urgent matters will take up much of his immediate focus. As a matter of fact, some analysts have criticized Obama for not taking a more direct stance on racism in the highly charged presidential campaign. Some believe that prominent black leaders, such as Jesse Jackson and Al Sharpton, put too much faith in the political process. Like the American labor movement, African Americans since the 1960s have been co-opted by the Democrats, working with an organization that at times seems more concerned with winning office than standing up for ideals. There is merit in sustained voter registration drives and raising money for candidates, but many believe that these tactics have still not brought racism to the forefront.

Many are hopeful that, just by seeing an African American and his family in the White House, racial barriers will become more eroded. Some, however, wonder when the next Martin Luther King Jr. or Malcolm X will appear. Neither of those leaders held political office or aligned too closely with a political party. They drew from religious backgrounds and followings but were able to bring their causes to the national stage.

It is clear to many that, for the good of the nation, racism must be quashed. Spike Lee's highly publicized *When the Levees Broke* documentary showed the nation that building a better world means retaining our collective humanity. Lee's provocative film revealed that, in today's polarized society, racial equality may seem out of reach, but it is an attainable aspiration. Although the decisive victory of Barack Obama belayed some of the fears that many white voters would not be able to bring themselves to vote for a black candidate, *New York Times* columnist Charles M. Blow talked about insidious racism in the summer of 2008:

> [In] a July *New York Times*/CBS News poll, when whites were asked whether they would be willing to vote for a black candidate, 5 percent confessed that they would not. That's not so bad, right? But wait. The pollsters then rephrased the question to get a more accurate portrait of the sentiment. They asked the same whites if most of the people they knew would vote for a black candidate. Nineteen percent said that those they knew would not. Depending on how many people they know and how well they know them, this universe of voters could be substantial. That's bad.[29]

THE ECONOMY

Innovation fuels America's power and culture. Yet, the constant demand for "more" and "faster" ratchets up anxiety as well. In the new millennium, general nervousness about the economy spreads a bit more each day. Signposts signal large problems on the horizon. Soaring gas prices, for example, serve as a daily yardstick. For sale signs and the empty homes they mock fill the nation's streets, cul-de-sacs, and suburban enclaves, constantly reminding hard-working (but scared) citizens that the other shoe could (and soon may) drop.

Despite individual stress, however, the country stands as the world's capital center. The United States is now in serious economic trouble, but when it is strong, people benefit across the board. The gain is felt across age, sex, demographics, and race. In 2007, for example, about 50 percent of all law and medical students were women, up from merely 10 percent in 1970. These kinds of socio-economic changes pull up the nation as a whole. Some 24 percent of adults in their prime working years live in households earning at least $100,000 annually. Between 1983 and 2004, median family net worth doubled from $49,700 to $99,300.[30]

On the downside, individual happiness has not kept pace with the technological innovation and abundance of consumer goods available.[31] In many respects, access and speed made life less enjoyable. Americans are not working fewer hours, living healthier, worrying less, or taking smaller quantities of medicines for smaller numbers of ailments. As employers search for ways to squeeze every penny out of overhead, increasing healthcare premiums for workers is an easy fix. By 2005, the average household spent $8,300 annually on health insurance and out-of-pocket health expenses annually.[32]

By mid-decade, many individuals and families floated their consumer habits on a sea of credit and debt. Historically low interest rates enabled homeowners to refinance, taking money out of their homes to use for other things, whether that meant renovations or buying a new plasma television. Across the nation, homeowners essentially gambled on pumped up home values and traded debt for greater debt, but at a lower interest rate. Banks and mortgage companies contributed to the system by offering sub prime loans and other creative financial packages that allowed people to buy a home with little money down and subsequent low payments over a set period of time. What many people did not realize, particularly those who are not financially savvy or have shaky credit reports, is that once the introductory period passed, the loans could increase significantly.

At the heart of the mortgage fiasco is people losing their homes, which, for most, is still synonymous with losing the American Dream.

Government reports indicated that, in the yearlong period from July 2006 to July 2007, foreclosures jumped 93 percent nationwide. Nearly 180,000 foreclosures took place in the latter month alone, a gaudy one filing for every 693 households. Nevada led the foreclosure market with one filing for every 199 homes. Taken as a whole, five states made up almost half the total foreclosures in the nation: California, Florida, Ohio, Michigan, and Georgia.[33]

Credit card debt also reached epidemic proportions in the new millennium. In the early 1970s, households carried about $600 in credit card debt in real dollars. In 2006, the average household balanced topped $7,300, a 1,200 percent increase.[34] Two years earlier, the Federal Reserve Board reported that revolving debt in the United States reached $800 billion, the majority comprised of credit card balances.

Recession Debate and the Teetering Economy

By late 2007 and early 2008, the subprime mortgage crisis placed an anchor around the neck of an otherwise teetering American economy already groping under the weight of a costly overseas war. Recession, the dreaded r-word, crept back into the national conscious. While the experts debated whether or not the country had already entered a recession or not, politicians devised stimulus packages designed to force spending money into the pockets of cash-strapped Americans. On a daily basis, the news never seemed to improve, ranging from massive layoffs at various global financial corporations to declining numbers of jobs created. People who turned to Wall Street for some indication of the nation's economic status found themselves in the midst of rollercoaster swings.

As with most aspects of popular culture, perception soon became reality. The more the media reported on the recession, the more steam the idea gained. People's fears about their jobs, the economy in general, and an unsettled situation in Iraq and Afghanistan made them apprehensive about spending money. Historically, when consumers turn off the spigot, the national economy is in big trouble. The gloomy national economic outlook forced President Bush to address the situation, stating, "Obviously the housing market is creating deep concern. And one of the real problems could be that if people, as a result of their value of their homes going down, kind of pull in their horns."[35]

A poll conducted by the Associated Press in February 2008 revealed that 61 percent of the public believed that the United States stood in the midst of its first recession since 2001. The facts provided evidence to the national mood. In 2007, the economy had its weakest year overall since 2002, expanding a mere 2.2 percent. The real estate fiasco triggered the anemic growth, with builders dropping their spending by almost 17 percent. People also took home less pay in 2007, with average weekly earnings actually falling 0.9 percent when adjusted for inflation.[36]

Despite mounting hard evidence, many economists joined President Bush in stating that the American economy was not in a recession. However, the threat of more fiscal challenges on the horizon led Congress and the president to work on an economic stimulus package that would provide tax rebates for individuals and tax cuts for businesses. In the rush to solve the nation's monetary problems, however, relatively few people questioned how we would pay for the $168 billion rescue package.[37]

The World is Flat

America remains the center of world finance, but its dependence on foreign nations to finance its growing national debt, Middle Eastern oil reserves, and Chinese imports, reveals the shaky nature of that position. *New York Times* columnist Thomas L. Friedman coined the phrase "the world is flat" to describe the consequences of globalization on the United States in his 2005 best seller The *World Is Flat: A Brief History of the Twenty-First Century.*

After visiting India, Friedman realized that globalization provided global nations a level playing field economically and removed many barriers to foreign trade that previously existed. One of Friedman's examples is the outsourcing trend occurring in corporate America. Companies sent jobs to overseas knowledge centers, which saved them money, instead of offering the same services using American employees. Companies like Dell, Microsoft, Citigroup, and many others outsourced IT and customer service functions to India, China, and other Far East nations. Despite the backlash against such practices, outsourcing provided a greater return on investment.

The International Association of Outsourcing Professionals estimated that American companies spent $4.2 trillion on outsourcing in 2006, up from $3.1 trillion just three years earlier. Obviously, with trillions of dollars being put into outsourcing, the trend is not going to stop. Rather, the question for U.S. corporations is how to best use it strategically. For example, some organizations are moving away from India, the traditional power base in the field, to places such as Russia, the Philippines, and Mexico. Any nation with a workforce strong in software and engineering and English-language skills is a potential hotbed for outsourcing.[38]

Enron and Corporate Crooks

From the mid-1990s until its financial collapse in late 2001, Enron stood as a darling of the business media, ranging from one of *Fortune* magazine's "World's Most Admired Companies" to a corporation studied in business schools nationwide for its innovation and success. Enron, led by chief executive Jeff Skilling and Chairman Ken Lay, also fooled finance professionals, receiving glowing reports from analyst firms that bought and sold enormous blocks of stock for investors, retirement funds, and 401Ks. Billions of dollars were at stake in these decisions, and Enron duped all the major players in perhaps the largest Ponzi scheme in history. Enron's stock, which, at one point, traded for $90 a share, plummeted to 50 cents a share, not really even worth the price of the certificate it would have printed on.

When the Enron collapse began, it unraveled faster than anyone could have imagined. Bankruptcy and mass layoffs took place quickly, while some employees lost their retirement funds in the meltdown. On May 25, 2006, a jury found Lay and Skilling guilty of conspiracy and fraud. For journalists Bethany McLean and Peter Elkind, who helped break the Enron fraud, the guilty verdicts had "positive implications," including offering "a measure of consolation—or retribution—for those employees who lost everything in Enron's bankruptcy. And it reinforces a critical notion about our justice system: that, despite much punditry to the contrary, being rich and spending millions on a crack criminal defense team does not necessarily buy freedom."[39]

At the heart of Enron's criminal activity was the deliberate manipulation of company stock to make the company more valuable on paper than in reality. Top executives then sold millions of dollars of essentially worthless stock for profit, when they knew the price was a sham. The unfortunate aspect of every underhanded financial plot is that someone is left holding the bag. In this case, it turned out to be Enron employees and investors.

The Enron scandal serves as the most shocking downfall in an era of high-profile corporate collapses. The others spanned a variety of industries and included some of the more prominent corporations in America. Like Enron, these were considered topnotch businesses. Accounting firm Arthur Andersen fell apart in the wake of serving as Enron's public accounting agency. Although the company collected revenues of $9.3 billion in 2001, some 85,000 Andersen employees either left the firm or lost their jobs in the downfall.

Adelphia Communications, founded by the Rigas family, grew into the fifth largest cable company in the United States. Members of the Rigas family hid debt and essentially allocated themselves millions of dollars in undisclosed loans. John and Timothy Rigas were found guilty of securities violations after federal officials determined that they stole $100 million in company money. Other stunning disintegrations included Tyco chief executive Dennis Kozlowski and WorldCom founder Bernard Ebbers. Both, seen as innovative leaders prior to the scandals, ended up in jail for bilking investors. Ebbers, for example, had $400 million in undisclosed loans.[40]

The outcome of Enron and other corporate shenanigans is that the public and government officials are less likely to give business leaders a free pass. In March 2008, the House Oversight and Government Reform Committee called executives largely responsible for the real estate bust to task for their roles in the crisis. Chief executives testifying before the committee included Angelo Mozilo of Countrywide Financial, Stanley O'Neal, formerly of Merrill Lynch, and Charles Prince, formerly of Citigroup. Rep. Henry Waxman, D-Calif., chairman of the committee, called the CEOs to task for their lavish compensation packages.

In 2006, on average, these leaders at the nation's largest 500 corporations made $15.2 million. Countrywide, which is well-known for its television commercials and Web advertising pushing home financing, paid Angelo Mozilo a $1.9 million salary and $20 million in stock awards based on performance, while he sold another $121 million in stock options. This took place as the company lost $1.6 billion in 2007, and its stock dropped 80 percent. Mozilo told the committee, "As our company did well, I did well." Waxman viewed the disparity between company results and CEO compensation as "a complete disconnect with reality."[41]

The Workplace

Americans have a love-hate relationship with work and the workplace. From an early age, people are taught to strive for the "American Dream," which places notions of hard work and meritocracy at the heart of one's cultural being. On the flip side, however, the constant agonizing over work- and money-related issues produces a nation full of uptight employees, basically unhappy with their status, wages, and position within workplace politics. Ironically, work provides a route to happiness and material comfort, while at the same time shackling individuals to their jobs and limiting freedom.

Cubicles across the nation are littered with Scott Adams's Dilbert cartoons. Adams turned the "cubiclization" of the workplace into a multimillion dollar industry. In essence, people lampoon themselves by tacking up the Dilbert episodes that seem to mirror their own lives as workers, but also express a degree of personalization at the same time. Others load their office space with knickknacks. Outside of family photographs, tchotchkes, or knick knacks, are perhaps the most common feature in America's "cube farms." Many tchotchkes are adorned with the company logo, such as miniature desk clocks and acrylic plaques touting the latest inner-office recognition.

Retaining personal space within a corporate setting gives workers a feeling of empowerment in a somewhat dehumanizing and powerless aspect of their lives. Surrounding oneself with the merchandise covered in logos shows a sense of pride in where one works, but the tacky displays scream of a mutated individualism allowed within the structured corporate setting. The company owns the cube, but employees individualize it as it becomes an extension of who they are.

There may be no better indicator of the duality of the corporate world than e-mail, a piece of technology that has the potential to make one's job infinitely easier, but at the same time, adds additional work to already long weeks. Basex Inc., a research firm in New York, estimates that 35 million e-mails are sent each day, which take up 2.1 hours daily for white-collar workers. This drain costs businesses money. In total, some 28 billion hours annually are spent on e-mail, with a price tag of $650 billion. Other efficiency experts place the figures even higher, with studies reporting that corporate workers get 50 to 100 e-mails a day, some even placing the total sent daily at upward of 142 billion.[42]

Another technology that is actually sapping efficiency is online video. A study released in early 2008 by Nielsen Online revealed that online video sites, such as market leading YouTube and others, receive most use on weekdays at lunchtime, usually between 12 P.M. and 2 P.M. The number of online videos consumed during the workday is astronomical: YouTube users accessed 674 million video streams in January 2008, while Yahoo had 157 million, and Fox Interactive Media nearly 93 million.[43]

Carriage Services Inc., a funeral services company in Houston, for example, told *The Wall Street Journal* that it discovered some 70 percent of 125 workers in the company headquarters watched online videos about an hour a day. As a result, the information technology executive blocked access to both YouTube and MySpace. But Carriage Services is just one of many companies confronting workers' Internet usage while on the job. Most corporations implemented policies against using work computers for personal e-mail, instant messaging, streaming music, and accessing inappropriate content.[44]

Another organization, Catholic Charities of Santa Clara County in San Jose, California, blocked video access so its network would not crash, ultimately leading to costly computer outages and potential loss of sensitive information. "It's a real issue when a network can't handle demand," said William Bailey, the nonprofit organization's IT manager. "Too much media, particularly video, is usually the reason why."[45]

Across the nation in Atlanta, a mid-sized real estate company grappled with similar issues, but it decided to block video sites because of bandwidth concerns. Without blocking the sites, the company faced a costly network upgrade—a difficult expense to swallow during a challenging real estate downturn. The downside of such decisions, however, is that employees may actually turn against management, particularly if they feel entitled to visit these sites during lunch breaks. "I know our people will say we're acting like Big Brother," explained another IT administrator. "But those pipes belong to the company. If management says we need to protect our resources, then that's what happens."[46]

Downsized...

If the real estate collapse and credit crunch did not do enough to make Americans fearful, corporations added to their anxiety through downsizing. In February 2008, employers laid off 63,000 workers, the highest figure since 2003. However, in the perverse world of unemployment calculations, the national rate actually dropped from 4.9 percent in January to 4.8 percent, as the Labor Department does not count those individuals who simply drop out of the job search altogether or those people collecting unemployment checks. As a matter of fact, the national unemployment rate is further skewed by the simple quantitative formula used to establish the number. There is no system in place to measure the real loss of a middle manager in Cleveland who earns $85,000 annually versus the addition of a fast food clerk in Florida who makes $8.50 an hour.[47]

The industries suffering the most widespread losses indicate the state of the overall national economy: construction, financial services, manufacturing, retailing, and business services. The snowball effect of the housing crunch, combined with costly overseas wars, is stretching the economy's stability. In an increasingly unstable environment, executives react by cutting overhead, which usually results in massive job losses. Repeated efforts by the Federal Reserve to manage the economy, through interest rate cuts and other cash-infusion measures, have little consequence on individual households affected by layoffs, credit challenges, and real estate woes.

The February 2008 job cuts followed about 22,000 losses in the previous month, setting 2008 on a record course for layoffs. The last time the nation suffered back-to-back cuts occurred in May and June 2003. At that time, the United States struggled to regain its footing after the 2001 recession. The Federal Reserve predicts a difficult year for workers in 2008, estimating that the unemployment rate will jump to 5.3 percent, versus an average of 4.6 percent in 2007. These figures are low when compared to other difficult economic times in modern American history, but the jobless rate has taken on a more important psychological role in the 2000s. The panic that would ensue if the jobless rate reached double-digits, as it did in the 1980s, would devastate the economy and begin a spiraling effect that would choke off consumer spending and corporate expansion, thus resulting in further job losses and eroding confidence.[48]

Some observers view the actions taken by the Federal Reserve as ineffective. Steven Lehman, an analyst at Federated Investors, explained, "There is a profound lack of understanding of markets and economies, and there is still persistent lingering faith that the authorities effectively have a magic wand they can wave to make everything fine. Economies and markets do go down—particularly after a multi-decade credit boom."[49]

LIVING CONDITIONS

In the 2000s, much of the national conversation about living conditions takes place in the context of marriage and the family. The public debate regarding gay marriage, for example, is wrapped within a wider discussion about marriage in general. Much of the talk follows a pessimistic viewpoint, either lamenting the decline of traditional marriages or questioning how the union can retain its sanctity, given the possibility of non-traditional marriages.

In 2007, a survey conducted by the Pew Research Center showed that the public's perception of a happy marriage changed dramatically from an earlier study done in 1990. The most telling information is that the perception of kids as a source for marital bliss dropped significantly, from 65 percent in 1990 to 41 percent in 2007, ranking eighth out of nine categories. At the top of the survey were faithfulness (93 percent) and a happy sexual relationship (70 percent). Interestingly, sharing household chores ranked third, reaching 62 percent, versus 47 percent in 1990. Some 53 percent of respondents claimed adequate income as a necessity in a successful marriage.[50]

The Pew researchers considered the 24-point drop in the children question and the jump for more day-to-day activities indicators of an overall shift in the way people view a happy marriage. When it comes to children, people are more open to unwed couples raising kids, adoption, and blended families than at any time in the past. "In the United States today," the report said, "marriage exerts less influence over how adults organize their lives and how children are born and raised than at any time in the nation's history."[51]

Picking Apart the Generations

Americans often define themselves (or are defined by cultural critics, corporations, marketers, and other entities) by generation. The 2000s are noted for two interrelated events: the start of retirement for Baby Boomers and the coming of age of Generation eXposed (also known as Generation Y or Millennials) group. In 2008, the first wave of Baby Boomers (born between 1946 and 1964) turned 62 years old, while the early Echo Boomers (born between 1977 and 1994) turned 31.

The sheer size of these generations spurs much of the resulting national culture, from what products are manufactured and marketed to the kind of television shows and films that get aired. Some 78 million people were born during the Baby Boom alone. The echo boom that defines their children refers primarily to the period between 1989 and 1993 when birthrates eclipsed 4 million per year.[52]

In some cases, it seems as if entire industries are devoted to selling to one of these two age groups. Certainly much of the television lineup, from the major networks to specialized cable stations, is geared toward these demographic segments. For example, TV shows like *The Office* and *How I Met Your Mother* appeal to and focus solely on Echo Boomer audiences, while *Without a Trace* and *CSI* are designed to attract all audiences, but they are favorites of older Baby Boomer audiences.

Recent studies reveal that Baby Boomers watch more television than younger segments of the population. In 2006, adults aged 45 to 64 watched 37 hours and 38 minutes of television each week. In contrast, those between 18 and 34 tuned in for just over 27 hours. For marketers, the positive aspect of this information is that Baby Boomers often watch shows targeted at younger viewers, such as *Grey's Anatomy* and *Desperate Housewives*.[53]

The power of the Boomers is in their immense size (nearly 24 percent of the population, or about 78 million) and their buying power (estimated at $3 trillion). Most of the nation's political and corporate leaders fall into this category, such as Hillary Clinton and Bill Gates. Marketing efforts at treating the demographic like one big happy family do not work, though. Marilynn Mobley, senior vice president at Edelman, a communications firm that conducted an extensive study of Boomers, explained, "Baby boomers have always been considered the 'me-generation,' and that doesn't change with age. We're still just as self-centered, and we want things very customized."[54]

Using Technology

One of the most glaring disparities between older and younger people is in how they use technology. In general, for someone in their later fifties or sixties, just being online is a sign of being hip, whereas for someone under the age of 25, sending e-mail is somewhat passé, as is waiting for more than a couple seconds for a Web page to load. Furthermore, while some people still resist owning a cell phone, the number of those holdouts is rapidly decreasing. It seems as if everyone, whether a senior citizen or middle school student, is connected.

One of the common denominators, according to journalist Chad Lorenz, is e-mail. In his interactions with a younger niece, it dawned upon him that e-mail, what seems like a necessity for those older than 25, really is not part of younger people's lives. His niece, "was too busy sending IMs and text messages to bother with e-mail," he explained. "That's when I realized that my agility with e-mail no longer marked me as a tech-savvy young adult. It made me a lame old fogey."[55]

For a generation of people raised (and raising themselves) on Facebook and MySpace, e-mail simply is not fast enough and requires too much work. While older people are firing away at their keyboards, the typical 20 year old is writing on a friend's Facebook wall, texting via cell phone, all while blogging on WordPress. According to Lorenz, teens are sending about 50 messages a day via cell phones, while being logged in to Facebook and/or MySpace during all hours outside of school. "When everyone's online," he said, "kids never have to leave the company of their pals. If you're not constantly plugged in, they say, you start to feel left out."[56]

One could merely chalk this behavior up to teens being teens. Is there really a difference between chattering away on Facebook and talking for hours a day on the telephone, like older people did when growing up? There is a reflective quality of e-mail that is falling by the wayside. Certainly composing an e-mail should not be equated with writing the next great American novel, but it is more serious and considerate than its cheap brethren the text message, with its clipped content and reliance on shorthand.

Another disconnect that younger users face is transitioning from the dorm room to the workplace, where e-mail still dominates. It is not like a young employee can simply turn on an understanding of etiquette when it comes to communicating with coworkers and bosses. One of the cutting-edge tools that Google introduced to combat this challenge is Gmail, which mixes e-mail with IM. This may be a future state for corporations as they cope with young workers who feel e-mail is too archaic to be part of the workplace of tomorrow.

The New Religious Zeal

Religion plays a critical role in American popular culture, just as pop culture exerts a significant influence on religion. On the conservative side, pop culture is something to be derided for its Hollywood (read "bad") morals and permissiveness. On the left, religion is the culprit, a codeword for the "simple" and unsophisticated people that some liberals look down on. Undeniably, both conservatives and liberals make assumptions about the spirituality of the other based more on stereotype than experience. And, like any issue that it can exploit, the mass media uses religion as a tool to sell television programs, newspapers, and magazines.

The most comprehensive information available about religion in the United States comes from the 2008 Pew Forum on Religion & Public Life *U.S. Religious Landscape Survey*, based on interviews with 35,000 American adults. The report indicates that the primary characteristics of American religion are fluidity and diversity. Some 28 percent of those surveyed left the faith that they were raised in and either chose another affiliation or left religion altogether. The number jumps to 44 percent if those who switched groups within Protestantism are included.[57]

Some 16 percent of people claim that they are unaffiliated with any particular faith, including 25 percent of those aged 18 to 29. These figures are surprising if one were to follow the political discussion of religion and its consequences on voting. Liberals paint a portrait of extreme right wing religious zealots running the Republican Party, while that side sees the left as godless. In fact, only 4 percent of those surveyed fall into the agnostic (2.4 percent) or atheist (1.6 percent) categories.[58]

Interestingly, the other major tenet of American religion is its fluidity. According to the study, "Constant movement characterizes the American religious marketplace, as every major religious group is simultaneously gaining and losing adherents. Those that are growing as a result of religious change are simply gaining new members at a faster rate than they are losing members." For example, the Catholic portion of the adult population has been around 25 percent for the past several decades. However, the undercurrent is those who have left the Catholic Church. Some 33 percent of those raised in the faith no longer describe themselves as Catholics. The survey explained that "roughly 10 percent of all Americans are former Catholics." The losses do not look more severe because of the large number of immigrants coming into the United States who are Catholic.[59]

Advertising of the 2000s

A century ago, advertisers plastered American towns and cities with signs, billboards, and brand names. It seemed as if every square inch of downtown areas contained some directive to potential buyers. Advertisers hoped to entice dollars away from consumers who, perhaps for the first time, had disposable income and sought new products designed to make their lives easier. At that time, a horse-drawn buggy with the Wrigley logo and slogan painted on the side was cutting edge innovation. Direct mail, such as the Sears catalog, served as the ultimate wish list for millions of families nationwide, particularly those isolated on farms and in rural communities. The advertising profession grew out of this need to connect consumers with goods.

Leap ahead a hundred years, and the lives of consumers are filled with similar forces—a constant barrage of commercials, billboards, ad banners, and displays in a multitude of mediums. The primary difference is that physical space is only one dimension of the way advertisers currently ply their trade. Just like in the earlier days, advertisers use the advanced technology at their disposal to reach consumers, through television, radio, film, and the Web. Today, advertising is part of the larger discipline of marketing or branding, representing the ubiquity of organizations, products, and services to consumers and organizations.

In the 2000s, businesses and manufacturers do not want people to simply buy products; rather, they want to form relationships with consumers, which will keep buyers returning again and again to trusted goods and those who provide them. Marketing is at the heart of building this relationship, whether it is redesigning a package to represent a product's place in the market or expounding on a company's social responsibility via a blog. Due to its influence and reach, advertising is a central function in marketing and branding.

DEVELOPING VALUES

Popular culture, technological innovation, and the power of the corporate world are the driving forces that dominated American life for the last 150 years. Standing at the intersection of the three and propelling them deep into people's daily lives is marketing—the umbrella term used to describe the communication fields of public relations, advertising, and marketing. Marketing has served as an important catalyst for the seismic societal transformations that have taken place in modern America, walking hand-in-hand with the nation's increasingly consumer-oriented culture. Because corporations speak to the public primarily through communications campaigns, advertising, public relations, and marketing play

ADVERTISING SLOGANS OF THE 2000s

"Can you hear me now?," Verizon, 2002

"I'm lovin' it," McDonald's, 2003

"Think outside the bun," Taco Bell, 2001

"What can BROWN do for you?," UPS, 2002

"Dude, you're getting a Dell," Dell Computers, 2001

"What happens in Vegas, stays in Vegas," Las Vegas Convention and Visitors Authority, 2004

"Life tastes good," Coca-Cola, 2001

"An Army of One," U.S. Army, 2001

"Army Strong," U.S. Army, 2006

"Look who we've got our Hanes on now," Hanes, 2005

a critical role in determining how people build their personal value systems.

Historically, the tendency has been to look at marketing as a corporate evil. The idea that companies push unnecessary or unwanted products on an unsuspecting public to gain profit seems wholly un-American. Acknowledging the fact that advertisers have a hold over the public somehow robs people of their autonomy or individuality. In addition, the omnipresence of marketing campaigns also works in favor of its critics. Spotting advertisements in poor taste or as being ineffective is an easy task, and the criticism of such work is an industry in itself. The monetary figures involved in orchestrating campaigns also make them convenient targets. One critic, historian Robert W. McChesney, said, "Modern marketing is clearly the greatest concerted attempt at psychological manipulation in all of human history."[1] He cites the advent of guerrilla marketing in the early twenty-first century as especially egregious. Guerilla marketing is the deliberate attempt to create a relationship with a consumer without that person knowing they are being marketed to, usually via grassroots, low-cost efforts, although the advent of social media sites enables large corporations to launch these campaigns through MySpace, Facebook, or other channels.

However, a deeper analysis of marketing reveals that there is also an educational aspect of the field that enables consumers to make informed, intelligent decisions about the products they purchase. In today's electronic age, for example, public relations keeps the lines of communications open between companies and the public (especially shareholders). Though the system certainly is not perfect, considering that scandals such as Enron still take place, imagine the corruption if public companies were not required to report important financial information like quarterly earnings. While corporations made this type of financial information available in earlier eras, in the new millennium, it is more readily accessible via the Internet than in previous eras, including the 1990s. Corporate marketing is a polarizing topic, but it deserves a broader examination, especially as it relates to how people use this influence to determine their own world views.

In the past, one could argue, elites drove much of the interaction between marketers and the public. Interestingly, however, the pervasiveness of Internet technology is significantly transforming the way the two sides deal with one another. Social media Web sites, such as MySpace, Facebook, and YouTube, have given consumers more power to choose the way they want to interact with those attempting to sell products or services to them. As a result, corporate America is scrambling to find ways to engage people via these channels.

Shaping Values

Turning on the television for five minutes or glancing through ads in a magazine, one finds countless examples of marketers attempting to dupe consumers. The most egregious examples seem to be diet- or health-related. The bold print or voiceover pushes a consistent message: "Take this pill and you'll become the thin, beautiful person you've always dreamed of being. You'll live a healthier, happier life, and people will love you."

The cultural historian Christopher Lasch chalked this thinking up as an addiction to consumption. In his view, advertisers solidify and expand the public's desire for acquiring goods, which makes them feel like they are important, worthy, and accomplished. According to Lasch,

"Consumption promises to fill the aching void; hence the attempt to surround commodities with an aura of romance; with allusions to exotic places and vivid experiences; and with images of female breasts from which all blessings flow."[2]

Advertising exists, in other words, to transform people into shopping machines, hell bent on erasing their insecurities through the power of acquisition. Critics of marketing pose a simple question: How can people develop a sense of value or their place in the wider culture if they are little more than ad-driven, brainwashed zombies? According to McChesney, "What such a commercial culture tends to produce—and what the avalanche of commercialism encourages—is a profound cynicism and materialism, both cancerous for public life."[3]

What has changed most dramatically since Lasch's era is that consumption has been subsumed by the public's celebrity obsession. The idea that everyone rightfully deserves their bit of fame is nearly universal in twenty-first century America. Marketers tap into this idea, presenting people with the image of a better, more beautiful self hidden somewhere behind the curtain while they trudge through their daily routines without any of the glamour they view thousands of times a day.

Whether portraying the latest age-resistant facial cream or a new, must-have luxury SUV, advertisements pull at a vein of insecurity that runs deep into the American psyche. While the results of this mindset are numbing, like the plethora of reality television shows and hundreds of millions of user-generated videos uploaded to YouTube, MySpace, and a host of smaller social media sites, the impact on popular culture cannot be understated. Despite the popularity of reality television shows, such as *Survivor* and *American Idol,* many contend that these programs are little more than extended commercials and opportunities for seemingly ordinary people to become celebrities. Mark Burnett, the powerful producer of *Survivor,* said that he viewed the show "as much as a marketing vehicle as a television show."[4]

Obviously, despite its long existence at the heart of popular and corporate culture, advertising is much maligned. The field is besieged by an age-old question: is advertising a good or bad thing for society? The notion that advertising influences the way people shape their values and the culture as a whole is now universal. What has changed in recent times is that messages are less likely to be completely driven from the top (agencies/corporations) down. Ideas, issues, and cultural meanings that bubble up from below, such as consumer-generated commercials and content strongly influence how marketers speak to their audiences.

Marketing as Public Education

Advertising's pervasiveness, in some respects, actually opens doors to public discussion about marketing efforts and one's place in the larger world. People use ads as a barometer for assessing their own values and roles as citizens. Consumers may also receive a useful information from companies through marketing campaigns. Bank of America, for instance, launched a new product in January 2005 called SafeSend that enabled Hispanic customers to remit money to Mexico free of charge. Previously, Hispanic consumers had to use costly payday loan establishments or wire transfers to send money back to Mexico, which topped $20 billion in total in 2005.

In examining Burrell Communications, a large African American-owned advertising firm, communications scholar Irene Costera Meijer sees client work that uses "positive realism" to show black consumers a view of life that is purposely thoughtful, engaging, and well-rounded. A McDonald's ad created by Burrell that showed a successful black father visiting his child's school, for instance, provides "a new story of responsible black male citizenship that can be a source of inspiration and guidance for men and women, whites and blacks."[5]

Meijer sees advertisements like this as providing a positive social impact. She explained that marketers should consider using positive images "that create so-called win-win situations, images which are good for the market and can change people's ideas about themselves and hopes for society."[6] According to Meijer, advertising can provide valuable stories of what it means to live the good life, which are otherwise hard to find in mainstream media channels. "Such stories should be seen as part of the wide array of practices and technologies with which individuals nowadays have to constitute their sense of self as—among other things—citizens of ever expanding communities."[7]

Of all the disciplines falling under the marketing umbrella, none is more essential to the education process than public relations. As a business function, public relations is driven by the bottom line, but professionals, as opposed to charlatans who do little more than produce spin, fluff, and puffery, conduct themselves ethically. Their goal is to inform consumers about the products and services of their clients. Public relations perhaps shines brightest in crises situations, when public education is most critical. The most important crises that public relations professionals handle deal with community disasters, such as plane crashes, fires, explosions, and major workplace accidents.

Public Reaction, Interaction, and Action

Unlike any other sporting event on the planet, the Super Bowl showdown is a spectacle of epic proportions. Interestingly, many viewers don't even care about the football game itself; they tune in to watch the commercials. The Super Bowl is advertising's main annual event. The buzz about the ads grows to a fever pitch each year, particularly when the price tag is revealed. In 2008, a 30-second commercial spot cost $2.7 million.[8] The stakes are high for the corporations willing to hand over that kind of money.

Before the Internet, Super Bowl ads were the hot topic at offices nationwide on Monday mornings, but the impressions had to be drawn from memory of the evening before. Marketers ran their commercials and then waited to get public reaction, perhaps from the morning newspaper. Cultural elites pushed their efforts at the public and received praise or criticism from media elites, like columnists or television news reporters.

With the Internet, however, groups of friends can gather around a computer screen and watch the advertisements over and over again, focusing on each one's strengths and weaknesses. They can also read countless blogs about the winners and losers, or post their own thoughts. The Web also provides greater reach for activist groups and industry watchdogs. Suddenly, ordinary people had a hand in determining the success or failure of commercials.

In 2007, Masterfoods' Snickers Super Bowl spot drew fire from gay rights groups for depicting two burly mechanics accidentally kissing, then reacting by doing "manly" things to prove their straightness, like ripping out chunks of chest hair. Almost instantly, activist groups, such as the Gay & Lesbian Alliance Against Defamation and the Human Rights Campaign, condemned the campaign, which they claimed promoted violence against homosexuals. These groups also criticized a Snickers Web site that ran alternative commercial endings and showed professional football players jeering as they viewed the ad. One ending featured the mechanics hitting each other with wrenches after the inadvertent lip lock.

Years ago, Snickers may have been able to wait out the criticism or quietly cancel the campaign. The fallout may have been minimal. However, the firestorm spurred by the ability for people to watch and re-watch the commercials via the Web forced the company to shutter the commercials and the accompanying Web site. In addition, the brand ignited a public relations nightmare. Mike McGuire, research director at Gartner, said, "For good or ill, the Internet dramatically increases awareness and reach. That's difficult to control and can be very dangerous."[9] The Snickers commercial withdrawal clearly shows that the Internet has changed the way people interact with marketers. Consumers use blogs, Web sites, and videos or podcasts to respond to marketing campaigns directly and may draw audiences as large as or larger than the campaign itself.

There is an important link between the marketing message and consumer reaction, interaction, and subsequent action, but it is not straight cause and effect. Advertising scholar Jerry Kirkpatrick said, "Advertising can make consumers aware of needs, it can stimulate their wants, it can stimulate demand, and it can make it possible for consumers to enjoy a greater and wider range of tastes. But tastes, needs, wants and demand all originate within the consumer."[10]

The real mystery seems to be where the original thoughts regarding tastes, needs, wants, and demand came from. These ideas are derived from a complex system of establishing one's world view, as much from parents, family members, and friends, as from mass media channels. Jib Fowles sees popular culture playing a critical role: "Based on their exposure to, and discriminating appropriation from, the advertising/popular culture mix, people are then able to purchase the items that give off desired symbols."[11] The flow of information goes both directions—from marketers, to consumers, and vice versa.

In reviewing historical case studies on marketing successes and failures, scholar Robert F. Hartley accepts that advertising's value is difficult to determine. Nike's use of celebrity endorsers, ranging from Michael Jordan to Tiger Woods, produces a Nike culture that permeates society, while other celebrity pitch campaigns that use those successes as a guide flop unceremoniously. Hartley sees the ultimate power resting in the hands of consumers. "There is no assured correlation between expenditures for advertising and sales success," he said. "But the right theme or message can be powerful. In most cases, advertising can generate initial trial. But if the other elements of the marketing strategy are relatively unattractive, customers will not be won or retained."[12]

SOCIAL MEDIA TRANSFORMATION

Technology forces change across society. Often, corporations are at the helm, pushing innovations out into the wider public. Sometimes, a groundswell of popularity surrounding a new technology bubbles up from below, propelled by users, before the business world leaps in and attempts to monetize the innovation. This age-old chicken-or-the-egg scenario dominates consumer culture, asking: What came first, the new product or the basic want/need for the innovation? In today's tech-heavy environment, the Internet (particularly the Web 2.0/social media craze) is intensifying the push/pull nature of consumer marketing.

Since launching in 2004, more than 100 million people have joined MySpace, a Web site that enables users to create their own personalized Web page filled with music, pictures, and messages. Each day, it receives one billion page views, making it one of the top Internet properties in the world. In July 2005, News Corp. CEO Rupert Murdoch bought MySpace for $580 million, at the time a staggering figure, but now what looks like a bargain.[13]

MySpace fills an interesting void. The site allows anyone with computer access to become the star of their own show, a kind of mini-celebrity, attracting friends, who are then listed on one's page. Journalists have dubbed the most popular users "MySpace celebrities," with some people acquiring more than one million friends. Many of these Web friends actually equate more directly as fans, thus the impulse to have as many as possible. Almost like an exaggerated, online version of the high school cafeteria, MySpace provides otherwise ordinary people with a taste of being a celebrity. Individual users then become their own brand with friends serving as their enduring fans.

MySpace is also increasingly commercial, not only as a place for marketers to interact with massive numbers of consumers, but for people to find content, whether a video from a little-known indie band or last week's episode of *24*. Part of the plan to make MySpace profitable is to build out its advertising function. A number of national advertisers are signed with the site, including Coke, Honda, and Procter & Gamble. An ad on the homepage runs at roughly $500,000 a day. Countless corporations have their own MySpace pages, which cost $100,000 or more, including Wendy's and Unilever. Several companies have already run successful viral marketing campaigns on MySpace. P&G, for example, launched a "Miss Irresistible" page for a new Crest toothpaste and drew almost 40,000 friends and more than three million page views.[14]

In October 2006, search engine behemoth Google made headlines by purchasing one-and-a-half-year-old YouTube for $1.6 billion. Though at the time wildly popular among teenagers and Web-savvy hipsters, YouTube was certainly no household name. Critics scoffed at the steep price and wondered if the tech geniuses at Google had finally made a big mistake. Since then, YouTube shows no signs of slowing down. In July 2006, more than 1.6 million U.S. visitors watched 21 million video streams per day. Google, however, is still trying to determine how to make the site profitable.

Given YouTube's vast reach and popularity, marketers have searched for ways to join the phenomenon. At this stage, though, the results have been mixed and point to a dramatic change in the way people will accept or reject advertisements. The strongest indication is that it will be on their own terms, not those dictated by the elites running advertising agencies or television networks.

For example, Unilever launched its Dove "Real Beauty" campaign, using real women as models, rather than the typical supermodel or actress that most beauty campaigns employ. As part of the campaign, the company placed a video, "The Evolution of Real Beauty," on the site in October 2006 that was an instant hit. The short ad became one of the most popular YouTube videos of all time, drawing more than 1.8 million views. However, Unilever's next attempt at creating social media buzz for Dove Cream Oil Body Wash fizzled. Unilever bought space for the video on YouTube's front page, which guarantees a large number of hits, but negative reactions ensued, including rebuttal videos discussing how the company does not understand the concept of user-generated video.[15]

The Dove success and failure left marketers shaking their heads and forcing them back to the drawing board in hopes of finding a better way to build brand equity. The challenge is that social media audiences are fickle and have a finely-tuned marketing meter. They are quick to label promotional videos "unauthentic" and stand up for the unwritten code that guides such sites. For corporations, viral marketing is a dicey proposition. Companies like Unilever, Coke, or Microsoft spend billions to build their brands. A great deal of equity can vaporize quickly when something like the Dove campaign goes wrong.

A surprising success that points to the breakdown of the wall between marketers and consumers is the user-created commercial. For example, in late 2006, Chipotle Mexican Grill ran a 30-second commercial contest for college students, offering $40,000 in prize money. The company posted the two winning entries on YouTube and received 17 million viewers the first month. Because Chipotle targets 18 to 34 year olds, the YouTube exposure hit their primary audience.[16]

Ultimately, what high tech has done is further remove marketers from what they most covet—control. Once a message reaches cyberspace, the corporation/agency no longer wields power over it. Web savvy consumers satirize ads, develop their own competing messages, and discuss its content without the originator having much, if any, recourse. A mocking image of a corporate logo or unintended use of a product sent out over YouTube or MySpace damages the efforts taken to build the brand. The popularity of these social media sites almost ensures an audience. For some videos that get the magical viral marketing bump, the number of viewers is staggering.

In late 2006, someone leaked a video to YouTube of a Bank of America employee singing a parody of the U2 song "One," but with the lyrics changed to reflect the Bank of America/MBNA merger. The over-the-top shtick and impassioned performance carried the video to Web screens worldwide. No one knows how many views it received, but estimates place it in the tens of millions range. Some even thought that Bank of America purposely leaked the video to create viral buzz. Regardless of how it came into the public eye, the resulting chatter had little to do with the bank's then-marketing slogan "Higher Standards."

While the available technology gives consumers greater control over how companies market to them, marketers are exploring ways to use social media to develop deeper relationships. One company, Utah-based Blendtec, a maker of high-powered blenders, created David Letterman-like videos of founder Tom Dickson blending a variety of odd items, like marbles and golf balls. Dickson's online grinding of an iPod alone garnered more than 3 million views. The media soon picked up on the company, which received press coverage and a feature on NBC's *Today* show. According to author Paul Gillin, "Online video is the most cost-effective tool ever invented to test and refine ideas and messages. If you're lucky, it may be a bonanza of free publicity."[17]

Gillin believes that public relations practitioners need to concede control if they want to use social media effectively, something that marketers are loath to do. "Once you put your video online, you've lost control of it. People will copy it, modify it, mash it up and have their way with it," he said. "Accept this, and don't try to control what they do. On the contrary, resolve to learn from the changes they make, because there may be a better product or marketing opportunity hidden there."[18]

Consequences

The age-old argument about marketing's role in society is too simplistic in today's media-saturated environment. The interaction between the public and marketers has consequences for society and democracy at large. Neither side can stand on the sidelines and cast stones at the other. Both the traditional corporation/agency (sender) and audience (receiver) of marketing campaigns play a role in determining how the information fuels the creation of values and culture. As shown above, even the idea of the sender-receiver relationship has undergone tremendous change as the Internet transcends boundaries.

Make no mistake, though, marketing is at a crossroads. Technology places more power in the hands of the people. This may make each person a kind of mini-activist able to reach mass audiences in reply to a campaign; a kind of ultra-democracy, where individuals truly work together within campaigns. In the future, perhaps the best scenario is that marketers will view the public as equal partners in the process. Consumers certainly have the tools at their disposal to prove that they are no longer brainless sheep being fed by marketing elites. Communications scholar Jib Fowles said, "Advertising is not a hail of commercial barbs inflicting damage on huddling consumers and their culture. Advertising is a buffet of symbolic imagery that advertisers hope will prove tempting and lead to the more difficult exchange of money for goods."[19]

Interestingly, the democratization of marketing via the Internet has made the relationship Fowles describes both more tenuous and intimate. Consumers—much more astute than commonly perceived—wander up to Fowles's buffet cautiously and take what they think they need based on deep-rooted values that have, in some way, been shaped by witnessing a lifetime of marketing campaigns. A person can use technology (i.e., TiVo) to either avoid many of the marketing messages being pushed at him or her, or choose his or her own method of interaction (i.e., YouTube). The realization must be made, however, that almost everything a person knows or cares about has been filtered through a marketing medium.

POLITICAL ADVERTISING

The prevailing wisdom of American politics is that campaign spending is at the heart of getting elected. The largest chunk of the money raised goes directly into advertising. While the new millennium brought Web-based advertising and marketing to the fore, hundreds of millions of dollars are still spent on television ads. As a result, political candidates place more emphasis on their Web sites, MySpace accounts, and other innovative (and less expensive) tools to reach out to voters, but also still rely heavily on television.

With Senator John McCain wrapping up the Republican nomination early, his campaign staff kicked fundraising into overdrive without actually having to spend that much on costly ads. In March 2008, for example, McCain raised $15.4 million. Although he trails the Democratic candidates greatly in terms of finances raised, his lock on the nomination means that he spent only $277,000 on TV ads between March 18 and April 16. In contrast, Senator Barack Obama spent $11 million on TV advertisements over the same timeframe, while Senator Hilary Clinton spent $4.5 million. The Obama campaign raised some $40 million in March, 2008, down from $55 million the previous month. Officials from the Clinton camp estimated that it raised $20 million in March.[20]

2004 Presidential Campaign

The most intriguing aspect of the 2004 presidential contest between George W. Bush and John Kerry is that there may never be a full accounting of the money spent on the battle. Journalist Chuck Todd said, "Billions of dollars were spent... on advertising, polls, mailings and campaign stops." Doubtless, as Todd explained, much of that money went toward advertising. The efforts to pay for the campaigns benefited from a change in finance law that allowed individuals to donate $2,000 per candidate, up from $1,000 in earlier elections.[21] While the public money a candidate collects is subject to election laws, the "soft money," or funds from private organizations, such as labor unions, veterans groups, and others, is what makes tallying a total nearly impossible.

One research agency estimated that television ad spending for the presidential campaign from March 3 to October 28 rang in at $575 million, or about $2 million spent for each of the 270 electoral votes needed for victory. More than half the TV money went to five key states: Florida, Iowa, Ohio, Pennsylvania, and Wisconsin. In Ohio, for example, with 20 electoral votes in the contest, the television figures equated to the Democrats spending nearly $3.4 million per electoral vote and the Republicans $1.8 million.[22]

2000 Presidential Election

Republicans enjoyed a 2-to-1 cash advantage in the 2000 presidential campaign, which they used to bolster advertising in key battleground states. In response, labor unions and liberal organizations increased their spending. The soft money financed a great deal of the election efforts. One research firm estimated that the major political parties raised a combined $393 million in soft donations in 1999 and 2000, with the Republicans accounting for about $214 million and the Democrats $179 million. In contrast, traditional donations accounted for another $430 million, with the Republicans outpacing the Democrats at $275 million to $157 million.[23]

With pollsters predicting that the 2000 presidential election would come down to the wire, both parties increased last-minute television ad spending. The Republicans spent $10 million in Pennsylvania, Florida, and California, while the Democrats allocated $9 million. With dozens of states in the balance—from Washington to Arkansas—both parties upped spending significantly, in addition to the various outside groups pushing for their respective candidates. The AFL-CIO spent $46 million on political activities to get out the vote for then-Vice President Al Gore, while the U.S. Chamber of Commerce raised $25 million to campaign for then-Texas Governor George W. Bush. Campaign finance experts predicted that the total combined spending for the presidential and Congressional races would exceed $3 billion.[24]

MEGA AGENCIES

Shockingly, a mere four multinational conglomerate advertising agencies—Omnicom, Interpublic, Publicis, and WPP—control more than 50 percent of the ad revenues worldwide. The reason for this is due to the fact that each one of these mega-firms owns dozens of smaller agencies (ranging from ads, to public relations and boutique firms), which conduct business under their own name. For example, the St. Louis-based public relations agency Fleishman-Hillard is owned by Omnicom, as is its competitors Brodeur Worldwide, Ketchum, and Porter Novelli. The consolidation that occurred over the last decade makes this new big-agency era completely different than in the past. The range of choices has diminished, which plays into the public mindset that a small number of nefarious firms control the means for selling goods to innocent consumers.

An unsuspecting business owner, without knowing the background of a firm, might believe that it is a local or regional agency, when in actuality, it is a subsidiary of one of the giants. In many cases, whenever a new business pitch occurs, different firms owned by the same mega-agency are competing against one another to win the business.

Omnicom

The 1986 merger of BBDO, Doyle Dane Bernbavck, and Needham Harper formed Omnicom. That year, combined company revenues hit $754 million. By 2006, the conglomerate posted worldwide revenue of $11.4 billion and a net income topping $864 million. About 43 percent of total revenue came from traditional advertising media, 36 percent derived from customer relationship management, another 10 percent from public relations, and 11 percent from specialty communications.[25]

The particular talent of the ad firms within the Omnicom umbrella is creativity, demonstrated by BBDO Worldwide, DDB Worldwide, and TBWA Worldwide consistently ranking as the top three most-awarded agency networks globally. Omnicom also benefits from having the resources to invest in cutting edge technology, increasingly demanded by its corporate clients.

At a New York industry summit in December 2007, Omnicom chief executive officer John Wren discussed innovative work conducted for corporate clients GE, Target, and Mars that shows the way traditional advertising is changing in the wake of the Web. Rather than talk about television commercials, Wren pointed to efforts that stretched across media channels, including video clips and Web sites.

For example, ad firm BBDO built a Web site (www.becomeanmm.com) for Mars's M&M candies that initially enabled users to insert real photographs into pictures with the brand's animated characters. From there, the site morphed into a place to play online games, make movies, create new animated characters, and send online greeting cards. The highlight of the "Inner M" campaign was that consumers could create an M&M of themselves, virtually melding into the Mars brand. This kind of cross-channel work points to a new kind of advertising that uses technology to extend a consumer's time with the brand. Wren told *AdWeek,* "We earn our fees working for clients by doing what we've always been doing and by pushing it through all sorts of media."[26]

Even a multinational conglomerate like Omnicom faces potential challenges. The firm earns nearly 50 percent of its revenue from its 100 largest clients. The loss of several of these, combined with general global cutbacks, could dampen future growth. Geographically, Omnicom generates about 54 percent of its revenue in the United States, with about 21 percent generated in Europe, 11 percent in the United Kingdom, and the remaining 14 percent in other markets, such as Asia.[27]

The mega agencies face a future that will most likely reward them for their size and scope, but perhaps also penalize them as well. The news media has responded to the threats it faces from declining readership and classified revenues by retrenching—shifting focus to hyper-local stories and programming. If this movement continues to develop, it is hard to imagine that the big firms will be able to compete in smaller locales scattered all over the nation and all over the world. In the mega agencies' favor, however, is that the transition to interactive, Web-based communications provides them with a way to use their resources to adapt. In addition, the mega agencies have the ability to go out and purchase the kind of expertise needed to thrive in a changing marketplace—in the form of hot startups, innovative firms, and local communications leaders, if necessary.

CELEBRITY ADVERTISING

The most enticing combination of popular culture and celebrity fascination takes place in advertising. Big money, iconic consumer brands, and famous individuals mean serious consequences for all parties involved. In the new millennium, celebrity advertising is growing more important. Even the stars themselves, who once shied away from shilling products in the United States, realize that serving as a spokesperson can have benefits in expanding one's own "brand." For example, this kind of thinking takes into account the entire Nicole Kidman brand, or all the aspects of the actress's star power, from films and modeling work to appearances and product endorsements.

Tiger Woods is one of the world's top celebrity pitchers, hawking everything from luxury Tag Heuer watches and Gillette razors to Gatorade Tiger sports drink and his own line of Nike golf clubs and accessories. Other top celebrity spokespeople include Kidman, Jessica Simpson, and Justin Timberlake. Some celebrities are less likely to appear in a commercial, but will still be heard; for example, George Clooney lends his voice to promote Budweiser.

A change in the 2000s is that advertising agencies, companies, and celebrities now view the relationship as a partnership, each hoping to benefit from the association with the other. Bill Cosby and Michael Jordan served as early innovators in this regard. Consumers actually liked them more after seeing them in commercials, whether for Gatorade or Jell-O. "Over the years, the trend has slowly shifted from using models to celebrities to endorse products because, regardless of what's going on in the world of luxury, celebrities sell," explained Ryan Schinman, president of Platinum Rye Entertainment, a firm that negotiates talent buys for companies and advertising agencies. "Of course, each celebrity has their own

Nicole Kidman is among the many celebrities who lend themselves to promoting products. Here she enters the Academy Awards ceremony in 2002. ©AMPAS/ABC. Courtesy of Photofest.

characteristics, so their image and lifestyle has to be in tune with the brand. Some are hits, some are misses."[28]

Kidman's work with Chanel No. 5 symbolizes the way a celebrity can transform a brand. The company made the actress the face of the fragrance in 2004 for $12 million. She later starred in a commercial directed by filmmaker Baz Luhrmann, shot for an estimated $46 million, making it one of the most expensive ads in history. The gamble paid off, however, when revenues jumped 16 percent after Kidman joined. Her appeal as a celebrity opened the fragrance to a different, younger demographic and translated into sales. The partnership certainly has a significant financial component, according to journalist Nicola Ruiz, "Endorsement money is key to a star's bank account. Celebrities, many of whom make between $10 million and $20 million for months of work on a movie set or while on a yearlong concert tour, are cashing in on ad campaigns that can pay as much as $3 million for a day's work."[29]

Another indicator of America's star-craze is that even most bad publicity doesn't really hurt the products the celebrities promote. A 2006 survey by the Luxury Institute revealed that 42 percent of respondents said that a damaged celebrity image would have no negative effect on future purchases. Perhaps this rationale explains why infamous celebrities, such as Pamela Anderson, Paris Hilton, Martha Stewart, and others continue to receive endorsement deals even after their reputations have hit the skids.[30]

THE FUTURE OF ADVERTISING

Although advertising and marketing play a critical role in getting products and services in the hands of consumers, advertising is still at the mercy of broader financial considerations, such as the looming recession late in the decade. As businesses respond to the growing crisis in the consumer real estate industry, many are pulling back ad expenses. This decision, however, is fraught with complications. For many executives, the move to Web-based ads is a way to hit their target demographics, but this comes at the expense of traditional mediums, such as newspapers, magazines, and radio.

According to Robert J. Cohen, senior vice president and director of forecasting at Universal McCann, ad spending reached $283.9 billion in 2007, a less than one percent gain over the previous year. This increase is the smallest since a recession rocked the industry in 2001. Between 2005 and 2006, for example, ad spending growth reached nearly four percent. If there is a bright spot in the storm, Internet expenditures grew by 20 percent from 2006 to 2007.[31]

Another bonus for the advertising industry is the dual-headed monster of the 2008 primaries and presidential election and the Summer Games Olympics in China. Steve King, worldwide chief executive at ZenithOptimedia, estimates that the Olympics will add an additional $3 billion in the global ad economy. He also sees another $2 billion derived from spending by the political candidates.[32]

Ultimately, corporations will push into every area they can if they feel that it will help them build the brand or sell products. Some of the iconic brands attempting to sell via social media sites have nothing to do with the Internet, such as Pepperidge Farms cookies, but that does not mean savvy marketers won't attempt to use new technology. Pepperidge Farms targeted women in its online campaign, emphasizing a message that cookies help women reconnect with their friends. On the other side of the spectrum, underwear and clothing company Jockey focused on young men. These disparate examples provide a glimpse into the future of advertising, one in which the push of an ad is replaced by the lure of a conversation and the excitement of interaction.

Architecture of the 2000s

Architecture is towering skyscrapers of twisting steel, gleaming glass facades stretching over multiple stories, and a rainbow of colors, shapes, and designs used to make buildings interesting. From another viewpoint, architecture is how a home fits into a subdivision, the type of roofing materials used based on locale, and the size of individual rooms. In other words, architecture encompasses a wide variety of topics that influences people's lives each day, ranging from their own home or apartment to the buildings where they work, shop, eat, and go for entertainment.

The biggest news in architecture in the 2000s was the explosion of the real estate market. As interest rates fell to historic lows, suddenly people all across the nation could buy and/or build their dream homes. Architects and homebuilders responded by changing the way residential homes looked. Big was in: great rooms, large chandeliers, oversized entryways, multi-car garages, giant picture windows, and other features dominated the "McMansions" of the day.

Then the real estate market crashed back down to earth and effectively took the national economy with it. What seemed like a minor correction in 2005 and 2006 suddenly took on epic proportions. The fall triggered widespread alarm and cast a shadow on every industry even loosely affiliated with real estate.

As the decade nears its end, no one is confident that the real estate business will turn around any time soon. Optimists point to 2009, but as each succeeding month reveals more mortgage defaults and foreclosures nationwide, the scenario looks worse and worse. Other observers predict that the housing market will never recover or gain back the value it lost in 2007 and 2008. Certainly, there are millions of Americans experiencing foreclosure, bankruptcy, and increased debt that are barely holding on. Some of these people will never recoup their losses or rebound from the black mark this debacle has placed on their credit history.

TRENDS

The United States is not one big architectural science lab churning out the same products over and over again. Instead, trends unfold regionally, meaning that what is taking place in New York may or may not resonate in Los Angeles, Atlanta, or Boston. What one is more likely to find is diversity and micro-trends based on a variety of factors, from the local economic picture to population density. As a result, Pittsburgh's focus may be on redesigning part of its waterfront based on new professional football and baseball stadiums being built, while San Francisco's efforts may concentrate on new public spaces and museums.

While celebrity architects, such as Frank Gehry and Renzo Piano will always attract international attention and significant media coverage, in most markets it is the smaller design firms that act as change agents. These local and regional architects are the ones designing and building new public buildings, educational centers, company headquarters, and perhaps most the most influential architectural work, people's homes and apartment buildings.

Thus, there is a balance in American architecture between the big-name architects usually working in the large metropolitan areas and the lesser-known activities taking place in the rest of the country. However, even within these categories, important influences cross boundaries, so one finds Gehry designing a new business school at Case Western Reserve University in Cleveland and a building spree taking over Clearwater, Florida, which is changing the way people interact with the waterfront and beaches. In Los Angeles, local architects and designers are recreating the city's former industrial areas, while at the same time, celebrity architects work on iconic public and private buildings.

City Trends

Many cities in the United States face a similar challenge: how to deal with the limitations of expansion. The large urban centers across the nation were built on waterways and at transportation hubs that now limit how they grow. For example, Los Angeles's problem in the new millennium is urbanism. People continue to move into the city, but L.A. can no longer continue to gobble up surrounding areas, and its western edge is the Pacific Ocean. Consequently, the city is redefining itself and taking measures to confront these challenges.

In a city notorious for sprawl, L.A. is taking steps to reconnect people. One effort involves studying potential mass transit options that will alleviate the traffic on the intricate highways surrounding the city. Another involves creating shared spaces, such as the plaza at the Nokia Theater, which allows for interaction and spontaneous growth.

Chicago, arguably the birthplace of the modern skyscraper and stomping grounds of Frank Lloyd Wright, confronts a series of urban issues that have little to do with big name architects. Rather, the city is in the midst of building community-centered projects, such as John Ronan's Gary Comer Youth Center. These buildings must take into account the needs of a diverse clientele who have specific needs.

According to journalist Blair Kamin, another problem Chicago and other cities across the nation face is the boom in often drab condominiums. "These are the buildings that are killing cities," he said, "and giving us this problem of density without urbanity."[1]

Tremendous growth in Atlanta forced city planners and developers to react to the city's changing face. The trendy Buckhead area, which used to be a near-suburb, essentially morphed into another part of the city. A local developer, Novare Group, purchased a nine-acre site in the area to build retail stores, offices, and luxury condos. Catherine Fox, an architecture critic and journalist, said, "The architecture isn't great, but the project shows the ambitions of the developer."[2]

While many cities struggle with confronting transportation issues, Atlanta is building BeltLine, a 22-mile transit line that will wrap around the city, connecting 45 neighborhoods. Included in the transit system are a series of parks, bikeways, and plazas. Developers are gobbling up areas near BeltLine, which holds great potential in revitalizing the already rejuvenated city core. "The BeltLine could become the city's civic symbol, linking the past and present even as it shapes the future," Fox explained. However, she is concerned: "There is no coherent design vision. The question now is: Will the BeltLine be more than just a transportation project?"[3]

As of early 2008, BeltLine is in the midst of a $60 million capital campaign to raise money toward its projected $2.8 billion price tag spread over 25 years. However, the Georgia Supreme Court ruled that school property tax money could not be used in building the transit system, eliminating $850 million that city officials expected to come from future school taxes. Atlanta Mayor Shirley Franklin and other civic leaders remain committed to the BeltLine, but the court decision makes implementation more difficult.

Homeownership Trends

The Joint Center for Housing Studies of Harvard University assesses the nation's housing situation with support from a variety of public and private sources, including the National Association of Home Builders, Freddie Mac, and the National Association of Realtors. Despite the gloomy news emerging from the real estate meltdown and credit crunch, it expects the long-term growth of homeownership between 2005 and 2015 to reach about 19.5 million units, compared to 18.1 million between 1995 and 2005. The factors contributing to this growth range from projected healthy income growth to the influx of immigrants and resulting boom in their native-born children.[4]

While the forecasted figures are encouraging, the report's analysis of housing affordability is not. In a single year, the number of households that spent more than 30 percent of total income on housing jumped by 2.3 million. Overall, in 2005, some 37.3 million households fell into this category, creating a new record. Once similar figures are released for the years since then, that record will surely fall as well. The simple fact of the matter is that income growth for most Americans cannot keep pace with home expenses, including insurance, taxes, and other components that make up the monthly mortgage payment.[5]

On the positive side of the equation, time is on the side of the housing market. In the next decade, Baby Boomers will enter a phase when many will purchase second homes, and the Echo Boomers (born 1981 to 2001) will recharge the market as they enter their prime home buying years. Immigration is expected to continue its growth patterns, and the offspring of recent immigrants will look to their slice of the American dream. In the new millennium, immigrants accounted for 14 percent of purchases, while another 18 percent of foreign-born renters stand poised to enter the real estate market.[6]

The real estate boom that ended in the mid-2000s essentially put a halt to the nation's rapid economic growth since the 2001 recession. According to the Harvard study, "The drop in home building was so drastic that it shaved more than a full percentage point off national economic growth in the latter half of 2006. As a result, residential fixed investment went from being a significant contributor to growth to a major drag on the economy."[7]

In attempting to find some way to benefit from the downturn, homeowners took advantage of low interest rates to refinance in 2005 and 2006. Some 85 percent of people who refinanced did so to draw cash out of their homes, the highest level witnessed since the 1991 recession. Between 2001 and 2005, home equity money grew by 31 percent, reaching $10.9 trillion. In the same period, investment and improvement figures jumped 23.6 percent to $228.2 billion. These numbers indicate that, while people realized that the housing meltdown prevented them from selling their homes, those with steady, secure incomes could use low interest rates to either remodel or refinance. However, if housing continues to depreciate, these options will not be factors for many households.[8]

REBUILDING AT THE WORLD TRADE CENTER

The terrorist attacks on September 11 destroyed one of the world's most recognizable buildings. The battle over what would replace it captured imaginations, eventually turning into the biggest prize in the industry. However, the decision regarding what to build on the World Trade Center (WTC) site also turned into a focal point of criticism and contempt. Acrimonious negotiations between local and regional authorities further delayed building. Over time, however, the controversy diminished, and construction began in late 2006 on the $2.4 billion, 1,776 foot Freedom Tower structure, scheduled for completion in 2012. The rest of the World Trade Center site includes four additional skyscrapers (Towers 2, 3, 4, and 5), the National September 11 Memorial and Museum, the World Trade Center Transportation Hub, a retail hub, and performing arts center.

Designed by David M. Childs of famed architectural firm Skidmore, Owings & Merrill, the Freedom Tower will be a 2.6 million square foot building that replaces the double towers of the original WTC with a single spire. The new building will feature a 50-foot-high public lobby rising up from the plaza level, followed by 69 office floors that lift the elevation to 1,120 feet. There will be a symbolic metal-and-glass parapet at 1,362 feet and 1,368 feet, the heights of the original twin towers. "The tower is an open, welcoming building that both radiates light and is filled with light. Our design team has achieved our goal of creating a great urban place—a building that serves the people who work in it, welcomes those who visit it, and plays an integral and vibrant role in the city that surrounds it," Childs said.[9]

WTC developer Larry A. Silverstein assembled a world-renowned team of architects to design the buildings and grounds of the site. Lord Norman Foster is designing Tower 2, while Lord Richard Rogers (Tower 3) and Fumihiko Maki (Tower 4) lead the efforts on the other primary skyscrapers. Michael Arad is designing the WTC Memorial, while Frank Gehry is heading work on the World Trade Center Performing Arts Center.

Emotions still run high concerning the design and construction on the site of the terrorist attacks. *The New Yorker's* Paul Goldberger calls the World Trade Center redesign at Ground Zero "a sad story." Rather than appeal to the sanctity of the area, he said, "In many ways, it merely reflects where we are today. It's a commercial development, not a civic place. And it isn't effective urban design." Goldberger sees the challenges with Ground Zero as emblematic of larger problems faced in the architectural profession today. He calls it, "withdrawal, even abandonment, of large-scale planning by the public sector." Corporate partners quickly step into the void, and in many cases, enable the private sector to overtake projects, ultimately deciding what gets built. "At the end of the day, it's not real planning," Goldberger said. "What we're seeing is the development of parallel infrastructures—one built by the private sector, and one by the public. I can imagine a time in the future when some people might have little interaction with the public infrastructure."[10]

One of the most critical challenges for the new WTC is safety, the same issue that confronts architects and designers worldwide in the post–September 11 era. Skyscrapers and other significant buildings serve as primary targets for terrorists. According to journalist Nicolai Ouroussoff, the new Freedom Tower represents the need for safety in a world filled with possible horrors, explaining that it "rests on a 20-story, windowless fortified concrete base decorated in prismatic glass panels in a grotesque attempt to disguise its underlying paranoia. And the brooding, obelisk-like form above is more of an expression of American hubris than of freedom."[11]

OFFICE SPACE(S) AND SKYSCRAPERS

People continue to be fascinated with the majestic buildings and skyscrapers business leaders build in homage to their companies (and often themselves). Complicit in these striking structures are the superstar architects that turned into celebrities over the last several decades. Leading the pack is Frank Gehry, who rose to international prominence with the design of buildings worldwide, including the Solomon R. Guggenheim Museum in Bilbao, Spain. As a matter of fact, Gehry arguably stands as the most famous living architect in the world in the late 2000s.

The famed designer's influence is seen nationwide in buildings that highlight curved features, warped steel, and extensive use of glass. The focal point of Gehry's buildings, such as the Peter B. Lewis Building (2002) at Case Western Reserve University in Cleveland, Ohio, showcase intricate ribbon patterns, which some observers liken to an exploding wrapped present. The beauty of a Gehry design is its ability to make brick, concrete, and glass come alive with a lightness that seems impossible. The sloped exteriors and bold uses of curves are Gehry's signature designs, so now clients who hire him expect that they will get the full Gehry treatment. On the flipside, however, the trademark style has led some critics to say that he just repeats his design of the Guggenheim over and over.

In the new millennium, Gehry's international acclaim led to projects across the globe. In the United States, he began the decade with the Experience Music Project in Seattle. Gehry designed another high profile venue in his home area, the Walt Disney Concert Hall (2003) in Los Angeles. On December 6, 2006, California Governor Arnold Schwarzenegger inducted Gehry into the California Hall of Fame.

In 2007, the IAC Building opened along the West Side Highway in New York City; it was

The Walt Disney Concert Hall in Los Angeles, designed by famed architect Frank Gehry. Sony Pictures Classics/ Photofest. ©Fernando Gomez. Courtesy of Photofest.

Gehry's first building in the Big Apple. As the corporate headquarters for the e-commerce conglomerate run by media mogul Barry Diller, the building reflects the cutting-edge nature of the Web giant, which includes Expedia.com, Ask.com, LendingTree, and HSN. The corporate interior of the building provides a view of the Hudson River, accentuating the waterfront appeal so desired by corporate bigwigs.[12]

From a distance, the IAC Building looks as if it is shimmering up out of the ground like sheer curtains blowing in the wind, but at the same time, it features a solid rectangular foundation that exudes strength. On closer inspection, the initial understanding of the building's compact power is underscored by its sloped and angled framework, so bent and at odds with the eye that one can hardly imagine that its underbelly is concrete.

FABRICATING "URBAN" CENTERS

Nostalgia for an imagined past drives much of the current architecture, particularly when it involves public spaces. One trend playing out across the nation is the movement to build urban-looking downtowns in suburban settings to mimic the appearance of an urban setting. These faux urban environments, often called town centers, are designed to provide consumers and/or residents with a feeling of a downtown center, yet within the safety net of the suburbs.

In Tampa, for example, many of these fake towns are actually disguised shopping malls, built to resemble quaint downtown areas. Typically, these centers are created near large (often gated) housing developments in the well-to-do suburbs, thus providing easy access to shopping, dining, and entertainment for the residents of the subdivision. Some have a small-town feel, while others are clearly derivative of Bourbon Street in New Orleans. Actually, many resemble a scene from Universal Studios or Disneyland.

In Lakewood, Colorado, the shopping center is dubbed a "lifestyle center," what journalist Jamie Reno called, "an idealized vision of an urban streetscape, with 22 open-air blocks of cafes, performance spaces, offices, housing, parks, and, of course, chain stores familiar to anyone who's spent time in the Galleria (can you say Sharper Image and Victoria's Secret?)."[13] Lakewood happened to be just one of several hundred such lifestyle centers going up around the nation, stretching from Washington, D.C., to Phoenix. The trend is pushed by large shopping mall developers to appeal to Baby Boomers, who are nostalgic for urban life, as long as it's in the safe confines of suburbia.

Otay Ranch Town Center opened near San Diego in Chula Vista, California, in late 2007 and drew a crowd of 80,000. The lifestyle center featured an outdoor fireplace, kids' areas, and a dog park, along with a slew of shopping outlets. Built by mall developer General Growth Properties, Otay Ranch also has a code of conduct that prohibits skateboarding, swearing, spitting, and congregating in large groups. In other words, restrictions designed to eliminate behaviors people do not like about city life. A man who bought a condo at the California site explained, "It gives you the feeling that you're in a city, but you don't worry about the drunks on the streets."[14]

The town center movement in the Pittsburgh region takes nostalgia one step further: building a small town feel within already preexisting small towns. In the suburbs east of the city, developers are building new communities that offer people an escape from modern life's hustle and bustle. Audrey Guskey, a professor at Duquesne University in Pittsburgh, explained: "Everyone is so busy in life—there's so many things to do—that people just want to have that community, that place to go, somewhere like *Cheers,* where everyone knows your name." Guskey views the town center movement in a positive light, saying, "A trend like this is perfect for Pittsburgh. Pittsburgh's like a small town, and people in this area like the feeling of being a part of a community. It's a fun trend... a great trend."[15]

In Irwin, a Pittsburgh suburb, the town center work focuses on revitalizing the business district using grant money that city planners hope will enhance the area and attract new businesses. Some of the decisions involved are aesthetic, such as installing all underground wires, thus eliminating potentially unsightly overhead lines. Others require more effort, like devising strategic plans that will attract younger residents. In Plum, a suburb spread out over 29 square miles, a town center built from scratch would draw the community together in ways never before possible. "I really think people are looking for that," said Rich Hrivnak, Mayor of Plum. "They want that sense of community. They want that one place they can go and come together as a community. I think of like Mayberry, with a town hall, an area with a quaint feel to it."[16]

THE AMERICAN HOME

Owning a home remains a fundamental tenet of the American Dream. Historically low interest rates and creative adjustable rate mortgage loans in the early part of the decade gave Americans the opportunity to purchase homes in record numbers. As more financiers artificially pumped money into the real estate market, the value of homes jumped, enabling even more refinancing and cashing out to occur. Often, people used the money to finance improvements or as a down payment on a second home or larger house in a better neighborhood. Either way, the increase in values, combined with low interest rates and creative financing, served as the tinder for the real estate fire sale taking place in the latter years of the decade. Despite the challenges people faced, homes still serve as an aspiration or statement of one's standing. Moreover, housing remains a critical component of the popular culture landscape.

In the early 2000s, people did not have to surf Internet realty sites or wait for the homes section of the Sunday paper to imagine living this fantasy. Instead, they could flip to any number of television programs and channels, such as *Trading Spaces* and *HGTV,* which featured young hip designers, planners, builders, and architects ready to help them vicariously realize their homeowner dreams. For those who preferred glossy magazines, they could visit the newsstand and pick up trendy remodeling and building magazines, like *Cachet, Real Simple,* and *Dwell.* Hundreds of other regional and city-specific home and luxury magazines gave everyone access to the notion that a home can be a piece of art, while still being functional and fun.

The TV shows and magazines brought the notion of upgrading and remodeling to the masses.

Also contributing to the craze, big box remodeling stores, such as Lowe's and Home Depot, became destination spots for weekend handymen and women, running seminars on topics from installing granite kitchen counters to upgrading bathroom fixtures.

The focus on remodeling served as a cornerstone of the housing craze leading up to the subprime mortgage meltdown later in the decade. The value of homes rose sharply as demand outstripped supply. Many millions of homeowners refinanced to take advantage of the low rates and used the cash from the transaction on their homes. This translated into room add-ons, upgrades across the board, and other additions.

While all these large forces swirled through the minds of homeowners and those attempting to buy into the American Dream, the idea of what a home meant changed after the September 11 terrorist attacks. Suddenly, the magical feeling of safety sleeping in one's own bed took on new urgency. According to journalist Bill Saporito, "The national tragedy of 9/11 reinforced a trend that was already under way: the home is not just everyone's castle, it's becoming a resort, an island of comfort in an ocean of insecurity. It's command central for the modern family in all its configurations, the place to huddle, socialize and strategize in an increasingly complex world."[17]

The renewed desire for safety and tranquility away from the chaotic nature of daily life increased the popularity of communal spaces where families could congregate. Floor plans for both pricey homes and those more modest in scale included great rooms, large, high-ceilinged rooms that were centrally located and viewable from several other parts of the house, most importantly the kitchen. Also, more builders included office spaces in new homes, providing residents with the option to work from home.

With families thinking about safety and togetherness, the kitchen served as the hub of activities,

A typical upscale kitchen in the 2000s: granite countertops, shiny stainless steel expensive appliances. Courtesy of Shutterstock.

after decades of secondary status in most housing designs. Kacey Fitzpatrick, a home designer and consultant based in California, called the kitchen "the meeting place, the eating place, the social gathering place, the communications exchange," adding that "the new layouts reflect the inherent need of family members to be near the headquarters."[18]

In previous decades, great bathrooms or additional square footage topped the homeowner wish lists. In the 2000s, however, gleaming, full-of-ego kitchens replaced those desires. Normal people who rarely cooked compared to their parents' generation suddenly had to have a Sub-Zero refrigerator and Viking Range. Designers knocked out walls to open the newly-luxurious kitchens up to the living or great room, usually adding a breakfast nook that enabled additional gathering opportunities.

The other trend in the American home during the decade transformed the master bedroom into a dazzling suite, with adjoining exercise rooms, sitting areas, computer areas, and multiple walk-in closets. Showers in the master bathroom also benefited from the opulence, with state-of-the-art showerheads and other gadgetry that changed bathing from a necessity to something fun, akin to an art form.

DESIGN

Economic prosperity and design walk hand-in-hand. The financial boom that occurred during the early years of the new millennium not only pumped money into the coffers of people in the upper income brackets, but also provided more disposable income in general. Suddenly, wealth meant more than being rich—appearing "wealthy" became the aim. People across economic groups wanted to seem well-to-do, whether that meant buying similar fashions as they saw on television or owning the same kind of sub-zero refrigerator as a celebrity.

Corporations recognized the public's fascination with wealth and eagerly stepped in to provide both real luxury items and faux knockoffs, depending on what individuals could spend. In one sense, wealth equaled democratization, giving more people access to items they deemed important. However, the fixation also turned the nation away from the more fundamental ideas of what constitutes a good life and replaced them with an obsession with money and fame.

In 2000, *Time* magazine dubbed America's obsession with faux wealthy style the "design economy." Explaining the term, it stated, "[Design] is the crossroads where prosperity and technology meet culture and marketing. These days, efficient manufacturing and intense competition have made 'commodity chic' not just affordable but also mandatory. Americans are likely to appreciate style when they see it and demand it when they don't, whether in boutique hotels or kitchen scrub brushes." According to Dziersk, president of the Industrial Designers Society of America, "This is the new Golden Age of design." Approximately 20 percent of the $6 trillion Americans spent on consumer goods in 1999–2000 went into purchases for their homes.[19]

An interesting aspect of the democratization of design is that people with money to burn did not necessarily buy designer name products in droves, like they did in the Wall Street-fueled 1980s. Instead, they attempted to fill their super-sized homes with kitschy items that expressed some level of individuality. As a result, designers and manufacturers designed items that represented certain ideas that people then bought to say something specific about themselves. For example, Apple introduced personal computers with splashes of color, replacing the staid beige traditionally used for monitors. Stores like Ikea and Pottery Barn mass produced home décor options, but offered enough varieties that shoppers felt that some degree of personalization and customization, yet at a more modest price. "Manufacturers recognize that consumers are looking for more than functional benefits," said Barry Shepard, co-founder of SHR Perceptual Management, the design consultancy that helped conceive the Volkswagen Beetle. "A product that matters needs to say something about the person who owns it."[20]

After decades of losing out in discount pricing wars with Wal-Mart, Target changed course and became the "it" store of the 2000s based on the seemingly simple notion that offering less expensive designer knockoffs would attract consumers.

The company launched product lines with famous designers such as Michael Graves, Isaac Mizrahi, and Mossimo Giannulli, which overhauled Target's reputation almost overnight.

Larger, Eco-Friendly, and Bold

Interior design in the late 2000s takes its cue from the larger culture, particularly the green movement and a desire for eco-friendly products. Popular trends include expanding the boundaries of the home outside the traditional interior space, filling homes with earth-friendly products, and using colors and patterns that represent a Californian or Southwestern flair.

Nationwide—even in cold climate regions—people are dressing up outside areas and essentially turning them into extra rooms. The focal point for many of these, just like the traditional home, is the kitchen. As a result, people are installing large, high-powered stainless steel grills that dwarf the kitchen stove, as well as outdoor fireplaces that are used for both atmosphere and cooking. Others purchase outdoor stoves and actually use it to replace their one inside. Cathy Whitlock, an interior designer in Nashville, said, "This trend to indoor-outdoor living seems to be going strong. I notice more and more homeowners wanting screened-in porches, particularly with outdoor fireplaces."[21]

The furniture used to decorate newly-minted outdoor living rooms is considerably upscale when compared to the weaved plastic and aluminum chairs and billowy lounges most people grew up with. Designers recognized the need for more luxurious outdoor furniture and responded with bright colors, use of tiled tabletops, and soft fabrics and cushions. In terms of the color palette of outdoor furniture, varieties of green (celadon to avocado) are popular. Many consumers are also turning to more natural sun shades, which combines one's desire to live a green lifestyle with the necessity for shielding outdoor sitting areas.

The move toward eco-friendly consciousness is one of the central themes in popular culture in the new millennium. The totality of the movement ranges from using natural fibers in pillows, to adding recycled materials to concrete and drywall. Consumers' demand for attractiveness in green living led many producers to reinvent their products for the new century. For example, GE and Sharp created new solar panels that do not detract from the picturesque nature of a home. Rather than sit on top of shingles, technological advances and a better understanding of today's customers enabled builders to streamline them into the roofing system seamlessly.[22]

Remodeling Meltdown

The remodeling boom that took place in the years leading up to the real estate meltdown seems like a distant memory in 2008. Across most of the nation, people are growing more cautious about big expenditures, even those at the top of the economic ladder. Wealthy homeowners are usually the last to halt remodeling projects because they have more disposable income and can weather financial instability better than those squeaking by or living month-to-month. As a result, some areas are bucking the trend and still have big-ticket remodels on the books. The Tampa-St. Petersburg area is one example of a region getting hit hard by the real estate crash, yet plowing money back into high-end homes.

According to Kermit Baker, director of the Remodeling Futures Program at Harvard University, people usually begin remodeling as soon as they buy a new home. Therefore, with less houses being sold, remodeling is taking a hit. Another critical factor is home value, which also drops during a period where inventory exceeds demand. Homeowners face little incentive to pump money back into their places when they do not foresee getting a substantial return on investment. Finally, the fact that home equity lines of credit and other loans traditionally used for remodeling are harder to get is swaying people away from such projects.[23]

In 2006, the residential remodeling industry hit $228 billion, a figure that doubled the total from the mid-1990s. In the South, remodeling projects jumped from $1,131 in 1996 to $1,566 in 2006, a 44 percent increase. Baker's research predicts that the remodeling industry will continue to drop at an annual rate of 2.6 percent through 2008.

A more concrete example comes from Home Depot. The giant hardware chain reported its first annual revenue decline, dropping from $79 billion in 2006 to $77.4 billion in 2007. Daniel E. Ashline, who owns a remodeling company in St. Petersburg, Florida, said, "Things are not as robust as they were 18 months ago. It's not like it was... 2005 was still good, and 2006 was better, but last year was just even. This year, we'll do 70 percent of what we normally do." Other Florida remodeling firms report sales drops of 50 percent and laying off workers as a result.[24]

Books

Newspapers, Magazines, and Comics of the 2000s

In 2000, after a disappointing theatrical run in which it made only $37 million (compared to production costs of $63 million), *Fight Club* came out on DVD. Released in two editions, the set revolutionized the medium because director David Fincher supervised its production, including now-commonplace "extras," such as commentary tracks, deleted scenes, and other special features. The immediate popularity of the DVD led to the film becoming an instant cult classic. All over the nation, actual fight clubs sprang up based on the popularity of the movie.

More importantly, the success of the DVD turned Chuck Palahniuk, author of the *Fight Club* novel, into a cult figure in his own right. Based on word-of-mouth popularity and a crazed fan base tuned into every known detail about him and his work on the Web, Palahniuk transformed from former diesel mechanic to one of the hottest writers in the world. Fast forward to 2007, with the release of *Rant: An Oral Biography of Buster Casey,* and Palahniuk's 10 books have sold more than three million copies.[1]

The hub of Chuck-related activity turned out to be "The Cult," his official Web site, created and run by Dennis Widmyer since 1999. Early in its existence, the site featured news and interviews with Palahniuk. However, members of The Cult soon took on more cultish activities (in some instances, peacefully replicating "Project Mayhem" from *Fight Club*), such as guerrilla marketing techniques in major cities around the nation, to publicize his books. As a result, the author scored a string of *New York Times* best sellers.

Palahniuk is one of literature's central figures in the new millennium, not only for his sales and dark subject matter, but also for the way he grew from unknown to global superstar. His upward trajectory is a combination of movie adaptation, quirky subject matter that appeals to readers across the spectrum, Internet mania, and highly effective marketing. Palahniuk, though now going on a decade of unparalleled success, represents the forces that come together in the twenty first century to propel winning writers into another stratosphere. There must be a mix of word-of-mouth marketing, Internet hype, differentiated content, and some modicum of luck. Palahniuk is a popular culture phenomenon in his own right, perhaps, in some circles, more famous than some of the celebrities that starred in *Fight Club,* except, of course, Brad Pitt. (See Entertainment of the 2000s.)

This chapter examines the literature of the new millennium—both epic, bestselling works and the highbrow fiction reserved for English literature graduate classes. Included is a discussion of the many forces that turn seemingly ordinary writers (fiction or nonfiction) into pop culture icons.

FICTION

Harry Potter Mania

No one could have predicted the worldwide phenomenon the Harry Potter books would set off when virtually unknown British author J. K. Rowling published the first book in the seven-novel series in 1997. By 2004, *Forbes* magazine estimated that Rowling parlayed the Potter fame into a billion dollar enterprise complete with movies, tie-in products, toys, and a variety of other related products. During the height of the series and subsequent films, the release actually led to increased business in affiliated industries. Observers estimated that the Harry Potter brand name is worth $15 billion.[2]

Warner Bros. is an example of Potter's influence in other media. The company benefited from the $2 billion the first two movies grossed worldwide. The fifth film, "Harry Potter and the Order of the Phoenix," drew $44.8 million on its Wednesday release, then the highest first-day sales figure in history. The summer blockbuster then went on to make a whopping $140 million in its first five days. The movie company plans to release the final film for the last book in two parts in the summers of 2010 and 2011.

Online bookseller Amazon.com also benefited both financially and in its branding efforts from the scope of the Potter series. The site allowed consumers to pre-order the last book, *Harry Potter and the Deathly Hallows,* in February 2007, and the book shot to the top of its bestselling titles some five months prior to publication. Amazon then partnered with the U.S. Postal Service and UPS to ship 1.3 million copies on its release date under unusually tight security measures. Potter mania grew to white-hot intensity, and the bookseller did not want to allow early copies to make their way into the public spotlight.[3]

Actor Daniel Radcliffe portrays boy wizard Harry Potter in *Harry Potter and the Sorcerer's Stone* (2001). Warner Bros./Photofest. ©Warner Bros. Courtesy of Photofest.

The Harry Potter phenomenon not only made Rowling rich and increased the profits of many partners tied to the brand, but the wizard also had a broader cultural impact, most notably increasing literacy rates among children. A 2006 report issued by The Kids and Family Reading Report and publisher Scholastic revealed that the series helped get more kids reading for fun and do better in school. Some 65 percent of respondents claimed that they performed better in school since starting the series, which 76 percent of parents also said. "Only once in a lifetime does a children's literary phenomenon like Harry Potter come along," said Lisa Holton, president of Scholastic Book Fairs and Trade Publishing. "Harry Potter has become part of our culture, and what it has done so magically is to prove that even in the digital age, well-written books are and will remain a great source of enjoyment and enrichment for adults and young readers."[4]

The Da Vinci Code

While Harry Potter received more media attention over a longer span, Dan Brown's *The Da Vinci Code* (2003) stayed parked atop the best seller list. In 2004, Brown's publisher, Random House, brought out a "Special Illustrated Edition" of the book, which also saw sales skyrocket. By mid-2006, more than 60.5 million copies were in print.

Few could have predicted such stellar heights for Brown, a moderately successful thriller writer up to that point in his career. *The Da Vinci Code* centers on Harvard professor Robert Langdon's investigation into a murder at the Louvre Museum in Paris. There are several secret societies involved, including the Roman Catholic Opus Dei.

Of course, any book that becomes so intimately ingrained in the popular mindset is also going to be turned into a movie. The big screen adaptation, directed by Ron Howard and starring Academy Award-winner Tom Hanks, debuted in May 2006 to decidedly mixed reviews. Still, the movie grossed $224 million worldwide its opening weekend. Over the next six months, the film drew $758 million.

Best Sellers

The book section of a Costco store is a sight to behold for book lovers. Seeing a couple hundred copies of a single popular title under one roof is like entering a fantasy world. Then, realizing that there are dozens of titles and hundreds of paperbacks available, one simply swoons. The discount price is the icing on the cake.

The person responsible for the Costco book section is its book buyer, Pennie Clark Ianniciello, According to one publishing insider, Ianniciello "has an uncanny knack for leading customers to buy books, for molding their taste. She seems to know what they'll enjoy discovering." Along with the traditional big name writers, the Costco team picks cookbooks, children's books, coffee-table books, reference works, and others that may appeal to the company's sometimes-quirky clientele.[5]

For admirers, the upside of discount retailers, such as Costco and Sam's Club, is that they make books affordable and available. For many people, the option of going into a bookstore, which houses hundreds of thousands of titles, and browsing around the stacks, simply rings too closely to forced library days at schools. Critics contend that big box bookstores, discounters, and online mega sites have too much control over what America reads. In cahoots with a small handful of publishing conglomerates, the booksellers more or less select which titles to get behind... and push hard.

On any given week, the likes of James Patterson, Stephen King, John Grisham, Danielle Steel, Nicholas Sparks, and Harlan Coben battle for the spot on the national best seller lists. Increasingly, these name brand authors live and die by the blockbuster mentality adopted by the movie and music industries. They release their books in hopes that the first week out scores that number one placement.

Each of Harlan Coben's books fight for the top of the best seller lists. Once a year, he publishes one thriller. It debuts at number one or somewhere near the top. The process is like clockwork. His novels are plot-driven. "I start with an idea, not a character," he explained. "I write about people who are living right, and wrong still finds them." This seemingly simple formula leads the reader on a wild ride, with multiple twists and turns, the book equivalent of riding a great rollercoaster ride.[6]

Book critic Chuck Leddy describes American's literary culture as "schizophrenic" because observers routinely criticize books that sell millions of copies or show up on the best seller lists for somehow being naturally inferior based on popularity. On the other hand, the title "artist" is reserved for the select few who have been deemed worthy by a select group of prize jury participants or members of university English departments. "Elitist prejudice against genre fiction is undemocratic and unfair—and misses the truth that genre writers have as much artistic aspiration as literary authors," Leddy said. "The schizophrenia that has fostered the false dichotomy between art and commerce should end. Commercial success isn't a curse, nor obscurity a perverse badge of honor."[7]

Literary Fiction

While the notion is that literary fiction does not sell, 2007 saw numerous critically-heralded books climb onto *The New York Times* Best Seller List. Some of the notable titles include: Michael Chabon's *The Yiddish Policeman's Union;* Ian McEwan's *On Chesil Beach;* Norman Mailer's *The Castle in the Forest;* and Ann Patchett's *Run.* Still, the market for literary fiction is shrinking as the nation continues its digital transformation. The squeeze is felt by publishers, agents, and writers themselves, who increasingly find difficulties getting published or noticed in a world filled with multiple James Patterson novels on the best seller list.

According to journalist Rachel Donadio, "The pride and joy of publishing, literary fiction has always been wonderfully ill suited to the very industry that sustains it. Like an elegant but impoverished aristocrat married to a nouveau riche spouse, it has long been subsidized by mass-market fiction and by nonfiction ripped for the headlines. One supplies the cachet, the other the cash."[8] As a matter of fact, the entire publishing system seems built to keep most novels from selling well, focusing on timing and volume first and foremost. This is strikingly ironic considering that the entire industry is built on sales. Like movies, DVDs, and music CDs, books destined for the best seller lists are shipped in huge quantities to satisfy the needs of the large retail chains. Grassroots marketing efforts and attempting to build an audience over time are tactics that used to work, but have lost their footing in the 2000s.[9]

In 2005, for example, nearly half of the literary fiction sales came from the top 20 books. This means that fewer literary works sold many copies at all, even from those with faithful fans and a minor following. Some established writers are pulling out all the stops to bolster sales. When promoting *The Plot Against America* in 2004, Philip Roth appeared on the *Today* show and PBS's *NewsHour,* his first American TV appearances since 1968. Even with the television tie-in, most observers believe that Roth's critique of the Bush Administration is what helped the book sell so well (more than 415,000 copies).[10]

Michael Chabon

Michael Chabon has the look of a serious writer—tall, with piercing blue eyes, and dark curly hair—though he could probably also pass for a former actor or musician. When he talks about writing, his face gives way to a radiant smile and a kind of deeply intellectual look around his eyes, adding gravitas to his voice. He is the type of person who really *listens* to a question, and then answers with wit and thoughtfulness, more interested in the interplay than just using it as a dramatic pause to hear his own voice, like so many successful people today. What is more important (even in our media frenzy world) is that Chabon backs it up with enormous talent. His accolades grow with each subsequent novel and include a then-record highest advance ever given for a first literary novel ($155,000), as well as the granddaddy of them all—the Pulitzer Prize in 2001 for his novel *The Amazing Adventures of Kavalier & Clay.*

Chabon's first novel, *The Mysteries of Pittsburgh* (1988), won him widespread acclaim as a kind of late 1980s Fitzgerald, even though he was only several years out of undergraduate work at the University of Pittsburgh and fresh off an MFA at University of California, Irvine. After a collection of short stories came out, however, Chabon stalled for a handful of years on a novel that he just couldn't finish. His frustration grew into the wonderfully quirky *Wonder Boys* (1995), later adapted into a critically-acclaimed movie starring Michael Douglas and Tobey McGuire, released in 2000.

The same year the film came out, Chabon published *The Amazing Adventures of Kavalier & Clay.* Set in the World War II era, the main characters—a Jewish Czech artist named Joe Kavalier and a Jewish American writer named Sam Klayman—create a comic book in the "Golden Age" of the industry, *The Escapist,* which draws on their fascination with real-life escape artist Harry Houdini. Using pieces of the real lives of many of the comic book industry's founders, Chabon tackles ideas about patriotism, Jewish folklore, exploitation, and discrimination. The big themes addressed in the novel, combined with Chabon's lush style, certainly led to the award, one of the most prestigious prizes a novelist can earn.[11]

Since winning the Pulitzer, Chabon has published two other adult novels: *The Yiddish Policeman's Union* (2007) and *Gentlemen of the Road* (2007), a novella *The Final Solution* (2004), and a young adult work, *Summerland* (2002). He also put out a collection of nonfiction essays and pieces in 2008, *Maps and Legends.* Like many fantastic American writers before him, Chabon ventured into the gates of Hollywood, pitching several movie ideas. The comic book aspect of *Kavalier & Clay* earned him greater credibility, as well as his association with director/producer Scott Rudin, who adapted *Wonder Boys* for the silver screen. He wrote for the 2004 sequel *Spider-Man 2,* which grossed more than $783 million worldwide.

Literary Lions

While highbrow critics lament the popularity of lowbrow novels and trashy autobiographies that capitalize on the often-fleeting fame of the latest sensational news story, many of the writers that have dominated the last four or five generations continue to pour out critically-acclaimed novels that provide insight into the American soul. Norman Mailer, who died in late 2007, published *A Castle in the Forest* earlier that year, which reached best seller lists nationwide. John Updike continues his prolific production, averaging a novel every other year, from 2000's *Gertrude and Claudius* to 2008's *The Widows of Eastwick.* In the decade, he also published a book of poetry, several short story collections, and two books of nonfiction.

Mailer's death marked one of many that slowly thinned the ranks of the nation's literary greats. Kurt Vonnegut, Hunter S. Thompson, Saul Bellow, and Susan Sontag also all died in recent years.

Although the dons of the American writing community keep in the public eye, many have taken on a quieter tone, which is a far cry from the situation at the beginning of the 2000s. The decade began with Tom Wolfe chiding John Irving, John Updike, and Norman Mailer. He labeled them "the Three Stooges" and Mailer and Updike "two piles of bones." Wolfe's attack centered on what he viewed as his fellow writers' unwillingness to address the world around them, that they were navel-gazers, wrapped up in their own lives. Wolfe, on the other hand, advocates a new brand of realistic fiction, like the kind written by Sinclair Lewis in the early years of the last century. The feud continues, albeit less dramatically, and with each new publication, the authors take another jab at one another.[12]

Many of the nation's literary lions gained new readers after being named selections of the Oprah Winfrey's Book Club. Toni Morrison had three books highlighted by Oprah, while a select handful of writers had two novels climb the best seller lists after being spotlighted by the powerful talk show personality. Others who benefited from the Oprah touch included such acclaimed writers as Jane Hamilton, Maya Angelou, Barbara Kingsolver, Joyce Carol Oates, and Cormac McCarthy.

Winfrey's impact on publishing in the late 1990s through the new millennium cannot be understated. "It's not true that Oprah Winfrey's

Oprah Winfrey is seen on her television program holding her new book club pick *The Road,* by Cormac McCarthy. AP Photo.

book club was the most important development in the history of literacy," explained journalist Richard Lacayo with tongue firmly in cheek. "For instance, there was the invention of the written word. Then there was movable type. So, Oprah comes in third. But no lower, at least not in the opinion of publishers and booksellers, who binge every month on the demand for whatever title she features on her show." Lacayo believed that Oprah's pick had the power of making serious fiction as popular as professional wrestling.[13]

With more than 25 million viewers who hinge on her every word, Winfrey continues to exert considerable force in publishing. In 2002, for example, when she shuttered the Book Club for a year, claiming that she could not keep up with the demands of a monthly pick, book experts thought it might spell doom for the industry. Upon returning the following year, Winfrey picked classic literature, beginning with John Steinbeck's *East of Eden.* As a result, the book spent weeks atop the *New York Times* paperback best seller list.

NOTABLE BOOKS

Harry Potter series, J. K. Rowling (U.S., 1998–2007)

Artemis Fowl, Eoin Colfer (2001)

Seabiscuit: An American Legend, Laura Hillenbrand (2001)

Fast Food Nation, Eric Schlosser (2001)

The Lovely Bones, Alice Sebold (2002)

The Purpose Driven Life, Rick Warren (2002)

The Nanny Diaries, Emma McLaughlin and Nicola Kraus (2002)

Hoot, Carl Hiaasen (2002)

The Da Vinci Code, Dan Brown (2003)

Eragon, Christopher Paolini (2003)

The Kite Runner, Khaled Hosseini (2003)

The Time Traveler's Wife, Audrey Niffenegger (2003)

The Jane Austen Book Club, Karen Joy Fowler (2004)

The Mermaid Chair, Sue Monk Kidd (2005)

Freakanomics, Steven D. Levitt and Stephen J. Dubner (2005)

An Inconvenient Truth, Al Gore (2006)

A Thousand Splendid Suns, Khaled Hosseini (2007)

In 2006, after being named an Oprah pick, author James Frey admitted that his book *A Million Little Pieces* contained half-truths and fabrications about his years as a recovering addict. He appeared on the show to apologize, and Winfrey, according to one journalist, "turned on him with calculated efficiency, using him to mop up the floor and clean up her reputation at the same time."[14] Many observers were in Winfrey's corner, as the pick helped Frey sell about 3.5 million copies.

In true digital age fashion, investigation Web site the Smoking Gun (www.thesmokinggun.com) exposed Frey's exaggerations, which Winfrey and others initially discounted. As more allegations came to light, however, the insurmountable mountain of evidence against Frey forced Winfrey and others to change their tunes. The Frey controversy followed on the less damaging scandal in 2001 when Winfrey chose *The Corrections* by Jonathan Franzen. He criticized some of her picks and asked that the Book Club stickers be removed from his book. Some observers saw Franzen's post-pick criticism as a way to generate further publicity (and sales).

NONFICTION

The combination of the war in the Middle East, an unpopular president, a general celebrity obsession, and the nation's diet and self-help craze propels the nonfiction market. In any given week, the books topping best seller lists range across these topics, from celebrity memoirs to investigative pieces that promise to go inside the war machine guiding the war in Iraq. The *New York Times* even began an advice list to shuffle these titles into their own category. The advice list is dominated by authors like Rhonda Byrne (*The Secret*), Joel Osteen (*Your Best Life Now*), and Deepak Chopra (*The Third Jesus*).

War Books

The wars in Iraq and Afghanistan generated enough books to fill a small library. Part of this glut resulted from journalists being embedded with troops in Iraq. The combination of on-the-ground reporting and the fascination with the war propelled many of these books. Another set of them came from Washington insiders, those with access to administration and military sources. The big change in terms of the publishing industry is that the more people who bought war books, the quicker publishers would get them out. Some books presented events that happened six to eight months previously. The hotter the topic, the quicker the book got into print.

The attraction of military books is obvious and continues a trend that takes place after each war, particularly with soldier memoirs. Journalist Chris Ayres, who wrote a book based on his experiences embedded with the Marines, said, "When you actually stand back a few paces, you see the absurdity of the embedded scheme, the horrible accommodations, the terror of being there, and the strain it puts on your psychology."[15]

MAGAZINES

A trip to the local Borders or Barnes & Noble bookstore reveals the power of magazines in the new millennium with shelves hundreds of feet long stretching entire walls displaying nothing but magazines. On closer inspection, it is almost impossible to imagine a consumer's niche that is not filled by some title, from *American Heritage* to *The World of Interiors.* One finds dozens of magazines devoted to home improvement, celebrity gossip, self-improvement, sports, and other interests, let alone the seemingly endless collection of Sudoku and crossword puzzles. Experts estimate that about 17,000 special interest consumer magazines exist in the United States today, and 22,000 total.

Magazines play a central function in mass media in the 2000s for the same reason they have for 200 years: people are interested in good content that is specific to their interests, and advertisers want to get their ads in front of those readers. The average magazine reader is educated and upscale, which is an attractive audience for advertisers. People even like magazine ads. A 2005 survey revealed that 61 percent of magazine readers view ads positively, while 48 percent claimed that the ads actually added to their enjoyment. In 2004, the top five consumer magazines with the highest advertising and circulation revenue were *People* ($1.27 billion), *Sports Illustrated* ($1.03 billion), *Time* ($1.02 billion), *TV Guide* ($918 million), and *Better Homes & Gardens* ($888 million). The top five advertiser categories were automotive, apparel and accessories, home furnishings and supplies, toiletries and cosmetics, and drugs and remedies.

The same forces that influence newspaper readership in terms of technology and the Internet are impacting magazines. One would be hard pressed to find a mainstream magazine that does not have an online edition. Many publishers, such as Rolling Stone and Time, offer additional content via the Web, as well as more interactive features and downloads of exclusive material. Internet Webzines are another compelling form of magazine that are vibrant in the new millennium. The satirical fictional news site *The Onion,* for example,

WORDS AND PHRASES

adorkable

adultalescence

-alicious

Axis of Evil

BFF (Best Friend Forever)

belly shirt

blog, blogger, blogging

bridezilla

chatiquette

crackberry (derogatory term for the addictive nature of a Blackberry device)

crunk

Facebook

fake bake (artificial tan)

fauxhawk (miniature, more styled Mohawk acceptable in some workplaces)

ginormous

Google

Googlegänger

Ground Zero

hook up (casual sex)

IM (instant messaging)

it is what it is

mashup

muffin top

off the hook

Pfish

pimp (verb meaning to dress up or make flashy)

Podcasting

"red is the new black," and similar (i.e., "fifty is the new forty")

shoe bomber

thugged out

tight (adjective to describe something cool)

tramp stamp (tattoo)

truthiness

waterboarding

Wi-Fi or WiFi

is a popular destination, though it started out as a free newspaper in Madison, Wisconsin, in the 1980s. Still available in print by subscription, most readers access it through its free, advertising-supported Web site.

NEWSPAPERS

The first decade of the new millennium brought significant change to the newspaper industry. On one hand, large publishers gobbled up smaller newspapers, as a wave of consolidation increased the reach of corporate conglomerates. At the same time, newspapers watched as readers increasingly turned to online sources for news. Many experts wondered if the influence and power of the Internet would ring the death knell for print newspapers. However, in response, newspapers brought out online editions and transitioned greater resources to the Web.

While pundits wrestle with the idea of newspapers disappearing, there are still some 9,800 newspapers in the United States, with a combined circulation of 56 million. If one counts the number of consumers who read the paper but did not actually purchase it, the number of readers jumps to 132 million daily and about 200 million each week who read weekly papers. Interestingly, about 77 percent of the nation's newspapers are weekly editions, which reveals a changing trend among newspapers in the 2000s: a push for hyper-local coverage, which differentiates print news from online sources.

The newspaper industry is also confronting changing demographics, particularly larger ethnic readerships. For example, Hispanics represent America's fastest-growing minority group. As a result, Spanish-language daily newspapers increased readers dramatically in the last three decades. In 1970, they had 140,000 readers, but today, that number skyrocketed to surpass two million. Hispanic readers are also loyal to their papers, which entices advertisers. Between 1990 and 2000, advertisers increased ad spending in Spanish-language dailies by 565 percent.

The biggest news of the new decade, though, is technology. How newspapers will make money from their online arms remains a critical issue, but there is no disputing the importance Web operations play in today's media landscape. All one needs to do is look at the way Web traffic to newspapers and news organizations spikes whenever there is a local, regional, or national crisis. Consumers understand that they can get breaking news from these sources.

A concern that keeps newspaper executives up at night is the exodus away from print by younger readers (who advertisers covet). A 2005 survey revealed that only 19 percent of those 18 to 34 years old read the daily newspaper, but 44 percent get their news from the Web. Many online news operations have combined with television stations to converge the best aspects of each medium into one powerful Internet news provider. The advent of blogging is also empowering online news organizations by giving readers additional methods of interacting with reporters and columnists.

Blogs

The intersection of technology and demand for 24-hour-a-day news combined to make blogs an important part of the nonfiction world in the 2000s. Blogs started as a type of online diary that enable the writer to post and publish almost instantly, but they have become more than diaries, with postings related to news, critical commentary on anything (usually, the nastier, the better), gossip, and all kinds of creative writing. Equally important, blogging involves receiving and responding to reactive or related comments to the original blog. With the advent of easy-to-use blogging tools, millions of people joined the online community. In recent years, users have added voice-based entries (dubbed podcasts) and video-based ones (vodcasts). In late December 2007, there were about 112 million blogs.

Much of the blogosphere is akin to digital diaries, family albums, and pages dedicated to celebrity or band worship. However, others have taken the medium more seriously, elevating it to a new mass media channel. Andrew Sullivan (www.andrewsullivan.theatlantic.com) and Arianna Huffington (www.huffingtonpost.com) are examples of mainstream journalists who used blogging to expand their reach. In addition to the online-only blog groups, virtually every newspaper and magazine has a cadre of designated bloggers who write exclusive or syndicated material for them.

Entertainment of the 2000s

In 2008, the New England Patriots carried a perfect regular season mark into the Super Bowl, television's biggest annual event, against the underdog New York Giants. The Patriots attempted to become the second team to ever finish undefeated. Star quarterback and budding pop culture icon Tom Brady led the Patriots. In the weeks leading up to the game, however, Brady filled more airtime, column inches, and computer screens for dating Brazilian supermodel Gisele Bündchen than his play on the football field.

The media frenzy chronicling what seemed like virtually every moment of the hoopla sparked even greater public interest. Money flowed into the tills of the gambling houses in Las Vegas, while global corporations placed their own bets by snapping up commercial time during the game at a whopping $2.7 million per 30-second spot. The American culture machine and the hyper capitalist system hummed as one.

The Retail Advertising and Marketing Association estimated that Americans spent $10 billion preparing for the big game. That figure includes the 3.9 million people who bought a new television, along with another 1.8 million new pieces of furniture. In response, companies such as Circuit City offered special incentives to pry people's money from their pockets. The retailer, for example, guaranteed delivery and installation for anyone purchasing a 32-inch or larger TV by the Wednesday before the Super Bowl. Anyone suffering from later delivery received a $50 gift card for their troubles.[1]

On the way to the coronation of the Patriots as the greatest team in NFL history, a stumble occurred... an unfathomable hiccup: the Giants scored in the game's closing minutes to upset New England, 17–14. While the sportswriters raced to rewrite their columns and come up with hyperbole big enough to capture the enormity of the victory, television aficionados soon learned that 97.5 million viewers in the United States watched the game, making it the second most viewed show in television history, behind only the 1983 *M*A*S*H* series finale. Television retained its hold on the national psyche.[2]

The super performance of the 2008 Super Bowl is not the only example of the way the performing arts steer popular culture, especially television and movies. For example, reality television first transformed its industry, and then swept through American culture as more and more people grew fascinated with the chance of becoming a celebrity. YouTube and MySpace enabled users to upload videos of themselves—a form of instant television—that actually gave them a platform for celebrity. Who could have imagined that a video of someone dancing to 1980s hits or wildly

HDTV MAKES LIFE BETTER

High-definition television (HDTV) is revolutionizing the quality of television programming sent into homes. HDTV has double the resolution of conventional broadcasts, which equates to a clearer, more detailed picture. The technological innovations over the last decade have led to HDTV becoming the standard television transmission system.

On February 17, 2009, HDTV becomes the standard for every TV station in America when television stations stop broadcasting on analog airwaves. Digital broadcasting allows broadcasters to offer improved picture and sound quality and additional channels. When the transition is made, all televisions must be HDTV-capable, or they will become obsolete. Analog TVs will need converter boxes to transform the HD signal for older TVs. The federal government and local broadcasters are spending millions of dollars to explain the change to consumers.

The picture quality is the factor that makes HDTV better. Lines that run horizontally make up the resolution (measured in progressive scan, with most HDTV sets running 1080p, the so-called true HD format), providing a crystal clear picture. HDTVs have either Plasma or LCD (liquid crystal displays) monitors. All HDTVs are wide-screen (a 16.9 ratio, like films at the theater) and have superior stereo qualities (Dolby surround-sound) compared to analog televisions.

singing off-key could lead to a form of fame and/or infamy?

As the decade progresses, traditional television shows made a comeback, but many rely on increased violence and gruesome scenes to draw viewers. It seems as if the boundaries have been eliminated in the 2000s. Then, just as it seemed a new era had dawned on the small screen, the Writers Guild of America went on strike, which placed the new television season in jeopardy and forced the networks to fill airtime with repeats, mid-season replacements, and reality shows.

In the movie business, studios grew even more reliant on blockbusters to carry the industry. For most big money flicks, opening weekend determines success or failure. In addition, more movies feature computer-generated graphics, revolutionizing the way people see films. At the same time, studios developed new and interesting ways to tie in films to other products, saturating the market with toys, clothing, video games, and an endless number of trinkets designed to help sell films. From a pop culture standpoint, these attempts are a fascinating aspect of the intersection of technology, media, and culture in the new millennium.

TELEVISION

Simultaneously, technology put televisions on steroids and shrunk them to sizes only considered worthy of science fiction in the not too distant past. In fact, it is difficult to even define what a television is in the new millennium. Is a person's video iPod a TV? What about one's computer screen? Do we need a new name for these devices that reflects their mobility? Regardless, viewers are increasingly turning to places away from home or outside the living room to watch television programming.

What remains constant is that television is a central component of American popular culture. The age-old debate about the merits or lack thereof (education versus entertainment) in watching TV continues in some segments of society. Many people even claim to never watch television, a kind of badge of honor worn by people one might meet in San Francisco or New York. For the rest of us, television serves a variety of purposes, from simple entertainment and news-gathering to education and even mindless background noise.

Since the beginning of the 2000s, the percentage of households with a television has held steady at 98.2 percent, or some 100.8 million in 2000 and 112.8 million in 2008. The growth aspect within homes is the length the television stays on, in 2006 topping out at 8 hours, 14 minutes daily. When broken down by gender, one sees that the average male watches about 4 hours, 35 minutes each day, while women view 5 hours, 17 minutes. Neither teens (3 hours, 22 minutes) nor children (3 hours, 26 minutes) watch as much as the average adult male or female.[3]

Advertising on television is another growing aspect. From 2000 to 2006, ad volume jumped from $60.3 billion to $71.9 billion. The latter

RADIO DEBUTS OF THE 2000s

"The Savage Nation with Michael Savage" (2000): strongly worded, frequently over-the-top right-wing opinion.

"The Sean Hannity Show" (2001): politics, call-in questions, and interviews hosted by the conservative commentator.

"The Laura Ingraham Show" (2001): political and current-events commentary with a satirical conservative take, featuring listener call-ins and guests.

"The Glenn Beck Program" (2002): conservative commentary, humor, and discussions of political and social issues.

"The Radio Factor with Bill O'Reilly" (2002): political talk with a conservative bent from the TV personality Bill O'Reilly.

"The Thom Hartmann Program" (2003): guest experts and listener call-ins on politics, economics, education, and social issues with a progressive point of view.

"The Clark Howard Show" (2003): consumer advocacy and money-management advice from the author and entrepreneur.

"The Alan Colmes Show" (2003): liberal commentary on politics and current events, hosted by the Fox News Channel's resident progressive.

"The Al Franken Show" (2004): comic Al Franken's satire, discussion, and commentary on the news of the day, with a left-wing slant.

"Theme Time Radio Hour" (2006): Bob Dylan-hosted satellite radio show exploring American music styles with a thematic approach.

figure represents more than 25 percent of the total advertising volume in the United States ($281.7 billion). Of the top 25 advertisers on television in 2006, the first five are automotive companies: General Motors Corporate Dealers Association ($528 million), DaimlerChrysler ($501 million), Ford Dealers Association ($439 million), Toyota Dealers Association ($384 million), and Honda ($377 million). Only AT&T cracked the top 10, placing sixth at $293 million.[4]

The Super Bowl remains the most costly advertising venue each year. The average 30-second commercial spot in prime-time on a major network, however, is creeping higher as the decade progresses, from about $82,000 in 2000, to $118,000 in 2007. Survey information confirms that the companies spending on television are benefiting. Some 81.8 percent of adults aged 18 and older feel that TV advertising is "most influential" versus newspaper (6.6 percent), radio (4.5 percent), Internet (3.7 percent), and magazines (3.5 percent).[5]

According to Susan Cuccinello, senior vice president of research at the Television Bureau of Advertising, "Television reaches more of an advertiser's prospects each day than any other medium, and adults spend significantly more time with television than with other media, in almost every major demographic segment." Not only is TV where adults say they learn the most about products and brands, but television still ranks as people's "primary news source, and as their primary source for local weather, traffic and sports news."[6]

The Magic of *American Idol*

Although it is difficult to fathom, *American Idol* almost never made it on air. Pitched in the early part of the decade to all the network stations by co-creators Simon Fuller and Simon Cowell, the execs all passed. Even Fox, which eventually picked up the show, gave the idea tepid interest early on. If it weren't for the intervention of Elisabeth Murdoch, daughter of News Corporation founder and CEO Rupert Murdoch, who loved the British version (*Pop Idol*) of the show, *American Idol* may never have existed. She urged her father to buy the rights to the show, and the rest is television history.

The real stars of *American Idol* are its judges: British record executive Simon Cowell, former pop star and choreographer Paula Abdul, and American producer Randy Jackson. Each judge plays an archetypical character. Cowell is the sarcastic, mean judge, while Abdul quirkily acts as the nice one, and Jackson is the outgoing, gregarious member. The chemistry between them propels the show, in addition to the showmanship of host Ryan Seacrest.

While the music takes over as the series progresses, the real star of stars is Cowell. According to journalist Bill Carter, Cowell transformed

Host Ryan Seacrest announces Kelly Clarkson's victory over Justin Guarini on the season one *American Idol* finale on television (2002), from left, Ryan Seacrest, Kelly Clarkson, Justin Guarini, Brian Dunkleman. FOX/Photofest. ©FOX. Courtesy of Photofest.

into a celebrity based on his work on the British version of the show, becoming "one of the most talked-about cultural figures in Britain in the winter of 2002. He was a tabloid newspaper's dream: seen by millions every week on television, saying something outrageously quotable ('You're a disaster.'), doing something unconscionably cruel (several young women left the auditions convulsed in tears after hearing his corrosive assessments of their talents) and tirelessly promoting his program (by doing every sort of interview in print and on television and radio)."[7]

In the first season of *Idol,* Cowell let loose, telling one contestant to get a lawyer and sue her vocal coach, while others were frankly labeled pathetic, horrible, and awful. His acerbic wit, mixed with genuine enthusiasm when they uncovered a talented singer, turned Cowell into an instant hit. Ten million people watched *American Idol* its first night and the second eclipsed 11 million. More importantly for Fox, the show topped the charts for viewers aged 18 to 34, the prime television demographic. According to journalist Ken Barnes, "It's conceivable that *Idol* may have ended up a middling success without the unprecedented candor and (at times) brutal wit he directs at contestants. No other vaguely similar show had such a consummate dasher of dreams, and none since has been able to duplicate the effect. (And how they have tried!)[8]

The Unreality of Reality TV

Imagine a 1 in about 20 shot at winning $1 million. The only catch is that you have to live in a desolate location, find your own food and water, and compete in physical and mental challenges. Not only does this include building shelter and gathering food (or facing hunger), but it could involve standing in the punishing sun on a small platform for as long as possible, wrestling in a pit of muck, or any variety of trivia challenges. As is now well-known, to win *Survivor,* a person must simply "outwit, outplay, and outlast" the other contestants.

When CBS launched *Survivor* in June 2000, no one predicted that the show would change the face of television for the rest of the decade. *Survivor* was not the first "reality" TV program. That honor is difficult to ascertain. One could argue that Allen Funt originated the genre with *Candid Camera,* while some would peg it to the series of wacky game shows of the 1950s, such as the decades-long running *Truth or Consequences. Survivor,* created by former British Army soldier Mark Burnett, caught the nation's attention, and each subsequent week, the excitement grew. As more viewers tuned in, the media picked up the trend and fed the hunger with countless articles, updates, and special sections. The Internet added to the anticipation. Web sites devoted to the show sprouted up, while others posted supposed spoilers or insider information claiming to know who would win. Certainly, the notion that "regular people," not actors, would win the $1 million played into the public's curiosity.[9]

Some 6,000 people filled out applications to appear on *Survivor* before that first season. CBS then added to the marketing effort by holding auditions in cities where it had stations, including Los Angeles and New York. The idea that something potentially dangerous might take place on the tiny island where the contestants were stranded added to the public fascination with the premise. Burnett also picked 16 players that mixed across demographic segments and backgrounds. "The early wave of media attention to the show paid off for CBS," explained journalist Richard M. Huff. "The network sold all of the advertising time on the show to eight companies—before the first episode aired."[10]

Interestingly, *Survivor* went head-to-head against ABC's immensely popular game show

The contestants row ashore on the fifth season of *Survivor: Thailand,* 2002. CBS/Photofest. ©CBS. Courtesy of Photofest.

Who Wants to Be a Millionaire, hosted by Regis Philbin. Although *Survivor* lost that night, the hype led to an even larger audience the next week, some 18.1 million viewers. Hosted by Jeff Probst, the reality program became a runaway hit, and it forced people across the nation to make sure they were home in time to watch. Internet sites and Web reports added to the popularity, as well as newspapers covering *Survivor* as if it were a sporting event. The most interesting marketing tactic CBS employed shrouded the outcome and events leading to up to it in mystery. The network threatened anyone who gave away secrets with a $5 million lawsuit and forced contestants to stay quiet until after the finale by withholding pay until the season ended.[11]

When Richard Hatch, an openly homosexual corporate trainer, emerged from the first season as victor, America had the role model for its first reality show villain. Hatch proved to be a master manipulator, and the audience both loved and hated to watch him pull the strings of other contestants, such as Rudy Boesch, a 72-year-old former Navy SEAL. Hatch stood as a fitting winner because much of *Survivor's* appeal came from the way people related their own lives to the antics players went through during the game. "A show's fundamental meaning must dovetail with the dominant meanings of its audience for it to be compatible with the lives of its viewers," explained media scholar Derek Foster. "As a microcosm of American values ... *Survivor* ... reflected and reinforced the Horatio Alger theme of the self-made individual whose hard work and self-reliance will invariably triumph in the face of adversity."[12]

As *Time* magazine noted shortly after the show's debut, *Survivor's* popularity prompted the rise of what it called voyeur television (VTV):

> Despite *Survivor's* gross-outs, its dark premise and its wall-to-wall cheesiness—the faux-Lion King sound track, the "tribal councils" held in what looks like a Holiday Inn Polynesian lounge circa 1963, the somber narration of Jeff Probst, former host of VH1's *Rock 'n' Roll Jeopardy!* and challenger to Regis for luckiest-man-in-America status—despite all this, viewers have embraced the desert-island soap with fascination and bemused contempt.[13]

NOTABLE TV SHOWS

Alias

The Amazing Race

American Idol

Cold Case

C.S.I.: Crime Scene Investigation

The Daily Show

Dancing with the Stars

Everybody Loves Raymond

Friends

Heroes

Law & Order franchise

Lost

The Office

Sex and the City

The Sopranos

Survivor

24

The West Wing

Who Wants to be a Millionaire

Will & Grace

A Time/CNN poll from mid-2000 revealed that 31 percent of adults would allow a reality television show film them in their pajamas, 29 percent kissing, 26 percent crying, and 25 percent having an argument. Only 8 percent said that they would be taped naked, while 5 percent said having sex. One wonders if the latter figures wouldn't be much higher in 2008.[14]

Cable Television

The economic woes facing consumers in 2007 and 2008 led to the unthinkable: people actually ditched cable television. True, some decided to move to satellite television for premium access, but cable companies across the country report losing subscribers to the bad economy. Comcast, for example, lost more than 73,000 customers in the first three months of 2008, while 21,000 dropped Time Warner Cable. In contrast, DirecTV and

Dish Network gained a combined 320,000 customers in the same timeframe. Most troubling for the big cable companies is that the difficult financial picture is leading to cutbacks in the ancillary services they offer, such as high-speed Internet and cable-based phone systems.[15]

At the same time, there is little love lost between most consumers and their cable television providers. Most operators have a virtual monopoly over their service area, so people are forced to accept whatever outrageous rate hike the company sends their way. In New York City, for example, Time Warner instituted a 9.6 percent hike, while Cablevision increased 4.7 percent. At the same time the bills increased, city officials reported that consumer complaints against the two cable companies jumped 41 percent. In most of the cable business, customers expect poor service, delays, incomprehensible bills, and outages. Despite the technological advances made in the industry, many basic challenges remain to be solved.[16]

While consumers balance cable bills with their other monthly expenses, the quality of television programming is getting stronger as the decade advances, particularly when considering the handful of acclaimed series running on the cable networks. Journalist Tim Goodman sees the storytelling element of TV setting it apart from other mediums, explaining, "Television is also different from film in that the storytelling is alive, the series are evolving (or devolving, as the case may be), and opinions can change with the content. A film tells a story in two hours or less most of the time and then history judges it. A television series tells 13 or 22 hours of a story and then comes back to do it again the next year—and if there's a noticeable drop-off in quality, then the critical perception also evolves (or devolves)."[17]

Not so many decades ago, Americans were happy with fewer television channels and whatever the major networks put out each year. Fast forward to the new millennium, however, and those antiquated ideas are out the window. Today's television landscape is crawling with niche channels that specialize in everything from specific college football conferences to an all-day menu of home improvement shows.

In the 2000s, the hottest commodities on cable TV have been the premium series, such as *The Sopranos* (HBO), *Deadwood* (HBO), *Sex and the City* (HBO), *Dexter* (Showtime), and *Weeds* (Showtime). In addition, basic cable stations are making their mark with original series, including *Mad Men* (AMC), *Breaking Bad* (AMC), *Monk* (USA), and *Psych* (USA).

Cable network executives realize that fewer consumers turn to them to see movies, as access to first-run films spans mail-order, the Web, demand television, and DVD rentals. As a result, they turn to original series to attract new viewers, even if such programming can be costly. Tony Vinciquerra, President and CEO of Fox Cable Networks, said, "Original programming helps build a brand." On Fox's FX channel, this idea worked on the back of critically-acclaimed shows, such as *The Shield, Rescue Me,* and *Nip/Tuck.* HBO built the blueprint for these networks by proving that viewers would tune in (and pay for) good shows on a premium channel. The basic cable networks are replicating that strategy and have the added benefit of drawing advertisers through commercials.[18]

Bringing in viewers and advertising dollars is critical, as production costs are increasing by about 10 percent per year. Dramas on basic cable run about $1 million per-episode, while costs at pay channels can be in the $3 million range. Marketing budgets are also increasing because it takes greater (and more costly) effort to reach potential viewers who are spending time online or playing video games.[19]

The Networks

With basic and premium cable networks upping the ante in both quality and quantity of shows, the networks have had to respond with better programming. However, like the cable networks, they have also relied heavily on reality shows to offset costs. As a result of the necessity for better quality, the networks produced shows such as *CSI* (CBS), *Heroes* (NBC), *24* (Fox), *Desperate Housewives* (ABC), *Grey's Anatomy* (ABC), and *Law & Order: SVU* (NBC). These shows feature strong writing, quality cinematography, and filmic production.

At the same time quality must be increased, the cost of network television is skyrocketing, probably the latter following from the former.

TOP ACTORS

Cate Blanchett, 1969–
Orlando Bloom, 1977–
Nicolas Cage, 1964–
Jim Carrey, 1962–
George Clooney, 1961–
Russell Crowe, 1964–
Tom Cruise, 1962–
Johnny Depp, 1963–
Leonardo DiCaprio, 1974–
Will Ferrell, 1967–
Tom Hanks, 1956–
Angelina Jolie, 1975–
Nicole Kidman, 1967–
Keira Knightley, 1985–
Heath Ledger, 1979–2008
Tobey Maguire, 1975–
Helen Mirren, 1945–
Brad Pitt, 1963–
Natalie Portman, 1981–
Will Smith, 1968–
Ben Stiller, 1965–
Hilary Swank, 1974–
Naomi Watts, 1968–
Reese Witherspoon, 1976–
Renée Zellweger, 1969–
Catherine Zeta-Jones, 1969–

ACADEMY AWARD WINNERS

2000 Picture: *Gladiator*

Director: Steven Soderbergh, *Traffic*
Actor: Russell Crowe, *Gladiator*
Actress: Julia Roberts, *Erin Brockovich*

2001 Picture: *A Beautiful Mind*

Director: Ron Howard, *A Beautiful Mind*
Actor: Denzel Washington, *Training Day*
Actress: Halle Berry, *Monster's Ball*

2002 Picture: *Chicago*

Director: Roman Polanski, *The Pianist*
Actor: Adrien Brody, *The Pianist*
Actress: Nicole Kidman, *The Hours*

2003 Picture: *The Lord of the Rings: The Return of the King**

Director: Peter Jackson, *The Lord of the Rings: The Return of the King*
Actor: Sean Penn, *Mystic River*
Actress: Charlize Theron, *Monster*

2004 Picture: *Million Dollar Baby*

Director: Clint Eastwood, *Million Dollar Baby*
Actor: Jamie Foxx, *Ray*
Actress: Hilary Swank, *Million Dollar Baby*

2005 Picture: *Crash*

Director: Ang Lee, *Brokeback Mountain*
Actor: Philip Seymour Hoffman, *Capote*
Actress: Reese Witherspoon, *Walk the Line*

2006 Picture: *The Departed*

Director: Martin Scorsese, *The Departed*
Actor: Forest Whitaker, *The Last King of Scotland*
Actress: Helen Mirren, *The Queen*

2007 Picture: *There Will Be Blood*

Director: Ethan and Joel Coen, *There Will Be Blood*
Actor: Daniel Day-Lewis, *There Will Be Blood*
Actress: Marion Cotillard, *La Vie en Rose*

*Highest grossing, as of December 31, 2007.

Jeff Zucker, President and CEO of NBC Universal outlined some of the challenges the networks face in trying to find programs. "Last year, the five broadcast networks spent more than 500 million dollars…more than half a billion dollars…on development of new series, scripts and pilots," Zucker said. "Some 80 pilots were made. Next fall, or whenever the next television season begins, at most eight of those series will return. 1 in 10. And of those eight, none could be considered a big success." In an era marked by increased competition for advertising dollars and viewer eyeballs, the old models no longer work as well for the major networks, Zucker's call to arms notwithstanding.[20]

Another jolt to the network model is that digital video recorder (DVR) technology enables viewers to bypass commercials, the lifeblood of the television economic model. Many observers see the DVR as just another innovation that provides the consumer with greater power than previous eras. "The amazing variety of choices consumers have today has important implications for consumer behavior. It's a shift from habit to choice...to individuals making choices when and how to consume media," Zucker said. "There is less and less habitual plopping down in front of the TV—and more and more media consumption made by conscious choice. This is a new kind of appointment TV, but where the appointment is made by the viewer, not by the network scheduling department."[21]

Watching Online

Technology plays a critical role for television, not only in its continuing central role as furniture in one's living room, but in expanding the ways people can watch their favorite programs when they are away from home. More frequently, primetime television viewing is occurring via the Web and

NOTABLE MOVIES

Almost Famous (2000)
Cast Away (2000)
Erin Brockovich (2000)
Traffic (2000)
Harry Potter and the Sorcerer's Stone (2001)
The Lord of the Rings: The Fellowship of the Ring (2001)
Shrek (2001)
Monsters, Inc. (2001)
Ocean's Eleven (2001)
Harry Potter and the Chamber of Secrets (2002)
The Lord of the Rings: The Two Towers (2002)*
My Big Fat Greek Wedding (2002)
Spider-Man (2002)*
Star Wars: Episode II–The Attack of the Clones (2002)
Finding Nemo (2003)
Pirates of the Caribbean: The Curse of the Black Pearl (2003)*
Mystic River (2003)
Shrek 2 (2004)*
Spider-Man 2 (2004)*
The Passion of the Christ (2004)*
The Incredibles (2004)
Harry Potter and the Prisoner of Azkaban (2004)
Fahrenheit 9/11 (2004)
National Treasure (2004)
Forty-Year-Old Virgin (2005)
Harry Potter and the Goblet of Fire (2005)
Wedding Crashers (2005)
Brokeback Mountain (2005)
Star Wars: Episode III–Revenge of the Sith (2005)*
Night at the Museum (2006)
Cars (2006)
The Departed (2006)
The Devil Wears Prada (2006)
Dreamgirls (2006)
Pirates of the Caribbean: Dead Man's Chest (2006)*
Spider-Man 3 (2007)*
300 (2007)
Hairspray (2007)
Juno (2007)
Superbad (2007)
Transformers (2007)
The Dark Knight (2008)
WALL-E (2008)

* Highest grossing as of December 31, 2007.

on smaller screens, such as cell phones and iPods. This move forces the major studios to rethink their use of technology and how to interact with consumers who want more of this programming.

Like other forms of online entertainment, once the brush fire has been lit, a raging inferno is soon to follow. The future of television viewing online already has role models for its growth based on what happened in the music industry. When consumers felt that they could get the content for free, they flocked to legal and illegal sites to access what they wanted.

According to Solutions Research Group, about 80 million Americans watched a TV show online, some 43 percent of the total online population. This is a significant increase over the 25 percent that claimed they viewed a show on the Web the year before. Perhaps more telling, and pointing to the future of primetime TV, some 20 percent of respondents said that they watch television via the Web weekly.[22]

One in five visitors to major network Web sites said that they did so to watch a specific show. However, the results of the specific shows they tuned into online do not automatically conform to the demographics one would imagine. Some of the top TV shows viewed on the Internet include: *Heroes, Grey's Anatomy, Dancing with the Stars, CSI, House,* and *Gossip Girl.*

Many online television viewers turn to the network Web sites to avoid commercials, though more skipping through ads is still done via a DVR. Examining the top 20 prime time shows, the study found that a whopping 55 percent of the shows were time shifted by DVR or by viewing online. Some 65 percent of DVR users say that they always skip commercials, up from 52 percent the previous year.[23]

FILM

In 2008, the Academy Awards turned somber with dark films winning major awards, as well as the actors and actresses who starred in them. *No Country for Old Men,* Joel and Ethan Coen's story of a battle resulting from a drug deal gone bad, won the Oscar for best picture. Daniel Day-Lewis won best actor for *There Will Be Blood,* his portrayal of a ruthless oil tycoon. In discussing the somber tones of the awards, two journalists noted that the contest turned into "a tug of war over sensibilities: Academy voters were being asked to choose between the nihilism of 'No Country for Old Men,' in which the serial killer prevails; the hopeful spunk of 'Juno,' in which a pregnant teenager forges her own solutions; or, perhaps, a saga of childhood betrayal and lives destroyed, in 'Atonement,' set against the backdrop of British retreat in the early days of World War II."[24]

In many instances, the tone of Academy Award-winning films either represents the feelings of the nation or counters the prevailing mood. The 2008 batch clearly struck a dark nerve in America's thinking, about itself, the ongoing overseas war,

Poster art for the hit teen movie *Superbad* (2007). It, along with several other successful comedies of the decade, such as the *Forty Year Old Virgin* (2005) were directed, written, and/or produced by Judd Apatow. Columbia Pictures/Photofest. ©Columbia Pictures. Courtesy of Photofest.

SPIDER-MAN

Spider-Man (Peter Parker) is a comic book superhero residing in the Marvel Universe. Created in 1962 by writer-editor Stan Lee and artist Steve Ditko, his first comic book appearance came in *Amazing Fantasy* #15. Since then, the character developed into one of Marvel's most popular and marketable figures—an American icon and global commodity.

The comic books spawned three blockbuster movies, numerous combined animated and live-action television series, and countless video games. His likeness can be seen on action figures, other toys, clothing, school supplies, house decorations, coffee mugs, breakfast cereal and candy, electronics, automobile accessories, and even human tattoos. The Spider-Man property single-handedly reinvented comic books in the new millennium after decades of relative obscurity.

The *Spider-Man* movie (2002), starring Tobey Maguire, broke box office records, becoming the highest grossing film of the year. The film earned nearly $115 million during its opening weekend and became the quickest to reach $100 million, doing so in only three days ($821.7 million worldwide). *Spider-Man 2* premiered two years later and made $783 million worldwide. Although released to mixed reviews in 2007, *Spider-Man 3* is the top-grossing of the series, earning $890.8 million worldwide.

There is too much money being made from the films to rule out further sequels. Early rumors indicate that *Spider-Man 4* will be released in 2010. Until then, Spider-Man fans can get their Spidey fix on the myriad of monthly comic books and endless array of products that feature the iconic character.

and the impending economic troubles facing the nation. For viewers, the difficulty is tuning into the Oscar telecast when such intense films are honored. In 2006, for example, when *Crash* won the best picture award, less than 39 million people watched. The 2008 version, hosted by *The Daily Show* star Jon Stewart, attracted a mere 32 million, earning the distinction of the least-watched Oscars ever.

Many experts attribute this disconnect to Hollywood snobbery, the awarding of movies that fewer and fewer people want to see. Journalist David Carr explained, "While there is much to be admired in the five Best Picture nominees, all told, they have pulled in around $313 million so far at the box office, a few million less than 'Transformers' did alone."[25]

DVD Sales

Innovation enabled DVDs to relegate VHS tapes to history's dustbin. In the new millennium, purchasing a movie on VHS seems archaic and perhaps most often done by those looking through a remainder bin at a big box superstore or on a dusty shelf in a used bookstore. However, the next iteration is on the launch pad—the high-definition DVD—which may someday destroy the traditional DVD business, which currently accounts for about 60 percent of studio profits. Sony introduced the Blu-ray disc, which has been named the industry standard. But, rather than cheer on this new innovation, studio executives worry that the hit the DVD business will take is going to disrupt their profits.

In 2007, for example, DVD sales in the United States fell 3.2 percent to $15.9 billion, the first time in the history of the business that sales dropped year-over-year. Adams Media Research anticipates a further decline in 2008 and 2009. Although the Blu-ray high-def disc is a formidable foe, the real challenge for DVD sales is competition with technology companies. Apple now offers movie downloads on iTunes, while broadband communications companies that pipe entertainment into people's homes are testing movie downloads. The threat is so steep that the movie studios responded by providing consumers with a digital file when they purchase a DVD. The file lets users burn the movie to a computer or transfer it to their iPod.[26]

George Clooney

Tom Hanks, Charlize Theron, and Johnny Depp are a few of the many fine actors and actresses working in the new millennium. Of this illustrious list, though, George Clooney may just

Actor George Clooney at the Golden Globe Awards televised in 2006. NBC/Photofest. ©Chris Haston. Courtesy of Photofest.

be the most important, not only for the kinds of films he has made, but as a throwback to a nostalgic age when those on the stage were charming, yet rugged; graceful, yet stereotypically manly. In recent years, Clooney used his star power to rally support for the struggling people of Darfur. In December 2007, he won a Summit Peace Award from the Nobel Peace Prize Laureates. In early 2008, officials at the United Nations appointed Clooney a U.N. peace envoy, recognizing his commitment to the region.

Clooney spent the years just prior to the new millennium (1994–1999) playing Dr. Doug Ross on *ER,* the highly-acclaimed television series created by bestselling writer Michael Crichton. After leaving the series to pursue movie work full-time, Clooney acted in a series of successful films, from the Coen Brothers' depression-era romp *O Brother, Where Art Thou?* (2000) to a trilogy of Las Vegas Rat Pack movies: *Ocean's Eleven* (2001), *Ocean's Twelve* (2004), and *Ocean's Thirteen* (2007).

Moving back and forth from blockbuster star to more serious roles, Clooney starred as a CIA operative in *Syriana* (2005), which won him an Oscar as best supporting actor. Journalist Caryn James places Clooney's star power at the nexus of his onscreen stardom and activism. She sees his popularity in this ability to "raise a question with an old-fashioned ring—'What's the right thing to do?'—and apply it to issues that are totally of the moment." As a result, she explained, "he avoids preachiness because his films don't pretend to answer tough moral questions; they simply insist the questions are worth asking."[27]

Clooney possesses the uncanny ability to be one of only three men to ever be named *People Magazine*'s Sexiest Man Alive twice (1997 and 2006), while also tackling parts that transform his handsome features into a kind of vulnerability or everyman. He is able to come off as overtly modest on one hand, but then own up to his stardom the next, and audiences love him for it even more. In *Michael Clayton* (2007), Clooney plays a faltering lawyer whose world is unraveling. In January 2008, he received a nomination for an Academy Award for Best Actor for it.

Brangelina: The World's Hottest Couple

The multimedia revolution sparked by the Internet made celebrity watching a 24-hour a day spectacle. Regardless of how much gossip, rumor, and misinformation is spooned out to the American people, it just seems as if they cannot get enough. Brad Pitt and Angelina Jolie symbolize the transformation in celebrity coverage, from media and photographers following them around when new movies came out to an environment where nothing is off limits. However, given the current craving for illicit gossip, it seems appropriate that Pitt and Jolie met while shooting the move *Mr. and Mrs. Smith,* while they were still both the Mr. and Mrs. in another relationship.

Prior to his relationship with Jolie, *Friends* sitcom star Jennifer Aniston and Pitt had a highly-public marriage, seemingly creating America's "perfect couple." The rumors of tryst between

Jolie and Pitt began in late 2004, on the set of the action movie they starred in as a married couple, secretly assassins, who are hired to kill each other. Shortly after the public announcement about his separation from Aniston, the weekly tabloids and Web sites buzzed with news of Pitt and Jolie. Then, the new couple took a very public vacation together in Africa, where photographers caught them frolicking in the surf and Pitt playing with Jolie's adopted son Maddox.[28]

In the ensuing years since they got together, Pitt and Jolie continue to dominate the tabloids and entertainment gossip. In what seems like collusion, since all the celebutainment magazines appear to feature the same stories each week, the couple lives in the public eye. In this age of media sensationalism, each photo of one of them alone is interpreted as a soon-to-be breakup or the end of their fairytale life. The headlines predict a marriage one week, a split the next, and constantly ponder the fate of poor Aniston, America's jilted sweetheart.

If there is a hidden benefit to the high-octane merger of two mega brands like Pitt and Jolie it is that the social justice causes they work for get more attention. Both entertainers have led efforts to gain recognition for conditions in Africa. Closer to home, Pitt started the Make It Right foundation to rebuild homes in New Orleans's ravaged Lower Ninth Ward. The organization teamed with 13 architects to design and then rebuild 150 houses with state-of-the-art features, such as solar heat and light, 5-foot elevated first floors, while in some designs, the homes even float. Pitt and Jolie also moved into a residence in New Orleans to keep the media spotlight on the city as it rebuilds in the deep wake of Hurricane Katrina.[29]

Pitt used his star power to coordinate rebuilding efforts after growing frustrated with the slow response of the national and local governments. After contributing $5 million of his own money to the cause, Pitt reached out to foundations, corporations, and other individuals to help. He explained his reasons for getting involved, saying, "I've always had a fondness for this place—it's like no other. Seeing the frustration firsthand made me want to return the kindness this city has shown me."[30]

Failure of Iraq Films

"Failure" is a stark word that boldly defines itself in its brashness. One need not ponder long and hard about what failure is. The word is tied to the American Dream so closely that we all know failure when we see it, touch it, or brush up against it. To say that films playing on the post–September 11 terrorist attacks and subsequent overseas wars have failed is to accuse them of not helping define what life should be like in this new age; rather, it says they merely play on patriotic stereotypes and racial intolerance.

On the surface, one could reject this notion of failure by pointing out that *United 93* grossed some $43 million after being made for just $15 million. This kind of limited viewpoint, though, just says that people are interested in the post–September 11 world, not that it has really transformed their lives. As journalist James Poniewozik explained, "saying that 9/11 has entered pop culture is not the same thing as saying that 9/11 has changed pop culture." He points to the Bush Administration for downplaying the force of the new world order on ordinary people. "The Administration's message to citizens since the attacks has been, believe that 9/11 changed everything when it comes to foreign and domestic policy and that 9/11 changed nothing when it comes to spending and living."[31]

Almost immediately after the September 11 attacks, critics proclaimed the end of irony, a notion that, according to *Time* magazine, "Our metaphors have expired. Pleasure seems mocking and futile . . . language that artists, comedians, storytellers and actors use to explain us to ourselves now seems frivolous, inappropriate or simply outdated."[32] Looking back from the vantage point of early 2008, these messages not only seem outdated, but ineffectual. What America learned in the post–September 11 world is that they should not stop the frantic national buying spree or worry too much about the war—pretty quickly, it would become news for the back page, not the headlines. The utter failure of films to reflect the world after September 11 or add to the national dialogue in a meaningful way proves the point that the talk of a world transformed was nothing more than that day's lead story.

Movie critic Richard Corliss sees the challenges in presenting filmic interpretations of the Iraq war in more artistic terms, saying, "this war is tragic but not inherently dramatic." Up to this point, there has not been the kind of stereotypical war movie aspects in the current campaign in the Middle East—clear cut good guys and bad guys and romance immediately standing out. Corliss also noted that it is difficult to present the United States in its World War II heroic sense when the country has bungled all its wars since then. "We may have to wait for Hollywood's definitive Iraq-war film," he said. "But that's the way the movie industry works. It took years for *The Deer Hunter, Coming Home,* and *Platoon* to appear and leave their indelible marks."[33]

NOTABLE THEATER

Aida, 2000 (1,852 perfs.)

The Producers, 2001 (2,502 perfs.)

Mamma Mia, 2001 (2,650+ perfs.*)

Hairspray, 2002 (2,300+ perfs.*)

Avenue Q, 2003 (1,900+ perfs.*)

Wicked, 2003 (1,800+ perfs.*)

42nd Street (revival), 2001 (1,524 perfs.)

Movin' Out, 2002 (1,303 perfs.)

Spamalot, 2005 (1,200 perfs.*)

The 25th Annual Putnam County Spelling Bee, 2005 (1,136 perfs.)

* Still running as of August 2008.

THEATER

Broadway is the gold standard of American theater. In late 2007, however, a 19-day stagehand strike crippled the industry. Although pundits worried that the strike would destroy the December holiday season, the Great White Way bounced back from the work stoppage. Sales Christmas week, which are usually good for Broadway in a typical year, went through the roof, topping $30 million. Some 14 shows brought in more than $1 million each, with *Wicked* topping the rush at $1.8 million.[34]

Although the strong holiday season helped Broadway regain its footing, the strike took a toll on grosses for the season (down 5% year-over-year) and attendance (dropping 4.5%). Both figures had been up prior to the strike, with grosses at 5.8 percent and attendance growing 5.5 percent. Producer Stewart Lane provided a personalized look at the strike's financial consequences, saying, "The profits we could have had during the second-most-important week of our business cycle is money we couldn't recapture. I have nightmares about how much we lost that weekend."[35]

Weekly sales figures provide observers with a glimpse of how Broadway is faring. In the week ending March 30, 2008, for example, some 26 musicals (attendance: 245,290) grossed $18.4 million or 87 percent of the Broadway total. The 7 plays (attendance: 39,418) accounted for $2.7 million. The overall paid admission price stood at $74.31 for all shows.[36]

Fashion

of the 2000s

In the new millennium, fashion is not just stereotypical, waif-thin runway models flaunting the latest Parisian styles. The idea of fashion goes well beyond these traditional limitations, though runways and haute couture are certainly a large part of the industry. Fashion in this decade may better be defined as a person possessing a sense of style, which is tied directly to the wider pop culture influences on one's daily life. As a result, fashion is currently a more important part of everyday life for most Americans than in the past.

Access to mass media certainly affects style choices, from television shows, films, and commercials to what one sees on the Internet. Drop into any upscale department store. The endless choices will either dazzle or depress the innocent shopper just looking for something to wear to work next Tuesday or for a night out on the town. Journalist Sharon Fink calls this phenomenon "fashion overload." She breaks the average woman's fashion needs down to its essentials, stating, "We want basics, kept stylish and up-to-date; a few well-chosen trends; and a couple of splurges. And we want it all to fit well."[1]

Perhaps the virtually unlimited access to fashion and trends via movies, television, and the Internet made designers think that they needed to expand the types of clothes available. They may have merely thrown many styles into the system and then waited to see what consumers picked, rather than offer a limited range of choices. Fink believes the fickle nature and quick boredom of shoppers is at the heart of the challenge. "We love to buy. We get bored easily. And once we got hooked on the fast turnover of styles at chains like Express and Target, everyone from top designers down were forced to crank out as much variety as possible to keep us interested and spending," she said.[2] Target has been particularly successful in hiring fashion designers, including Isaac Mizrahi, Liz Lange, Rogan Gregory, Richard Chai, and others, to produce affordable but highly stylish clothes and design household products.

DISCOUNT SHOPPING

Novato, California, is located 30 miles north of San Francisco, straight up Highway 101 after crossing over the Golden Gate Bridge. The town's nearly 50,000 inhabitants occupy the northernmost section of well-heeled Marin County, one of the richest areas in the United States. Despite the countless million dollar homes that dot its hillsides, Novato is actually a blue-collar oasis in the heart of this affluent madness. Nestled between the city and Napa Valley wine country to the north, the town is certainly the closest thing to "normal" in Marin, if not the entire San Francisco Bay area.

Actress Amy Smart arrives with fashion designer Rogan Gregory at the "Rogan for Target" clothing line debut in Beverly Hills, California, in 2008. AP Photo/Dan Steinberg.

Just about any day of the week, the most hopping spot in Novato is Vintage Oaks Shopping Center, a couple miles south of the city, and a convenient exit just off busy 101. By mid-morning on any given weekend, a sea of bright, shiny SUVs pushes latecomers to the farthest nether regions of the parking lot, forcing them to trudge through a multitude of orphaned shopping carts and dodge other dawdlers on the way to the door.

What's all the fuss at Vintage Oaks? Among its 50 stores, the colossal plaza is home to the two-headed discount shopping monster of Target and Costco. These stores have come to define Novato. Target and Costco give the town an identity distinct from its wealthy neighbors in the southern portion of the county, not only openly inviting a different economic class of shopper to the area, but also a melting pot of workers to staff the stores.

The Target experience is all about brand and image. Drop a shopper in front of any Target across the nation, and that person should have a similar experience and feeling as they walk through the shiny red doors. The famous Target Bullseye is about more than the merchandise within the store; it is about branding the franchise itself, thus giving shoppers a uniquely Target experience on every visit.

Earlier in its history, Target attracted shoppers searching for bargain merchandise, such as the special on the 300-ounce Tide laundry detergent for $16.88. Over the last decade, however, Target's unique ability to redefine itself as a central point for hip culture enabled it to become a destination for consumers searching for the latest fashion styles and trends.

The Novato Target is a jumble of scurrying workers, shoppers streaming by with red-orange carts, kids crammed into the snack bar, and packed checkout lanes. Target has spent billions of dollars branding its bullseye logo and unique, apple-red tint. The result is a constant sea of red everywhere you turn.

A quarter mile down the strip, past the Old Navy, various small beauty shops, and the sporting goods store sits Costco, the king of discount warehouses. The Novato store, like others across the nation, is a cultural wonderland.

There are few assurances in life, and most of them are bad, like DMV lines will always be long and the mechanic's bill will always total at least $500. In Novato, like places around the nation that have a Costco, there is another certainty: the Costco lot is always full. Nothing slows down Costco shoppers, not a freak blizzard, torrential downpour, or beautiful summer day in which they should be out enjoying the sunshine.

The scene at Costco is utter chaos. Here comes a middle-aged woman who must be 5-foot-4-inches tall and not much more than 100 pounds pushing an oversized cart filled with giant jugs of olive oil, cases of wine and Diet Coke, various hardcover books, large stacks of boxed food, and just like 90 percent of the people exiting Costco, the ever-present, mammoth package of toilet paper precariously balancing on top. The cart must weigh in at about 200 pounds, easily doubling her weight. She's not only struggling against the weight of the cart on its little frail wheels, but she can't see over the mountain of merchandise. This is a lawsuit waiting to happen—perhaps the smartest thing to do is park far, far away.

Inside, Costco is a Spartan warehouse. The emphasis at Costco is on products and prices. Every nook and cranny is filled with something to buy, whether stacked from cement floor to ceiling on simple metal shelves or on barebones tables that look like they survived your Aunt Elma's last trip to the flea market.

At the end of each row, shoppers may find jars of peanut butter as big as buckets or cases of off-brand shampoo amassed on wooden skids. The Costco experience is shopping stripped to its essence. The message is direct, screaming, "bargain" to the masses picking over its wares. No wonder more than 25 percent of American households are card-carrying Costco members.

While Costco doesn't make its customers work to find a deal, they do have to pile up the mileage as they wander through the aisles thick with merchandise. Each twist and turn not only provides a new opportunity for finding a treasure, but also for saving money. This combination is a powerful incentive for middle class shoppers, despite the bare surroundings and long checkout lines that fly in the face of usual demands for high standards of customer care and pampering.

The magic in the Costco experience—making it worthwhile to put up with the crowds and cramped parking—is that it provides grownups with the feeling of a genuine treasure hunt. The "wow" factor, like finding the latest James Patterson novel for less than half price or saving hundreds of dollars on the family's grocery bill through bulk purchases, makes Costco an exciting place to shop. Perhaps some members get slightly woozy when their bill is totaled, but even the shock of plopping down $300 or $400 is softened by the cherished perception that the word "bargain" can be slapped on every item. Costco makes people feel like they got their money's worth.

And what becomes of our friend from the parking lot, the woman valiantly struggling against the weight of her purchases? After loading up her sleek, black Chevy Tahoe, she eventually makes her way back to her subdivision, listening to a message on her cell phone from her daughter about ballet practice. Arriving home, her son, Jordan, is playing basketball with his friends in the driveway. As she pulls into the garage, the middle school boys flip open the hatch and take turns carrying boxes and other loose items into the kitchen.

Once Mom gets the haul corralled, the boys go back to their game, each with a can of pop and a handful of cookies from the trip. Letting her mind wander as she fills the pantry and cupboards, she begins to tick off how much she saved on each item. A little smile forms as she realizes that the total surpasses $250. She can't wait to tell her husband once he gets home from the office.

Not only did Mom save money, she feels great about her Costco trip. She bought the staples essential to running her household, planned family meals, and even picked up a few small gifts for the holiday season. Most important, however, she uncovered bargains. The extra money can be put toward the family's next vacation or into the costs of raising kids quickly approaching their teenage years.

This scenario isn't unique, but it reveals a trend being played out in homes from coast to coast. Over the years, our consumer thought process has changed. The shopping ritual has developed into more than merely acquiring life's essentials. Quite the contrary, shopping gives people hope and a sense of control over their lives. They choose items that reflect their own self-image and call out to their dreams and aspirations.

According to shopping guru Paco Underhill, "If we went into stores only when we needed to buy something, and if once there, we bought only what we needed, the economy would collapse, boom." Instead, a shopping revolution took place, fueled by the nation's increased wealth since World War II. "The economic party," Underhill said, "has fostered more shopping than anyone would have predicted, more shopping than has ever taken place anywhere at any time."[3]

Discount shopping, whether it is at Wal-Mart, Costco, or The Dollar Store, takes the experience one step further. A person ventures into Wal-Mart for several reasons, but the primary draws are widespread selection and "everyday low prices." The variety of items fulfills the aesthetic craving, while the lower cost appeals to the feelings of vindication consumers attain when they've saved a buck.

Discount shopping triggers some inherently American values—the availability of an endless assortment of goods and the notion of tracking down the best bargain available, thus saving money and outsmarting the other guy. For many consumers, this notion turns shopping into a new competitive sport, neatly falling into the habit we Americans have of treating most aspects of life as a contest or battle.

A perfect example is the local mall on the day after Thanksgiving with the early bird sales, which usually begin before the sun rises. The parking lot is packed, and impatient, sleepy people are waiting for the doors to open—all this effort to get wrapping paper for half price or to save 10 bucks on a sweater.

Rescuing the Economy

Conditions were ripe for an economic "Perfect Storm." The collective weight of the dot.com implosion that began in early 2001, the September 11 terrorist attacks, and the successive wars in Afghanistan and Iraq resulted in a faltering economy, millions of people losing their jobs, and widespread insecurity.

Stories of retirees losing their life's savings as the stock market tanked and millions of high tech jobs disappearing as companies went belly-up turned the economic boom of the late 1990s into ancient history. Pundits filled the airwaves with chatter about a possible global depression. Republicans and Democrats took turns blasting one another for the dire conditions, bemoaning the lack of leadership necessary to get the economy back on track. All the while, consumers ignored the calamity and went right on shopping.

In a time when common sense dictated that people should save every spare penny and carefully plan for the (gloomy) future, shoppers barely flinched. Unlike other recessions, they continued to spend, despite the economic doldrums. Without consumer willingness to keep on shopping in the face of a troublesome economic situation, the country could have tumbled deeper into an economic quagmire.

On the surface, it seemed as if shoppers had lost their minds. A closer look, though, reveals that consumers did not go crazy during the recession that followed the dot.com bust in the early years of the twenty-first century. Spending habits were not based on a hope and a prayer. The federal government, under the leadership of Federal Reserve Chairman Alan Greenspan, took steps to put money back into people's hands by dropping interest rates to historic lows. More than a dozen cuts have been made since January 2001. For people who had taken out large mortgages in earlier decades, the new rates enabled them to consolidate debt under one low interest umbrella or roll the money they saved into other areas.

The combination of the low interest rates and increased consumer spending propped up the economy, even as corporations dramatically cut spending and began downsizing millions of workers (estimated at 2.6 million in a two-year span beginning March 2001). For the first time since 1948–1949, however, consumer spending rose throughout the recession, buoyed by low rates and favorable finance terms, such as zero percent financing on new cars and big-ticket items like washing machines and big-screen televisions. Many people still felt pinched by the 2001 recession, but it "officially" ended after a mere eight months due to these factors.

Household spending now accounts for about 70 percent of the economy. Therefore, tracking consumer spending is increasingly important. Every fluctuation has become a defining moment, worthy of front-page news. Policy makers keep an eye on consumer confidence polls on the lookout for trends that show the economy is improving. Monthly sales figures from Wal-Mart and Target provide a glimpse into American households, revealing the state of the economy on a personal level.

The downside, however, is that all the rampant consuming pushed household debt to record numbers in the early 2000s, estimated at a then-staggering $8.9 trillion. Mortgage debt alone jumped to more than $6 trillion in 2001, a 60 percent jump over the previous five years. In addition, overall family net worth fell considerably as the stock market plunged from dot.com boom highs.

Home equity lines of credit and refinancing enabled many people to transfer high-interest credit card and automobile debt to their mortgage, thus paying down debt in one hand but increasing it in another. In essence, these maneuvers put cash in people's pockets and provided the disposable income that ultimately ends up in the coffers of Wal-Mart, Target, and their discount brethren. The Bush Administration used the same tactic at several times during its reign, basically giving people a check from the federal government in hopes that they would spend it on big ticket goods. The 2008 relief efforts, for example, were meant to offset the real estate woes and credit crunch many people experienced.

Consumers saw a significant bump in their paychecks from the Bush Administration's tax cuts and from their employers as bigger raises started to be doled out as the nation began its rocky road to recovery. In September 2003, nationwide retail sales rose 5.9 percent, representing the largest jump since March 2002. Individually among the discount retailers, Wal-Mart's sales rose 6 percent, Kohl's 5.5 percent, and Target saw a whopping 14.8 percent gain. This trend indicated that continued growth was on the horizon. A robust holiday shopping season awaited retailers—good news for the companies and the nation as a whole.

The Wal-Mart Effect

Given that household spending represents 70 percent of the economy, Wal-Mart's enduring strength comes as no surprise. With billions of dollars being pumped into retail coffers, Wal-Mart continued to grow despite the widespread economic woes, not only propping up the limping economy, but also putting it in a strong position to capitalize on the inevitable rebound.

Wal-Mart's command is simply staggering, ranging from 2002 revenues of $245 billion to the mind-boggling reality that 82 percent of American households made at least one purchase there last year. Each week, 138 million shoppers visit one of Wal-Mart's 4,750 stores, almost half of the country's population. Today, net sales for the fiscal year ending on January 31, 2008, reached $374.5 billion, an increase of 8.6 percent over fiscal year 2007. Income from continuing operations for the fiscal year ended January 31, 2008 increased 5.8 percent to $12.9 billion, up from $12.2 billion in the prior year.[4]

As a matter of fact, Wal-Mart is so pervasive that economists and business analysts coined the "Wal-Mart effect" on the global economy. On one hand, the company's growth through the recession played a role in suppressing inflation. However, each productivity gain it squeezes out of a vendor or distributor ripples across the global economy. To do business with Wal-Mart, vendors must transform the way they operate to conform to the giant's processes.

On a global scale, Wal-Mart's policies affect the economies in many of the world's developing nations. Several countries in Central America and South Asia are dependent on the company, which in turn, relies on cheap manufacturing to produce low priced goods. Wal-Mart and its vendors are forced to continually search for ways to cut costs out of production, which means heavy use of workers in developing nations who will work much cheaper than their American counterparts.

Because of its sales prowess, Wal-Mart controls large shares of business done by its vendors, including some of the America's largest corporations. In the early part of the decade, Wal-Mart accounted for 28 percent of Dial's total sales, 24 percent of Del Monte Foods, 23 percent of Clorox, and 23 percent of Revlon. Wal-Mart has been almost single-handedly responsible for saving Levi's by signing a deal to sell blue jeans at discount prices. As a matter of fact, Wal-Mart is so powerful that it is considering offering banking services at the same time it is beginning the largest global expansion in company history.

In the early 2000s, Wal-Mart operated 1,309 stores in 10 nations. By 2008, those figures grew to 3,125 stores in 13 markets. It is already the largest single retailer in both Canada and Mexico. In 2003 alone, Wal-Mart added another 130 new stores in foreign markets. In comparison, Target spent $3.5 billion in 2003 to expand in the United States. Many of its new outlets will be SuperTargets, melding the grocery store with the discount store, just like Wal-Mart's highly successful Supercenters.

If Wal-Mart maintains its current growth rate of 15 percent, the company will record sales of $600 billion by 2011. The retailer is also going to top 2 million employees, up from its current 1.4 million. This record expansion and growth is taking place while the national economy is stumbling along due to unemployment concerns and fears regarding the global geo-political situation, including further fighting in Iraq and future acts of terrorism.

The challenge in a world so thoroughly dominated by Wal-Mart, according to labor rights experts, is that its workers simply cannot fulfill the American dream (and in many cases, feed their families) on the salaries it pays. Furthermore, as the company puts the screws to its vendors and distributors, these companies are forced to lower their costs, which most often involves outsourcing work overseas and shedding American workers.

There is a Catch-22 that may ultimately play out: someday workers and those who have lost their jobs because of Wal-Mart's tactics will no longer be able to afford to shop there. When sales get sluggish at Wal-Mart, the slowdown will have a ripple effect across the global economy, with the potential for cataclysmic consequences. The international economy will not be able to absorb Wal-Mart's stumble—as it did with the fall of Woolworth's and, more recently, Kmart—because there has never been a company as pervasive and powerful as Wal-Mart.

The Bentonville behemoth and its discount brethren are not the only companies that expanded during the recession in the early 2000s. Some would argue that the truest heirs to the legacy of Woolworth's and other long lost five-and-dimes are the deep discount or closeout retailers, like Save-A-Lot, Big Lots, and Dollar General. This slice of the discount shopping pie has grown into a $20 billion market and experienced tremendous growth over the last several years.

These stores sell a limited selection of groceries and general merchandise aimed at lower-income shoppers. Their prices are 20 to 40 percent below those of Wal-Mart and remain competitive because they limit operating costs. Hard discounters try to siphon off the bottom third of Wal-Mart shoppers, typically those who earn $30,000 or less annually.

Big Lots, the largest of the closeout retailers, alone had sales eclipsing $3.8 billion in its 1,400 stores in 45 states in the early years of the decade. The company's stores are smaller than the average Wal-Mart or Target, but are located in more diverse areas, often closer to city centers and in strip malls that low-income shoppers patronize. Each location, however, averages $2.85 million in annual sales.

The combination of high interest retail charge cards and less stringent requirements for bankcards sent consumer debt through the roof in low-income households. Predatory credit card companies target these families, and studies reveal that lower-income households have seen their revolving debt skyrocket 184 percent in recent years. Expanding the credit pool by blanketing this segment of consumers with high interest cards has pushed the average credit card debt in the United States to $12,000 per household, according to Federal Reserve estimates.

Purchasing goods by credit card—even if charged a prohibitive interest rate—has enabled lower-income families to mimic their middle class neighbors. Closeout stores carry brand name merchandise, though a toy may be last year's craze or a blouse may be slightly irregular.

On the psychological front, dollar stores offer the same wonder as other discounters, but at considerably reduced prices. Shoppers still get the same treasure hunt feeling, never quite sure of the bounty they may uncover, but always knowing that it will be inexpensive.

Economic Rocket

In the summer of 2003, while the news headlines focused on wildfires ravaging California, which destroyed hundreds of thousands of acres around Los Angeles and San Diego, taking nearly two dozen lives, the nation's gross domestic product growth soared to 7.2 percent, a 19-year high.

Given the increasing criticism over its handling of the situation in Iraq, the Bush Administration immediately pointed to its tax cut program as the driver. Good economic news and positive signs of a full recovery from the latest recession would help the president counter his critics. Tax rebates—whether or not they are good for the nation's long-term economic health—put about $100 billion back into the hands of consumers just before the school shopping season began. In addition, the record number of individuals who refinanced their mortgages in the spring spent the money over the summer.

Once again, the willingness of millions of people to hit the shopping centers fueled this dramatic growth. The sequence of events is almost predictable—any time consumers are given an extra fistful of dollars, they dash off to Wal-Mart to spend the bounty. What George Bush Sr. called "voodoo economics" has been reborn during his son's reign, essentially a trickle-down effect that works because people are not afraid to spend.

Clearly, the seemingly illogical notion that increased consumer spending could dig an entire nation out of economic turmoil has sustained the United States over the last several years. Without the combination of low interest rates and increased consumer spending, there is no doubt that the recession would have lasted much longer, while the residual effects would have devastated countless families and communities.

The prominent role consumers have played in keeping the economy afloat reveals the importance of America's discount retailers. While department stores and upscale merchandisers struggled, the discounters grew more powerful and more central to the economic health of the nation.

Wal-Mart's sprint to become the largest company in the world proves how critical cheap shopping is in today's society. The company's growth also points to America's transition from a manufacturing power into a service economy, a profound transformation for a country historically dominant in heavy industry. Philosophically, Americans view themselves as builders, not manning stores with little nametags and bright blue vests.

Wal-Mart plays such a critical role in the nation's economy that the company has moved beyond mere economic importance (particularly for a company that has no direct military or intelligence ties, like a Northrop Grumman or Boeing). Retail analyst Tom Rubel surmised that if Wal-Mart, "ever stumbles, we've got a potential national security problem on our hands." The downfall of Wal-Mart could potentially destroy the American economy, triggering chaos worldwide. "They touch almost everything," he explained. "If they ever really went into a tailspin, the dislocation would be significant and traumatic."[5]

Wal-Mart, that corporate giant, the one that people either love or hate, is now America's bellwether. No barometer of leading economic indicators is complete without taking into account the Wal-Mart effect.

FASHION AND CLOTHING STYLES

Daily fashion in the new millennium is as jumbled and chaotic as the rest of popular culture. What people wear around the country is based on a complex web of local customs, climate, proximity to New York and Los Angeles, and the hottest television shows, rock bands, and movies. Fashion is a melting pot, just like the nation itself. If there is any unifying theme when examining a national

FASHION TRENDS OF THE 2000s

The emphasis on fashion in the 2000s is casual and comfortable. Layering thin separates is popular, particularly among females. Most workplaces allow employees to wear business casual year round.

Women/girls: low rider jeans; belly shirts and cargo pants; capris; miniskirts and long skirts; cropped jackets; bare legs (no pantyhose); hoodies (hooded pullovers); layering with thin separates; bootleg jeans; sleeveless dresses; empire waist blouses and dresses; tunic tops; pantsuits for work; flip flops, Ugg boots, and Croc clogs; large handbags.

Men/boys: jeans and T-shirts; some layering; button-down shirts with tails untucked; cargo pants; soul patches (tiny patch of beard) for young men.

fashion, it is that the industry is driven by celebrities (including celebrity, name brand designers themselves) and young people.

Early in the decade, fashion shook off the baggy, grunge days of the 1990s, as well as the hipster cool of Northern Californian dot.coms, reveling in more revealing styles. Women ditched their traditional Levis blue jeans for a new style, cut low at the waist (dubbed "low-rise") and tight everywhere else. Other female styles were punctuated with strategically placed tattoos, piercings, and undergarments worn outside clothing. Midriff-bearing tops were hot among some young women, almost always accompanied by a pierced bellybutton.

The most influential and enduring fashion statement to emerge from the early decade vaulted into the national conscious piggybacking off the pop hit "Thong Song" by Sisqó. The catchy tune became the virtual national anthem of college students venturing to the beach on spring break and received heavy airplay on MTV. "Thong Song" did more than elevate a piece of women's underwear to the national spotlight; the hit reinvigorated the idea that undergarments could be the most important visible piece of clothing. In its new public role, the underwear industry introduced a variety of new styles that drew inspiration from the thong. The women's underwear industry achieved sales of about $2.4 billion, and the thong garnered a quarter of that market. Writing in 2004, journalist Alex Kuczynski explained, "The thong underpant became a cultural touchstone, the very symbol of the tease. It caught on at a time when lad magazines like *Maxim* and *FHM,* with their photographs of panty-clad but never entirely nude women, took over... [and Brittany] Spears, the celebrity perhaps most associated with the thong, embraced the virgin/temptress paradox with cutting accuracy. Audiences could look, but they could never touch. The thong is an invitation, not a promise."[6]

For men in that period, hip hop influenced daily wear, from the urban cool of Sean "Diddy" Combs to the urban aggressive oversized pants, white T-shirts, and backward baseball cap with a bandana underneath look sported by Eminem. Business casual remained a part of the workplace. Button-downed, short-sleeved shirts cut square across the bottom and worn not tucked in (a modified version of the traditional Hawaiian shirt, minus the gaudy prints) became a foundation in the evolving business wear market. Neckties became more and more a thing of the past, especially wearing them to work. According to a Gallup Poll in October 2007, only six percent of men reported wearing a tie to work every day, compared with 10 percent in a poll in 2002.[7]

By mid-decade and later, the fashion world became more muddled as a variety of new styles grew out of the influences of the previous years, with inevitable backlashes. Many women, for example, resorted to the cleaner, more professional look of 1950s and 1960s fashion after growing weary of the scantier styles dominating the industry. Also jumbling the fashion marketplace are the traditional style categories that remain consistently popular, such as preppy clothes, 1980s styles, and the hippie, 1960s look. Perhaps the best aspect of American fashion, at least as it is worn by the hundreds of millions of regular people in the country, is that it is so fluid that one does not have to make wholesale modifications of a personal style often, if at all.

Celebrity Fashion

For celebrities, having one's own clothing line now seems to be part of the "platform" used to build the iconic brand that stars desire. What seemed like a crazy idea decades ago (for example, when actress Jaclyn Smith launched a clothing line with Kmart) appears like a natural part of the fashion world. In the 2000s, there are actually so many celebrities who have their own lines that a complete list would fill many pages.

In early 2007, for example, Madonna launched a clothing and accessory line, dubbed "M by Madonna," with Swedish retailer H&M, while Jennifer Lopez followed up her hit fragrance and Sweetface line with clothes aimed at juniors, called "justsweet." Other celebrities to launch clothing deals include Sarah Jessica Parker, Venus Williams, Mary-Kate and Ashley Olsen, Ashley Judd, and Victoria Beckham. David Wolfe, a creative director at the Doneger Group, said, "The consumer is desperate for some guidance to sort out the crowded retail landscape. Because the media tells us so much about celebrities, people have an idea of what their image means in terms of fashion, and if they can connect a name to an image and merchandise, it makes shopping so much easier."[8]

An important question as the decade draws to a close is whether or not the fashion industry can constantly sustain itself with new celebrities entering the fray. Some celebrities have track records to show the power of their brands, such as Combs, whose Sean John line made $450 million in 2002. Some experts estimate that the celebrity-licensed products market accounted for $3 billion in sales that year. Brian Dubin, head of WMA's East Coast commercial division, said, "Your client, whether they are an athlete or an actor or an actress, has intangible assets: a name, a reputation, a credibility, and an image. All of those attributes may be combined into something that could be made into a brand. When they are turned into a product or a service, then they become tangible assets."[9]

A NIP HERE . . . A TUCK THERE

In today's "expose all" society, America's obsession with youthful vigor transformed plastic surgery from a behind-closed-doors topic to one discussed on the front pages of celebrity tabloids and at family dinner tables. Not only were the uses and misuses of augmentation by celebrities from Michael Jackson and Cher to Meg Ryan and Ashley Simpson aired for public consumption, but a whole industry of reality television "makeover" shows attempted to change the way people looked (and viewed themselves) through extreme surgical measures.

In 2004, doctors performed approximately 9 million plastic surgery operations, up 25 percent from 7.4 million in 2000. Three years later, in 2007, the number nearly doubled to 16 million. While the vast majority of these surgeries take place under the care of trained professionals, a growing number are performed quickly, cheaply, and at great risk of complications. In 2004, for example, more than 4,000 teenagers less than 18 years old had breast implants, even though the FDA only approved the surgery for those over 18. Another 6,000 teens underwent liposuction, a dangerous and painful procedure for eliminating body fat.[10]

As the number of augmentation surgeries increased, two related results also skyrocketed—either those unhappy with the results and/or people enduring botched procedures. So many people fell into one or both of these categories that it spawned an entirely new segment of the industry: surgeons specializing in fixing errors or mistakes—called "undo-plasties" commonly.

The challenge for professional, trained plastic surgeons is that the business is largely unregulated. In many instances, any licensed physician can perform plastic surgery. In some states, dermatologists and even dentists can do nose jobs and other procedures. They may or may not have had much exposure to the field during their internships. Adding to the challenge is that many surgeries are taking place in a physician's office to cut down on costs that would incur from a hospital stay. Because most procedures are paid for up front, and most insurance companies don't cover them, there is little a patient can do in the event of a bad outcome.

Debra Dunn, a New York woman in her forties, grew despondent after two nose jobs wrecked her self image and left her feeling like she did not resemble herself. She avoided going out in public and had several additional procedures done in an attempt to regain her former nose. The additional work cost more than three times the initial amount. Dunn, however, is not alone in feeling regret over her plastic surgery. Celebrities from Courtney Love to Julio Iglesias publicly lamented their procedures. "Such dramatic surgeries can make people feel as though their permanent self is not their genuine self—at least on the outside," explained Kathy Kater, a St. Paul, Minnesota-based psychotherapist. "That can lead to a real feeling of internal discontent or even a very deep grief for a self who now seems to have disappeared."[11]

Fueled by Television

Like so much of pop culture in the 2000s, reality television contributed to the burgeoning popularity of cosmetic surgery, resulting in the mass marketing of the specialty. Soon, just like with fast food joints and drugstores, it seemed as if plastic surgeons stood at every street corner hocking their services. Television shows, such as *Dr. 90210, Extreme Makeover,* and *The Swan,* demystified augmentation, as well as the pain, suffering, and post-surgery swelling that goes hand-in-hand with such work.

As a result, the potential growth of the industry reduced the cost so that anyone who grew up dreaming of having a nose just like their favorite movie star or celebrity could go under the knife in search of their idealized perfection. In 2004, the average cost of the 10 most popular cosmetic surgery procedures (from liposuction to lip augmentation) cost about $4,000, making it affordable for just about anyone.

In 2003, ABC launched *Extreme Makeover,* a show that gave everyday people the opportunity to undergo a series of procedures to basically become a new person. While the program offered a variety of services, including counseling, personal trainers, and dieticians, the focus revolved around the "reveal" when the contestant debuted his or her new look to the gasps and cheers of family and friends. By 2005, the show averaged approximately seven million viewers each week. The success launched two high-profile knockoffs: Fox's *The Swan* and MTV's *I Want a Famous Face.*

The contestants after receiving plastic surgery makeovers on the "reality" television show *The Swan* (Fox Network) season one, May 24, 2004. 20th Century Fox/Photofest. ©Robert Voe.

Each show revolved around participants undergoing a variety of cosmetic procedures.

Critics of this programming pointed to the consequences such an emphasis on appearance would have on young females and others who may strive for perfect looks. Lou Gorfain, executive producer of *Extreme Makeover,* countered that his show gave people a new lease on life. "It's therapeutic. The lesson is empowerment," he said. "People have the power to change their appearance." The debate on altering one's life by changing one's outward appearance continues, though by the late 2000s, the emphasis on safer means does seem to be taking hold. ABC cancelled *Extreme Makeover* in May 2007.[12]

Botox: The Fountain of Youth?

Created in 1989 and approved by the FDA in 2002, Botox is a liquid made from purified botulism toxin that is injected into facial wrinkles. The toxin paralyzes the muscles, thus "smoothing out" wrinkles, and lasts approximately 120 days. After that, additional injections on a regular basis are necessary to keep up the illusion of wrinkle-free skin.

Even before FDA approval, doctors used Botox in cosmetic procedures. The American Society of Plastic Surgeons estimated that 800,000 injections took place in 2000, while the FDA believes that the number doubled by the next year. By 2004, about three million Botox procedures took place in the United States.[13] Two years later, Botox became the most popular cosmetic drug in the world.

Despite the number of references to Botox in popular culture, the typical customer is a man or woman from 50 to 65 years old, though the trend is picking up in younger age groups. The availability of the drug helps its popularity. Botox can be injected by nurse practitioners at a doctor's office, clinic, or spa.

Some cities are even holding Botox parties, such as the one held in Boise, Idaho. In late 2007, a spa threw the party at a local nightclub, handing out cosmetic products and the chance to buy the drug for use when visiting the facility, though no one underwent an actual injection at the bash. Boise cosmetic surgeon Michael R. Bailey sees the use of Botox spreading like wildfire. "Are we seeing more of the common American person having cosmetic surgery? Yes, I've done people who drive vans for a living, are housekeepers," he said. "Cosmetic surgery improves your quality of life. Nothing more, nothing less. It's not going to get anyone a new girlfriend or boyfriend. But it makes people feel better about themselves."[14]

Across the country in Manhattan, Smoothmed opened in early 2007, a Botox-on-the-go store offering injections to busy New Yorkers. Drs. Andrew I. Elkwood and Michael I. Rose teamed to launch the store near Bloomingdale's. Despite concerns from critics that offering Botox in the model of a convenience store or Starbucks is potentially dangerous, Rose and Elkwood see competitive pricing and location as a means to broaden the market. "Botox is the female yuppie heroin," Rose said. "It's like electricity: If you want to keep it on, you have to keep paying." The pair developed a computerized system for mapping each patient's face, thus ensuring that the exact procedure is duplicated on subsequent trips.[15]

Food

of the 2000s

Food plays an interesting and important role in popular culture. In the new millennium, the meaning of food shifts depending on one's perspective. Sometimes, food revolves around the chef's preparations, and at other times, it is about what foods to eat and which to avoid. The focus also turns to the presentation of food, whether it is handed through a car window or served on fancy, hand-painted dinnerware at a five-star restaurant. Sometimes, we are highly critical of food and food producers and marketers, and other times, we pay homage to the artistry and usefulness of food.

We give our foods many labels, which also reflect our feelings about eating and weight in general. Even our restaurant choices have specific names, from the "fast-casual" experience at Chipotle or Panera Bread to the "sit-down" chains of Chili's, Applebee's, and TGI Fridays. The hottest moniker in the late 2000s is "organic," though certainly few people could provide an exact definition. Aisles upon aisles at grocery stores across the nation feature organic foods, from non-bleached, whole wheat flour to free-trade coffee beans.

On an even more personal level, Americans are counting carbohydrates, good fats, bad fats, sugars, sugar substitutes, and a myriad of other factors that may or may not explain the healthiness of a particular food. We know to look at the list of ingredients and at the nutritional information chart, but the scientific terminology used to mask good things from bad makes it a guessing game at best.

One of the central roles of food in the 2000s is actually about eliminating bad foods and replacing them with healthier choices. The decade could be labeled "the diet decade," actually eclipsing the fitness-crazed 1980s as the real "me" era. Our popular culture reflects this dieting fascination. One needs to look no further than Jared the Subway Diet Guy to the multitude of low-carbohydrate diet books that litter the *New York Times* best seller list. The NBC series *Biggest Loser* pits average people in a race to lose weight, coached by a variety of fitness experts and dieticians. VH1 is preparing for its sixth season of *Celebrity Fit Club,* which follows the weight loss regiments of eight celebrities divided into two teams. Past participants include film actor Gary Busey, rapper BoneCrusher, 1980s pop singer Tiffany, and television actress Maureen McCormick. The 2008 version of Celebrity Fit Club will feature alumni of previous seasons and some newcomers, including *Saved by the Bell* actor Dustin Diamond, *Joanie Loves Chachi* and *Happy Days* actress Erin Moran, and *Family Ties* actress Tina Yothers.

The good health/healthy eating kick grabs the public's attention, but whether or not these fads actually help people get healthier is up for debate. One thing is for certain, though: in the late 2000s, more food producers, manufacturers, and restaurants are adopting healthier menu options. The leading indicator of the magnitude of this change is McDonalds, which began offering health conscious options after surviving the scathing documentary *Super Size Me,* in which an otherwise healthy man eats only from McDonald's menu for 30 days and winds up several steps closer to death's doorstep. On another front in the food wars, entire cities and states outlawed trans fat in restaurants.

Certainly, mass media performs a critical role in the nation's fixation on food. Cooking segments are a staple on local news shows and the big national, morning programs, such as NBC's *Today Show.* Food aficionados and chefs are a staple on cable television. Some celebrity cooks, such as Rachael Ray, transformed from minor figures in the celebrity world to megastars based on cooking-themed programs. They then build their early successes into media empires that span across multiple channels, all based on using themselves and their image as a brand name. The modern model for this kind of meteoric rise is Martha Stewart, who overcame many obstacles, including her much-publicized jail sentence for insider trading, to regain her position atop the heap of lifestyle mavens.

Newspapers devote a great deal of space to health issues, more or less covering every report and study that presents some bit of new information about our wellbeing. Without a doubt, the Internet's role in pushing health news, misinformation, gossip, and facts keeps the subject in front of interested viewers. Reality television provides consumers with even more food-related programming. The perfect example of this is the Food Network, owned and operated by E. W. Scripps Company, which also owns HGTV, DIY Network, and Great American Country. The Food Network reaches more than 90 million American households through cable and satellite television subscription packages.

"MCSHAKES" AND "MCGURGLES"

In early 2003, a healthy (6 feet, 2 inches tall and roughly 185 pounds), young documentary filmmaker named Morgan Spurlock began a journey that revolutionized the way the world viewed fast food. Over a 30-day period, he lived (and gorged) only on McDonald's food, living by the motto that if a restaurant employee offered to "super size" his meal, he would. Using the visual power of film, Spurlock, who directed, wrote, and starred in the documentary, revealed the total devastation that McDonald's could have on an otherwise fit

RISE OF THE ORGANIC FOOD INDUSTRY

The rise of organic foods, foods that are produced with little or no chemical influence or genetic alteration, occurred in response to two of the nation's leading health issues: cancer and obesity, but it also came about in pursuit of better-tasting food. As a backlash to previous decades' popularization of convenience foods that capitalized on cheap chemicals to preserve the shelf life of foods and kill plant-eating pests in farms, 1990s food manufacturers advertised their organic products as the natural solution to America's declining health and lifestyles. Many Americans—those who could afford to do so—jumped on the trend and ditched the bygone products of yesterday with unpronounceable ingredients and moved toward purchasing only those foods that were labeled whole, fresh, organic, and natural, evidence of which could be found on the "certified organic" sticker placed on every piece of produce in specialty stores. Longtime established supermarkets did not buy into the trend until later in the decade and into the 2000s, causing a slew of specialty super markets, such as Whole Foods Market, Fresh & Easy, Sunflower Market, Fresh Market, and Trader Joe's, to pop up all over bigger U.S. cities. Now, most "regular" grocery stores include a section specially designated for organic products. The cost of organic foods is often at least 50 percent higher than non-organic foods, leaving those with lighter pocket books, less access to specialty stores, or less interest to depend on more chemically enhanced foods. (Unless they grow their own organic fruits and vegetables, of course.)

person. The film naturally leads to questions regarding the restaurant chain's understanding of the health consequences of its menu, as well as the impact of placing profits above nutrition.

Super Size Me (tagline: "A Film of Epic Proportions") catalogs Spurlock's physical and mental transformation, which left him 24.5 pounds heavier and decidedly less healthy. He suffered from mood swings, liver damage, and sexual dysfunction during the month devoted to eating McDonald's meals. The film features lengthy interviews with his personal physician, who tells him that if he doesn't stop the fatty diet, he might die, and his girlfriend, who elaborates on his sexual failings. Spurlock's hair even starts to fall out.[1]

The visceral images alerted the audience to the considerable health risks associated with consuming fast food. Viewers not only saw Spurlock's body mass gain, but they also watched him throw up out the window of his vehicle after eating a Double Quarter Pounder with Cheese after complaining about the "McGurgles" and "McShakes" the food produced. At one point late in the experiment, Spurlock even experienced heart palpitations.

The movie opened at Robert Redford's Sundance Film Festival to widespread acclaim in May 2004 and eventually grossed more than $28 million, making it one of the top-selling documentaries of all time. Spurlock received a nomination for an Academy Award for Best Documentary but did not win.

Morgan Spurlock changed the way people viewed the fast food industry in his documentary *Super Size Me* (2004). Roadside Attractions/Photofest. ©Avi Gerver. Courtesy of Photofest.

Journalist Richard Schickel finds the true power of *Super Size Me* in its uncovering of the hypocrisies of the fast food industry. Spurlock discusses the mass seduction of children, lured into fast food chains by happy meals and playground equipment. But the deceit runs deeper.

"Government at every level is complicit," Schickel said. "The feds ship sloppy Joe makings to grateful school-lunch programs—it's the cheapest grub available. Other schools contract for pizza and sodas from corporate purveyors while cutting back on phys ed classes. And everyone starts getting fatter younger."[2]

HEALTHY FAST FOOD

In an attempt to combat potential lawsuits and increasingly negative media coverage, fast food chains began offering healthier alternatives in the 2000s. Restaurants such as McDonalds, Burger King, and KFC started offering smaller portions and foods lower in fat and calories to overcome potential public relations nightmares and consumer backlash. Still, the effort might be too little, too late. The $105 billion fast food industry is at a crossroads, and some innovative chains are attempting to create a new kind of fast food for the future.

Since 2000, several restaurants introduced organic fast food, many with catchy, nutrition-friendly sounding names, such as Healthy Bites Grill and HeartWise Express. The Tampa-based EVOS, for example, uses hormone-free chicken and hormone and antibiotic-free free range beef and serves Airfries with a fat content 50 to 70 percent lower than deep-fried ones. O'Naturals opened its doors in 2000 and expects to have hundreds of locations nationwide by 2012.

Many industry observers simply do not think that McDonald's and its brethren can overcome their greasy fast food pasts. Gary Hirshberg, Chairman and CEO of Stonyfield Farm Yogurt, said that, within a decade, the fast-growing fast food chains in the nation will be more focused on organic and natural foods.

The Fast Food Response

McDonald's openly criticized Spurlock and *Super Size Me.* The company complained that anyone eating a 5,000-calorie-a-day diet without exercise would gain weight. The restaurant also claimed that its typical customer did not eat there as frequently as Spurlock or gorge themselves when they did. As the film's popularity increased, McDonald's did remove the "super size" option from the menu. However, the company claimed that it did so independent of the documentary.

In 2006, McDonald's introduced wrap sandwiches, featuring chicken wrapped in tortillas, and other healthier food options. Although most criticism the company receives is for its red meat, McDonald's currently sells as much chicken as beef, which is 150 percent more than in 2002.[3]

Notwithstanding *Super Size Me,* McDonald's global sales increased 6.7 percent in 2007 (3.3% in the United States) and 6.3 percent in 2006. Revenues also reached a record high of $22.8 billion. Some 56 million customers visit the fast food restaurant each day.[4] Political commentator George Will calls McDonald's new menu items part of the "Snack Wrap Era," where fast food restaurants responded to "consumer appetites for something to eat between meals and with one hand on the steering wheel."[5]

OBESITY

In the United States, some two-thirds of American adults are considered overweight, while one-third fall into the obese category. In addition to the psychological and self-image challenges being overweight and obesity magnifies, the condition carries serious health risks, such as an elevated risk of heart disease, diabetes, and even an increase in some types of cancer. Some experts have labeled the nation's obesity challenge an epidemic, particularly when one considers the public and private health costs associated with treating overweight or obese people and the overwhelming majority of people who fall into one of the categories.

Obesity and overweight are not new problems, but they are becoming more problematic. Since 1988, the number of overweight individuals has significantly increased. In 2003 to 2004, 67 percent of adults aged 20 to 74 fell into the category. The obesity rate, however, has remained relatively consistent since the early 1960s, comprising about 32 to 34 percent of the adult population (30% of men and 34% of women). These figures alone prove that the multitudes of diet fads simply have not made a real impact on the overweight and the obese.

The numbers of children who fall into these categories are more shocking and frightening. From 2003 to 2004, about 17–19 percent of children (aged 6 to 11) and adolescents (12 to 19 years old) fell into the overweight category. Most disheartening, the number of overweight children two to five years old doubled from 7 to 14 percent between 1988 and 2004.[6]

Food Portions, Cravings, and Bingeing

One of the primary culprits in America's losing battle with the bulge is the sheer size of foods today. Visit a grocery checkout lane and face the wall of "king size" candy bars, or go to Sam's Club or Costco, and every food item available is its own monster portion. All the fast food chains have some version of a larger portion menu, with Wendy's even naming its foods "Biggie." Lisa Young, a New York University nutrition researcher, dubs this phenomenon "portion creep," and it leads to overweight and obesity. The simple fact of the matter, as Young said, is that people eat whatever is in front of them. The more a person gets his hands on, the more he will stuff it down. So what if it's the restaurant size tortilla chips accompanied by a vat of salsa. One can see the wheels turning: "We're Americans; we eat everything on our plates." This is the land of the endless all-you-can-eat buffet from coast-to-coast. "Americans have grown proportionally to increased portion sizes," Young said.[7]

Young found that portion sizes increased over time and that many food items doubled or tripled, leading to an exorbitant caloric intake. For example, in 1955, McDonald's sold one size of fries, which weighed 2.4 ounces. Today's large fry order is 6 ounces. The first Hershey's milk chocolate candy bar offered a mere 0.6 ounce in 1908 and 1 ounce in 1960. Today, a person can buy an entire bag or individual bars ranging from 2.6 ounces to 8 ounces.

Restaurants are central to the portion challenge as well. The public assumes that the portions at Applebee's or Macaroni Grill are healthy, but restaurants actually want to please customers, and the larger sizes give people a better feeling about the establishment. Young explained that consumers should not automatically think that the restaurants are watching their portion sizes for them. The slab of meat that arrives at one's table may represent three or more properly sized portions all in one.

When it comes to drinking soda, portion is out of control. In 1973, 7-Eleven convenience stores introduced 12-ounce and 20-ounce soda drinks. By 1978, it added the 32-ounce Big Gulp, and 10 years later, the 64-ounce Double Gulp (equivalent to half a gallon). In 2003, 7-Eleven eliminated its 16-ounce size and offered soda ranging from 20 ounces to 64 ounces. The chilling fact is that all these calories add up. While people may not worry as much about what they drink (because they don't feel it the same way they do a greasy burger or fries), the calories, sugar, and caffeine in soda, energy drinks, fancy coffee drinks, and sweetened teas is costing them their health. University of North Carolina researcher Barry Popkin found that soda, milk, juice, beer, and other beverages accounted for 21 percent of the calories people consumed, up from 16 percent in the 1970s. Add that to the fact that Popkin's study took place before the real explosion of energy drinks, which often contain twice the caffeine and calories of other drinks.[8]

Both men and women are affected by food cravings and binge eating. A groundbreaking 2007 study by the McLean Psychiatric Hospital, an affiliate of Harvard, disclosed that Binge Eating Disorder (BED) is America's most common eating disorder, more common than the more publicized disorders of bulimia and anorexia combined. The study defined bingeing as uncontrolled eating at least twice a week for at least six months. The primary feeling one gets during a bingeing spree is the total loss of control over eating. Some scientists go as far as labeling the craving/bingeing issue an epidemic. According to Roger Gould, MD, a professor at the University of California, Los Angeles, some five million women (the majority are women) suffer from clinical bingeing disorder, while another 15 million experience moderate bingeing levels.[9]

Health.com conducted a survey of 1,000 women to learn more about the reasons for bingeing. Some 26 percent claimed boredom and loneliness triggered them; 20 percent felt overwhelmed; 17 percent cited depression, anger, or anxiety; 15 percent were tempted by a favorite food; and stress caused 10 percent to binge. Experts say that at the heart of bingeing is emotion, whether it is insecurity, self-doubt, or anger. "Food helps change our conscious experience. We go into a bubble. Everything feels alright, and nothing can get to us," Gould said. In many cases, however, food becomes like a medication, but it soon wears off, or another part of the emotion picks up, forcing the person to start the cycle all over again. Under these conditions, bingeing is more like a food addiction. One 36-year old Health reader said, "I eat when I'm bored or lonely as a way to 'make up' for what I'm missing. Then, I get mad at myself for doing so, which causes me to eat more, which causes me to get mad again."[10]

A challenge for binge eaters is that temptation and fulfillment are all around. America caters to those who eat too much for whatever reason by providing oversized portions, easily accessible junk foods, and no real rationale for not living a sedentary lifestyle. Even people who are actively dieting find reasons to binge. Experts say that this deprivation can actually lead to cravings and binge episodes that sabotage the diet altogether. When Health.com asked its readers what foods they craved during a binge, 36 percent said anything they could get their hands on; 24 percent said sweets; 11 percent said chips; and 9 percent said fast food and chocolate.[11]

DIET AMERICA: HIGH PROTEIN, LOW CARBS, LITTLE COMMITMENT

Americans are addicted the idea of dieting, but they are fat and getting bigger each year. Best seller lists overflow with diet or psychological/self image-related books that focus on getting people to lose weight, but few actually work. Even if a person experiences some short-term weight loss, none of the diet fads really help keep the weight off for the long-term. Until a pill is invented that magically turns obese people into waifs and flab into washboard abs, dieting will remain a central focus in the home and for American popular culture.

The American Institute for Cancer Research reports that about 25 percent of men and 40 percent of women are actively dieting. Jana Klauer, MD, a weight-reduction specialist in New York City, acknowledges that some diets are necessary and potentially life-saving. Diets help in this regard. "There's a psychological benefit as well as a physical one to losing weight in the early stages. People are encouraged because they see improvements in their appearances, or because they feel lighter and maybe are more comfortable exercising," she said. The downside is that dieting is just the first step. She explained, "To keep the weight off, you need a healthy eating style."[12]

The perennial favorite diets of most Americans are both low-carb lifestyles: Atkins and the South Beach Diet. Dr. Robert Atkins introduced his high-protein, low-carb diet in 1972. The reintroduction of his findings, *Dr. Atkins' New Diet Revolution,* topped the best seller lists and set off a nationwide dieting craze. Observers estimate that at one point, about 17 percent of the total American population followed Atkins's weight loss prescription. The controversial plan includes eliminating vegetables and fruit from one's diet and replacing them with high-protein substitutes.[13] Arthur Agatston, MD, introduced the South Beach Diet, another low-carbohydrate plan, but one that allows for certain fruits and vegetables, sustained over three phases. The South Beach Diet mainly advises that dieters eliminate processed carbs, saturated fats, hydrogenated oils, and trans fats.[14]

The fat epidemic stretches far and wide, cutting across age groups, demographics, and ethnicity. About the only dieting "facts" that experts agree on is that obesity and overweight is costing the nation dearly and the culprit is "bad" fats, such as trans fats that make up the bulk of processed foods. In 2002, after issuing a report that estimated that obesity costs the United States some $117 billion annually and is linked to 67 percent of deaths, President Bush launched a national dieting initiative with the simple message: eat right and exercise daily.[15]

The enemy in the war on fats is trans fat, sometimes called "Franken-fats" because they are laboratory created. In most foods, trans fats appear on the ingredients label as hydrogenated or partially hydrogenated oils. The sad fact is that these oils are everywhere and almost impossible to avoid. Trans fats, according to journalist Gail Gorman, "are created artificially by heating liquid vegetable oil in the presence of metal catalysts and hydrogen." Trans fats are popular among food manufacturers because they "extend the shelf life of most of the processed foods we consume ... not only in almost all commercial products that contain fats but also in almost all fast foods, which are usually cooked in partially hydrogenated oil."[16]

Companies solve many challenges with trans fats, such as providing a longer shelf life, reducing transportation costs, and eliminating waste byproducts. Despite the scientific studies that show the general harm of all these trans fats in today's foods, the government has not intervened in a dramatic way to eliminate them. Some observers would blame this on the food industry lobbyists and lawyers who help elect politicians with large campaign contributions.

DRINK NATION

At any point prior to the mid-1990s, coffee served as a setting, usually as a way to ask someone out on an informal date ("Would you like to get a cup of coffee?"). Since then, however, coffee has taken center stage, a point of cultural reference, in addition to its brazen, more aggressive tone ("Let's go get coffee"). Consumer goods take on this kind of iconic quality whenever they become a kind of cultural wallpaper—such a part of everyday life that they are no longer really discernable unless one takes a deep look. Over the last couple decades, coffee has assumed this role in American society. No one blinks twice at coffee or the daily trips to refill or fill up, whether it is at a local diner, national chain, convenience store, or communal workplace pot.

Interestingly, coffee is just the chief beverage in America's national obsession with drinks. Even humble water grew in pop culture prestige as bottled water became a must-have accessory, first for movie stars and celebrities, before moving on to soccer moms and just about everyone else. In the ongoing soft drink wars, Coke and Pepsi continue to battle, but their lineups have added virtually every other kind of drink one can imagine, hedging that if one brand falters, then another will rise up to take its place. On college campuses, a plethora of high caffeine, additive-laden energy drinks, such as Red Bull and Vault, are highly popular, despite health warnings about excessive caffeine intake.

Coffee Culture

Only in America could a consumer's decision regarding where to buy a cup of coffee be turned into a discussion of political beliefs, yet that distinction serves as a marker in the new millennium. According to writer Conor Clarke, a 2005 poll found that those who leaned left were "twice as likely to go to the world music-playing, fair trade-embracing, Seattle-based coffee chain [Starbucks] as they were to patronize Dunkin' Donuts—a well-known peddler of red-state values."[17] For example, Clarke points to Fox political television show host Bill O'Reilly, who told *Newsweek* that he will not go in a Starbucks, preferring to purchase his cup of Joe in mom-and-pop coffee shops.

Regardless of politics, the argument that one's choice for a caffeine fix matters in defining identity indicates the importance people place on coffee in our collective consciousness. The simple fact is that coffee matters in America, not only what kind a person prefers, but where it is bought and how the bean is grown and imported. Coffee and coffeehouses play a central role in mass media, from the multi-Emmy winning show *Frasier* (1993–2004) set in the coffee-rich confines of Seattle to Bob Dylan selling CDs on the Starbucks music label, which the chain decided to dump in early 2008.

Starbucks is the coffeehouse most people imagine when they think about coffee. However, the coffee industry itself is so large that many others have entered into the high-end market, from McDonald's (dubbed McCafés) to Dunkin' Donuts. Examining the shelves of the local grocery store, one finds that Folgers, Maxwell House, and the in-store labels have upgraded the flavors they offer, offering more bold and exotic blends.

The combination of increased competition and the idea that the company moved too far away from its core business of selling coffee has hurt Starbucks at the end of the decade. In 2007, company stock dropped 42.8 percent and another 14.7 percent through the beginning of 2008. The dramatic fall, both financially and in reputation, forced founder Howard Schultz to return to Starbucks as CEO. Since returning to the job he left eight years ago, Schultz is focusing on returning the company to its roots: selling coffee that tastes good and being more customer-friendly. The challenge is getting consumers interested in high-priced coffee when they face a disastrous economy, including massive real estate foreclosures and potential job losses. Suddenly, a $4 cup of coffee seems a bit excessive, no matter how fancy the creation.

Schultz said, "I think when you get large and very successful, you have to balance creativity and entrepreneurship with process and strategy. We got a little out of balance, and we weren't as creative and entrepreneurial as we were when we were smaller. And what I'm trying to do is infuse the company with the kind of spirit and innovation [we had] when we were younger."[18] Company research, according to Schultz, reveals that people are simply not going to Starbucks (or a competitor) as frequently as they did prior to the economic turmoil the nation faces. To counter this challenge, Schultz said, Starbucks must show consumers that it is an "affordable luxury" through "surprise and delight."[19] Whether the public buys into this philosophy will define how the corporation fares into the next decade.

Liquid Energy

PepsiCo made headlines when it purchased the rights for its Amp energy drink to become one of the main sponsors of Dale Earnhardt Jr. Nascar's most popular driver, Earnhardt made a high-profile move to a new team owned by Rick Hendricks for the 2008 season and switched to number 88. Amp, the fifth-leading drink in the $10 billion energy drink market, launched a national marketing campaign starring the driver, which included a slew of new products and collector items. Amp and the National Guard (the other co-sponsor) were rumored to have spent $95 million a year to sign Earnhardt. Included in the deal were the naming rights for the fall race (the Amp Energy 500) at Talladega, a legendary track where Earnhardt has won multiple times.[20]

When initially introduced to the marketplace, energy drinks were targeted at college students and teens. There were some concerns about the consequences of high caffeine intake, but that seems to have leveled off over time. As the industry matures and become more competitive, efforts are underway to link them to a much-needed power boost for busy people. The larger impact is that the formerly-fringe status of these drinks has basically disappeared, while at the same time, reordered the carbonated-beverage industry. "In convenience stores, the only people going to the fountain and pulling a Coke are old people," said Mark Hall, creator of Monster Energy and president of Hansen Beverage Co. "If we've been able to do anything, it's to make soft drinks cool for young people."[21]

Monster leads the energy drink market with a 27 percent market share, while Red Bull stands second, Rock Star is third, and Full Throttle (owned by Coca-Cola) is fourth.[22] Created by Hall, Monster launched in spite of Red Bull's then-dominant lead in the market. The upstart overtook the giant through successful marketing and branding tactics, including the name of the product itself, placing it in 16-ounce cans, versus Red Bull's 8.3 ounces, and including the aggressive claw marks on the label. Next, going after the young male demographic, Hall sponsored extreme athletes from the X Games, mostly in motorized sports. A $25,000 initial investment has grown into a $15 million athlete payroll.[23]

FOOD HIGHLIGHTS OF THE 2000S

2000 Krispy Kreme Doughnuts holds an initial public offering of its stock.

2002 To celebrate the 100th anniversary of its ever-popular animal crackers, Nabisco uses online and mail-in consumer voting to select a new animal to add to boxes of Barnum's Animals. The koala handily beats out the penguin (48% to 33%), with the cobra making a dismal showing (only 9%).

2003 Mini Melts Inc. uses liquid nitrogen to flash freeze ice cream and sells it in the form of small, popcorn-like globules.

2003 In Washington, D.C., menus in several congressional cafeterias change "French fries" to "freedom fries" after France refuses to support the war in Iraq. Makers of French's Mustard promptly issue a press release affirming their patriotism and noting that their brand is based on a family name.

2005 Kraft Foods rolls out an array of South Beach Diet-branded products tied in to the bestselling South Beach Diet created by Miami cardiologist Arthur Agatston.

2005 Produce distributors begin employing a laser tattooing process to label their fruits and vegetables. Industry workers and consumers alike hope the technology may soon do away with tiny adhesive labels. After a particularly grueling session of peeling stickers, 76-year-old Jean Lemeaux of Clarksville, Texas, complained, "I got up the next morning and looked in the mirror, and there were two of them up in my hair," (*New York Times*, July 19, 2005).

2007 In *The Sushi Economy,* Sasha Issenberg examines the sushi craze that began in America in the early 1970s and predicts that China will be the cuisine's next big frontier.

2008 The city of Needles, California, continues a $10 million restoration of El Garces, part of the Fred Harvey chain of hotel restaurants that extended along the Santa Fe Railroad to provide a "civilized" dining experience to rail passengers. El Garces was considered the "crown jewel" of the entire Harvey House chain, and in addition to excellent food, boasted linen tablecloths, distinctive china, and fresh flowers daily.

FAST-CASUAL DINING

With budgets tightening in the early years of the new millennium, busy Americans turned away from traditional fast food items (burger, fries, and a shake) to embrace a new way of combining quickness with value: fast-casual chains. In the late 2000s, with budgets once again shrinking in a post-*Super Size Me* world, restaurants such as Panera Bread, Chipotle Mexican Grill, and Quiznos Sub Sandwich Shop are once again offering an alternative to McDonald's, Wendy's, and Burger King. Less money to spend on dining excursions also means trouble for sit-down restaurants, such as Chili's, Applebee's, and Outback Steakhouse. The fast-casual establishments capitalized on a family-friendly environment (many offering "kids eat free" nights), health consciousness, and price to gain an even stronger foothold in an ever-tightening economy.

According to Darren Tristano, executive vice president of Technomic Information Services, a food industry consulting firm, the immediate drop is seen at major chain restaurants, which face slowing sales growth, down to 4.2 percent in 2007, after hitting 6 percent a year earlier. As a result, chains across the industry are rethinking their menus and attempting to drive home the value at a low cost message. One option is for restaurants to introduce dollar and/or value menus. "This is something all chains should consider if they want to stay competitive. Price is king right now," Tristano said.[24]

Another aspect of the fast-casual experience that customers demand is dubbed "food with integrity," by Janelle Barlow, coauthor of *Branded Customer Service.* According to Barlow, "food with integrity speaks to the trust that a customer places in the consistency of the food" and offers consumers a snack or meal that looks, tastes, smells, feels, and delivers the same experience again and again. Mimicking Bill Clinton's "It's the economy, stupid" phrase, Barlow claims, "It's the food, stupid." She explained, "When most urban dwellers have hundreds of fast-casual restaurants within a five-mile radius of them, standing out from the crowd is the first imperative not only for success, but for survival."[25]

Named the top fast-casual dining establishment in 2007 by *Fast Casual* magazine, Denver-based Chipotle exemplifies the qualities that consumers want from this kind of dining service: better ingredients and affordable food. Since opening in 1993, Chipotle now operates 670 stores all owned and operated by its corporation, unlike the franchise-based management of most fast food chains. Chief executive officer Steve Ells credits the company's growth and success to focusing on high quality food, healthful ingredients, and consistent, same-store growth, including technology and equipment upgrades.[26]

In 2007, for example, Chipotle stopped serving cheese linked to cows treated with recombinant bovine growth hormone (rBGH) and became the top U.S. restaurant seller of naturally raised meats. In addition, the company opened 88 new locations, while recording a 10.9 percent same-store sales increase through third quarter 2007. "We believe that these results are evidence that people appreciate our continued focus on improving the customer experience in our restaurants," Ells said. "We believe we are the only restaurant committed to making better tasting, socially responsible gourmet food available and affordable so that everybody can eat better... this sets us apart."[27]

IS OUR FOOD SAFE?

In February 2008, the USDA initiated the largest meat recall in its history, demanding that some 143 million pounds of beef from Chino, California, meatpacking company Hallmark Meat Packing and distributor Westland Meat be pulled from the shelves. The total represented two years' worth of production.

Ironically, the governmental agency demanded that the meat be recalled even though officials believed that the product posed little threat to consumers and had been eaten by countless people. The USDA deemed the move necessary after a videotape of employees at Hallmark revealed that they allowed sick and improperly inspected animals to be slaughtered.[28]

Like in a good corporate espionage movie, an operative for the Humane Society of America posed as a slaughterhouse worker to shoot the video, which showed sick cows (referred to as "Downer Cows") being prodded with electric shocks and lifted via forklift to be taken off to slaughter. He then turned the tape over to the Humane Society in fall 2007.

The danger with meat recalls is that some of the product may have already made its way into people's bellies by the time the action is taken. For example, about 37 million pounds of meat went to school lunch and public nutrition plans. Ron Vogel, a USDA official, explained, "Almost all of this product is likely to have been consumed."[29] Subsequently, 150 school districts and a couple of fast-food restaurant chains banned Westland beef from their kitchens.

The consequences of tainted food may seem remote, but historically, many outbreaks have led to illness and death. In September 2007, the USDA recalled 21.7 million pounds of Topps Meat ground beef. However, that occurred after about 30 people got sick from *E. Coli* bacteria in the meat. Another threat on the minds of consumers is mad cow disease (bovine spongiform encephalopathy, BSE), which can lead to fatalities.

FOOD AFICIONADOS

The explosion of cable television channels devoted to cooking and food intensified the already growing cooking addiction taking place on local, regional, and national daytime talk shows for decades. Julia Child may have brought cooking to the masses, but today's crop of celebrity chefs expands the notion to an entirely new plane. Much of this expansion is based on the advent of technology, such as new cable channels, the Internet, and greater multimedia opportunities.

In today's media-saturated world, a celebrity chef such as Emeril Lagasse not only has his own shows on the Food Network, but has coined catchphrases ("BAM!" and "kick it up a notch") that extend him as a brand name. He appears as himself in Crest toothpaste commercials, so excited by the product's minty-fresh flavor that he exclaims, "BAM!" Lagasse also has a string of 11 Emeril restaurants, does other celebrity appearances, and he has a slew of books, cookware products, and food products.

In early 2008, Martha Stewart Living Omnimedia purchased much of the Lagasse empire for $45 million in cash and $5 million in stock. The merger eliminates one of Stewart's primary competitors, acquiring the rights to Lagasse's TV shows, Web site, licensed products, and cookbooks. In return, Lagasse benefits from Stewart's deep ties to Kmart, Costco, and Macy's. Stewart explained, "His tastes are very different from mine, as is his food, and I think that's good. Being complementary and different is better than being competitive."[30]

Rachael Ray

Rachael Ray's rise from the grocery store cooking classes to international celebrity is the stuff of legend and a virtual embodiment of the American Dream. She was raised in upstate New York in a family with a vast cooking experience, exposing her to the industry in a variety of food service roles. After moving to New York City, she launched a successful career as a gourmet food manager and buyer. Returning to upstate New York, Ray taught cooking classes, hoping that they would lead to increased sales at the gourmet market where she worked as chef. The popularity of the classes led to weekly appearances on a CBS station in the Albany, New York, area. The success of the segments featuring 30-minute meals and a subsequent cookbook launched her next endeavor: the Food Network.[31]

Ray hosted several shows on the Food Network, including her signature programs: *30 Minute Meals* and *$40 A Day*. With the success of her cooking show, which led to a 2005 Daytime Emmy Award for Outstanding Service Show and a nomination for Outstanding Service Show Host, she launched a series of cookbooks that filled the best seller lists, all built around the 30-minute theme.[32]

One of Ray's greatest successes occurred when she launched the magazine *Every Day with Rachael Ray* in October 2005. In short order, the magazine sold out a total print run in excess of 1 million copies, including 20,000 at Barnes & Noble, which set a record for the chain. Ray possesses what one publishing insider calls "consumer connectivity," and it is this ability to understand what people want from her that drives the cooking guru's accomplishments. Explaining her vision of the magazine, Ray said, "The title, to me, means getting more out of every day. Even though you have to work, even though we're all busy, even though we don't have a ton of time, we're not sacrificing the time we do have. That time we're going to have fun with, we're going to make these wonderful meals; we're going to take fun little weekend jaunts."[33]

On September 18, 2006, Ray debuted an hour-long syndicated show *Rachael Ray,* produced by CBS and Oprah Winfrey's Harpo Productions. Combining elements of a talk show with her typical everyday cook mentality, the show garnered seven Daytime Emmy nominations in its first year on the air.

The Internet is credited with helping many celebrities gain an audience, but the medium also provides an avenue for criticism that did not exist prior to the mid-1990s. Like Martha Stewart before her, Ray is roundly denounced—and in some cases, even hated—by a legion of critics who have taken to the Web with sites such as the "I Hate Rachael Ray" blog and the "Rachael Ray Sucks Community," which garnered mentions in *The New York Times, USA Today, The Boston Globe,* and *Slate.* Even a 2005 *Newsweek* article about her couldn't help but stir up the anti-Rachael soup.

Many critics find fault with Ray's general over-exposed celebrity, pitching everything from Ritz crackers to GE appliances. She even posed for centerfold-like pinups for the notorious FHM magazine, much criticized for its objectification of women. Ray's reply was, "I think it is kinda cool for someone who is goofy, and a cook, just a normal person, to be thought of in that way."[34]

Ray also gets denounced for adopting what is called an obviously fake "aw shucks" persona to explain her rise from local cooking workshop leader to international celebrity. Journalist Florence King wrote that Ray's "Recent consecration by Pope Oprah has resulted in so much overnight world-class fame that her face is on everything but the cover of *Tool & Die Quarterly.* TV is now all Rachael, all the time. There's her cooking show, her eating show where she samples restaurants, her own talk show, guest appearances on other people's talk shows, books, book tours, and so many tie-ins and endorsements that she's all over the commercials too." She describes the anti-Ray foes on the Internet as "ready to do battle against

Perky food show host turned domestic diva Rachael Ray, host of *30 Minute Meals* (2002). Food Network/Photofest. ©Food Network. Courtesy of Photofest.

Martha Stewart, popular culture's reigning domestic doyen. NBC/Photofest. ©NBC. Courtesy of Photofest.

the cult of mediocre celebrity."[35] The tie to Oprah Winfrey launched Ray's solo career in ways that accentuated what she achieved on the Food Network, but the push to the next level of stardom required Oprah's anointed touch.

Martha Stewart

Already in her late sixties, Martha Stewart shows few signs of slowing down. By the dawn of the new millennium, she already had numerous bestselling books, a television show, and many endorsement and design deals, in addition to a publicly-traded company that bore her name. At the time, it truly seemed like Martha's World. In 2004, however, Stewart's world took a nasty turn when she was convicted of insider trading and sentenced to a five-month jail term and five months of home confinement, what one journalist called "a spectacular public disgrace."[36]

Her status as a public figure brought out pundits for and against her. Some argued that the Securities and Exchange Commission made Stewart a scapegoat for the corporate wrongdoing going on at the time. Others believed she should pay the price for her criminal activity, just like anyone else who would have done the same. Regardless of one's stand on Stewart's conviction and imprisonment, almost nobody thought she would be able to regain her status upon release. For her part, Stewart had no doubts, announcing from the courthouse steps after being sentenced, "I will be back."[37]

After being released from the federal prison in West Virginia and serving her house arrest at her 153-acre home in Bedford, New York, Stewart immediately plotted her comeback. Her return to Martha Stewart Living Omnimedia helped the stock price level off after years of falling in her absence. Stewart's main priority, though, was regaining her place on television. She launched a new daily program, *The Martha Stewart Show,* which earned five Emmy nominations in its first year on the air, and hosted a Martha version of Donald Trump's *The Apprentice* on NBC. The show failed to capture the public's imagination, but it did place Stewart back in the limelight. Next, she worked to jumpstart *Martha Stewart Living* magazine and began a radio channel on Sirius satellite radio.[38]

In a career that spans decades and includes everything from designing homes to pillow sets and bath towels, Stewart is not cowering from the competition from the likes of Ray and others grasping for her throne. In 2006, she summed up Ray's daily talk show for *Business Week,* stating, "Her daily show is much less appealing than her Food Network show. It's very disjointed and loud, and I don't learn anything." This was made at a time when Ray's show averaged 2.3 million viewers, or about 46 percent more than Stewart's, according to Nielsen Media Research.[39]

By all accounts, Stewart has been on a tear since leaving prison. Her renewed vigor cuts across media platforms to include a Martha version of the Internet, several magazines, and many merchandising projects. Among the many endorsement deals are a line of 1,400 branded plates, linens, and home accessories for Macy's; a 350-color paint line at Lowe's; and the continued association with Kmart. Although the retailer is struggling, Stewart is guaranteed $60 million in the deal, regardless of the amount of product she pushes.[40]

Music

of the 2000s

From Thomas Edison's invention of the wax cylinder phonograph in 1877 to the latest Web-based innovations, technology is at the heart of the music industry. Technological innovation and change go so completely hand-in-hand that one can chart the advance over time from records and phonographs, to MP3s. Each subsequent invention builds on its predecessor and revolutionizes music performance and consumer response. The intersection of performance (the music itself) and consumer response (people listening and/or purchasing) defines the music business.

In the new millennium, divergent forces compete with each album, new video, or ring tone: media convergence and the white noise produced in a culture that churns nonstop. The idea behind convergence is that the lines between media channels no longer exist. For instance, where does viral marketing for a new band begin and how does that intersect with traditional forms of advertising?

In the music business, convergence provides greater opportunities for artists and management to compete in the battle for consumers across all mediums. However, the sheer volume of messages produced in a converged society also leads to information overload, or a seemingly endless cloud of marketing, advertising, sales, and informational touch points demanding something from consumers—their attention, money, memory, or actions. Therefore, every artist in a converged culture operates in a setting that enables constant interaction with consumers across numerous media outlets, but the idea that everyone is always adding to the system creates a crisis situation in which people cannot decipher or distinguish the messages.

The search for a footing in the slippery, converged world really defines what popular culture is all about in the new millennium. For most artists and the corporate marketing efforts supporting them, convergence leads to a blockbuster mentality, or an all-out program designed to create huge release day sales that will then lead to greater exposure, thus greasing the marketing gears that keep the pop culture industry churning.

In 2006, Epic Records built such a program around "A Public Affair," the new single from pop singer and actress Jessica Simpson, who is a virtual case study on how to build a celebrity in the new millennium. Already a well-known singer, Simpson developed into a megastar based on her highly-publicized MTV reality television show with then-husband Nick Lachey, which portrayed her as less-than-intelligent, but somewhat normal. She rode that momentum into starring roles in several films, including the remake of

The Dukes of Hazzard, playing Daisy Duke. Epic produced two videos for the song, one a big budget typical video, while the second was pieced together from fan clips. The fan angle also led Epic to provide customizable versions of the song on Yahoo! Music, which it then followed with a poster that provided a text message for people to sample the song. Epic marketing executive Lee Stimmel explained the need for such a comprehensive program, saying, "It's hard to break a record these days—it takes a lot more avenues of exposure."[1]

Pulling the fans into the creative process and then giving them a chance to interact with their submissions plays on the general narcissism of Americans today. With outlets like YouTube, people know that they can create their own version of their favorite songs, so record companies and artists attempt to bring them into the process earlier through such contests.

A constant yearning for fame—almost a feeling of being entitled to it—gripped the nation in this decade. As a result, young people would do just about anything to have their moments in the public eye. For a tiny minority, the payoff takes place, but the vast majority either never get their bit of fame, or they wash up on the wreckage that is a natural byproduct of the reality industry. For example, *American Idol* has ruled the television airwaves for most of the decade, despite being little more than a televised talent show. The payoff is that a "normal" person will survive the process and achieve the American dream. However, even the runaway success of the series cannot overshadow the impact of technology on two primary fronts: the widespread theft of digital music and Apple's iPod.

Another curious phenomenon that points to the intersection of music and technology is the out-of-this-world success of interactive rock video games, such as Guitar Hero and Rock Band. Since being released in 2005, Guitar Hero I and II grossed more than $360 million. The video games, perhaps fueled by the idea that the player gets to morph into a celebrity for a couple of minutes, sparked a renewed interest in classic rock by a younger generation that does not instinctively know The Sex Pistols, ZZ Top, or the Ramones.[2]

APPLE'S IPOD

A Google search for "iPod" in early 2008 returned 319 million hits. While a search engine is hardly a scientific indicator, the figure certainly reveals how deeply the iPod rests in our national psyche. Not only has the term "iPod" become virtually synonymous with "digital music player," but the device has also led to an entire industry of other products to support it, from Bose headphones to combination speaker/base systems to turn an iPod into a complete home entertainment unit. The iPod also influenced styles of dress, necessitating that designers and manufacturers come up with clothes that enable one to easily carry it.

In 2006, the iPod celebrated its fifth anniversary, and in many regards, the rebirth of Apple as one of the world's great consumer goods companies. Steve Levy, author of a book about the device, *The Perfect Thing,* practically gushed, "The iPod nano was so beautiful that it seemed to have dropped down from some vastly advanced alien civilization. It had the breathtaking compactness of a lustrous Oriental artifact." In addition to changing the way people interact with their personal music library, the iPod also presented music lovers a way to download music legally, a far cry from the days of Napster.[3]

On October 23, 2001, Apple chief executive Steve Jobs launched the first iPod, saying "With iPod, listening to music will never be the same again." Even Jobs, however, could not have realized the impact the music player would have on Apple. When he made the announcement, shares sold at around $9 per share. In April 2008, the stock stands at $147 a share, an astronomical increase in such a short time frame. Furthermore, though Microsoft and SanDisk launched their own MP3 players to compete, Apple dominates with more than 70 percent of the market.[4]

DOWNLOADING MUSIC: FREE AND OTHERWISE

The rise of the Web in the mid- to late 1990s led to the popularity of the MP3, a new kind of compressed music file condensed enough that it could be swapped online. Although compressing the file reduced the sound quality, manageability trumped aesthetics. For the most part, only true aficionados could tell the difference between an MP3 file and an audio CD track. Depending on a person's computer modem speed, an MP3 could be downloaded in minutes or as quickly as a couple seconds.

The ability to trade music over the Internet had a mushrooming effect culturally. First, users essentially violated copyright rules when swapping music online. Then, as is typical of a capitalist system, innovation runs with money-making potential. A number of file-sharing companies formed, the most infamous being Shawn Fanning's Napster, which became synonymous with free downloading. Soon, however, consumers seemed to believe that the ease of downloading music from Internet sites somehow made the music free.

In the early days of file-sharing, most users stored the music on their computer hard drives, either using their computers as a sound system or burning the files onto CDs to play on the go. Later, with the rise of portable MP3 players, most notably the iPod, people uploaded the files to the device directly.

Despite rampant file-sharing and the music industry's weak initial reaction, the courts eventually caught up with Napster. In 2001, the U.S. Supreme Court ruled against the company, declaring free music swapping illegal and in violation of music copyrights. Although the music industry shut down Napster as an illegal file-sharing site, others such as KaZaA and LimeWire used a new innovation, called peer-to-peer (P2P) networking, to continue the practice in which a decentralized file-swapping service enables users to download from computer to computer without housing music or video at a central location, thus making the files harder to track to their original source.

CD Sales Plummet

Despite the challenges the music industry faced from online piracy, full-length CD/album sales reached 785.1 million units in 2000. Optimists chalked the figure up to listeners basically previewing songs and bands online and then purchasing CDs afterward. At that time, the music business seemed like it would weather the online theft storm, though sales dropped to 762.8 million in 2001.

Nevertheless, as the decade progressed, industry watchers realized the complete devastation music piracy was inflicting on the business. The pessimistic viewpoint—that piracy would kill album sales because consumers would not pay for what they could download for free—came to fruition.

In 2002, total album sales fell to 681.4 million, more than 100 million less than two years earlier. Three years later, the number dropped to 618.7 million. By 2007, CD sales dropped to 500.5 million units, a 36 percent plummet over the course of the decade. The 2007 figure stands as the lowest sales number since Nielsen began estimating the data in 1993.

While music piracy decimated the CD business, the ubiquitous MP3 player led to burgeoning sales of digital singles. Overall music sales, including singles and digital songs, jumped 14 percent to 1.4 billion units from 2006 to 2007. Though these numbers seem encouraging on the surface, most of the new transactions were digital tracks. In addition, the total sales year-over-year figure was less than the previous year, down from 19 percent. Even digital track sales fell from a 65 percent increase in 2006 to 45 percent in 2007.

The primary challenge for the industry, according to Kenneth Kraus, a music attorney in Nashville, is that "we've lost a whole generation of kids" who grew up illegally downloading music,

Josh Groban performs at the 2006 American Music Awards. ABC/Photofest. ©Craig Sjodin. Courtesy of Photofest.

Total Album Sales, 2000–2007

Year	Total (millions)
2000	785.1
2001	762.8
2002	681.4
2003	656.3
2004	666.7
2005	618.7
2006	588.1
2007	500.5

Source: Nielsen SoundScan

HIT SONGS OF THE 2000s

"Beautiful Day"—U2 (2000)

"Bootylicious"—Destiny's Child (2001)

"Landslide"—Dixie Chicks (2002)

"In da Club"—50 Cent (2003)

"Hey Ya!"—OutKast (2003)

"This Love"—Maroon 5 (2004)

"Hollaback Girl"—Gwen Stefani (2005)

"Hips Don't Lie"—Shakira featuring Wyclef Jean (2006)

"Umbrella"—Rihanna featuring Jay-Z (2007)

"Bleeding Love"—Leona Lewis (2008)

and CD sales may never regain the losses from earlier in the decade.[5]

Perhaps revealing the depths of the battle the music industry faces regarding online piracy, the top two selling albums in 2007 were not by hip hop, rock, or rap artists. Instead of rap impresario Kanye West or timeless rocker Bruce Springsteen at the top of the charts, adult contemporary singer Josh Groban charted the bestselling CD in 2007, reaching 3.7 million units. The second ranked album was the soundtrack to the Disney Channel TV movie *High School Musical 2,* which sold 3 million units. In contrast, Usher's album *Confessions* sold about 8 million copies in 2004.

In 2007, CD sales also fell in every major music genre, from hip hop (30%) to country (16%). Only three rock groups sold more than half a million CDs: Fall Out Boy, the White Stripes, and Paramore. With the music labels in a free fall, retailers who sell CDs turned to alternatives to get into the fan's wallet, including selling more DVDs and computer games, such as the incredibly popular Guitar Hero. Classic rock icons The Eagles circumvented the labels altogether, selling their album *Long Road Out of Eden* directly via Wal-Mart. The gamble paid off, with the band charting the third highest selling CD of the year, totaling 2.6 million copies.[6] (See "Total Album Sales, 2000–2007.")

AMERICAN IDOL

Determining whether *American Idol* is more a music or a television topic would be a difficult (if not impossible) task. The show has changed both industries. From a music viewpoint, a slew of new pop singers (ironically, not just the winners) have emerged based on the show's popularity. The biggest names include first season victor, Kelly Clarkson, second season runner-up Clay Aiken, and fourth season winner Carrie Underwood. Other performers have launched surprisingly strong careers based on their *Idol* work, while others who were considered sure-fire successes have fizzled after the show's glaring lights went dim.

The successes and failures of *Idol* contestants shows the difficulty of breaking big in the music business, even when handed the keys to one of the industry's strongest franchises. For example, Taylor Hicks did not parlay his fifth season victory into a major debut, stalling at the lower rungs of the sales list. His album sold more than 700,000 copies, a respectable figure for a new artist, but not so much after considering that the final episode drew more than 33 million viewers. However, Chris Daughtry used his experience as a springboard, selling more than 3 million records and reaching number one on *Billboard.* In fact, some of the singers who scored big on their first albums after victory, found rougher roads on their follow-up efforts.

Some *Idol* singers find themselves on independent labels after the season ends. For some, it is a risky move, but it has an upside if fans respond. Elliott Yamin, who scored a third-place finish, signed with new label Hickory Records. His debut has sold more than 300,000 copies. "I don't have any gimmicks. I wanted to be genuine, I wanted to cross over," Yamin said. "I wanted to make a singer's type of record, and it is selling. People are responding to it."[7]

NEW ORLEANS SURVIVES KATRINA

Hurricane Katrina destroyed much of the Ninth Ward district in New Orleans. Among those losing their homes stood legendary rock and roll pioneer Fats Domino, who had lived there for nearly 50 years. The news of his rescue gave music fans something to cheer about, after initial reports indicated that he went missing as the flood ravaged the region.

All over New Orleans, similar rescues took place as other areas slipped deeper and deeper underwater. The levees holding back Lake Pontchartrain gave way, obliterating much of the city's musical heritage. Thousands of small bars, nightclubs, and music venues were devastated in the flood, what some observers believed to be New Orleans's true gift to music history. In addition, countless New Orleans musicians, from band leaders to recording session players, lost their homes and livelihoods in Katrina's wake.

As the musicians of New Orleans regrouped, others put together benefit shows to help the residents of the Big Easy. A giant show put together by MTV, VH1, and CMT, featured the Rolling Stones, Paul McCartney, and many others. BET offered its own relief effort, led by Russell Simmons, Jay-Z, Chris Rock, and Stevie Wonder. Master P, a New Orleans resident and founder of No Limit Records, discussed the ruin: "All of the houses are gone—everything people worked for and sacrificed for. Most of the stuff washed away."[8]

HOW OTHERS SEE US

Hip Hop Nation: Brazil

By the early 2000s, American hip hop culture was established as the default soundtrack and style of the world's youth—so much so that the government of Brazil set up a federal program to teach it to the nation's teens.

Launched in 2003 by Minister of Culture (and popular singer/songwriter) Gilberto Gil, the Culture Points program provided grant money to community groups that aimed to spread the hip hop ethic to Brazil's young people, giving them a voice and a vocabulary for self-expression. With Culture Points funding, artists taught teens the finer points of graffiti art, music producers supplied recording equipment and engineering expertise to nascent rappers, choreographers helped break-dancers learn new moves, and small publishers printed books of rap and street poetry.

The program made some Brazilians uncomfortable. American rappers who portrayed themselves as gangsters or as ostentations fashion hounds were scorned by music fans in Brazil, who tended to prefer political or "message" artists like Public Enemy. The idea of using taxpayer money to encourage a culture of lawlessness and bling was disturbing. Gil, however, sought to explain that, for large portions of the Brazilian population, hip hop represented "the only connection to the larger world." Inclusive programs like Culture Points would "keep young people from being diverted to criminality or consigned to social isolation." Within a few years, the government's seed money (and its tax breaks, too) had encouraged major corporations to underwrite rap concerts, break-dancing performances, and even hip hop recordings.

RAP AND HIP HOP

A 2007 survey conducted by the Pew Research Center revealed that a significant number of Americans view rap and hip hop as a bad influence on society, citing offensive language, violence, and negative portrayals of women. Some 64 percent of whites and 61 percent of blacks think hip hop is a bad influence, while 74 percent of whites and 71 percent of blacks say the same about rap music. Among Hispanics, 59 percent perceive hip hop negatively, while 48 percent view rap similarly.[9]

When examined by gender, there are significant differences. The report shows that, "Among whites, men are much more likely than women to say hip hop and rap have a bad influence on society. Among blacks, however, the gender relationship tilts in the opposite direction—women are more likely than men to say these forms of music are having a bad influence."[10]

Blacks (45%) and Hispanics (40%) are far more likely to listen to hip hop than whites (23%). Those who listen to hip hop often or sometimes tend to be younger; some 79 percent of blacks ages 18 to 34 listen to hip hop, while 64 percent listen to rap. However, young whites also listen to hip hop (56%) and rap (47%).

In 2007, radio shock personality Don Imus served as an unlikely catalyst for public outrage against rap lyrics by calling the Rutgers women's basketball team a derogatory phrase used for prostitutes and linking the phrase to race. The media frenzy against Imus transformed into a more general demand that rap and hip hop musicians clean up their work. Bill Cosby, Oprah Winfrey, and the Reverend Al Sharpton led the demand for change. They aimed their outrage at the ostentatious displays of wealth in hip hop videos, the objectification of women in the songs and videos, and the virtual nonstop use of the word "nigger" in their lyrics.[11]

Despite hip hop's negative image among the general population, young people are avid fans and consumers. Both album and singles charts are constantly filled with the work of rap, hip hop, and other entertainers that fall somewhere in between. It would not be a great stretch to say that hip hop and rap have defined the music of the new millennium so much, in fact, that many now claim these music genres are now the mainstream.

Rap artists consistently top the charts. For example, 50 Cent (a.k.a. Curtis Jackson) scored 2005's top selling CD and had four songs in the top ten on *Billboard's* pop chart—the first artist to do so since the Beatles.

Hip hop's centrality to the nation's popular culture is seen in an exhibit held at the Smithsonian Institute in 2008, featuring portraits of hip hop stars, such as LL Cool J, as well as music. Artist Kehinde Wiley painted the four original pieces in the exhibit in 2005 as part of a VH1 tribute program. Assistant Curator of Photographs at the Smithsonian Frank

Top-selling Rap Artists, 2006

Artist	Album
1. T.I.	King
2. Lil Wayne	Tha Carter II
3. Eminem	Curtain Call: The Hits
4. Ludacris	Release Therapy
5. The Notorious B.I.G.	Duets: The Final Chapter
6. Chamillionaire	The Sound of Revenge
7. Yung Joc	New Joc City
8. Rick Ross	Port of Miami
9. Juelz Santana	What the Game's Been Missing!
10. Busta Rhymes	The Big Bang

Sean Combs (P. Diddy). Courtesy of Photofest.

Goodyear said that the mainstream has attempted to push hip hop from the center; however, "There's nothing marginal about hip hop at all. Hip hop is at the center of our culture. It's the most influential cultural phenomenon that extends beyond the music."[12]

Yet, while hip hop maintains its cultural importance, actual album sales have fallen off over the past several years. Rock music continues to lead in market share, with country music placing second. In 2006, rap and hip hop slipped to third place, accounting for 11.4 percent of the market at about 131 million.[13] Certainly, when discussing rap and hip hop, once must acknowledge that the cultural influence surpasses the actual popularity in terms of sales, indicating that hip hop is a lifestyle, perhaps to an even greater extent than it is a music genre.

Hip hop's influence crosses into other areas that show the genre's increasing cultural importance. Sean "P. Diddy" Combs, for example, is an internationally-acclaimed fashion designer, with his Sean John clothing line that extends him as a brand name. At the same time, Combs continues to produce other young stars and perform. He is also a budding actor, not only starring in the movies *Made* and *Monster's Ball,* but also appearing in the 2004 Broadway version of *A Raisin in the Sun,* which followed with a televised adaptation in 2008. Combs even owns a movie production company and restaurants. (See "Top-Selling Rap Artists, 2006.")

Top Ten Classic Rock Ring Tones, 2006

Artist	Song
1. AC/DC	"Back in Black"
2. Lynyrd Skynyrd	"Sweet Home Alabama"
3. Ozzy Osbourne	"Crazy Train"
4. Pink Floyd	"Wish You Were Here"
5. Journey	"Don't Stop Believin'"
6. Def Leppard	"Pour Some Sugar on Me"
7. Steppenwolf	"Born to Be Wild"
8. AC/DC	"Hells Bells"
9. Van Morrison	"Brown Eyed Girl"
10. AC/DC	"Thunderstruck"

Source: T-Mobile.

Music

PERFORMERS

Timeless Rockers

Although pop music grabs a great deal of attention, particularly from those under the age of 25, rock and roll remains a lynchpin of American culture. However, at the same time, the music industry is moving toward a blockbuster mentality in which musicians are judged by their hits, with much less emphasis on their careers. In an era of downloads and ringtones, the traditional idea of a rock star may soon disappear.

The notion that the rock star is at an end really proves the greatness of timeless rockers such as the Rolling Stones, Neil Young, Aerosmith, and Bob Dylan. The subsequent generation has also proved its longevity, with artists like Madonna, Prince, U2, and Bruce Springsteen still making groundbreaking and popular records. For example, Springsteen's 2007 album *Magic* debuted at number one, a great feat for an icon who released his first album before many of today's music listeners were even born. The Rolling Stones' *A Bigger Bang* tour, which lasted from 2005 to 2007, became the biggest tour in music history, grossing $558 million. (See "Top Ten Classic Rock Ring Tones, 2006.")

Bob Dylan

Bob Dylan remains a prolific singer/songwriter and iconic figure in popular culture. In the new millennium, he has released a series of groundbreaking CDs, including "*Love and Theft*" (2001) and *Modern Times* (2006). His reissues have been just as prolific, including *The Essential Bob Dylan* (2000), *Live 1975* (2002), *Live 1964* (2004), *No Direction Home* (2005), *The Best of Bob Dylan* (2005), and *Dylan* (2007). In 2000, he won both a Golden Globe for Best Original Song and an Academy Award for Best Song for "Things Have Changed," which appeared on the *Wonder Boys* soundtrack.

In addition, as he approaches 70 years old, Dylan has taken a more public role than any time in the recent past, doing advertisements for Cadillac, Victoria's Secret, and Apple. He also hosts a highly acclaimed radio show (*Theme Time Radio Hour*) on XM Satellite Radio. Dylan published *Chronicles: Volume One* in late 2004, the first of

Bob Dylan continued to redefine himself as a performer in the new millennium. Columbia/Photofest. ©Columbia Records. Courtesy of Photofest.

a rumored three-volume memoir. Dealing with the early years the singer spent in New York City and flashes of later years, he took a nonlinear path through his career that enticed readers. The book spent many weeks atop best seller lists, both nationally and regionally, and got nominated for a National Book Award.

In 2003, the film *Masked & Anonymous,* which Dylan co-wrote (using a pseudonym) with television writer/producer Larry Charles made its way into theaters, starring Luke Wilson, John Goodman, Mickey Rourke, and a host of well-known actors. Most thrilling for "Dylanologists" was that Dylan himself starred as former rock legend Jack Fate, who is bailed out of jail to perform a one-act benefit concert in a society spiraling out of control. People either loved or hated the film. In typical Dylan fashion, the movie either confounded viewers or just presented another of the musician's unique views of a nation at the end of its rope.

Dylan served as the subject of two other projects in the new millennium. Famed director Martin Scorsese released a two-part documentary, *No Direction Home,* in 2005. The film, which featured taped interviews with the singer himself, focused on his early rise to fame through his near-fatal motorcycle accident in 1966. In 2007, the film *I'm Not There,* written and produced by Todd Haynes, used six different actors to represent various parts of Dylan's life, including Marcus Carl, a 13-year-old African American actor and Academy Award-winning actress Cate Blanchett, who won widespread praise for portraying Dylan's mid-1960s "mod" phase. The daring film earned critical acclaim and spots as one of the year's 10 best films at *The Washington Post, Premiere, The Village Voice,* and many others.

U2

Two titans of the music business came together in 2004 when U2 and Apple teamed to launch an ad campaign for the iPod. That project, which Apple dubbed the fusion of "Art, Technology & Commerce," cemented Apple's place at the center of the digital music revolution and helped keep the Irish rock band in the forefront of consumers' minds. The early iPod U2 Special Edition digital player held up to 5,000 songs and had unique features, such as a red click wheel and signatures of each member of U2 engraved on the device. For Bono, the new player took him back to the early days of listening to music with headphones via a bulky cassette player. "We want our audience to have a more intimate online relationship with the band, and Apple can help us do that," he said. "With iPod and iTunes, Apple has created a crossroads of art, commerce and technology which feels good for both musicians and fans."[14]

In addition to the stylistic innovations, the U2 iPod launched as the band prepared to release its new album *How to Dismantle an Atomic Bomb* and gave fans access to its first single, "Vertigo," through the iTunes Music Store. Even more directly, however, U2 starred in a television commercial for the player and the new song, silhouetting images of band members against a red background.[15]

The ad received heavy rotation on network and cable television, ensuring that the player and the band's new CD would be successful. The partnership between the corporation and U2 may have seemed pretty typical in terms of using celebrities and music to sell goods and services, but the key attribute of the U2-Apple campaign served to further legitimize digital music, downloaded legally, and the iPod's centrality in the music industry. Before long, brokering deals with Apple became more important than virtually every other retail outlet.

Although it is hard to believe, given their enduring popularity, U2 formed more than 30 years ago. The four-man group (Bono, The Edge, Larry Mullen Jr., and Adam Clayton) rose to prominence in the early 1980s as a wave of European groups broke big in the United States. Back then, U2's sound was alternative rock, emerging as an underground favorite of college students. In 1987, however, U2 released *The Joshua Tree,* a landmark album that sold millions of copies, produced number one hit singles, and propelled the band into the upper echelon of rock stardom. They sold out arenas across the country, and U2 videos played continuously on MTV. In 2007, celebrating the 20-year anniversary of the groundbreaking album, the band re-released *The Joshua Tree,* digitally remastered, along with a DVD from the accompanying tour and footage of the recording process.

In 2000, U2 released *All That You Can't Leave Behind,* a monumental CD that earned the group seven Grammy Awards, including Record of the Year. The album reflected the spirit of the early decade, examining ideas about individual and collective contributions to the greater good and the enduring love of family. "It's an album about essence, about the casting away of the nonessential things and realizing what those essential things are: family, friendship," Bono explained, reflecting on the album in 2005. "I wanted to make a really raw record about the things you just cannot live without." Interestingly, Bono had a health scare during the recording of the album, a possible throat cancer that remained secret at the time. His facing mortality may help explain the lyrical content involving family/friendship bonds.[16]

U2 followed up the success early in the decade with *How to Dismantle an Atomic Bomb.* Accolades followed, and the band's fame rose on the back of the Apple partnership and Bono's increasingly public work as a peace ambassador, particularly for African nations and AIDS victims in those regions and worldwide. In 2005, the singer raised some $15 billion by working with government leaders from around the world, including George W. Bush. Bono's work in Africa and for eradicating AIDS even began rumors about him possibly winning a Nobel Peace Prize—high praise for a singer who has taken on a much higher calling by using his fame for good in an era where there is little benefit in doing so. (See "Top Concert Tours in 2007.")

Top Concert Tours in 2007

Year	Total (millions)
The Police	$133.2
Justin Timberlake	$70.6
Van Halen	$56.7
Rod Stewart	$49
Genesis	$47.6
Bon Jovi	$41.4
Dave Matthews Band	$41.1
Billy Joel	$39.1
Roger Waters	$38.3
Bruce Springsteen and the E Street Band	$38.2

Source: Pollstar.

Music

MUSIC BUSINESS GURUS

Rick Rubin

Rarely do music producers become as famous as the stars they help shape. Rick Rubin is an exception. Sporting his distinct shaggy hair and long, unruly beard, Rubin led the comeback efforts of Johnny Cash and Neil Diamond and infused new life into groups such as the Red Hot Chili Peppers and the Dixie Chicks. As a record company executive, Rubin signed Public Enemy and the Black Crowes.[17]

Initially, Rubin gained fame as a rap and hip hop producer, working with LL Cool J and Run-DMC. In the late 1980s, he went from underground prodigy to mainstream star after shaping the Beastie Boys' debut *Licensed to Ill,* which sold 9 million copies and virtually launched rap music commercially. He parlayed that success into a series of high-profile ventures with other artists, though it was his work with legendary country star Cash that showed the full power of his artistic vision. "I don't think I have a sound. I think it's more about capturing the most direct sound of the artist—what they're supposed to sound like," Rubin said. "I would say my production tends to be sparse, and it tends to be minimal."[18]

In 2007, Time magazine called Rubin "the most widely accomplished record producer of the past 20 years," which he accomplishes with "teddy-bear sensitivity that defies every stereotype of his profession."[19] That year, he had albums nominated for a Grammy in rock, country, and pop/soul categories. At least part of Rubin's magic with artists is getting them to realize their artistry again, as writers, vocalists, or whatever else he can pull from their souls. "I try to get them in the mindset that they're not writing music for an album," he said. "They're writing music because they're writers and that's what they do."[20]

Sports

and Leisure of the 2000s

American popular culture is tied closely to the way people play and relax, whether that is attending a Pittsburgh Steelers football game or watching the X Games on a 46-inch high definition flat screen television. Leisure time encompasses a broad sweep of sporting events and other fun activities designed to take us outside the drudgery represented by the work world and often harsh realities of everyday life. However, leisure activity also includes sitting around the house, watching a sporting event or movie on one's home theater system.

In the new millennium, social media is a new popular leisure activity. Social media Web sites give users a way to broadcast news and information about themselves that appeals to the general narcissism of young people (though a surprisingly large number of adults over the age of 30 participate as well).

From a popular culture perspective, many of the traditional sports have been eclipsed by activities scoffed at in earlier times. If measured by spectators and television ratings, NASCAR, for example, is certainly more popular than any pro sport outside football. Professional wrestling remains highly popular. More and more viewers are interested in the no-holds-barred world of ultimate fighting, surpassing boxing on most people's radars.

The rising popularity of video games, bolstered by the confluence of technology and culture, has significant consequences. Many young people would much rather spend their days playing games online or via the hottest video console in front of the television or computer screen than go outside to play or engage in a sport. Although critics bemoan video games for contributing to childhood obesity and diverting young people's attention away from schoolwork, the gaming industry is big business. Journalist Laura M. Holson reported on the growth of video games versus movies based on 2004 revenue totals: "Video games are among the fastest-growing, most profitable businesses in the entertainment world. In the United States, domestic sales of video games and consoles generated $10 billion in revenue, compared with movie ticket sales of $9.4 billion."[1]

Cultural transformations are also changing the way people look at the sports they play. Golf, for instance, is losing players at an alarming rate, considering that Tiger Woods is the dominant professional athlete in the world, both on the course and as a celebrity spokesperson. The fact is that many younger, married men just will not spend four to six hours away from their families on a weekend morning like their fathers did. As a result, even Woods's incredible fame is not enough to attract new players to the sport.

The unfortunate fact is that actual physical activity during leisure time is declining and being replaced by time spent in front of the computer or television. For example, a poll conducted in early 2008 revealed that watching television served as the favorite leisure activity for women, with some 23 percent identifying it as such, followed by 16 percent who said they enjoyed using the Internet, with 10 percent saying that they liked to play free Web-based games. Only 4 percent claimed that playing sports or exercising was their favorite leisure activity. No other individual physical activity made the top 10 list.[2]

In the 11- to 17-year-old demographic, only 10 percent claimed they enjoyed playing sports or exercising. They preferred either using the Web or talking on the phone, both at 19 percent. In contrast, women aged 55 to 64 most enjoy watching television (22%) or playing free Web-based games (18%). According to one observer, "More women than men say TV is their favorite leisure activity—almost one-third more. And TV scores as the favorite activity for women, while with men, the Internet edged it out for first place."[3]

The declining amount of physical activity (and the many health challenges that come with being overweight and obesity) may harm the nation (see Food of the 2000s), but forcing people off the couch is not realistic, even if it makes sense. One thing is certain: the Web-based technology that people love to use has a downside; Pandora's Box has been opened, and the Internet has been unleashed.

SPORTS

In the summer of 2007, with ESPN cameras rolling, 32-year-old professional skateboarder Jake Brown fell 45 feet while performing at the X Games in Los Angeles. In the famous "Big Air" competition, competitors took turns dazzling the crowd and television viewers with aerial stunts on the 62-foot-tall, 293-foot-long Mega Ramp. After the fall, spectators and other skateboarders in the games thought Brown had died, but he walked off the ramp with assistance several minutes after the disaster. He wound up in an L.A. hospital with a liver injury, two sprained wrists, a bruised lung, whiplash, and a concussion. Luckily, Brown survived his brush with death. In fact, he became more famous after the fall, particularly as the video spread via the Internet.[4]

This kind of willingness to push boundaries is a central tenet of the way people approach leisure time in the new millennium—at least among those who perform their leisure activities by getting up off the couch. What one might have assumed to be the limits are now just another goal for fitness-crazed people, whether than means doing yoga in a studio with the heat cranked up to 110 degrees or running sub six minute miles at 40 years old. However, the unfortunate truth in America is that the fitness buffs are a vocal minority among an otherwise sedentary population.

Between 1999 and 2004, a study concluded that summer leisure time in the United States increased from five hours a day to six-and-a-half hours daily. However, this extra time is being eaten up primarily by computers, television, and video games. Also taking up a great deal of leisure time is food (either eating out, cooking, or baking) and "me time" (e.g., reading, religion, or pets). Gardening, for example, jumped 60 percent from 2000 to 2004. The greatest growth over that span, however, was watching a movie at home.[5]

Since the late 1990s, some 20 million people stopped being active, many of them aging Baby Boomers. Those older than 45 who still do fitness programs, are more likely to be women than men (81% versus 66%). Baby Boomers often turn to swimming as a primary form of exercise, while people under 45 years old prefer running and jogging. About 80 percent of those considered active live in the Western United States, where a healthier lifestyle is a given more than a task.[6]

NASCAR Speeds to the Top

Everything about NASCAR is larger than life. The drivers buzz along super speedways at speeds eclipsing 200 miles per hour with just inches between them. The stands at the massive racetracks shoot up several hundred feet, seemingly straight into the air. And, just for good measure, nearly every inch of the cars, drivers, and fan areas are covered with corporate logos from the most important brand names in the world. Of course, when racing at high speeds, what seems like a

NASCAR race day at Martinsville Speedway, Martinsville, Virginia. From the film *Nascar 3D: The IMAX Experience* (2004). Warner Bros./Photofest. ©Warner Bros. Courtesy of Photofest.

simple fender bender can turn into a multi-car pile up with billowing smoke, fire, and near fistfights among drivers and fans alike. That is the beauty of NASCAR—its fans are as passionate about the sport and the teams they root for as the teams themselves.

Cost to Run a NASCAR Nextel Cup Team

Feature	Cost (millions)
Engine Program	\$3.5–\$4
Cars (15–18 per team)	\$2–\$3 (\$150,000 per car)
Tires	\$1
Travel	\$1.5
Team Salaries	\$3–\$4
Driver Compensation (salary, winnings, bonuses)	\$2–\$12
Total	\$13–\$23

The overwhelming fan support pays dividends for NASCAR. In terms of dedicated spectators and corporate sponsorships, no other sports come close to professional football and stock car racing. The NFL and NASCAR have a stranglehold on American culture, grabbling headlines whether in season or out. Racecar drivers such as Dale Earnhardt Jr., Jeff Gordon, Tony Stewart, and Jimmie Johnson are celebrities, growing larger than the sport itself.

Gordon, for example, made headlines nearly as often during 2007 for the birth of his daughter as for his racing. In the past, the popular four-time champion also appeared on both the *Regis and Kelly* morning show and *Saturday Night Live.* On November 29, 2007, more than 100,000 fans watched two-time Nextel Cup champion Johnson take his car on a victory lap around Times Square in New York City. The driver then made appearances on several national morning news programs.

If there is a chink in racing's armor, it is that the sport's tremendous growth over the last decade makes it difficult to keep up the pace. Regardless of its popularity, at some point, the numbers will start to level out, particularly with every other sport in the world gunning for its audience. Television ratings, historically one of stock car racing's tried and true strengths, are leveling off, dropping 12 percent from 2005 to 2007. This figure is in line with other major professional sports, but it is still a sign of potential pitfalls ahead.

Another challenge NASCAR faces is that the cost of participation is escalating, whether it is for the top-tier teams or lesser contenders. Top organizations like Hendrick Motorsports or Joe Gibbs Racing have large facilities filled with engineers, software specialists, and technicians that cut into operating margins. Estimates show that the cost of fielding a team can eclipse $20 million. Granted, corporate money offsets team cost, but given the dicey national economy, some companies are cutting back.

Primary team sponsorship, by the likes of Office Depot, Mountain Dew, or DuPont costs about $15 to $20 million. A secondary sponsorship, which may mean a small decal on a top driver's car, is $2 to $4 million. Teams are not the only ones to gain in the relationship, though. A marketing firm estimated that each sponsor received $5.2 billion in television exposure during the 2007 season. Larry DeGaris, president of Sponsorship Research & Strategy, explained: "There's a lot of competition for sponsors right now. Teams are going to be selling against each other."[7]

NASCAR's coffers certainly are not empty, even though some aspects of the business have stagnated. Nextel signed a $700 million, 10-year deal in 2004 for the primary naming rights, and NASCAR-licensed merchandise sales topped $2 billion each year from 2004 to 2006.

A survey of stockcar fans revealed that 71 percent "almost always" or "frequently" choose products or services because of their NASCAR affiliation. So, a Jimmie Johnson fan chooses Lowe's over Home Depot, while a Jeff Gordon supporter will drink Pepsi versus Coke. In more than any other professional sport, NASCAR fans buy the products endorsed by their favorite teams.[8] (See "Cost to Run a NASCAR Nextel Team.")

Football

Football's inherent violence carries weight on and off the field. Between end zones, the game is full of career-threatening traumas, from multiple concussions to ruptured tendons and knee ligaments. After the game has ended, the violent nature of the game presents itself in the situations some players find themselves, from college stars getting into fights outside bars to professionals encountering gunplay. These kinds of stories dominate the news headlines and serve as fodder for radio and television talk shows. When a big name star is confronted with such challenges, the question becomes whether the game can survive or will fans turn their backs after reaching a breaking point.

In 2007, the NFL came under fire for the dog-fighting allegations and indictment of Michael Vick, the star quarterback of the Atlanta Falcons. A search of the three-time Pro Bowl player's property in rural Virginia uncovered more than 50 pit bulls and the graves of dogs killed in an extensive dog-fighting ring sponsored by Vick. After a lengthy trial and protests by animal rights organizations nationwide, the judge sentenced Vick to 23 months in prison. Although he could be released early, the former star also faces state dog-fighting charges that could result in additional jail time.[9]

Pundits wondered whether the NFL could withstand having one of its highest-paid and most prolific players jailed for such cruel charges. However, after the verdict and the authorities carted Vick off to jail, the media machine turned to other stories. Vick became old news, as stale as a week-old donut. The 2007 and 2008 football seasons went off without a hitch, though when Atlanta Falcons games were televised nationally, one could see many number 7 jerseys in honor of Vick. Commentators made the obligatory remark or two, but they basically avoided the topic, and the game continued. Despite the Vick verdict, football remains the most popular American sport. By the time the 2007 season ended, there were fewer and fewer mentions of Vick.

Football, however, continues to thrive. Millions of people participate in fantasy football leagues across the nation, while betting action in Las Vegas picks up dramatically during the season, culminating in the college bowl games and Super Bowl. When the Pittsburgh Steelers beat the Seattle Seahawks in the 2006 Super Bowl, people bet $94.5 million in Vegas, a record at the time. Experts estimated that the latest game between the New York Giants and New England Patriots topped $100 million. While it is impossible to pinpoint, pro football is thought to generate about $10 billion in gambling, both legally and illegally. In contrast, the NFL makes about $7 billion in revenues each year.[10]

Basketball: The LeBron James Era

A handful of years ago, on the playgrounds in and around Cleveland, whispers circulated about a young kid in nearby Akron who might be the next Michael Jordan. He possessed otherworldly athletic ability with attributes that cannot be taught: size, speed, vision, and a natural feel for the game. The budding superstar's name was LeBron James. When sketchy rumors turned into hard facts, the story seemed too typically rags-to-riches to be true, like the creation of the perfect athlete by some shoe company for marketing purposes. He helped lead his team to the state championship—despite a tumultuous home life and being raised by a single mother in Akron's toughest ghetto.

Two events changed James's young life forever: appearing on the cover of *Sports Illustrated* in early 2002 (when only a junior in high school) christened "The Chosen One," and, seven months later, the nationally televised ESPN2 game against perennial high school champion Oak Hill Academy. The *SI* magazine article and flurry of copycat stories that followed put him on the national radar screen. The hype machine included another cover story, this time for *ESPN The Magazine*, revealing a much different James dealing with his newfound fame and the subsequent avalanche of publicity. As the region's largest newspaper, The *Cleveland Plain Dealer* took over the James watch, virtually covering his every move, including "The James Journal," a compendium of all things LeBron.

The attention of the print media placed James on a pedestal. Before the rise of the Internet and countless new media outlets (from talk radio shows to cable television programming), this degree of buildup would have been reserved for a mere handful of proven superstars. However, in the twenty-first century, when many celebrities are famous for little more than being famous, a high school superstar can grab the interest of the world. And yet, despite all the hype, relatively few people had actually seen James play basketball.

That all changed, however, in late 2002 when ESPN2 televised the Saint Vincent-Saint Mary match-up with Oak Hill Academy. The network then followed the first broadcast with an early 2003 game against Mater Dei High School at the famed Pauley Pavilion on UCLA's campus, a basketball temple. Befitting a legend in the making, James responded to the limelight in both games, thus cementing his position as the next big thing in the sports world.

Against Oak Hill, a crowd of more than 11,500 spectators packed Cleveland State University's Convocation Center, some paying more than $100 for courtside seats. Also in the mix were dozens of NBA scouts and officials and even a couple players from the Cleveland Browns, all out to judge the skills of the 17-year-old high school phenomenon. More importantly, for the television network, the game drew a 1.97 rating, which equates to 1.67 million homes tuning into the high school basketball contest. James's star power made the telecast ESPN2's highest rated program in the two years since it covered the death of NASCAR legend Dale Earnhardt.

The final box score revealed SVSM's utter dominance over the former number one high school basketball team in America, 65–45. James lit it up for 31 points, 13 rebounds, and 6 assists in his television debut. After the Oak Hill game, LeBron James would no longer be an urban legend, like playground heroes from yesteryear. His national debut and astounding success against one of the country's best high school teams turned skeptics into believers. The James hype machine went into overdrive.

Many of today's sports and entertainment heroes have an edge. They appear a little dangerous, often just half a step away from a good brawl or jail cell. This hardcore image appeals to the MTV generation. Teenagers always seem to fall for the kind of corporate-sponsored rebellion MTV peddles, whether it is the latest rap single providing a glimpse of street life, the bling lifestyle, or violence-filled videogames and movies. As a matter of fact, many young people would rather sit around playing videogames than actually play a particular game itself, so the videogame companies fill their wares with action and graphics that are cartoon-like. Basketball games feature crazy dunks, high-flying acrobatics, and little, if any, fundamentals. Why shoot a 15-foot jump shot when a dunk could be had?

What may make LeBron James the perfect NBA idol for the twenty-first century is that he combines the style and grace of Michael Jordan with a healthy dose of urban culture, personified by young rappers and sports stars, such as Nelly, Jay-Z, Ludacris, Allen Iverson, and the late Tupac Shakur. James has that big smile and natural good looks, which appeals to consumer product marketers, while at the same time possessing the skills and toughness that draws in the free-spending teenage demographic.

While a combination of talent and personality fueled Jordan's rise to icon status, James differs in that he is from the ghetto, thus naturally possessing more "street cred." James also more readily identifies with black urban culture. Unlike Jordan, who lived a middle class lifestyle growing up in Wilmington, North Carolina, James has risen from the ghettoes of Akron, a rough town in the aging Rustbelt, under pressure to stay vibrant as the manufacturing-based economy vanished, leaving high unemployment rates and many people struggling to survive.

James and his mother (who gave birth to him when she was only 16 years old) jumped from apartment to apartment when he was little, always searching for a little better way of life, but unable to escape the vicious cycle of poverty. Like many young black men across the nation, James has never met his biological father.

Unlike some athletes who embellish the tough times of their youths to gain respect among their peers, James does not have to exaggerate about his experiences in the roughest sections of town. He told *Sports Illustrated,* "I saw drugs, guns, killings; it was crazy. But my mom kept food in my mouth and clothes on my back."[11]

On the court, James personifies the popular culture influences that shape today's teenagers. He wears it on his skin, in the form of multiple tattoos (which he had to cover with white athletic tape while in high school according to SVSM school rules) to the dress code teens follow—the ever-present headband, armband, droopy shorts and oversized jersey. In the videogame and cable show world of spectacular dunks and highlight reel plays, James excels at symbolizing his generation, even though his individual game is about more than freewheeling acrobatics. For corporations looking for a fresh face, the youngster will appeal with his good looks and bright smile.

On the streets, and particularly in the African America community, respect is a key tenet of an individual's social mindset. The idea of respect among young black males has been portrayed in numerous popular culture vehicles, from a slew of television shows and movies to the lyrics of slain rapper Biggie "Notorious B.I.G." Smalls and other hip hop stars. James shows his respect for those who have given him guidance and support by publicly thanking God and showing his reverence for his mother. In return, James asks for the community to respect him for turning raw ability into brilliance.

James is not immune to the chest pounding, trash-talking style that pervades basketball, whether on the blacktop behind the local high school or in NBA arenas around the country. After dunking on an opposing player, James ferociously yells, "King James," or "You sorry," reported a writer who has covered James.[12] At one time, this kind of behavior would have been punished or scorned, but now popular culture glorifies displays of individual self-importance that give athletes a kind of signature gesture that kids can then mimic. Showing up an opponent not only ensures an athlete "gets his," but it can also make him more famous (or infamous).

There are many similarities between James and Michael Jordan (circa the 1980s and 1990s) in addition to the familiar number 23 they each wear. On the court, both have tremendous quickness and jumping ability. When the game ends, they each flash a similar multimillion-dollar smile and display an innate, natural charisma. Like the youthful Jordan before him, James is even criticized for having a weak jump shot—about the only Achilles' heel that can be found in his game.

Because he is routinely compared with Jordan and seemingly destined for NBA superstardom, James faces incredible pressure every single day of his life. These demands intensified when he became the first pick in the 2003 NBA draft. Observers expect James to single-handedly resurrect the hometown Cleveland Cavaliers, despite the franchise's history of underperformance and disappointment.

In fact, this level of anticipation and expectation separates Jordan and James. Over the last several years, James has already experienced Michael Jordan-level attention. Every move he makes on and off the court is up for public consumption and scrutiny. Jordan, on the other hand, did not face this pressure as a rookie because the NBA was a different place then. Jordan certainly did not have much of a grace period, but there was a time when he still had some measure of privacy. Of course, as the team's number one draft pick, Jordan was expected to help the club right away. No one, however, expected the scrawny kid out of the University of North Carolina to become the Michael Jordan that he developed into.

In contrast to the way James's star has risen, there is almost an innocence to Jordan's ascent to global icon status, even though he became a star in his freshman year at the University of North Carolina after hitting the game-winning jump shot against Georgetown in the NCAA Championship game. Observers who watched Jordan realized that he had the potential to be a special player, but no one thought he would develop into the greatest player to ever live. The general public gradually recognized Jordan's immense talent, hand-in-hand with seeing his face on television in Nike ads.

One NBA Western Conference scouting director explained how James would have to push himself to achieve the level of Kobe Bryant, Tracy McGrady, and the handful of top pro stars. "He's able to get by on his physical ability right now," the scout told sports writer Marc Stein. "The question is, what happens when he can't just get by on physical ability alone? The mental side, the emotional side, those are unknowns. In high school, the only thing we're seeing is the physical ability."[13]

James is already considered the game's next great marketing hope. Experts estimate that his first shoe contract—signed with Nike after a long battle with Adidas—approached or exceeded $90 million over five years. Although he waited until after the draft to sign the Nike deal, college was never really an option for the youngster. He had been marketed too long to be put on the shelf while competing for any major college program.

Jordan took a liking to James, inviting him to Chicago to play together and giving the youngster his top secret cell phone number. It is a role Jordan has taken with other young, African American superstars, such as his close friendship with golf sensation Tiger Woods. Critics, however, view the James-Jordan relationship with a grain of skepticism, thinking that the move was intended to get James on the Nike payroll, like his basketball idol.

As James's on the court exploits continue to electrify and his jumper has started dropping on a regular basis for the Cavaliers, thus muting the one criticism of his game, the only issue that concerns basketball experts is how the young man will deal with the fanfare. An NBA Eastern Conference scout explained the way a high school player affects a team, stating, "The problem with taking on a high school player is that, for the coach, you're dealing with a lot of things you don't normally deal with. And it takes up a lot of time." Summing up the challenge of easing a teenager into the game, the scout explained, "These kids don't even know how to keep a checkbook when they get to the NBA."[14]

In the years since joining the NBA, James developed into one of the league's most popular players and one of its fiercest competitors. He won Rookie of the Year after the 2003–2004 season, in which the Cavaliers tallied 18 more victories than the preceding year. The following year, James averaged more than 27 points per game, then surpassed that figure at 31.4 points per game in 2005–2006. That season, the team made its first playoff appearance since 1998, and James won the All-Star MVP.

In 2006–2007, James led the Cavaliers to the NBA Finals for the first time in team history, though they were swept in the best of seven series by the San Antonio Spurs, the closest thing the NBA has had to a dynasty in the last decade, winning four championships. The ability to lead his somewhat undermanned team to the championship round evoked comparisons to Michael Jordan, the same one James faced since bursting on the national scene as a teenager. According to Howard Beck, "What James does best, other than win, is make the game look simple. He can fill a box score and dominate on the court without ever looking as if he is trying to do either. The greatest measure of an NBA star is how much he lifts up his teammates, and James excels in this category."[15]

Tiger Woods in the TV golf match Lincoln Financial Group Battle at Bighorn, Bighorn Golf Club, Palm Desert, California. ABC Sports, July 29, 2001. ©2001 ABC, Inc. Courtesy of Photofest.

Golf

There is a serious conflict in the world of golf today. On one hand, Tiger Woods is possibly the greatest golfer who ever lived and draws the sport huge television ratings in addition to his global fame. However, Woods's wins and winning personality have done little to popularize golf or draw more people into the game. One could argue, however, that the true measure of Woods's work in this regard will not be reflected for another decade, but the numbers as they currently exist reveal that golf is dropping in popularity.

Woods is not only the best golfer in the world, but he is the king of endorsements. His phenomenal popularity led to a wide range of gigs as celebrity spokesperson, from Gillette razors and Nike to management consulting firm Accenture and Buick. In early 2008, *Chicago Sun-Times* columnist Jay Mariotti went as far as to declare that, as measured by "his impact on sport and fashion and popular culture and the American condition," Woods has now surpassed the legendary Michael Jordan. When combining the level of excellence on the playing field with the carefully managed aura in the celebrity world, it does seem that Mariotti's statement rings true.[16]

In pro golf, the ultimate measure of success is the number of major tournaments won. Woods stands in second place on the all-time list with 13 majors, behind Jack Nicklaus who owns 18. Some 11 of Woods's major wins took place in the new millennium, as well as many of his other notable achievements, including winning 11 tournaments in 2000 and possessing all four major trophies at one time by winning over the 2000–2001 timeframe. Through 2007, Wood earned $76.6 million on the PGA Tour and $94 million overall.[17]

While Woods won tournaments, drove revenues for corporate partners and the PGA Tour, and brought in countless millions for charity, the number of people who played golf in America either stayed flat or declined since 2000. The National Golf Foundation and the Sporting Goods Manufacturers Association estimates that the total number of people who play golf dropped from 30 million to 26 million over the decade. More troubling than this figure is the significant drop in the number of people who play 25 times a year or more (6.9 million in 2000 to 4.6 million in 2005) and eight times or more (17.7 million in 2000 to 15 million in 2006). "The man in the street will tell you that golf is booming because he sees Tiger Woods on TV," said Jim Kass, research director of the National Golf Foundation. "But we track the reality. The reality is, while we haven't exactly tanked, the numbers have been disappointing for some time." Kass is optimistic, but the combination of an aging population in the United States and a less active younger generation spells real trouble for golf and many other recreational sports.[18]

Ironically, given golf's link to consumerism and corporate sponsorship, the difficult economy is the primary factor people claim keeps them from playing more often, if at all. According to Kass, the surveys show that people are working more, making less in real wages, and corporations are cutting back golf-related perks, such as country club memberships. In the early part of the 2000s, observers believed that the retiring Baby Boomers would actually increase the number of golfers. Playing on this hunch, many additional golf courses were built, with more than 3,000 created between 1999 and 2003. The surplus actually resulted in a glut and many facilities are up for sale or gone bankrupt, mainly in Arizona, Florida, Michigan, and South Carolina.[19]

JUICED: BASEBALL'S STEROID CHALLENGE

In February 2008, Roger Clemens—by nearly all accounts the most dominating pitcher in his era and one of the all-time greatest—appeared before a Congressional panel investigating steroid use in baseball. For fans that grew up idolizing Clemens and other big name legends, the day crushed dreams. For cynics already skeptical about the state of the national pastime, Clemens's testimony (shown live on ESPN) sounded phony; it was another nail in baseball's coffin. A survey conducted shortly after the pitcher's testimony revealed that a majority of baseball fans (57%) did not believe his claim that he never used performance-enhancing drugs.[20]

Clemens is the most recent legend caught up in the steroid scandal that has rocked baseball for years. Standing at home plate is Barry Bonds, baseball's all-time homerun champion, the virtual poster boy for illegal performance-enhancing drugs in the game, allegations that have dogged him for a decade. Sitting on the bench are other stars (for instance, Andy Pettite and Rafael Palmeiro), mid-level players (like Brady Anderson and Jason Giambi), and ordinary players (like John Rocker and Brett Boone) who are accused of using steroids to elevate their games in an era in which drug use seemingly runs rampant.

Few players have admitted to using steroids or growth hormones, though much of the current debate about drug use can be traced to a tell-all book by former all-star Jose Canseco, *Juiced* (2005). Although widely ridiculed at the time of publication, Canseco's book foreshadowed much of what followed over the next three years. Taking a different approach, Jason Giambi, for instance, publicly apologized to New York Yankee fans without ever specifically stating what he had done to warrant such an apology.

The Clemens accusations came to light in the final report of an investigation commissioned by Major League Baseball and headed by former Senator George Mitchell, dubbed "The Mitchell Report." A media circus erupted after the release of the findings, though a deeper read revealed that much of Mitchell's juiciest information came from disgruntled trainers and other peripheral people loosely affiliated with the game. This information diminished the report somewhat, but it did not stop the wall-to-wall coverage of the names involved, including the big fish caught in the expedition: Roger Clemens.

Journalist Tom Verducci called the reaction to Clemens part of the "perpetual, multimedia cycle in the Britneyfication of events," which included live events and a nationally-televised interview on *60 Minutes*. However, Clemens deserves a special place in the history of steroid investigations because he chose to publicly defend himself. According to Verducci, "Hundreds of ballplayers have used performance-enhancing drugs. Only a

WORLD SERIES

2000 New York Yankees (AL), 4 games; New York Mets (NL), 1 game

2001 Arizona Diamondbacks (NL), 4 games; New York Yankees (AL), 3 games

2002 Anaheim Angels (AL), 4 games; San Francisco Giants (NL), 3 games

2003 Florida Marlins (NL), 4 games; New York Yankees (AL), 2 games

2004 Boston Red Sox (AL), 4 games; St. Louis Cardinals (NL), 0 games

2005 Chicago White Sox (AL), 4 games; Houston Astros (NL), 0 games

2006 St. Louis Cardinals (NL), 4 games; Detroit Tigers (AL), 1 game

2007 Boston Red Sox (AL), 4 games; Colorado Rockies (NL), 0 games

fraction of them have been publicly identified as users. None have gone anywhere near the lengths Clemens has to defend themselves. He even asked to appear before Congress."[21]

The Mitchell Report grew out of a series of events that dominated the headlines in the 2000s, including the 2003 raid of the Bay Area Laboratory Cooperative (BALCO), which revealed that Giambi and Bonds were clients. A series of congressional hearings in 2005 featured testimony by Mark McGwire and Palmeiro. The former refused to say much of anything about possible steroid use, while the later angrily declared his innocence in a video clip that has been played countless times since then. That Palmeiro tested positive for illegal drugs just months afterward forced Major League Baseball to act, thus leading to the formation of the Mitchell Commission. According to professor Abraham Socher, "The pharmacological genie has long been out of the bottle... still, the report is valuable for the wealth and specificity of its detail."[22]

BREAKING INTO THE MAINSTREAM

Mixed Martial Arts

In the early years of the new millennium, Ultimate Fighting Championship (UFC) dominated the then-underground sport of mixed martial arts, a modified street fight that took place in an octagonal ring in which contestants either submitted or were knocked unconscious. The fights, unlike professional wrestling, were real and often bloody. The gritty realism of splattering blood, forced submission, or true knockouts gave the sport a brutality that fans desired, even as commentators and legislators questioned the legality of such fights. The payoff for Ultimate Fighting and other sanctioning mixed martial arts organizations was the dream 18- to 34-year-old male demographic that large companies battle to attract.

Back then, fans who wanted to see UFC were basically limited to pay-per-view events, which some states would not even allow to take place in their jurisdictions. Quickly, however, mixed martial arts moved from the extreme fringes of the sports world to center stage. The spectacle of watching two men basically knock the snot out of each other captured the interest of fight fans growing weary of mismatched boxing matches and the deterioration of the heavyweight division, most notably by the seemingly-invincible Mike Tyson and the bland fighters that blundered through the weight class after Lennox Lewis retired.

From these rather auspicious beginnings, mixed martial arts grew into a force in the sports world. By 2007, cable network Showtime aired matches, and in early 2008, CBS announced that it would become the first major broadcast network to show mixed martial arts fights. The network said that it would place bouts on Sunday nights, which is the least watched night on television. The goal is to draw in young viewers who have traditionally shied away that night. Not incidentally, CBS owns Showtime, which is helping with production.[23]

The Ultimate Fighting Championship is the elite organization for mixed martial arts. In the 1990s, the company had been marred in legislative and regulatory battles at the hands of critics who lamented the sport's violence, including Arizona Senator John McCain. The move to the mainstream began in 2001 when Dana White and two old sparring partners bought the company for $2 million. By 2006, UFC had pay-per-view sales of $223 million and sold out arenas across the nation. White bought out Pride, an Asian competitor, for $70 million in 2007. The company also started a reality television show on Spike TV, a Viacom-owned cable network directed at young males. In June 2007, the season finale of The Ultimate Fighter 5 drew 2.6 million viewers.[24]

Some commentators believe that mixed martial arts is the perfect vehicle for attracting young male viewers who have been raised on ultraviolent video games. Others point to the UFC's real fights, a far cry from the scripted world of professional wrestling. At least in part due to the power of the Web and online videos as a distribution channel, a number of mainstream and underground no-holds-barred sites exist, ranging from the illegal to the outlandish. In early 2008, on YouTube alone, thousands of amateur fight videos are available, from *Fight Club*-style matches to high school females squaring off in suburban locations. And, of course, clips from UFC and other companies are freely available online.[25]

OLYMPICS

2004 Olympics

Coming together under the motto "Unity," more than 10,500 athletes from 600 nations met in Athens for the 2004 Summer Olympic Games. NBC won the rights to cover the Olympics on television in the United States, but the Athens event marked the first time the games would be broadcast via the Internet as well. The United States took home the most medals (102, including 36 gold), followed by Russia (92, 27), and China (63, 32).

The United States did well in track and field at the Athens games, but lanky swimmer Michael Phelps stole the show, winning four individual gold medals and two more as part of winning relay teams. Phelps's amazing performance placed Mark Spitz's all-time record of winning seven gold medals in one games (at the 1972 Munich Olympics) in jeopardy and built expectations for the 2008 Olympics.

In contrast, the men's basketball team disappointed fans around the globe by settling for a bronze medal. With young superstars, such as LeBron James and Dwayne Wade, complimenting all-stars Tim Duncan, Allen Iverson, and others, the team seemed a lock for the gold. An 89–81 loss to eventual gold medal-winning Argentina in the semifinals derailed the American team.

2008 Olympics

The 2008 Beijing Olympics transformed from a global competition into the Michael Phelps show almost from the start. The 23-year-old swimmer from Baltimore stood so dominant in his sport at the start of the games, that many believed he could break Spitz's mark. Phelps did not disappoint, winning eight gold medals. For his career, Phelps earned 16 Olympic medals (14 gold and 2 bronze). In the process, the young man set seven world records—five on his own and two more on a team relay.

By the time Phelps left China, the only question left on most peoples' minds was where the swimmer stacked up against the best athletes of all time. While this question may be argued for the next 100 years, it is certainly a given that he will become one of the great celebrity endorsers ever. One of Phelps's first stops was the cover of *Sports Illustrated* with all eight gold medals draped from his neck, mimicking the picture Spitz made famous. Marketing experts estimate that Phelps upped his earning potential to about $10 million annually, placing him among the richest Olympic pitchmen ever. "Right now, the guy's got the world on a string," said one marketing analyst. "He's in that upper realm, not in terms of income but in terms of profile, with Tiger Woods and LeBron James and Lance Armstrong."[26]

Seemingly minutes after Phelps won the eighth gold, for example, Visa aired a commercial narrated by Academy Award winning actor Morgan Freeman thanking the young man for his feats. In addition to Visa, Phelps has deals in place with Speedo, Omega, Hilton, and AT&T. There are even rumors that Phelps is on his way to Hollywood to play an underwater superhero. Perhaps such a casting would make sense, given that more than one million people have already signed up to be Phelps fans on Facebook.[27]

Beyond Phelps, the biggest story about the Beijing Games was China and how well the Chinese athletes performed. While many observers thought that the Olympics would be marred by protests regarding China's human rights abuses, there were few disruptions. Furthermore, Beijing itself was decked out with fantastic architecture and buildings specifically for the Olympics. Few viewers will forget the sight of "The Cube" swimming arena or the "Bird's Nest" track and field stadium.

TECHNOLOGY

Social Media

The rebirth of the Internet after the spectacle flameout early in the decade came at the hands of Web users themselves who started to explore the Internet's capacity for linking people in a personal way, yet with the distance that online communication provides. Upstarts such as Friendster, Classmates, MySpace, and Facebook, gave users the freedom to build profiles, a kind of online billboard that provided a public face for anyone who wanted to participate. Observers labeled these outlets "social networking" sites.

Web sites enabling regular users to build their own free homepages and share content, pictures, and other information without first learning intricate programming skills developed relatively early in Internet history. AOL, GeoCities, and others served as early pioneers in the effort to get users their own tiny space on the Web. None of these sites, however, caught the user's imagination like MySpace and Facebook. Within a year of their launching in 2003 and 2004, respectively, each social media site changed the way people talk about the Internet. People nationwide could be heard saying, "Do you have a Facebook?" or "Check out my MySpace."

Founded in 2003 by Tom Anderson and Chris DeWolfe, MySpace grew quickly into the leading social network site. Launched as an online hub to showcase upcoming bands and musicians, MySpace rapidly evolved into a phenomenon, acquiring more than 106 million profiles by 2006. The ability to list and link to MySpace friends (i.e., other users) provided the gimmick that caught people's attention. In addition, users could manipulate their profiles to reflect their personalities, or at least the persona that they wanted other MySpace users to see.

MySpace's centrality in the Web 2.0 universe attracted Rupert Murdoch, the magnate who owns the media conglomerate News Corporation. In 2005, Murdoch purchased MySpace's parent company (Intermix Media Inc.) for $580 million. While many users and critics railed against the new corporate owner, MySpace continued to grow and expand, moving into 24 countries by 2007. Under the guidance of its corporate parent, MySpace also charged into new content areas, forming its own record label and producing online video series. With its vast and deep user base, MySpace also developed into an advertisers' dream. Corporations flocked to the site to hock their wares to the predominantly young demographic. Industry observers estimate that MySpace will draw about $800 million in revenue in fiscal 2008, primarily from advertising.[28]

The success or failure of MySpace's transformation from an independent site to more of a mainstream media outlet may be an indicator of how the Web will evolve in the future. Will independent-minded users keep coming back to the site as it becomes more of a media portal as its slogan claims, "a place for friends?" DeWolfe, the founder who runs the business aspect of MySpace, said, "Some people still perceive MySpace like it was in early 2004, as a niche place for scenesters in New York and Los Angeles. That's how it started, but it's become very mainstream. It's about consuming content and discovering pop culture."[29]

Founded in 2004 by Harvard undergraduate Mark Zuckerberg, Facebook is MySpace's primary competitor in the social networking arena. Originally a tool to link college students at elite universities, Zuckerberg later expanded the site to other colleges and high schools, and then eventually opened to those outside universities. Facebook's strengths are its clean layout style and the ability to track friends' actions on the site, whether it is adding a gadget that ranks favorite movies or merely updating an online photo album.

Journalist Michael Hirschorn sees the site's ability to thwart spammers and porn site offers as a key to its popularity and continued expansion. In addition, Zuckerberg opened the site to outside developers, which enabled them to embed widgets that increase the user's experience. For example, members can send one another virtual gifts and challenge one another to music or film trivia contests. The key is that this interaction is contained among Facebook friends, which is more selective than the MySpace version. The exclusivity is an attractive quality for today's more discerning Web users. "If the overall trend on the Internet is the individual's loss of control as corporations make money off information you unwittingly provide, Facebook is offering a way to get some of that control back," Hirschorn said. "In Facebook's version of the Web, you, the user, are in control of your persona."[30]

MySpace and Facebook continue to battle for supremacy among social media sites in the United States. In December 2007, for instance, MySpace logged 69 million unique visitors, versus 35 million for Facebook. The numbers jump geometrically when examined by page views, with MySpace totaling 38 billion and Facebook 13 billion.[31]

When looked at from a global perspective, however, Facebook is actually much closer to MySpace. In November 2007, MySpace had 105 million unique visitors worldwide, while Facebook rang up

93 million. The site also surpassed its rival in the total minutes users spent on the site at 21 billion minutes versus 17 billion minutes.[32]

Online Videos

The Internet fulfilled its destiny in the mid- to late 2000s, finally becoming a kind of on-the-go television or theater. Spurred by technology, such as wider access to broadband Internet connections, and the popularity of social media networks, the Internet moved from a primarily text-based mass media channel to one dominated by video. If a single entity can be credited for this shift, it is YouTube, owned by parent company Google.

The pervasiveness of online video is demonstrated by its astronomical growth. In November 2007, for example, more than 75 percent of Internet users in the United States watched a video online, averaging 3.25 hours per person during the month. Powered by YouTube, Google is the dominant force in the video market. The company increased its market share in this category to 31 percent. In total, U.S. Internet users viewed approximately 9.5 billion videos in November, with 2.9 billion of this figure coming from YouTube.[33]

When examined individually, these statistics reveal that YouTube's 74.5 million users averaged 39 videos per person over the course of the month. In contrast, MySpace tallied 389 million videos watched by 43.2 million people, or 9 videos per user. The 3.25 hours per viewer is a 29 percent increase from January 2007.

From a demographic viewpoint, the typical online video consumer is a male (53% versus 43% female), aged 18 to 29 (70%), with at least some college education (54%). Interestingly, some 60 percent of online video watchers claim a household income exceeding $75,000, while another 53 percent fall in the $50,000 to $75,000 segment. In race or ethnicity, users break down as follows: English-speaking Latino (55%), African American (46%), and white (45%).[34]

The results of the survey, conducted by the Pew Internet & American Life Project, confirm the preconceived notions of who uses the Internet most often and who frequently visits sites such as YouTube. However, there are other interesting aspects of the survey that show the true pervasiveness of online video. Some 30 percent of those 50 to 64 years old said they visited video sites, and 16 percent of those were older than 65. The findings regarding household income show that either viewers themselves are well off, or that the children of upper middle class families are the most likely to go to these sites. The large number of English-speaking Latinos who visit YouTube and other video pages confirms recent research that reveals astronomical Internet usage growth in the Hispanic community.[35]

In December 2007, with the writers' strike crippling television, statistics show that Americans turned to the Web to fulfill their viewing needs, with 141 million people watching more than 10 billion videos that month alone. This served as the heaviest month of online video consumption since comScore Video Metrix began tracking video hits. Market leader Google accounted for 3.3 billion videos, or nearly 33 percent of the total. The time spent watching videos also increased in December, reaching 3.4 hours (203 minutes) per person over the course of the month. That trend shows no sign of slowing, with the figure jumping 34 percent over the course of 2007.[36]

Video Games

Some critics shrug off the video game industry. The reality is that gaming is big business and a major player in the worlds of technology, consumer goods, and entertainment. The industry has morphed from a niche category into an $18 billion enterprise. The names that dominate the field include a who's who of global corporations, including Microsoft and Sony, as well as divisions of all the major film studios.

The biggest transformation in video games in the new millennium centers on making games more accessible to a wider audience. Teenage boys, while still important to the overall picture, are no longer the only market in town. Games like Guitar Hero and Dance Dance Revolution prove that video game companies are designing games that appeal to people of both sexes and all ages. According to journalist Seth Schiesel, "Companies that are making games more accessible are growing like gangbusters, while traditional powerhouses with a traditionally limited strategy of building around

HOW OTHERS SEE US

YouTube and Facebook: All the World's On Stage

When an amateur opera singer wowed the judges on a British TV competition, millions of music fans got word of his performance via blogs and instantly could see it for themselves.

When a Norwegian comedian's prank on a New York City politician provoked a profanity-laced tirade, viewers the world over could watch and debate who had been in the wrong.

When protests erupted anywhere in the world—Teheran or Tibet, London or Lebanon—news broadcasts and eyewitness cell phone videos were soon posted for international viewing. Another social network site helped create a massive protest against the leftwing guerilla group, the FARC, when Oscar Morales created a group against FARC on Facebook. That group and others were then able to mobilize a crowd estimated from 500,000 to 2 million in Bogota to protest the FARC's tactics of kidnapping and guerrilla warfare.

For issues both serious and silly, and interests both broadly popular and painfully arcane, YouTube has become the world's video town square. Founded in 2005 in San Mateo, California, YouTube provides the technology for people to share video clips regardless of the formats they were filmed in. Within months of its launch, YouTube was ranked among the fastest-growing sites on the Internet. Its popularity spread via word-of-mouth (and e-mail), and soon it featured not only homemade music videos but also commercial ones. By 2007, YouTube postings included authorized promotional material from television networks, and the Web site was co-hosting U.S. presidential primary debates with CNN.

Several governments, including China, Turkey, Saudi Arabia, Thailand, and Iran, have locally banned or blocked all or part of YouTube. When Pakistan, citing videos that were offensive to Islam, attempted to block its citizens from accessing the site in February 2008, it instead shut YouTube down completely for several hours. The resulting outcry from users elsewhere cast a harsh spotlight on the repressive tactics of Pakistan's ruling elite.

See "Colombians in Huge FARC Protest," BBC News, http://news.bbc.co.uk/2/hi/americas/7225824.stm.

the same old (if you will) young male audience have stagnated, both creatively and on the bottom line."[37] The move is toward social gaming, in which people interact with each other in front of the television. Then, gaming develops into a party atmosphere, a big hit with college students and players in their 20s, who want the social aspect along with the online experience. Nintendo's Wii console is a prime example of this trend, as is Guitar Hero. Nintendo cannot keep up with Wii demand, shipping 1.8 million units a month globally.

Clearly, social gaming is driven by technological innovations and a more robust broadband network, which reveals the tight relationship between culture and technology. Online PC games, for example, allow people to interact on the screen, eliminating physical distances, but they also necessitate high-speed Internet connections and exceptional computer graphics and processors. While these systems still appeal primarily to lone gamers, the numbers of subscribers are in the tens of millions.[38]

Concurrently, an even faster segment of the market is enabling interaction in front of the screen and bringing in families, older users, and females. The Wii symbolizes this revolution, outselling more advanced systems, such as Microsoft's Xbox 360 and Sony's PlayStation 3. Wii Play ranked number two on 2007's bestselling video games. The game enabled interactive, yet simple, play among people using the system, which appealed to those not interested in learning codes or pressing multiple buttons in some arcane sequential order to win. "If new acceptance by the masses is one pillar of gaming's future, gaming's emergence as a social phenomenon is the other," Schiesel said. "Hard-core gamers are still willing to spend 30 hours playing along through a single-player story line, but most people want more human contact in their entertainment."[39]

SCRABULOUS

Scrabble, the American crossword board game that was first marketed in the 1950s, enjoyed a global burst of popularity in 2007. Far from being pleased by the renewed interest, however, the game's manufacturers began to threaten lawsuits: the version being played by 700,000 people a day was digital, and it was created and run by someone else.

The electronic game, Scrabulous, was a program written by brothers Jayant and Rajat Agarwalla in Kolkata, India. The Agarwallas grew up in an upwardly mobile family believing that education and English-language proficiency were the keys to success. To improve their English, their mother encouraged them to play Scrabble. They remained dedicated players into adulthood, and in 2005, they combined their programming skills with their love of the game to create an online version.

Mimicking the physical Scrabble in all but name, Scrabulous used a 225-space playing grid, 100 letter tiles, and identical scoring. Because it was virtual, however, far-flung players could challenge one another to games, and there were no time limits. (It also allowed for unlimited cheating opportunities, another attraction for some.) When the Agarwalla brothers made their game available to Facebook users, millions added a Scrabulous feature to their pages on the popular social-networking site, making it a worldwide phenomenon.

All those new eyeballs earned the Agarwallas substantial advertising revenues (a reported $25,000 a month) for their site, and Hasbro, Scrabble's American owner, accused them of copyright infringement. But in the Internet's freewheeling, borderless culture, that idea seemed to have little meaning. To Scrabulous players, the idea of Scrabble is as classic and free wheeling as checkers or poker; to Hasbro's lawyers, copyright law may let anyone use an idea, but the expression of that idea must be provably unique. It may take a court to decide.

Online Shopping

The most pervasive consequence of the Internet is arguably its function as yet another outlet for Americans to shop. When given overcrowded malls and outrageous gas prices, many people choose to shop online, particularly during the Christmas holiday shopping season. Further enticing reticent mall-goers, many Web-based companies dropped shipping prices or eliminated them altogether. Others guaranteed pre-Christmas delivery for orders placed by a given date.

From November 1 to December 27, 2007, consumers spent about $29.2 billion online, a 19 percent jump over the 2006 total. Many shoppers purchased video games and consoles via the Internet, with Sony PlayStation and Nintendo Wii driving sales.

Citing convenience as the primary reason for purchasing products online, two-thirds of American consumers who use the Internet told the Pew Internet & American Life Project team that they have bought an item online. This equates to about 49 percent of all Americans, up from 22 percent in June 2000. Although people enjoy the time-saving and ease of purchasing online, the Pew study found that people are concerned with the safety of their financial and personal data. Some 75 percent of Internet users do not like giving this information online. Another sticking point is that nearly 60 percent of Internet shoppers have felt frustrated, confused, or overwhelmed by the online experience.[40]

Although these worries are a natural effect from the online experience, the tremendous pace of Web-based shopping grew quickly over the decade. In comparison, 22 percent of Americans said they had bought a product online in 2000, while 35 percent claimed to have used the Web for product-related research. The latter figure jumped to 60 percent in September 2007. Furthermore, while Internet users conduct transactions in increasing numbers, the amount of money spent is growing even faster. The Census Bureau estimates that online revenues have skyrocketed nearly 500 percent, from $7.4 billion in 2000 to $34.7 billion in the third quarter of 2007.[41]

CELEBRITY OBSESSION

Americans are not only obsessed with celebrities, but many actually act like mini-celebrities in their own daily lives. This fascination with following celebrities and mimicking their moves is a constant reminder of Andy Warhol's prediction that someday everyone will be famous for 15 minutes.

Across the nation, people are imitating celebrities when choosing their clothing, hairstyles, sunglasses, accessories, and (most important) attitude. One merely needs to walk through a crowded mall to see the consequences of this fixation. For faux-celebs, life is a barrage of people bringing their formerly private lives into public view, just as tabloid journalism has done to celebrities on television shows like *Access Hollywood* and in magazines ranging from *Us Weekly* to *People.*

In the 2000s, self-promotion is essential. In many respects, Web sites such as Facebook and MySpace and the never-ending stream of reality television shows actually teach people to expose themselves at every turn. On social networking sites, for example, a user can describe a current mood, and then have it blasted out to all his or her friends, thus making a broadcast statement and forcing others into the emotion in some small way. Then, when the mood changes, that new information is sent again, just as the changes a user makes to his or her profile and group memberships are posted for all to see. Users can even list their top friends and compare where they are in the lists of their friends—a vicious cycle of self-absorption.

As it now stands, the United States is a country full of people loudly carrying on via cell phone, bottled water in hand, wearing a T-shirt emblazoned with the message: "It's Always About Me." We do not look away in horror or subject these kinds of people to ridicule, as past generations might have done to those who tried a bit too hard to be the center of attention. We're all too busy trying to be the center of attention. These displays of nihilism are commonplace occurrences: new millennium America is self-fascination at its zenith. Millions of people go through life with the feeling that they are one coincidental event from being discovered and becoming the celebrity they all dream of becoming. Ironically, many Hollywood celebrities are fighting just as hard to remove themselves from the public eye... at least until their next picture is released.

Britney Spears

The headlines scream: "Last Day with Mommy," "Brit's Fight to Get Well," and "Inside Her Ordeal." The subject is Britney Spears, pop singer, celebrity, and popular culture icon. Americans cannot get enough Spears news, particularly when it focuses on her meltdowns, brushes with the law, hospitalizations, or battles with the paparazzi. She graces the covers of "celebtainment" magazines such as *People, InTouch,* and *Us Weekly* with alarming frequency. Her every move seems to be captured on film nightly on *Entertainment Tonight, E! News,* and *The Insider.* Spears always ranks among the top-searched names on various Internet sites, and a recent Google search returned 80.2 million hits.

Britney-mania even found its way into the venerable *Atlantic Monthly* in early 2008. Reporter David Samuels spent time with the paparazzi as they stalked Spears in and around Hollywood (ironically, as wildfires threatened to burn large chunks of L.A. and Hollywood). Samuels explained Spears's importance: "History's best-publicized celebrity meltdown has helped fuel dozens of television shows, magazines, and Internet sites, the combined value of whose Britney-related product easily exceeds $100 million a year." Part of the Britney Economy is driven by an underground network of spies, tipsters, and photographers, who all pocket stipends for their work charting her every move, including "500 or 600 parking-lot attendants, club kids, and shop girls in and around L.A."[42]

In late February 2008, *The New York Times* chimed in, speculating about the status of Spears's net worth, estimated at anywhere from $50 million to $125 million. The article came on the heels of a series of involuntary treatments at the UCLA Medical Center. Jamie Spears, her estranged father, became co-conservator, assuming de facto control over her daily life. A team of lawyers set out to protect her financial interests, along with several family members, including her brother.[43]

As events in her life spiraled out of control, from allegations of heavy drinking, to her failed marriage to former backup dancer Kevin Federline, Spears squandered a myriad of endorsement deals, said to have earned her $12 million, from the likes of Toyota, Nabisco, Clairol, Sketchers, McDonald's, and Pepsi. She has an ongoing relationship with Elizabeth Ardin for Britney perfume. Despite the steady stream of chaos and uproar that surrounds Spears, she is already mounting a comeback with a recurring role on the hit CBS comedy *How I Met Your Mother.* One insider explained her continued star power, saying, "Because we're so incredibly fickle as a society, the perfect entertainment is someone who's in the bottomless pit and rising again. If she's together, fit, beautiful and on her game, it'll be just printing money."[44]

Paris, Lindsay, and Anna Nicole

Since the birth of mass media, people have longed for news of celebrities, particularly those who shine bright, while at the same time appear somewhat dangerous. Paris Hilton, Lindsay Lohan, and Anna Nicole Smith each symbolize the celebrity obsession of the new millennium. Hilton is famous for being a mega-rich heiress and Los Angeles party girl; Lohan parlayed an early acting career into teen stardom; and Smith embodied the rags-to-riches story of a poor girl who transforms into a star.

Unfortunately in the world of celebrity, death actually propels a star's legend. In the case of Smith, she rocketed to success in the 1990s after appearing in Playboy and in several high-profile advertisements. She could not sustain the success and by the beginning of the new decade, her star power fizzled. But, Americans love it when a celebrity makes a comeback. The E! cable network provided Smith with such a vehicle in 2002, *The Anna Nicole Show,* which centered on her bizarre behavior and interactions with an entourage of hangers-on. The show ran for two years and put Smith back in the spotlight.

While Smith appeared in several films after her celebrity rebirth, her fame grew exponentially when she became a spokesperson for the diet company TrimSpa. On the diet plan, she dropped about 70 pounds. Her outlandish behavior continued in late 2004 when she appeared at the American Music Awards, slurring her words and speaking incoherently. The next three years of Smith's life turned out to be a whirlwind of triumphs and tragedies, including the death of her son by an accidental overdose, marriage to longtime attorney Howard K. Stern, and the birth of a baby girl.

On February 8, 2007, a friend found Smith passed out in her hotel room in Hollywood, Florida, where she later died. Officials determined that it was a drug overdose that killed her, a combination of medications. Smith lived in a media circus for most of her life, but after her death, the frenzy intensified significantly.

Cameramen and reporters fought for space outside her hospital after news of her death hit the airwaves. Enterprising journalists filed stories from Mexia, Texas, her tiny hometown. Smith news then hit the accelerator when the dispute over her daughter's biological father played out in the national media. Soon, questions about her state of mind, her battle with drugs and alcohol, and the multimillion dollar fortune she left behind were topics of discussion on celebrity news shows, Web sites, and magazines.[45]

In the 24-hour-a-day world of modern popular culture, it is difficult to determine whether the antics of celebrities such as Lohan and Hilton are the mindless deeds of young women who symbolize their generation, or the carefully plotted actions of media smart celebrities who understand that the goal is to stay in the news at all costs. Hilton, for one, hardly warrants the title of celebrity, as her early fame derived from being rich and possessing a famous name. However, since getting in front of the paparazzi, she has built herself into a one-woman brand empire, from a singing career and reality television show to illicit video propelled by the Web and a short stay in jail.

Lohan is more difficult to understand, though her repeated stints in and out of rehab clinics makes one less certain that these are planned publicity stunts, resulting in a sinking film career and detrimental party girl image. If she meant to stay in people's minds this way, the effort certainly backfired. However, Lohan launched another offensive in March 2008, appearing in *New York* magazine as Marilyn Monroe and on the cover of *Bazaar,* looking innocent and clean, not at all like she just stepped out of a detox clinic. Such appearances sell magazines and provide celebrities with the chance to redeem themselves. "Scandal-craving readers snap up the issues, which often promise a star's first on-the-record account of her troubles," journalist Ruth La Ferla said. "Ms. Lohan's Marilyn Monroe-inspired striptease for New York was the magazine's biggest selling issue of the past four years."[46]

Travel of the 2000s

In 2000, the future looked bright for the travel industry. The Internet enabled airlines, hotels, and car rental agencies to interact and sell to customers in a whole new way. Big name Web-only companies, such as Priceline, Expedia, and Travelocity, used extensive advertising and branding campaigns to become household names. For consumers, the Internet allowed people to find less expensive means of travel and to do so themselves, virtually eliminating the need for travel agents. Self-service travel reigned supreme in the industry.

The online sites tackled astronomical growth. For example, in early 1998, research firm Jupiter Communications predicted that online travel sales would reach $11.3 billion by 2002. At the time, the organization considered this a gutsy call, as online sales accounted for less than a billion dollars the year before. As it turned out, Jupiter could have been bolder in its prediction. Forrester Research, another analysis firm, estimated that nearly 19 million households made travel purchases on the Web in 2001 and accounted for $16.7 billion in revenues. Despite the many challenges faced immediately after the terrorist attacks on September 11, 2001, the Internet companies rebounded.

The attacks initially devastated the airline industry, forcing some carriers (barely holding on before the tragedy) into bankruptcy. Furthermore, the entire travel and tourism market suffered as the uncertainty following the attacks led people to reexamine their priorities, including whether business travel could be done safely. Experts estimate that the travel and tourism industry lost some $30 billion after September 11.

Even a national tragedy could not destroy the travel industry. Travel, particularly air travel, had become a normal part of everyday life for too many people in and out of the corporate world. Low-cost carriers, most notably Southwest Airlines, made air travel seem more convenient than packing up the car and kids for a long road trip. Consequently, passengers did not stay away for long, even as security measures, threat assessment codes, safety procedures, and long lines made it more time-consuming and difficult to board planes. The travel agency community also rebounded by refocusing on specialized and luxury travel.

By the late 2000s, airlines faced a different set of challenges, including rising fuel costs, which translated into higher fares, and a weakened economy that forced consumers to rethink trips and travel. By the summer of 2008, most airlines had begun to charge fees for traveling with more than one bag, and for food and drinks served on the flight, including soft drinks. Still in the late 2000s, people generally see travel and tourism as a regular aspect of their lives. Thus, they are not going to stop, despite the rising costs and problems associated with travel, just like the need to drive regardless of gasoline prices. The proof is in the numbers, which reveal that, by 2010, online travel planning is estimated to reach $150 billion.

ONLINE TRAVEL SITES

Way back in the ancient days of 1995—we're talking about the Web here—a *Brandweek* article asked rhetorically: "Are Travel Agents Dinosaurs?" Despite the industry's $93.5 billion in yearly billings at the time, most onlookers assumed that the Internet would make travel agents obsolete.

Six years later, travel agents still roamed the earth. They were a bit disgruntled but they were also empowered by the demons sent to smite them. As it turns out, travel agents plugged into the latest and greatest technology, which helped them retain a competitive edge, just like savvy headhunters who listed job openings on Monster.com or HotJobs.

However, the success of online travel sites doesn't prove that there are still travel agencies. Unquestionably, travel is one of the industries that benefited most from the Web. Analysts estimated that the online travel industry hit $17 billion in 2001 and grew to $68 billion by 2005. Even though most of the big names in the online travel game initially focused on air travel, such as Priceline.com, Travelocity, Expedia, and Orbitz, the public soon learned to shop for travel savings across different kinds of travel-related sites.

In early 2001, the Travel Industry Association of America released two reports detailing America's fascination with online travel. The association concluded that more than 59 million travelers used the Internet to get information or check prices, while 25 million from that group purchased travel products or services on the Internet. The kinds of items they purchased varied as well:

- 84 percent bought airline tickets;
- 78 percent purchased lodging;
- 59 percent rented vehicles;
- 51 percent bought tickets for amusement parks, sporting events, and other occasions;
- 17 percent purchased travel packages;
- 8 percent purchased a cruise.

Ben Cutler, senior analyst of the Internet consumer practice at research firm Cyber Dialogue, said online travel "is the first e-retail category to be shopped by a majority of online adults." Cutler estimated that 43 million online adults shopped for travel via the Web in the early years of the new millennium, which represented 51 percent of the total people on the Net. These figures were significantly higher than 1999's numbers, which revealed 17.2 million people shopped for travel online, or 28 percent of the total online population.[1]

Most online companies failed to revolutionize business or live up to a sliver of the incredible hype brought on during the dot.com feeding frenzy. The stories of failure, unfortunately, are more abundant than the stories of success. However, several travel sites broke the mold and made money on the Internet, such as Expedia, which morphed into an online travel bazaar, and Hilton Hotels, which married its Web site and back office functions so well that some analysts believed that the company had the best e-commerce organization in the world.

Turbulence at Takeoff

Like so many other businesses in the mid-1990s, travel companies did not know what to make of the Internet. Some early pioneers realized the medium's potential, but back then, the technology had not caught up with the inspiration. No one really knew what a good Web site should or shouldn't do or even how it ought to look. As a result, the first travel sites were balky and difficult to use. Years of trial and error ensued before truly good travel sites developed. By early 1996, most American businesses raced to establish a presence on the Internet, but they rushed headlong into Internet projects before really understanding how the medium could help them. There were few people who understood how a site should be designed and even fewer who could articulate a Web strategy.

A pioneer in the online travel game was the Raleigh-based PC Travel, which launched in June 1995. Founder and president George Newsom put up the site as an extension of his 25-year-old travel business and estimated that users filled out 1,000 reservation profile forms a day. PC Travel focused on selling discounted airline tickets, vacations, and cruises. The firm also gave extra discounts and bonus frequent flier miles to travelers who joined its Web-Net Traveler Club, at an additional cost of $49.95.

As soon as online travel started to show promise, many critics sprung to action, determined to prove that using travel agents still resulted in better savings. In 1996, magazines from *Popular Science* (concluding that the sites were "long on information, but short on savings") to *Fortune* (warning "don't dump your travel agent just yet") ran stories hopeful about the future of online travel but cautioning the reader to still keep an agent's number handy. The *Fortune* article also discussed a major problem for all Web users in the mid-1990s: the time it took to get the computer booted, signed on to a service provider, and then navigate to the individual sites. Back then, dealing with a travel agent by phone was probably a much easier task.

The critics made some good points in the short term and only cautiously explored the future implications of online travel. Booking travel via the Internet challenged even the most patient early users because many corporate Internet sites had no e-commerce capabilities. For example, the Avis car rental site did not offer online reservations. Instead, if one wanted to use Avis, one sent the company an e-mail and waited for a response.

Although detractors had their knives sharpened, surveys from the mid-1990s showed that 70 percent of Internet users used the medium to get travel information, while 15 percent booked airline tickets via the Internet. In 1997, Internet users booked $900 million in travel, an impressive figure, but less than 1 percent of the total travel market, so obviously, if online travel sites could meet customer needs at a better price, then they could continue to build on these numbers. The proof of online travel's potential clearly existed.

What travel sites like Expedia and Travelocity needed was more people online and the technology to gain wider acceptance with the general public. Once that happened, it would not take a large spark for online travel to ignite. The leading sites took the time to build technology to meet customer expectations, and then waited for enough users to go online to form a critical mass. In a short while, the explosion of venture capital money and publicity hype combined to set off that spark. Before long, people could not even remember what it was like before the Internet. As the Internet became omnipresent, travel developed into its first killer category.

Erik Blachford, an executive at Expedia, believes travel is the ideal Internet industry and sees the reasons falling into three neat little buckets. First, travel-related information is difficult to aggregate offline. Basically, there isn't a traditional way to gather all the disparate content into one location better than the way it can be done online. Second, information is electronic-based, so there is no need for warehousing or a supply chain and other necessities that tripped up so many Web companies. Finally, there are tremendous cost savings because no one is sitting around waiting for customers to walk in the door or call on the phone, as is the case with traditional travel agencies.

Companies have to use technology to deliver information correctly the first time and every time thereafter that a customer goes to the site. One of the biggest cultural changes brought on by the Web is the expectation of perfection. Zero tolerance is commonplace, especially because the competition is a click or two away. This heavy reliance on technology is the first exposure of Expedia's roots as a Microsoft company. As the company originated within the Redmond-based software giant, it had top-notch talent working on what was essentially an online startup.

The second instance of Expedia revealing its heritage occurred among senior management. Richard Barton founded the company while working on a travel CD-ROM that Microsoft founder Bill Gates wanted him to develop. Barton realized the CD idea would fail, but an online travel site had a chance for greatness. Like Barton, Expedia's other leaders cut their teeth in Microsoft's highly competitive environment, so they developed a quasi-Microsoft culture.

As a matter of fact, Blachford explained, Expedia leaders also modified the culture to fit their startup mentality. "We kept our discipline and style, but changed what we didn't like about Microsoft. As Expedia developed, it was definitely not Microsoft, but its foundation stones were Microsoft." Blachford views this as a distinct advantage over the willy-nilly startups being led by college students and MBA dropouts. "You can't just invent that culture," he said. "We had skilled product development people, good training, and a commitment to technology."[2]

The success of Expedia in almost immediately carving out a sizeable market share poses interesting questions about the role of startups launched by corporate parents. Like Monster.com, backed and financed by the power of TMP Worldwide, Expedia had an almost unfair advantage from the start. "Could we get where we are today without Microsoft?" Blachford asked. "Probably, but that foundation made it much better. Look at Travelocity; it also grew up with Sabre in the background." Microsoft's technical resources also helped Expedia overcome the severe engineer drain that tech companies faced in 1999. Microsoft attracted the talent and could assign people to work on the travel site. "In the long run," Blachford pointed out, "sites differentiate on service, which comes down to technology. The customer doesn't see it, but technology plays into the overall customer experience."[3]

The technology push by Microsoft had a key impact early in Expedia's life. From the start, Expedia planned to become a one-stop travel hub in cyberspace, so it used Microsoft's connections with resorts, hotels, and other travel-related companies to offer discounts that no one else offered. Certainly, every advantage Microsoft could deliver was important for Expedia in the dogfight that broke out between the company and archrivals Travelocity and Priceline.com. Launched in April 1996, Priceline had more than one million visitors to its site within its first week. The auction mentality, so popular on the Internet, helped Priceline become an early leader in the New Economy. Founder Jay Walker was even likened to an electronic age Thomas Edison in a 1999 article in *Forbes* magazine. Priceline went public in March 1999 at $16 a share and rocketed to $88 its first day and then soon jumped higher to trade at $130 a share. Priceline's market cap reached an extraordinary $18.5 billion, and Walker's share of the pie equaled a tidy $9 billion. Walker's status as a New Economy paper billionaire was a far cry from Edison, who gained and lost several fortunes over the course of his life.

In March 2000, just before the Internet bubble economy popped, Travelocity went public by merging with Preview Travel, then the distant third company behind Expedia and Travelocity. The combined entity immediately became the ninth largest travel agency in the United States and the leader in market share among online travel agencies. More importantly, the new Travelocity jumped to number three among online commerce firms, right behind Amazon and eBay.

After the merger, the company's market capitalization reached $2.54 billion, but it gradually dropped down to about $700 million—much of the drop due to the NASDAQ crash that spring. With Preview Travel's long-term marketing deals with AOL, Excite, Lycos, and Snap (the leading portals in early 2000), the combined entity (with more than 6.2 million monthly visitors) worked to convert visitors into paying customers, a challenge that plagued online travel firms from the start. Less than 10 percent of people who went to the site ended up purchasing anything.

By late 2000, Travelocity extended its lead to account for more than 21 million users. The company's market share hit 35 percent, compared with Expedia's 25 percent. Both companies also turned a profit faster than anyone expected. Expedia beat its own predictions for profitability by five quarters, while Travelocity did the same one quarter early.

Orbitz Flies into Battle

In an unprecedented display of solidarity, the five largest U.S. airlines (Delta, United, Northwest, Continental, and American Airlines) came together to form Orbitz, a $145 million online travel site to rival Expedia and Travelocity. Orbitz attracted quite a buzz when it launched in June 2001, as observers noted its potential antitrust implications and the site's chances at knocking off its main competitors. It may be telling that Orbitz began life as a project code-named "T2," supposedly either after the Arnold Schwarzenegger movie of the same name or the more ominous "Travelocity Terminator."

As a matter of fact, Orbitz found its way on the radar screens of attorneys at the Justice and Transportation Departments, state attorneys general offices, and among various consumer advocacy groups even prior to going live. Critics felt that Orbitz would collude to set ticket prices and form a monopoly over its rivals. In an interesting twist, Orbitz CEO Jeffrey G. Katz believed much of the lobbying against Orbitz came from supposed consumer alliances that actually represented the interests of Expedia and Travelocity. There is plenty of evidence that he was at least partially right.

Katz promised Orbitz would offer consumers a better search engine and many more choices than they currently enjoyed. The immediate benefit of using the Orbitz engine is that it delivered fares from more than 20 major airlines. The results, laid out in a user-friendly manner, could range from a dozen to hundreds of options. The public responded favorably with 3.7 million unique users visiting in the first month. The company turned these Web surfers into $100 million in reservations. These statistics vaulted Orbitz into third place behind its two main rivals.

Orbitz was a latecomer to the online travel industry, so it had to fight to catch up with the market leaders. To beef up name recognition, each of the site's 35 charter members also committed to spending about $2 million a year on marketing opportunities for Orbitz.

Expedia: Cyberspace Travel Hub

Expedia strengthened its hub strategy by purchasing Travelscape.com and Vacationspot.com for $177 million. The deal gave Expedia access to discount hotel reservations and luxury vacation packages, which broadened its scope in important strategic ways, Blachford said. "We decided to act as a retailer rather than as a travel agent and diversified into other areas to decrease our dependency on air. Our business model allows us to make tactical pricing decisions and offer better prices to customers," he explained.[4]

Blachford estimated that technology would remain vital. Just as the banks had to determine how important ATMs would become and then scale to that figure, online sites had to scale to the number of users they forecasted. "One hundred percent of tickets will never be sold online," he said, "but what is the magic number that will? My guess is that it will reach 40 to 50 percent, which means there are still huge opportunities waiting to be realized." That kind of penetration required an ongoing commitment to technological upgrades and innovations, as online firms only accounted for about 14 percent.

The primary benefit of online travel is that people want a one-stop shopping experience and will use the site that can give them the most services in a central location. For example, someone traveling to Cozumel, Mexico, will want to reserve airfare and a hotel, but they also might want to rent snorkeling gear, plan an excursion to the Mayan ruins at Chichen Itza, and make dinner reservations at several restaurants in Cancun. "In the long run, users will be able to reserve everything online," Blachford said. "They will have an entire itinerary booked and reserved online. Today's world is piecemeal; tomorrow's will present everything all at one place."[5]

Expedia served as Microsoft's first successful spin-off, going public on November 10, 1998, at $14 a share, and like most Net stocks, jumped to $53.44, resulting in a $2 billion market cap, with Microsoft retaining a 70 percent ownership. On July 16, 2001, Microsoft sold Expedia to Barry Diller's USA Networks for $1.5 billion. Diller is a master at convergence; he built USA into a media powerhouse, with tentacles in television (USA), vacation packaging (National Leisure Group), hotel reservations (Hotel Reservation Network), discount shopping (Home Shopping Network), and ticketing (Ticketmaster). He owned a database of about 30 million customers, and Microsoft desperately needed access to them. "USA Networks has a broad reach, which Microsoft can leverage to reach consumers," said Microsoft vice president Yusuf Mehdi.[6]

Hilton Books Room on the Web

Bruce Rosenberg vividly remembers the day Hilton Hotels launched its Web site, which enabled customers to make reservations online. "We launched a site that cost $50,000 to build, and that was a big bet," he said. "The reservation system concluded with an e-mail sent to the reservation site, but the people there didn't know how to operate e-mail. We set up a bell to alert them an e-mail was coming in."[7] The bell rang three times, and Rosenberg was ecstatic. However, it wasn't the number of orders that got him excited; it was where they came from: one each from Europe, Asia, and the United States. A bell then went off in Rosenberg's mind.

The next day he walked in to his boss's office and told him about the orders. "You've got to be kidding," his boss replied, not knowing whether to be incredibly happy or extraordinarily sad. Rosenberg had seen the light (and heard the bell); he immediately asked his boss for $500,000 to build an e-commerce Web site. Luckily, the three orders were enough for him to agree.

When it came to the Internet, Rosenberg, the Senior Vice President of e-business, knew the early metrics, but he wondered to himself, "How do you turn it into a real business?" From the first day, he decided to keep a major tenant as his guide: leverage the brick and mortar assets to compete online. Hilton focused on customer service and internal discipline, so these values would be kept as the company plunged into e-commerce.

Immediately, Rosenberg realized that Hilton could have great ambitions on the Web, but it didn't want to become a travel agency. He worked internally to set the proper expectations, both for those who expected miracles and others who didn't want to be bothered with the Web. The Web challenge intensified when Hilton acquired the Promus Hotel Corporation in late 1999, which brought Hampton Inn, DoubleTree, and Embassy Suites into the fold. All the disparate brands had to be brought under one umbrella that leveraged the power of the Hilton name.

After conducting numerous user surveys and doing other forms of research, Hilton executives saw that when customers called the Hilton help line, they only stayed on an average of two minutes. On the Web, however, customers initially stayed eight minutes, and that number fell gradually down to five. Rosenberg determined that the Hilton homepage had to be the best point of access to the company in the world.

With this idea in mind as a rallying point, bells then started ringing all over Hilton. The company realized that a customer accessing the Web site cost Hilton eight times less than a voice conversation. Using internal tech tools, Rosenberg calculated a return on investment (ROI) for the homepage and charted it daily. Using the services of a research firm, he then began forecasting how revenue and expenses would change for the site over the next three years. Rather than trying to grab market share or get big fast—the common mania of pure Web companies—Hilton used statistics and forecasting to reinforce the accuracy of its strategy.

At one point, Rosenberg worried about all the venture capital money flowing to competitors and how it would affect Hilton's efforts. In retrospect, he said that it actually kept the company on its toes. "Instead of focusing on competitors, we concentrated on executing on our plan," he said. "We did not want to overspend or have any write-offs from our e-business efforts." In fact, Rosenberg said that Hilton is already collecting $500 million in revenue from business on its Web site, which will approach five percent of the company's total by the end of 2001.[8]

After Hilton built a world-class external site, it then used Web technology to shave costs off its backend, such as having an integrated reservation booking and call center. Tony Nieves, Senior Vice President of Purchasing at Hilton, organized a team to build an internal e-business marketplace to get suppliers hooked directly into the Hilton system. The procurement site began with 500 Hilton hotels and their suppliers, but Nieves expects it to expand to Hilton's 1,600 managed and franchised hotels in the next year. In total, the exchange includes more than 3,500 suppliers, with about 1,000 of these being active participants. Nieves said that the hotels on the system are spending 60 percent of their procurement budgets on the site.

Rosenberg believes the Web is the best place to interact with Hilton. It provides content, personalization, and transaction capabilities across all the company's properties. Hilton's early success on the Web proved that brick and mortar companies could not only compete when it comes to e-commerce, but they actually had the infrastructure to dominate.

As we near the end of the new millennium, online travel is a ubiquitous part of consumer culture.

Travelocity, Expedia, and others no longer have to spend tens of millions of dollars on marketing campaigns because people automatically turn to the sites to fulfill their travel needs. The irony of the former upstart online travel companies is that they are now mainstream. For instance, in early 2008, Priceline sold for $127 a share, while Expedia shares were a more modest $25.

In today's Web 2.0 world, the stalwarts of online travel are adapting to consumer demands. Expedia, for example, owns TripAdvisor, a social travel site that features user-generated travel reviews. "The influence of social networking and community services is growing significantly for online travel," said one industry analyst. "Seeking information and looking for perspective—like-minded experience and judgments—are currently trumping the straightforward hunt for the best price. Services that facilitate a purchasing decision by aggregating or filtering content make [online travel information] relevant to the user."[9]

SEPTEMBER 11

Terrorism and Online Travel

It is clear that Expedia, Travelocity, and Orbitz developed different strategies, despite the similarity of their products. Internet users were trained to expect huge savings online, and the travel sites fulfilled this need. However, with the uncertainties that lingered as a result of the September 11 terrorist attacks, the brakes were applied to the phenomenal growth of online firms. Expedia dropped from trading in the mid-30s per share to the low 20s, lowering its market cap to $1.18 billion, while Travelocity fell from the low 20s down to about $13 a share, which valued the company at $650 million.

The chaos surrounding the airlines resulted in massive layoffs in that business and billions of dollars lost in travel and tourism, which had a ripple effect on the main travel Web sites. Expedia and Travelocity reported that bookings dropped by 50 percent after the attacks. If there was a saving grace for the online firms, it was that they had cash in reserve to carry them through the downturn. Expedia, for example, had $225 million in the bank, and because it carried no inventory, it could weather the storm better than many of its online brethren.

ECO-FRIENDLY TRAVEL

Checking into a room at the Quorum Hotel-Tampa, guests immediately notice a tag hanging on the back of the door and others strategically placed throughout the suite. The place cards feature beautiful pictures of sandy beaches and sunsets, perfectly appropriate for the Tampa Bay area, which features some of the world's greatest

THE ROOTS OF ECOTOURISM

The United States environmental movement has roots in the nineteenth century, but it wasn't until the 1960s and 1970s when environmentalism made the leap into public consciousness. In the late 1960s, new scientific discoveries and high-profile environmental accidents, including a widely publicized incident in 1969 when the polluted waters of the Ohio River caught fire, brought environmental issues to the political foreground. In 1970, a nationwide celebration of conservation and environmentalism, known as Earth Day, was established as a focal point for the movement. Until the mid-1970s, funding for environmental protection was obtained through government grants and public donation. As environmental concern entered the mainstream, enterprising individuals saw the potential for combining conservation and tourism. By 1989, tourist agencies were offering environmentally-friendly trips to a variety of exotic locations, from Africa to Antarctica, where visitors could engage in snorkeling, scuba diving, hiking, and photography. Now a multi-million dollar industry, ecotourism and environmentalism proved to be more than a simple fad. With a dwindling supply of natural resources, the sake of the world's natural areas is dependent on creative fundraising and cooperation between state and public organizations. By combining recreation with environmental protection, ecotourism provides a prime example of how to simultaneously address public and private interests for mutual benefit.

beaches. However, the message contained on each is more serious: "We invite you to join with us to conserve water by using your towels more than once," the notice reads. "In addition to decreasing water and energy consumption, you help us replace the amount of detergent waste water that must be recycled within our community."[10] The marketing effort to educate guests at the hotel is part of the Southwest Florida Water Management District's (Swiftmud) program to conserve water. Initiated in 2002, the move is one of many nationwide that focuses on reaching people with an eco-friendly message. Consumers in the new millennium demand these types of programs, and the travel industry is one of the most innovative in meeting this need.

As a primary tourist destination, Florida is a leader in the eco-friendly travel movement. The state began a "Green Lodging" program in 2004 within the Florida Department of Environmental Protection's waste management division to promote hotels and motels that meet a number of criteria built around environmental awareness. From 2004 to 2008, the number of hotels participating grew from 10 to more than 100, with another 275 in the application process. Companies achieving the Florida Green Lodging certification have learned that it is also a financial benefit, according to journalist Ted Jackovics, "realizing conservation can become a marketing tool as well as a cost-savings effort."[11]

Nationwide, the eco-friendly movement at hotels began in the 1990s by giving guests the opportunity to opt-out of linen and towel service, which saved on water and electricity expenses. The Texas-based Green Hotels Association estimated that hotels could save $6.50 or more a day per room if guests participated. In the Tampa region, since 2002, Swiftmud's plan is estimated to have saved participants about 20 percent to 30 percent in laundry expenses and one billion gallons of water.[12]

In addition to Florida, where Governor Charlie Christ signed an executive order requiring state agencies and departments to hold meetings and conferences at Green Lodging companies, similar programs are underway in California, Michigan, North Carolina, Pennsylvania, Vermont, Virginia, and Wisconsin. According to Penny Heudorf, Director of Sales and Marketing at Quorum Hotel-Tampa, businesses are also using the eco-friendly designation in making decisions about where to permit business travel and meetings. "These days, when we go through a process with business clients to negotiate rates, the clients are asking what we are doing in terms of environmental initiatives," she said.[13]

"WHAT HAPPENS IN VEGAS . . ."

In the new millennium, destinations and tourism groups that represent geographic regions banded together in the battle to win travelers in a heated industry based on cutthroat competition. In 2005, Las Vegas, which many people equated with Sinatra's Rat Pack, gambling, and Sin City, embraced its outlaw heritage with a new slogan, "What happens here, stays here." The motto—part of a risky $75 million advertising campaign—struck a chord with adult travelers, who flocked to Vegas, viewing it as a kind of adult playground. The campaign also flew in the face of the city's attempt to mimic Disney with its former "It's anything and everything" family-friendly slogan.[14]

In early 2008, building off the success of "What happens here . . . ," Las Vegas tourism executives introduced a complimentary tagline: "Your Vegas is Showing," meant to work with the now-iconic slogan. Erika Pope of the Las Vegas Convention and Visitors Authority explained that Vegas in the new millennium represents the "adult freedom experience." Each year since the original campaign launched, the number of visitors broke the record of the previous year. Some 38.9 million people visited in 2006, topped by the 39.2 million in 2007.[15]

Although its slogan is catchy, Las Vegas reinvented itself on more than just a catchphrase. At the heart of the transformation is a building boom on the Strip and a steady infusion of celebrities. In early 2008, for example, the gold-covered Trump International hotel opened, capitalizing on "The Donald's" popularity. Rapper and budding business tycoon Jay-Z opened a nightclub (dubbed 40/40) inside The Palazzo, another of Vegas's new hotels. The glitz of potentially rubbing elbows with a real life celebrity at a new club or at a boxing match draws many tourists to Vegas. At

Las Vegas at night. The spectacularly glittering skyline indicates how much of a popular vacation destination the city has become. Courtesy of Shutterstock.

the same time, the average room rate has nearly doubled over five years, from $80 to $139 a night. The new hotels begin rates at $200 and quickly go up from there. Similarly, tickets to shows in Vegas are pricey, from $95 to $250 to see Bette Midler to $94 to $160 for tickets to Cirque du Soleil's tribute to the Beatles at the Mirage.[16]

LUXURY TRAVEL

For wealthy people, travel means exclusivity and privacy. The difference between these high-end consumers and everyone else is that the rich have unlimited resources to pay for those features. Often for the wealthy, travel is one of the best ways they can enjoy their money; after all, there are only so many cars, boats, planes, or houses one can own. Milton Pedraza, CEO of the Luxury Institute in New York, explained: "The widening number of affluent travelers around the world are increasingly willing to spend their wealth on *experiences* like travel instead of *things* like cars or second and third homes." From 2005 to 2006, for example, luxury hotel revenue increased 10 percent.[17]

For business travelers on the road, more are opting for higher-end digs and upgrading from the lesser pack of discount chains. In response, some hotels are remodeling and expanding services to lure in corporate money. According to consulting firm PricewaterhouseCoopers, about 136,500 hotel rooms began construction in 2006, a 64.2 percent increase in one year and the single-biggest jump since 1994.[18]

Little upgrades, such as a larger bed and nicer bathrooms, are enough to get business road warriors hooked. Hampton Hotels designed a program called "Cloud Nine," which attracts people by making sleep more enjoyable with 200-thread-count comforters and jumbo-sized down or foam pillows. Realizing that business people have specific work needs, most hotels offer high-speed Internet access.

HOW OTHERS SEE US

Globalization = Americanization?

During the twentieth century, the expansion of mass media, the increasing ease of travel, and the burgeoning communications industry made far-flung cultures more closely interlinked. In the early years of the twenty-first century, this process has only accelerated with the Internet and wireless technologies. Are these trends a threat to local cultures that will inevitably be swamped by the homogenizing, commercialized tide of globalization? And, as many contend, does this coming global culture wear an American face?

Certainly, the power and reach of American business is tremendous. As columnist Thomas Friedman has written, "globalization wears Mickey Mouse ears, it drinks Pepsi and Coke, it eats Big Macs." Resentment of this "soft power," coupled with anger over U.S. foreign policy and the Iraq War, led to a perceptible rise in anti-American sentiment in the mid-2000s.

On the other hand, the flow of international communication goes both ways, and American popular culture itself is globalizing, incorporating more outside influences more quickly than ever before. In pop music, Caribbean styles like dub and reggaeton have been a major factor on the American charts; in fashion, Australia's Ugg boot sparked an American craze; in food, formerly exotic flavors like Thai and Vietnamese cooking are becoming positively mainstream; in film, genres like Japanese horror have attracted large audiences and inspired Hollywood remakes.

Some historians look back to Japan in the early twentieth century for clues about how to incorporate the best or most useful aspects of technology and global culture while maintaining the integrity of local culture. And, as international relations theorist Joseph Nye posits, perhaps the Internet itself—with its ability to enable the formation of virtual, idea-based communities without regard to borders or distances—will be the means by which cultural traditions and niche interests will survive and thrive in a globalized age.

Visual Arts of the 2000s

The Biennial art show at the Whitney Museum of American Art is a showcase of young talent and presents a kind of state of the union of contemporary art. The 2008 Biennial, according to journalist Leslie Camhi, reveals the depths in which "we're living at the end of the American empire" and how that might make an observer "feel nostalgia for a not-so-distant past when our nation's art seemed in the vanguard, formally or politically."[1]

The show featured many versions of the trendy "dystopic video art and sculptural installation," but only one painter, which Camhi claims might be "a thing of the past, a relic from a preceding generation." Other artists put together works strewn together from pieces of garbage. Phoebe Washburn built an "ecosystem" of different objects rising up from "beds of neon-yellow golf balls." Other artists—81 in total—worked in video or via video screen. Many pondered the dual wars in Iraq and against terror and the consequences.[2]

Taken as a whole, the 2008 Biennial may not fulfill some grand vision of American art as we near the end of the first decade of the new millennium, but the kinds of work and what is considered art make a statement about the direction visual arts is charting. Many of the artists featured video installations, which points to the way art is both following and leading the broader culture. Taking cues from music videos, reality television, and film, among other factors, artists who work with video are showing how their work reflects broader societal implications. These artists also point toward a future where art is unfixed, whether in a flat-screen frame or concealed some way within the fabric of a home. Glimpses of this future already sit on mantles in people's homes and on the shelves of retailers in the form of picture frames loaded with digital images that change at the viewer's discretion. How long before this kind of technology transforms art and how people interact with artwork?

Undoubtedly, technology infiltrated the visual arts in the decade as the computer and its peripherals took center stage in American life. For example, computer software and programs enabled graphic artists to create designs that were more sensual and expressive of the democratic impulse. These works, unlike a static painting, allowed for interaction with the audience and a unique viewer experience. In addition, visual arts delivered a greater degree of freedom to the art world by making the Internet an important component. With the Web, more people entered into the art world, primarily through purchasing art online or participating in an auction at a site like eBay. However, enabling transactions to occur in the virtual world also carried some risk. Art collectors and museums face the real possibility that a rare find purchased through a middle man may actually be a stolen treasure or a fake.

While new artists are breaking onto the scene in the 2000s, few, if any have, achieved the iconic or popular status of their predecessors, such as Jackson Pollack, Andy Warhol, or Ansel Adams. Artists whose work dominated the art houses of the 1980s and 1990s still receive most of the attention in the world of visual arts. The old masters still receive the lion's share of public attention, even though traditional paintings are much less influential in today's digital world.

An important trend in the 2000s is that more cultures are now participating in the art world, if only on a local or regional scale in some cases. For instance, Native Americans put on arts festivals to showcase their work, as do African Americans and other groups. Most of the smaller programs won't get much more publicity than a blurb in the hometown paper, but the millions of people collectively that flock to these community-building events have the opportunity to gain insight into the artwork of cultures outside their own.

At the Smithsonian Institution's National Museum of the American Indian, for example, the professional staff enlisted community curators to help them with framing the last 500 years of native history. These helpers came from different tribes and aided the staff in gaining a better understanding of artifacts and displays. Kevin Gover, Director of the museum and a Pawnee, explained, "Our philosophy is to give voice to the native community, to give them an opportunity to tell their story. In the mind of Indian people, they've never been able to tell their story. Their story is told by others."[3]

ONLINE ART AND AUCTIONS

The Internet revolution extends to the art world and stands poised to increase its importance in the future. The Web offers some critical benefits to potential art buyers: the ability to participate in auctions across physical space and additional research opportunities that did not exist as easily before the wired world. Perhaps the most compelling feature is that the Internet delivers direct access to artists. Collectors are already using this link to buy directly from rising stars. In the near future, such exchanges may eliminate the auction house model, though posthumous sales do necessitate a middle person role to some degree.

For the larger auctions that generate global interest, Bonhams (bonhams.com), Christie's (Christies.com), and Sotheby's (sothebys.com), all have online sites that attract new audiences who either enjoy the anonymity of the Web experience or may be intimidated by the stuffy atmosphere of an in-person auction.

eBay

Web-based auction site eBay has had a central role as a popular culture phenomenon in the new millennium. Though its traditional auction model waned a bit as the novelty of the site wore off, the company created new revenue streams that simultaneously expanded its influence. In the art world, eBay Live Auctions enabled auctions to take place in the virtual world with or without a simultaneous one in the physical realm. After registering to be an online bidder, a person simply makes bids via the site.

In early 2008, Wildwood Antiques Center near Toledo, Ohio, hosted an auction that included prominent works owned by Owens-Illinois Inc., a local corporation that manufactures glass containers. The auction took place at Wildwood's location, as well the eBay site, with online bids projected onto a 20-foot-by-10-foot screen. The on-site bids were also registered on eBay, so both groups had the information simultaneously.[4]

Green Valley Auctions of Mount Crawford, Virginia, sold $368,000 in its annual winter catalogued and uncatalogued sale of eighteenth- and nineteenth-century glass and lighting in January 2008, with more than 3,500 pieces sold over 4 sessions. The firm eclipsed its 2007 winter figure, which president and senior auctioneer Jeffrey S. Evans said is due to its online component. "In this auction," he said, "about 31 percent of the sales over the three days went through eBay Live. We think that's interesting and significant." Using eBay, Evans said, opened the sale globally, with buyers in Egypt, Malta, South America, and the Netherlands, in addition to the firm's traditional European buyers. Others merely watched the action via the Internet.[5]

Along with eBay's successes, some gallery owners and observers criticize the company for focusing too much on the bottom line and moving further away from its roots as a place where small businesses and individuals could buy and trade freely. Chuck Hamsher, owner of the Purple Moon gallery in Charleston, West Virginia, had a long and fruitful relationship with the online seller dating back to 1999. By 2001, he opened an eBay store. In 2008, however, he closed the virtual location and stopped doing business with the auctioneer after it lowered listing fees but increased commission fees. The company also altered its famous feedback/rating system, the backbone of the transaction model.[6]

Hamsher wrote in his blog on why he left eBay and received hundreds of e-mails in response from other small business sellers. With tighter profit margins and cost controls, small businesses have more to lose under eBay's new commission setup. The company bumped its fee from 5.25 percent to 8.75 percent. Perhaps even more debilitating to eBay users is that sellers will no longer be able to post negative feedback to buyers, which opens the site to additional fraud. "The feedback system has worked because it was mutual. The system is worthless without being mutual," Hamsher wrote in his blog.[7]

MUSEUMS

Though most museums focus on displaying great works of art by the acknowledged masters—a distinctly historical outlook—the art world competes with all the other forms of entertainment available to consumers in the modern world. In response, museums launch marketing plans that include family nights, limited-run exhibits that will attract significant attention, and other programs that will draw people off their couches and away from the computer.

Science and technology museums, such as the Museum of Science and Industry (MOSI) in Tampa and the Carnegie Science Center in Pittsburgh, have been particularly successful in marketing to families and children. MOSI has an entire wing designed for kids to interact with science and technology through exhibits that enhance motor skills, logic, and creativity as children play. In some instances, these institutions are willing to take risks to gain exposure. Both centers hosted the controversial "Bodies" traveling exhibit, which featured preserved human bodies and internal organs on display. Despite public outcry from religious organizations and human rights activists, MOSI increased membership and used the money raised from ticket sales to fund operations and new exhibits.

In an attempt to uncover what patrons want from the museum experience, institutions nationwide are using technology. The Museum of Modern Art in New York completed a $450 million expansion in 2005 and simultaneously compiled information on visitors to put into a database. The Detroit Institute of Arts conducted research into patron preferences and uncovered statistics that overturned common perceptions, including that only 7 percent of visitors actually read wall plaques and spent a mere 4 or 5 minutes in any gallery, much less than the 20 minutes that officials assumed. Museum executives realize that these kinds of studies help them determine who visits, why they come, and what will make them return. In implementing the findings, museums are changing everything from the types of music played to hours of operation. Nancy Price from the San Francisco Museum of Modern Art said, "People want to know that what they're seeing is relevant to their life. This might sound simple, but it's important for us to hear."[8]

The challenge for museums is balancing the presentation of so-called high brow versus low brow exhibits. According to journalist Carol Vogel, "While serving up what audiences want may be a smart business move, there is a fear by curators that things can go too far, that catering to public opinion could dumb down a museum and supplant curatorial wisdom. Are museums for high culture or low? Places to see Ralph Lauren's car collection and 'Star Wars' costumes, props and drawings rather than Vermeer and Renaissance tapestries?" This kind of equilibrium remains elusive, yet critical, for museum curators, particularly in an era dominated by digital communications. It is not an easy task to get people into museums.[9]

Museums work hard to market their exhibitions to the public and to encourage attendance. Courtesy of Shutterstock.

Michael Govan

In the not-so-distant past, the Los Angeles County Museum of Art (LACMA) had little consequence on the artistic scene, locally or nationally. In 2006, backers brought in Michael Govan to turn around the ailing museum. In the years since, Govan led that transformation, basically turning LACMA into LA's foremost art institution. This is pretty heady stuff for a formerly second-tier museum in a city that is home to Hollywood and the Getty.

Govan represents a new breed of museum chief executive, both strategic and with the artistic flair to make people take notice. Similar to the rock star architects and artists of the last 20 years, Govan takes on high-profile projects and essentially becomes the face of the organization. In 2003, he drew national attention for turning an abandoned biscuit factory into the Dia Art Foundation museum in Beacon, New York.[10]

The first step in the makeover included a physical expansion and upgrade. LACMA opened the $56 million Broad Contemporary Art Museum, designed by Italian architect Renzo Piano, to house the collection of its most prominent backer, Eli Broad. The new facility contains 56,000 square feet of exhibition space, which serves as the focal point of the museum's transformation.

But, Govan's real strongpoint is in having a knack for exhibit design. Artist Alexis Smith outlined Govan's work in bringing neon artist Dan Flavin to the museum. "The Flavin exhibition was beautifully selected, installed and almost choreographed," Smith said. "Its level of visual sophistication was doubly interesting because it was done not by a museum curator but by a museum director."[11] Govan also orchestrated the remodeling of the museum's entrance, bringing in artist Robert Irwin to create a garden of palm trees, Chris Burden to install vintage street lamps, and for phase two of the renovation, a Jeff Koons-designed 70-foot train replica dangled from a crane.

Today's young museum leaders are able to wow corporate sponsors and celebrities. Govan brought Barbara Streisand into LACMA as a trustee. He also strengthened ties with Hollywood, adding Michael Lynton, the chief executive of Sony Pictures Entertainment, as a director. These ties are critical in running a museum in the new millennium. Govan and his colleagues at other institutions must delicately mix corporate sponsorship and dollars into growth and sustainability plans. For example, the global oil company BP funded the new $25 million solar-powered entrance pavilion and will have its name adorned to the structure. This move led to some criticism, but it seems to be a necessity in today's art world. Museums need large endowments and LACMA's $170 million is miniscule compared to more well-known places like the Museum of Modern Art ($650 million).[12]

Another central figure in the LACMA's renovation is Broad, its benefactor and namesake for the new building. The list of pieces he is donating reads like a who's who of contemporary art: Koons, Cindy Sherman, Roy Lichtenstein, and Robert Rauschenberg. "I'd like to make the largest gift, and I liked to help raise a lot of money," Broad said. "But now that we've got other, younger trustees of some prominence and wealth, I'm delighted that they're very engaged. And we've got a great leader in Michael, so it all feels pretty good to me."[13]

Scams, Fakes, and Fraud

The culmination of a five-year probe into art fraud took place on January 24, 2008, when teams of federal agents from the Internal Revenue Service, National Park Service, and Immigration and Customs Enforcement descended on four California museums: The Mingei International Museum in San Diego, the Los Angeles County Museum of Art, the Pacific Asia Museum in Pasadena, and the Bowers Museum in Santa Ana. The raids came after the agencies investigated possible theft and tax schemes after the institutions allegedly accepted looted cultural treasures from Thailand. According to journalists Jeff McDonald and Jeanette Steele, the action taken in California "has drawn new attention to an unwelcome fact of the art trade: An increasing amount of pillaged property is finding its way into museums and private collections."[14]

With no federal agency providing oversight into the art theft challenge, even the best museums and collectors in the world face reproach. The stakes are high for all parties involved in complex art purchasing and trades. Often, the transactions seem more like they are from a James Bond movie than between real-life international dealers and museum representatives. In the 2000s, developing countries are most susceptible to looting.

In the California case, Robert Olson, a Los Angeles smuggler, sold items stolen from grave sites in the Ban Chiang region of northeast Thailand. At the Mingei, federal officials believe that 70 objects were acquired illegally, and they seized 23 in the January search. The artifacts in question are mainly earthenware pieces, some that date back to 3000 B.C. Similarly, in 2007, the J. Paul Getty Museum in Los Angeles returned 40 pieces that Italian officials said were stolen. Both The Metropolitan Museum of Art in New York and the Museum of Fine Arts in Boston also returned stolen Italian artwork.[15]

Investigators at Immigration and Customs Enforcement's Office of Investigations conduct extensive analyses of potentially illegal art sales, citing the general political instability in some parts of the world as a catalyst for such crimes. Some 50 agents watch the Web and investigate international shipping records hoping to minimize illegal trafficking. The office focuses on returning pilfered pieces to their rightful owners, not necessarily convicting the looters and/or middlemen involved in the transactions. Putting the criminals in jail is difficult in these cases, so prosecutors concentrate on getting the items returned.[16]

PHOTOGRAPHY

Ian Allen

Photographer Ian Allen and his friend documentary filmmaker Jeremy Blakeslee snuck into an abandoned Bethlehem steel mill in eastern Pennsylvania to look around and capture images of the empty plant, once teeming with life and hot, molten metal. Soon to be demolished and replaced with a casino, the men dodged security guards and jumped fences to get at the heart of the deserted mill. Of Allen's photography, journalist Jami Attenberg said, "The cavernous images have a mournful air; one can feel the staleness in the place. In some shots, the abandoned machinery looms as if it were wounded. The photos capture what is absent as much as what remains."[17]

Taken from inside and outside the abandoned mill, Allen's photographs underscore desertedness and the immensity of the place. Some of the shots are taken from rooftops as a sheen of snow covers the ground. They reveal depth, represented by the rail lines indicating distance and the blue-gray sky that extends out forever. The rusty buildings preview the work of demolition crews that will pull the plant apart piece by piece. In another shot, a section of the mill's roof in the foreground accentuates the run-down town built on a stark hillside just beyond its gates. These are the people the mill left behind, and their homes are multicolored, but worn: a hodgepodge of misshapen buildings filled with people as abandoned as the mill itself.

Originally from Seattle, and educated at the School of Visual Arts in New York, the 27-year-old Allen epitomizes visual arts in the new millennium. He is not limited to one medium, working in both photography and design. Allen also represents the kind of fluid globalization that younger artists embody. On a trip to Asia, Allen contrasted the chaotic street life in Tokyo with the rural solitude of Tibet. Unlike artists of past generations, Allen is focused on his work first, rather than the money he can generate. "At this point in my career, I'd rather be stuffing my portfolio and wait to stuff my wallet later, if ever," he said. "I'm trying to avoid the ever-increasing salary-equals-success mentality that young designers can get trapped in."[18] Allen's client list represents his interests across popular culture. They range from MTV and HBO, to the advertising firm Ogilvy & Mather and *New York* magazine.

Gregory Crewdson

Director, production manager, or choreographer—rather than photographer—might be better labels for what Gregory Crewdson creates on film. Rather than the traditional stereotype of a barren, white room containing little more than a photographer, model, and camera, Crewdson stages elaborate scenes, sometimes on a soundstage and others in the field, often small towns in Massachusetts. Regardless, the result is an image that tells a story of humanity, particularly in the American suburbs. Sometimes, these photographs capture the lurid details people hope to keep from their neighbors, while others the focus on the elegance in ordinary lives.

Born in Brooklyn, New York, in 1962, Crewdson teaches photography at Yale University, where he received his MFA. He gained attention in the 1990s for several series that mixed the mundane and outrageous into a surreal view of life in Lee, Massachusetts, where his family had a cabin when he was a boy. The town serves as the backdrop for many of Crewdson's works. In his artist's biography from the Guggenheim, one gets the sense of the scope and filmic vision of Crewdson's works, which are "Decidedly cinematic images reminiscent of the films of Steven Spielberg. These recent photographs have become increasingly spectacular and complex to produce, requiring dozens of assistants, Hollywood-style lighting, and specially crafted stage sets."[19]

One is thrown off when first examining Crewdson's stills. They require a second, deeper look because it is almost impossible to believe that the lush colors aren't from a painting. Crewdson's *Twilight* series (1998–2001), for example, shows typical family scenes, bathed in deep hues of reds and grays. Then, there is an added fantastical aspect of the photograph that completely changes the viewer's perception of the piece. Crewdson explained his fascination with that instant where normal and abnormal collide, saying:

> In all my pictures what I am ultimately interested in is that moment of transcendence or transportation, where one is transported into another place, into a perfect, still world. Despite my compulsion to create this still world,

> it always meets up against the impossibility of doing so. So, I like the collision between this need for order and perfection and how it collides with a sense of the impossible. I like where possibility and impossibly meet.[20]

In a 2006 photo, *Untitled (north by northwest)*, a woman sits in the passenger seat of an automobile, its lights on, stopped in the middle of a desolate street at a yellow light. There is no visible sign of the driver or that the person even existed—the only option is that the character literally ran out of the frame. But how did the driver get out of the picture before the passenger could react? True to Crewdson's style, the photograph looks like a color movie still, and the dawn sky and light mist in the background have sucked the color out of the picture, which allows the faint yellow of a crosswalk in the foreground and the overhead traffic light to sizzle. Upon first glance, the viewer would be hard pressed to believe that such perfection could be staged.

The tension, however, is always the focus in Crewdson. Describing Crewdson's style as a chronicler of suburban America, a recent reviewer said, "Rather than depicting suburbia as a place of expectation, his photographs show the suburbs as a shadowy world where strange and even surreal things happen; in one image showing here, a middle-aged man watches absently as clouds of smoke billow from a backyard shed. You sense that some dark truth lies below the scene's otherwise calm surface." The artist asks the audience to reexamine life both hidden and exposed in the seemingly boring suburbs and perhaps question the stereotypes associated with suburbia.[21]

PAINTING

Mark Bradford

Arts

Over a six year span, Mark Bradford achieved the American Dream. At the beginning of the journey, he ran his mother's hair salon in South Los Angeles with hopes of someday becoming an artist. Fast forward a little more than a handful of years later, and his paintings sell for $250,000. He is a featured artist at shows around the country and enjoys global fame, including winning the 2006 Bucksbaum Award, a $100,000 prize given to a participant at the Whitney Biennial.

Like any great American success story, Bradford's did not come without some heartbreak. In 2001, he sold his first piece, titled *Enter and Exit the New Negro* to the Studio Museum in Harlem. For the next two years, some of his work met with criticism, including shows at Art Basel Miami and the Whitney Altria space. In 2003, however, Bradford bounced back at a show called "Bounce." Curator Eungie Joo pushed him to "work big" and bought him the canvas to do so. Bradford came back strong, including the piece *Los Moscos,* later one of his works at the 2006 Whitney Biennial.[22]

In September 2007, his first solo show, "Neither New nor Correct," opened at the Whitney. It featured scenes from his hometown Leimert Park neighborhood in Los Angeles. Bradford's influences extend beyond his African American roots to include his place as a third generation small business owner. He explained:

> Early on, I was interested in using material that came from my merchant roots. My mother was a hair stylist; I was a hair stylist. But then I started thinking, "Where is what I do?" It doesn't sound right, but that was my question. And the answer to where? was community. Once I looked out of the hair salon and became interested in the environment around me—and the language of that environment—everything that I had been trying to talk about was already there...I wanted to engage that material more directly. The conversations I was interested in were about community, fluidity, about a merchant dynamic, and the details that point to a genus of change. The species I use sometimes are racial, sexual, cultural, stereotypical. But the genus I'm always interested in is change.[23]

Like many other twenty-first century artists, Bradford works across many forms of media, not just painting. He is well-regarded as a "found" artist, or one who takes things he finds on the streets (in Bradford's case, signage and advertising) and turns it into art. "Bradford incorporates elements from his daily life into his canvases: remnants of found posters and billboards, graffitied stencils

Adam Weinberg, director of the Whitney Museum of American Art, New York, stands in front Mark Bradford's *Los Moscos* as he addresses reporters during a press preview of the Whitney Biennial 2006: "Day for Night," February 28, 2006 in New York City. AP Photo.

and logos, and hairdresser's permanent endpapers he's collected from his other profession as a stylist," the experts at The Saatchi Gallery said. "In *The Devil is Beating His Wife,* Bradford consolidates all these materials into a pixelised eruption of cultural cross-referencing. Built up on plywood in sensuous layers ranging from silky and skin-like to oily and singed, Bradford offers abstraction with an urban flair that's explosively contemporary."[24]

ENDNOTES FOR THE 2000s

OVERVIEW OF THE 2000s

1. Jack Loechner, "It's a Wrap: The Internet Year 2007," *Research Brief,* Center for Media Research (February 6, 2008), http://blogs.mediapost.com/research_brief/?p=1634 (accessed February 6, 2008).
2. Loechner, "It's a Wrap."
3. Associated Press, "Data Breaches Climb in '07," *St. Petersburg Times,* December 31, 2007, 5A.
4. "The $1.7 Trillion Dot.Com Lesson," *CNNMoney* (November 9, 2000), http://money.cnn.com/2000/11/09/technology/overview (accessed November 15, 2000).
5. "UN Report Cites Global Internet Growth Despite Economic Woes," *USA Today* (November 18, 2002), http://www.usatoday.com/tech/news/2002-11-18-global-net_x.htm (accessed November 19, 2002).
6. Samantha Levine, "News in the Hands of Too Few?" *U.S. News & World Report,* 144, 1 (2008): 23–25. Academic Search Premier, EBSCOhost (accessed March 22, 2008).
7. "Business: The Anti-Mogul," *The Economist* (November 10, 2007), http://www.proquest.com.proxy.usf.edu (accessed March 20, 2008).
8. Matt Smith, "Bush: I Will Work to Earn Your Respect," *CNN.com Election 2000* (December 13, 2000), http://archives.cnn.com/2000/ALLPOLITICS/stories/12/13/bush.ends.campaign/index.html (accessed December 14, 2000).
9. "Looking Back, Looking Forward: A Forum," The Nation (December 2, 2004), http://www.thenation.com/doc/20041220/forum/3 (accessed December 2, 2004).
10. Sean Wilentz, "The Worst President in History?" *Rolling Stone,* May 4, 2006, 32–33; Robert S. McElvaine,

"Historians Vs. George W. Bush," *History News Network* (August 20, 2005), http://hnn.us/comments/66933.html (accessed August 20, 2005).

11. Richard Willing, "Ex-CIA Spy's Account Unveiled," *USA Today* (October 21, 2007), http://www.usatoday.com/news/washington/2007-10-21-plame-book_n.htm (accessed April 18, 2008).
12. "President Bush—Overall Job Rating in National Polls," *PollingReport.com,* http://www.pollingreport.com/BushJob.htm (accessed March 15, 2008).
13. Wilentz, "The Worst President in History?," 34.
14. Richard Wolf, "Bush Has Big Plans for His Last Year," *USA Today,* January 28, 2008, Academic Search Premier, EBSCOhost, http://search.ebscohost.com/login.aspx?direct = true&db = aph&AN = J0E332403812708&site = ehost-live (accessed March 17, 2008).
15. Wolf, "Bush Has Big Plans for His Last Year."
16. Wilentz, "The Worst President in History?," 35.
17. James Poniewozik. "The Big Fat Year in Culture: So much for the post-9/11 Warm-and-Fuzzies. In 2002 the Pop World got Weird Again." *Time,* December 30, 2002, Expanded Academic ASAP. Thomson Gale. University of South Florida. http://find.galegroup.com.proxy.usf.edu/itx/infomark.do?&contentSet = IAC-Documents&type = retrieve&tabID = T003&prodId = EAIM&docId = A95739763&source = gale&srcprod = EAIM&userGroupName = tamp59176&version = 1.0 (accessed June 9, 2007).
18. *The Complete 9/11 Commission Report* is available at http://govinfo.library.unt.edu/ 911/report/index.htm.
19. Jack Devine, "An Intelligence Reform Reality Check," *Washington Post* (February 18, 2008), http://www.washingtonpost.com/wp-dyn/content/article/2008/02/17/AR2008021701733.html (accessed March 30, 2008).
20. "Bush's 'Bannergate' Shuffle," *Time* (November 1, 2003), http://www.time.com/time/columnist/dickerson/article/0,9565,536170,00.html (accessed November 15, 2005).
21. "Public Attitudes Toward the War in Iraq: 2003–2008," Pew Research Center (March 19, 2008), http://pewresearch.org/pubs/770/iraq-war-five-year-anniversary (accessed April 17, 2008).
22. Lizette Alvarez and Andrew W. Lehren, "Six of the Fallen, in Words They Sent Home," *The New York Times* (March 25, 2008), http://www.nytimes.com/2008/03/25/us/25dead.web.html?pagewanted = all, (accessed March 30, 2008); "U.S. And Coalition Casualties," Forces: U.S. & Coalition/Casualties, Special Reports from CNN.com, http://www.cnn.com/SPECIALS/2003/iraq/forces/casualties (accessed March 30, 2008).
23. "Public Attitudes Toward the War," Pew Research Center.
24. Dana Priest and Anne Hull, "Soldiers Face Neglect, Frustration At Army's Top Medical Facility," *Washington Post* (February 18, 2007), http://www.washingtonpost.com/wp-dyn/content/article/2007/02/17/AR2007021701172.html (accessed March 30, 2007).
25. Priest and Hull, "Soldiers Face Neglect, Frustration At Army's Top Medical Facility."
26. Paul Elias, "Veterans Accuse Government of Mishandling Medical Care," *The Mercury News* (San Jose) (April 19, 2008), http://www.mercurynews.com/breakingnews/ci_8984799 (accessed April 19, 2008).
27. Quoted in Bob Batchelor, "Unspeakable Tragedy: Race and Katrina," *PopMatters* (August 29, 2006), http://www.popmatters.com/features/060829-katrina.shtml (accessed August 29, 2006).
28. George Bush, "President Bush Addresses NAACP Annual Convention" (July 20, 2006), http://www.whitehouse.gov/news/releases/2006/07/20060720.html (accessed July 21, 2006).
29. Charles M. Blow, "Racism and the Race," *New York Times* (August 8, 2008), http://www.nytimes.com/2008/08/09/opinion/09blow.html?_r=1&scp=1&sq=chalres%20m.%20blow&st=cse&oref=slogin.
30. Pat Regnier, "Are You Better Off?" *Money: 35th Anniversary Special 110* (October 1, 2007): http://www.proquest.com.proxy.usf.edu (accessed November 3, 2007).
31. Yang Yang, "Social Inequalities in Happiness in the United States, 1972 to 2004: An Age-Period-Cohort Analysis," *American Sociological Review* 73.2 (2008): 204–26, http://news.uchicago.edu/images/ assets/pdf/Happinesspaper.pdf.
32. Yang, "Social Inequalities in Happiness in the United States, 1972 to 2004."
33. Darla Mercado, "Foreclosure Filings Up 93% this Year," *InvestmentNews,* August 21, 2007.
34. Regnier, "Are You Better Off?"
35. Quoted in Jeannine Aversa, "Many Believe US Already in a Recession," *Associated Press* (February 10, 2008), http://ap.google.com/article/ALeqM5hJjzb-73g6-mEmgvyixbf7Vzw2lgD8UNNUBO2 (accessed February 11, 2008).
36. Aversa, "Many Believe US Already in a Recession."
37. Aversa, "Many Believe US Already in a Recession."
38. "Outsourcing Trends to Watch in 2007," *Fortune,* September 3, 2007, S2.
39. Bethany McLean and Peter Elkind, "The Guiltiest Guys in the Room," *Fortune* (July 5, 2006), http://money.cnn.com/2006/05/29/news/enron_guiltyest/index.htm (accessed September 15, 2006).
40. Penelope Patsuris, "The Corporate Scandal Sheet," *Forbes.com* (August 26, 2002), http://www.forbes.com/2002/07/25/accountingtracker.html (accessed November 15, 2007).
41. Quoted in "CEOs Defend Their Paychecks," *St. Petersburg Times,* March 8, 2008, 2D.
42. "You've Got Mail (Lots of It)," *St. Petersburg Times,* January 27, 2008, 1F.
43. Bobby White, "The New Workplace Rules: No Video-Watching," *The Wall Street Journal,* March 4, 2008, B1.

44. White, "The New Workplace Rules."
45. Quoted in White, "The New Workplace Rules."
46. White, "The New Workplace Rules."
47. Jeannine Aversa, "Employers Slash Jobs by Most in 5 Years," *AP* (March 7, 2008), http://biz.yahoo.com/ap/080307/economy.html (accessed March 7, 2008).
48. Aversa, "Employers Slash Jobs by Most in 5 Years."
49. Quoted in Tim Paradis, "Stocks Turn Mixed in Early Trading," *AP* (March 7, 2008), http://biz.yahoo.com/ap/080307/wall_street.html?.v=19 (accessed March 7, 2008).
50. "Empty-Nesters, Unite," *Atlantic Monthly,* October 2007, 33.
51. Quoted in "Empty-Nesters, Unite."
52. Jerry Adler, "The Boomer Files; Hitting 60." *Newsweek* (November 14, 2005), 50. Expanded Academic ASAP. Thomson Gale. University of South Florida. http://find.galegroup.com.proxy.usf.edu/itx/infomark.do?&contentSet=IAC-Documents&type=retrieve&tabID=T003&prodId=EAIM&docId=A138452122&source=gale&srcprod=EAIM&userGroupName=tamp59176&version=1.0 (accessed June 9, 2007).
53. Lorne Manly, "TV's Silver Age," *The New York Times Magazine* (May 6, 2007), http://www.nytimes.com/2007/05/06/magazine/06tvland-t.html?pagewanted=1&_r=1 (accessed February 10, 2008).
54. Quoted in William Hupp, "The Misunderstood Generation," *Advertising Age* (February 5, 2008), http://adage.com/sendopinion?article_id=124865 (accessed February 5, 2008).
55. Chad Lorenz, "The Death of E-Mail," *Slate* (November 14, 2007), http://www.slate.com/id/2177969/pagenum/all/#page_start (accessed November 18, 2007).
56. Lorenz, "The Death of E-Mail."
57. "Summary of Key Findings," *U.S. Religious Landscape Survey,* Pew Forum on Religion & Public Life, http://religions.pewforum.org/reports (accessed March 20, 2008).
58. "Summary of Key Findings."
59. "Summary of Key Findings."

ADVERTISING OF THE 2000S

1. Robert W. McChesney, *The Problem of the Media: U.S. Communication Politics in the Twenty-First Century* (New York: Monthly Review Press, 2004), 161.
2. Christopher Lasch, *The Culture of Narcissism: American Life in an Age of Diminishing Expectations* (New York: W.W. Norton), 137–38.
3. McChesney, *The Problem of the Media,* 166.
4. Quoted in McChesney, *The Problem of the Media,* 149.
5. Irene Costera Meijer, "Advertising Citizenship: An Essay on the Performative Power of Consumer Culture," *Media, Culture & Society* 20 (1998): 242.
6. Meijer, "Advertising Citizenship."
7. Meijer, "Advertising Citizenship," 247.
8. Stuart Elliott, "This Year's Super Bowl Ads to Be Gentle and Sweet," *The New York Times* (January 31, 2008), http://www.nytimes.com/2008/01/31/business/media/31adco.html?fta=y (accessed January 31, 2008).
9. Quoted in Gavin O'Malley, "Snickers Scrubs Super Bowl Ad Site," *MediaPost Publications* (February 7, 2007), http://publications.mediapost.com/index.cfm?fuseaction=Articles.showArticle&art_aid=55165&passFuseAction=ublicationsSearch.showSearchReslts&art_searched=nickers&page_number=0 (accessed February 7, 2007).
10. Jerry Kirkpatrick, "A Philosophic Defense of Advertising," *Advertising in Society: Classic and Contemporary Readings on Advertising's Role in Society,* eds. Roxanne Hovland and Gary B. Wilcox (Lincolnwood, IL: NTC, 1989), 517.
11. Jib Fowles, *Advertising and Popular Culture* (Thousand Oaks, CA: Sage, 1996), 49.
12. Robert F. Hartley, *Marketing Mistakes and Successes,* 8th ed. (New York: Wiley, 2001), 352.
13. Patricia Sellers, "MySpace Cowboys," *Fortune* (September 4, 2006): 73–74.
14. Sellers, "MySpace Cowboys," 73–74.
15. Brian Morrissey, "Inside the Promise and Peril of YouTube," *ADWEEK* (January 29, 2007): 10.
16. Ron Ruggless, "Students' Low-Cost Chipotles Ads Draw 18 Million Online Viewers," *Nation's Restaurant News* (December 4, 2006): 4.
17. Paul Gillin, "The World's Watching: So Why Aren't PR Pros Using Viral Video?" *Bulldog Reporter's Daily Dog* (March 29, 2007), http://www.bulldogreporter.com/dailydog/issues/1_1/dailydog_barks_bites/index.html (accessed March 29, 2007).
18. Gillin, "The World's Watching."
19. Fowles, *Advertising and Popular Culture,* 165.
20. Leslie Wayne, "McCain Reports Improved Fund-Raising, but Still Lags," *The New York Times* (April 21, 2008), http://www.nytimes.com/2008/04/21/us/politics/21campaign.html (accessed April 21, 2008).
21. Chuck Todd, "Campaign by the Numbers," *The New York Times* (November 3, 2004), http://www.nytimes.com/2004/11/03/opinion/03todd.html?scp=103&sq=campaign+advertising+bush+kerry&st=nyt (accessed March 30, 2005).
22. Todd, "Campaign by the Numbers."
23. Don Van Natta Jr. and John M. Broder, "With Finish Line in Sight, An All-Out Race for Money," *The New York Times* (November 3, 2000), http://query.nytimes.com/gst/fullpage.html?res=9901E5D61F30F930A35752C1A9669C8B63&sec=&spon=(accessed April 20, 2008).
24. Natta and Broder, "With Finish Line in Sight, An All-Out Race for Money."
25. Omnicom, 2006 Annual Report, Omnicom Group (April 2007), http://www.omnicomgroup.com/investorrelations/financialoverview/financialperformance.

26. Andrew McMains, "OMC Shows New Creative Tactics," *AdWeek* (December 5, 2007), http://www.adweek.com/aw/national/article_display.jsp?vnu_content_id=1003681472 (accessed December 20, 2007).
27. Omnicon, 2006 Annual Report.
28. Quoted in Nicola Ruiz, "Can A Star Sell You Style," *Forbes* (April 18, 2008), http://www.forbes.com/style/2008/04/18/style-star-ad-forbeslife-cx_nr_0418style.html (accessed April 21, 2008).
29. Ruiz, "Can A Star Sell You Style."
30. Ruiz, "Can A Star Sell You Style."
31. Stuart Elliott, "Forecasters Say Madison Avenue Will Escape a Recession, Just Barely," *The New York Times* (December 4, 2007), http://proquest.umi.com/pqdweb?did=1392567101&sid=4&Fmt=3&clientId=20178&RQT=309&VName=PQD (accessed January 8, 2008).
32. Quoted in Elliot, "Forecasters Say Madison Avenue Will Escape a Recession, Just Barely."

ARCHITECTURE OF THE 2000s

1. Quoted in Russell Fortmeyer, "The State of American Architecture: Chicago," *BusinessWeek* (February 11, 2008), http://www.businessweek.com/innovate/content/feb2008/id20080213_872885.htm (accessed March 1, 2008).
2. Quoted in Clifford A. Pearson, "The State of American Architecture: Atlanta," *BusinessWeek* (February 11, 2008), http://www.businessweek.com/innovate/content/feb2008/id20080213_006669.htm (accessed March 1, 2008).
3. Quoted in Pearson.
4. Joint Center for Housing Studies of Harvard University, *The State of the Nation's Housing: 2007,* Cambridge, MA: Harvard College, 2007, 1.
5. Joint Center for Housing Studies, *The State of the Nation's Housing,* 1.
6. Joint Center for Housing Studies, *The State of the Nation's Housing,* 4.
7. Joint Center for Housing Studies, *The State of the Nation's Housing,* 5.
8. Joint Center for Housing Studies, *The State of the Nation's Housing,* 6–7.
9. "Freedom Tower," World Trade Center Web site, Silverstein Properties, http://www.wtc.com/about/freedomtower (accessed March 31, 2008).
10. Quoted in Clifford A. Pearson, "The State of American Architecture: New York," *BusinessWeek* (February 11, 2008), http://www.businessweek.com/innovate/content/feb2008/id20080211_678597.htm (accessed March 1, 2008).
11. Nicolai Ouroussoff, "Medieval Modern: Design Strikes a Defensive Posture," *The New York Times* (March 4, 2007), http://www.nytimes.com/2007/03/04/weekinreview/04ouroussoff.html?_r=1&scp=2&sq=%22david+childs%22&st=nyt&oref=slogin (accessed March 1, 2008).
12. Nicolai Ouroussoff, "Gehry's New York Debut: Subdued Tower of Light," *The New York Times* (March 22, 2007), http://www.nytimes.com/2007/03/22/arts/design/22dill.html?pagewanted=1&_r=1&hp (accessed January 31, 2008).
13. Jamie Reno, "Scenes From a New Mall," *Newsweek* (October 15, 2007), http://www.newsweek.com/id/43924 (accessed February 1, 2008).
14. Reno, "Scenes From a New Mall."
15. Quoted in Stephanie Hacke, "Town Centers Help Create Sense of Community," *Woodland Progress* (February 27, 2008), http://www.gatewaynewspapers.com/woodlandprogress/92658 (accessed March 7, 2008).
16. Quoted in Hacke, "Town Centers Help Create Sense of Community."
17. Bill Saporito, "Inside the New American Home," *Time* (October 14, 2002), http://www.time.com/time/magazine/article/0,9171,1003432,00.html (accessed January 29, 2008).
18. Quoted in Saporito, "Inside the New American Home."
19. "The Redesigning Of America," *Time* 155 (March 20, 2000), http://find.galegroup.com.proxy.usf.edu/itx/infomark.do?&contentSet=IAC-Documents&type=retrieve&tabID=T003&prodId=EAIM&docId=A60588201&source=gale&srcprod=EAIM&userGroupName=tamp59176&version=1.0/ (accessed June 9, 2007).
20. Quoted in "The Redesigning Of America."
21. Quoted in Candace Ord Manroe, "Hot Home Trends 2008," *At Home with Century 21,* January/February 2008, 17.
22. Manroe, "Hot Home Trends 2008," 18.
23. Judy Stark, "Remodeling Makeover," *St. Petersburg Times,* March 1, 2008, 5F.
24. Quoted in Stark, "Remodeling Makeover."

BOOKS, NEWSPAPERS, MAGAZINES, AND COMICS OF THE 2000s

1. Jordan E. Rosenfeld, "Shock and Awe," *Writer's Digest,* October 2007, 47.
2. Julie Watson and Tomas Kellner, "J.K. Rowling And The Billion-Dollar Empire," *Forbes.com* (February 26, 2004), http://www.forbes.com/maserati/billionaires2004/cx_jw_0226rowlingbill04.html (accessed September 15, 2005).
3. "Pottermania Unleashed," *Forbes.com* (July 20, 2007), http://www.forbes.com/business/2007/07/20/potter-scholastic-books-biz-cx_0720potter.html (accessed September 15, 2008).

4. Quoted in "New Study Finds that the Harry Potter Series has a Positive Impact on Kids' Reading and their School Work," Press Release, July 25, 2006, Scholastic Web site, http://www.scholastic.com/aboutscholastic/news/press_07252006_CP.htm (accessed April 1, 2008).
5. Quoted in Julie Bick, "Seattle Helps Shape What Nation Reads," *The Seattle Times* (March 11, 2008), http://seattletimes.nwsource.com/html/businesstechnology/2004273751_seattlebookczars.html (accessed March 15, 2008).
6. Quoted in Liz Ruiz, "Coben Tried to 'Grab You on Page One,'" *The State* (South Carolina), February 17, 2008, E2.
7. Chuck Leddy, "Loot vs. Literature: Genre and Literary Fiction," *Writer* 121 (2008): 8–9.
8. Rachel Donadio, "Promotional Intelligence," *The New York Times* (May 21, 2006), http://www.nytimes.com/2006/05/21/books/review/21donadio.html?sq=&pagewanted=all (accessed September 15, 2006).
9. Donadio, "Promotional Intelligence."
10. Donadio, "Promotional Intelligence."
11. "Meghan Holohan, "An Active Voice," *Pitt Magazine,* Summer 2003, 29.
12. Craig Offman, "Tom Wolfe Calls Irving, Mailer and Updike 'the Three Stooges,'" Salon.com (January 21, 2000), http://archive.salon.com/books/log/2000/01/21/wolfe/index.html (accessed August 29, 2001).
13. Richard Lacayo, "Oprah Turns the Page," *Time* (April 15, 2002), http://www.time.com/time/magazine/article/0,9171,1002228,00.html (accessed November 15, 2002).
14. David Carr, "How Oprahness Trumped Truthiness," *The New York Times* (January 30, 2006), http://www.nytimes.com/2006/01/30/business/media/30carr.html?ex=1296277200&en=1c0e8843da5b43d6&ei=5088&partner=rssnyt&emc=rss (accessed April 27, 2006).
15. Randy Dotinga, "Iraq War Books Do A Quickstep into Print," *The Christian Science Monitor,* http://www.csmonitor.com/2005/1130/p14s03-bogn.html (accessed April 1, 2008).

ENTERTAINMENT OF THE 2000S

1. Sarah Mahoney, "Super Bowl-Related Sales Approach $10 Billion," *MediaPost Publications* (January 24, 2008), http://publications.mediapost.com/index.cfm?fuseaction = Articles.showArticle&art_aid = 74959 (accessed February 1, 2008).
2. Paul Thomasch, "Giants and Patriots Draw Record Super Bowl Audience," *Reuters* (February 4, 2008), http://www.reuters.com/article/topNews/idUSN0420266320080204?pageNumber=1&virtualBrandChannel=0 (accessed February 6, 2008).
3. "TV Basics: Television Households," *TV Basics: An Online Brochure,* Television Bureau of Advertising, http://www.tvb.org (accessed February 8, 2008).
4. "TV Basics: Television Households."
5. *2006 Media Comparisons Study,* Television Bureau of Advertising, http://www.tvb.org (accessed February 9, 2008).
6. *2006 Media Comparisons Study.*
7. Bill Carter, "How A Hit Almost Failed Its Own Audition," *The New York Times* (April 30, 2006), http://www.nytimes.com/2006/04/30/business/yourmoney/30idol.html?pagewanted = all (accessed April 30, 2006).
8. Ken Barnes, "Long Live 'American Idol,'" *USA Today,* March 10, 2008, L3.
9. Richard M. Huff, *Reality Television* (Westport, CT: Praeger, 2006), 2–3.
10. Huff, *Reality Television,* 6.
11. Huff, *Reality Television,* 7.
12. Derek Foster, "Jump in the Pool: The Competitive and Collegial Culture of *Survivor* Fan Communities," in *Understanding Reality Television,* ed. Su Holmes and Deborah Jermyn (London: Routledge, 2004), 280.
13. "We Like To Watch: Led by the Hit *Survivor,* Voyeurism has become TV's Hottest Genre," *Time,* June 26, 2000, Expanded Academic ASAP. Thomson Gale, http://find.galegroup.com.proxy.usf.edu/itx/infomark.do?&contentSet=IAC-Documents&type=retrieve&tabID=T003&prodId=EAIM&docId=A62880218&source=gale&srcprod=EAIM&userGroupName=tamp59176&version=1.0 (accessed June 9, 2007).
14. "We Like To Watch."
15. Yinka Adegoke, "Cable Loses Subscribers, Satellite Gains in Q1," *Reuters* (April 28, 2008), http://www.reuters.com/article/marketsNews/idUSN2846199920080428?sp=true (accessed April 29, 2008).
16. Chuck Bell, "Time for New Yorkers to Strike Back Against Big Cable," *NYDailyNews.com* (April 16, 2008), http://www.nydailynews.com/opinions/2008/04/16/2008-04-16_time_for_new_yorkers_to_strike_back_agai.html (accessed April 28, 2008).
17. Tim Goodman, "TV's Best of 2007," *San Francisco Chronicle* (December 31, 2007), http://www.sfgate.com/cgi-bin/article.cgi?file=/c/a/2007/12/31/DDDGU66SJ.DTL (accessed April 1, 2008).
18. Quoted in Ronald Grover and Tom Lowry, "Spending Like Mad Men on Cable TV," *Business Week* (April 24, 2008), http://www.businessweek.com/magazine/content/08_18/b4082054975746.htm?chan=top+news_top+news+index_businessweek+exclusives (accessed April 30, 2008).
19. Grove and Lowry, "Spending Like Mad Men on Cable TV."
20. Jeff Zucker, "A Time for Change," *Vital Speeches of the Day,* May 2008, 205.

21. Zucker, "A Time for Change," 207.
22. "Prime Time is Anytime," Digital Life America survey, Solutions Research Group, February 4, 2008, 1.
23. "Prime Time is Anytime."
24. David M. Halbfinger and Michael Cieply, "'No Country for Old Men' Wins Oscar Tug of War," *The New York Times* (February 25, 2008), http://www.nytimes.com/2008/02/25/movies/awardsseason /25osca.html?ref=awardsseason (accessed March 30, 2008).
25. David Carr, "In Oscars, No Country For Hit Films," *The New York Times* (March 3, 2008), http://query.nytimes.com/gst/fullpage.html?res=9C01E3D6143BF930A357 50C0A96E9C8B63 (accessed March 30, 2008).
26. Brooks Barnes and Matt Richtel, "Studios Are Trying to Stop DVDs From Fading to Black," *The New York Times* (February 25, 2008), http://www.nytimes.com/2008/02/25/business/media/25dvd.html (accessed February 25, 2008).
27. Caryn James, "A Movie Star for All Eras, Even the Present," *The New York Times* (January 6, 2008), http://www.nytimes.com/2008/01/06/movies/awardsseason/06jame.html (accessed February 1, 2008).
28. Michelle Tauber, et al., "And now . . . Brangelina," *People* 63 (2005): 56–61, Academic Search Premier, EBSCOhost (accessed February 26, 2008).
29. Alec Appelbaum, "Pitt Unveils Sustainable Housing for New Orleans," *Architectural Record* 196 (2008): 12, Academic Search Premier, EBSCOhost (accessed February 26, 2008).
30. Quoted in Robin Pogrebin, "Brad Pitt Commissions Designs for New Orleans," *The New York Times* (December 3, 2007), http://www.nytimes.com/2007/12/03/arts/design/03pitt.html?sq= (accessed December 3, 2007).
31. James Poniewozik, "The Day That Changed . . . Very Little," *Time*, August 7, 2006, Expanded Academic ASAP, Thomson Gale (accessed January 24, 2007).
32. "What's Entertainment Now?" *Time*, October 1, 2001, Expanded Academic ASAP, Thomson Gale (accessed June 9, 2007).
33. Richard Corliss, "Why the Iraq Films Are Failing," *Time* (November 15, 2007), http://www.time.com/time/magazine/article/0,9171,1684509,00.html (accessed February 21, 2008).
34. Miriam Kreinin Souccar, "Broadway Strike Shows No Lasting Effects," *Crain's New York Business*, January 14, 2008, LexisNexis Academic (accessed May 1, 2008).
35. Quoted in Souccar, "Broadway Strike Shows No Lasting Effects."
36. "Seasons Greeting B'Way," *Variety*, April 7–13, 2008, LexisNexis Academic (accessed May 1, 2008).

FASHION OF THE 2000s

1. Sharon Fink, "As the Fashion World Churns," *St. Petersburg Times*, February 2, 2008, E1.
2. Fink, "As the Fashion World Churns," E3.
3. Paco Underhill, *Why We Buy: The Science of Shopping* (New York: Simon & Schuster, 1999), 31.
4. "Wal-Mart Reports Record Fourth Quarter Sales and Earnings," Wal-Mart Stores Web site (February 19, 2008), http://www.walmartstores.com/FactsNews/NewsRoom/7950.aspx (accessed February 25, 2008).
5. Quoted in Anthony Bianco and Wendy Zellner, "Is Wal-Mart Too Powerful?" *Business Week*, October 6, 2003, 102.
6. Alex Kuczynski, "Now You See It, Now You Don't," *The New York Times* (September 12, 2004), http://www.nytimes.com/2004/09/12/fashion/12THON.html (accessed January 5, 2005).
7. Joseph Carroll, "'Business Casual' Most Common Work Attire. Gallup Poll, October 4, 2007. Gallup. http://www.gallup.com/poll/101707/Business-Casual-Most-Common-Work-Attire.aspx (accessed June 4, 2008).
8. Quoted in Marc Karimzadeh, "The Delebrities," *Women's Wear Daily* (December 11, 2007), http://www.wwd.com/article/print/120803 (accessed February 20, 2008).
9. Quoted in Angela Phipps Towle, "Celebrity Branding," *The Hollywood Reporter* (November 18, 2003), http://www.hollywoodreporter.com/hr/search/article_display.jsp?vnu_content_id=2030984 (accessed July 2, 2007).
10. Jane Friedman, "Cosmetic Surgery." *CQ Researcher*, April 15, 2005, 319.
11. Quoted in Kirsten Sharnberg, "After Plastic Surgeries, More Do An About-Face," *Chicago Tribune* (January 21, 2008), http://www.chicagotribune.com/news/nationworld/chi-plastic_regrets_21jan21,0,506282.story?coll=chi_tab01_layout (accessed January 21, 2008).
12. Friedman, "Cosmetic Surgery," 323.
13. Friedman, "Cosmetic Surgery," 332.
14. Jeanne Huff, "Botox: In Search of Youth," *Idaho Statesman* (January 12, 2008), http://www.idahostatesman.com/life/story/261770.html (accessed January 21, 2008).
15. Natasha Singer, "The Little Botox Shop Around the Corner," *The New York Times* (April 19, 2007), http://www.nytimes.com/2007/04/19/fashion/19skin.html?pagewanted=1 (accessed January 21, 2008).

FOOD OF THE 2000s

1. *Super Size Me*, DVD, directed by Morgan Spurlock (New York: Showtime Networks, 2004).
2. Richard Schickel, "Pigging Out to Make a Point," *Time* (June 7, 2004), http://www.time.com/time/magazine/article/0,9171,994386,00.html (accessed February 18, 2008).
3. George Will, "Make Big Macs and Millionaires," *The Tampa Tribune*, December 30, 2007, C2.

4. Press Release, "McDonald's Business Momentum Drives Strong Results for 2007," McDonald's Corporation, http://www.mcdonalds.com/corp/news/fnpr/2008/fpr_012808.html (accessed February 25, 2008).
5. Will, "Make Big Macs and Millionaires," C2.
6. National Center for Health Statistics, "Health, United States, 2007 With Chartbook on Trends in the Health of Americans," Hyattsville, MD: 2007, 40.
7. Quoted in Nanci Hellmich, "Portion Distortion," *USA Today,* June 23, 2005, 8B.
8. Kim Painter, "A Gluttony of Glug-Glugging," *USA Today,* April 10, 2006, 6D.
9. Leslie Goldman, "Our Dirty Little Secret? We Can't Stop Bingeing," *Health,* June 2007, 129–30.
10. Quoted in Goldman, "Our Dirty Little Secret?" 130.
11. Goldman, "Our Dirty Little Secret?" 131, 194.
12. Quoted in Christina Le Beau, "Diets Compared," *Better Nutrition* 66 (2004): 37.
13. Katherine Hobson, "Still No Perfect Diet," *U.S. News and World Report,* March 19, 2007, 59.
14. Le Beau, "Diets Compared," 38–39.
15. Gail Gorman, "The Big Fat Lie," *The Consumer's Medical Journal,* 2005, 2.
16. Gorman, "The Big Fat Lie," 4.
17. Conor Clarke, "Hill of Beans," *The New Republic,* November 20, 2006, 8.
18. Maria Bartiromo, "Howard Schultz on Reinventing Starbucks," *Business Week,* April 21, 2008, Academic Search Premier (accessed April 28, 2008).
19. Bartiromo, "Howard Schultz on Reinventing Starbucks."
20. Kenneth Hein, "PepsiCo Positions Amp as Everyman's Drink," *Brandweek,* January 21, 2008, Academic Search Premier (accessed April 20, 2008).
21. Quoted in Gerry Khermouch, "Canned Heat," *Brandweek,* October 8, 2007, Academic Search Premier (accessed March 30, 2008).
22. Hein, "PepsiCo. Positions Amp as Everyman's Drink."
23. Khermouch, "Canned Heat."
24. Quoted in Jen Haley, "Consumers Pinching their Pennies," *CNN* (March 10, 2008), http://www.cnn.com/2008/LIVING/personal/03/07/consumer.spending (accessed March 11, 2008).
25. Janelle Barlow, "Top Brands," *Fast Casual* 14 (2007/2008): 7.
26. Valerie Killifer, "Chipotle Sizzles at No. 1," *Fast Casual* 14 (2007/2008):18.
27. Quoted in Killifer, "Chipotle Sizzles at No. 1."
28. David Brown, "USDA Orders Largest Meat Recall in U.S. History," *Washington Post,* February 18, 2008, A01.
29. Quoted in Brown, "USDA Orders Largest Meat Recall in U.S. History."
30. Quoted in Brian Stelter, "Celebrity Chef Sells His TV Shows and Products to Martha Stewart," *The New York Times* (February 20, 2008), http://www.nytimes.com/2008/02/20/business/media/20martha.html?_r=1&ref=media&oref=slogin (accessed March 11, 2008).
31. "Rachael Ray's Official Biography," Rachael Ray's Official Web site, http://www.rachaelray.com/bio.php (accessed March 1, 2008).
32. "Rachael Ray's Official Biography."
33. Alec Foege, "The Rachael Way," *Brandweek* 48, Academic Search Premier, EBSCOhost, http://search.ebscohost.com.proxy.usf.edu/login.aspx?direct=true&db=aph&AN=24269226&site=ehost-live (accessed March 11, 2008).
34. Quoted in Jill Hunter Pellettieri, "Rachael Ray," *Slate* (July 13, 2005), http://www.slate.com/id/2122085 (accessed March 11, 2008).
35. Florence King, "Our Last Nerve," *National Review,* March 5, 2007, 42.
36. Jenny Allen, "Martha Comes Clean," *Good Housekeeping* 244, 9: 152–232. Academic Search Premier, EBSCOhost, http://search.ebscohost.com.proxy.usf.edu/login.aspx?direct=true&db=aph&AN=27047795&site=ehost-live (accessed March 11, 2008).
37. Quoted in Allen, "Martha Comes Clean."
38. Allen, "Martha Comes Clean."
39. Diane Brady, "The Reinvention of Martha Stewart," *Business Week* 4008 (2006): 76–80. Academic Search Premier, EBSCOhost, http://search.ebscohost.com.proxy.usf.edu/login.aspx?direct=true&db=aph&AN=22910974&site=ehost-live (accessed March 11, 2008).
40. Brady, "The Reinvention of Martha Stewart."

MUSIC OF THE 2000s

1. Brian Hiatt, "How to Sell a Smash Hit," *Rolling Stone,* September 7, 2006, 19.
2. Brian Hiatt, "Rock Games Strike A Chord," *Rolling Stone,* October 18, 2007, 19–20.
3. Dan Barkin, "He Made the iPod: How Steve Jobs of Apple Created the New Millennium's Signature Invention," *Knight Ridder Tribune Business News,* December 3, 2006, ProQuest Database (accessed January 1, 2007).
4. Grace Wong, "Apple's iPod is Turning 5," *CNNMoney.com* (October 20, 2006), http://money.cnn.com/2006/10/20/technology/apple_ipod/index.htm (accessed October 25, 2006).
5. Dean Goodman, "Album Sales Plunge in '07 as Digital Growth Slows," *Reuters Online* (January 3, 2008), http://www.reuters.com/article/internetNews/idUSN3053893220080104 (accessed January 4, 2008).
6. Steve Knopper, "2007: From Bad to Worse," *Rolling Stone,* February 7, 2008, 15.
7. Quoted in Shirley Halperin, "American Dreams," *Entertainment Weekly,* July 27, 2007, Lexis-Nexis Academic (accessed January 1, 2008).

8. Brian Hiatt, "Lost in the Flood," *Rolling Stone*, September 22, 2005, 13–14.
9. *Blacks See Growing Values Gap Between Poor and Middle Class*, Pew Research Center, November 13, 2007, 6, 42.
10. *Blacks See Growing Values Gap Between Poor and Middle Class*, 42.
11. Peter Katel, "Debating Hip-Hop," *CQ Researcher*, June 15, 2007, 531.
12. Quoted in "Hip-Hop Comes Alive at Smithsonian Exhibit," *Newsday* (March 21, 2008), http://www.newsday.com/travel/ny-f5619682mar23,0,7919095.story (accessed March 21, 2008).
13. Katel, "Debating Hip-Hop," 532.
14. "Apple Introduced the U2 iPod," Apple Press Release, October 26, 2004.
15. "Apple Introduced the U2 iPod."
16. Quoted in Jann S. Wenner, "Bono: The *Rolling Stone* Interview," *Rolling Stone*, November 3, 2005, 61.
17. Mark Binelli, "The Guru," *Rolling Stone*, September 22, 2005, 74, 76.
18. Binelli, "The Guru," 76.
19. Josh Tyrangiel, "The Dude," *Time* 169 (2007): 62–65, Academic Search Premier, EBSCOhost (accessed March 1, 2008).
20. Quoted in Tyrangiel, "The Dude."

SPORTS AND LEISURE OF THE 2000s

1. Laura M. Holson, "Lights, Camera, Pixels... Action!" *The New York Times*, October 24, 2005, C1.
2. Mike Vorhaus, "Favorite Leisure Activities Among Females," *Advertising Age*, February 11, 2008, Academic Search Premier (accessed April 27, 2008).
3. Vorhaus, "Favorite Leisure Activities Among Females."
4. Matt Higgins, "Dramatic Fall Exposes the Risk in Extreme Sports," *The New York Times* (August 4, 2007), http://www.nytimes.com/2007/08/04/sports/othersports/04xgames.html?scp=5&sq=extreme+sports&st=nyt (accessed September 15, 2007).
5. Jodai Saremi, "Leisure Fun Facts," *American Fitness*, March/April 2008, 41.
6. Saremi, "Leisure Fun Facts."
7. Quoted in John Goff, "A Wild Ride," *CFO*, August 2007, 41.
8. Goff, "A Wild Ride," 45.
9. Juliet Macur, "Vick Receives 23 Months and a Lecture," *The New York Times* (December 11, 2007), http://www.nytimes.com/2007/12/11/sports/football/11vick.html?_r=1&oref=slogin (accessed December 25, 2007).
10. Joe Drape, "The Official Line vs. the Betting Line," *The New York Times* (January 31, 2008), http://www.nytimes.com/2008/01/31/sports/football/31gambling.html?scp=9&sq=football+popularity&st=nyt (accessed January 31, 2008).
11. Grant Wahl, "Ahead of his Class," *Sports Illustrated*, February 18, 2002.
12. Tom Friend, "Next: LeBron James," *ESPN The Magazine*, December 23, 2002.
13. Marc Stein, "Breaking Down LeBron James' Game," *ESPN.com*, December 12, 2002.
14. Stein, "Breaking Down LeBron James' Game."
15. Howard Beck, "Ready for N.B.A. Throne, but Not Like Mike," *The New York Times* (June 6, 2007), http://www.nytimes.com/2007/06/06/sports/basketball/06lebron.html?_r=1&oref=slogin&pagewanted=all (accessed June 6, 2007).
16. Jay Mariotti, "Sorry, MJ, but Tiger has Trumped You," *Chicago Sun-Times* (February 26, 2008), http://www.suntimes.com/sports/mariotti/812610,mariotti022608.article (accessed March 12, 2008).
17. "Tiger Woods Profile," Official Web site for Tiger Woods, www.tigerwoods.com (accessed February 26, 2008).
18. Quoted in Paul Vitello, "American Players are Abandoning the Courses," *International Herald Tribune* (February 25, 2008), http://www.iht.com/articles/2008/02/25/sports/GLUT.php (accessed March 13, 2008).
19. Vitello, "American Players are Abandoning the Courses."
20. "Poll: Majority of Fans Think Clemens is Lying," *USA Today*, February 27, 2008, S1.
21. Tom Verducci, "Believe Him or Not," *Sports Illustrated* 108 (2008): 38–41, Academic Search Premier, EBSCOhost (accessed March 24, 2008).
22. Abraham Socher, "No Game for Old Men," *Commentary*, March 2008, 56.
23. Michael Hiestand, "Mixed-Martial Arts Gets Fighting Chance on CBS," *USA Today*, February 29, 2008, S3.
24. Paula Lehman, "Offbeat Thrills Now, Big Money Later?" *Business Week* 4049 (2007): 64–66, Academic Search Premier, EBSCOhost (accessed March 17, 2008).
25. Greg Beato, "Bleeding Into the Mainstream," *Reason* 39 (2007): 16–18, Academic Search Premier, EBSCOhost (accessed March 17, 2008).
26. Childs Walker, "Companies Vie to Hand Phelps Money," *The Baltimore Sun*, August 20, 2008, http://www.baltimoresun.com/sports/olympics/bal-phelps820,0,1121086.story (accessed August 21, 2008).
27. Quoted in Walker, "Companies Vie to Hand Phelps Money."
28. Brian Stelter, "From MySpace to YourSpace," *The New York Times* (January 21, 2008), http://www.nytimes.com/2008/01/21/technology/21myspace.html?_r=2&pagewanted=1&oref=slogin (accessed January 23, 2008).
29. Quoted in Stelter, "From MySpace to YourSpace."
30. Michael Hirschorn, "About Facebook," *The Atlantic Monthly*, October 2007, 155.

31. Erick Schonfeld, "MySpace May Still Dominate in the U.S., But (Surprise!) Facebook is Catching Up Fast Worldwide," *TechCrunch* (January 16, 2008), http://www.techcrunch.com/2008/01/16/myspace-may-still-dominate-in-the-us-but-surprise-facebook-is-catching-up-fast-worldwide/ (accessed January 16, 2008).
32. Schonfeld, "MySpace May Still Dominate in the U.S."
33. Gavin O'Malley, "YouTube Continues to Grow Video Share," *Online Media Daily* (January 18, 2008), http://publications.mediapost.com/index.cfm?fuseaction=Articles.showArticle&art_aid=74597 (accessed January 18, 2008).
34. "Video Sharing Web Site Audience Doubles in a Year," *Research Brief*, Center for Media Research (January 22, 2008), http://blogs.mediapost.com/research_brief/?p=1623 (accessed February 1, 2008).
35. "Video Sharing Web Site Audience Doubles in a Year."
36. "10 Billion Video Views Online in December," *Research Brief*, Center for Media Research (February 22, 2008), http://blogs.mediapost.com/research_brief/?p=1646 (accessed February 26, 2008).
37. Seth Schiesel, "As Gaming Turns Social, Industry Shifts Strategies," *The New York Times* (February 28, 2008), http://www.nytimes.com/2008/02/28/arts/television/28game.html?sq=&pagewanted=all (accessed February 28, 2008).
38. Seth Schiesel, "In the List of Top-Selling Games, Clear Evidence of a Sea Change," *The New York Times* (February 1, 2008), http://www.nytimes.com/2008/02/01/arts/01game.html?fta=y (accessed February 1, 2008).
39. Schiesel, "In the List of Top-Selling Games, Clear Evidence of a Sea Change."
40. John B. Horrigan, *Online Shopping*, Pew Internet & American Life Project, February 13, 2008, i.
41. Horrigan, *Online Shopping*, iii, iv.
42. David Samuels, "Shooting Britney," *The Atlantic*, April 2008, 37.
43. David M. Halbfinger and Geraldine Fabrikant, "In the Drama of Britney Spears, a Show Business Fortune Is at Risk," *The New York Times* (February 25, 2008), http://www.nytimes.com/2008/02/25/business/media/25britney.html?sq= (accessed February 26, 2008).
44. Quoted in Halbfinger and Fabrikant, "In the Drama of Britney Spears."
45. Hilary Hylton, "Anna Nicole Smith, 1967–2007," *Time* (February 8, 2007), http://www.time.com/time/arts/article/0,8599,1587535,00.html (accessed September 15, 2007).
46. Ruth La Ferla, "A Glossy Rehab for Tattered Careers," *The New York Times* (March 9, 2008), http://www.nytimes.com/2008/03/09/fashion/09magazines.html?_r=2&pagewanted=all&oref=slogin (accessed March 30, 2008).

TRAVEL OF THE 2000s

1. Ben Cutler, "Online Travel: The Internet's Biggest Retail Sector Gets Even Bigger," *Internet Consumer Trend Report*, 2001.
2. Erik Blachford, interview by Bob Batchelor, April 15, 2001.
3. Blachford interview.
4. Blachford interview.
5. Blachford interview.
6. Jay Greene, "Microsoft's First-Class Deal," *Business Week*, July 30, 2001, 37.
7. Bruce Greenberg, interview by Bob Batchelor, May 20, 2001.
8. Greenberg interview.
9. Wendy Tanaka, "Travel Web Sites Get Personal," Forbes.com (March 28, 2008), http://www.forbes.com/technology/2008/03/27/social-network-travel-tech-personal-cx_wt_0328travel.html (accessed March 28, 2008).
10. Quoted in Ted Jackovics, "Accommodations for the Environment," *The Tampa Tribune*, February 24, 2008, B8.
11. Jackovics, "Accommodations for the Environment."
12. Jackovics, "Accommodations for the Environment," B7.
13. Jackovics, "Accommodations for the Environment."
14. Michael McCarthy, "Vegas Goes Back to Naughty Roots," *USA Today*, April 11, 2005, 6B.
15. Kitty Bean Yancey, "$40B Thrown into Vegas Development Kitty," *USA Today*, January 18, 2008, 7D.
16. Ellen Creager, "New Glitter Adds Gold to Vegas," *St. Petersburg Times* (FL), April 13, 2008, 4L.
17. Quoted in Chris McGinnis, "The Pampered Traveler," *Fortune*, October 29, 2007, S2.
18. McGinnis, "The Pampered Traveler," S6.

VISUAL ARTS OF THE 2000s

1. Leslie Camhi, "The 2008 Whitney Biennial and the Failure of an Empire," *Village Voice* (March 11, 2008), http://www.villagevoice.com/art/0811,374042,374042,13.html (accessed March 12, 2008).
2. Camhi, "The 2008 Whitney Biennial and the Failure of an Empire."
3. Quoted in Robin Pogrebin, "For American Indians, A Chance to Tell Their Own Story," *The New York Times* (March 12, 2008), http://www.nytimes.com/2008/03/12/arts/artsspecial/12indian.html?ex=1206072000&en=409ca01dc3bc767f&ei=5070&emc=eta1 (accessed March 12, 2008).
4. Tahree Lane, "Diverse Collection to be Sold on Sunday," *Toledo Blade* (February 21, 2008), http://toledoblade.com/apps/pbcs.dll/article?AID=/20080221/ART03/802210318 (accessed March 1, 2008).
5. Quoted in W.A. Demers, "Galle Vase Emerges at $20,340 at Green Valley Auction," *Antiques and The Arts Online* (February 26, 2008), http://antiquesandt

hearts.com/Antiques/AuctionWatch/2008-02-26__11-47-50.html (accessed March 11, 2008).

6. Sarah K. Winn, "Local Retailer Boycotts eBay," *The Charleston Gazette* (March 2, 2008), http://sundaygazettemail.com/News/Business/200803010319 (accessed March 12, 2008).
7. Quoted in Winn, "Local Retailer Boycotts eBay."
8. Quoted in Carol Vogel, "Museums Refine the Art of Listening," *The New York Times* (March 12, 2008), http://www.nytimes.com/2008/03/12/arts/artsspecial/12visitors.html?ex=1206072000&en=4173627bbdd5b2a7&ei=5070&emc=eta1 (accessed March 12, 2008).
9. Vogel, "Museums Refine the Art of Listening."
10. Barbara Isenberg, "Thinking Out of the Box," *Time* (November 19, 2007), http://www.time.com/time/magazine/article/0,9171,1685661,00.html (accessed February 22, 2008).
11. Quoted in Isenberg, "Thinking Out of the Box."
12. Edward Wyatt, "To Have and Give Not," *The New York Times* (February 10, 2008), http://www.nytimes.com/2008/02/10/arts/design/10wyat.html?scp=8&sq=govan+los+angeles&st=nyt (accessed February 22, 2008).
13. Quoted in Wyatt, "To Have and Give Not."
14. Jeff McDonald and Jeanette Steele, "Balancing Art, Ethics," *The San Diego Union-Tribune* (February 17, 2008), http://www.signonsandiego.com/news/metro/20080217-9999-1m17art.html (accessed March 12, 2008).
15. McDonald and Steele, "Balancing Art, Ethics."
16. McDonald and Steele, "Balancing Art, Ethics."
17. "New Visual Artists 2008," *Print,* April 2008, 109.
18. Quoted in "New Visual Artists 2008," 111.
19. "Gregory Crewdson Biography," Guggenheim Museum, http://www.guggenheimcollection.org/site/artist_bio_172.html (accessed March 15, 2008).
20. "Crewdson Interview," Egg The Arts Show, n.d., http://www.pbs.org/wnet/egg/210/crewdson/interview.html (accessed March 15, 2008).
21. Benjamin Genocchio, "The Soul of Suburbia, Captured on Film," *The New York Times,* http://query.nytimes.com/gst/fullpage.html?res=9B0CE5DF1F3BF930A25752C0A96E9C8B63&sec=&spon=&pagewanted=2 (accessed March 15, 2008).
22. Brian Keith Jackson, "How I Made It: Mark Bradford," *New York Magazine* (September 24, 2007), http://nymag.com/arts/art/features/37954/ (accessed March 1, 2008).
23. "Interview: 'Market > Place,'" *Paradox,* Season 4, 2007, Art:21–Art in the Twenty-First Century, PBS, http://www.pbs.org/art21/artists/bradford/clip1.html (accessed March 15, 2008).
24. "Selected Works by Mark Bradford," The Saatchi Gallery: London Contemporary Art Gallery, http://www.saatchi-gallery.co.uk/artists/mark_bradford.htm (accessed March 15, 2008).

Resource Guide

PRINTED SOURCES

Batchelor, Bob, ed. *Basketball in America: From the Playgrounds to Jordan's Game and Beyond.* Binghamton, NY: Haworth Press, 2005.

Battelle, John. *The Search: How Google and Its Rivals Rewrote the Rules of Business and Transformed Our Culture.* New York: Portfolio, 2005.

Benedict, Jeff. *Out of Bounds: Inside the NBA's Culture of Rape, Violence, & Crime.* New York: HarperCollins, 2004.

Berman, Morris. *Dark Ages America: The Final Phase of Empire.* New York: W. W. Norton, 2006.

Bernstein, Michael A., and David E. Adler, eds. *Understanding American Economic Decline.* New York: Cambridge University Press, 1994.

Bigsby, C.W.E. *Modern American Drama, 1945–2000.* Cambridge: Cambridge University Press, 2000.

Bilstein, Roger. *The Enterprise of Flight: The American Aviation and Aerospace Industry.* Washington, D.C.: Smithsonian Institution Press, 2001.

Blakely, Edward and Mary Gail Snyder. *Fortress America: Gated Communities in the United States.* Washington, DC: Brookings Institute Press, 1997.

Brooks, David. *Bobos in Paradise: The New Upper Class and How They Got There.* New York: Simon & Schuster, 2000.

Brown, Jane D., Jeanne R. Steele, and Kim Walsh-Childers, eds. *Sexual Teens, Sexual Media.* Mahwah, NJ: Lawrence Erlbaum Associates, 2002.

Browne, Ray B., ed. *Profiles of Popular Culture: A Reader.* Madison: The University of Wisconsin Press, 2005.

Deardorff, David II. *Sports: A Reference Guide and Critical Commentary, 1980–1999.* Westport, CT: Greenwood Press, 2000.

De La Haye, Amy, and Cathie Dingwall. *Surfers Soulies Skinheads & Skaters: Subcultural Style from the Forties to the Nineties.* Woodstock, NY: Overlook, 1996.

Dixon, Wheeler Winston, ed. *Film Genre 2000: New Critical Essays.* Albany: State University of New York Press, 2000.

Duany, Andres, and Elizabeth Plater-Zyberk. *Suburban Nation: The Rise of Sprawl and the Decline of the American Dream.* New York: North Point Press, 2000.

Duncan, Russell, and Joseph Goddard. *Contemporary America.* 2nd ed. London: Palgrave Macmillan, 2005.
Dylan, Bob. *Chronicles: Volume One.* New York: Simon & Schuster, 2004.
Dyson, Michael Eric. *The Michael Eric Dyson Reader.* New York: Basic Civitas Books, 2004.
Faludi, Susan. *The Terror Dream: Fear and Fantasy in Post-9/11 America.* New York: Metropolitan Books, 2007.
Fishwick, Marshall William. *Probing Popular Culture: On and Off the Internet.* New York: Haworth Press, 2004.
Franklin, John Hope. *Mirror to America: The Autobiography of John Hope Franklin.* New York: Farrar, Straus and Giroux, 2005.
Friedman, Thomas L. *The World is Flat: A Brief History of the Twenty-First Century.* New York: Farrar, Straus and Giroux, 2005.
Frith, Katherine Toland, ed. *Undressing the Ad: Reading Culture in Advertising.* New York: Peter Lang, 1998.
Gimlin, Debra L. *Body Work: Beauty and Self-Image in American Culture.* Berkeley: University of California Press, 2002.
Gray-Rosendale, Laura, ed. *Pop Perspectives: Readings to Critique Contemporary Culture.* New York: McGraw-Hill, 2008.
Heller, Dana, ed. *The Great American Makeover: Television, History, Nation.* New York: Palgrave Macmillan, 2006.
Hischak, Thomas S. *American Theatre: A Chronicle of Comedy and Drama, 1969–2000.* New York: Oxford University Press, 2001.
Holtzman, Steven. *Digital Mosaics: The Aesthetics of Cyberspace.* New York: Simon & Schuster, 1997.
Hoyle, Russ. *Going to War: How Misinformation, Disinformation, and Arrogance Led America into Iraq.* New York: Thomas Dunne Books, 2008.
Johnson, Haynes. *The Best of Times: America in the Clinton Years.* New York: James H. Silberman, 2001.
———. *Divided We Fall: Gambling with History in the Nineties.* New York: W. W. Norton, 1994.
Kaufman, Robert Gordon. *In Defense of the Bush Doctrine.* Lexington: University Press of Kentucky, 2007.
Kilbourne, Jean. *Deadly Persuasion: Why Women and Girls Must Fight the Addictive Power of Advertising.* New York: The Free Press, 1999.
Levitt, Steven D., and Stephen J. Dubner. *Freakonomics: A Rogue Economist Explores the Hidden Side of Everything.* New York: William Morrow, 2005.
Light, Alan, ed. *The Vibe History of Hip Hop.* New York: Three Rivers Press, 1999.
Mackiewicz Wolfe, Wojtek. *Winning the War of Words: Selling the War on Terror from Afghanistan to Iraq.* Westport, CT: Praeger, 2008.
Montgomery, Bruce P. *The Bush-Cheney Administration's Assault on Open Government.* Westport, CT: Praeger, 2008.
Mooney, Chris. *Storm World: Hurricanes, Politics, and the Battle Over Global Warming.* Orlando, FL: Harcourt, 2007.
Nunn, Joan. *Fashion in Costume 1200–2000.* 2nd ed. Chicago: New Amsterdam, 2000.
Oermann, Robert K. *A Century of Country: An Illustrated History of Country Music.* New York: TV Books, 1999.
Owen, Rob. *Gen X TV: The Brady Bunch to Melrose Place.* Syracuse, NY: Syracuse University Press, 1997.
Roberts, Sam. *Who We Are Now: The Changing Face of America in the Twenty-first Century.* New York: Henry Holt, 2004.
Rubinstein, Ruth P. *Society's Child: Identity, Clothing, and Style.* Boulder, CO: Westview Press, 2000.
———. *Fighting Back: The War on Terrorism from Inside the Bush White House.* Lanham, MD: Regnery, 2002.

Sammon, Bill. *Misunderestimated: The President Battles Terrorism, John Kerry, and the Bush Haters.* New York: Regan Books, 2004.

Schlosser, Eric. *Fast Food Nation: The Dark Side of the All-American Meal.* New York: Houghton Mifflin, 2001.

Schneider, Barbara, and David Stevenson. *The Ambitious Generation: American Teenagers, Motivated but Directionless.* New Haven, CT: Yale University Press, 1999.

Smith, George, and Nicola Walker Smith. *New Voices: American Composers Talk About Their Music.* New York: Amadeus Press, 1995.

Springhall, John. *Youth, Popular Culture and Moral Panics: Penny Gaffs to Gangsta-Rap, 1830–1996.* New York: St Martin's, 1998.

Steel, Jon. *Truth, Lies, and Advertising.* New York: John Wiley & Sons, 1998.

Stewart, Jon, David Javerbaum, and Ben Karlin. *America (the Book): A Citizen's Guide to Democracy Inaction.* New York: Warner Books, 2004.

Twitchell, James B. *Twenty Ads That Shook the World: The Century's Most Ground-breaking Advertising and How it Changed Us All.* New York: Crown Publishers, 2000.

Vise, David A., and Mark Malseed. *The Google Story.* New York: Delacorte, 2005.

Warde, Alan, and Lydia Martens. *Eating Out: Social Differentiation, Consumption and Pleasure.* New York: Cambridge University Press, 2000.

Wellner, Allison S. *Americans at Play: Demographics of Outdoor Recreation and Travel.* Ithaca, NY: New Strategist Publications, 1997.

Yeffeth, Glenn, ed. *The Man from Krypton: A Closer Look at Superman.* Dallas: BenBella Books, 2005.

Zeff, Robbin, and Brad Aronson. *Advertising on the Internet.* 2nd ed. New York: John Wiley & Sons, 1999.

Zegart, Amy B. *Spying Blind: The CIA, the FBI, and the Origins of 9/11.* Princeton, NJ: Princeton University Press, 2007.

MUSEUMS, ORGANIZATIONS, SPECIAL COLLECTIONS, AND USEFUL WEB SITES

America at War. The Washington Post Web site. http://www.washingtonpost.com/wp-srv/world/specials/iraq. The Washington Post Company, 2008.

A compendium of information about the wars in Iraq and Afghanistan, the site features photographs, multimedia resources, and articles about the conflicts overseas, military and political leaders, and citizens affected by the wars. The site also has interactive maps and other features that provide quick information. There is also an updated list of casualties in both wars, including a photograph and biographical information about the fallen.

Iraq. U.S. Department of State Web site. http://www.state.gov/p/nea/ci/c3212.htm. The Office of Electronic Information, Bureau of Public Affairs, U.S. Department of State, 2008.

The Web site compiles information about the war in Iraq, including remarks by the president, top-ranked military leaders, and other governmental officials. The site also contains government reports on the military and rebuilding efforts in Iraq, as well as photographs and related links.

The Surprising Legacy of Y2K. American RadioWorks. http://americanradioworks.publicradio.org/features/y2k/index.html. American Public Media, 2008.

A Web site that contains a series of radio broadcasts (and transcripts) investigating the Y2K computer challenge that gripped the nation in the late 1990s. For the fifth anniversary of Y2K, America Public Media examines the history and the legacy of the millennium bug. After the hoopla and warnings about Y2K, many dismissed it as a hoax, scam, or non-event. Not only was Y2K a real threat narrowly averted but it also still has important effects on the economy. It continues to change how people look at technology.

Whitley, Peggy, et al. American Cultural History 1990–1999. Kingwood College Library Web site. http://kclibrary.lonestar.edu/decade90.html, 2007.

A Web site dedicated to examining American cultural history in the 1990s, Whitley provides an overview of the decade and extensive links to additional resources. The site is filled with statistics about the 1990s and photographs of the era.

William J. Clinton Presidential Library. 1200 President Clinton Avenue, Little Rock, Arkansas, 72201. http://www.clintonlibrary.gov/.

The archival and museum holdings at the Clinton Presidential Library and Museum are the largest within the Presidential Library system. Included in these collections are approximately 76.8 million pages of paper documents, 1.85 million photographs, and over 84,600 museum artifacts. Official records, as well as donated materials, will be made available to researchers. In addition to the archival collection and research facilities, the library and museum features exhibits, special events, and educational programs. The museum includes replicas of the Oval Office and the Cabinet Room. Permanent exhibits utilize documents, photographs, videos, and interactive stations. A timeline and alcoves highlight domestic and foreign policy, as well as life in the White House.

VIDEOS/FILMS

Bowling for Columbine. Directed by Michael Moore. 119 minutes. Distributed by MGM Home Entertainment, 2003. VHS. Documentarian Michael Moore examines the root of violence involving firearms in the United States. He focuses on the shootings that took place at Columbine High School in Littleton, Colorado.

Fahrenheit 9/11. Directed by Michael Moore. 122 minutes. Distributed by Columbia TriStar Home Entertainment, 2004. DVD. Through archival footage, interviews, and declassified documents, Michael Moore illustrates the connections President George W. Bush has to the royal house of Saud of Saudia Arabia and the bin Ladens, how the president got elected on allegedly fraudulent circumstances, and then proceeded to blunder through his early presidency. When terrorists struck on September 11, Moore explains how Bush failed to take immediate action to defend the nation.

Fight Club. Directed by David Fincher. 139 minutes. Distributed by 20th Century Fox, 2000. DVD. The film captures the zeitgeist of the late 1990s and early 2000s by examining the power of consumerism on modern American society, particularly in emasculating men. Filled with anarchist overtones and riveting performances by Brad Pitt and Edward Norton, *Fight Club* had widespread influence on filmgoers searching for existential meaning.

Hip-Hop: Beyond Beats and Rhymes. Directed by Byron Hurt. 61 minutes. Distributed by Media Education Foundation, 2006. DVD. A provocative examination of the conceptualization of masculinity and hypermasculinity in hip-hop culture. Includes interviews with prominent rappers, music industry executives, and social critics, including Mos Def, Fat Joe, Chuck D, Jadakiss, Busta Rhymes, Russell Simmons, and Michael Eric Dyson.

No End in Sight. Directed by Charles Ferguson. 102 minutes. Distributed by Magnolia Home Entertainment, 2007. DVD. Presents an insider's observations of the 2003 invasion of Iraq and the subsequent occupation, featuring commentary from high-ranking officals, Iraqi civilians, American soldiers, and analysts. The documentary examines U.S. policy decisions surrounding the invasion and their consequences in Iraq, including such issues as low U.S. troop levels, the uncontrolled looting of Baghdad, the purging of professionals from the Iraqi government, the disbanding of the national military, and the subsequent surge of civil and political chaos.

Rap: Looking for the Perfect Beat. Directed by Susan Shaw. 53 minutes. Distributed by Films for the Humanities, 2000. Featuring pioneering rap artist Melle Mel, the documentary describes the history of rap and hip-hop from its roots in earlier oral and musical traditions to its full flowering in the mid-1990s. The video contains interviews with rappers Ice Cube and Snoop Doggy Dogg.

Road to the Presidency: Inside the Clinton Campaign. Directed by Scott Jacobs. 164 minutes. Distributed by Facets Video, 2004. DVD. An unprecedented view of the 1992 presidential election. The documentary provides an inside look at Bill Clinton's path through the primaries, the Democratic convention, and the televised debates with President George H. W. Bush. The film provides insight beyond simple campaign reporting and gives a compelling view that is funny and poignant, as well as instructive.

Star Wars. Episode III, Revenge of the Sith. Directed by George Lucas. 140 minutes. Distributed by 20th Century Fox Home Entertainment, 2005. DVD. The final piece of the *Star Wars* puzzle, the film examines how Anakin Skywalker becomes Darth Vader. Torn between loyalty to his mentor, Obi-Wan Kenobi, and the seductive powers of the Sith, Skywalker ultimately turns his back on the Jedi. This begins his journey to the dark side and his transformation into Darth Vader.

Super Size Me. Directed by Morgan Spurlock. 100 minutes. Distributed by Samuel Goldwyn Films and Showtime Independent Films, 2004. DVD. Filmmaker Morgan Spurlock embarks on a journey to find out if fast food is making Americans fat. For 30 days he eats or drinks only from the McDonald's menu. The film includes visits to doctors and nutritionists and details Spurlock's spiral toward obesity and stunning metamorphosis.

The War Room. Directed by Chris Hegedus and D. A. Pennebaker. 96 minutes. Distributed by Vidmark Entertainment, 1994. VHS. Documentary about the Clinton presidential campaign, from the New Hampshire primary to the victory party 10 months later. Featured are the two men credited with getting Clinton elected: James Carville, the campaign manager, and George Stephanopoulos, the communications director.

Cost of Products from 1900–2000

Cost of Products 1900–2000

Product	1900s	1910s	1920s	1930s	1940s
Food					
Flour (cents per pound)	16	21	30.5	21	34.7
Bread (cents per pound)	3	7	9	7.9	11
Round steak (cents per pound)	14	23	36.2	39.3	65
Butter (cents per pound)	29	35.8	55.2	39.5	54.3
Eggs (cents per dozen)	27.2	34.1	55.4	38.3	56.1
Milk (cents per half gallon)	14.4	17.6	27.8	26.3	31.2
Potatoes (cents per 10 lbs.)	17	15	36	24.7	49.3
Coffee (cents per pound)	35	30	50.4	25.7	41.9
Sugar (cents per pound)	30	33	35	28.9	38.6
Clothing					
Women's blouse (each)	$0.98	$1.00–$1.98	$1.98	$0.39	$2.90–$7.98
Women's shoes (per pair)	$1.50	$1.95	$2.50	$2.95–$10.50	$8.95–$16.95
Men's suit	$3.98–15	$13.95–$15	$12.50	$14.95–$26.75	$27.95–$44.95
Child's coat	$2.48–$7.98	$5.98	$14.50–$16.50	$8.69–$11.98	$8.50–$13
Travel/Leisure					
Gas (dollars per gallon; yearly averages)	N/A	N/A	$0.21–$0.30	$0.17–$0.20	$0.18–$0.27
Ford Model T	$825	$360	$290	$495 (used)	$625 (used Deluxe Sedan)
Theater ticket	$0.35–$0.75	$0.10–$0.25	$0.20–$3.00	$2–$5 (opera)	$1.20–$3
Home Furnishings and Appliances					
Refrigerator	$8.92 (wooden ice box)	$900	$195–$245	$174.50–$250	$159.95
Bedroom set	$39.50–$60	$236.50–$355	$1,450	$68.75–$99.50	$100
Living Room set	NA (Sofa, $4.50–$10.98/each)	$154–$171.50	$160	$88 (3 pieces)	$269 (3 pieces)

The statistical data presented in this section are compiled from a number of sources and meant to be representative of the indicated decade. The sources include: Proquest, *New York Times Historic,* (1851–present) database; U.S. Bureau of Labor Statistics (BLS), *Retail Prices of Selected Foods in U.S. Cities, 1890–1970;* Morris County Library, *How Much Did It Cost in Morris County, New Jersey?* http://www.gti.net/mocolib1/prices; and Energy Information Administration (EIA), Department of Energy, "Retail Gasoline Historical Prices," http://www.eia.doe.gov/oil_gas/petroleum/data_publications/wrgp/mogas_history.html, as well as information derived from the works cited in the volume.

1950s	1960s	1970s	1980s	1990s	2000s
51.8	56.7	39 (5 lb. bag)	69 (5 lb. bag)	99 (5 lb. bag)	99 (5 lb. bag)
17	22.3	39 (22 ounce loaf)	99 (2 20 ounce loaves)	99 (22 ounce loaf)	284 (per loaf)
98.8	116.1	179 (London Broil)	297 (prime rib)	289 (boneless sirloin)	600 (prime rib)
74.1	80.8	70	173	150	349
56.7	59.4	69	87	99	229
45.9	59	49	93	115	319
56.4	80.8	49.5	38	189 (5 lb. bag)	69 (per lb)
94	83.2	99	225	299 (13 ounce can)	799
53.5	61.5	49.8	43	43	43
$1.99	$8	$9.75–$20	$29.99–$119	$9.99–$48	$19.99–$49.99
$7.99–$18.95	$5.90–$19.97	$8.99–$30	$19.99–$68	$28.99–$89.99	$29.99–$129
$59–$85	$29.90–$42.95	$35–$60	$159–$265	$187.50–$475	$250–$495
$7.80–$42.98	$19.99–$37.99	$23–$55	$30–$180	$29–$116	$42–$115
$0.27–$0.31	$0.30–$0.35	$0.36–$0.90	$0.93–$1.38	$1.06–$1.23	$1.36–$4.50
$598 (used Victoria)	$2,199 (new Custom Sedan)	$2,895 (new Pinto)	$13,499 (new Mustang convertible)	$15,988 (new Taurus)	$32,080 (Explorer, Eddie Bauer edition)
$1–$1.50	$1.25	$3–$9	$10–$30	$10–$60	$26.50–$99.50
$249.95	$288.88	$348	$429.99–$699	$449.97–$1,999	$399–$1,449
$59.95–$72.96	$399–$599	$895 (6 piece)	$697–$1,267 (4 piece)	$2,799 (7 piece)	$1,500–$2,199
$129	$198.99–$299 (2 piece)	$488–$855 (3 piece)	$1,300	$499–$1,999 (3 piece)	$999–$3,199

Appendix: Classroom Resources

This section includes an assortment of ideas for teachers and others who wish to use *American Pop* in classroom assignments. Each activity has two versions: one for the teacher and one for the student.

Advertising Messages and Stereotypes

FOR TEACHERS

ESSENTIAL QUESTION

How do today's ads use stereotypes in order to sell products to consumers?

OBJECTIVES

- Students will identify persuasive advertising techniques.
- Students will analyze how stereotypes are presented by popular advertisements.
- Students will debate about the appropriateness of advertisements.

RATIONALE

Students see so many advertisements daily that they *almost* believe they have tuned them out, until you ask them to name products they've seen advertised recently, and suddenly, they can list enough to fill a page. Although it's obvious to students that advertising has a persuasive purpose, it's only upon investigation that students can really analyze the messages advertisements send by portraying (or not portraying) people in specific ways. This lesson allows students to explore advertisements in the media both historically and today.

DISCIPLINE

This lesson could be used to study media literacy in multiple courses, including American history (modern history), government/citizenship, sociology, journalism/media studies, and/or English Language arts (to study persuasion).

STANDARDS

- Students will plan and present an oral presentation that demonstrates appropriate consideration of audience, purpose, and the information to be conveyed.
- Students will identify, analyze, and apply knowledge of the conventions, elements, and techniques of advertising and provide evidence from the works (print and/or broadcast ads) to support their understanding.

PACING

Project should take 2 to 3 days or 4 to 5 days if it includes Activity Extension.

LESSON

Activity 1 (Lesson Introduction)

Students should work with a partner. In a 10-minute timed session, ask students to generate (with their partners) a list of as many advertisements as they can remember, describing the product, the ad itself, and any messages the ad seemed to send about the product.

Activity 2: Studying ads by time period

Students will work in pairs or groups (depending on class size) to investigate a decade of American history and its advertising techniques and the productions advertised. After reading the advertising chapters from *American Pop* about the decade, students should fill out the Student Worksheet to synthesize ideas about their decade's advertising.

- Team 1: 1900s
- Team 2: 1910s
- Team 3: 1920s
- Team 4: 1930s
- Team 5: 1940s
- Team 6: 1950s
- Team 7: 1960s
- Team 8: 1970s
- Team 9: 1980s
- Team 10: 1990s
- Team 11: 2000s

Students may also bring in magazines and/or newspapers they read or have at home (assuming they are appropriate for school). The activity can also be extended by finding examples of real ads from the time period, through public or school library collections of old newspapers and magazines. Working in groups, students will select ads to evaluate based on the criteria on the Student Worksheet.

Activity 3

Divide students into teams for a debate. Although many aspects of advertising can be brought up by students during the debate, all arguments should stay focused on the overall question of whether advertising is harmful or not:

- Advertising can be harmful and images used by advertisers contribute to negative stereotyping;

- Advertising is not harmful, but it is instead a tool used by companies to sell products.

Activity Extension

Students should watch one or two hours of their favorite network or basic cable channel (because those two have commercials) and analyze the advertisements. Students should write a short paper on their findings, using the prompt on the Student Worksheet.

Assessment

Suggested Weighting

Partner-based advertising and class discussion (Activity 1), 10 points; Group advertising evaluation activity (Activity 2), 30 points; Debate (Activity 3), 20 points; Paper analyzing television ads (Activity Extension), 30 points.

Rubric: General Performance Scoring Rubric

Rubric: Debate Rubric

STUDENT WORKSHEET

Name____________________________

LESSON TITLE: STUDYING ADVERTISING MESSAGES AND STEREOTYPES

Mission

Advertising is an essential component of revenue for newspapers and magazines. However, very often, the people depicted in advertisements do *not* look like the average American, and the products themselves are not nearly as attractive in real life as they appear in the advertising. We *know* this, yet we still buy products. What messages do ads really send if we study them critically? This activity will help you investigate ads and will prepare you for a debate about whether ads are harmful or not.

For homework, read the advertising chapters from American Pop, *from the 1900s through the 2000s. [Your teacher may also ask you to research old ads in newspapers or magazines available in digital or hard copy at libraries.] If possible, try to find different types of magazines. You will break into groups to study the advertisements and report on them as follows:*

Students will work in pairs or groups (depending on class size) to investigate a decade of American history and its advertising icons. After reading the advertising chapters from *American Pop* about the decade, students should fill out the Student Worksheet to synthesize ideas about their decade's advertising. [Note: this assignment could also be made by groups of decades, by volumes of *American Pop;* thus, volume 1, 1900s–1920s; volume 2, 1930s–1950s; volume 3, 1960s–1980s; and volume 4, 1990s–2000s.]

- Team 1: 1900s
- Team 2: 1910s
- Team 3: 1920s
- Team 4: 1930s
- Team 5: 1940s
- Team 6: 1950s
- Team 7: 1960s
- Team 8: 1970s
- Team 9: 1980s
- Team 10: 1990s
- Team 11: 2000s

1. As a group, study the collection of advertisements you have obtained. What are the most interesting ads you have? Choose a few and explain them below. Why did you select them?

2. Some ads appeal to a particular group, such as women, men, mothers, or children. Find an example of an advertisement that appeals to a particular group. Describe the ad and then explain why you think it's meant to reach a particular age group.

3. Whether purposeful or not, many ads send messages about men and women. Find indications in advertisements that seem to display a female stereotype. How do they express this stereotype? For whom do you think the ads are designed and why?

4. Find an advertisement that seems to display another stereotype. How does it express this stereotype? For whom do you think the ad is designed for and why?

5. As a group, look for ways that the ads reflect the culture and history of the time. For example, how do the ads of the 1920s differ from the ads of the 1930s? What qualities of life do the ads appeal to: order, cleanliness, prejudice, excitement, freedom, security, fun, success, status, etcetera?

Now get ready for the next part of this lesson: a debate about advertising. Prepare for a debate by reading the instructions below and answering the three questions that follow.

Order of Today's Debate

Round 1: Each group will have 1 minute to present its findings in a planned speech to the class.

Round 2: Each group will have 30 seconds to give an impromptu response back to the opposing viewpoint. While this isn't fully planned ahead of time, you will jot down potential notes to use (see the worksheet below).

Choose one of these two opinions:

A. Advertising can be harmful and images used by advertisers contribute to negative stereotyping;
B. Advertising is not harmful instead a tool used by companies to sell products.

1. What is your group's topic and opinion about the topic?

2. As a group, brainstorm ideas about why your group's opinion is correct. What casual evidence (evidence from the ads you saw today or ads in general) helps you defend your topic?

3. As a group, prepare how you will refute your opponents' argument about advertising? What evidence or examples might make their argument weak?

Activity Extension

For homework, turn your attention to television advertisements. Choose a TV show that you watch or your family watches regularly and carefully observe the ads that appear during the show. Write a short paper (1–2 pages) describing and analyzing the television ads in the show. Think about the following:

- What was the primary demographic (e.g., age group, gender group, etc.) the ads aimed at? Why do you think so?
- How did the ads depict men and women? What stereotypes about men or women did the ads seem to perpetuate? How?
- What messages did the ads send about some of the following: Age? Popularity? Success? Family?

Check:

a. Did you fully respond to all the questions about your group's advertisements?

b. Did you choose a topic for the debate and come up with logical evidence to defend your group's position?

c. Did you find reasons to explain why your opponents' arguments might not be well thought-out or accurate?

d. In the extension activity, is your paper supported by details of the advertisements you saw on your selected television show?

Advertising Products and Slogans: Images That Represent America

FOR TEACHERS

ESSENTIAL QUESTION

What do products and their advertisements teach us about America?

OBJECTIVES

- Students will identify key products and slogans from the past century.
- Students will analyze how iconic products help represent the time period when they were created.
- Students will identify and analyze their own "key products and slogans" of modern-day America and present their findings to the class in an analytical paper and class project.

RATIONALE

Some teenagers admit they go to the movies just for the previews. Many Americans watch the Super Bowl for the advertisements. On *Jeopardy,* most students would do better on "Advertising Slogans" than on "Famous Quotes from Literature." Studying historical advertising helps students understand more about America at the time when the ads were made, and studying advertising today helps students reflect on our country's priorities. This project helps students study the past and present through the advertising icons that pervade our lives.

DISCIPLINE

This lesson could be used to study media literacy in such courses as American history (modern history), government/citizenship, journalism/media studies, and English language arts.

STANDARDS

- Students will organize, write, and successfully use standard English conventions.
- Students will identify and comprehend the main ideas of a work of nonfiction and use the main ideas to form an understanding of an historical event or time period.
- Students will deepen their understanding of an advertisement or advertising icon by studying its historical context and making connections between the advertisement and the events that were occurring at the time it was created.
- Students will plan and present an oral presentation that demonstrates appropriate consideration of audience, purpose, and the information to be conveyed.

PACING

Project should take 3 to 4 days or 5 to 6 days if it includes Activity Extension.

LESSON

Activity 1 (Lesson Introduction)

Students will write a 1-page journal entry answering the following questions: How has advertising affected you? What products do you currently have on you (e.g., iPod, Nike shoes, etc.) that you've seen advertising for? What products have you tried just because of advertising? What's your favorite ad on television and why? What's the importance of advertising in your life? After writing in their journals (about 10 minutes), students should talk about their answers in a class discussion.

Activity 2

Students will work in pairs or groups (depending on class size) to investigate a decade of American history and its advertising icons. After reading the research from the advertising chapters about the decade, students should fill out the Student Worksheet to synthesize ideas about their decade's advertising. The source material for students to study will be the advertising chapters below from *American Pop.*

- Team 1: 1900s
- Team 2: 1910s
- Team 3: 1920s
- Team 4: 1930s
- Team 5: 1940s
- Team 6: 1950s
- Team 7: 1960s
- Team 8: 1970s
- Team 9: 1980s
- Team 10: 1990s

Note: Students may opt for the 2000s in an activity extension, below.

Activity 3

After completing the Student Worksheet, students (working in pairs or groups) should make an informational poster for a presentation about the decade's main advertising components. They can sketch products discussed or find photos online or from their research and write key concepts on their poster. Give students time (at least 1 day) to create their poster and determine how they're going to teach the class about their assigned decade. The Student Worksheet will guide students. Groups will then present their illustrated poster to the class and discuss their assigned decade.

Activity Extension—Icons and Products of the 2000s

After students finish presenting the major advertising icons of the 1900s–1990s, they'll now create a project (paper, illustrated poster, or PowerPoint project) to examine advertising icons of the 2000s. Students should work on this independently at home. If students choose to create an illustrated poster or PowerPoint project, they should still turn in a written explanation that analyzes why they chose the icons they did to represent current advertising and what it says about America.

Assessment

Suggested Weighting

Journal response (Activity 1), 10 points; Research worksheet (Activity 2), 20 points; Class presentation (Activity 3), 20 points; Icons and Products of the 2000s (Activity Extension), 30 points.

Rubric: General Performance Scoring Rubric

STUDENT WORKSHEET

Name___________________________

LESSON TITLE: PRODUCTS AND SLOGANS: ADVERTISING IMAGES THAT REPRESENT AMERICA

Mission

You'll be studying iconic advertising images from a decade that has been assigned to you. By studying the advertising of a decade, you can learn a lot about the country and the time period. Your first step is to research your assigned decade. Read the material from the advertising chapters in *American Pop* and answer the following questions. Then read the directions on the bottom of this page about how to make an illustrated poster to help with your presentation.

1. What decade will you be researching? __________

2. What were the strangest advertising icons for your decade? What made them seem strange? List a few interesting icons and some information about each:

3. Which advertising icons listed for your decade are still used today? Have they changed through time? If so, how? If not, why?

4. As a whole, what statement can you make about your decade based on the advertising from that era? What do think were the country's priorities at that time? What were the hot new products? What does this show about America?

Designing an Illustrated Poster

As a pair (or group) you'll be presenting your decade to the class, using an illustrated poster as your visual aid. Draw or sketch some of the products/icons listed, or find images of these products online. In addition to the collage of products you show on your poster, write key concepts and descriptions of the products. Be ready to explain to the class the images you have selected to highlight.

Activity Extension—Icons and Products of the 2000s

Now that you've studied a decade from the 1900s through the1990s, it's time to study America today. Working by yourself, you'll now create a project (paper, illustrated poster, or PowerPoint project) to show advertising icons of the 2000s. What does it mean to be an icon today? What products are the most iconic or have the most recognized logos, and what types of consumers do they appeal to? Are these icons all positive? Possible ideas for your project include:

- An illustrated poster
- A PowerPoint presentation

- A collage
- No matter what format your project takes, you also need to turn in a 1-page written explanation that analyzes why you chose the icons you did, how they represent current advertising, and what they show us about America.

Check:

- Did you fully complete the questions about the advertising icons of the decade you were assigned or chose?
- Did you construct an illustrated poster and then label or explain these illustrations to the class?
- Did you complete a project on your own (in the Activity Extension) about the advertising icons of today?
- Did you write a short analysis paper to accompany your poster or PowerPoint project (in the Activity Extension) that explains your advertising icons?

Film, Music, and Popular Culture Images of the Vietnam War

FOR TEACHERS

ESSENTIAL QUESTION

How does popular culture help tell the story of the Vietnam Era in America?

OBJECTIVES

- Students will analyze how music lyrics help describe and define the Vietnam era.
- Students will investigate how filmmakers have portrayed the Vietnam War.
- Students will use research from *American Pop* to gather information about songs, novels, and films of Vietnam.

RATIONALE

Years ago, many schools avoided the topic of Vietnam in curriculum, but more recently, schools have embraced studying it. One easy way to reach students is to have them study the music of the time period and the more recent films made about the time period. This lesson allows students to study one particular piece of media (a song) about Vietnam and then, working in groups, choose an additional song, film, or novel about Vietnam to research and explore.

DISCIPLINE

This lesson is primarily for an American history or world history course but could be used to study media literacy in multiple courses, including government/citizenship, sociology, journalism/media studies, and/or English Language arts. The lesson also connects well with Vietnam-era novels taught in American literature courses.

STANDARDS

- Students will organize, write, and successfully use standard English conventions in their writing.
- Students will deepen their understanding of an historical event by studying media (songs, film, or photography) of the time period and about the time period.
- Students will gather information from their research, evaluate the quality of the information they obtain, and use it to write a research paper or create a media (Power Point, etc.) presentation.
- Students will identify and analyze the impact of the Vietnam conflict on soldiers and on the home-front.

PACING

Project should take 3 to 4 days or 5 to 6 days if it includes Activity Extension.

LESSON

Activity 1 (Lesson Introduction)

Students will write a 1-page journal entry answering the questions: What comes to mind when thinking of the Vietnam War? Describe what you know of the war from history, films, novels, music, or stories you have heard. How have movies or songs shaped your view of the war? After writing in their journals (about 10 minutes), students should share their answers in class discussion.

Activity 2

In Volume 3 of *American Pop,* students should read the 1960s and 1970s chapters "Overview," "Entertainment," and "Music." Working in groups, students should select a Vietnam-related song, novel, or film to study. Suggestion for possible topics include: *Apocalypse Now; Born on the Fourth of July; The Deer Hunter; Going after Cacciato; The Green Berets; In Country; Platoon; Rambo: First Blood, Part II; The Things They Carried; We Gotta Get Out of This Place;* or *Winners and Losers.* Working in groups, students should analyze their choice of topic and complete the Activity 2 section of the Student Worksheet.

Note: Although widely viewed by students, some films on the Vietnam experience are rated R. Please determine appropriateness of the films for some audiences or check with your school's video policy and/or retain parental authorization before approving student choices of R-rated films.

Activity 3

Students present their choice of topic to the class, explaining what they learned from their research and their own analysis of the piece. If possible, students could play a song, show an appropriate film clip, or read a passage (depending on whether they have chosen a song, film, or novel).

Activity Extension—Photography, Letters, and Poetry of Vietnam

After studying how novels, music, and film depicted Vietnam, students should work in groups to gather research on primary source history of Vietnam. Groups should choose either photography of Vietnam (and the home front), letters from Vietnam War soldiers back home, or poetry of soldiers and nurses serving in the war. Using the library or online research, students should acquire materials and then study the materials, coming up with a presentation (poster, PowerPoint, etc.) that highlights their findings.

Assessment

Suggested Weighting

Journal response (Activity 1), 10 points; Analysis of additional song, novel, or film (Activity 2), 40 points; Class presentation on group's choice of topic (Activity 3), 30 points; Photography, letters, or poetry analysis presentation (Activity Extension), 30 points.

Rubric: General Performance Scoring Rubric
Rubric: Multimedia Performance

STUDENT WORKSHEET

Name___________________________

LESSON TITLE: FILM, MUSIC, AND POPULAR CULTURE IMAGES OF THE VIETNAM WAR

Mission

It can be overwhelming learning about the complexity of the Vietnam War and its effects at home and abroad, but one easy way to gain insight about the era is to study the music and literature from the time period, as well as recent films about the Vietnam experience. This lesson allows us to study one particular song, film, or novel about Vietnam to research and explore.

Working as a group, choose another song, piece of literature, or film about Vietnam to explore. Suggestions for possible topics include: *Apocalypse Now; Born on the Fourth of July; The Deer Hunter; Going after Cacciato; The Green Berets; In Country; Platoon; Rambo: First Blood, Part II; The Things They Carried; We Gotta Get Out of This Place;* or *Winners and Losers.*

1. What work will your group be studying? ________________________________

Carefully analyze the work. Select the bullet points below that apply to your work and begin analyzing it (after reading it, hearing it, or watching it):

- What does the work show us about soldiers? Explain.
- What does the work show us about Americans back home? Explain.
- What does the work show us about attitudes toward the government? Explain.
- Is the work positive, negative, or both? Explain.
- What are the overall messages or themes of the work?
- What stands out the most … what are the "sound bites" or strongest aspects of the work?
- What information about the time period did you find in *American Pop?*

As a group, discuss and record some thoughts about how to communicate what you learned (including the answers to the bullet points above that are applicable to your work) to the class in a short presentation. Spend time planning your group presentation. Depending on the work selected, see if you can play your song, show a short (appropriate) film clip, or distribute a photocopied passage or two of a book to help the class understand your work and understand your analysis of it.

Activity Extension—Photography, Letters, and Poetry of Vietnam

After studying how novels, music, and films depict Vietnam, now gather (in groups) primary source materials on the history of Vietnam to analyze deeper. Choose photography of the Vietnam War (and the home front), letters home from soldiers in Vietnam, or poetry by soldiers and medical personnel serving in the war. Using the library or online research, gather resources, and then share your findings with your group. As a group, present these findings to your class.

Check:

- Did your group fully analyze the song, film, or literary work about Vietnam that you chose?
- Did you create a presentation that was informative and based on research from *American Pop?*
- Did your presentation show careful analysis of the time period and content of your work (from the bullet points listed above)?
- Did your Activity Extension show careful analysis of the time period and help bring alive to the class the issues facing those living in Vietnam-era America?

Literature Links to Music: Creating a Soundtrack for a Novel

FOR TEACHERS

ESSENTIAL QUESTION

How can creating a soundtrack for a novel help students better understand and convey the characters, events, and themes of the novel?

OBJECTIVES

- Students will analyze a novel's characters, events, and themes.
- Students will choose songs to represent the novel and write a paper explaining their choices.
- Students will design an album/CD cover with an artistic image that reflects the novel.
- Students will present their findings to the class.

RATIONALE

A wonderful way to have students study major aspects of a novel is for them to relate music of today with the novel they have just read. Most of our students listen to diverse types of music, so creating an album for a work they have just read is interesting and meaningful. Whether connecting characters, events, and themes by lyrics or by the type and tone of music, students will gain confidence in reading and interpreting literature and a deeper understanding of the music and words they listen to every day.

DISCIPLINE

This lesson is designed primarily for English or music classes, although any class in which students read literature could use this lesson.

STANDARDS

- Students will organize, write, and successfully use standard English conventions in their writing.
- Students will identify and comprehend the main ideas of a work of nonfiction and use the main ideas to form an understanding of an historical event or time period.
- Students will deepen their understanding of pieces of music (songs) by studying their historical context and making connections between the songs and the events that occur within a novel.
- Students will plan and present an oral presentation that demonstrates appropriate consideration of audience, purpose, and the information to be conveyed.

PACING

Project should take 5 to 6 days (suggested time is for students to complete the project at home, not during class instruction days), with 1 to 2 class share days (for Activity Extension).

LESSON

Activity 1

Give students the Student Worksheet that explains the assignment. Students are to think about the novel they have just read and choose 8 to 10 songs to make up the album soundtrack for the novel. Depending on the era of the novel, students can research the music that was popular during that period and use that music, or current music, to illustrate the novel. If they are not familiar with music from older periods, they may be able to find it at the public or school library or by asking older relatives, neighbors, or friends. Teachers, especially music teachers, may also have some music. *Note: This does not actually mean the students have to CREATE the album—just explain (in words) what the album would include. Some students may not have the ability or technology to make a CD, and the chief value of this assignment is in the explanations of why they'd choose the particular songs. Still, if students wish to make a CD and have the technology to do so, this should be encouraged as it may help to motivate them. Do remind students not to download songs illegally in order to create their album, however.* Students should choose a dozen songs from a variety of artists that convey the characters, events, and themes of the novel. The first step for students is brainstorming about the novel itself and possible songs that would connect to the novel. This is the front side of the Student Worksheet.

Activity 2

After brainstorming, students choose the 8 to 10 songs that they believe most connect to the novel and list these songs (the artist and the song title) on the back of the Student Worksheet. Then they write a paper explaining each of their song choices with a well-argued paragraph. Each paragraph should explain why they chose the song—how it connects to a character, event, or theme of the novel. Students should cite examples of song lyrics or orchestral movements of the music to explain their choices and cite examples from the novel that seem to match the song. Instead of typing this out and printing it on computer paper, offer students the option of actually making an 8- to 10-page CD booklet, with each page giving the song title and the paragraph explaining why they chose the song.

Activity 3

After choosing the 8 to 10 songs and explaining them in their papers, students should design an album/CD cover (hand-drawn or computer-designed) that creatively conveys the novel as well as the soundtrack choices. This is turned in with the paper that they write. Or, if they have chosen to create the 8- to 10-page CD booklet (see Activity 2), this can serve as the cover for that booklet.

Activity Extension—A Soundtrack Share Day for the Novel

Although students are not required to physically make a CD for this album, one option is to ask students to find and locate at least one 1 of their 8 to 10 songs on the album and bring the song to class (on a CD or cassette, etc.). Each student can play one of their songs (or, if that would take up too much time, a part of the song) from their soundtrack (make sure it is classroom-appropriate). The students in class then can guess why that song was chosen, and the person sharing the song can explain whether or not the class made the correct link to the novel or if there were different reasons the song was chosen.

Assessment

Suggested Weighting

Brainstorming portion of Student Worksheet, 20 points; Paper explaining each of the 8 to 10 song choices, 50 points; Short presentation of one song and explanation (Activity Extension), 20 points.

Rubric: General Performance Scoring Rubric

Rubric: Generic Writing Rubric

STUDENT WORKSHEET

Name____________________________

LESSON TITLE: LITERATURE LINKS TO MUSIC: CREATING A SOUNDTRACK FOR A NOVEL

Mission

Your goal is to find 8 to 10 songs to make up an album that musically represents a novel you have been reading in class. There are four steps (and a related Activity Extension) that you need to complete in order to do well on this project. Your first step is to brainstorm a list of the key characters, events, and themes of the novel. You will be connecting the music you choose for this project with your novel in three ways. Each song should fit one of three categories:

- Songs that represent characters;
- Songs that represent critical events of the novel;
- Songs that represent important themes of the novel.

For each song, you will write a paragraph explaining why you selected the song. If your song has lyrics, why do the lyrics of the song remind you of the characters, events, or themes of this work? Be specific and use examples from the song. If the song does not have lyrics, how do the musical movements of the song mirror the characters, events, or themes of the novel? Be specific in your explanation. Use your brainstorm lists below to determine your songs and then begin writing your 8 to 10 paragraphs of explanation.

Step 1: Brainstorming

1. Brainstorm about the main characters of the novel:

Character name	Words to describe character	Possible song

2. Brainstorm about the major events of the novel:

Major event	Words to describe this event	Possible song

3. Major themes of the novel:

Theme	Explanation of theme	Possible song

4. Research the music of the era:

Depending on the era of the novel, you can research in *American Pop* within the "Music" chapters for each decade, which include the music that was popular during that period. You may use older music or current music to illustrate the book. If you are not familiar with music from older periods, you may be able to find it at the public library or by asking older relatives, neighbors, or friends if they have the music.

Step 2: Writing

After completing the brainstorming chart above, begin writing your paper explaining each of your song choices with a well-argued paragraph. Each paragraph should explain why you chose the song—how it connects to a character, event, or theme of the novel. Cite examples of song lyrics or orchestral movements of the music to explain your choices and cite examples from the novel that seem to match the song.

Creative Idea: Instead of typing and printing this out on standard size paper, you can instead actually make an 8- to 10-page CD booklet, with each page showing the song title and featuring a paragraph explaining why you chose the song.

Step 3: Album/CD Cover Design

After choosing the 8 to 10 songs and explaining them in your paper or CD booklet, create artwork (hand-drawn or computer-designed) that creatively conveys the characters, events, and themes of the novel as well as your soundtrack choices. This should be turned in with your paper that analyzes the 8 to 10 songs you've chosen. Or, if you have chosen to create the 8- to 10-page CD booklet (explained in Step 2 above), this artwork can serve as your cover for the booklet.

Activity Extension—A Soundtrack Share Day for the Novel

Find at least one of your songs on the album and bring the song to class (on a CD or cassette, etc.). You will be asked to play one of your songs (or, if that would take up too much time, a part of one of your songs) from your soundtrack (make sure it is classroom-appropriate.) The students in class then must guess why that song was chosen (how it might relate to the characters, events, and/or themes of the novel). You will then share whether or not that is how you explained your song.

Check:

- Did you successfully complete the characters-events-themes brainstorm list as part of generating ideas for how to construct your soundtrack for the novel?

- Did you write 8 to 10 well-explained paragraphs analyzing why you chose each particular song for inclusion in your soundtrack?

- Did you design an effective cover for your album/CD that helps convey the characters, events, and/or themes of the novel?

- Did you choose a song (or a section of a song) to share with the class to help them guess (and then hear from you) how the song relates to the novel?

Music Controversies: A Debate

FOR TEACHERS

ESSENTIAL QUESTION

How do current issues in the music industry affect musicians and music lovers?

OBJECTIVES

- Students will research and understand controversial issues relating to the music industry.
- Students will prepare a short persuasive speech about a topic that interests them.
- Students will analyze how music controversies impact both the industry and the consumer.

RATIONALE

Whether it's using ringtones on a cell phone or their iPods and other MP3 players as they walk through the hallways at school, students use music throughout the day. Music downloading and questions about music censorship are prevalent in their lives and the world around them. This lesson allows students to investigate and then debate issues facing the music industry, allowing the class to gain multiple perspectives on controversial issues.

DISCIPLINE

This lesson could be used to study media literacy in such courses as American history (modern history), government/citizenship, journalism/media studies, and the speech and debating standards of English language arts.

STANDARDS

- Students will organize, write, and successfully use standard English conventions in their writing.
- Students will identify and comprehend the main ideas of a work of nonfiction and use the main ideas to form an understanding of an historical event or time period.
- Students will plan and present an oral presentation that demonstrates appropriate consideration of audience, purpose, and the information to be conveyed.

PACING

Project should take 2 to 3 days or 5 to 6 days (at home, not in class) if it includes Activity Extension.

LESSON

Activity 1 (Lesson Introduction)

Students will write a 1-page journal answering the following questions: "Should people be allowed to download music for free, or is it only fair for artists to charge money for each download? Should the music industry sue people who improperly use file-sharing programs? Why or why not?" After writing their journal entry (about 10 minutes), students should talk about their answers in a class discussion.

Activity 2

Students will work in groups to investigate a controversial issue in the music industry. Six potential groups are listed below. (You could also allow students to create their own topic for debate.) In these groups, students should brainstorm to gather evidence and reasons for their side of the debate and use the Student Worksheet as a guide to stimulate discussion within their groups. Students can use informal evidence based on their own experiences and research.

Suggested source: "Music of the 2000s," volume 4, *American Pop.*

- Group 1: Downloading and file-sharing of music should be legal
- Group 2: Downloading and file-sharing of music should be illegal
- Group 3: Music should be censored, and it's OK if major stores do not sell music with offensive lyrics
- Group 4: Music should not be censored, and major stores should sell all kinds of music, even if the music contains offensive lyrics
- Group 5: MP3 players should be allowed in high schools
- Group 6: MP3 players should be banned in high schools

Activity 3

Each group will present their topic for 1 minute in a debate. The opposing group will then have 1 minute to present their topic, followed by a 30-second rebuttal for each of the groups. Then the class members who are not in either of the debating groups will vote on a winner between the two opposing groups, based on their various arguments.

Activity Extension—Music Industry in Current Events

After the debate activity, students can continue to follow issues related to the music industry in print news and online news for the following week, with an instructor either requiring a short paper or offering the paper option as extra credit. See Student Worksheet for more information.

Assessment

Suggested Weighting

Journal response (Activity 1), 10 points; Pre-debate worksheet (Activity 2), 20 points; Speech/debate (Activity 3), 40 points; Activity Extension (paper), 20 points.

Rubric: General Performance Scoring Rubric

Rubric: Debate Rubric

STUDENT WORKSHEET

Name________________________

LESSON TITLE: MUSIC CONTROVERSIES: A DEBATE!

Mission

Your group will study and take a position on a controversial topic related to the music industry. Another group will argue the opposite opinion. You'll look for different types of evidence to prove your point and help formulate an argument. Then your group will have exactly 1 minute to make your point to the class. After the opposing group has its turn to present, you'll have a chance to make an impromptu reply.

Order of today's debate:

- Round 1: Each group will have 1 minute to present its findings in a planned speech to the class.
- Round 2: Each group will have 30 seconds to make an impromptu response. While this isn't fully planned ahead of time, you'll jot down potential notes to use (see the worksheet below).

1. What is your group's topic and opinion about the topic?

2. As a group, brainstorm ideas supporting why your group's opinion is correct. What casual evidence (evidence from your own experiences or stories you've heard) supports your opinion?

3. Use research from volume 4 of *American Pop* and other sources to support your assigned opinion. What research would support your opinion?

4. Part of any debate is the ability to refute your opponent's argument, and you'll need to do this for the second round of the debate. What do you think is the strongest evidence the opposing group will have about this topic? Brainstorm a way to refute your opponents' evidence in the second round of the debate.

Activity Extension—Music Industry in Current Events

In the week following the debate, track any articles about the music industry that you find in national newspapers and magazines or through research on the Internet. Keep a folder of the articles you find during the week. At the end of the week, use your articles to write a paper (1 to 2 pages) about music in the news. Try to answer the following:

- Did you find any articles on controversies related to music or the music industry? If so, what are they?

- Did you find any articles on technology's impact in the music industry? If so, explain.

- What artists were in the news during the past week?

- What other interesting topics related to music did you read about this week?

Check:

- Did you prepare for your debate by fully answering the questions on the Student Worksheet?

- Did you speak clearly and persuasively during the debate in order to articulate your points and convince your audience?

- Did you create a folder of articles about music in the news (Activity Extension)?

- Did you write a well-argued paper (using examples) that discusses the music industry in current events?

- Did you proofread your paper and check for grammar and punctuation errors?

Sports Controversies: Newspaper Editorial/ Opinion Column

FOR TEACHERS

ESSENTIAL QUESTION

How do sports controversies affect not only sports but society itself?

OBJECTIVES

- Students will study and discuss controversial issues in the world of sports.
- Students will understand how to write a persuasive newspaper column or editorial.
- Students will research information related to their topic in order to formulate an opinion.

RATIONALE

Now more than ever, people love to express their opinions about issues involving sports in America. From callers on sports talk radio discussing gambling to analysts on ESPN arguing about performance enhancing drugs, sports talk revolves around two clear ingredients: being opinionated and knowing your information. In this lesson, students investigate important controversial issues in the world of sports and then write a persuasive opinion based on the evidence they have gathered.

DISCIPLINE

This lesson could be used in English, journalism, modern history, citizenship, or physical education courses.

STANDARDS

- Students will identify and comprehend the main ideas of a work of nonfiction and use the main ideas to form an understanding of the concept.
- Students will organize, write, and successfully use standard English conventions in their writing.
- Students will gather information from their research, evaluate the quality of the information they obtain, and use it to write a persuasive paper that is supported by research.

PACING

Project should take 2 to 3 days or 4 to 5 days if it includes Activity Extension.

LESSON

Activity 1 (Lesson Introduction)

Give students an interesting sports column from a local or national paper that is written about a current event in sports and have them read it to themselves. They will then write a 1-page journal entry answering the following questions: What is the author's main argument in this sports column? What evidence do you feel is the strongest in the column and why? What else do you notice about the author's writing style? Do you agree with the columnist's opinions on this issue? Why or why not? After writing their journal entry (about 10 minutes), students should discuss answers with their peers.

Activity 2

Randomly assign students one of the topics below and have them read the "Sports and Leisure" chapters in each decade. This will take about a day (in class) or can be assigned for homework (depending on how quickly you want to accomplish the lesson). While students are reading, they should take notes on the key facts presented regarding their controversial issue in the sports world.

Read the "Sports and Leisure" chapters, especially concentrating on these topics: 1900s, Ty Cobb; 1910s, the Black Sox scandal; 1920s, Shoeless Joe and the Negro League; 1930s-1960s, racism in sports and protests at the Olympics; 1970s, sexism, (Billie Jean King and Title IX); 1980s, the Olympics boycott and diver Greg Louganis, HIV positive and competing in the 1988 Olympics; 1990s, Mark McGuire and Sammy Sosa alleged cheating; and 2000s, steroids and congressional testimony.

- Group 1: Breaking Down Barriers; topic: racism in sports
- Group 2: Breaking Down Barriers; topic: sexism in sports
- Group 3: Bribery in Sports; topic: Black Sox scandal and more recent instances
- Group 4: Pumping Up; topic: steroids or other performance enhancers and sports

Activity 3

After researching their topics, students should complete the Student Worksheet, which helps them formulate an opinion on their topic, and then write a persuasive editorial/column about it. Students then briefly discuss what they've written with the class before turning it in.

Activity Extension—Publishing an Opinion on a Sports Issue

Have students research another controversial issue in the world of sports and write another editorial/column. Have them publish this on a school Web site or class blog, if your school has the technology available. If not, encourage students to submit their sports opinion as a letter-to-the-editor of a local or national paper.

Assessment

Suggested Weighting

Journal response (Activity 1), 10 points; Reading notes (Activity 2), 20 points; Sports editorial (Activity 3), 40 points; Publishing an opinion (Activity Extension), 30 points.

Rubric: Newspaper Article Rubric

STUDENT WORKSHEET

Name____________________________

LESSON TITLE: SPORTS CONTROVERSIES: NEWSPAPER EDITORIAL/ OPINION COLUMN

Mission

You will be writing a persuasive opinion column for a newspaper. Sometimes these are called "editorials," although usually these are written by the editorial board of a newspaper. If you are simply representing yourself, usually a persuasive opinion is called a "column." A good sports column is a miniature persuasive essay, complete with the following elements:

- An interesting lead or "hook" for the reader of your column
- Your clearly stated opinion on a controversial issue
- Clear evidence and examples to support your information
  - Some examples can be factual (proven facts, statistics)
  - Some examples can be emotional (arguments designed to appeal to emotion)

Research the scandals and controversies that have occurred in sports from the 1900s to today. Read the "Sports and Leisure Activities" chapters from *American Pop* and other sources as needed. and consider these topics:

- In the 1900s, the unpopular and racist baseball player, who was, nonetheless, a major star: Ty Cobb.
- Scandal in baseball: the 1910s Black Sox scandal (ending in 1920).
- Racism: the founding of the Negro League in the 1920s due to racism in sports because African Americans were not allowed to play professional team sports until the 1940s; the controversies in the 1960s over Muhammad Ali, Arthur Ashe not being able to enter South Africa, and the protests of medalists Tommie Smith and John Carlos at the 1968 Olympics.
- Olympics and politics: the cold war.
- Sexism in American sports, both professional and amateur. The start of Title IX and Billie Jean King plays Bobby Riggs.
- Controversy at the Olympics: the 1980s Olympics summer games are boycotted by the U.S.; Diver Greg Louganis is HIV positive and his competing in the 1984 Olympics is questioned.
- Steroid use: the suspicion of McGuire and Sosa in the 1990s; steroids in the 2000s and congressional testimony.

1. What topic have you been assigned ______________________________

2. Does your topic have two different sides? Multiple aspects? What are they? Write some detailed notes in the space below. You will use these in your column.

3. What is your opinion on this issue? Formulate a very specific argument detailing your opinion. Write one strongly worded sentence that will be the thesis or main point of your persuasive column.

4. What evidence (facts from your article, anecdotes, or other evidence meant to elicit emotional responses from the reader) will you use in your column to prove your point?

After completing question 4, you are ready to write your editorial.

Remember, when you write your editorial/column, you will be judged on:

- How thoroughly you discussed the topic;
- How clear your persuasive argument was;
- How many examples and how much evidence you used to thoroughly prove your point (evidence should be from the article you read);
- How effective your writing style was in your paper (which includes your ability to organize your editorial, make it clear to the reader, and use proper grammar and punctuation). See the Newspaper Article Rubric before you begin to write your editorial/column.

Activity Extension—Publishing an Opinion on a Sports Issue

Although for your most recent assignment you were assigned a controversial topic in the sports world, now is your chance to become a sports columnist or blogger and have complete control of what you write. Choose another controversial issue in the world of sports and write a persuasive column about that topic (based on your own knowledge and/or any research you wish to conduct). Publish this on a school Web site or class blog (if your school has the technology available) or turn it in as a persuasive column (in printed format) to your teacher. Your persuasive article will be graded with the same criteria as your assigned column.

Check:

- Did you successfully research and take notes on your assigned controversial issue in the world of sports?
- Did you write a well-organized persuasive column that used factual evidence (from the article) and emotional evidence (if applicable) as you made your persuasive point?
- Did you write in an effective style (making clear points to the reader, using proper grammar and punctuation, and powerful persuasive language)?
- Did you choose an issue (for the Activity Extension) of importance to the sports world and write an effective, well-organized, and well-supported persuasive sports column?

Televised Reality: Is Reality Television Real?

FOR TEACHERS

ESSENTIAL QUESTION

If reality television is real, then what does it reveal about America today?

OBJECTIVES

- Students will research how reality television has been criticized for not being real.
- Students will analyze what reality television shows us about society today.
- Students will investigate whether reality television needs to be real or if it serves some other purpose.

RATIONALE

Many stories in the media focus on reality television and its growing place in American society. This lesson allows students to look at source material that explains elements of reality television and discusses charges that some reality television is staged. Students then will have the opportunity to discuss current reality shows and trends and reach conclusions about the genre's validity and purpose.

DISCIPLINE

This lesson could be used to study media literacy in such courses as American history (modern history), psychology, sociology, journalism/media studies, and English language arts.

STANDARDS

- Students will organize, write, and successfully use standard English conventions in their writing.
- Students will identify and comprehend the main ideas of a work of nonfiction and use the main ideas to form an understanding of a concept.
- Students will identify, analyze, and apply knowledge of the conventions, elements, and techniques of television and provide evidence from the works to support their understanding.

PACING

Project should take 1 to 2 days or 5 days (with time at home, but not in class) if it includes Activity Extension.

LESSON

Activity (Lesson Introduction)

Students will write a 1-page journal answering the following questions: Why do Americans love reality television? What is real about reality television and what isn't? What reality television shows do you, or people you know, watch? Why? After writing their journal entries (about 10 minutes), students should talk about their answers in a class discussion.

Activity 2

Working in groups, students will brainstorm about reality programs they have watched in the past few years and record their notes. Each group will present their findings to the class.

Activity Extension—Close Interpretation of a Reality Program

For an additional project, students could choose one current reality television program and watch it at home (on their own), taking notes throughout the show in order to write a paper. Students should focus on how real the program was in their own opinion, citing evidence from throughout the show. In addition, students could explain how people were portrayed and just what the show seemed to reveal about America (e.g., stereotypes, trends, or other topics).

Assessment

Suggested Weighting

Journal response (Activity 1), 10 points; Short group presentation, 20 points; Activity Extension (individual paper analyzing reality program), 30 points.

Rubric: General Performance Scoring Rubric

Rubric: Generic Writing

STUDENT WORKSHEET

Name______________________________

LESSON TITLE: TELEVISED REALITY: IS REALITY TELEVISION REAL?

Mission

How real is reality television? What do some scholars say about this genre? Today, you'll investigate the role of reality television and the messages it sends to viewers and work in groups as you contemplate the current state of reality television and what it shows us about America. The Activity Extension allows you to focus on one particular reality show and write a careful analysis.

You may wish to read the television section of the "Entertainment" chapter in the 2000s section of volume 4 of *American Pop* from the beginning to the end.

Activity (Lesson Introduction)

Write a 1-page journal answering the following questions: Why do Americans love reality television? What's real about reality television and what isn't? What reality television shows do you, or people you know, watch? Why? Following journal-writing time (about 10 minutes), you should talk about your answers in a class or group discussion. In a group, brainstorm ideas about the current state of reality TV shows and report back to the class.

Activity Extension—Close Interpretation of a Reality Program

Choose one current reality television program and watch it at home (on your own), taking notes throughout in order to write a paper. Write a short paper (1 to 2 pages) analyzing the show. Here are a few issues to consider as you watch:

- How real or staged does this program seem? What examples from this episode seem to make this real? What examples could suggest that parts of this show are produced, staged, or not spontaneous? Explain.
- Are there stereotypes—gender, racial/ethnic, or age—reinforced on the show? Are there specific types of reality contestants? If so, explain.
- Are these average people? How does the cast reflect (or not reflect) the average American? What messages does this show seem to be sending to its audience?

Check:

- Did you fully complete the research questions about reality television?

- Did you brainstorm ideas about the current state of reality television in Part 2 of the Student Worksheet?

- Did you write a well-detailed paper (in the Activity Extension) that analyzes one particular reality show and the messages it sends about America?

- Did you proofread your paper and check for grammar and punctuation errors?

Television and Society: Research, Write, and Present a Television Analysis Project

FOR TEACHERS

ESSENTIAL QUESTIONS

- How has television changed through time?
- How do television shows present similar ideas in different ways?
- What does television today tell us about American culture?

OBJECTIVES

- Students will conduct research about a television topic of their choice.
- Students will compose a research paper analyzing a topic of their choice.
- Students will present their findings to the class in a multimedia presentation.

RATIONALE

If the average teenager today spends more time watching television than completing homework, there is very little a teacher can do to change that habit. Yet, teachers can use this interest in television to help students research and study the genre of television, with students becoming experts on some phase of television, past or present. This lesson provides a framework for students to become the teachers, by choosing, exploring, and presenting a television-related research project. By the end of the class presentation days, students will have heard a mix of different projects that thoroughly investigate the genre of television.

DISCIPLINE

Although primarily designed for a journalism or media studies classroom, this lesson could be used to study media literacy in multiple courses, including American history (modern history), government/citizenship, sociology, or English Language arts, as the core component involves writing a research paper.

STANDARDS

- Students will identify, analyze, and apply knowledge of the conventions, elements, and techniques of television and provide evidence from the works to support their understanding.
- Students will gather information from their research, evaluate the quality of the information they obtain, and use it to write an organized research paper.
- Students will organize, write, and successfully use standard English conventions in their writing.
- Students will plan and give an oral presentation that demonstrates appropriate consideration of audience, purpose, and the information to be conveyed.

PACING

Activity 1 (journal writing and sharing with class) will take one day. The paper should take about a week (depending on whether your class will research in or out of school) to research and write. The Activity Extension is designed to take 2 to 3 days in class.

LESSON

Activity 1 (Lesson Introduction)

Students will write a 1-page journal entry answering the following questions: What type of television shows are your favorites and why? What is the best television show you have ever seen? Do you have a "guilty pleasure" television show? Why do you enjoy it and why do you think you should not like it? What is your favorite television show and why? What interests you most about television? After writing in their journals (about 10 minutes), students should share their answers in a class discussion.

Activity 2

Each student will choose a topic related to television for a research project and class presentation. Projects may focus on issues that interest the student but should fall into one of the following categories:

- **Project Choice A: Genre Study:** Students analyze the current state of the television drama, television sitcoms, television animated programs, or television reality shows.
- **Project Choice B: Historical Approach:** Students study how television has changed over a period of time by narrowing the topic. (Example: how police shows have changed from *Dragnet* to *CSI* or how women in sitcoms have changed from *I Love Lucy* to *The New Adventures of Old Christine* or another current program.) The "Overview" and "Entertainment" chapters from the 1940s through the 2000s in *American Pop* should help illuminate issues of the day.

- **Project Choice C: Comparative Approach:** Students study two or more shows that present a different view of the same theme. (Example: the role of family in *Friday Night Lights* vs. *Heroes,* or the medical drama in *ER* vs. *Grey's Anatomy,* or even a comparison of *America's Top Chef* versus *Hell's Kitchen.* Other shows can be substituted.)

Note: The Student Worksheet for this lesson gives students a detailed explanation of how to research, write, and present this project. Students should be given time in and/or out of the classroom (at the instructor's discretion) to plan, library/computer lab time to research, and time to write the paper.

Activity 3

After choosing a topic, students should spend time researching their topic using resources in the school library, public library, and online. They should also spend time (as part of their research) finding and viewing TV shows that are related to their topic and choose a 5-minute clip from the TV show(s) to help highlight the findings of their paper. Instructors may want to pre-approve these clips to make sure they are classroom-appropriate. Students should complete the paper following the format outlined on the Student Worksheet. The "Entertainment" chapters from the 1940s through the 2000s in *American Pop* are good starting points for research.

Activity 4

On the day that their research paper is due, each student will briefly present his or her findings to the class, quickly summarizing the topic and presenting a 5-minute (or shorter) TV clip to the class that highlights his/her findings. In large classes, you might wish to schedule film presentations over a 2- or 3-day period in order to have enough time for all students to present.

Activity Extension

After learning so much about television, students now have their turn at becoming producers. Place students into groups of 5 or 6, with each group choosing a television show type (game show, sitcom, talk show, reality show, drama, etc.) to write and produce a 10-minute segment. Students should have 2 to 3 days in class to work on writing and rehearsing their show and then one day to perform their show for the class. Note: Some instructors may prefer to have students film their show on their own as homework.

Assessment

Suggested Weight

Research paper, 100 points; Class presentation with media/film clip, 40 points; Activity Extension, 40 points.

Rubric: Research Report

Rubric: General Performance Scoring Rubric

STUDENT WORKSHEET

Name______________________________

LESSON TITLE: TELEVISION AND SOCIETY: RESEARCH, WRITE, AND PRESENT A TELEVISION ANALYSIS PROJECT

Mission

You will pick a topic to study for a TV and society paper. This is an individual research paper that will include an in-depth paper, a class presentation, and a multimedia film clip.

Your project should be about television and include an in-depth study of television. Choose one of these patterns as the focus of your paper:

- **Project Choice A: Genre Study:** Analyze the current state of the television drama, television sitcoms, television animated programs, or television reality shows. Choose the genre that most interests you and find currently airing shows (not just reruns) to research and study within your genre.
- **Project Choice B: Historical Approach:** Study how television has changed over a period of time by narrowing down your topic. (Example: How police shows have changed from *Dragnet* to *CSI* or how women in sitcoms have changed from *I Love Lucy* to *The New Adventures of Old Christine.*)
- **Project Choice C: Comparative Approach:** Study two or more shows that present a different view of the same theme. (Example: the role of family in *Friday Night Lights* vs. *Heroes,* or the medical drama in *House* vs. *Grey's Anatomy,* or even a comparison of *America's Top Chef* versus *Hell's Kitchen.*)

Media Clip Requirement: You *must* use at least one media clip in your presentation: a VHS taped television show or a DVD of a television show (see back of this worksheet for more details). If you have difficulty obtaining a television clip, ask your teacher or see if you can make a visual aid (poster presentation, etc.) instead of using a clip.

Instructions for Creating Your Paper and Presentation

Introduction: (½ page)

In your introduction, explain your concept/idea (for example, the portrayal of women in television dramas today) and explain why you chose the topic, why it is worth studying, and any other background about the topic you feel is important.

Part I: Research (includes Internet and article research) (1 ½ to 2 pages)

Discuss the history of your topic and the historical background. This is where you use your notes on the history of the show(s), information about the shows' casts, writers, etcetera. What did critics say about the movies or genres you are studying? Use your Internet research, magazine articles, and journal articles, and explain what the show is like, what people have written about it, how it relates to your topic, and so on.

Part II: Analysis (3 to 4 pages)

After discussing the research you found, analyze your topic. In roughly 3 pages, write your own section of this paper where you explain what you discovered about your topic, why the TV shows you chose are important in investigating your topic, and what your shows highlight about America. Remember, this project is called "television and society," so in this section of the paper, explain what these shows suggest about American viewers. What messages do the shows' writers/producers send to us? Do they reinforce existing stereotypes or create new stereotypes? Do they entertain? Inform? Persuade? This analysis section will be very different, depending on the topic you chose. For example, if you are writing about the role of television animation and how it has changed over time, this section will include research of when different animated shows aired and what they were like. You would also include your analysis of how animation has changed. If your topic is comparative, such as the portrayal of two different medical shows currently on TV, your section here will focus on a case-by-case comparison/contrast of differences you see in how these two shows use their setting to create TV drama. Because research is still required, you would find facts about the shows to add to your paper.

Brief Conclusion (½ to 1 page)

Provide a quick summary of your findings and explain any last thoughts you have about your topic. Your conclusion should also serve as a short reflection: what did you like or not like about the project, what was most interesting to you, what surprised you, what frustrated you, and so on. What did you learn about film from this project?

Works-Cited Page

Add a works-cited page where you list (alphabetically) your sources of your research, using an appropriate style, as explained by your instructor.

Media Clip Requirement

Remember that you must have a TV clip or visual aid when you present your paper to the class. Please have your clip cued (if it is a VCR tape) or memorize exactly where it is on a DVD. Your clip must be pre-approved by your instructor and should not be any longer than 5 minutes. If you'd like to show two quick film clips (from different TV shows), this is possible as long as the clips do not add up to more than 5 minutes. The clip should reinforce a major point you make in your paper. Make sure you have a sound reason for showing the clip you choose.

Check:

- Did you follow the step-by-step directions for the organization of your research paper?
- Did your paper contain both research and your own analysis of television?
- Did you properly cite your research according to the rules given by your teacher?
- Did you proofread your paper and check for grammar and punctuation errors?
- Did you prepare a short TV clip or visual aid to show to the class for your presentation?

General Bibliography

See also the Resource Guide at the end of of each volume for more suggestions of print resources, Web sites, and videos for further research.

Alexander, Charles C. *Our Game: An American Baseball History.* New York: Henry Holt, 1991.

Allen, Frederick Lewis. *Only Yesterday: An Informal History of the 1920s.* 1931. New York: Harper and Row, 1964.

Batchelor, Bob, ed. *Basketball in America: From the Playgrounds to Jordan's Game and Beyond.* Binghamton, NY: Haworth Press, 2005.

Battelle, John. *The Search: How Google and Its Rivals Rewrote the Rules of Business and Transformed Our Culture.* New York: Portfolio, 2005.

Benson, Susan Porter. *Counter Cultures: Saleswomen, Managers, and Customers in American Department Stores, 1890–1940.* Urbana: University of Illinois Press, 1986.

Berman, Morris. *Dark Ages America: The Final Phase of Empire.* New York: W. W. Norton, 2006.

Bigsby, C.W.E. *Modern American Drama, 1945–2000.* Cambridge, MA: Cambridge University Press, 2000.

Blackford, Mansel G., and K. Austin Kerr. *Business Enterprise in American History,* 2nd ed. Boston: Houghton Mifflin, 1990.

Boyer, Paul. *By the Bomb's Early Light: American Thought and Culture at the Dawn of the Atomic Age.* New York: Pantheon Books, 1985.

Branch, Taylor. *Parting the Waters: America in the King Years, 1954–1963.* New York: Simon and Schuster, 1988.

Brinkley, Douglas. *Wheels for the World: Henry Ford, His Company, and a Century of Progress, 1903–2003.* New York: Viking, 2003.

Brooks, David. *Bobos in Paradise: The New Upper Class and How They Got There.* New York: Simon & Schuster, 2000.

Browne, Ray B., ed. *Profiles of Popular Culture: A Reader.* Madison: The University of Wisconsin Press, 2005.

Cashman, Sean Dennis. *America in the Age of the Titans: The Progressive Era and World War I.* New York: New York University Press, 1988.

———. *America, Roosevelt, and World War II.* New York: New York University Press, 1989.

Chafe, William H. *The Paradox of Change: American Women in the 20th Century.* New York: Oxford University Press, 1991.

Chambers, John Whiteclay II. *The Tyranny of Change: America in the Progressive Era, 1890–1920,* 2nd ed. New Brunswick, NJ: Rutgers University Press, 2000.

Chandler, Alfred Jr. *Giant Enterprise: Ford, General Motors, and the Automobile Industry.* New York: Harcourt, Brace and World, 1964.

Chernow, Ron. *Titan: The Life of John D. Rockefeller, Sr.* New York: Random House, 1998.

Clark, Clifford Edward Jr. *The American Family Home, 1800–1960.* Chapel Hill: University of North Carolina Press, 1986.

Cohen, Lizabeth. *Making a New Deal: Industrial Workers in Chicago, 1919–1939.* Cambridge, MA: Cambridge University Press, 1990.

Cooper, John Milton Jr. *The Pivotal Decades: The United States, 1900–1920.* New York: W. W. Norton, 1990.

Cremin, Lawrence A. *American Education: The Metropolitan Experience, 1876–1980.* New York: Harper and Row, 1988.

Dickstein, Morris. *Gates of Eden: American Culture in the Sixties.* 1977; Cambridge, MA: Harvard University Press, 1997.

Diggins, John Patrick. *The Proud Decades.* New York: W. W. Norton, 1988.

Dubofsky, Melvyn. *The State and Labor in Modern America.* Chapel Hill: The University of North Carolina Press, 1994.

Dylan, Bob. *Chronicles: Volume One.* New York: Simon & Schuster, 2004.

Ewen, Stuart. *Captains of Consciousness: Advertising and the Social Roots of the Consumer Culture.* New York: McGraw-Hill, 1976.

Ewen, Stuart, and Elizabeth Ewen. *Channels of Desire: Mass Images and the Shaping of American Consciousness.* New York: McGraw-Hill, 1982.

Faludi, Susan. *The Terror Dream: Fear and Fantasy in Post-9/11 America.* New York: Metropolitan Books, 2007.

Fishwick, Marshall William. *Probing Popular Culture: On and Off the Internet.* New York: Haworth Press, 2004.

Fox, Stephen. *The Mirror Makers: A History of American Advertising and Its Creators.* New York: William Morrow, 1984.

Franklin, John Hope, and Alfred A. Moss. *From Slavery to Freedom: A History of African Americans.* 8th ed. New York: Knopf, 2000.

———. *Mirror to America: The Autobiography of John Hope Franklin.* New York: Farrar, Straus and Giroux, 2005.

Friedman, Thomas L. *The World is Flat: A Brief History of the Twenty-First Century.* New York: Farrar, Straus and Giroux, 2005.

Garraty, John A. *The Great Depression.* New York: Harcourt Brace Jovanovich, 1986.

Gitlin, Todd. *The Sixties: Years of Hope, Days of Rage.* Rev. ed. New York: Bantam, 1993.

Goodrum, Charles, and Helen Dalrymple. *Advertising in America: The First 200 Years.* New York: Harry N. Abrams, 1990.

Harrington, Michael. *The Other America: Poverty in the United States.* New York: Macmillan, 1962.

Heinrich, Thomas, and Bob Batchelor. *Kotex, Kleenex, Huggies: Kimberly-Clark and the Consumer Revolution in American Business.* Columbus: Ohio State University Press, 2004.

Hill, Daniel Delis. *Advertising to the American Woman, 1900–1990.* Columbus: Ohio State University Press, 2002.

Jackson, Kenneth T. *Crabgrass Frontier: The Suburbanization of the United States.* New York: Oxford University Press, 1985.

Jacobs, Jane. *The Death and Life of Great American Cities.* New York: Random House, 1961.

Johnson, Haynes. *The Best of Times: America in the Clinton Years.* New York: James H. Silberman, 2001.

Karnow, Stanley. *Vietnam: A History.* Rev. ed. New York: Penguin, 1991.

Kennedy, David M. *Freedom from Fear: The American People in Depression and War, 1929–1945.* New York: Oxford University Press, 1999.

Kessler-Harris, Alice. *Out to Work: A History of Wage-Earning Women in the United States.* New York: Oxford University Press, 1982.

Kowinski, William S. *The Malling of America.* New York: Morrow, 1985.

Leach, William. *Land of Desire: Merchants, Power, and the Rise of the New American Culture.* New York: Pantheon Books, 1993.

Lears, T. J. Jackson. *Fables of Abundance: A Cultural History of Advertising in America.* New York: Basic Books, 1995.

Levitt, Steven D., and Stephen J. Dubner. *Freakonomics: A Rogue Economist Explores the Hidden Side of Everything.* New York: William Morrow, 2005.

Marable, Manning. *Race, Reform, and Rebellion: The Second Reconstruction in Black America, 1945–1990.* 2nd ed. Jackson: University Press of Mississippi, 1991.

May, Elaine Tyler. *Homeward Bound: American Families in the Cold War Era.* New York: Basic Books, 1988.

Miller, James. *Flowers in the Dustbin: The Rise of Rock and Roll, 1947–1977.* New York: Simon and Schuster, 1999.

Patterson, James T. *Grand Expectations: The United States, 1945–1974.* New York: Oxford University Press, 1996.

Schlosser, Eric. *Fast Food Nation: The Dark Side of the All-American Meal.* New York: Houghton Mifflin, 2001.

Shilts, Randy. *And The Band Played On: Politics, People and the AIDS Epidemic.* New York: Penguin, 1987.

Sklar, Robert. *Movie-Made America: A Cultural History of American Movies.* New York: Vintage, 1975.

Southern, Eileen. *The Music of Black Americans: A History.* 3rd ed. New York: W. W. Norton, 1997.

Stewart, James B. *Den of Thieves.* New York: Simon and Schuster, 1991.

Toll, Robert C. *On with the Show: The First Century of Show Business in America.* New York: Oxford University Press, 1976.

Troy, Gil. *Morning in America: How Ronald Reagan Invented the 1980s.* Princeton, NJ: Princeton University Press, 2005.

Wiebe, Robert H. *The Search for Order, 1877–1920.* New York: Hill and Wang, 1967.

Wilentz, Sean. *The Age of Reagan: A History, 1974–2008.* New York: Harper, 2008.

Wiseman, Carter. *Shaping a Nation: Twentieth-Century American Architecture and Its Makers.* New York: W. W. Norton, 1998.

Zinn, Howard. *A People's History of the United States, 1492-Present.* New York: Harper Perennial, 1995.

Index

About the Editor and Contributors

SET EDITOR

Bob Batchelor teaches in the School of Mass Communications at the University of South Florida. A noted expert on American popular culture, Bob is the author of: *The 1900s* (Greenwood, 2002); coauthor of *Kotex, Kleenex, and Huggies: Kimberly-Clark and the Consumer Revolution in American Business* (2004); editor of *Basketball in America: From the Playgrounds to Jordan's Game and Beyond* (2005); editor of *Literary Cash: Unauthorized Writings Inspired by the Legendary Johnny Cash* (2006); and coauthor of *The 1980s* (Greenwood, 2007). He serves on the editorial board of *The Journal of Popular Culture*. Visit him on the Internet at his blog (pr-bridge.com) or homepage (www.bobbatchelor.com).

CONSULTING EDITOR

Ray B. Browne is a Distinguished University Professor in Popular Culture, Emeritus, at Bowling Green State University. He cofounded the Popular Culture Association (1970) and the American Culture Association (1975) and served as Secretary-Treasurer of both until 2002. In 1967 he began publishing the *Journal of Popular Culture*, and in 1975 the *Journal of American Culture*. He edited both until 2002. He has written or edited more than 70 books and written numerous articles on all fields in literature and popular culture. He currently serves as Book Review Editor of the *Journal of American Culture*.

CONTRIBUTORS

David Blanke, author of *The 1910s* (Greenwood, 2002), is currently Associate Professor of History at Texas A&M University, Corpus Christi. He is the author of *Hell on Wheels: The Promise and Peril of America's Car Culture, 1900–1940* (2007) and *Sowing the American Dream: How Consumer Culture Took Root in the Rural Midwest* (2000).

Kathleen Drowne, coauthor of *The 1920s* (Greenwood, 2004), is Assistant Professor of English at the University of Missouri, Rolla.

Patrick Huber, coauthor of *The 1920s* (Greenwood, 2004), is Assistant Professor of History at the University of Missouri, Rolla.

Marc Oxoby, PhD, teaches English and Humanities classes for the English Department at the University of Nevada, Reno. He has worked as a disc jockey and as the editor of the small-press literary journal *CRiME CLUb.* A regular contributor to the scholarly journal *Film and History* and *The Journal of Popular Culture,* he has also written for several other periodicals as well as for *The St. James Encyclopedia of Popular Culture, The International Dictionary of Films and Filmmakers,* and *New Paths to Raymond Carver.*

Edward J. Rielly, Professor of English at St. Joseph's College in Maine, has taught on Western film and the history of the west for many years. He is author of several nonfiction books, including *F. Scott Fitzgerald: A Biography* (Greenwood 2005) and *The 1960s* (Greenwood, 2003). He has also published 10 books of poetry.

Kelly Boyer Sagert is a freelance writer who has published biographical material with Gale, Scribner, Oxford, and Harvard University, focusing on athletes and historical figures. She is the author of *Joe Jackson: A Biography* (Greenwood, 2004), *The 1970s* (Greenwood, 2007), and the *Encyclopedia of Extreme Sports* (Greenwood, 2008).

Robert Sickels, author of *The 1940s* (Greenwood Press, 2004), is Assistant Professor at Whitman College, Walla Walla, Washington.

Scott F. Stoddart, coauthor of *The 1980s* (Greenwood, 2006), is the Dean of Academic Affairs at Manhattanville College, New York, where he currently teaches courses in cinema and musical theatre history.

Nancy K. Young, is a researcher and independent scholar. She retired in 2005 after 26 years of a career in management consulting. With her husband, William H. Young, she has cowritten three recent Greenwood titles, *The 1930s* (2002), *The 1950s* (2004), and *Music of the Great Depression* (2005).

William H. Young, author of *The 1930s* (Greenwood, 2002) and coauthor of *The 1950s* (Greenwood, 2004), is a freelance writer and independent scholar. He retired in 2000 after 36 years of teaching American Studies and popular culture at Lynchburg College in Lynchburg, Virginia. Young has published books and articles on various aspects of popular culture, including three Greenwood volumes cowritten with his wife, Nancy K. Young.

ADDITIONAL CONTRIBUTORS

Cindy Williams, independent scholar.

Mary Kay Linge, independent scholar.

Martha Whitt, independent scholar.

Micah L. Issitt, independent scholar.

Josef Benson, University of South Florida.

Ken Zachmann, independent scholar.